The Woman's Hand

Gender and Theory in
Japanese Women's Writing

The Woman's Hand

Gender and Theory in
Japanese Women's Writing

PAUL GORDON SCHALOW

JANET A. WALKER

Editors

Stanford University Press
Stanford, California

Stanford University Press
Stanford, California
© 1996 by the Board of Trustees of the
Leland Stanford Junior University

Printed in the United States of America

CIP data appear at the end of the book

The costs of publishing this book
have been supported in part by an
award from the Hiromi Arisawa
Memorial Fund (named in honor
of the renowned economist and the
first chair of the Board of the University of Tokyo Press) and fi-
nanced by the generosity of Japanese citizens and Japanese
corporations to recognize excellence in scholarship on Japan.

Stanford University Press publications
are distributed exclusively by Stanford
University Press within the United States,
Canada, Mexico, and Central America;
they are distributed exclusively by
Cambridge University Press
throughout the rest of the world.

The editors dedicate this volume of essays to

Howard Hibbett

Acknowledgments

This volume of essays emerged from the Rutgers Conference on Japanese Women Writers, which was organized by the editors and Nina Cornyetz and held at Rutgers University on April 9–10, 1993. The essays by Chieko M. Ariga, Doris G. Bargen, Lynne K. Miyake, Sharalyn Orbaugh, John Whittier Treat, and Meera Viswanathan were originally presented as papers at the conference. Additional essays by Nina Cornyetz, Joan E. Ericson, Noriko Mizuta, Livia Monnet, Maryellen Toman Mori, and Michiko Niikuni Wilson, and a selected bibliography by Joan E. Ericson and Midori Y. McKeon were solicited later, giving the volume its present form. The editors express their heartfelt thanks to the essayists for their outstanding contributions and for their unwavering support of the project.

Others who contributed to the conference and, indirectly, to this volume also deserve our thanks: Phyllis I. Lyons, Susan J. Napier, Lucy North, H. Richard Okada, and Ann Sherif acted as respondents at the conference. Noriko Mizuta (Lippit) presented the keynote address. Brett de Bary led a roundtable discussion among the conference speakers and gave useful advice at various stages of the project. The distinguished contemporary writer Kōno Taeko served as a special respondent. Katsuyo Motoyoshi interpreted for Kōno Taeko at the roundtable discussion. Chie Satō Roden gave a musical dimension to the conference with a performance of contemporary piano works by Japanese and American women. Ryōko Toyama, Director of the Archibald S. Alexander Library at Rutgers University, first suggested that we invite Ōba Minako to Rutgers University and acted as go-between in our initial contacts with her.

Ōba Minako graciously accepted our invitation to come to Rutgers University and presented a special address, "Without Beginning, Without End," which opens the volume. No one who attended the conference will ever forget the uncanny power of the words of the address as she spoke them that day.

The editors are especially grateful to the Japan Foundation for its funding of the conference and for the additional support the conference received from the following sources: the Dean of Rutgers College, James W. Reed; the Dean of Douglass College, Mary S. Hartman; the Associate Provost for Academic Affairs in Social Sciences, Barbara J. Callaway; the Chair of the Department of East Asian Languages and Cultures, Ching-I Tu; and the Associate Dean of Douglass College, Louise Duus.

We offer special thanks to Doris G. Bargen for suggesting the title of the volume and to Nina Cornyetz for her valuable contributions at various stages leading to its completion. We also owe a particular debt of gratitude to the anonymous reviewer of the manuscript for Stanford University Press, whose comments aided the authors and editors immeasurably in shaping the essays into a coherent whole, and to John Ziemer of Stanford University Press, whose editorial expertise was invaluable in bringing this sometimes daunting project to fruition.

We acknowledge Livia Monnet for allowing us to reprint her essay on Tsushima Yūko's "The Chrysanthemum Beetle," which appeared in different form in *Japan Review* 4 (1993); the University of Chicago Press for giving us permission to use parts of John Whittier Treat's study of Hayashi Kyōko from his *Writing Ground Zero* (Chicago: University of Chicago Press, 1995); Doris G. Bargen, Maryellen Toman Mori, and John Whittier Treat for their selection of illustrations to accompany their essays; Akiba Yūko, Assistant Curator at the National Museum of Modern Art, Kyoto, for her assistance in locating the cover art by Mitani Toshiko; and the following museums and individuals for permission to use the illustrations that appear in the volume:

The Art Institute of Chicago, for an untitled woodblock print by Utamaro

The British Museum, for the ivory and wood *netsuke* by Minkō of Tsu

The Harvard University Art Museums, for the drawing by Aubrey Beardsley, "The Woman in the Moon" (for *Salome*)

The Maruki Gallery, for the detail of mother and child from the Hiroshima mural entitled "Mizu" (Water) by Maruki Iri and Maruki Toshi

Mitani Aoko, for the painting by Mitani Toshiko, entitled "Asano" (Morning fields), in the collection of The National Museum of Modern Art, Kyoto

Ōba Minako, for the photograph of herself.

The editors dedicate the volume to Howard Hibbett, The Victor S. Thomas Professor of Japanese Literature, Emeritus, at Harvard University.

P.G.S.
J.A.W.
Highland Park, New Jersey

Contents

Preface

It has been twenty years since Anglo-American critics launched the revisionist project of recovering a feminine tradition of literature with the publication of Ellen Moers's study of Anglo-American and French literature, *Literary Women: The Great Writers* (New York: Oxford University Press, 1976), Elaine Showalter's *A Literature of Their Own: British Women Novelists from Brontë to Lessing* (Princeton: Princeton University Press, 1977), and Sandra M. Gilbert and Susan Gubar's *The Madwoman in the Attic: The Woman Writer and the Nineteenth-Century Literary Imagination* (New Haven: Yale University Press, 1979). Later critics of Anglo-American literature and of European literatures have continued this project, and in the past few years books that have as their goal the extension of this project still further afield, to cultures outside the West, have appeared.

A collection of essays edited by Thelma B. Kintanar, *Women Reading: Feminist Perspectives on Philippine Literary Texts* (Manila: University of the Philippines Press, 1992; distributed by University of Hawaii Press) examines the Filipino woman's writing traditions from precolonial, colonial, and postcolonial times. Several modern generations of women writing in Arabic are discussed by Joseph T. Zeidan in *Arab Women Novelists: The Formative Years and Beyond* (Albany: State University of New York Press, 1995). And Farzaneh Milani's *Veils and Words: The Emerging Voices of Iranian Women Writers* (Syracuse, N.Y.: Syracuse University Press, 1992) rediscovers a long-buried tradition of Iranian women poets and storytellers. Susie Tharu and K. Lalita's *Women Writing in India: 600 B.C. to the Present*, vol. 1, *600 B.C. to the Early 20th Century* (New York: Feminist Press, 1991); vol. 2, *The 20th Century* (1993) is an ambitious anthology of women writers of the Indian subcontinent. Far more than an anthology, it includes lengthy interpretive essays that position the writers socially, historically, and ideologically, and it interrogates the topics of "woman" and "literature" in ways that challenge eurocentric feminist criticism.

The Woman's Hand belongs, then, to a wider inquiry into women's traditions of writing worldwide and is offered specifically in the context of the critical scrutiny of women's writing that has been occurring within the field of Japanese literary studies in North America in the past decade. The essays in the volume represent the first fruits of a newly emerging movement within Japanese literary studies to apply feminist and gender criticism to Japanese texts in theoretical ways. The selected bibliography at the end of this volume attests to the significant accumulation of works by Japanese women writers now available in English translation, as well as the relative paucity of critical studies that problematize the issue of gender as an element in women's writing. Three monographs including translations are available that focus on individual modern women writers: Higuchi Ichiyō (1872–96) in Robert Lyons Danly, *In the Shade of Spring Leaves: The Life and Writings of Higuchi Ichiyō, a Woman of Letters in Meiji Japan* (New Haven: Yale University Press, 1981); Uno Chiyo (1897–) in Rebecca L. Copeland, *The Sound of the Wind: The Life and Works of Uno Chiyo* (Honolulu: University of Hawaii Press, 1992); and Kōda Aya (1904–90) in Alan M. Tansman, *The Writings of Kōda Aya, A Japanese Literary Daughter* (New Haven: Yale University Press, 1993).

Among general discussions, chapter 26 of Donald Keene's history of modern Japanese literature, *Dawn to the West: Fiction* (New York: Holt, Rinehart, & Winston, 1984), introduces several modern women writers, and Masao Miyoshi's essay "Gathering Voices: Japanese Women and Women Writers" in *Off Center: Power and Culture Relations Between Japan and the United States* (Cambridge, Mass.: Harvard University Press, 1991) interprets the role of women writers in contemporary Japan. But the only book-length study of a number of women writers is that by Victoria V. Vernon, *Daughters of the Moon: Wish, Will, and Social Constraint in Fiction by Modern Japanese*

Women (Berkeley, Calif.: Institute of East Asian Studies, 1988), which explores themes in fiction by five women writers and two male writers of the twentieth century. Otherwise, H. Richard Okada's *Figures of Resistance: Language, Poetry, and Narrating in "The Tale of Genji" and Other Mid-Heian Texts* (Durham, N.C.: Duke University Press, 1991) discusses women writers of the Heian period (794–1185) in terms of their contribution to the literary tradition at its inception. Haruo Shirane's *Bridge of Dreams: A Poetics of "The Tale of Genji"* (Stanford: Stanford University Press, 1987) and Norma Field's *Splendor of Longing in "The Tale of Genji"* (Princeton: Princeton University Press, 1987) in particular provide valuable insights in *The Tale of Genji* as a woman's text. Ironically, the legacy of the Heian period, when women wrote using the native script in what was called "the woman's hand" (*onna-de*), may have contributed to the lack of rigorous critical scrutiny of gender issues up to now, since the literature by women is so thoroughly integrated and naturalized within the Japanese literary tradition—what Alan M. Tansman calls "a female canon embedded in a male literary culture" (*The Writings of Kōda Aya*, 9).

The present volume builds upon and extends the efforts of these critics by providing a series of essays demonstrating different approaches to the tradition of Japanese women's writing—from consideration of issues of gendered writing in classical and modern literature to analysis of the themes and styles of a number of contemporary writers of stature. *The Woman's Hand* is not structured around a specific theoretical approach; rather, it represents a pluralistic inquiry into women's writing in Japan. Since Japanese literature is much less widely known to a Western audience than the Anglo-American and some European traditions, the volume as a whole represents the kind of effort undertaken by feminist scholars in the Anglo-American tradition during the early stages of feminist criticism: to recover a feminine tradition erased in the predominant focus of translators and critics on male writing. But the collection mirrors also the concerns of later waves of criticism: the French feminist concern with a feminine language and the female body as sites of resistance, and the postcolonial concern with woman as defined by aspects of acculturation such as ethnicity and class. What the essayists share is a close and extensive knowledge of women's texts, and a critical methodology that honors the links between life and text. Except for the opening essay by Ōba Minako, who is a contemporary novelist, critic, and short-story writer, all the essays are by scholars of Japanese or comparative literatures who locate their work within North American academic discourse and who share a belief that the self-critical study of Japanese women's writing holds great significance for intellectual inquiry in the world today.

(*Note*: Japanese names appear in Japanese style, surname first, except in the case of individuals writing in English who have chosen to adopt the Western order.)

Contributors

Chieko M. Ariga is Associate Professor of Japanese Literature at the University of Utah. Her research interests include gender theory, cultural criticism, women's literature, and literature of the Edo period. She is the author of *Jendaa kaitai no kiseki* (Nichibei Josei Shuppan, 1996), and her articles have appeared in *Journal of Asian Studies*, *Monumenta Nipponica*, and *IRIS: A Journal About Women*. She is Associate Editor of *U.S.-Japan Women's Journal*.

Doris G. Bargen has published articles on classical and modern Japanese literature in *Harvard Journal of Asiatic Studies*, *Mosaic*, and *Monumenta Nipponica*. Her forthcoming book from the University of Hawaii Press is *A Woman's Weapon: Spirit Possession in "The Tale of Genji,"* and her next project is a study of *kaimami* in *The Tale of Genji*. She is Visiting Assistant Professor of Japanese at the University of Massachusetts at Amherst.

Nina Cornyetz is Assistant Professor of Japanese at Rutgers University. Her recent publications include a cultural analysis of contemporary Japanese racialism and critical essays in Japanese and in English on the modern writers Enchi Fumiko, Nakagami Kenji, Yamada Eimi, and Shimada Masahiko. She is presently completing a book manuscript entitled "Dangerous Women: Phallic Fantasy and Modernity in Izuki Kyōka, Enchi Fumiko, and Nakagami Kenji."

Joan E. Ericson is the author of a book (forthcoming from the University of Hawaii Press) on the modern Japanese woman writer Hayashi Fumiko that includes a translation of *Diary of a Vagabond*. Her current research focuses on the issues of conformity and resistance in women's journals of the 1920's and 1930's. She is Assistant Professor of Japanese at Colorado College.

Midori Y. McKeon is Assistant Professor of Japanese at San Francisco State University. She is currently doing research on modern Japanese women writers and on gender representation in Japanese folk tales.

Lynne K. Miyake is Associate Professor of Japanese at Pomona College. Her research is in the areas of feminist and post-structuralist theory and narratology, and she has published several articles on classical Japanese narrative.

Noriko Mizuta is President/Professor of Comparative Literature and Director of the Center for Inter-Cultural Studies and Education at Jōsai University, as well as editor of the Center's annual English-language publication, *Review of Japanese Culture and Society*. She is co-editor and co-translator, with Kyoko Iriye Selden, of *Japanese Women Authors: Short Fiction* (M. E. Sharpe, 1991) and the author and editor of several books of feminist literary criticism in Japanese, the most recent of which is *Monogatari to hanmonogatari no fūkei: Josei hyōgen no shinsō*.

Livia Monnet is the author of articles on the modern Japanese women writers Tsushima Yūko, Ishimura Michiko, and Takahashi Takako. She has a book entitled *Gender and the Performance of Culture: Reading Contemporary Japanese Fiction* forthcoming from Stanford University Press. Her current research is on the role of race, culture, and identity in the writings of Bessie Head, Saegusa Kazuko, and Unica Zürn. She is Associate Professor of Japanese and Comparative Literature at the University of Montreal.

Maryellen Toman Mori is Associate Professor of Japanese Language and Literature at Santa Clara University. She teaches regularly in the Women's Studies Program and is the author of articles on the modern Japanese women writers Takahashi Takako and Okamoto Kanoko. She is working on a translation of Takahashi Takako's short-story sequence *Lonely Woman* for the MLA series Texts and Translations.

Ōba Minako is a contemporary fiction writer, essayist, and critic. She made her debut in the Japanese literary scene by winning the Akutagawa and Gunzō awards for her "Sanbiki no kani" (The three crabs) in 1968. She has since won numerous other literary awards. Her experience of Hiroshima immediately after the atomic bombing and her decade-long residence in Sitka, Alaska, are often noted by critics as influences on her unique literary perspective. Ōba was inducted into the prestigious National Academy of Arts (Geijutsuin) in 1991.

Sharalyn Orbaugh's essays on women in Japanese literature engage cultural theory with an emphasis on the body—politic, material, and as social construct—as well as build on feminist and postcolonial film theory to address vision, the gaze, and visibility in the social construction of gender and race. She explores issues of race, linguistic identity, gender, and caste in a forthcoming book from Stanford University Press on fiction produced during the Allied Occupation of Japan. She is Assistant Professor of Japanese at the University of California–Berkeley.

Paul Gordon Schalow teaches at Rutgers University and is a member of the East Asian, Comparative Literature, and Women's Studies faculties. The 1993 Rutgers Conference on Japanese Women Writers was an outgrowth of a course he has taught on Japanese women's writing since 1988. His publications include a study and translation of Ihara Saikaku's *The Great Mirror of Male Love* (Stanford University Press, 1990). His current project is a study of male love and friendship in Japanese literature.

John Whittier Treat is Professor of Japanese at the University of Washington and the author of *Writing Ground Zero: Japanese Literature and the Atomic Bomb* (University of Chicago Press, 1995). He has also published essays on the Japanese women writers Ōta Yōko and Yoshimoto Banana. His latest book, on homosexuality and the Western study of Japan, is forthcoming from Oxford University Press.

Meera Viswanathan's research interests are Japanese literature and Japanese thought; she is currently working on a book on modern Japanese aesthetics in the work of Kuki Shūzō, Watsuji Tetsurō, and Origuchi Shinobu. She is Associate Professor of Comparative Literature and East Asian Studies at Brown University.

Janet A. Walker is Associate Professor of Comparative Literature at Rutgers University. She is the author of *The Japanese Novel of the Meiji Period and the Ideal of Individualism* (Princeton, 1979) as well as essays on the classical Japanese woman writer Izumi Shikibu, Japanese autobiography, and the modern non-Western novel. She is currently working on a book on landscape in Meiji fiction.

Michiko N. Wilson is Associate Professor of Japanese and Comparative Literature at the University of Virginia. She has published *The Marginal World of Ōe Kenzaburō: A Study in Themes and Techniques* (M. E. Sharpe, 1986) and is finishing a book on the writings of Ōba Minako. She is the editor of the series Japanese Women Writers in Translation, from M. E. Sharpe, in which her translation of Ōba Minako's novel *Birds Crying* will appear.

The Woman's Hand

Gender and Theory in
Japanese Women's Writing

Introduction

PAUL GORDON SCHALOW
JANET A. WALKER

A collection of essays that takes women's writing as its primary subject assumes a link between gender and discursive practice. Such a linkage has existed from the very beginning in Japanese literature, with the distinction made in the Heian period (794–1185) between vernacular writing (what H. Richard Okada calls "hiragana discourse") done in "the woman's hand" (*onna-de*)[1] and Chinese writing done in "male letters" (*otoko moji*). Although the project of describing how the sex/gender system affects Japanese women's and men's writing has only just begun in North American scholarship, the application of gender criticism to Anglo-European literatures is well under way. Critics have generally defined women's discursive practice in terms of four major gender-related categories or contexts: literary-historical, biological, experiential, and cultural. Accordingly, we have divided the thirteen essays in this volume into four parts. Part I locates women writers within Japanese literary history, Part II shows ways in which modern women writers have "written the body" in Japan, Part III gives examples of tropes and genres used to write about female experience, and Part IV depicts how gender intersects with other social and cultural contexts in Japanese women's writing.

Some three decades ago, feminist and gender criticism began with a set of what now seem like naive assumptions: that one can define a self-evident category called "woman," that women share certain experiences, and that discursive practices proceed from lived experience. The ongoing poststructuralist and deconstructionist critical debates that began in the 1980's called many of these assumptions into question. Experience, authenticity, voice, writer, even "woman" itself—all have been scrutinized, qualified, and sometimes all but abandoned as no more than metaphorical positions. As a result of that critical process, established notions of female identity, history, and culture are rightfully being contested. The aim of this volume is twofold: to inquire into the question of a female perspective and literary practice in Japan in a way that will contribute cross-culturally to a reconceptualization of old notions, and to suggest how theories derived primarily from Western discursive practice can be fruitfully applied in a description of the linkages between gender and writing in Japan.

While respecting the notion that literature is not an unmediated expression of the writer's inner truths and recognizing that women can hardly be called unified, essential beings, we take the critical position that "woman" remains an important and valid idea within literary criticism. The fact that the essays in this volume insist on gender as a critical context for understanding the meaning(s) of texts by women does not suggest that other important contexts do not exist; gender joins race, class, nationality, and history—both personal and national—as one of the many strata in need of excavation for interpreting literary texts. And, although most of the chapters in this volume focus primarily on women's texts, we recognize that both women's and men's texts are the proper subject of gender criticism. We recognize, too, that critical inquiry is a process, not an outcome. It is not our aim that readers of the volume should draw definitive conclusions about the nature of women's writing in Japan from the essays presented here. Rather, we would hope that readers come away with an appreciation of the critical positions the essayists have taken and with a more sophisticated ability to read the complex traces of the sex/gender system in Japanese writing by both women and men.

One often-noted danger of pursuing gender-based readings of texts is that such readings are to some extent inevitably implicated in a limited (and limiting) binary model of maleness and femaleness and that the very concern with gender may inadvertently be a critical playing out of aspects of the sex/gender system that support male domination. Further, gendered readings of texts sometimes make the

Morning Fields (Asano), 1976, by Mitani Toshiko (1904–92). In a long and prolific career, Mitani was known for her distinctive style and for painting only the figures of women and girls. The painting shows two female figures seated back-to-back and looking outward at a field of blooming grasses. In what serves as a fitting metaphor for this volume, their gaze suggests a field expanding limitlessly around them. (National Museum of Modern Art; Kyoto; reproduced by permission of Mitani Aoko)

differences between women and men seem inevitable and essential. But, as Ann Sherif notes in a review of two recent studies of modern Japanese literature that completely ignore women's writing, "considerations of gender can also take the form of bringing to light aspects of literature and culture previously ignored in intellectual inquiry" (202).[2] In its most thoughtful applications, then, gender criticism does not replay or perpetuate the problems it addresses, but works to make the literary history we chart more accurate by bringing the ideas and discursive activities of women into the scope of critical consideration.

The impact of women's practice of literature on literary culture as a whole is, of course, a multifaceted phenomenon, and only a portion of it can be described in a single collection of essays.[3] The present volume concentrates largely on postwar contemporary fiction by women. This focus is linked to the historical dominance of fiction worldwide in the modern era and to the privileging of fiction in modern Japanese literary criticism.[4] The modern critical emphasis on fiction has meant in the case of Japan that women have been described as discursively "silent" during the many centuries between the great efflorescence of writing by court women in the Heian period and the introduction of nineteenth-century European ideas of literature in the Meiji period (1868–1912). If looked at in terms of women's larger relationship to literary culture, however, Japanese women were far from quiet. During the so-called silent centuries, it was itinerant Buddhist nuns who recited the tale of the Soga brothers' vendetta, turning mothers and wives into central heroines of the tale.[5] In the Edo period (1600–1868), numerous women composed *renga* (linked-verse) in competitions independent of men's; dozens of diaries by women survive from the period; and townswomen in the urban centers were ardent readers of literary works of all types.[6] Thus, although women were certainly underrepresented in the production of fiction at the time, other important sorts of relations that women have to literary culture survived and even flourished. The larger relationship of women to literary genres besides fiction may be outside the scope of this collection, but it is our hope that the volume will spur others to give the topic the critical attention it deserves.

Part I: Situating the Woman Writer in Japanese Literature

Each of the three essays in Part I seeks to explain some aspect of the important role of women writers in Japan's literary history dating back to the Heian period. The section begins fittingly with a special address by the prominent contemporary woman writer Ōba Minako (1930–), originally presented at a conference at Rutgers University on Japanese women's writing held in 1993.[7] It describes her lifelong response, first as a reader and then as a writer, to the Heian tradition of women's writing.[8] Her reading of Heian canonical works by women goes against the male critical tradition in its revisionist inter-pretation of *The Kagerō Diary* and *The Pillow Book of Sei Shōnagon*, and it concludes with an appreciation of Murasaki Shikibu's *The Tale of Genji*. For Ōba, the Heian past is a living tradition that both validates her desire to write and provides a model for her exploration of women's experience in her writing.

Ōba's works could be what Noriko Mizuta Lippit was referring to when she noted that "in the context of Japanese literature, the works of modern women writers are the legitimate successors of the literary diaries developed by women writers in the Heian Period" (quoted in Heinrich, 408). But this link to the Heian past has not re-sulted in the acknowledgment of modern women writers as a domi-nant current in modern Japanese literature. In fact, their position is little better than that of American and English women writers, who have no such glorious legacy to draw on. As Masao Miyoshi has stated, "By the time modern Japanese women began their practice in the late nineteenth century, they were as deprived of tutors of their gender as their Euro-American sisters of the eighteenth century. They had to scratch and wrench their space from a male-dominated literary world" ("Women's Short Stories in Japan," 370). Neverthe-less, elements of the Heian legacy have carried over, as the works of a writer like Ōba amply testify. Most significantly, the legacy gives modern women writers a strong proprietary sense toward the Japa-nese literary language, a sense that differs markedly from the often-noted discomfort of European and American women who struggle with an alien, male-dominated language when they write. It would seem that in Japanese women writers' confident ownership of a "woman's language," their discursive experience most diverges from that of non-Japanese women writers.

As many critics have noted, modes of vernacular writing in Japanese were essentially invented by court women in the Heian pe-riod at a time when women were largely excluded from the benefits of literacy in Chinese.[9] Lynne K. Miyake's essay describes the prob-lems and possibilities the association of women with vernacular writing posed for the male courtier Ki no Tsurayuki when he tried to write *The Tosa Diary* in his native Japanese. Tsurayuki's text was more than an attempt to break away from Chinese, the language of the male sphere, and appropriate for his own uses the vernacular, associated with the female sphere; Miyake argues that the text chal-lenges the fundamental dichotomy of male/female and Chinese/

Japanese as gender and linguistic binary opposites and instead inscribes a new literary language that moves fluidly between the two poles. Miyake's provisional acceptance of the dual poles of male and female languages not only is a strategic use of essentialist notions of male and female as two bounded, inviolate entities, but also argues for the inadequacy of the binary scheme and describes *The Tosa Diary* as a challenge to it.

Joan E. Ericson's essay places the emergence of a concept of "women's literature" (as connoting a distinctive style) within its historical and literary context and describes the problematic and shifting relationship of Japanese women writers to the rubric "woman writer." Typically, modes of defining and categorizing writing by women worldwide have been built upon ideas of gendered difference that privilege men's writing and that are constructed and maintained by an overwhelmingly male literary establishment. The predictable result of this situation is that writing by women is marginalized and made to seem substandard or irrelevant. The experience of women writers in modern Japan has been no different in this regard. Ericson's essay shows that a distinct category called "women's literature" was the product of a confluence of social and literary forces in the 1920's and that the category served to promote a certain limited kind of writing by women while discouraging other kinds. The essay concludes that, especially in the past decade, women are increasingly writing and being read in ways that defy categorization by gender.

Part II: Narrating the Body

Some of the most powerful contemporary theories of the link between gender and women's discursive practice emphasize female biology. In the early years of the contemporary feminist project, feminist critics recoiled from biology because of its associations with a severely limited destiny for women; in their view, patriarchal ideology had for too long defined women's bodies so as to support its own narrow concerns, particularly reproduction and child-rearing. But many theorists have since encouraged women to look at biology "as a resource, rather than a destiny" (Rich, 62); they stress the importance of the female body as a sensual ground and a source of imagery for women's writing. Hélène Cixous, in particular, has articulated the critical need for women to write with, and about, their bodies: "Write your self. Your body must be heard. Only then will the immense resources of the unconscious spring forth" (284). Linda Singer, noting that women's experience has until now been largely written by men, seconds Cixous's call to "write the body" and break the silence upon which women's suppression depends:

> Given the relatively monolithic history of masculine hegemony over the sexual, despite variations in the apparatus which secure it, women's sexuality has been represented either as a lack, or as a series of self-interested masculine projections. This has allowed men to construct women in their absence, constructing and re-constructing sexual difference in a way that perpetuates men's position of dominance. By resisting this repressive dynamic through writing, women's discourse can disrupt or subvert a sexual order that has historically depended on our silence. (148)

The three essays in Part II on narrating the body discuss writers in the 1960's and 1970's who broke the silence and claimed the right to self-formulation by "writing the body."

In writing the bodily self, many women writers have been led by their frustration with women's social subordination and their disempowered status to turn inward and to inscribe their own inner worlds or, sometimes, to inscribe a mythic outside world more to their liking. As Patricia Waugh has commented, "Given the acute contradictoriness of women's lives, and sense of subjectivity, it is not surprising that many contemporary women writers have sought to displace their desires, seeking articulation not through the rational and metonymic structures of realism but through the associative and metaphorical modes of fantasy" (171).[10] The dual appeal of fantasy and imagination in women's writing is apparent in these essays on the body. Sharalyn Orbaugh's essay suggests the centrality of the female body in her interpretations of several short stories by Kanai Mieko (1947–), describing how Kanai, as Lucy North puts it, "makes the actuality of female bodies manifest by insisting on the concrete and physical nature of bodies' properties."[11] Orbaugh argues that, through the construction of a fantastic world of violence by and against women that exaggerates and literalizes aspects of the "gender-based power economies," Kanai succeeds in revealing mechanisms of female subordination that would be less obvious in a realistic narrative. Doris G. Bargen, in her discussion of Enchi Fumiko (1905–86), shows that Enchi's story "A Bond for Two Lifetimes: Gleanings" offers women a body-centered spiritual experience that had not been imagined before for women, one that is equivalent to the male experience of entering a trance to circumvent death in Buddhist ascetic self-mummification. And Maryellen Toman Mori's essay on the contemporary writer Takahashi Takako (1932–) demonstrates how Takahashi creates a pseudo-utopian critique of erotic relations between men and women by blurring even bodily boundaries.

Kanai, Enchi, and Takahashi all are shown to employ fantasy or discourses of the imagination to deconstruct gender binarism in their stories. Kanai's rejection of gender dichotomy appears to be highly political: her works create a multidimensional female subjectivity that makes it essentially impossible to identify the polarities of "complicity with" or "subversion of" the existing gender order. Whereas Kanai's bold act of writing the body serves to expose and deflate male (phallic) power, Enchi's literary project in "Gleanings" seems to have been designed more to adopt and subsume male power. By rewriting a classical text by a male author, Enchi takes over male textual prerogatives and thereby demonstrates that, for women, the ability to reproduce *textually* is a subversive alternative to the *sexual* reproduction commonly associated with women. By contrast, Takahashi's subversion of gender dichotomy is accomplished by creating fictional characters who defy categorization as social or sexual agents; they fall outside dichotomous categories such as male and female, heterosexual and homosexual, or they combine elements of several categories in unfamiliar ways. By destroying the binary model, Takahashi allows women to discursively seize phallic power without seizing the phallus and enables them to experience the thrill of a specially feminine bliss (*jouissance*) associated with discomfiture and loss.

In the same way that the fictional works by these Japanese women writers employ discourses of fantasy and imagination to deconstruct gender binarism, all three essayists reject the critical dichotomization of women and men — and the ideology of value associated with it — as inadequate to explain women's writing. Instead of valuing writers (or their fictional characters) on the basis of how subversive they are of male power, as many critics — male and female — of Japanese women's writing have done, Orbaugh asks us to look instead "at the ways women have behaved or could be imagined to behave in the power contexts in which they have found themselves, the ways they have manipulated the discursive elements they found imposed upon them, the strategies they have used to survive and encode their own subjectivities within even the most restrictive of circumstances." Employing the discourse of subversiveness, Masao Miyoshi has argued that the writer Enchi Fumiko "is not an articulate strategist for feminism, nor is she an intellectual speculator on social history. She is thus finally incomplete, inasmuch as she refuses to confront the material historicity of contemporary Japan, taking refuge instead in erotic daydreaming and unresolved discomfiture located in transcendental personalism and aesthetic culturalism" ("Gathering Voices," 209–10). Bargen's analysis of Enchi, however, shows the writer to be far more "complete" (and complex) in her writing of the body than critics searching for subversiveness of male power can realize, given the limits of the subversive/complicit critical model. Finally, Mori's study reveals Takahashi Takako's works as constituting not mere critiques of male power and female subordination but full-fledged deconstructions of the binary gender system, to the extent that they announce both gender identity and individual subjectivity to be based on a set of false distinctions. Just as Takahashi's female characters seize male power only to divest themselves of it, Mori seizes the critical model that values subversion only to abandon it for a model that challenges traditional feminist criticism by collapsing and integrating sexual and gender binarisms.

Part III: Defining the Female Voice

The three essays in Part III explore the expression of women's experience in literature. Meera Viswanathan's essay continues the challenge begun in the previous section to the notions of complicity and resistance, turning now to the haunting figure of the *yamamba* ("mountain witch") as an emblem of thwarted female existence. Viswanathan shows that the literary trajectory of the yamamba leads from the comical and pathetic to the evil and finally to the unredeemed. In both female- and male-authored texts, this movement is motivated by unbearable social constraint and leads to expressions of female self-empowerment through grotesque deformations of "woman." Viswanathan contrasts the contradictory nature of the yamamba's meaning for women with Cixous's "laughing Medusa," who represents a much more positive figure for achieving authentic female being through bodily self-empowerment.

John Whittier Treat's essay on Hayashi Kyōko (1930–) locates the core of her literary imagination in her concern, as a survivor of the atomic bombing of Nagasaki, with the biological future of humankind. The notion that Hayashi, as a woman writer, is logically concerned with reproduction and motherhood suggests the existence of a female imagination, equated here with female biology. As Elaine Showalter notes with regard to English women writers, "The 'female imagination' cannot be treated by literary historians as a romantic or Freudian abstraction. It is the product of a delicate network of influences operating in time, and it must be analyzed as it expresses itself, in language and in a fixed arrangement of words on a page" (12). Treat's essay shows that Hayashi's specific response to the atomic aftermath is ultimately rooted in the irredeemable historical moment of "ground zero," and he further raises the possibility that the soil of ground zero nourishes the woman writer of atomic bomb literature in ways different from the male writer.

The idea of a female *Bildungsroman*, or "novel of development," has received considerable critical attention in recent years.[12] Michiko Niikuni Wilson looks at the genre of the Bildungsroman to explore the issue of resistance as a specifically female mode of development. Analyzing two major novels by Ōba Minako, Wilson argues that whereas the traditional novel of development culminates in a male character's integration into society, the telos of Ōba's female-centered Bildungsroman is one of ongoing resistance to social integration. Wilson concludes that in literature and in life a woman becomes herself by continually and continuously "unbecoming" what others would have her be.

All three essays identify historically sanctioned modes within the Japanese literary tradition for the expression of women's experience. Viswanathan points to the yamamba trope, which had its origins in preliterate storytelling traditions and entered the literary genres of high narrative, popular song, and drama (as well as the visual arts) from late Heian onward. The trope was revived in the fiction of several modern women writers, in particular Ōba Minako, who, according to Mizuta Noriko, "has written in several works about those aspects of female sexuality and existence that defy containment within the system by contrasting 'domesticated' women who live in villages with yamamba-like women who live deep in the mountains" (Ōba and Mizuta, 141). Wilson demonstrates that another aspect of Ōba's work — namely, its focus on private experience — is a conscious return to the expression of the personal, especially concerning female-male relations, first found in tales (*monogatari*) and diaries (or memoirs, *nikki*) by women of the Heian court. If modern women writers such as

Ōba can be said to have given new life to the yamamba trope and women's genres of writing from the Heian period, Hayashi Kyōko can be said to have reached back even further into the historical and tribal past, for Treat shows that she has consciously resuscitated the ancient communal function of the ritual reciter (*kataribe*), who speaks repetitively and sonorously of the historical events of the tribe, lest they be forgotten.

Each of these essays suggests that there are profound implications for literature when women, not men, write about women's lives. The yamamba confronts male-centered social and literary ideology with a literary image of the deformed female creatures that such an ideology breeds; she is a reminder to the body politic of what happens to a certain kind of woman, and perhaps (as Ōba's interpretation of the trope suggests) to *every* woman, in a world where women cannot speak their minds. Hayashi's atomic bomb literature critiques the achieving of war's goals by means that court biological catastrophe and gives a woman's reasons why nuclear war must happen "never again." Finally, Wilson's essay demonstrates that Ōba's vision of men and women willing to abandon traditional gender roles and to work instead to nurture each other has literary implications; if women and men step beyond the gender binarism of male discourse, it may eventually lead to conditions that will allow a fuller expression of female (and male) experience, as yet unimagined in literature.

Part IV: Locating "Woman" in Culture

The essays in Part IV discuss women in various cultural contexts beginning with immediate postwar Japan and extending into the 1990's. Each of the essays raises interesting critical problems that result when women's texts are considered in the light of the intersection of gender and other ideological structures. Noriko Mizuta's essay explores women's experience in colonial, wartime, and postwar contexts, arguing that the ideology of gender binarism creates separate destinies for men and women both as colonizers and as citizens of a defeated nation. Whereas Mizuta is concerned with the intersection of gender and the ideology of imperialism, Chieko M. Ariga reveals how gender interconnects with male critical hegemony. Ariga shows how a critical establishment that is almost exclusively male consistently employs a discourse of universalism in reading women's texts, and how that discourse serves to erase the specificity of women's experience. Livia Monnet uses Tsushima Yūko's (1947–)

story "The Chrysanthemum Beetle" to critique the centuries-old patriarchal construction of female jealousy; at the intersection of gender
and jealousy, Monnet discovers philosophical questions regarding
victimhood and subjectivity. Nina Cornyetz's essay foregrounds the
link between gender and racial ideologies by focusing on Yamada
Eimi's (1959–) depiction of relationships between Japanese women
and African-American men, and she suggests that Yamada's exercise
of female discursive power may serve to objectify others in the same
way that women have been objectified in male power relations.

Mizuta's essay continues the critical exploration begun by Treat's
essay into the impact of war on women, this time in the fiction of Hayashi Fumiko (1903–51). It also explores the question of female personal and literary development in regard to the genre of the Bildungsroman. In contrast to Wilson's essay on Ōba Minako, in which
Ōba's *Birds Crying* is described as a successful woman-centered
novel of development, Mizuta concludes that Hayashi Fumiko saw
no potential for female development within male discourse in the
immediate postwar period, and identifies Hayashi's *Drifting Clouds*
as a female anti-Bildungsroman.

Both Monnet and Cornyetz return in their essays to the issue of
fantasy, a mode of women's writing first discussed in Part II with regard to the fiction of Kanai Mieko, Enchi Fumiko, and Takahashi
Takako. In the case of Cornyetz, Yamada Eimi's fiction is shown to
fetishize African-American men as a fantasy "other," who, by virtue
of being unrooted in the Japanese context, can be inscribed as easily
as a blank slate. Monnet, too, addresses the question of fantasy and
otherness and shows how, within an essentially realistic mode of fiction, Tsushima uses fantasy (and especially the fantasy of humans
becoming insects) to critique modern humanistic subjectivity and encourage readers to view their place in the world from outside themselves, in the margins.

✄

In conclusion, the thirteen chapters in this volume represent an
exercise in the gendered reading of texts. Each chapter affirms that
the idea of "woman" is important within literary criticism, yet each
also works to show how little about that category can be taken as
self-evident. In this volume, Japanese women's texts (and subtexts)
are discussed not only in relation to maleness (textual and otherwise)
but on their own terms and with a sure sense of relevance that is
usually reserved for writing by men. What emerges is not a mono-

lithic or essentialist image of the feminine in Japanese literature, but an image characterized by such variety and difference that it opens and defamiliarizes the very notion of gender around which the volume is organized. The volume clarifies the impact of the sex-gender system on women's writing in Japan and introduces the specific literary contexts in which Japanese women have historically found themselves, but—and most important—it embodies a multidimensional sense of "woman" that brings with it a critical framework less implicated in the existing gender order. When critics practice gendered reading while simultaneously questioning the ideology of gender binarism, as they have in this volume, they are able to chart a new and fuller history of gender's impact on discursive expression.

Notes

1. Elsewhere, the term *onna-de* (sometimes read *onna-te* or *onna no te*) has been rendered as "the female hand" (Bowring) and "the feminine hand" (Okada; see esp. chap. 6, "Situating the Feminine Hand," 159–182).

2. The studies addressed in Sherif's review article, "The Canon with a Critical Difference," are David Pollack's *Reading Against Culture* (1992) and James A. Fujii's *Complicit Fictions* (1993).

3. For a broad discussion of the relation of Japanese women writers to their social and literary milieu, see Vernon, esp. Part II, "Texts and Contexts," 33–134.

4. The focus on fiction is true also of most Anglo-American feminist critics of women's writing. Besides the ground-breaking studies of Showalter, Moers, and Gilbert and Gubar noted in the Preface, notable studies include Carby; Christian; De Jean; Miles; Spencer; Spender; and Todd. For a theoretical account of how the novel came to dominate "world" literary culture, see Moses. For a brief comparative account of the rise of the novel form in several countries of the non-Western world, including Japan, from the last century or so, see Walker.

5. For the early oral transmission by Buddhist nuns of the Soga story, see Kominz.

6. For further discussion of these exceptions during the centuries when women were "silent," see Chapter 3, by Joan E. Ericson, in this volume, pp. 74–115.

7. See McKeon for a summary of the conference, known as the Rutgers Conference on Japanese Women Writers, and its significance for the field of Japanese literary studies.

8. The Meiji period writer Higuchi Ichiyō responded to the Heian tradition in a very different way; see Danly, esp. 19–20, 60–61.

9. For an exciting and provocative essay on the philosophical implica-

tions for Japanese culture as a whole of having a literary tradition founded by women, see Miller. In contrast to the widespread acknowledgment of the important role of women writers in shaping vernacular fiction in its early stages in Japan, Joan De Jean, in her study *Tender Geographies*, has to work against the European assumption of the masculine origins of literary forms when she argues that aristocratic women writers of the seventeenth century invented the French novel.

10. Susan J. Napier brought this quote to our attention in her response to Meera Viswanathan's paper, "In Pursuit of the Yamamba," at the 1993 Rutgers Conference on Japanese Women Writers.

11. Lucy North, respondent's remarks on Sharalyn Orbaugh's paper "The 'Body' in Fiction by Japanese Women" at the Rutgers Conference on Japanese Women Writers. North went on to argue that Kanai's stories do not stop with presenting the female body and sexuality literally, but "in fact *open themselves out* to psychoanalytic interpretation" through their "*literalizing* of a psychoanalytic theory" (author's emphasis).

12. For a useful introductory essay and annotated bibliography, see Fuderer.

Works Cited

Bowring, Richard. "The Female Hand in Heian Japan: A First Reading." In *The Female Autograph: Theory and Practice of Autobiography from the Tenth to the Twentieth Century*, ed. Domna C. Stanton. Chicago: University of Chicago Press, 1987, 49–56.

Carby, Hazel V. *Reconstructing Womanhood: The Emergence of the Afro-American Woman Novelist*. New York: Oxford University Press, 1989.

Christian, Barbara. *Black Women Novelists: The Development of a Tradition*. Westport, Conn.: Greenwood Press, 1980.

Cixous, Hélène. "The Laugh of the Medusa." Trans. Keith Cohen and Paula Cohen. In *The Signs Reader: Women, Gender & Scholarship*, ed. Elizabeth Abel and Emily K. Abel. Chicago: University of Chicago Press, 1983, 279–97.

Danly, Robert Lyons. *In the Shade of Spring Leaves: The Life and Writings of Higuchi Ichiyō, a Woman of Letters in Meiji Japan*. New Haven: Yale University Press, 1981.

De Jean, Joan. *Tender Geographies: Women and the Origins of the Novel in France*. New York: Columbia University Press, 1991.

Fuderer, Laura Sue. *The Female Bildungsroman in English: An Annotated Bibliography of Criticism*. New York: MLA, 1990.

Fujii, James A. *Complicit Fictions: The Subject in Modern Japanese Prose Narrative*. Berkeley: University of California Press, 1993.

Heinrich, Amy Vladeck. "Double Weave: The Fabric of Japanese Women's Writing." *World Literature Today*, special issue: *Contemporary Japanese Literature* 62, no. 3 (Summer 1988): 408–14.

Kominz, Laurence R. *Avatars of Vengeance: Japanese Drama and the Soga Literary Tradition.* Ann Arbor: University of Michigan, Center for Japanese Studies, 1995.

McKeon, Midori Yamamoto. "Amerika ni okeru Nihon josei bungaku kenkyū no dōkō." *Nichibei josei jānaru* 14 (1993): 35–52.

Miles, Rosalind. *The Female Form: Women Writers and the Conquest of the Novel.* London: Routledge & Kegan Paul, 1987.

Miller, Mara. "Canons and the Challenge of Gender: Women's Voices in the Japanese Canon." *The Monist: An International Journal of General Philosophical Inquiry* 76, no. 4 (Oct. 1993): 477–93.

Miyoshi, Masao. "Gathering Voices: Japanese Women and Women Writers." *Off Center: Power and Culture Relations Between Japan and the United States.* Cambridge, Mass.: Harvard University Press, 1991, 189–216.

———. "Women's Short Stories in Japan." *Mānoa* 3, no. 2 (Fall 1991): 33–39.

Moses, Michael Valdez. *The Novel and the Globalization of Culture.* New York: Oxford University Press, 1995.

Ōba Minako and Mizuta Noriko. *Yamauba no iru fūkei.* Tokyo: Tabata shoten, 1995.

Okada, H. Richard. *Figures of Resistance: Language, Poetry, and Narrating in "The Tale of Genji" and Other Mid-Heian Texts.* Durham, N.C.: Duke University Press, 1991.

Pollack, David. *Reading Against Culture: Ideology and Narrative in the Japanese Novel.* Ithaca, N.Y.: Cornell University Press, 1992.

Rich, Adrienne. *Of Woman Born: Motherhood as Experience and Institution.* New York: W. W. Norton, 1976.

Sherif, Ann. "The Canon with a Critical Difference." Review of *Complicit Fictions: The Subject in Modern Japanese Prose Narrative*, by James A. Fujii; and *Reading Against Culture: Ideology and Narrative in the Japanese Novel*, by David Pollack. *Journal of the Association of Teachers of Japanese* 28, no. 2 (Nov. 1994): 195–208.

Showalter, Elaine. *A Literature of Their Own: British Women Novelists from Brontë to Lessing.* Princeton: Princeton University Press, 1977.

Singer, Linda. "True Confessions: Cixous and Foucault on Sexuality and Power." In *Erotic Welfare: Sexual Theory and Politics in the Age of Epidemic*, ed. and intro. Judith Butler and Maureen MacGrogan. New York: Routledge, 1993, 145–62.

Spencer, Jane. *The Rise of the Woman Novelist: From Aphra Behn to Jane Austen.* Oxford: Blackwell, 1986.

Spender, Dale. *Mothers of the Novel: 100 Good Women Writers Before Jane Austen.* Oxford: Blackwell, 1986.

Todd, Janet. *The Sign of Angellica: Women, Writing, and Fiction, 1660-1800.* London: Virago, 1989.

Vernon, Victoria V. *Daughters of the Moon: Wish, Will, and Social Constraint in Fiction by Modern Japanese Women.* Japan Research Monograph 9. Berkeley: University of California, Institute of East Asian Studies, 1988.

Walker, Janet A. "On the Applicability of the Term 'Novel' to Modern Non-Western Long Fiction." *Yearbook of Comparative and General Literature* 37 (1988): 47–68.

Waugh, Patricia. *Feminist Fictions: Revisiting the Postmodern*. London: Routledge, 1989.

Part I

Situating the Woman Writer in Japanese Literature

1

Special Address:
Without Beginning, Without End

ŌBA MINAKO

I have come to Rutgers University today to speak about a literature written by women in Heian Japan almost 1,000 years ago.* I am
now sixty-two years old, and as I discuss women's writing from that
period, I will be remembering the events of almost fifty years ago,
when I was a schoolgirl of twelve or thirteen.

In those days, the whole world was caught up in war. As a result, schoolgirls like myself were forced to perform physical labor for
eleven hours a day, sewing military uniforms. We had little or no
interest in the great war itself, and perhaps because we were so
young, we had no idea what the war was all about. But one thing we
did know: under no circumstances were we to talk honestly about
what we were thinking or feeling. I also knew that the books we
were allowed to read and talk about in public were of absolutely no
interest to me; I found books written 1,000 years earlier to be far
more interesting, books such as Murasaki Shikibu's *Genji monogatari*
(The tale of Genji).

At the time, literature from the West was banned in Japan. I remember once being roundly scolded for bringing copies of Thomas
Hardy's *Tess of the D'Urbervilles* and Flaubert's *Madame Bovary* to

---

*Editors' note: This essay was originally presented in Japanese with English translation as a
special address at the Rutgers Conference on Japanese Women Writers in New Brunswick,
New Jersey, April 10, 1993. Japanese title: "Hajime mo naku, owari mo naku." English translation by Paul Gordon Schalow.

school. The books were confiscated, for they were thought to be immoral, dangerous works. The Japanese authorities were ignorant of their own country's literature, however, and thus thought nothing of allowing us schoolgirls to read far more dangerous works, such as *The Tale of Genji*. Perhaps they were unaware of the work's subversive power because of its venerable history of being used to teach etiquette and manners to young ladies.

From an early age, I spent most of my time reading the old romances, myths, and novels of world literature. I suppose that I was fairly sophisticated in that regard. In contrast, when it came to conventional social values, I was a bit of a simpleton. What concerned me as a child was what motivated the people in my life. I was sensitive to how they were feeling—whether they were sad or suffering, happy or angry, satisfied or not—but other issues escaped me entirely. Looking back on it now, I guess you could say that I was fundamentally out of touch with the values of the day. And my sense of alienation only increased, for I soon reached the age when adolescents begin to doubt the conventions by which adults live their lives.

The war ended when I was fourteen. By then, much of the Japanese landmass was scorched earth. Shortly thereafter, I went to Tokyo to attend college. My favorite book during this period was *Makura no sōshi* (The pillow book) by Sei Shōnagon. Several chapters from *The Pillow Book* have come to mind at various times throughout my life, each time awakening new responses in me in keeping with my age and experience. The process of finding new meaning in passages read long ago continues to this day.

Among the wonderful passages that take on deeper meaning with every passing year are these:

Chapter 167: Things that are near, though distant: relations between a man and a woman (*The Pillow Book*, 181).

Chapter 260: Things that pass unnoticed: the years of one's life; spring, summer, autumn, winter.

Chapter 261: Things that we are apt to forget: a mother who has grown old.

I see something timeless in these passages, and I recognize myself in them. No matter how many times I read such passages, they always remain vivid and fresh.

As a girl of fifteen or sixteen, when I first read chapter 63, which describes a man leaving the side of a woman the morning after making love, I glossed over it because it made no sense to me. But now, having reached my present age, I burst out laughing every time I read it:

> A lover who is leaving at dawn announces that he has to find his fan and his paper. "I know I put them somewhere last night," he says. Since it is pitch dark, he gropes about the room, bumping into the furniture and muttering, "Strange! Where on earth can they be?" Finally he discovers the objects. He thrusts the paper into the breast of his robe with a great rustling sound; then he snaps open his fan and busily fans away with it. Only now is he ready to take his leave. What charmless behavior! "Hateful" is an understatement.
>
> A good lover will behave as elegantly at dawn as at any other time. He drags himself out of bed with a look of dismay on his face. The lady urges him on: "Come, my friend, it's getting light. You don't want anyone to find you here." He gives a deep sigh, as if to say that the night had not been nearly long enough and that it is an agony to leave. Once up, he does not instantly pull on his trousers. Instead he comes close to the lady and whispers whatever was left unsaid during the night. Even when he is dressed, he still lingers, vaguely pretending to be fastening his sash.
>
> Presently he raises the lattice, and the two lovers stand together by the side door while he tells her how he dreads the coming day, which will keep them apart; then he slips away. The lady watches him go, and this moment of parting will remain among her most charming memories.
>
> Indeed, one's attachment to a man depends largely on the elegance of his leave-taking. When he jumps out of bed, scurries about the room, tightly fastens his trouser sash, rolls up the sleeves of his court cloak, overrobe, or hunting costume, stuffs his belongings into the breast of his robe and then briskly secures his outer sash — one really begins to hate him. (*The Pillow Book*, 49–50)

Each of the famous scenes and phrases in *The Pillow Book* represents an aesthetic response to a variety of objects, contrived by nature or man, such as flowering trees, birds, grasses, trees, temples, islands, or flutes; and Sei Shōnagon makes of her response a twofold narrative, which she tells with spontaneity and ease. One is the narrative of the fading, changing world of man and nature; side by side with this is the story of our unchanging human response to that world. It is a timeless technique, for even now, in modern-day Japan, we find ordinary people from their teens to old age who read *The Pillow Book* with great pleasure a thousand years after it was written.[1]

The past several decades have been characterized as the age of feminism, a brilliant new age of revolution in the way women live their lives; yet listen to what Sei Shōnagon had to say in chapter 21 regarding the way women should live:

> When I think of women who live dependent on their husbands—women without a single hopeful prospect in life yet who believe that they are perfectly happy—I cannot help but feel impatient and upset with them. Often they are of quite good birth, yet have had no opportunity to find out what the world is like. I wish they could live for a while in society, even if it should mean taking service as an attendant at court, so that they might come to know the delights life has to offer.
>
> Men believe that women serving in the palace are bound to become corrupted by it, but court service provides a woman with opportunities to meet the imperial majesties, high court nobles, senior courtiers, and other gentlemen of rank; and to learn about the world.[2]

In a flash, 1,000 years have flowed by, and now most modern-day women suddenly find themselves living in a way once reserved for women in court service.

There are many examples in Sei Shōnagon's writing where the intensity of her gaze makes it possible to visualize what she sees with a startling clarity. Unlike the writer Murasaki Shikibu, whose genius lies in her ability to depict the interior world, Sei Shōnagon is especially skilled at making the exterior world come alive. Her writing has a striking vitality and freshness that hints at the very essence of life. Surely, it is this freshness and vitality that has made *The Pillow Book* so beloved of the Japanese people.

Sei Shōnagon was born in the middle of the Heian period, in about the year 965 or 966, into the Kiyowara clan of middle-ranking courtiers. From her late twenties, starting in about 993, she served the sixty-sixth emperor, Ichijō, and his consort, Teishi (Sadako), for a period of approximately eight years. The thoughts that she jotted down during her term of service were collated (possibly by herself, or someone close to her) and circulated at court from about the year 1001 as "The Pillow Book of Sei Shōnagon."

The Pillow Book consists of over 300 chapters, some diary-like, others essayistic, still others made up of lists of things such as the names of flowers or trees. Some chapters are a mere sentence or two in length; others go on for pages. They are organized with great skill in what would seem to be a deliberate attempt to avoid unity and predictability.

In *The Pillow Book,* Sei Shōnagon never once mentions the politically difficult situation of the consort, Teishi, whom she served. Instead, she depicts court life as sumptuous and bright, in a style overflowing with intelligence and wit. By doing so, she creates a counterpoint for the deep tragedy of her consort's existence.

What Sei Shōnagon most wanted to do in *The Pillow Book,* it seems to me, was to comment on the peculiar position of highborn women in her day, as exemplified by the consort Teishi. I am referring here to the custom among Fujiwara clan heads of marrying their daughters to emperors in order to consolidate control over future emperors, their grandsons. A Fujiwara woman thus became an imperial consort to suit her father's political ambitions, and any consort who suffered the misfortune of losing her powerful father immediately became vulnerable to the ambitions of rival clansmen and was in danger of displacement. This is exactly what happened to Teishi.

Teishi was the daughter of Fujiwara Michitaka, eldest son of the powerful Fujiwara chieftain, Kaneie. After Michitaka's death in 995, Teishi's eldest brother, Korechika, lost out in a power struggle with their uncle Michinaga for leadership of the Fujiwara clan. Along with leadership of the clan came de facto control of the court and nation. Michinaga promptly made the bold move of naming his own daughter Shōshi (Akiko) consort to Emperor Ichijō, creating a rivalry that continued until Teishi's death in 1001 at the tender age of 24. Teishi left behind a royal prince who was prevented from ever becoming emperor, whereas the two sons born to Shōshi later became the emperors Go-Ichijō and Go-Suzaku. Readers of the day would have been aware of these events as they read *The Pillow Book.* It is the beauty of the textual world, juxtaposed simultaneously in the reader's mind with the tragedy of the extra-textual world, that gives *The Pillow Book* its resonance and power.

This is not to say that Sei Shōnagon's depiction of the court is completely positive, however. There are hints of shadows in even the brightest world. Chapter 9, for example, tells the story of a dog named Okinamaro who is nearly beaten to death for chasing the imperial cat. Chapter 87 shows a forlorn Teishi living in seclusion in the palace after her father's death, making a game of guessing when a mountain of snow in her garden will melt away; and there is the haunting story of a beggar nun who comes repeatedly to the empress's quarters. Each of these scenes is symbolic of a peculiar terror lurking in the background. Undoubtedly, Sei Shōnagon intended for readers to draw a parallel between Teishi's fate and the depiction of singular events beyond her control.[3]

Next, I turn to *Kagerō nikki* (The kagerō diary; trans. as "The Gossamer Years" by Edward Seidensticker), which preceded *The Pillow Book* by one generation. The author of *The Kagerō Diary* is known to posterity only by the name Michitsuna no Haha (the Mother of [Fujiwara no] Michitsuna). She was a secondary wife of Fujiwara Kaneie, the Fujiwara clan head and father of Michitaka and Michinaga. (Kaneie was therefore the grandfather of the consorts Teishi and Shōshi mentioned earlier.) The Mother of Michitsuna died in 995, situating her one generation before Sei Shōnagon.

Kaneie was, as we have seen, the most powerful man of his day. As you may know, polygyny was not unusual in those days. The position a wife held vis-à-vis her husband's other wives was determined by a number of factors, including her father's prominence, her own intelligence and education, and the number of worthy children she bore. It was on the basis of such factors that her position as wife was established, both by her husband and by popular opinion at court. Their judgment, and therefore her relative position as wife, was fluid and capable of shifting over time. Similarly, wives had the right to judge a husband based on his merits, and they were free to leave him and marry someone more powerful or more successful, if they so desired. At the point when Kaneie married Tokihime and the Mother of Michitsuna, the two women were on an equal footing; only later did Tokihime come to occupy the position of principal wife.

The secret of Tokihime's success lay in the fact that she bore many children, among them two sons of great talent, Michitaka and Michinaga; and a daughter, Senshi, who became consort to the Emperor En'yū and the mother of the Emperor Ichijō. Consequently, Kaneie's love for her was great. By contrast, the author of *The Kagerō Diary* had only one child, Michitsuna, and thus could not compete successfully for the top position as Kaneie's principal wife. Kaneie had taken the author of *The Kagerō Diary* as wife when already married to Tokihime, and he would have relations with several other women in the course of his twenty or more years with her.

The author of *The Kagerō Diary* was the first to take her internal

Ōba Minako, 1994 (Photograph courtesy Ōba Minako)

struggle and suffering as a woman and make of it a literature of the self, characterized by a strong sense of personality and individuality. It has been said that the origins of the *shishōsetsu* ("I-novel") in Japan can be traced to *The Kagerō Diary*. In the history of Japanese literature, it is at any rate the first prose work to vividly record a woman's interior world.

A poem from the work is included in the thirteenth-century waka collection, *Hyakunin isshu* (Single poems by 100 poets):

> To lie alone the whole night through, waiting for dawn;
> how slowly time passes — do you know how it feels?[4]

The poem is the complaint of a neglected woman, and even today many Japanese women can recite it from memory (it is a handy phrase for confronting a man with one's feelings of anger). The Mother of Michitsuna sent the poem to Kaneie one morning shortly after their marriage; she had refused to open the door to him the night before because she had just learned that he was seeing another woman, known as the "woman in the back alley."

In those days, marriage simply meant that the man accepted as a son-in-law would visit a woman at her parents' home, at least at the start; if his visits became infrequent or stopped entirely, the marriage was dissolved. A man who had achieved prominence socially sometimes established a separate household where he lived with his wife, but it was rare for newlyweds to live together in a separate household.

Kaneie's response to the poem is remarkable in its own right:

> Of course I know how it feels: It is no pleasure to
>   wait endlessly
> at a door that never opens — winter night or not.[5]

This response by Kaneie is set late in the tenth or early in the eleventh month, just when temperatures were beginning to get cold, and it shows the disarming, possibly insincere, qualities that made him the outstanding leader he would become. In any case, the poem by the Mother of Michitsuna shows the courage and pluck of a woman who dares to compete as an equal with a man who might be called the political star of his day; what is even more intriguing, it overflows with her clever ability to excite her husband's interest.

The numerous poetic exchanges between Kaneie and the Mother of Michitsuna, of which this one is representative, are thrilling to read. They remind me of a one-on-one ball game, where one side lobs the ball and the other side tries desperately to return it. With Kaneie busy with his other women and seeming to have forgotten her, the Mother of Michitsuna sets off on a pilgrimage to remote Hatsuse (Hasedera, a temple south of Nara founded in 686). On the way home, who should meet her halfway but Kaneie and his retinue, coming as far as Uji, midway on the trip, to escort her back to the capital. This grand display of attention from Kaneie was possible because of his position as a political star, and surely the Mother of Michitsuna was eager to preserve the moment in her writing, since such attention from him enhanced her own status.

During her pilgrimage to the Narutaki Temple at Nishiyama, in the northern part of Kyoto, a rumor makes the rounds that the Mother of Michitsuna intends to take the tonsure and become a nun, an action she has indeed begun to consider seriously. In the female protagonist's innermost mind, the anger and pain she feels toward her husband over his treatment of her for the almost twenty years of their marriage affect her so deeply that her health begins to suffer. Severely ill, she goes so far as to write a last will and testament. Even after her recovery, days pass when all she wants to do is die. Constantly beset by worry over Kaneie's latest affair, she reflects back on her years of dissatisfaction, when she was forced to listen as Kaneie's carriage passed by her gate without stopping. Small wonder that she should consider becoming a nun in order to escape such suffering. Her retreat to the temple is cut short, however, by Kaneie's ostentatious arrival to take her home; his grand display of power, plus the continuous stream of gifts he sends to her at the temple, convinces her to return to the sad life she had been living in the capital.

Eventually, Michitsuna's mother agrees to take in and raise a daughter of Kaneie's by another woman. The female protagonist is nearly forty years old when she moves back to her father's home. Her relationship with Kaneie has quietly come to an end. He still sends her his sewing, indicating that perhaps he continued to provide her with some sort of financial support.

Be that as it may, we as readers are left with two questions: Why does such a talented woman spend her days in an agony of resentment toward her husband? As a woman of such high status and intelligence, couldn't she have figured out a better way to live her life, even if it meant serving at court as a lady-in-waiting? The story is written is such a way as to suggest that she chose to spend her days in this manner and to cling to her position as the wife of a man of power and influence.[6] *The Kagerō Diary* is the honest and courageous confession of a woman's experience. Without it, we would know virtually nothing about the reality of a high-born lady's inner life in this period.

Of the three writers, the Mother of Michitsuna, Sei Shōnagon, and Murasaki Shikibu, the author of *The Kagerō Diary* was the earliest. One could say that, within the flow of history, Sei Shōnagon and Murasaki Shikibu studied the way this pioneer lived her life, and chose to live theirs differently. Perhaps it is because of the diary's powerful message, "A woman's life should not be spent this way," that it has been so greatly appreciated over the centuries. The Mother of Michitsuna's literary depiction of her jealousy, that primal human emotion, reveals the impact of Heian Japan's polygynous marriage structure on male-female relations and hints at a larger movement away from ancient matriarchal social forms toward patriarchal ones.

This brings us, finally, to *The Tale of Genji*, written by a woman and acknowledged worldwide as Japan's most celebrated literary achievement. The author of *The Tale of Genji*, Murasaki Shikibu, was born, like the Mother of Michitsuna and Sei Shōnagon, into a family of the provincial governor class. She is thought to have been only in her forties when she died, probably between the years 1014 and 1025. She was married late for her day, when she was 27 or 28, to a man much senior to herself, who was also from the provincial governor class. The man died soon after, and about the year 1004 she entered the service of Emperor Ichijō's consort Shōshi. Shōshi, you will remember, was the daughter of Michinaga, who had been in competition with Emperor Ichijō's other consort, Teishi, whom Sei Shōnagon served. By this time, Teishi and her father Michitaka had already died, and political power had passed into Michinaga's hands.

Keep in mind that a woman writer such as Murasaki Shikibu did not appear on the scene spontaneously, any more than Ōba Minako spontaneously appeared on today's literary scene. She was nurtured on the dreams dreamed by her foremothers, the women writers who came before her.

In her diary, Murasaki Shikibu left the following well-known criticism of Sei Shōnagon:

> Sei Shōnagon has the most extraordinary air of self-satisfaction. Yet, if we stop to examine those Chinese writings of hers that she so presumptuously scatters about the place, we find that they are full of imperfections. Someone who makes such an effort to be different from others is bound to fall in people's esteem, and I can only think that her future will be a hard one. She is a gifted woman, to be sure. Yet if one gives free rein to one's emotions even under the most inappropriate circumstances, if one has to sample each interesting thing that comes along, people are bound to regard one as frivolous. And how can things turn out well for such a woman? (quoted in *The Pillow Book*, 9)

For years, these comments have been widely discussed by scholars, but I would like to reconsider their significance today. Although Murasaki Shikibu disparages Sei Shōnagon in this passage, a comparison of *The Pillow Book* and *The Tale of Genji* reveals the extraordinary debt that she owes Sei Shōnagon as a writer.

The Tale of Genji depicts the inner workings of the human mind with an almost frightening accuracy and subtlety. Murasaki Shikibu was able to write in this way because she was extremely sensitive to the part that her predecessor Sei Shōnagon had carefully kept hidden: namely, the dark side of human nature, which Sei Shōnagon may have wanted to write about but could not. It was this extraordinary sensitivity that allowed her to discern the hidden patterns of the human psyche that Sei Shōnagon had felt compelled to record in *The Pillow Book*. Moreover, in the structure of her literary works, the influence of the even earlier *Kagerō Diary* is clearly visible. That is to say, when the woman's anger and suffering in *The Kagerō Diary*, which was born from her powerful, individual need to speak for herself, is superimposed on the apparently civilized, aestheticized world of *The Pillow Book*, what emerges is this masterpiece, *The Tale of Genji*.

It is commonly said that Murasaki Shikibu had a dark, complex, introverted nature, whereas Sei Shōnagon was by nature a bright, uncomplicated extrovert, but I for one would argue that, in terms of complexity and intelligence, Sei Shōnagon has a thoroughness and precision that is, if not superior, then at least equal to that of Murasaki Shikibu.

Perhaps we can call *The Tale of Genji* a literary blend of what preceded it, since it carries within it the echoes of *The Kagerō Diary*, *The Pillow Book*, and other works. The work is divided into two parts, the first part being the story of a "shining" superhero, Hikaru Genji, and his loves. Genji was born a royal prince but was destined to live his life outside the imperial succession as a high-ranking courtier. The second part of the work, the final ten Uji chapters, is the story of two men and their loves: Kaoru, thought to be Genji's son, is in fact the product of Genji's wife the Third Princess's illicit union with Kashiwagi; the other man is Niou, Genji's grandson. The pleasure of this section is less in the plot of the story than in the murmuring voices of ancient female spirits audible here and there between the lines — lines written by a medium, Murasaki Shikibu, whom they have entered.

When I came to the United States for the first time in the late 1950's (and in those days, it was not as easy to go back and forth between the two countries as it is now), the only two Japanese books I carried with me were *The Tale of Genji* and Bashō's *Oku no hosomichi* (The narrow road to the deep north).[7] While I lived in this country, I would open these books and read at random from them whenever I had the chance. Each time I did so, I discovered something new.

The Tale of Genji is that kind of book. It has a strange newness that touches one beyond time and place. In fact, in Japan today, the most avid readers of *The Tale of Genji* are not scholars and researchers, but ordinary housewives, young girls, middle-aged women, and elderly men and women.[8]

To get back to the main point, the heroines who appear in the pages of The Tale of Genji stand uncomfortably within the value system of their time. In the way they are narrated, they appear as sad, seductive, and sometimes humorous, in a blending of the eternal and the changing. None of the depictions of the women in Genji's life strikes the reader as a characterization of a happy woman: not Genji's official wife, Lady Aoi; nor, after Aoi's death, his second official wife, the Third Princess; nor his unofficial wife, Lady Murasaki, who for all practical purposes acts as his principal wife. On the surface Genji seems to care for these women, but in actuality they suffer constantly from Genji's infidelity; they exist for mere decoration, like pretty flowers, to enhance the prestige of a man of power.

The female characters who have a brilliance, a strange beauty, and a romantic quality befitting the heroine of a monogatari (tale) are those who lived outside the values and conventions of their time: Oborozukiyo, Lady Rokujō, Yūgao, and Ukifune. Oborozukiyo is engaged to marry the crown prince, but nevertheless pursues an affair with Genji. Lady Rokujō is an aristocrat of impeccable breeding and good taste, but she is jealous of Genji's relations with other women, and in life and in death, her spirit becomes a possessive demon that takes possession of Genji's women, killing Aoi and Yūgao. Later, it even possesses Murasaki.

A woman's jealous hatred transforms itself into a murderous demon, becomes detached from the jealous woman herself, and takes on a life of its own, capable of making Lady Rokujō herself cringe in terror. Most important, others imagine that such a thing can occur, and spirit possession thereby becomes an important theme in Japanese literature. In other words, when Lady Aoi is possessed, her attendants believe it is the living spirit of Lady Rokujō that is killing her, and Lady Rokujō looks at herself in horror and disgust, wondering if indeed it isn't her spirit that is possessing and finally killing Aoi. Not only in the case of the living spirit or dead spirit of Lady Rokujō, but throughout anything called a monogatari, subjectivity and objectivity coexist in a complex blend; the author's face emerges eerily at odd moments, then disappears. The lack of grammatical subjects is a special characteristic of this writing. Things are expressed in a way that blends hearsay and the author's imagination, through phrases such as "they say that" or "apparently" that convey with extreme vagueness the origin of the tale or the identity of its narrator.

As a child I grew up reading old tales such as this, and at a certain point I came to believe that the strange beauty of this narrative mode was especially suited to the Japanese disposition. Now and then, I, too, believed that I could feel a spirit, like Lady Rokujō's, living inside me.

In any case, *The Tale of Genji* is an extremely long and complex work of 54 chapters, and any number of scholars over the centuries have spent their entire lives studying it. It is not my intention to make scholarly statements regarding this work; rather, I want only to tell you how I, as a writer active in the latter half of the twentieth century, have read this work over the years, what I have learned from its traditions, and what it is I am trying to include in my own writing that I hope will be passed on to future generations. With this in mind, time will allow us to take a close look at just one or two of the many heroines in *The Tale of Genji*.

Murasaki Shikibu inserts apparently innocent comments about Hikaru Genji everywhere in *The Tale of Genji*. She seems at first glance to be praising the man, but on closer inspection we see how cool and penetrating her gaze is. For some reason, the tale is written in such a way that readers feel pleasure when the Shining Prince is treated cruelly by his ladies, or is betrayed by them, or when they have affairs behind his back. I would like to quote just a few points in the text that have special meaning for me, and I hope that you will try to imagine what it is that Murasaki Shikibu was trying to say in them and what it is that I am feeling when I read the lines.

The hero of the tale is, of course, the superhuman lover, Hikaru Genji. In the course of the story, he makes advances to one woman after another and has sexual relations with them. In chapter 8, on his way home after a banquet at the palace on a spring night when the moon is covered with mist, he meets a woman (who becomes known as "night of the misty moon," Oborozukiyo) in a garden of the imperial palace and carries her into an adjoining room. When she raises her voice in alarm, he tells her, "My status allows me to do whatever I please. Just keep silent," or something to that effect.[9] She then realizes that he is Genji and does as he says. For the modern reader this section is somewhat hard to accept. As I see it, Murasaki Shikibu was obliquely asking the reader of her day to question such goings-on. Of course, other readers over the years may have interpreted the scene differently, since Oborozukiyo seems to be a daring sort of girl who enjoys the thrill of making love with Genji. The fact that a character's motives are open to various interpretations is one of the special characteristics of the narrative.

In the scene where Genji encounters Utsusemi in chapter 2, he picks her up and carries her into a room, but he is challenged by a lady-in-waiting to the woman. His blunt reply is, "Come for her in the morning." Utsusemi scolds him, saying that a man of rank ought not to behave in this manner.[10] Her words, and her insistent and successful rejection of Genji, must have resounded in Murasaki Shikibu's day as a pleasant and invigorating new voice for women's self-assertion, and this spirit echoes throughout the entire book.

The reason the Yūgao chapter (chapter 4) has long been appreciated as one of the best in *The Tale of Genji* could be because of the charming, even seductive quality of its heroine, Yūgao. This is the poem she writes when Genji first reveals his face to her:

> Your face seemed quite to shine in the evening dew;
> but perhaps I was dazzled by the evening light.[11]

Although expressing herself with superficial sweetness, she has injected a good deal of bitterness into the poem (suggesting that the handsome appearance of his face was a trick played by the evening light). The reader cannot help but enjoy her clever jab at Genji.

That night, after spending the day with Genji in lovemaking, Yūgao is possessed by a demonic spirit and dies. At dawn, Genji summons his closest confidant, Koremitsu, and has him wrap her dead body in a robe and dispose of it in secret. The hushing up of the scandal is addressed by a shadowy authorial figure that makes an eerie appearance: "I had hoped, out of deference to him, to conceal these difficult matters; but I have been accused of romancing, of pretending that because he was the son of an emperor he had no faults. Now, perhaps, I shall be accused of having revealed too much" (*The Tale of Genji*, 83). It is a fitting way to conclude the strange and mysterious Yūgao chapter.

There is no end to the number of passages I could cite for you, but I will conclude here. The reason for *The Tale of Genji*'s popularity over many generations has to do with something hinted at in subtle ways throughout the book: namely, the dissatisfactions of real-life people who are neither docile about nor blind to the problems of the society in which they live. Strangely, these dissatisfactions are shared by people at the cutting edge of every era in human history and have been a stimulus to the writers of every age. If I were asked what single literary work has had the greatest impact on my life since my childhood, I would probably have to say *The Tale of Genji*.

Heian women's writings have acted ever since as guidebooks for how women observe men: "This is how men deceive women"; or, perhaps, "They are incapable of deceiving women; this is just how they are, neither innocent nor guilty"; or perhaps, "This is how they fill us with pity, how they are selfish, agreeable, foolish, wise, despicable, even noble." With such thoughts, women have since the beginning of time loved men and been disappointed by them. *The Tale of Genji* contains the wisdom of its age, but it was recorded with a cool and penetrating gaze that transcends the wisdom of the age. If it had been written purely from the viewpoint of the time when it was written, it would rapidly have become outdated, along with everything else from the period, and there would be no readership for the book today. In every age, people possess the power to cross over and expand the boundaries of space and time inhabited by this living creature called humankind, by living close to the very source of life that transcends the wisdom of their day, and by looking critically at a warped and imperfect world.

This tale begins with the question "In which emperor's reign was it?" and ends in the Uji chapters with the realization by Kaoru that Ukifune is alive and hiding somewhere: "As he examined the several possibilities, a suspicion crossed his mind: the memory of how he himself had behaved in earlier days made him ask whether someone might be hiding her from the world" (*The Tale of Genji*, 1090). It is not an ending as such; the tale comes to an end like the glittering trail of a broken thread swaying in the breeze.

The nature of this tale, without beginning and without ending, is the nature of this world in which we live. I recognize myself in it, and it provides me with the powerful underpinnings that make the writings of Ōba Minako what they are today.

ɔ

Translator's postscript: In a 1994 collection of fictionalized autobiographical essays titled Mukashi onna ga ita *(Long ago, there was a woman), Ōba Minako mentions the preceding address presented at "a foreign university" (Rutgers University) in an essay in which she reflects on what it means, for her, to be a Japanese woman who writes. Since the essay allows*

the reader added insight into Ōba's thinking as a writer, I include a transla-
tion of it here. The translation consists of chapter 26 in its entirety.

The heroine ("a woman") of the essays in Long Ago, There Was a
Woman *represents Ōba's creation of a female persona paralleling the male
hero of the tenth-century poem-tale* Ise monogatari *(Tales of Ise), long
identified with the courtier/poet Arihara no Narihira (825–80; see McCullough,* Tales of Ise, *for a translation). The title of Ōba's collection derives
from the fact that many of the poetic episodes in* Tales of Ise *begin with the
phrase* mukashi otoko arikeri *"long ago, there was a man." Like* Tales of
Ise, *Ōba's essays are episodic, contain poetry, and depict issues involving
male-female relations, this time from a woman's perspective.*

The essays in Long Ago, There Was a Woman *were serialized in the
literary magazine* Nami *between July 1991 and December 1993 (with a
seven-month break from January to July 1993, while Ōba was Writer-in-
Residence at Rutgers University). The cover of the conference bulletin bore
the words, in Ōba's calligraphy,* Mukashi onna ga ita, *which thus became
the Japanese title of the conference, known otherwise as "The Rutgers Conference on Japanese Women Writers."*

Chapter 26: "Long Ago, There Was a Woman"
(Ōba, Mukashi onna ga ita, 147–53)

Long ago, there was a woman. From the time she had reached
the age of reason, she began to experience unexplained feelings of
anger. She wondered why this should be and came to believe that it
was because she had had the misfortune of being born a woman.
Eventually she started to write those feelings down, and one day she
was surprised to discover that she had become a writer.

It occurred very naturally; and perhaps it was just as natural that
women active in the feminist movement began to discuss the works
she had written, since what the woman had written was written by a
woman. At that time, women all over the world had begun to complain in unison about their years of unfair treatment, and the movement called feminism became widespread in society. Everything
seemed to fit together like slowly turning gears.

But the woman herself was not an activist, for she had no agenda
in her mind. She just wrote down the things she experienced in her
life each day that made her feel that way, and then presented them
only because she had been given the opportunity to present them. At
some point, the woman came to believe that it was not that she

would rather die than live in silence, but rather that living itself meant speaking her mind, despite the dangers.

When she was very young, the woman had somehow done what people conventionally do and had married a man in a manner that was typical at the time. One day, this man, her husband, had told her: "Do you expect to be able to say whatever is on your mind? If you think you can do that and survive, you are wrong."

This was her husband's response, not to an especially extravagant outburst during a quarrel between them but to some trivial thought she had casually expressed. Her husband's tone of voice was equally nonchalant, almost soothing, and she might easily have overlooked his words, but instead they stabbed her to the depths of her being, opening a wound that would be with her for as long as she lived.

For decades to follow, the woman would recall those words hundreds of times with a fresh, blood-spattering intensity. And each time she would say to herself: "I expect that someday, somehow, this man and I will separate. Until that day, I will show him that I can say what is on my mind and still survive."

On another occasion, he had once criticized an unmarried woman for bearing a child. "She cannot even earn enough to feed herself!"

It is possible that the man's words were intended more to assure himself than to attack the woman, but the shamelessness of the man's words darkened her world like a great white swan blotting out the sky.

In any case, the woman clung to the memory of those words in anticipation of a final day of reckoning with that man and lived thereafter thinking only of how best to express herself so as to capture people's attention and, having done so, to survive. And so, writing bit by bit the things that were on her mind, she discovered one day that she had become a novelist.

Most likely, the reason the feminist movement had spread throughout the world was that there were other women, many others, who carried inside a similar wound that festered within.

One day, because she was a woman writer from Japan, the woman was invited to a foreign university to speak at a conference entitled "Long Ago, There Was a Woman," where scholars of women's writing were gathered from around the world. She gave a rambling talk, resuscitating the image of women and men that writers such as the Mother of Michitsuna, Sei Shōnagon, and Murasaki Shikibu had observed so intently over 1,000 years earlier.

As she spoke, she looked out the window at the figures of two students, a young man and a young woman caressing each other, leaning against an oak tree. The young woman's shining blond hair glowed like a shower of burning sparks in the evening light of early spring. With both hands, the young man had buried his fingers in the lush golden tresses that cascaded over her shoulders. He whispered something, his forehead pressed to hers. The girl's eyes were closed; in one hand, she held a magnolia blossom.

Observing their actions, the woman writer from Japan recalled a poem from long, long ago.

> If tied, it would slip off;
> And untied, it was too long, —
> Ah, that hair of yours! —
> Is it all disarranged
> Now while I see you not?
> *The Man'yōshū*, 65[12]

It is a poem that evokes the fragrance of loose, cascading tresses. The blond-haired young woman had sky-blue eyes the color of forget-me-nots. Soon their color faded to pale blue, and then with nightfall her hair and eyes turned black as jet. "It is a black-haired beauty standing there," thought the woman novelist who had come from Japan.

The maiden and the young man were students who attended a seminar in which the woman participated now and then.

The young people in that country always spoke as if to say, "So, what conclusions are we supposed to draw, anyway? Can you explain it to us simply and clearly?" Then they would wait expectantly for an elaborate response from the speaker.

The affectionate young couple sat in the classroom with the same, expectant look. "That's me, forty years ago." The thought came from somewhere to the woman's mind. And then she recalled those words the man had once spoken to her: "Do you expect to be able to say whatever is on your mind? If you think you can do that and survive, you are wrong."

Although they said nothing aloud, the young people's eyes seemed to say, "The way you ramble on, we have no idea what you are talking about."

Then a male student spoke: "The era now belongs to women, doesn't it? We have no choice but to nod our heads in agreement, no matter what demands women make of us. It doesn't pay to fight the trend."

A female student answered with a scornful laugh: "Men love to mechanize everything, and that's how they ended up cutting their own throats. Nowadays muscle power and physical strength are unnecessary, so men have no function anymore. Lesbians can have children through artificial insemination, and men don't have anything to do. Unless men are gangsters or hoodlums, women aren't even intimidated by them anymore. Women used to get pleasure from playing up to men, but that doesn't happen nowadays.

"There are no more animals to hunt, or fields to till. Men go on and on at their interminable meetings, saying the most stupid things. Are we supposed to just sit there and act impressed? Forget it. It's a shame, but we can't coddle men the way we used to. If we do, they take advantage of it. We can't afford to forget the things men made us endure in the past."

The steady sound of cars passing outside was audible. Also, the distant sound of an elevator, and another unidentified mechanical noise. In the hallway, the occasional sound of foreign words, the echoes of a foreign tribe. In the distance, the barking of a dog, birds singing, the sound of the wind.

"Yes, women in the country of my birth have been scrutinizing men and writing down what they've observed with their own eyes for over a thousand years. Of course, they've also written about women's lives. There was one woman who had an affair with a man who wielded great power, and yet when she finally looked at his face, which seemed to her so handsome as to glow with light, she impudently said that her vision must be betrayed by the deepening dusk. The story of her sudden death and the hurried disposal of her corpse was also written down, for the sake of people in later ages who needed to hear the truth."[13]

The woman rambled on about one thing and another. "Face it, there are no conclusions. You ramble on about what you have seen, and then your time in this world is up."

At some point, the figure of the young man with his fingers buried in the girl's long hair disappeared into the darkness of the night.

Several days passed, when one morning the girl with long blond hair sat all by herself in the classroom.

"Where is your boyfriend?"

"He got sick and had to return to his native land. But I am worried that he will never be able to return to this country. It's politically unstable there, and he may not be able to get out . . ."

The girl tossed back her long hair, damp with sweat, and smiled. "It's gotten warm, and I'd like to tie it up, but this is how he liked it . . ."

> 'Do it up!'
> 'It is now so long!'
> So say they all.
> But as you saw it, I will keep
> This hair of mine, dishevelled though it be.
> *The Man'yōshu*, 65–66[14]

Without our knowing why, certain things change, while other things remain the same.

—Trans. Paul Gordon Schalow

Notes

1. When I was a girl, since there were no translations of *The Pillow Book* into easy-to-read modern Japanese, we read the original text with the aid of a few simple explanatory notes. Remembering the difficulties I had with the original, in 1991 I wrote a modern-language version of *The Pillow Book*, which Kōdansha published. It has sold remarkably well, and I am delighted that at the dawn of the twenty-first century there are still large numbers of high school students and their parents who read this work with such pleasure. It seems amazing to me that a work of classical literature such as this should still be read widely by nonspecialist readers in their native language, in a form not too different from the original. I wonder how many other such examples there are in world literature.

The sections I quote from *The Pillow Book*, and others like it, are deeply embedded in the language and consciousness of the Japanese people and are commonly quoted in everyday conversation, much the way lines from a Shakespeare play might come up in English conversation.

2. *Trans. note*: For a variant of this passage, see Ivan Morris's translation in *The Pillow Book*, 39.

3. *Trans. note*: The "brightness" of Sei Shōnagon's depiction of the court has sometimes led readers to conclude that Sei Shōnagon was superficial and elitist, that she pandered to the aristocracy and especially to the empress she served, and that she was incomplete as a writer because she was unable to write with complexity about the multiple dimensions of life, un-

like the more "talented" Murasaki Shikibu. By contrast, Ōba's reading of *The Pillow Book* here emphasizes the subtle presence of dark elements in Sei Shōnagon's writing and describes its textual "brightness" as an intelligent writerly response to a political and personal tragedy Sei Shōnagon felt she could not address more directly.

4. *Trans. note*: Seidensticker's translation reads "Do you know how slow the dawn can be / when you have to wait alone?" (*The Gossamer Years*, 38). Seidensticker notes that "a pun on *akuru ma*, 'the interval before dawn' and also 'the interval before the door opens,' indicates to Kaneie that she knew he was there and purposely kept him out. This is a rather daring poem" (*The Gossamer Years*, 170n19).

5. *Trans. note*: Seidensticker's translation reads, "Though perhaps not as stubborn as a winter's dawn, an unopened gate means cruel waiting, too" (*The Gossamer Years*, 38). This rendering of the poem makes Kaneie seem rather conventional. Ōba's interpretation emphasizes a complicating element in the poem: Kaneie claims that being barred from his wife's rooms would be unpleasant in any season, which may have been meant to flatter her.

6. *Trans. note*: Seidensticker's translation of *The Kagerō Diary* does not lend itself to being read the way Ōba argues here, as a woman's self-realization of having clung to an unhappy marriage for the wrong reasons. In the translation, the protagonist reveals little insight into her unhappiness, and there is little evidence that she considers a solution to her dilemma to be within her own powers, except to the extent that turning to religion for comfort is an act of will on her part. Sonya Arntzen's new translation of *The Kagerō Diary* (University of Michigan, Center for Japanese Studies, forthcoming) may reveal the dimensions of the story that Ōba sees in it to an English readership.

7. *Trans. note*: There are two translations of this work by Matsuo Bashō: Nobuyuki Yuasa's "The Narrow Road to the Deep North"; and Earl Miner's "The Narrow Road Through the Provinces."

8. I spend about half of each year near Kyoto, and recently I joined a group of readers of *The Tale of Genji* for a picnic on the banks of the Uji River where the Uji chapters of *Genji* take place. *The Tale of Genji* has that sort of powerful hold on us.

9. *Trans. note*: For the scene of Genji's initial encounter with Oborozukiyo, see *The Tale of Genji*, 152–53.

10. *Trans. note*: For Genji's encounter with Utsusemi, see *The Tale of Genji*, 42–43.

11. *Trans. note*: This is a reworking of Seidensticker's translation of the poem; see *The Tale of Genji*, 70.

12. *Trans. note*: *Man'yōshū*, poem no. 123, by Mikata Shami to his wife: takebanure / takaneba nagaki imo ga kami / konogoro minu ni kakagetsuramu ka. His wife's response follows in poem no. 124. The headnote reads "Composed during an illness of Mikata shortly after his marriage to a

daughter of Sono Ikuha" (*The Manyōshū*, 65). See also Sato and Watson, *From the Country of Eight Islands*, 41.

13. *Trans. note*: The reference is to Yūgao's poem addressed to Genji, and to her subsequent death at the hands of a possessing spirit, depicted in the Yūgao chapter (chapter 4) of *The Tale of Genji* and recounted in Ōba's "Special Address," above.

14. *Trans. note*: *Man'yōshū*, poem no. 124, by the wife of Mikata Shami: Hito wa mina ima wa nagashi to take to iedo / kimi ga mishi kami midaretari tomo. Composed in response to her husband's poem, no. 123. See also Sato and Watson, *From the Country of Eight Islands*, 41.

Works Cited

The Manyōshū: The Nippon Gakujutsu Shinkōkai Translation of One Thousand Poems. New York: Columbia University Press, 1969.

Matsuo Bashō. "The Narrow Road to the Deep North" (*Oku no hosomichi*). In *The Narrow Road to the Deep North and Other Travel Sketches*. Trans. Nobuyuki Yuasa. Middlesex, Eng.: Penguin Books, 1966, 97–143.

———. "The Narrow Road Through the Provinces" (*Oku no hosomichi*). Trans. Earl Miner. In Miner, *Japanese Poetic Diaries*. Berkeley: University of California Press, 1969, 157–97.

McCullough, Helen Craig. *Tales of Ise: Lyrical Episodes from Tenth-Century Japan*. Stanford: Stanford University Press, 1968.

Mother of [Fujiwara no] Michitsuna. *The Gossamer Years: The Diary of a Noblewoman of Heian Japan* (*Kagerō nikki*). Trans. Edward G. Seidensticker. Rutland, Vt.: Tuttle, 1964.

Murasaki Shikibu. *The Tale of Genji* (*Genji monogatari*). Trans. Edward G. Seidensticker. New York: Knopf, 1976.

Ōba Minako. *Makura no sōshi*. By Sei Shōnagon. Shōnen shōjo koten bungakukan, 4. Tokyo: Kōdansha, 1991.

———. *Mukashi onna ga ita*. Tokyo: Shinchōsha, 1994.

Sato, Hiroaki, and Burton Watson, trans. *From the Country of Eight Islands: An Anthology of Japanese Poetry*. Seattle: University of Washington Press, 1981.

Sei Shōnagon. *The Pillow Book of Sei Shōnagon* (*Makura no sōshi*). Trans. Ivan Morris. New York: Penguin Books, 1967.

2

The Tosa Diary:
In the Interstices of
Gender and Criticism

LYNNE K. MIYAKE

Tosa nikki (The Tosa diary), written in 935 by a prominent male poet and courtier, opens with a provocative statement:

> Otoko mo sunaru niki to iu mono o, onna mo shite mimu tote, suru-nari.

> I intend to see whether a woman can produce one of those diaries men are said to write.[1]

As a feminist scholar trained in the United States (albeit more than a millennium later), I am struck by the male diarist Ki no Tsurayuki's (ca. 870–945) use of a woman persona[2] and its implications for narratology and gender studies. *The Tosa Diary* challenges the conventional models of narration, gender, and genre and manipulates the textual conventions of orthography, perspective, and language that determined gender identity in the Heian period (794–1185), when the diary was written, thereby creating a multi-voiced, multi-gendered, revolutionary work. The diary subverts the culturally determined styles creating man or woman in literary texts (especially notions of what constitutes a diary written by a [male] courtier) and in the process exposes gender as a product of narrative convention and not an ontological fact or an entity existing before the act of narration. Most Japanese scholars acknowledge *The Tosa Diary* as a milestone in the development of Japanese prose and the institution of a new literary genre, *nikki bungaku* (diary literature), a genre that influenced prose for generations to come, but few see the woman persona as anything more than a tool to free Tsurayuki from the social and textual constraints imposed on a male courtier. Fewer still would pursue the provocative suggestion that the merger of the woman persona with that of Tsurayuki's discursive construction, the male courtier / provincial governor in the text produces a not-entirely-male, not-entirely-female, gender- and genre-bending text.[3] In the West, too, the diary's multi-voiced text has been found baffling and incongruous.

The problem surrounding *The Tosa Diary*'s reception on both sides of the Pacific results, I believe, from the diary's position in the interstices of Heian male and female textual production and of Japanese and Western literary and critical scholarship. Japanese critical practice cannot adequately discern the diary's revolutionary, new, gender-bending aspects, because it does not consider gender central to the diary.[4] It does not recognize that, with the creation of a female yet male persona, *The Tosa Diary* subverts what Heian tradition considered suitable "male" and "female" literary modes of production — that it deconstructs the binary polarities of male and female reproduced in literary texts (classical Chinese *kanbun* poetry and diaries versus Japanese *hiragana/wabun*[5] poetry, and later, prose); in spheres of activity (the public versus private arenas); education (Chinese poetry and classics versus Japanese *waka*[6] poetry); and language (Chinese versus native Japanese). In short, the Japanese scholarly world fails to see that gender is crucial in shaping literary production in Heian Japan, and it simply reads the woman persona as functional and the diary as primarily a historical document that illuminates the life and creative process of its author.

From its position in the interstices of Japanese and Western scholarship, *The Tosa Diary* also poses a challenge to Western assumptions concerning voice/persona, point of view, subject position, and gender that inform a Western critic's reading of any text. A Western reader perhaps unconsciously expects the point of view to be singular, unchanging, and anchored in one persona at one time[7] — but, when it constantly shifts, is multiple, and is less clearly delineated between personas, it causes disruption and discomfort.[8] *The Tosa Diary* creates this disjunction by providing space for double, even multiple "voices" — not just one (the provincial governor/male) or the other (the woman persona/female) but some composite of the two — to share the same textual moment. This notion of multiple, undifferentiated voices finds a basis in the different perceptions of personal names and the so-called personal pronouns that exist in Japanese. The classical Japanese *wa ga/ware* (translated as variants of "I" but not equivalent to the English "I," as will be argued below) are not "repositories of personhood, agency, and personal identity" (Kondo, 27)[9] as is the case in English, but are more contextually or relationally (deictically) defined. There is no sense that there is an unchangeable, essence of a *ware* ("I") outside and beyond the context (i.e., formal/informal, the specific participants, time, place, power relationships) that forms the ground for its creation. *Wa ga/ware*, then, are more open-ended and undifferentiated than their English counterparts and do not function as exclusive referents of one persona alone; they can be appropriated by a character, a narrator, or even a reader who is willing to assume the experiencer perspective from which the event or emotion is being described. The absence of pronouns in instances where the referent is clear—a situation not normally found in the English language, which usually requires that sentences have subjects—provides for more ambiguity and for a space where other voices can reside jointly. This notion of a "loose" narrative point of view and undifferentiated pronouns, in turn, finds support in the Japanese concept of the self. Conceived of as unbound, shifting, multiple, and contextually and relationally defined, the self in reality has many selves, each created—crafted, in Dorinne Kondo's words—to fit and respond to the specificities of the situation.

The Tosa Diary also undermines Western assumptions about how gender and gender identities are constituted and marked. In most instances, Western readers regard gender identity to be either male or female, or at least expect to find the delineation between them clear. A multitude of merged identities that are neither entirely male nor entirely female but move along a continuum between the two is not what Western readers would find familiar. Further, personas are usually considered "on stage" and in the act of narration when they are in sole possession of the narrator position and/or actively narrating in their own voice. *The Tosa Diary*, however, provides a different scenario, allowing orthography, perspective, and language to mark the presence of the female persona. Because of gender differentiation in the Heian period in language, education, and spheres of activity, *hiragana* is the "female hand" (*onna-te*) in opposition to *kanbun*, the "male hand" (*otoko-te*); its use constitutes the presence of the woman persona even if the content, perspective, and narrating voice at that time is male. (I am, of course, not saying that in these instances the woman persona effaces the male persona, but rather that both personas are present at the same time.)

No doubt, many Western readers may feel a "sense of unfamiliarity" and "discomfort" vis-à-vis *The Tosa Diary* and may attempt to explain away its difference by "domesticat[ing] or neutraliz[ing its] exoticism" and by "exaggerat[ing] the familiar aspects of the text . . . thereby dispers[ing] its discreteness in the hegemonic sphere of First World literature" (Miyoshi, 9).[10] But it is the *Diary*'s "unfamiliarity" and "exoticism" that are central in highlighting our Western assumptions about gender, narratology, and self/selves/personal identity, and in urging us to develop "a native [Japanese] taxonomy," "an alternative methodology for reading" (Miyoshi, 27–28)[11] that would explain its complexity. Until now, *The Tosa Diary*'s position in the interstices of Heian female and male literary production and Japanese and Western scholarship has prevented it from gaining recognition as a revolutionary, gender-, and genre-bending work in either tradition. I believe, however, that its textual challenges to both will prove invaluable in creating a notion of gender, self/selves, narratology, and literature that will be broad enough to encompass non-Western as well as Western works.

♨

The Tosa Diary, as we know it today, documents a 55-day journey from the province of Tosa (in Shikoku prefecture) to the Capital (present-day Kyoto) taken in 934 by Ki no Tsurayuki as he completed his four- to five-year term as provincial governor. Composed of 54 entries, the diary follows the format of a Chinese-style, courtier's diary, with the date for each entry acting as a kind of subheading. Some entries are as simple as a notation of the weather (for example, "The weather was too bad for the boat to leave," Nineteenth Day of First Month [276]), or a ditto-mark-like repetition of the entry of the day before ("Same as the day before," Sixth Day of First Month [268]). But others are more elaborate records of impromptu poetry-composing sessions (Eighteenth and Twenty-ninth Days of First Month [275–76, 280–81, respectively]), of visits by those who had come to bid the departing party farewell (Twenty-sixth and Twenty-seventh Days of Twelfth Month [264–67]), and of private thoughts and sorrows, such as lamenting the death of a child (Fourth, Ninth, and Sixteenth Days of Second Month [283, 287–88, 289–91, respectively]). Composed of poetry and prose, the diary records literary evocations of poetic sites, anxiety over traveling by boat, the excitement of going home coupled with a disappointment upon finding home as unreceptive as the provinces, and a parent's lament for a deceased child left behind in Tosa. The most striking things about this diary/travelogue, however, are the fact that Tsurayuki, the provincial governor figure in the diary, elects to tell his story from the perspective of a woman in his entourage and the implications of this phenomenon for both Japanese and Western scholarship.

Most conventional scholarly Japanese readings of the woman persona, perhaps because they stem from a historical, biographical, and philological critical tradition,[12] tend to downplay the importance of the woman persona and to draw on the actual events of Tsurayuki's life to discern personal motives for the utilization of this persona. I do not find fault with such an approach per se (and I agree in part with some of the conclusions drawn by Kikuchi Yasuhiko and other scholars discussed below), but in this instance the exclusive privileging of historical fact and situation obscures the fictional and gender significance of the woman persona. Some of the earliest theories from the Tokugawa period (1600–1868), for example, stress biographical reasons and claim that since it was unmanly for a courtier to mourn the loss of a daughter (however prominent this theme in the diary, there is no historical verification that Tsurayuki did lose a daughter), the woman persona became the perfect foil. Others contend that the adoption of the female guise was peripheral and purely for amusement, or was necessary only to dispel Tsurayuki's sorrow over the loss of his patrons at court and his dissatisfaction with being relegated to the provinces.[13] A second group of scholars views the female persona as little more than a rhetorical flourish in the humorous, unconventional style of Heian *haikai* poetry, interpreting Tsurayuki's use of the incongruous female persona as the best stratagem by which to challenge the hegemony of Chinese poetry and prose and Japanese *waka* poetry.[14] Both sets of theorists, nonetheless, view the woman as peripheral to Tsurayuki's enterprise and do not recognize the gender implications of her interventions.

A third group, although its explanations vary considerably, argues that the adoption of the female guise enabled Tsurayuki to free himself from the strictures imposed upon him by both the *kanbun* Chinese diaries and his position as a male courtier and to establish a forum in which to express his personal, private feelings more freely.[15] All of them consider this new and innovative and see it as the factor that transformed *The Tosa Diary* from a utilitarian record-keeping diary into literature. But they, too, see the woman persona as nothing more than a stylistic tool.

More provocative for its gestures toward gender issues is the analysis presented by Kikuchi Yasuhiko (123–27). In his examination of Tsurayuki's use of a female persona, Kikuchi focuses on the first line of the diary, "I intend to see whether a woman can produce one of those diaries [I have heard that] men write" (263), identifying the phrases "one of those diaries [I have heard] that men write" (*otoko mo sunaru*) and "a woman will attempt [it]" (*onna mo shite mimu*) as crucial. From these lines Kikuchi deduces that what is at issue is the relationship of men and women to diaries and to the writing of diaries, and not just the gender of the writer. Accordingly, Kikuchi argues that the phrase "diaries [I have heard that] men write" indicates diaries written by male courtiers in the daily-entry format—rather than longer, fuller, more autobiographical accounts without clear demarcation of time characteristic of what later became known as *nikki bungaku*, or diary literature, prose narratives written almost exclusively by women. Male courtier diaries would also be written in *kanbun* Chinese and would record actual events, whereas "a woman will attempt [writing such a work]" entails a woman's utilization (and interpolation) of the textual conventions ascribed to her by the period—that is, recording actual events in Japanese but maintaining the daily-entry format of a Chinese diary. Thus, the combining of the formula for the production of a male text with that for a female text, as the opening line of the diary seems to suggest, can only result in "a new text," a text that is neither "a woman's diary" nor "a man's diary" (Kikuchi, 124). The first line of *The Tosa Diary*, then, according to Kikuchi, signals that the diary intends to (1) shed the conventions imposed by diaries written by men, (2) use Japanese instead of Chinese, but (3) retain the daily-entry format. However, since Tsurayuki is not writing a "true" man's, record-keeping diary, fictionalized settings, personages, and poems would be interwoven with descriptions of actual events.

In his reading of the diary, Kikuchi includes some analysis of gender and even credits the third-person perspective of the woman persona with being *the* catalyst that engenders "a new world of a [new] work" (Kikuchi, 124). In the end, however, he views the woman persona only as a springboard, positioned at the inception of the enterprise, and no more. What remains essential is not that the persona is a woman but that she maintains a third-person point of view. Although Kikuchi recognizes that it is the woman persona who enables Tsurayuki to combine two traditions to produce a new work, he nonetheless negates the implications of his findings by contending that the woman's presence is limited—found only in the first six out of the 55 days of the journey at most, or in the first line, at the least (Kikuchi, 124)[16]—and does not pursue the significance of his conclusions.

As the preceding discussion indicates, for most Japanese scholars, gender is not central to the reading of the diary. In fact, they view the woman persona as having a limited significance: most (Imai, Akiyama, Hagitani, Hisamatsu, and even Kikuchi)[17] see the woman persona merely as a tool, indispensable but a device, nonetheless, whose only purpose was to free Tsurayuki from the social constraints imposed on a male courtier. For this reason, they contend that Tsurayuki did little to maintain the perspective of the woman persona and certainly did not consider the female guise central to his enterprise. Perhaps one reason for the minimization of the woman persona is the fact that *Tosa* scholars (largely male, but female scholars are included) tend to be unversed in gender issues and, therefore, do not see that their position in relation to the *Diary* is necessarily marked "male." Perhaps as a consequence, there is, to my knowledge, no study emphasizing the significance of where and how in the text the woman persona's presence is documented. Rather, *Tosa* scholars view the woman persona through an overdetermined "male" gaze that does not recognize language (the "female" as opposed to the "male hand"), male appropriation of female creativity, and other such methods as marking her presence.

ᔕ

In contrast to the Japanese situation, research in the West includes many studies on the gender implications of male literary (Daniel Defoe, Samuel Richardson, Charles Dickens, James Joyce, Henry James) and non-literary (professional female [drag] impersonators; transvestites) performances in female guise. These studies have yielded such critical terms as "narrative transvestism" (Madeleine Kahn), "(metaphoric) transvestism" (Sandra M. Gilbert), "literary masquerade" (Anne Taylor), "drag" or "female impersonator" (Esther Newton), and "transvestite" and "cross-dressing" (Suzanne Kessler and Wendy McKenna), but none appears applicable to

Tsurayuki's performance. As with all theoretical terms, these code historically situated performances and betray ethnocentric assumptions about the self/subject, sexual identity, and eroticism. They, therefore, cannot readily be applied to the Heian example. Drag, for example, as discussed by Esther Newton in her informative study *Mother Camp: Female Impersonators in America* is a highly political and eroticized act performed by those who, because of their sexual desire, are most marginalized and oppressed in society.[18] Transvestism also necessitates the overt presence of a powerful eroticism that practitioners experience when they don the clothes of the opposite sex (see Madeleine Kahn for further discussion). Although the gender blending in *The Tosa Diary* shares some similarities with drag performance, the historical and contextual disjunction is too great to make any comparison or application meaningful. This is especially true in the case of eroticism. Eroticism is very much present in Heian texts but manifests itself through innuendo and indirection (extreme indirection, by twentieth-century standards), and intensifies its effect through elision.[19] The issue is further complicated by the term's implication in such notions as love, desire, and sex—all concepts with powerful cultural connotations in the English language that do not readily transfer to Japanese. Even in masquerade and cross-dressing, where eroticism is less of an issue, assumptions involving the wholeness and completeness of the self and sexual identity make these terms unsuitable as theoretical tools for examining *The Tosa Diary*.

Judith Butler's article "Performative Acts and Gender Constitution: An Essay in Phenomenology and Feminist Theory" and her subsequent book *Gender Trouble: Feminism and the Subversion of Identity* mark an important turning point in the study of gender identity. Butler's argument that (1) gender is not "a stable identity or locus of agency from which all various acts proceed" but something "instituted through a *stylized repetition of acts*" (a performative act) that creates "the illusion of an abiding gendered self"; and (2) that this then opens up the possibility of "gender transformation," a different kind of repeating that breaks or subverts the repetition of culturally determined styles creating man or woman ("Performative Acts," 519–20), is the first theoretical position that might help in explaining what *The Tosa Diary* attempts to do. Butler's analysis, however, does not move beyond certain eurocentric parameters, nor does it problematize the larger contexts—the institutional, political, ideological, economic, historical, to name a few—that implicitly form the backdrop against which her theory is formulated. Thus, Butler's analysis loses much of its applicability for a non-Western text like *Tosa*. Butler further limits her argument by examining identity only in terms of gender. Not surprisingly, Butler's conceptualization of the self also retains culture-specific (i.e., English-language) assumptions about proper names and personal pronouns, viewing them as repositories of personhood, agency, and personal identity. Thus, although Butler does constitute the self as instituted in time and, therefore, changing, she does not acknowledge the role that contexts—those mentioned above, and specifically the context of power—play in the shaping of the self. This results in her viewing the self as singular and not plural or relationally defined. As Dorinne Kondo points out through her analysis of the various terms used to indicate "I" in modern Japanese, "individual" identities have not *one* self but a plurality of selves, which are molded and shaped in and by the specificities of each situation. It is this plurality and fluidity of selves that provide the ground for more than one persona to occupy any single textual moment/space in *The Tosa Diary*, and what enables the diary's multi-voiced and gender- and genre-bending act—something left unexplained in Butler's formulation of the self.

The failure of Western criticism to form a suitable theoretical framework for the examination of gender in *The Tosa Diary* highlights once again the difficulty—or even the impossibility—of transferring concepts across historical, cultural, and geographic contexts. It is a dilemma that constantly confronts those of us who study non-Western cultures. How are we to engage in meaningful research on a topic like gender, which is still accorded little legitimacy in Japan, and whose delineations in *The Tosa Diary* do not neatly fit within Western categories? In creating and situating our readings, how do we avoid aggrandizing the issue and "re-naming" its significance in our own image, thereby depriving "the non-West" of even its "imaginary products" (Chow, xiii)?

In short, how do we/I situate our interventions? For one, we must be aware that there are no inviolate, apolitical spaces of critique. As a critic working in the West, I am always already implicated in the First World, eurocentric theoretical stances of the United States and must consciously avoid becoming trapped by the intellectual parameters within which Western ideology orders knowledge. I must use the specificities of *The Tosa Diary* and the history, geography, and politics that produced it to critique and refashion the theories I bring from the West. By the same token, I must be aware of how the strictures and limitations placed upon me by Japanese scholarship shape my reading. Most of all, however, I must give voice to my position in the interstices of Japan and the West: partial readings—stories—by either the West or Japan cannot be allowed to stand. Complex, multiple, but locally engaged oppositional stories/ positions—which often lie in the interstices—must go on record as alternative readings to the dominant, hegemonic storytelling/writing of knowledge.[20]

⌀

My first step, then, must be to examine the historical ground that produced *The Tosa Diary*. Although Japanese scholarship does not acknowledge the functioning of gender in the diary, gender and gender differentiation played prominent roles during the Heian period, an aristocratic age in which literary production revolved around a highly circumscribed, court-centered society that shared a standard, corporate body of knowledge. Political power during the period, however, resided largely with the men, and on the whole, women remained marginalized.[21] Relegated to the private, domestic sphere, women had little opportunity of formally participating in government and politics and were, therefore, not allowed to acquire the tools of governance: Chinese language and culture. Interestingly, however, women's exclusion from Chinese discourse provided a space for them to become literate and to engage in literary production in Japanese. This phenomenon, coupled with certain historical and social conditions expanded upon below, stimulated a dual system of literacy—one largely for men (Chinese) and the other for men and women (Japanese)—creating two literary, if not real-life, traditions, that were not totally mutually exclusive but overlapped in the private arena of courtship, love, and everyday matters.[22] I am not contending that only men participated in the public arena and that women did not engage in power struggles at court (cf. Empress An-shi [927–64], consort of Emperor Murakami) or that women never acquired knowledge of Chinese (the author of *The Tale of Genji*, Murasaki Shikibu, was known for her ability to read Chinese), but the official practice was that women were not to concern themselves openly with governance or politics or to give voice to such matters in their literary endeavors.[23] Also, although men of Tsurayuki's day were supposed to limit their prose musings to Chinese, they did write fictional prose tales (such as *Utsuho monogatari* [The tale of the hollow tree; late 10th c.]), but these remain anonymous, because few men would publicly claim authorship of what many Confucians proclaimed frivolous and not worthy of the attention of a Heian courtier.

Political power, however, resided in the hands of men, but unequally. Males of the Fujiwara clan came to command unprecedented authority by establishing themselves as maternal relations to the imperial house and ruling as regents. Those not born into this privileged family often advanced themselves by marrying their sisters and daughters to a Fujiwara male. Thus, a young girl was groomed from birth to become a desirable wife; her training included the arts of poetry, music, and literature as well as such domestic duties as dyeing, sewing, and incense making. A suitable wife, then, received training in the arts as well as household management—the reason for a woman's education and literary expertise. Despite these talents and accomplishments, however, women were often, in Gayle Rubin's words, pawns in the "traffic in women" (157, 174).

This "marriage politics" is evidence of the oppression under which women lived, but within its parameters women received an education, although mainly in Japanese language and poetry, and became highly skilled producers of literature. Men, however, used Japanese largely for informal, more private interactions,[24] reserving Chinese for the more formal, and more prestigious, public functions at court. A partial explanation for this state of affairs lies in the peculiar position of honor the Heian court accorded China—so much so that Chinese even became the vehicle for official communications, much like Latin in the European Middle Ages. For all practical purposes, Chinese became the "male hand," the *otoko-te*, the exclusive domain of the educated, elite, male courtier, tailored to serve him in his sphere of influence—the public arena. Official records, laws, the emperor's pronouncements, and communications with Chinese courts[25] were composed in Chinese. Chinese became the language of clarity, rationality, and elegance—and the means by which men maintained their position of privilege vis-à-vis women.

Barred from Chinese and the public arena, women turned to their native Japanese, known as *onna-te* or the "female hand," and the private and personal world of Japanese *waka* poetry. This is not to say that Japanese *waka* and *wabun* were the sole domain of women, but the fact that these were the conventional media of expression open to women, whereas men utilized both *waka* and *wabun* on the one hand and the *shi* (Chinese poetry) and Chinese prose (*kanbun*) on the other, colors the kind of text each produced. For example, an examination of two male-authored and two female-authored works, one of each from the genres of diary literature (*nikki bungaku*) and the historical tale (*rekishi monogatari*), reveals that during the Heian period gender was a decisive factor in fashioning the text.[26] In short, gender determined not only the mode of expression but the kind of education a person received, the scope of an individual's life experiences, his/her world, and, ultimately, the language that a writer used to describe the world. A male courtier like Tsurayuki, for example, (1) received training in both the Chinese classics and the art of the Japanese *waka*; (2) participated formally in both the public (court, official) and private (domestic) spheres of life; (3) saw the world as a series of court rituals and public gatherings, interspersed with romantic tête-à-têtes; (4) was openly conversant in both Chinese (*kanbun*) and Japanese (*hiragana/wabun*); and (5) wrote poetry and prose in Chinese and poetry in Japanese. (It is true, however, that Tsurayuki was trying to champion the cause of *hiragana* and did write one of the prefaces of the *Kokinshū* in *hiragana*.) The dual nature of a man's training — the private and public aspects of his education, experience, perception, and even mode of expression — colored his understanding and, consequently, his depiction of the world.

In contrast to this male-courtier orientation, a woman writer like the author of *Kagerō nikki* (The Kagerō diary) found her discursive world circumscribed in various ways: (1) she received training almost exclusively in Japanese poetry and hid any expertise in Chinese for fear of being ridiculed by both male and female contemporaries should her knowledge become known; (2) she was supposed to immerse herself in the private, nonpolitical sphere (taking care of domestic concerns, waiting patiently for her husband's/lover's visits, participating in her mistress's/master's salon); (3) she usually composed in *hiragana/wabun*; and (4) she found literary expression in *waka*, and rarely, if ever, in Chinese poetry or prose. There were exceptions to this scheme, but few references to them have been preserved. Furthermore, surviving textual evidence argues for a "party" line: clear-cut gender differentiation in perception and content in literary production, and a rather strict adherence to this differentiation by men and women writers.

♫

It appears, from this brief survey of the Heian period, that differentiation in textual expression and production along gender lines did exist, as did the possibility for its manipulation and subversion. As a successful "performance" of a woman by a man, *The Tosa Diary* accomplishes this subversion. As a diary, which normally would have been in *kanbun* Chinese and by a man, in *hiragana* Japanese, the text exploits the conventional expectation of *hiragana* as the "female hand" and utilizes it to constitute a performance that produces woman. The opening passage invokes a woman persona: her presence is then sustained by a stylized performance of composition in Japanese. The performative acts of naming a woman as persona in the first line and of writing the diary in Japanese, then, are all that were needed to establish a woman's presence in the diary. There are other indications of the woman persona, which I will discuss below, but the gender-infused equations of Chinese constituting male prose writing and, perhaps to a lesser degree, Japanese prose equaling woman's writing — or at least not male-courtier writing — allow for the establishment of a woman's voice.

The textual "performance" recorded in *The Tosa Diary*, therefore, serves as a stunning example of gender transformation (Judith Butler). Subverting the usual repetition of gender identity production as only male or only female, the text combines the woman persona with the male-courtier / provincial governor presence, as manifested in the diction, style, and perspective of the diary, and succeeds in creating a multi-voiced narrative. It is not merely a question of engaging in female impersonation to valorize woman and "her hand" in an age when women were often disempowered as mere pawns in marriage politics. Nor was it even a matter of using woman to validate man, as Japanese scholars contend happens in *The Tosa Diary* and as Elaine Showalter argues occurs in the film *Tootsie*, whose central character, Michael Dorsey, a down-and-out actor, becomes the actress Dorothy Michaels only to advance his acting career and to stage his re-emergence as a hierarchically superior male (120–23). Neither empowering women nor disenfranchising men, as is said occurs in Bakhtinian carnivalization (see *Rabelais and His World*), *The Tosa Diary* uses woman to stimulate a new and different literary production.

One important way in which the two voices — the woman persona and the male presence — interact and succeed in producing their complex merger is appropriation.[27] There are four ways in which the woman's voice is appropriated and interwoven with the male persona to craft a multi-voiced textual persona. The first is as a vehicle through which the text can present experiences that would normally be inappropriate in a courtier's Chinese diary. One such experience is the personal sorrow and disappointment the author Tsurayuki felt at his lack of advancement at court and at the death of his imperial patron, Emperor Daigo, in 930, the year Tsurayuki was sent to Tosa province. Although Tsurayuki is highly acclaimed as a talented poet and the author of the renowned Japanese *hiragana* preface of the first imperial poetic anthology, because he was not a member of the ruling Fujiwara hegemony, he remained a low-ranking courtier all his life. To add insult to injury, Tsurayuki suffered personal defeat even in his forte, the realm of poetry, with the unfavorable reception of his newer, simpler approach to Japanese poetry between 923 and 931 (Konishi, 2: 284). It is the woman persona, however, who helps translate Tsurayuki's sorrow and defeat into a moving portrayal of mourning for a deceased child and, ultimately, creates the text of *The Tosa Diary*. It is she, after all, who affords the diary the latitude to challenge successfully the prose conventions of the day, and it is she who provides the means to contest the stranglehold Chinese had on the diary form. Without the appropriation of the woman persona, the experiment might have been far less successful. Situated outside the cultural and literary establishment of Chinese literature, the marginalized woman persona was the perfect stratagem for, and perhaps the only method of, infiltrating tradition and subverting its conventions.

The second function that the woman persona performs in the diary is as validator of the accomplishments of Tsurayuki's alter ego, the governor and later the chief passenger. The woman persona faithfully spends pages describing the magnificent parties, the gifts, and the countless people who come to bid the departing provincial governor a splendid farewell. On the Ninth Day of the First Month, for example, the reluctance with which the people of Tosa bid the governor farewell reflects the high regard in which they held him.

> Of the many people who had come separately to say good-bye, eager to see the Governor as long as he was still in the district, the most faithful had been Fujiwara Tokizane, Tachibana Suehira, and Hasebe Yukimasa, who had followed him from place to place ever since his departure from the official residence. Those three had hearts as deep as the ocean. Knowing that the boat was to set out across open water from Minato, they had come for a final farewell. (271)

These self-laudatory remarks, however, are more palatable

coming from the mouth of a third person, a woman, perhaps a lady-in-waiting figure — a figure whose writings often included tributes to her master or mistress.[28] The presence of the woman persona also makes it easier for the governor, Tsurayuki's discursive construction, to be the center of focus without appearing self-serving (see the Ninth Day of the First Month [271] for an example).

Thus, although the governor / chief passenger is criticized for his lack of poetic talent on two occasions, he is portrayed as a man of some consequence, refined in his tastes, adept enough at poetry to perform in crucial situations, such as the exchange of farewell poems with the newly appointed governor, and genteel enough to warrant a series of farewell parties. The humorous depictions of his unsuccessful attempts at poetry and other less than flattering portrayals of the governor can be viewed, instead, as the third form of appropriation: the gaze of a man who in the later years of his life is gently poking fun at all that he had held sacred and close to his heart, through the guise of a woman. One such incident is recorded on the Seventh Day of the Second Month.

> The chief passenger was still feeling ill. Furthermore, he was an unrefined man, ignorant of the art of composition. But he decided to try a poem — possibly from a combination of admiration for the old lady's feat and relief at being near the capital. This was the rather eccentric result of his labors: [a poem follows]. . . .
>
> He must have been thinking of his indisposition when he composed it. Since a single poem was not enough to express all his sentiments, he produced another: [a second poem follows]. . . .
>
> The poem was probably inspired by a desire to show his joy at the proximity of the capital. Recognizing that it was inferior to the Awaji woman's, he was impatient with himself for composing it. (286)

A previous attempt, occurring on the First Day of the Second Month, also results in disparaging comments: "It would seem that those who heard his [the chief passenger's] composition began to remark privately on its lack of ingenuity" (282). The chief passenger is labeled "unrefined" and "ignorant of the art of composition," and his poetic attempts are deemed "eccentric," "lacking in ingenuity," or so clumsy that they need to be excused by his illness — appraisals far from the truth, if the chief passenger were indeed a representation of the historical Tsurayuki. The commentary by the editors of the Japanese text used for this study claims that these negative depictions are mere fabrications, but I contend that they serve as an ironic look at Tsurayuki's life from the perspective of old age[29] and act as further insurance against charges that Tsurayuki aggrandized the portrayal of himself in the diary.

The fourth and final means of appropriation is the use of the woman persona as a covert source of creativity—a kind of male co-option of female creativity. Sandra M. Gilbert argues that donning the costumes specific to the "opposite" gender and capitalizing on the contradictions and challenges such cross-dressing poses to the usual order of things is an oft-used strategy in this kind of appropriation. However, this concept, too, must be modified to fit *The Tosa Diary*, for, unlike the metaphorical male transvestite in male modernist writings (e.g., Leopold Bloom in James Joyce's *Ulysses*) as outlined by Gilbert (199–200), Tsurayuki does not feel any "humiliation" in taking on the female guise, nor does he express relief when he returns to his position as a hierarchically dominant male. *The Tosa Diary* does not operate under the traditional Western premise that male and female are separate and opposite entities, with little possibility of merger or that when contact is made, one entity must ultimately dominate the other. In the *Diary*, male and female merge and coexist in the same textual moment without effacing or dominating the other. *The Tosa Diary*, then, does not accept the categories of difference and polarity established in the West and combines seeming opposites into new and dynamic entities.

ⱷ

Thus, like the metaphorical male transvestites in male modernist writing, *The Tosa Diary* is energized by the male to female textual conversion and uses the stance to advantage, but it is not necessarily utilization with a disdain for the female gender. There is no sense, for example, that being "male" is better; in fact, the textual options made available through the woman persona are readily exploited into the text. The fact that the diary does not allow the female voice to stand alone and conflates her with the male persona, however, discloses that more can be gained by merger than by the woman persona's solo performance. Thus, the *Diary* combines the woman persona with that of Tsurayuki's discursive construction, the provincial governor / chief passenger and begins its challenge of the two-gender system.

Never composed entirely of only one or the other but moving back and forth along a continuum between the two personas, *The*

Tosa Diary problematizes the binary polarity of male and female
gender identities and creates something new — what Kessler and
McKenna call multiple genders. The two voices of the diary, one
male, the other female, merge without effacing each other or dissolving into a single androgynous state. Both voices remain on stage
at all times and appear in different modulations of intensity, thereby
creating a multitude of gender possibilities. Both share the same
textual space without disappearing into the oblivion of a single new
gender or into only the male or only the female gender. This multiplicity is accomplished through the use of language, orthography,
perspective, point of view, spheres of activity, and the foregrounding
of the historical author. Note the manipulation of male expressions
and female language and orthography in this passage:

> Sore no toshi no, shiwasu no, hatsuka amari hitohi no hi no, inu no
> toki ni kadode su. Sono yoshi, isasakani, mono ni kakitsuku. (29)

> The departure took place during the Hour of the Dog [7:00 P.M.–9:00
> P.M.] on the Twenty-first of the Twelfth Month in a certain year. I
> will set down a few notes about the journey. (263)

As mentioned above, the writing of the diary in *hiragana* marks
the presence of the woman persona. The use of *kanbun*[30] expressions
like *sore no toshi no* (in a certain year) and *isasakani* (a few [inconse-
quential], a bit) rather than their Japanese counterparts, *itsuka no toshi*
and *isasaka*, respectively, however, indicate a male persona. This
seamless merger of *kanbun* expressions written in *hiragana* Japanese
orthography marks one instance of the simultaneous presence of
both male and female narration. (This is not a solitary occurrence —
kanbun expressions are liberally sprinkled throughout the text.)

A similar kind of conflation occurs when Chinese-style couplets
(e.g., First Month, Ninth Day [Matsumura et al., 39]) and rhetorical
flourishes based on Chinese poetry (e.g., Second Month, Sixth Day
[Matsumura et al., 60]) — other indicators of the male hand — are introduced into the prose. Allusions to Chinese poetry are still other
examples. Some instances such as the reference to two Chinese sing-
ers, Yu Gung and Qin Qing ("The cabin dust has scattered and the
clouds are standing still"), on the Twenty-seventh Day of the Twelfth
Month (267) can be explained away as common knowledge, but
other citations such as the two lines of poetry by the Tang poet Gu
Dao ("The oar strikes through the moon on the waves; / The boat
presses against the sky in the sea") on the Seventeenth Day of the

First Month (275) cannot be dismissed as part of the repertoire of both male and female members of the court. Further, because the content of both passages is nonetheless Chinese, and thus, exhibits a masculine orientation, both reflect a merger of the male and female — the male sphere of activity or expertise with the female orthography, language, and narration.

The recitation and exchange of Chinese poetry, as in the following passage (Twenty-sixth Day, First Month), also represents a conflation of male content with female perspective: "There was another grand banquet at the Governor's residence, with presents for everyone including the servants. People chanted Chinese poems, and the host, the guest of honor, and others exchanged Japanese poems. I cannot record the Chinese ones" (264). The event recorded, the composition of Chinese poetry, is a male activity, not usually open to women. However, with the line "I cannot record the Chinese ones [poems]," the woman narrator swiftly reappears on stage, causing the reader to backtrack a few lines and attempt to find the point at which the female voice entered the description of what until that point had been a "masculine story."

Matters become even more ambiguous and intertwined when, in the following example, the woman persona weaves into her prose an allusion to a Chinese text without the usual caveat that she really does not have much knowledge of things Chinese: on the Ninth Day of the Second Month, the grieving mother of the deceased child recites a poem mourning her loss and begins to weep. The narrator concludes: "Such poems are not composed for pleasure. Both in China and in our land, they spring from emotion too strong to be borne" (288). Matsumura et al. (64) and Hagitani (373) concur that the second sentence "Both in China and in our land, they spring from emotions too strong to be borne" is based on the Mao preface to *The Book of Songs* (2d c. B.C.E.; *Mōshijo* in Japanese) and, thus, would not be within the purview of a female narrator. Some would say that the quoted line echoes the Japanese preface to the first imperial anthology and even that *Mōshijo* was common knowledge among both men and women, but, nevertheless, the passage would still be male rather than female in orientation. Thus we again witness a closely knit merger of male and female — female language and orthography juxtaposed to male content, education, and erudition.

As the diary progresses, the female narrator becomes less visible amid the use of *kanbun* expressions, *kanbun* rhetorical flourishes, and allusions to Chinese poetry. The woman narrator, however, covertly establishes her presence through language, orthography, and the utilization of third-person description, hearsay, suffixes of conjecture, and honorifics vis-à-vis Tsurayuki's discursive construction, the chief passenger. The occurrence of these devices indicates that the chief passenger is not telling the story from his perspective; rather, a narrator of some kind is describing the event utilizing the so-called third-person point of view, thus eliminating the possibility that (Tsurayuki's) male voice is the narrator. In these instances, then, we have a merger of male content/activity with female language, orthography, and perspective, creating voice(s) that are neither male nor female but that move along a continuum between the two.

Through the author's manipulation of language, orthography, content, perspective, and grammatical elements, then, the woman persona and the provincial governor persona function not as bound, separate entities, one female, the other male, but as two traveling nodes on a continuum of "maleness" and "femaleness,"[31] the one influencing the manifestation of the other at any given moment in the text. Determination of where one ends and the other begins is not possible; the persona(s) establish(es) new locations of gender/identity, crafted by the circumstances in which it/they is/are placed. The social, historical, power — and literary — contexts, then, cause the "self"/persona to shift and change as conditions necessitate, so that the woman persona and the provincial governor persona blend in and out of each other, much as the narrator and the character Kashiwagi do in Richard Bowring's analysis of a passage from the "Kashiwagi" (Oak Tree) chapter of *The Tale of Genji* (*Murasaki Shikibu: The Tale of Genji*, 61–66). The passage, depicting the male courtier Kashiwagi's state of mind as he prepares to die for the transgressions he has committed against the Third Princess and her husband Genji, reveals the interconnectedness of the discourses of the narrator and the character Kashiwagi to such an extent that at times they are indistinguishable. A certain line, for example, may be ascertained as a presentation of Kashiwagi's thoughts; the sudden appearance of the word *kaku* (like this) or an honorific verb, however, signals the narratorial presence.[32] Yet when we try to determine exactly where the narrator's comments began, we are unable to do so.

In much the same way, the interconnectedness of the male and female personas in *The Tosa Diary* can be witnessed in its most complex manifestation in the following passage from the end of the diary

(Sixteenth Day, Second Month), when the travelers return home, only to find the house in disrepair and, even worse, merely a painful reminder of the child left buried in Tosa.

Sate, ike meite kubomari, mizu tsukeru tokoro ari. Hotori ni matsu mo ariki. Itsutose mutose no uchi ni, chitose ya suginikemu, katae wa nakunarinikeri. Ima oitaru zo majireru. Ohokatano mina midare ni tareba, "Aware" to zo, hitobito iu. Omoiidenu koto naku, omoi-koishiki ga uchi ni, kono ie nite umareshi omunago no, morotomo ni kaeraneba, ikaga wa kanashiki. Funabito mo, mina ko takarite nonoshiru. Kakaru uchi ni, nao kanashiki ni *taezushite, hisokani* ko-koroshireru hito to *ierikeru* uta,

"umareshimo kaeranu mono o waga yado ni komatsu no aru o miru ga kanashisa"

to zo ieru. Nao *akazu ya aramu,* mata kaku namu.

"Mishi hito no matsu no chitose ni mimashikaba tōku kanashiki wakare semashi ya." (67–68)

There had been a stand of pine trees beside a pond of sorts, but half of them had died, and new ones had crowded in. One wondered if their thousand-year lifespans had somehow been exhausted in five or six years. The sheer desolation of the scene evoked exclamations of grief and despair.

Memories came flooding back. Among many sad, nostalgic thoughts, the most poignant were of the little girl, born in that house, who had not returned with the party. The children of others from the boat, chattering and shouting in noisy groups, made the grief of a certain person more unbearable than ever, and he murmured a poem to someone who understood his feelings:

umareshi mo	What sadness to see
kaeranu mono o	how young pine trees have sprung up
wa ga yado ni	inside the garden
komatsu no aru o	of one who is bereft
miru ga kanashisa	even of a child once born.

He also composed this, possibly because his feelings still demanded expression:

mishi hito no	If the child's lifespan
matsu no chitose ni	had been a pine's thousand years,
mimashikaba	that distant parting,
tōku kanashiki	that sad, eternal farewell,
wakare semashi ya	would never have take place.

(290–91)

Here we have a complex merging of characters and personas, male and female. The passage is in *hiragana*, signaling a female persona, but the appearance of the *kanbun* expressions (italicized in the passage above)—the *shite* in *taezushite* ("without ending, stopping"; the native Japanese equivalent being the continuative *de*) and *hisokani* ("quietly, surreptitiously"; the native Japanese equivalent being *misokani, shinobite, shinobiyaka ni*)—quickly brings to the fore a male presence. The most surprising and rapid juxtapositions, however, occur a few lines later, directly preceding the poems that identify the composer of each poem. The verb before the first poem, *ierikeru*, does not utilize an honorific and, thus, appears to refer to the narrator, speaking in her own voice and signaling the first poem as her composition. The verb before the second poem, *akazu ya aramu*, however, includes the conjecture suffix *mu* (probably, possibly) and therefore signifies that the narrator is describing the action of a third person, presumably that of the chief passenger. Grammatically speaking, then, the composer of the first poem is the female narrator, and that of the second is Tsurayuki's discursive construction, the chief passenger. Most commentators, including Helen McCullough (290–91), Hagitani (425), and Matsumura et al. (68n1) conclude that *both* poems are by Tsurayuki. Matsumura and his colleagues simply note that since both poems appear to be by the same personage, the discrepancy in narrating voices results from Tsurayuki's attempts to make the diary appear to be written in a woman's voice. Although McCullough does not explain why she chooses the chief passenger as the composer of both poems (this can be deduced from the use of "he" as subject in both instances), she seems to do so to provide symmetry to the passage. Hagitani, however, resolves this dilemma of shifting perspectives by contending that the deceased child's father (presumably, Tsurayuki's discursive construction) is identical to the child's mother, who is in turn equated to the narrator. (He, however, does not provide any basis for his interpretation.) Thus, all voices are one and the same for Hagitani, as he glosses over the different perspectives and places them under one voice, that of the male historical author, Tsurayuki.

I choose, however, to be more faithful to the text and to acknowledge the presence of shifting perspectives—a phenomenon similar to the seamless "maleness" to "femaleness" continuum found in the Kashiwagi/narrator passage. At the outset of this passage from *The Tosa Diary*, someone faces a stand of pine trees and laments the loss of his/her child. The persona at this juncture appears to be female (either the narrator or the deceased child's mother, we cannot be sure) and this fact, plus the presence of the *wabun* discourse and orthography, indicate a female presence, but the occurrence soon after of the *kanbun* expressions *(taezu)shite* and *hisokani* denote a male presence. After acquiescing to this change, the reader is suddenly confronted a few words further by a verb with no honorifics *(ieri-keru)*, indicating that the persona is again female. One poem and two verbs later, the utilization of a conjecture suffix *(mu* in *aramu)* again turns the narration male. The passage, then, moves in and out of the perspectives of male and female with no indication as to exactly when and where the switches occur. Is it male or female at any or all of these points? I suggest that it is neither totally one nor the other. Rather, the point of view is a conflation of maleness and femaleness, each narrative moment producing a different gendered perspective, neither entirely male nor entirely female but, depending upon the "strength" or "weakness" of each perspective, located somewhere along the continuum between the two.

Even in the first line of the diary, where it appears clear that the perspective is female, indicators of maleness occur. The language, orthography, and the hearsay suffix *naru* in "otoko mo sunaru niki" indicate female, but the word "diary," a foreign loanword in the Heian period, was probably written in *kanji* (Chinese characters) (Hagitani, 52), marking male expertise. Further, the readers' knowledge that the historical author was Tsurayuki, a male courtier, had as great an effect in producing maleness as the opening statement, the language, and the orthography had in producing femaleness. Thus, even in the first line of the diary, which most Japanese commentators would say denotes a woman persona, we find a not-entirely-female, not-entirely-male persona.

This shifting back and forth between male and female perspectives in *The Tosa Diary* is possible because of the lack of a clear morphological distinction between direct and indirect discourse in classical Japanese (Bowring, *Murasaki Shikibu: The Tale of Genji*, 63; Fowler, chap. 2). Since few if any pronouns are included and no changes for person or tense are marked when the text moves from direct to indirect quotes, classical Japanese does not permit definitive rendering into either a first- or a third-person narration. This opens the way for the blending and merging of two voices, allowing both to share the same textual space. A second, and, for the purposes of this chapter, more provocative reason for the ambiguity lies in the nature of the so-called personal pronouns, especially those for "I" (e.g., *watashi* in modern Japanese, *wa ga/ware* in classical). Taking its cue from the narrative persona of Japanese poetry (*waka*), the classical Japanese "I" is more open-ended and undifferentiated than the conventional first-person "I" in Western poetry and narratives.[33] As noted earlier, the Japanese "I" is open-ended and undifferentiated, because Japanese "personal pronouns" are not equivalent to personal pronouns in English. Unlike their English counterparts, the modern Japanese *watashi* and the classical Japanese *ware* are not expressive of person-hood, agency, and personal identity but are defined relationally (insider to outsider, senior to junior member) and contextually (formal versus informal, court versus home). Thus the *ware* in a Japanese poem or a diary can have room for more than the desig-nated fictive character; it can include the narrator, as we saw in the Kashiwagi-narrator analysis above, and even the reader, as my study on the narrative triad in *The Tale of Genji* argues. The "I" in the West-ern novel *The Confessions of Felix Krull*, in contrast, refers to no one but the title character Felix Krull, and a reader will always identify the "I" as indicating Felix (because the work is narrated in the first person). The Japanese poem—and diary—persona, however, is often not even marked by *ware*, and, even when it is, it does not function solely as referent to a designated fictive persona.

With seldom any delineation of person, gender, or social status, and lacking the exclusivity of personal pronouns in English, the *ware* in the Japanese poem and the diary is "referentially empty, shifting, and contextual[ly based]" (Kondo, 26–30). The stance of the *ware* per-sona is that of an experiencer/witness of an event or an emotion, its non-gender-differentiated, multi-persona voice remaining fluid and shifting. It is not a first-person point of view that represents only a single, particular persona. Chiyuki Kumakura considers this per-spective pervasive in Japanese literature and labels it the "speaker's point of view." Inscribing few indices of difference, the *ware* persona encourages multiple participation in the fictive world, inviting all—whether character, reader, or another narrator-persona—who are willing to assume the stance of experiencer/witness of the events re-counted to share the fictive moment. The contextually implied per-sona of the Japanese poem—and of the diary—is fluid and open-ended; the presence of the character does not preclude a sharing by narrator and reader, and the presence of one narrator-persona does not eliminate the presence of another.

As briefly alluded to above, the affinity present between narrator and character, and among reader, character, and narrator, can also occur between narrator and narrator (that is, between the woman and the provincial governor / chief passenger personas). Since *The Tosa Diary* persona is more contextually and relationally defined, it, like the Japanese poetic persona, does not necessarily function exclusively as referent of the female persona. In the absence of an "I" in most textual moments, and in the Japanese pronoun's capacity to be more open-ended and undifferentiated even when present, other indicators of the gender — and, therefore, the identity — of the persona, such as the perspective from which the story is told and the use of Chinese or Japanese locutions, undercut the identification of the persona as solely that of the woman persona or the surrogate governor.

The female voice, then — that of the narrator introduced in the first line — provides the frame and the basic perspective. She chronicles the poems and the events of the trip and narrates the personal: the bereavement for a dead child left buried in a strange land, the private fears of a journey by sea, the shock at the state of disrepair of the house left several years earlier, the disillusionment at finding that the home to which she had long dreamed of returning was as alien and unwelcoming as the provinces and only assailed her/them with memories of the deceased child. The other voice, the male-courtier voice, perceptible largely at the level of style and diction, however, is present at all times as well — so much so that Japanese scholars have privileged the male voice to the exclusion of the female voice. The content may be personal and private, closer to Japanese poetry than to the Chinese courtier diaries or even to Chinese poetry, but the diction and style in which it is phrased often reflect the touch of the male courtier, as we saw in the use of Chinese terms in the passage ironically following directly on the introduction of the woman persona. (Watanabe Minoru, in his informative book *Heianchō bunshōshi*, discusses several other instances.)[34] Even at the level of content, however, the interests and perspective are often more public and "male-based," as the numerous descriptions of parties and public composition of (especially) Chinese poetry indicate. Thus, although the "official" voice of the narrative belongs to the woman persona, the male courtier voice conflates with and participates in her performance at every juncture.

♨

Why did the text utilize two voices? No doubt the use of only the male courtier / provincial governor persona would have limited the content largely to precedents and rules of court and family rituals, injunctions to descendants, and perhaps notations of what transpired during the day — the stuff of male-courtier Chinese diaries. Utilizing a woman persona permitted the discussion of more private topics, a practice primarily associated with Japanese poetry, but total adherence to such an agenda would have meant the effacement of male-courtier concerns. The maintaining of both voices, neither totally effacing the other, however, resulted in a new text — a rich multi-voiced, multi-gendered text. By manipulating the narrative conventions of the day, then, *The Tosa Diary* created a gender- and genre-bending text that cut across the culturally determined textual boundaries delineated by the period. This, of course, meant that the gender-differentiated barriers that normally separated the textual productions of men and women had to be crossed and gender-based elements refashioned to "craft" personas that would more sensitively embody its story. It is remarkable that a text as early as the tenth century recognized that the identities of "man" and "woman" are created through convention and belief, that these conventions could be subverted, and that the blending and merging of the two produces not androgyny but a multitude of possibilities. In the process of this discovery, *The Tosa Diary* engaged in a remarkable performance of a narrative production of multi-gendered selves.

Despite this phenomenal feat, *The Tosa Diary* has remained, in my opinion, greatly underrated and misunderstood, due largely, no doubt, to the fact that it resides in the interstices of Heian male and female textual production, as well as of Japanese and Western literary and critical scholarship. Only when the discrepant audiences who "read" the narrative understand that knowledge is situated and not disembodied (Haraway), that we all speak from particular positions and agendas, that it is position and location that produce specific modes of reading and knowing (Mohanty), and that these can engender alternative readings (Mani, 25–26) which can act as powerful critiques of the traditions between which they exist — only then will the cross-cultural significance of a work like *The Tosa Diary* be fully appreciated.

Notes

I express my appreciation to Steven Carter, Dorinne Kondo, C. T. Nishimoto, and Eri Yasuhara for their insightful readings of this paper.

1. The passage can also be translated: "I intend to see whether a woman can produce one of those diaries that I have heard (that) men write." I have used the edition of *Tosa nikki* in Matsumura Seiichi et al., 29–68. There are two English translations of *The Tosa Diary*: Helen C. McCullough's "*Tosa Nikki*: A Tosa Journal" in *Kokin Wakashū*, 263–91, and Earl Miner's "*The Tosa Diary*" in *Japanese Poetic Diaries*, 57–91. All quotations in this paper are from the McCullough translation, although I have made some modification in the first line. Hereafter, page references in the text are to McCullough's English translation or to Matsumura et al.'s edition of the diary in Japanese.

2. As will become evident, the term "persona" may not be suitable in talking about the narrating presences in *Tosa*, and the less person-oriented term "voice" may be better; for lack of better terms, however, I will use "persona" and "voice" to indicate both the female and the male (governor) narrating figures in the diary.

3. My appreciation to Dorinne Kondo for coining this phrase.

4. In Japan, gender and feminist scholarship has been introduced into some (i.e., French and English) literature departments, into sociology (largely through the work of Ueno Chizuko), and history, but it has gained little credence in the field of classical Japanese literature (*koku bungaku*) and has not firmly established itself in the Japanese scholarly world. Masao Miyoshi points out that there are still taboos on serious discussion of sex and gender matters even today and that feminism has yet to take hold in Japan. He does conclude, however, that feminism cannot be contained indefinitely. See Chapter 8, "Gathering Voices: Japanese Women and Women Writers," especially 205–6 and 211–12, in Miyoshi's instructive book, *Off Center*. Some change has been taking place, as is seen in the appearance of special editions on feminism and of a section on feminism in a recent issue of a mainstream literary journal discussing theoretical approaches to literature.

5. *Kanbun* is a Japanese version of classical Chinese in which a line of Chinese is written in the Chinese word order (subject-verb-object) with special marks that enable the reader to transpose it into Japanese syntactic order (subject-object-verb), thereby rendering it into a kind of Japanese. Narrowly defined, *hiragana* (or Japanese, in my discussion) is the orthographic system used to record the Japanese language, but it can be used, as in the term *wabun*, to indicate "native" (as opposed to the foreign classical Chinese) discourse, used by the members of the court for everyday, private activities such as letter writing and the composition of Japanese poetry (*waka*; see note below).

There is some dispute over the gender coding of *kanbun* as *otoko-te* or the "male hand" and *hiragana/wabun* as the *onna-te* or the "female hand," for it is not clear to what extent these conventions of literary production were upheld or to what extent all men but not women became conversant in both *kanbun* and *hiragana*, especially as the period progresses. I would argue, however, that at least in *Tosa* these literary conventions seem operative, and a dichotomous opposition is set up between them. Most studies of *The Tosa Diary* would concur.

6. During the Heian period, *waka* referred most narrowly to the 31-syllable *tanka* (short poem), but, used in a broader sense, it meant court poetry in all its forms, including the *chōka* (long poem) and the *sedōka* (head-repeated poem), in contrast to popular songs, religious hymns, and other later derivative forms. I also use it in its general sense of Japanese, as opposed to Chinese, poetry.

7. This, of course, characterizes the classic realist Western novel and not its avant-garde manifestations in the twentieth century, which attempt to subvert this expectation.

8. Even though it is widely recognized in gender research that gender is not just male or female (as attested to by the presence of transsexuals and gender-blenders) and that gender is a social construct rather than a biological or philosophical fact, a multi-gendered, not-entirely-male, not-entirely-female persona still remains implausible to many Western readers. See Kessler and McKenna; and Devor.

9. See also Bachnik.

10. Miyoshi points out that Japan may have gained status economically and can therefore no longer be considered a Third World nation on that ground, but that it has not done so culturally. He cautions (246n1) that the terms "First and Third Worlds" do not represent "single regional entities but are assemblies of complexly diversified and differentiated nations and societies." He nonetheless feels that "in terms of social and cultural development" and "economic and military domination throughout history and at present," these terms are useful in certain contexts. My use of "First World" and "Western" elicits similar concerns for caution and elasticity. In other essays, I have tried to convey this caution and elasticity by leaving "west/western" in the lower case. See also Okada, "Introduction."

11. Miyoshi further cautions against the danger of constructing Japan as "ontologically exceptional" and argues for placing Japanese literature in its proper context, i.e., that of Korean and Chinese literature. See also Okada, "Introduction."

12. The present literary-critical scene is changing for a segment of Japanese critics, who are attempting to incorporate Western scholarship on narrative into the reading of *monogatari* (tale narrative), but on the whole such movement is not yet discernible among those working on *The Tosa Diary* and *nikki bungaku* (Chiyuki Kumakura, pers. comm., Aug. 13, 1992).

13. Katō Umaki (1721–77), a scholar and a poet, and Ueda Akinari (1734–1809), a prominent prose writer and scholar, are cited in Shinagawa (289) as proponents of this second theory and as having presented these views in a book entitled *Tosa nikki kai*, but no date of publication is given. To

further complicate matters, under a list of major reference works Shinagawa records this title as having been authored by someone else; it is not clear whether a separate volume with the same title is being indicated or not. Hagitani (514) verifies the positions of both Katō Umaki and Ueda Akinari, but makes no reference to a book title. Kishimoto Yuzuru proposed a similar view in *Tosa nikki kōshō* (Tokyo, 1815). See Shinagawa, 289–92, and Hagitani, 511–17, for an overview of research done on *The Tosa Diary*.

14. Konishi, 285–87; Imai, 105. Kagawa Kageki, a poet of the Tokugawa period (1600–1868), was probably one of the first to formulate this theory in *Tosa nikki sōken* (Tokyo, 1823). See Hagitani (514) for an overview of research on *The Tosa Diary*.

15. Hagitani Boku, in his extensive commentary on *The Tosa Diary*, for example, views the woman persona as integral to the fictionalization of the work but more as a mask that allowed Tsurayuki to express his true feelings. Another noted scholar, Hisamatsu Sen'ichi, sees the woman persona largely as an indispensable third-person *monogatari* perspective through which Tsurayuki could disclose his innermost thoughts. Shigetomi Tsuyoshi, Mezaki Tokuei, and, to a certain extent, Imai Gen'ai retool the *haikai* theory presented above, contending that Tsurayuki used the woman persona—an unconventional, somewhat humorous (in its disparity with Tsurayuki's actual identity) guise—to plumb the depths of his soul. Lastly, Akiyama Ken and Kimura Masanori argue that the female persona was merely employed to enable Tsurayuki to "find" himself—to explore, search out, and, ultimately, put down on paper the disparate and fragmented aspects of his self.

16. Others such as Hisamatsu (275) and Hagitani (491) agree. Strictly speaking, these scholars and the commentary by Matsumura et al. do record instances of the woman persona throughout the work, but many, especially Hagitani, do not consider that the diary is written strictly from the point of view of the woman persona beyond the Twenty-sixth Day of the Twelfth Month. My argument contests this reading.

Recently, Kikuchi has revised his statement (pers. comm., June 26, 1994), arguing that the woman persona reappears at the end of the diary as reciter of the last two poems. Kikuchi contends that since Tsurayuki began with the woman persona, it is only fitting that he close with her. Kikuchi has written an article on the matter, and it is being considered for publication.

17. Imai, 105; Akiyama, "Nikki bungaku no seiritsu to tenkai," 39; Hagitani, 491; Hisamatsu, 274; Kikuchi, 124.

18. My thanks to David Roman (pers. comm., Nov. 21, 1992) for pointing this out.

19. Unfortunately, little research has been done on this fascinating topic.

20. I thank Lata Mani (pers. comm., Nov. 6, 1992) for helping me refine my ideas on the function of criticism in the interstices.

21. Okada feels that women, by their use of *hiragana* writing, "locked"

men out both literally and figuratively and were the true cultural power brokers during the Heian period. I concur that women were not entirely powerless, but I do not believe that the picture is as rosy as the one Okada paints. Although women may have had some "scriptive dominance" in terms of prose, the production of waka, especially the compilation of imperial anthologies, was a male-dominated enterprise, presided over by male compilers and commissioned by [male] emperors. Further, many of the diaries and narratives of the period record tales of women at the mercy of male erotic whim in a polygamous society — ultimately not a position of power for women. Thus, I would conclude that the situation was a much more complex one, with the contradictory poles of agency and victimization existing side by side. As Mani points out in her discussion of the status of Indian women, it does not necessarily have to be one or the other but a combination of the two, both co-existing at the same time, often in contradictory relationship to each other. See Mani, 37; and Okada, chap. 6.

22. This is a much too simplistic model and does not take into consideration a third segment of the population, the monastic world of career clerics and those who took the tonsure in adult life (Steven Carter, pers. comm., Oct. 15, 1992). Further, it does not fully account for the fact that many women had knowledge of both kanbun and the Chinese classics and referred to them in their writings, although many of them acknowledged that it was considered improper to do so. Nonetheless, it appears that Tosa presents kanbun and wabun as alternative discourses and places them in opposition to each other.

23. In The Murasaki Shikibu Diary (trans. Bowring), for example, Murasaki Shikibu explains that her father always lamented the fact that she had not been born a boy, for she was much quicker at learning Chinese than her brother. On another occasion, Murasaki Shikibu talks about teaching her mistress, the empress, Chinese in secret, because many were gossiping about how unbecoming it was for them, as women, to be studying Chinese. In The Kagerō Diary (trans. Seidensticker, The Gossamer Years), the author, Michitsuna no Haha, discusses the banishment of a prominent member of court but feels compelled to explain why she includes matters of governance in her work, for such matters were not acceptable topics for women's diaries. In The Tosa Diary itself the woman persona remarks: "People chanted Chinese poems, and the host, the guest of honor, and others exchanged Japanese poems. I cannot record the Chinese ones" (264) — precisely because as a woman the woman persona was not suppose to be able to understand Chinese. It cannot, however, be denied that in practice, as noted above, some women had knowledge of both kanbun and the Chinese classics.

24. Men did, however, compose poetry in Japanese for the often more formal (and public) uta-awase contests.

25. From 607 to 894 the Japanese court frequently dispatched official embassies to the Sui and later Tang dynasties (Watson, 4–5).

26. The following conclusions are taken from a paper presented at the

Association for Asian Studies in 1988, in which I compared two male-authored works (*The Tosa Diary* and *The Great Mirror* [*Ōkagami*]) and two female-authored works (*The Kagerō Diary* and *A Tale of Flowering Fortunes* [*Eiga monogatari*]). Interestingly, Japanese scholars of classical literature seem fairly confident about the gender of the authors of tales and other works even when the identities of the authors are unknown. Only works of corporate authorship such as *Tales of Yamato* (*Yamato monogatari*) have posed any difficulty, although most scholars consider another work of corporate authorship, the *Tales of Ise* (*Ise monogatari*), to be male-authored.

27. The term "appropriation" comes from Western theory and must be modified to fit the Heian example: my use of the term, therefore, presupposes male use of female/woman but without male being dominant over female and without masculine disdain of the female as inferior and undesirable.

Of interest, but not directly related to my thesis, is Richard Bowring's discussion of Tsurayuki's writing of the diary as an attempt to reappropriate the female into the male sphere. According to Bowring, as men in the tenth century began to realize that through their obsession with Chinese they were losing control of their own language, they commissioned the compilation of the *Kokinshū*, a poetic anthology with an underrepresentation of women, to return Japanese poetry to the public arena and the male domain. The writing of *The Tosa Diary*, too, was supposed to have been done in the same spirit and "signified a reappropriation of the female into the male sphere" (*Murasaki Shikibu: The Tale of Genji*, 11). Bowring's point is well taken, but I do not think that we can necessarily assume, as he does, that by Tsurayuki's time the production of diary literature or even *wabun* prose was already a well-established, woman-dominated field that men felt compelled to reclaim. Women appear as the predominant consumers of *wabun* prose works, but it is not as clear that they are as yet its primary producers. I, too, believe that a reappropriation of the female does take place, but I am of the opinion that it occurs after the writing of *The Tale of Genji*. See Bowring, *Murasaki Shikibu: The Tale of Genji*, 11–12.

28. See, e.g., Bowring, *Murasaki Shikibu: Her Diary*; and Morris.

29. The modern novelist Tanizaki Jun'ichirō followed a similar strategy in two works of his later years, *The Key* and *Diary of a Mad Old Man*, which parody his lifelong obsession with femmes fatales.

30. It may be difficult to claim categorically that these expressions could indeed be considered *kanbun* and, therefore, male-marked, but, just as the earliest usage of French expressions in English was at first marked as new, innovative, and/or upper-class, these expressions have been identified as more *kanbun* than *hiragana* in their usage by Matsumura et al. and others. Until there is research to the contrary, I will follow their lead for the purposes of this paper. The same can be said for what Matsumura et al. identify as Chinese-style couplets, rhetorical flourishes based on Chinese poetry, and allusions to Chinese poetry in the following discussion.

31. See Kondo, chap. 1.

32. Suffixes of reasoning and interpreting, honorifics (a complex set of verbs, nouns, and related expressions that establish the relative social standing of speaker, listener, and referent), and the like reveal the presence of a mediating persona, often a narrator.

33. For further discussion of this point, see Miyake. Some work has been done on the nature of personal pronouns in Japanese, but much more needs to be undertaken, especially in terms of how they affect narration and the narrative production of self.

34. Watanabe, sect. 4, chap. 1. See Hagitani, 491, for a discussion of the gradual demise of the woman's voice in the diary, and 495–99, for a catalog of Chinese-style expressions. See also Tsukishima.

Works Cited

Akiyama Ken. "Nikki bungaku no seiritsu to tenkai: *Tosa nikki* to *Kagerō nikki.*" In idem, *Ōchō no bungaku: Heian kyūtei no hikari to kage.* Tokyo: Ōbunsha, 1982, 38–44.

———. "Nikki bungaku ron." In idem, *Ōchō joryū bungaku no sekai.* Tokyo: Tokyo daigaku shuppankai, 1972, 166–92.

Bachnik, Jane. "Deixis and Self/Other Reference in Japanese Discourse." In *Working Papers in Sociolinguistics 99.* Austin: Southwest Educational Development Laboratory, 1982, 1–36.

Bakhtin, Mihail. *Rabelais and His World.* Trans. Hélène Iswolsky. Bloomington: Indiana University Press, 1984.

Bowring, Richard, trans. *Murasaki Shikibu: Her Diary and Poetic Memoirs: A Translation and Study.* Princeton: Princeton University Press, 1982.

———. *Murasaki Shikibu: The Tale of Genji.* Cambridge, Eng.: Cambridge University Press, 1988.

Butler, Judith. *Gender Trouble: Feminism and the Subversion of Identity.* New York: Routledge, 1990.

———. "Performative Acts and Gender Constitution: An Essay in Phenomenology and Feminist Theory." *Theatre Journal* 40, no. 4 (1988): 519–31.

Chow, Rey. *Woman and Chinese Modernity: The Politics of Reading Between West and East.* Minneapolis: University of Minnesota Press, 1991.

Devor, Holly. *Gender Blending: Confronting the Limits of Duality.* Bloomington: Indiana University Press, 1989.

Fowler, Edward. *The Rhetoric of Confession: Shishōsetsu in Early Twentieth-Century Japanese Fiction.* Berkeley: University of California Press, 1988.

Gilbert, Sandra M. "Costumes of the Mind: Transvestism as Metaphor in Modern Literature." In *Writing and Sexual Difference,* ed. Elizabeth Abel. Chicago: University of Chicago Press, 1980, 193–219.

Hagitani Boku. *Tosa nikki zenchūshaku.* Tokyo: Kadokawa shoten, 1967.

Haraway, Donna. "Situated Knowledges: The Science Question and the

Privilege of Partial Perspective." *Feminist Studies* 14, no. 3 (1988): 575–99.

Hisamatsu Sen'ichi. *Zōho shinpan Nihon bungakushi: chūko.* Tokyo: Ibundō, 1981.

Imai Gen'ai. *Nikki bungaku no kenkyū.* Tokyo: Hanawa shobō, 1935; reprinted—1981.

Kahn, Madeleine. *Narrative Transvestism: Rhetoric and Gender in the Eighteenth-Century English Novel.* Ithaca, N.Y.: Cornell University Press, 1991.

Kessler, Suzanne, and Wendy McKenna. *Gender: An Ethnomethodological Approach.* Chicago: University of Chicago Press, 1978.

Kikuchi Yasuhiko. "Tosa nikki." In idem, *"Kokinshū" igo ni okeru Tsurayuki.* Tokyo: Ofūsha, 1980, 121–70.

Kimura Masanori. "Nikki bungaku no honshitsu to kōsaku shinri." In *Kōza Nihon bungaku no sōten 1: chūkohen.* Tokyo, 1973, 99–126.

Kishimoto Yuzuru. *Tosa nikki kōshō.* Tokyo, 1815.

Kondo, Dorinne. *Crafting Selves: Power, Gender, and Discourse of Identity in a Japanese Workplace.* Chicago: University of Chicago Press, 1990.

Konishi Jin'ichi. *A History of Japanese Literature,* vol. 2, *The Early Middle Ages.* Trans. Aileen Gatten; ed. Earl Miner. Princeton: Princeton University Press, 1989.

Kumakura Chiyuki. "Interpersonal Speaker: The Point of View in Japanese Narrative." Paper presented at the Colloquium, Center for Japanese Studies, University of California at Berkeley, 1986.

Mani, Lata. "Multiple Mediations: Feminist Scholarship in the Age of Multinational Reception." *Feminist Review* 35 (1990): 24–41.

Matsumura Seiichi et al., eds. "Tosa nikki." In *Tosa nikki, Kagerō nikki. Nihon koten bungaku zenshū* 9. Tokyo: Shōgakukan, 1973, 29–68.

McCullough, Helen, trans. "Tosa Nikki: A Tosa Journal." In idem, *Kokin Wakashū: The First Imperial Anthology of Japanese Poetry with "Tosa Nikki" and "Shinsen Waka."* Stanford: Stanford University Press, 1985, 263–91.

Mezaki Tokuei. *Ki no Tsurayuki. Jinbutsu sōsho* 73. Tokyo: Yoshikawa kobunkan, 1961.

Miner, Earl, trans. "The Tosa Diary." In idem, *Japanese Poetic Diaries.* Berkeley: University of California Press, 1969, 57–91.

Miyake, Lynne K. "The Narrative Triad in *The Tale of Genji*: Narrator, Reader, and Text." In *Approaches to Teaching Murasaki Shikibu's "The Tale of Genji,"* ed. Edward Kamens. New York: MLA, 1993, 77–87.

Miyoshi, Masao. *Off Center: Power and Culture Relations Between Japan and the United States.* Cambridge, Mass.: Harvard University Press, 1991.

Mohanty, Chandra Talpade. "Feminist Encounters: Locating the Politics of Experience." *Copyright* 1, no. 1 (1987): 30–44.

Morris, Ivan, trans. *The Pillow Book of Sei Shōnagon.* Suffolk, Eng.: Penguin Books, 1967.

Newton, Esther. *Mother Camp: Female Impersonators in America.* Englewood Cliffs, N.J.: Prentice Hall, 1972.

Okada, H. Richard. *Figures of Resistance: Language, Poetry, and Narrating in "The Tale of Genji" and Other Mid-Heian Texts.* Durham, N.C.: Duke University Press, 1991.

Rubin, Gayle. "The Traffic in Women: Notes on the 'Political Economy' of Sex." In *Towards an Anthropology of Women*, ed. Rayna Reiter. New York: Monthly Review Press, 1975, 157–210.

Seidensticker, Edward G., trans. *The Gossamer Years (Kagerō nikki).* Rutland, Vt.: Tuttle, 1964.

Shigetomo Tsuyoshi. "*Tosa nikki* ni tsuite." *Kokugo to kokubungaku* 25, no. 6 (1948): 14–24.

Shinagawa Kazuko. *Zenyakuchū: Tosa nikki.* Tokyo: Kōdansha, 1983.

Showalter, Elaine. "Critical Cross-Dressing: Male Feminists and the Woman of the Year." In *Men in Feminism*, ed. Alice Jardine and Paul Smith. New York: Methuen, 1987, 116–32.

Tanizaki Jun'ichirō. *Diary of a Mad Old Man.* Trans. Howard S. Hibbett. New York: Berkeley, 1971.

———. *The Key.* Trans. Howard S. Hibbett. New York: Berkeley, 1971.

Taylor, Anne. *Male Novelists and Their Female Voices: Literary Masquerades.* Troy, N.Y.: Whitston, 1981.

Tsukishima Hiroshi. "*Tosa nikki* to kanbun kundoku." In *Heianchō nikki I: Tosa nikki, Kagerō nikki*, ed. Nihon bungaku kenkyū shiryō kankōkai. Tokyo: Yūseidō, 1971, 113–20.

Watanabe Minoru. *Heianchō bunshō shi.* Tokyo: Tokyo daigaku shuppankai, 1981.

Watson, Burton, trans. *Japanese Literature in Chinese*, vol. 1, *Poetry and Prose in Chinese by Japanese Writers of the Early Period.* New York: Columbia University Press, 1975.

3

The Origins of the Concept
of "Women's Literature"

JOAN E. ERICSON

Japanese women writers occupy a pre-eminent position in the classical literary canon, a phenomenon that many observers, both Japanese and Western, have noted as an anomaly in world literatures (Morris, 211; Katō, 170–88). Literary histories also commonly mention that after an earlier period of dominance, Japanese women writers were eclipsed, and virtually silenced, before their re-emergence in the modern era (Vernon, 17–32; Keene, *Dawn to the West*, 1113). Today, any sizable Japanese bookstore contains a section dedicated to women writers, usually promoting the latest winners of the Women's Literary Prize or current bestsellers, as well as an impressive array of works, principally fiction, by women. Furthermore, the wide selection of stories by modern Japanese women writers translated into English since the early 1980's attests to the recognition that even modern women writers are now beginning to receive outside Japan.[1] But a Western reader might easily miss the specific connotations that the terms "woman writer" (*joryū sakka*) or "women's literature" (*joryū bungaku*) have conveyed, at least until recently, in the modern era.[2]

The implications of Japanese gender-based literary categorizations are difficult to summarize, both because of ambiguities and inconsistencies in the ways the terms are employed in literary criticism, and because of the conflation of literary aesthetics with far more pervasive and deeply rooted social attitudes toward gender differences. Although many modern literary critics have treated the categories "women's literature" and "woman writer" as value-neutral terms whose substance is self-evident (Yoshida, 10; Ikari, 53–54; Kikuta; Muramatsu, *Kindai joryū sakka no shōzō*, 258), they have assumed that "women's literature" is a specific literary style—principally characterized by sentimental lyricism, and impressionistic, non-intellectual, detailed observations of daily life—and that a "woman writer" writes in this fashion. Although popular, this style is often critically disparaged. Even among those critics who denied any explicit disapproval of the style, the net effect of categorizing the works of modern Japanese women writers by the gender of their author was to segregate this body of work from the modern literary canon.

In the past decade, the terms "women's literature" and "woman writer" have come under increasing criticism for their limiting and derogatory connotations; Japanese feminists have substituted the term *josei* (female) for *joryū*, to avoid the implication of a specific "style" (a literal translation of *ryū*) (Tomioka, 107–8; Yuri, 74; Endō Orie, 36). Although "women's literature" (*joryū bungaku*) previously had been applied mainly to works written in the modern period,[3] in the contemporary feminist usage, *joryū bungaku* is relegated solely to the classical canon, where, it is argued, "women's literature" does mean a specific, and highly regarded, style of writing (Negoro, 1; Kanai, 1–10; Muramatsu and Watanabe, 1). In the early 1990's, the far-reaching reappraisal by feminist critics (see, e.g., Ueno et al.; Egusa and Urushida; Saegusa; and Yamashita) of modern literary classics as "male literature" (*danryū bungaku*) provoked a firestorm of reaction.[4] This essay contributes to the contemporary debate by examining the modern origins of the practice of categorizing literature by gender— how "women's literature" (*joryū bungaku*) came to be the predominant characterization of literary works by women—treating the concept as a set of institutional practices that crystallized in the 1920's, and briefly illustrating its complex, and not wholly detrimental, impact on women writers.

The contradictory legacies of the categorization by gender are visible in the curious mix of reactions toward these concepts among the women writers I interviewed. Setouchi Harumi (1922–) advocated the elimination of all such distinctions, including not only the literary concept but the special prizes and societies honoring women writers that developed over the past fifty years and played an important role in promoting many women's literary careers. Sata Ineko (1904–) denied that there was a stigma to the term, yet mentioned, parenthetically, that she was pleased when critics wrote that she did not seem like a woman writer. Tsushima Yūko (1947–) observed that the notion of "women's literature" as a specific style no longer reflected the diversity of approaches employed by women writers. She also expressed annoyance at the continued existence of a segregated space in bookstores for women's literature, separate from general literature, yet she gave as a reason for this that perhaps readers simply were used to this division, and admitted to haunting these sections herself to see what has been newly published.

Tsushima expressed the dominant interpretation: that the segregation of women's literature cannot be understood as a case of contemporary discrimination but reflects an immutable tradition, harking back to classical antiquity, deeply rooted in the public's mind. When women writers point to the obvious exceptions to a systematic categorization of women writers, or particular works by women, solely by gender, they are certainly correct. There has always been a permeability to the concept of women's literature, for it never applied to all women writers or to all the works of those who were thought to write in that style. This selective application of the term poses the initial problem for the contemporary reader. Since those few women who have received the highest critical praise are generally not characterized as "women writers," nor is their work viewed as "women's literature," for most "women writers" are these labels earned, rather than being merely ascribed because of the writer's sex? Such a categorization is significant, for at its core is a judgment of the merits of a writer's literary aesthetics. Women may publish in prestigious journals, but the categories through which their work is discussed prejudge their contributions as marginal and outside the literary mainstream. Why women have remained marginal within the modern Japanese canon cannot be explained without serious consideration of the institutional practices and social processes that determine who gets published, who constitutes the readership, how a work is received—in addition to how the literary aesthetic is conveyed.

The following discussion of the codification of women's literature in the modern era is not meant to be a complete or exhaustive coverage of women writers; rather, the treatment is selective, designed to illustrate how categorization by gender became the predominant means of assessing women's literary efforts in the middle half of the twentieth century.

When Was Women's Literature?

Women's contributions to the classical Japanese canon were considerable, far greater than women's contributions to, for example, English or French literatures. In the Nara period (685–793), the *Kojiki* (Record of ancient matters; 712), the earliest extant book in Japan, is said to have been recited by Hieda no Are, a female royal attendant, and transcribed by the male scholar Ō no Yasumaro (Konishi, 1: 161).[5] Perhaps the greatest of all Japanese poetic anthologies, the *Man'yōshū* (The ten thousand leaves; ca. 759), includes selections by more than 130 women poets. For their enduring influence on succeeding generations, the accomplishments of women writers during the Heian period (794–1185) stand above all others. The centrality of women to this era's literary canon may be explained, in part, by the crystallization of a poetic aesthetic that elevated pure *yamato kotoba* (native Japanese language), even as it sought to mirror the ideals of classical Chinese. The *Kokin wakashū* (Anthology of ancient and contemporary Japanese poems; 905) illustrates this emerging aesthetic; it was written, probably, in *hiragana*, the "woman's hand" (*onna no te*, or *onna-de*) that, by the tenth century, was considered to be the sole script suitable for women (Konishi, 140–42; Bowring, "The Female Hand"). Prose classics by Heian court women, such as Michitsuna no Haha's *Kagerō nikki* (The gossamer years, or Kagerō diary; ca. 974), Sei Shōnagon's *Makura no sōshi* (The pillow book; ca. 996), Murasaki Shikibu's *Genji monogatari* (The tale of Genji; ca. 1010), Takasue no Musume's *Sarashina nikki* (As I crossed a bridge of dreams, or Sarashina diary; ca. 1050), are held up as exemplary standards for Japanese literature.[6]

The interplay of language and gender in classical Japanese literature both confirms and qualifies Wittgenstein's dictum that "the limits of my language mean the limits of my world" (115). In the court literature of the Heian period, language demarcated the boundaries of gender-specific divisions between two literary arenas. Realms restricted to men consisted of official documents and literary works, such as poetry, prose, and diaries written in literary Chinese. A notable exception was *waka* poetry, which was written in *hiragana* and often signed. Because the conventions of men's formal sinified styles often permeated unacknowledged works, literary scholars have been able to attribute the sex of the authors of anonymous Heian texts based on gender markers in the language.[7]

Having been denied formal education—specifically, the extensive training needed to write in classical Chinese—highborn women employed a written form that more closely approximated the spoken Japanese word and, moreover, enabled them to express their private emotions and perceptions in both fiction and poetic diaries in ways that were intimate, immediate, and lyrical. Thus, the very conventions utilized to exclude women from government and so-called serious matters gave them the use of a vehicle that facilitated the portrayal of the nature of social relations and the subjectivity of experience.

The boundaries between gender-divided literary realms were, however, permeable. A few women, such as the Empress Shōtoku (718–70) and Princess Uchiko (807–47), wrote Chinese poems, and most literary women, despite their limited education, learned and utilized some Chinese characters (Keene, *Anthology of Japanese Literature*, 162–64). Yet for women to flaunt their erudition was a breach of court etiquette. Murasaki Shikibu chafed at the sobriquet Our Lady of the Chronicles, earned because of the sophistication of her literary style and her reading of literary Chinese.[8] And she herself was not above disparaging her contemporary Sei Shōnagon for littering her writing with Chinese characters (Bowring, *Murasaki Shikibu*, 131). Women were expected to restrict themselves to informal means of expression and highly personal observations or emotions—expectations that must have prompted Ki no Tsurayuki (870?–945?), the main editor of the *Kokin wakashū*, to adopt a female persona in his *Tosa nikki* (The Tosa diary; 934–35), a travel account that begins: "Diaries are written by men, I am told. I am writing one nevertheless, to see what a woman can do" (trans. Keene, *Travelers of a Hundred Ages*, 20).[9] Despite the artifice of a female identity—"the author declares 'she' cannot understand poetry composed in Chinese, the language of men" (Keene, *Travelers of a Hundred Ages*, 21)—the diary has a formal sinified structure and lacks the introspection characteristic of Heian women's writings. Employing a female narrator, nevertheless, allowed the author to include a collection of *waka* poems and, perhaps more important, to express the narrator's grief over the death of a daughter.

Wittgenstein's "limits" can perhaps be qualified when considering gender roles in literature. Despite the inescapable influence of social and literary conventions, an author's choice of language is also determined by intention and "affiliation" that link the work to other literary and intellectual traditions.[10] However sharply delineated and closely watched, boundaries remain porous, in part because of their fundamentally artificial character; women may be expected to act in specific, limited ways, but, like all people, they remain capable of expressing their own creativity in ways that may challenge or subvert expectations. Trespassing — or simply "passing" — and impersonation are not unique to the Japanese experience. Henry Louis Gates, Jr., has written of the long tradition in American letters of adopting a language and identity to present, often with painstaking verisimilitude, supposed firsthand accounts of lives and cultures only imagined, notably in the ersatz slave narratives written by whites or free blacks for the abolitionist press (27).

Despite women's pre-eminent position in classical Japanese literature, and despite the importance of the heavily feminine tradition of poetry and diaries, a strong female voice seems to have died out in Japanese literature before the modern period.[11] The apparent absence of women writers from the mid-fourteenth through the mid-seventeenth centuries has often been explained by the growing codification and integration into Japanese society of Neo-Confucian precepts (Vernon, 27–28; Chabot). But the change in the nature of women's role in literature appears to be rooted in the earlier medieval era, when transformations in the legal structure of individual inheritance and property rights increasingly subordinated women (Mass, 9, 49, 101–6). Although on occasion women's names can be found in linked-verse (*haikai no renga*) poetry and travel diaries of the Edo period (1603–1868), what has survived in the literary canon from this period was written almost entirely by men.[12] However, for the most part, the female poets existed outside male circles and composed in separate women's poetry matches. The term characterizing their poetry, "women's linked verse" (*nyōbō renga*), denotes something distinct and different from the work of their male counterparts.

The scarcity of female authors in the literary histories of this period thus does not preclude the existence of writing women. Anthologies from the first decades of the twentieth century remind us of the variety and diversity of women's literary efforts during the Edo period. In 1901, two anthologies devoted to women writers were published. One of these, *Joryū bungaku shi* (A history of women's literature), included biographies and excerpts of works by women from the early medieval era up to the end of the Edo period. The four-volume *Joryū bungaku zenshū* (Collection of women's literature), which was edited by Furuya Tomoyoshi and produced in 1918-19 by the same publisher as that of the earlier anthology, included tales (*monogatari*), histories, essays (*zuihitsu*), travel diaries, and poetry by 30 women writers from the Edo period. This collection emphasized the importance of poets of *waka* and *haikai*, especially Kaga no Chiyo (1703-75) and Chie no Uchiko (1745-1807), as well as the diverse accomplishments of Arakida Reiko (1732-1806).[13] But in neither of these anthologies were women writers treated as sharing a common literary style. Instead, the terms for women's literature (*joryū bungaku*) or woman writer (*keishū sakka*) referred simply to the sex of the authors.[14]

The early twentieth-century attempt to recover literary works by Edo-period women could not rely on the standard histories or interpretations, for most women represented in the aforementioned anthologies merely shared their work within a circle of friends and acquaintances and relied on hand-copied, not printed, texts. Interestingly, in 1916, the woman poet Yosano Akiko (1878-1942) wrote a biography of Reiko, whose extensive *oeuvre* had not been published during her lifetime. As one of the handful of prominent women in the literary world of the 1910's, Yosano Akiko sought to establish a literary lineage of women writers in the recent past, building a bridge between the widely heralded, but distant, literary achievements of classical antiquity and the contemporary world where female authors were rare.

From the end of the nineteenth century, women writers began to publish and were received enthusiastically in some circles. In 1895, the literary magazine *Bungei kurabu* (Literary club) published a special issue entitled "Keishū shōsetsu" (Women's fiction) devoted to contemporary women writers (Mawatari, 35); this publication was so popular that two years later a second issue appeared under the same name.[15] But the treatment of critically acclaimed women writers as exceptions revealed the scarcely veiled disdain for women's abilities shared by many critics. For example, Tanabe (later, Miyake) Kaho's novel *Yabu no uguisu* (Nightingale in the grove; 1888) was praised by a critic as "surprisingly complex (considering the author [is] a woman)" (Keene, *Dawn to the West*, 167). And Hoshino Tenchi, a critic who reviewed Higuchi Ichiyō's (1872-96) story "Umoregi" (A buried life; 1892), commented that "not only is the conception unusual, but the style is so incisive it makes one doubt the work was written by a woman" (*Jogakusei* [Schoolgirl, Dec. 1892], trans. Keene, *Dawn to the*

West, 173-74). Moreover, the prominent novelist Tsubouchi Shōyō (1859-1935) praised Miyamoto Yuriko's (1899-1951) first published story "Mazushiki hitobito no mure" (A flock of the poor; 1916) as "unwomanish," since it had few short sentences (Miyamoto Kenji, 7).

Some have viewed such assumptions about women's abilities and styles in the modern era as emblematic of the emerging segregation of women's literature. Akiyama Shun, for instance, in his 1980 essay "Ima joryū bungaku to wa nani ka" (What is women's literature today?), argued that "the concept of 'women's literature' was first used in modern Japanese literature, as seen in references to Higuchi Ichiyō, because women's thinking was thought to be far different in character from the so-called male writer's 'intellect' [*chisei*], a Western scholastic intellect" (125). Akiyama suggested that the disparagement of women writers by Meiji (1868-1912) intellectuals such as the author Kunikida Doppo derived not from a feudalistic patriarchy but from a Meiji (male) elitist attempt to monopolize Western intellectual work. The constellation of attitudes women writers confronted directly affected the nature of their published work. Recent research has uncovered how Higuchi's male mentor, Nakarai Tōsui, edited early drafts of her stories to conform to expectations, in terms of language and characterization, of how a woman should write (Seki, 48-51).

However, the specific characteristics attributed to the work of women writers, and assessments of whether any given writer conformed to those expectations, changed rapidly beginning in the 1890's. Despite the acuity of his observation on the reshaping by the founders of modern Japanese literature of the particular prejudices that confronted women writers, Akiyama failed to cite specific examples of the use of the concept "women's literature" that would allow us to assess how the term was meant. Aside from Akiyama, most other literary critics and historians, including her American biographer Robert Lyons Danly, have not categorized Higuchi Ichiyō as a writer of "women's literature" (Okazaki, 174-78; Keene, *Dawn to the West*, 165-185; Karatani, 135). References to "women writers" or "women's literature" may not have suggested a common style but, as in the anthologies of Edo era women writers, may simply have served to note their gender. By arguing for the existence of a separate and distinct literary category from the 1890's, Akiyama presumed a continuity in the perception of women's writing that stands in sharp contrast to the enormous transformation of social attitudes, including those on gender, of aesthetic tastes, and of institutional dynamics in commercial publishing that characterized the succeeding decades. The specific attributes of this categorization of women's literature and its relation to shifting attitudes toward women and to the tenor of national politics are better explained by the crystallization of social, intellectual, and literary trends of the 1920's and early 1930's.

The Emergence of a Modern Categorization of Women's Literature

For the purposes of this study, the most curious question is one of timing: Why did the concept of women's literature, as something that denoted a specific style, emerge when it did? It is not possible to answer this query by simply examining what women wrote and how their writing changed, for example, during the 1920's; to do so would assume that the label was earned, rather than ascribed, and would tend to separate the production and reception of literature from its broader historical and social context. The segregation of women writers, the categorization by gender, is not simply attributable to an endemic sexism, however deeply rooted that may be in Japanese society. Why women's literature acquired its modern meaning when it did is best attributed to the growth of women's literacy and to the emergence of journals targeted at a female audience, as well as to the reaction to shifting gender roles of the Taishō (1912–26) period.

Women Readers

Literacy—the ability to read *kana* (the Japanese syllabary) and simple *kanji* (Chinese characters)—was widespread by the early twentieth century, even among women. The proportion of girls completing the compulsory four-year primary education rose dramatically from 18 percent in 1875 to 72 percent in 1900 to 97 percent in 1910 (*Nihon kindai kyōiku shi jiten*, 93). The consequences of this rapid transformation to near universal elementary literacy for young women are too often neglected in discussions of the social changes of the Meiji era, but evidence from other areas of the world demonstrates the enormous significance of women's literacy in empowering women and improving the quality of women's lives.[16] Most newspapers and journals printed the phonetic *kana* alongside *kanji*, making reading material accessible even to those with a modest education.

However, access for women to most forms of higher education

remained limited until the 1920's, and even then, professional or university training was extremely rare. Women were not allowed to enter standard high schools but were tracked into either special women's high schools (whose enrollment soared nationwide from 12,000 in 1900 to over 300,000 in 1925) or vocational and normal schools (total enrollment in both types of school reached almost 23,000 by 1925). Universities first admitted women in 1915 (by 1930 there were only 81 women enrolled) and restricted their entrance to a very small, if often extremely talented, few (*Nihon kindai kyōiku shi jiten*, 108).[17] Nevertheless, the educational and social reforms of the Meiji era established, by the 1920's, a mass female readership.

This new female reading public, swelled by the numbers of matriculates and graduates in high schools for girls, was increasingly capable of reading moderately sophisticated literary works. Moreover, while the higher educational institutions remained largely sex-segregated, the quality of young women's education improved following the educational reforms of the 1910's. By the mid-1920's, graduates of girls high schools constituted 10 percent of their age cohort in the general population. Maeda Ai (651) has argued that these graduates constituted the core of the readership of the women's journals.

The market for these journals has conventionally been seen as the growing middle class; however, surveys conducted by the women's journals showed that their readership was not limited to the metropolitan middle class but included provincial residents of modest means. A profile of subscribers published in the December 1925 issue of *Fujin sekai* (Ladies' world) suggested that a small but significant portion (roughly 4–5 percent) of salaried, middle-class family budgets was devoted to purchasing journals or newspapers. Maeda (652) concluded that in the mid-1920's the middle-class norm, defined as an annual income of 800 yen, was to subscribe to one newspaper, one or more magazines for the husband, and at least one women's magazine.

The growth of women's magazines coincided with women's advancement into urban white-collar occupations. Fields such as nursing or elementary-school teaching had been open to women since the Meiji era, but the trends accelerated during the 1910's and 1920's; the number of women in nursing increased from 14,000 in 1914 to over 42,000 a decade later, and the proportion of elementary-school teachers who were women rose from 37.5 percent in 1912 to 47.5 percent in

1922. Although exceptional women such as actresses, physicians, or reporters, who broke barriers to gain entrée into more glamorous or well-paid fields, were often profiled in the journals, the bulk of white-collar female workers were employed in more conventional sex-segregated jobs. A survey of "working women" in Tokyo published in 1923 found 18,274 clerk/typist/office workers, 8,500 telephone operators, 5,000 waitresses, 2,445 schoolteachers, and 1,500 actresses and entertainers (Tōkyō shi shakai kyoku, 16).[18] Margit Nagy (202) reminds us that white-collar women were a distinct minority: of the 27 million women in the nation in the year of the survey, 3.5 million were members of the paid labor force, and 2.6 million of these engaged in manual labor.[19] The majority of wage-earning women in the modern tertiary sector (as opposed to those working in family-run shops) were single, between school and marriage, and contributed to their parental household income.[20] Their wages gave them disposable income and the ability to make discretionary purchases of items such as women's magazines.

A 1924 survey of the reading habits of 900 women workers, principally office workers, clerks, nurses, and telephone operators, conducted by the Tokyo Social Affairs Department found that 800 of the women subscribed to a newspaper and 740 to a women's journal (Maeda, 653). This underlines the striking degree to which urban wage-earning women in the tertiary sector constituted a core of devoted readers and a significant market for journals that promoted writing by women. This finding is at odds with the stereotype advanced by the prominent Marxist critic and advocate of proletarian literature Aono Suekichi (1890–1961), in a 1925 article entitled "Women's Demands on Literature," that the consumption of women's magazines was largely to fulfill the fantasies of housewives and housebound middle-class daughters—"to imbibe the intoxicating freedom of women's liberation in the world of fiction . . . [specifically] in popular literature in women's magazines" (quoted in Maeda, 814).[21]

Women's Journals

The category of "women's literature" was created, in part, by the changing nature of the publishing business as editors and publishers tailored their publications to target specific market niches, either the women's market in general or a selected part of it (Tokura; Minemura). This trend was encouraged by the continuing notion that women had a distinct and separate place in society. Two kinds of women's journals developed: one advocated the "good wife and wise mother" concept of the "traditional" Japanese family;[22] the other provided forums for advocates of social and political reform or took as their mandate the education of women, and often served as serious literary venues for women.

The embryonic women's movement facilitated the publication of many early works of fiction. Several of the early women's journals, such as *Jogaku zasshi* (Women's education magazine; begun in 1885), a Christian journal oriented toward elevating the status of women, or *Sekai fujin* (The world of ladies; established 1907), dedicated to women's education and rights, were launched with a reforming mission. But the reforming zeal often waned, particularly in the face of official hostility (*Sekai fujin* was banned within two years), and these journals generally failed to provide an effective artistic forum. However, the editors of *Jogaku zasshi* were able to establish a mainstream literary journal entitled *Bungakkai* (The world of literature), a forum that later helped to promote the popularity of the writer Higuchi Ichiyō.[23] The first feminist journal got its start in 1911 when the college-educated Hiratsuka Raichō (1886–1971) used the money intended for her dowry to found the journal *Seitō*, or "Bluestocking." It declared its mandate to be "to gauge the progress of women's literature, to exhibit natural talent, and hereafter to give birth to women's genius" (quoted in Inoue, 182). This journal lasted only four and a half years before it was banned for "disrupting good morals and manners," but during its short life span, it challenged pervasive conventions about marriage and the role of women in Japanese society (Sievers, 181). Although some critics, even those sympathetic to women writers such as Inoue Yuriko (182) dismiss its literary contributions, this publication, particularly in its first two years, provided a much-needed venue for publications by women writers. In a somewhat similar fashion, in 1928, the female playwright Hasegawa Shigure (1879–1941) founded the journal *Nyonin geijutsu* (Women's arts), which helped launch the careers of several women writers.[24]

But the majority of "women's magazines" were unconnected to the feminist movement or an activist editor. Women's journals that targeted the broadest cross section of women readers grew rapidly in the early 1920's. *Fujo kai* (Women's world), begun in 1910, had achieved a modest circulation of 12,000–13,000 per issue by 1913. By 1926, its circulation reached 250,000. *Shufu no tomo* (The housewife's friend), begun in 1917, was already publishing 230,000–240,000 copies by 1924. Other journals, such as *Fujin sekai, Fujin kōron* (Ladies' forum), and *Fujin kurabu* (Ladies' club), also had print runs of at least 100,000 copies by the mid-1920's. *Fujin kurabu* had grown since its establishment in autumn 1920 to 150,000 copies by January 1927. In that same year, *Fujin sekai*'s twentieth anniversary issue ran to 600,000 copies (Mawatari, 40). Maeda Ai (650) estimated the total number of copies of January 1925 issues of women's magazines sold nationwide at 1.2 million.

The impact of women's magazines in promoting what was considered "popular" as opposed to "pure" literature in the 1920's might best be viewed as the culmination of trends that extended well back into the Meiji era. Mass-market magazines explicitly targeted at women grew steadily from the turn of the century (Maeda, 651; Mawatari, 40–42); fourteen women's magazines were published monthly by the mid-1920's, and together these publications established a critical mass that constituted a new reading public for literary work, and they influenced what was being written and by whom.

Publishing in women's journals helped promote women writers' visibility and strengthen their reputation, but it was the serialization of their work in newspapers or in other mass-circulation journals that established them as household names. The growing status and legitimacy of women's journals among the reading public were reflected in the literary pages of at least two newspapers with national circulation: the *Asahi* and the *Yomiuri*. By summer 1930, the *Asahi* ran regular features on contemporary women writers, and the *Yomiuri* presented monthly reviews of the articles in forthcoming issues of major women's journals. This coverage of women writers and the journals in which they published no doubt helped to secure their popular recognition, but the newspapers did not invent the interest or the audience. They covered the story and mirrored, even if their spotlight stimulated, the public's newfound admiration for women's literature.

Women's journals opened new possibilities for publishing and income that changed the nature of literary careers, and not just those of women. Ōya Sōichi (1900–1970), an influential social commentator, was one of the first to assert the impact of women's journals on the literary establishment (*bundan*, or literary guild);[25] in a 1926 essay, "Bundan girudo no kaitai ki" (The dismantling of the literary guild), he compared women's magazines to new colonial markets in the way they opened up opportunities:

> What one must call the remarkable phenomenon of the increase in women readers in recent years has influenced popular writing in much the same way that the discovery of a vast new colony might influence the country. Thus the sudden development of women's magazines influenced Japan's *bundan*, much as the growth of the spinning industry's China market reconstituted the Japanese financial system. Popular writers' incomes rose proportionately in relation to the development of women's magazines. (80)

Yet in his view, increased incomes and circulation served only to debase the value of the literary works, as the new venues for publication catering to popular tastes unleashed a flood of "slipshod works." Ōya blamed the declining standards of writers on the fact that they could now publish popular literature without the self-discipline needed to write in the style of "confessional" fiction that dominated the literary high-ground. Thus, new outlets for publication undermined the literary hierarchy and the tight control over access and acceptable styles in journals that had characterized the *bundan*.

Ōya was not alone in criticizing literature that focused on the thoroughly modern and faddish facets of life, particularly the atmospheric stories on "places of assignation, geisha, cafés, waitresses, cards, *shōgi*, mah-jongg, billiards, and baseball . . . [that] flooded the market" (Ōya, 80).[26] The writer and critic Satō Haruo had voiced a similar opinion about the debasement of the *bundan* several months earlier in an essay "On the Life of the Literary Man." Yet Ōya stood apart in emphasizing the central role of women's journals in promoting the surge of popular literature of the early 1920's. However, Ōya also placed the responsibility for the supposed decline in standards on the *bundan* itself, on its system of distinguishing between serious works of literature and those written explicitly for honoraria or wages, suitable for popular consumption. "Short pieces of confessional fiction in general magazines [*sōgō zasshi*] or literary magazines and popular novels [*tsūzoku chōhen*] in newspapers or women's magazines — these were the general rule of thumb for the inhabitants ·of the *bundan*" (quoted in Maeda, 650). In Ōya's view, the *bundan's* allowance for "hack writing" by established authors, distinguished principally by the venue of publication, undermined the literary establishment's foundations when women's magazines flooded the market and provided a lucrative alternative to "serious" literary efforts.[27]

The literary critic Muramatsu Sadataka reflected the sort of sentiments still widely held in the 1950's in his disparagement of literary work published in mass-circulation venues:

> Many of the readers of newspaper fiction are women. It is not an exaggeration to say that they are represented in particular by housewives who, after having seen their husbands off to work, are satisfied with reading the next newspaper installment at the kitchen table. They have this in common with readers of women's magazines. For these women, the most appealing subject matter is family-based, particularly that fraught with the complications of love affairs of a married woman or a married man. ("'Onna de aru koto' ron," 175)

Gender Roles

Sharp distinctions between appropriate spheres for men and women were hardly invented in the modern era. However, as the pace of social change accelerated from the Meiji period on, and as the norms of family organization, occupations, schooling, and government were increasingly challenged, the boundaries between the sexes were policed with increased vigor. Intellectuals were recruited for a state-sponsored campaign to promote a separate sphere for women in the roles of "good wives and wise mothers" (ryōsai kenbo) (Nolte and Hastings, 158–59; Garon, 10–15). But efforts to elaborate distinctions between the roles of men and women in the institutions of politics, education, work, and the family tended, in the long run, to founder in the sea change of social transformation; or, perhaps we should say that concepts of masculinity and femininity, particularly the ways in which power was linked with gender—notably in the declining norms of domesticity and submissiveness—changed in ways that were beyond the capacity of the state or its minions to control.

Although the blurring of gender norms, as well as campaigns to reinvent them, were evident from the 1880's, they escalated during the first decades of the twentieth century. Donald Roden writes of the growing gender ambivalence during the 1920's that it "captured the imagination of a cross section of the literate urban population in a manner that was simply unthinkable in the heyday of 'civilization and enlightenment' [in the Meiji period]" (43). He argues that this process was rooted in shifting attitudes in the late Meiji period that subverted the conventional notions of male "household head and stalwart provider" and fueled the image of a "new woman [who] exuded . . . a firm self-confidence [*kakko taru jishin*] and an emotional independence from the patriarchal family" (43). The shifting ground of gender identities was projected in the popular media and dissected monthly in mainstream and, especially, in women's magazines, not only in *Seitō* and later *Nyonin geijutsu*, but also in less activist-oriented, more long-lived publications.[28]

The rapid accession of women to new occupations during the boom years of World War I fueled the new image of working women. The independence, self-confidence, and self-sufficiency of many young working women shattered conventional gender roles. In the decade following the great earthquake of 1923, the media fixated on the symbol of the *moga*, or *modan gāru* (modern girl), to represent not only a decadent libertine but also, in a broader sense, a threat to the social order:

> The trumpeted promiscuity of the Modern Girl, who moved from man to man, was thus but one aspect of her self-sufficiency. She appeared to be a free agent without ties of filiation, affect, or obligation to lover, father, mother, husband or children—in striking counterpoint to the state ideology of family documented in the Civil Code and in the ethics texts taught in schools. (Silverberg, "The Modern Girl," 246)

It was in the context of such shifting gender norms that the call of conservative critics for a return to the "natural" distinctions between men and women began to have significant influence. Nogami Toshio, for example, warned of the degeneration that would follow from a blurring of "spiritual differences" between the sexes and from the "deviant conditions that have arisen . . . [where] women who perform men's work have significantly increased in number" (quoted in Roden, 44). In 1922, General Ugaki Kazushige decried "the feminization of men and the masculinization of women and the neutered gender that results [as] a modernistic tendency that makes it impossible for the individual, the society, or the nation to achieve great progress. Accordingly, [he argued] since the manliness of man and the femininity of woman must forever be preserved, it is imperative that we not allow the rise of neutered people who defy nature's grace" (quoted in Roden, 52). Such sentiments were not entirely original, but it was only in the 1920's that the reaction gained a critical mass. As described by Roden, educators and representatives of government ministries

> waged a vociferous campaign—in the name of bourgeois gentility, natural order, and civilized morality—against the perceived distortions and excesses of Taishō culture. These included feminism, homosexuality, recreational sex, and the blurring, whether intended or not, of the sacred and inviolate lines between the masculine and feminine. The defenders of respectability spared no effort in championing the immiscibility of the sexes with long-winded explanations of male aggression and female passivity, of male rationality and female hysteria, of man's destiny to work outside and woman's to stay at home, and of the necessity to prevent the "masculinization" of feminine language. (52)

It was in the wake of the rising tide of reaction that the hitherto vague concept of a separate "women's literature" took form.

The Crystallization of a Category

The dominant trend in Japanese literature in the first decades of the twentieth century was to emphasize the interiority of the author in what came to be known as the I-novel, or I-fiction (*watakushi-shō-setsu*, or *shishōsetsu*). Although it has not been uncommon to attribute this fixation on the "self" to an emulation of Western tradition, Edward Fowler (28–29) has traced its roots to classical literary traditions as well as to the structure of the Japanese language itself. In particular, the confessional diaries of women writers in the classical Japanese tradition constituted a wellspring for this pre-eminent genre of modern Japanese letters. It is not surprising, then, given greater opportunities for education and the growth of a sizable female readership, especially among the urban middle classes, that women should adopt similar confessional forms to express their world. In fact, the most successful modern authors, both male and female, were influenced by this "feminine" tradition. Women writers were quite candid about themselves, revealing secrets about their lives, loves, and search for survival, in a manner as sensational and indiscreet as that of their male counterparts.[29]

The root of interiority and modern psychological narration were tied to a transformation of literary language through the *genbun itchi* movement, which aimed to create a written form of Japanese based on modern colloquial speech. Karatani Kōjin (69–75) has characterized this profound rupture in literary traditions, which occurred in the 1890's, as a prerequisite for modern realism and confessional forms, in that it erased the immense diversity of Chinese-influenced literary styles and genres (*kanbungaku*). But the triumph of the *genbun itchi* movement also made literature far more accessible to women readers and writers, who could increasingly appreciate it and even participate in it through a language that did not have to be learned. Modern women's writing has often been linked to this transformation of literary style: Tanabe Kaho's *Yabu no uguisu* is said to have been inspired by Tsubouchi Shōyō's *Tōsei shosei katagi* (The characters of modern students; 1885–86), a work that advanced the cause of *genbun itchi*; and Higuchi Ichiyō's initial stories (1892) were inspired by the financial success of Tanabe's novel (Danly, 28; Keene, *Dawn to the West*, 167). However, the emergence of women's literature as a distinct style in itself crystallized only in relation to the principal conceptual antinomies of literary criticism in the 1920's.

The term "I-novel," a literal translation of *watakushi shōsetsu*, which may more appropriately be rendered as "confessional or personal fiction," was coined in the early 1920's as a slightly derogatory term for a literary tendency that began in the late Meiji era. In a 1921 issue of the literary journal *Kaizō*, the *watakushi shōsetsu* was described as "no more than an extension of a chronicle, lacking in reflection" (Chiba, 185). Yet in a few short years, in the hands of influential writer-critics such as Kume Masao, the *watakushi shōsetsu* (including the *shinkyō shōsetsu*, or mental-attitude fiction) became the preeminent measure of literary merit.[30] The works of emerging proletarian writers were found lacking, according to this new standard, and dismissed as mere popular entertainment compared to confessional literature, which was validated as "pure literature."[31] By the early 1930's, a preoccupation with the "national character" or "uniquely Japanese features" as the essence of artistic expression began to restrict permissible literary forms, and in the wake of state repression, proletarian literature ceased.[32] Despite their roman à clef quality, which presumed a familiarity with the people and personalities of the members of the literary guild that populated these stories, and which might be expected to limit their readership, works in the I-novel form assumed, by the mid-1930's, an unassailable place at the center of the contemporary canon (see Kobayashi).

Women writers of the 1920's also often favored a confessional style; however, their works were generally categorized not as *watakushi shōsetsu*, but rather as *jiden shōsetsu* (autobiographical fiction) (Itagaki, "Shōwa no joryū sakka," 32; Yoshida, 16; Kōra, 110). The notion that "women's literature" constituted a distinct style must have derived from the presumption that women's confessional auto-biographical fiction (*jiden shōsetsu*) was somehow different from the *watakushi shōsetsu* composed by men. The implications of such a distinction deserve to be spelled out, even though they were not widely perceived at the time. Only a few observers—such as Shintō Junko, who argued that literature labeled in a way that indicated it was written by women implied that the works were "poor pieces of writing" (*dasaku*) or "inferior pieces of writing" (*akusaku*) (48–49)—have noted the negative connotations attributed, through this division, to "women's" writing.

"Women's literature" cannot be viewed as constituting a literary school in the same sense as the Ken'yūsha group (1885–1903) with its journal, *Garakuta bunko* (Rubbish library); the Romantic writers (1889–1904) with their journal, *Bungakkai* (The world of literature); or the White Birch Society (1910–20) and its organ, *Shirakaba* (White birch).[33] Nor did the "women" of "women's literature" constitute an informal group like Natsume Sōseki's coterie, in which aspiring male writers gathered around an established master. Women writers grouped by critics under this heading shared no unifying tradition, no school, and no journal, and consequently the term did not do justice to their diversity of perspectives and approaches. To be so categorized said nothing of an author's relation with other literary, intellectual, social, and political trends. Moreover, the seeming simplicity of the term facilitated a conflation between references to an author's sex and aesthetic judgments of her style. The ease of this conceptual slippage could make the attribution indelible. That an author was a "woman writer" suggested an inevitable destiny; the label suggested a permanence when, as a critical assessment, it should only have been taken as a contingent association. The fixity of the categorization could only lead to a neglect of any transformation or change in an author's style and obscure artistic maturation and development.

Women's literature as a distinct style of writing developed as a residual category, defined not so much by intrinsic criteria as by its relation to other principal conceptual distinctions in the criticism of the 1920's. Although some women writers wrote short, simple sentences and gave realistic, concrete portrayals of subjects near at hand, so did many men. The variability in language and style among individual male and female writers was at least as great as the presumed variability between the two groups. The boundaries of women's literature were thus demarcated by a set of conceptual antinomies, the pure and the popular, the confessional and the autobiographical. These oppositions were always imperfect, and allowances were made for exceptions. But their combined effect implicitly devalued the work of women writers as merely popular and aesthetically second-rate.

It was enough that a distinctly separate identity be firmly cemented in the critical discourse, for separate did not suggest equal. Remarkably, even though the work of women writers changed enormously in the subsequent half-century, this segregated classification remained the prevailing characterization of what women wrote and the dominant concept through which women's literary work was perceived. As I will discuss below, it also influenced how many women wrote, as some authors internalized these expectations and others adopted perspectives to satirize or resist them.

A separate women's style was neither universally acknowledged nor encouraged by male critics and writers; a questionnaire in the January 1, 1949, issue of a resurrected *Nyonin geijutsu* elicited a range of responses to the question "What are your expectations for women's arts?" The critic Ara Masato wrote, "Separating men from women must be stopped as quickly as possible." The poet Kimata Osamu, a student of the poet Kitahara Hakushū, replied, "I look forward to the birth of a woman artist who does not need the special designation 'woman' [*joryū*]." And the poet Horiguchi Daigaku answered, "To become an artist who overcomes being female [*josei*]." Although a few respondents celebrated women's difference, most either challenged the concept of gender-based art or disparaged what was perceived as female. The artist Suda Kunitarō wrote, "I look forward to art that is not imitative. That is because I believe that women especially have this imitative nature." Takii Kōsaku, a writer and follower of the confessional writer Shiga Naoya, anticipated that once women secured higher education, they (like men) would produce sensitive, detailed, and beautiful works. Hinatsu Kōnosuke, a poet, thought that women writers up until that point had been coddled, and inferior work had been accepted "because they were women" (Joryū bungakusha kai, 67).

In the same questionnaire, the query "What literary work could have been written only by a woman?" prompted the answer "none" or titles of Western works. Kimata Masato was the only respondent to identify specific works by a Japanese woman (Sata Ineko's [1904–] recently published "Michi" [Road] and "Kyogi" [Falsehood]). The dismissal of the question's premise was common: "I do not think there are any exceptional works in that category" (Odagiri Hideo), and "There are none among high-quality works" (Fukuda Tsuneari) (Joryū bungakusha kai, 127).

Champions of women's artistic sensibilities often have been equally categorical. In the early 1970's, Okuno Takeo (15) asserted that men needed to assume a woman's voice to write. He viewed Japanese fiction since the Meiji era as feminine (*josei-teki*), and even went so far as to suggest creating a literary prize for "men's style" (*danryū*) as men's talent decreased. Such a prize would parallel the separate prizes for women writers already in existence and presume that such special recognition should be granted only to the second-rate. Okuno concluded (259–60) that women were best suited for writing fiction, since their capabilities are analogous to those of shamanistic mediums, and they can change into the characters they portray.

Female writers and critics have also argued that women writers possess unique characteristics. Itagaki Naoko assumed that women naturally write simpler, less intellectual fiction (*Meiji, Taishō, Shōwa no joryū bungaku*, 2). Kumasaka Atsuko began her article on Hayashi Fumiko (1903–51) and Okamoto Kanoko (1889–1939) with the premise that certain sensations are "inherently feminine," notably the *on-nen* (hatred) that comes from "a consciousness of being a victim" (79). And many have reflected assumptions about separate men's and women's styles of language that have been conventions, so the presumption went, since classical antiquity. However, a study in the May 1967 issue of *Kokubungaku* that compared vocabulary in literary works by men and women concluded, contrary to expectation, that the women's works contained fewer expressions of emotion (*kanjō-teki hyōgen*) and more examples of independence and objectivity (*jiritsusei kyakkansei*) than did the works of male authors (cited in Tsukada, 31).[34]

Presumptions of Difference

The biography of the writer Miyamoto Yuriko written by her husband, Miyamoto Kenji, a Communist Party leader, to accompany the fourteen volumes of his wife's collected works published soon after her death in 1951, was designed to distance her from the category of women's literature. Miyamoto Kenji presented his wife not as a woman writer (*joryū sakka*) but as an important figure in the literary canon and as an intellectual writer of the Proletarian school, and carefully located each of her works within the broader literary and political framework of the time. He used the terms *josei* (female) or *fujin* (lady), rather than *joryū* (implying a woman's style), in reference to both Yuriko and other women whose works he discusses in the book, such as Tsuboi Sakae (1899–1967), Sata Ineko, Nogami Yaeko (1885–1985), and Hayashi Fumiko.[35] In giving background information on the milieu of female writers, he argued that women who did not have strong personalities or a distinctly individual writing style were grouped together with other women, as if by default, even though there were no literary groups of female writers or established literary journals for their work. Nevertheless, the biography illustrated the gender stereotypes that determined whether and where a woman could publish and the ways in which women authors could internalize those expectations. For example, Takita Tetsutarō, the editor of *Fujin kōron*, initially rejected Yuriko's work because she did not write simply enough for the readership of a magazine targeted at women; significantly, Yuriko was elated by this rejection, for she took it as a vote of confidence in her artistry (7–8). Women writers themselves often shared disparaging preconceptions. For example, Yosano Akiko praised Yuriko at the outset of her career for her "rationality, in contrast to the sentimentalism of so many fledgling women writers" (quoted in Miyamoto Kenji, 137).

Even female literary critics such as Itagaki Naoko, who challenged the conventional critical neglect of and condescension toward women writers in the early Shōwa era, nevertheless set them apart from the mainstream literary trends and tendencies in a 1931 essay "Genkon Nihon no joryū bundan" (The women's literary guild in Japan today). Yet it was precisely from the 1920's that a veritable renaissance of women writers from many different strata of society, such as Hayashi Fumiko, Hirabayashi Taiko, Miyamoto Yuriko, Sata Ineko, Tsuboi Sakae, and Uno Chiyo, caught the popular imagination. Their writing was not limited to any particular literary genre or form and included autobiographies, histories, and dramas, as well as poetry and fiction. However, despite the diversity of styles, temperaments, and approaches, a perception took root among the public, critics, and even the writers themselves that most women wrote women's literature (*joryū bungaku*) and that any female author could be labeled *joryū sakka rashii* (a typical woman writer).

Itagaki wrote a history of women's literature from the vantage point of the mid-1960's, in which she demonstrated the immense range and considerable accomplishments of women writers in the 1920's. She argued that despite the close mirroring by women of the dominant styles in the mainstream literary arena, they wrote within a separate sphere. "The women writers of the Taishō period . . . dealt with typical women's material and worlds and brought out characteristic feminine qualities. Therein was born the appeal of women writers and their *raison d'être*" (*Meiji, Taishō, Shōwa no joryū bungaku,* 106). In her view, the women writers of the 1920's distinguished themselves from earlier women writers by their characterizations, albeit in largely apolitical terms, of contemporary social problems (*Meiji, Taishō, Shōwa no joryū bungaku,* 117). This focus would be echoed, with a more didactic edge, in Proletarian literature.

Writing in the early 1970's, the leftist critic Odagiri Hideo echoed some of Itagaki's themes and illustrated the entrenched reluctance to use the same terms for women writers as for men. Odagiri praised the "socially conscious" confessional fiction of several well-known women writers, but he continued to characterize them as a single group and saw them as having commonalities that separated their work from men's (172).

The critic Nakamura Mitsuo presented the clearest characterization of the established conventions of women's literature as they existed until recently, in his 1953 analysis of Hayashi Fumiko and women writers in general. Nakamura separated women writers into two groups: those similar to men and those having a "female sensibility" who write women's literature.[36]

> There are generally two types of women writers [*joryū sakka*]. On the one hand are those who are closer to men or who give the reader the feeling of outdoing men, rather than being women. Presently such writers as Miyamoto Yuriko are of this type. I think that Hirabayashi Taiko also belongs to this pattern. Even male readers, when we read these writers, do not need to be conscious of the fact that they are pieces written by women.
>
> Furthermore, the writers themselves do not wish to be so considered. And female readers too, while they recognize feminine elements in those works, no doubt sense in the writer a certain degree of masculinity and admire the writer for completely separating herself from the weaknesses of her sex. There is more of a sense of sexual attraction than sisterly affection in their admiration.
>
> However, the special characteristic of Hayashi Fumiko as a

writer is found in the opposite situation, in the fact that she remains feminine throughout, and that feminine quality is at times so strong as to be overpowering. . . . Hayashi Fumiko had an unusually strong female sensibility and female faults, but without discarding those elements, she let them mature to fruition. ("Hayashi Fumiko ron," 95)

Perhaps because he presumed common conventions that the audience would accept as natural and self-evident, Nakamura failed to define what constituted masculine or feminine qualities, faults, or styles.

In keeping with the permeability in the categorization of women's literature since the 1920's, Nakamura did not equate sex with gender. But the objections to Nakamura's characterization of Hayashi Fumiko as quintessentially feminine, a judgment shared by his contemporaries,[37] is not simply due to a lack of specificity in the definition. Such an approach gives no indication of the fluidity of gender distinctions and treats differences as fixed and unchanging. And whereas women writers may be either masculine or feminine, these traits appear imbedded in any given individual; femininity is not treated as a conscious choice, an identity that authors adopt or shed according to intentions or objectives. A brief review of Hayashi's literary career will illustrate not only several of the inadequacies of gender-based categorizations but also the ways in which a woman writer could subvert as well as invoke literary conventions.[38]

Hayashi burst onto the literary scene with her immensely popular, ostensibly autobiographical account of the hardships and travails of a young aspiring woman writer in *Hōrōki* (Diary of a vagabond; 1928–30), serialized in *Nyonin geijutsu* (Women's arts), and published as a separate volume in Kaizōsha's Shin'ei bungaku sōsho (A library of new literary faces) in July 1930. Purporting to be excerpts from an unnamed author's diary, *Diary of a Vagabond* mirrored the structure of a classical *uta monogatari* (poetic tale) through its frequent inclusion of poetry and letters.[39] The general theme of a female protagonist who suffers from loneliness, having been neglected and discarded by a succession of lovers, also replicated a common motif in classical diaries. At the same time, there is an undeniable modernity in its approach and subject matter and its frequent references to Western writers and themes. The protagonist's drive to write, and her unvarnished encounters with an assortment of literary figures, follows the roman à clef style of a *watakushi shōsetsu*. However, the originality and power of the work were rooted not so much in the mix of literary allusions as in the clarity and immediacy with which Hayashi was able to convey the humanity of those on the underside of Japanese society. Hayashi excelled in her portrayal of women on the margin, those with a tenuous hold on employment, residence, or relationships, who often found themselves cut loose and scrambling to survive, women whose interests and experiences were neglected by contending political ideologies and ignored by male literati.

After *Diary of a Vagabond* made Hayashi a public figure, she wrote for an audience that wanted to learn more about her. A sequel (*Zoku Hōrōki*; Diary of a vagabond II), published in November 1930 employed roughly the same structure and language, and covered the same period, returning to many of the same incidents, but often with more graphic elaboration and incriminating detail.[40] The style was similar to works by other confessional writers, who revealed their humiliating exploits and flights of fancy to a well-informed audience and were under public scrutiny by choice. Hayashi next serialized a fictional portrayal of an unhappy homeless young woman abandoned by her husband in the *Tōkyō Asahi shinbun*, but when it failed to secure either critical or popular success, she returned to writing in an autobiographical voice that would be the hallmark of her career. Hayashi would also continue to suggest the revelation of personal experiences by using in the titles of her later books such terms as diary (*nikki*), chronicle (*ki*), record (*shofu*), scribbling (*rakugaki*), and biography (*den*), even though these works were clearly fictional.[41]

From the mid-1930's, Hayashi chronicled her concerted effort to change from an autobiographical/confessional style of writing to an "objective" (*kyakkan-teki*) fiction: "to separate myself from the gut-wrenching confusion of the autobiographical *Diary of a Vagabond*."[42] In her later fiction, Hayashi departed from the lyrical sentimentality that characterized *Diary of a Vagabond*. Her language, as a whole, reflected her transition toward more standard, composed, and complex grammatical constructions. However, perhaps the most striking change in her style was the shift from the fragmented, discontinuous narrative that left many incidents either partially or wholly unresolved toward a more clearly delineated structure, with a standard beginning, middle, and end that unfolded to reveal a tightly rendered story line. Even in those later works that purported to be autobiographical, incidents were presented as a continuous narrative, in chronological order, within a discrete time frame.

Hayashi gained considerable notoriety in the late 1930's for her war reportage in China, as well as for her participation in the first Pen Squadron—a group of popular writers who toured the front to write about the circumstances and sacrifices of soldiers for the readers back home. This collaboration with state-sponsored wartime propaganda was the focus of considerable postwar criticism. However, in contrast to some other writers, such as Sata Ineko, Hayashi never apologized, or even rationalized, her participation in the war effort. When the war ended, she returned to Tokyo, and just as she had seemed to join in the general enthusiasm of the war effort, she would voice her opinion against the death and misery caused by war. Her *Uzushio* (Swirling eddies; 1947), the first serialized long fiction by any writer to appear in postwar newspapers, focused on the problems of women, widowed by the war after often fleeting relationships with their spouses and left to fend for themselves. Despite the evolution of her literary style, Hayashi's themes of wandering, abandonment, and bare subsistence, as well as disillusioned intimacy, tempered by irrepressible resiliency, exhibit considerable continuity with the best of her earlier works.

The response to Hayashi's aesthetic transformation varied considerably, even among women writers. In 1947, Miyamoto Yuriko (177) criticized Hayashi for having abandoned the natural, volatile quality found in *Diary of a Vagabond* and for adopting a more refined taste. In her view, Hayashi's later writing contained unnecessary nihilistic and sentimental excesses. Miyamoto indicted both Hayashi and Uno Chiyo as women writers (*fujin sakka*) who embraced the progressive spirit only for personal advancement, not for larger political or aesthetic interests.[43] Miyamoto saw their work as overly individualistic and, at the same time, pandering to issues of gender. Both Hayashi and Uno, she argued, postured as "women writers" and shamelessly promoted their gender to secure press coverage and titillate consumers. "The success that they gained as a result served instead to create the boundaries of their literature" (178). In contrast, Shibaki Yoshiko (1914–), a 1941 recipient of the Akutagawa literary prize and a 1961 recipient of the Women's Literary Prize, contended that Hayashi's "early works were full of poetic sentiment and feeling, and that lyricism eventually excessively sweetened her writing, but in her later years she was able to escape magnificently from this sphere. The war proved to be the opportunity for her literary style to face the shift in harsh reality directly and singlemindedly" (218). In 1963, in an article published in Japanese, Edward G. Seidensticker celebrated Hayashi's later fiction: "An all too typical woman writer [*joryū sakka*] in her early career, Hayashi Fumiko abandoned her former feminine fixed outlook with the experience of Japan's defeat. . . . Hayashi wrote some of the best postwar short stories, probably the best by women" (129).

Hayashi's career was shadowed by the notion that she was a "woman writer," but it was advanced by this designation as well.[44] Through the women's journal *Nyonin geijutsu*, Hayashi found an outlet that allowed free rein for her *Diary*'s originality and its successful blend of underclass circumstances with idioms and themes of classical women's diaries. In the wake of its enormous commercial success, Hayashi quickly moved to publish in mainstream literary journals and newspapers. She utilized all the opportunities that prominence as a woman writer could afford — tours, lectures, even participation in a plane relay across Japan — to preserve her celebrity status and garner offers for publication. Even as she tried to establish herself as a writer of serious "objective fiction" in the mainstream press and literary journals, Hayashi also continued to publish ostensibly autobiographical works that catered to the expectations of her audience.[45] For over twenty years, her embracing of the identity of a "woman writer" secured her a status that allowed her to provide for herself and an increasing retinue solely through her publications.[46]

The persistent categorization of Hayashi as a "woman writer" of "women's literature" assured that although she might be especially prominent, her work would also be considered marginal to the canon and would rarely receive sustained critical scrutiny. Even those who closely read and evaluated more than a smattering of her work were hobbled by the received wisdom about "women writers." For example, the critic Fukuda Hirotoshi dismissed Hayashi's early works (including *Diary of a Vagabond*) as girlishly sentimental but characterized "Bangiku" (A late chrysanthemum; 1949) — the work that secured her the Women's Literary Prize — as more masculine or "androgynous" (*chūsei*) and therefore more mature and serious. The irony of his presumption — that works by women writers merit critical attention and "women's literary prizes" to the extent that they distance themselves from characteristics of their gender — only underscores the stigma associated with "women's literature."

The inadequacies of the "woman writer" designation for Hayashi are twofold: it fails to capture what is specific to her distinct, somewhat idiosyncratic voice, and it fails to reflect what evolved in her work as she matured. Hayashi may have lacked a larger vision—she eschewed directly addressing societal contradictions and profound philosophical or existential questions—but her work merits continued scrutiny on several grounds. She was a chronicler of a largely unilluminated world of the underclass, of people who existed on the margin, and sympathetically captured the ever-resurgent tenacity of those for whom modernity was experienced as an unrelenting catastrophe. Her characters, predominantly women, embody a dogged determination, perseverance, and resilience, despite the unrelenting woes that besiege them. For many, including Muramatsu Sadataka, it is for her portraits of the everyday life of this stratum that she will be remembered. But for others, such as Edward Seidensticker (125–26), her fictional imagination, notably in her postwar stories, succeeded not only in capturing the spirit of the era, the nihilistic disaffection against a backdrop of austerity and injustice, but also in transcending circumstances to present the individual's personal exercise, however inadequate, of choice and self-determination.[47] Her contributions merit a place in Japanese literary history, a place obscured by the misguided categorization of her work as "women's literature."

Gender and Literature

Modern Japanese women writers confronted a specific constellation of attitudes toward their gender that shaped not only their prospects for publication and critical reception, but, in some circumstances, even how the women themselves wrote. Attributes presumed to be natural in a woman's voice—sentimental lyricism, and impressionistic, nonintellectual, detailed observations of daily life—were the result of a confluence of social and literary trends that, in the 1920's, crystallized the notion of a distinct "women's style." However misguided the characterization of "women's literature" was, it was historically bounded and, by the 1980's, no longer conveyed, at least not to most writers and critics, a distinct literary style. This concluding section addresses the relevance of gender, and this historically grounded approach, to women's literature in Japan.

Murō Saisei's *Ōgon no hari* (Golden needles; 1961), which surveys the work of nineteen Taishō and Shōwa women writers, is emblematic of the essentialism that segregates and subordinates even as it rescues these writers from relative obscurity. Murō depicts the essence of women writers, which in his view is fatally flawed, as their capacity to sew. Just as when women sew a kimono, he argues, when they write, they leave nothing left over, resolving everything. In Murō's view, this resolution is inappropriate for fiction, which should leave some loose ends (3). Murō also compares several women writers to fish: Nogami Yaeko and Kōda Aya (1904–90) hide in deep recesses after making a name for themselves, whereas Hayashi Fumiko, flashy and highly visible, ascends to the surface of the pond (89).

Murō's approach, arguing by means of analogy and relying on comparisons between authors, embodies a fundamental fallacy. He suggests that because some women sew, all women writers adopt the habits of sewing and then transfer those specific skills to an entirely different arena. Of course, the presumption that sewing is somehow naturally feminine would be contradicted by any survey of such practices worldwide.[48] And the domestic imagery reveals a hostility toward boundary crossing: skills appropriate to the female domain are inappropriate in male spheres. But the basic fallacy is the logic of Murō's analogies. His logic is similar to this: since women are neat dressers, they cannot write as convincingly, given the disheveled state of everyday existence; or since women are shorter, they cannot reach the literary heights of male authors. Such assertions are absurd, but the logic is the same as Murō's: the reader must accept the attributions as given or natural and agree with the linkage to literary creation. His characterization of Hayashi as an eye-catching surface swimmer similarly substitutes an essence, however fitting, for the kind of historical context and close textual scrutiny necessary to locate her work precisely in relation to modern Japanese literature as a whole.

The codification of the concept of "women's literature" was a corollary and an outgrowth of the dominant literary movement and genre of the 1920's, naturalism and the I-novel. The naturalist-influenced confessional mode of expression enabled women, even those without much education, to represent their personal experiences in a way that captured the attention and imagination of a considerable portion of the reading public. But the capacity of women, as writers, to achieve a degree of prominence and economic independence through their publications reflected broader changes in Japanese society, where the growth of women's education and the increase of discretionary income enabled them to become both producers and consumers of literary commodities. The growth of the women's market in the publishing industry, and of women's journals in particular, followed the rapid growth in women's literacy. By the 1910's, literacy was virtually universal among young women at an elementary level. A market niche that mirrored the sex-segregated world of higher education and gender-specific conventions of composition — employing, principally, a written-as-spoken, rather than a self-consciously intellectual voice — came to be styled "women's literature." Such broad characterizations of style cut across gender lines of both writers and readers. But the conventions were codified, even as anomalies were allowed. Those women, or those works by women, that failed to meet these expectations were treated as "masculine" exceptions.

This essay points, particularly, to the mediating role of institutional structures, notably the publishing industry, in shaping the creation and reception of literary works by women. But it also underscores the crucial importance of each woman writer's intentions and affiliations, which confirm, subvert, or even reconstruct the norms associated with literary works. As indicated in the opening statement of the problem, "women's literature" no longer conveys the same sense of a specific style as it did by the 1920's and early 1930's. Women are now or, rather, are increasingly becoming recognized as writing in a variety of perspectives and voices that are not simply reducible to their gender. "Women's literature" was, then, historically bounded, but its limited, transitory character remains only partially recognized by literary critics and even women writers themselves.

The stigma of "women's literature" continues to haunt women writers today. Tsushima Yūko claimed in 1991 that she was trying to eradicate sentimentality from her own writing style, as if to distance herself from the tradition, if not the derogatory label, of "woman writer." And she distinguished contemporary women writers, such as Ariyoshi Sawako and Sono Ayako, from those prominent women writers of the 1920's who relied on passion or enthusiasm (*jōnetsu*) to be successful; Ariyoshi and Sono, she argued, were brilliant, nonemotional, and intellectual.[49] Along with Kurahashi Yumiko and Kusaka Yōko, they have been described as representative of the first generation of postwar, college-educated women writers, and their work has been characterized as "intelligent, ironic, and [full of] black humor" (Okuno et al., 92–94). Such new approaches by women writers might suggest the complete passing of the term "women's literature" from the contemporary literary lexicon. On the other hand, an array of institutional sinews supportive of women writers — women's journals, prizes, lecture circuits, marketing networks — is well established and helps to present such writers and works to the public. To refuse the label risks losing hard-won recognition and rewards. However, there is no reason to presume that the connotations associated with the term need be fixed or frozen. The pace of change may be gradual, or even glacial, but the process of reproducing literary conventions in successive generations inevitably requires an accommodation to the broader social contexts, as well as to the concerted efforts of the women writers themselves to recast how they are perceived and appreciated.

In an era when so much has been written on the issue of gender in literature, I hesitate to rush in with a sweeping summary of the relevance of the specific circumstances of the Japanese experience. On this side of the Pacific, gender has become one of the central concerns of literary studies. The institutional mechanisms that shape the critical reception of women's writing have been transformed by the rapid increase in conferences, associations, publishing houses, and review journals dedicated to works by women. Equally important has been a more self-consciously inclusive policy of more mainstream literary institutions. Women's journals, in particular, celebrate a neglected tradition and offer an enthusiastic response to women's voices, if not to every woman writer, and feminist critics have proposed their own alternative canon, as illustrated by Sandra Gilbert and Susan Gubar's *Norton Anthology of Literature by Women*. However, to adopt a separate feminist canon, complete with its own hierarchy, risks imposing, anachronistically, criteria that, for many women, would be no less artificial or exclusive than the existing standards of conventional literary histories. But to enfold women wholly within the larger male-dominated tradition risks neglecting their specific experience and voice and replicating the same patterns that have subordinated women in the wider social sphere. The Japanese experience suggests a resolution to this conundrum.

One contribution that the long lineage of Japanese women writers and the varying reception of their works can make to the study of the role of gender in literature is to establish the inherent mutability of the substance and consequences of terms such as "women's literature." If we understand that the connotations and impact of such a concept are not fixed or frozen but historically determined and subject to change, then we must approach the issue of gender as a heuristic problem to be investigated. The objective cannot be to collate and codify what women have written: rather, it must be to reconsider the work of both men and women in light of a new set of questions and priorities. Such an approach must be historical, but it also requires greater attention to the institutional factors and the broader patterns and pace of social change that shape the context in which a work is created and received. To suggest that women constitute a separate and unbroken tradition grossly distorts their work and its relation to their times. But it would be equally a distortion to neglect the significance of gender in shaping the content and quality of what is written and read.

Notes

1. For examples of translations into English, see the Selected Bibliography, pp. 461–92.

2. The term *joryū bungaku* has previously been translated as "female-school literature" (Lippit and Selden, xiv) or "feminine-style literature" (Vernon, 137), but I have chosen "women's literature" because it conveys some of the ambiguity in Japanese usage that facilitates a conflation of an author's gender with a specific literary style.

3. Classical literature (*ōchō bungaku*) was not conventionally categorized according to the gender of the author, and the reference for women writers of the court was usually "female" (*josei*) or "court lady" (*nyōbō*) rather than *joryū* (Fujii, 87–89).

4. A sampling of the recent debates can be found in special issues of journals such as "'Dansei' to iu seido" (The institution called "male") in *Nihon bungaku*; "Feminizumu no kotoba" (The vocabulary of feminism) in *Kokubungaku*; "Feminizumu no shinpuku" (Feminism's pendulum) in *Gunzō*; and "Masei to bosei" (Witches and mothers) in *Shin Nihon bungaku*. See the list of works cited for complete bibliographic information.

5. The sex of Hieda no Are remains contested. The original Japanese edition of this book does not unequivocally state that Hieda no Are was a woman. The recitation by Hieda no Are has been linked by many, including nativist philosopher Hirata Atsutane (1776–1845) and folklorist Yanagita Kunio (1875–1962), to the role that women have historically played in oral traditions in Japan.

6. None of the names of these authors is known: two of the authors are identified only by their relations to historically identified men (the Mother of Michitsuna and the Daughter of Takasue), and even the most renowned of classical authors, Murasaki Shikibu, is called by her father's court title (*shikibu*) and the appellation of a principal character in *The Tale of Genji*: Murasaki, or "lavender."

7. For insight into this matter, see Miyake; and Bundy.

8. She was tagged with this particular label because she had dared to

read the *Nihon shoki* (The records of Japan; 720), which was written in literary Chinese (Bowring, *Murasaki Shikibu*, 137–39).

9. See Chapter 2, by Lynne K. Miyake, in this volume, pp. 41–73.

10. For the notion of affiliation as a means of asserting choice and continuity, see Gilbert and Gubar, *No Man's Land*, 171.

11. Keene (*Travelers of a Hundred Ages* 175, 264) observes that there was a hiatus of about three centuries (ca. 1358–1681) in works by women writers.

12. Notable exceptions include Inoue Tsūjo (1660–1738), Iseki Takako (1785–1845), and Takejo, whose *Kōshi michi no ki* (1720) was published in 1807 (Keene, *Travelers of a Hundred Ages*, 328–40, 376–82). Yanagawa Kōron (wife of Yanagawa Seigan, 1789–1858) stood out for her compositions of *kanshi*, or Chinese poetry (Keene, *World Within Walls*, 555).

13. Arakida Reiko's work — *renga* poetry, histories written in *kana*, classical fiction (*gabun*), travel diaries, and love stories — occupies all of the second and part of the third volumes in the four-volume set. Reiko's love stories, such as *Goyō* (Five leaves) and *Hama chidori* (Plover), have a Heian setting. Other authors also evoked Heian themes and models: Takabatake Tomi (d. 1881) chose the pen name Takabatake Shikibu, reminiscent of Heian writers such as Murasaki Shikibu or Izumi Shikibu, who are known to us today only by the court title *shikibu* and a given name not their own. Uden no Yonoko's travel diary (1806) was described as having the literary form and excellence of Sei Shōnagon's *The Pillow Book* (Furuya, 3: 5).

14. *Keishū sakka* (a woman gifted in the arts; literally [one from the] bedroom [who] excels), a predecessor to *joryū sakka*, was more widely used in the Meiji (1868–1912) and Taishō (1912–26) eras. The term came to viewed by women writers and critics as outmoded and even pejorative, but it did not suggest a specific style of writing.

15. See Shioda, 261–62, for a list of authors included in these two special issues.

16. Increased literacy among women is associated with declining maternal mortality and physical vulnerability, improving nutrition and health, and greater real income. For a disturbing account of the costs associated with low literacy, among other factors, see Sen.

17. These figures represent women attending the institutions designated "universities" (*daigaku*) under the old educational system and do not include women enrolled in Normal schools for teacher training, women's colleges, or other specialized schools.

18. Note that some white-collar jobs, notably nursing, are absent in the survey results.

19. The 900,000 non-manual working women were classified as *chi-teki rōdōsha* or mental laborers.

20. On the marital status and motivations of the women in this survey, see Nagy, 205–9.

21. For Aono, see Keene, *Dawn to the West*, 598–99; and Arima, 183–88.

22. Although this "good wife and wise mother" (*ryōsai kenbo*) charac-

terization derived from deep-rooted patriarchal practices, the Ministry of Education popularized the formula in the last decade of the nineteenth century, "exhort[ing] women to contribute to the nation through their hard work, their frugality, their efficient management, their care of the old, young and ill, and their responsible upbringing of children" (Nolte and Hastings, 152). See also Garon, 11–15.

23. See Brownstein for a discussion of this rare exception to the rule that publishers and editors of general interest journals established women's magazines to supplement their flagship publication.

24. For a brief history of *Nyonin geijutsu*, see Kōno. The journal ran from July 1928 to June 1932, and published a total of 48 issues. The debut prose of both Hayashi Fumiko and Enchi Fumiko (1905–86) appeared in its initial issues. Hayashi achieved considerable prominence almost immediately, but it was not until after Hayashi's early death in 1951 that Enchi Fumiko gained similar recognition.

25. For a discussion of the *bundan* in this period, see Fowler, 128–45; Keene, *Dawn to the West*, 546–52; and Chapter 11, by Chieko M. Ariga, in this volume, pp. 352–81.

26. *Shōgi* is a Japanese board game, roughly equivalent to chess.

27. Even in the 1960's, though embarrassed about his popular fiction, Mishima Yukio "devote[d] about one-third of his time each month to writing popular fiction and essays in order to be able to live comfortably and to spend the remaining time on serious fiction and plays" (Keene, *Dawn to the West*, 1188–89).

28. See also Rodd.

29. For confessional fiction by men in English translation, see Tayama; and Shiga. For works by women in this confessional tradition, see the English translations of Hirabayashi Taiko; Hayashi Fumiko; and Uno Chiyo, listed in the Works Cited.

30. "Watakushi shōsetsu to shinkyō shōsetsu" by Kume Masao, originally published in Jan. and May 1925 in *Bungei kōza*; reprinted in Miyoshi and Sofue, 50–57.

For Kume, while it was possible for Europeans to achieve the confessional standards of the I-novel, it was rare: "For example, a work such as Tolstoy's 'My Confessions' is of course not devoid of artistic passages, but it is not personal fiction. Rousseau's confessional records also contain various fictional scenes, but this cannot really be called personal fiction either. However, when we come to Strindberg's *The Confession of a Fool*, that is clearly personal fiction" (51).

31. In the 1920's, proletarian literature attracted a large number of proponents, writers (Kobayashi Takiji, Hayama Yoshiki, Hayashi Fusao, Kuroshima Denji) as well as critics (Aono Suekichi, Nakano Shigeharu). Recent observers have often found it wanting—hobbled by a "stylistic immaturity and awkwardness of techniques" (Keene, *Dawn to the West*, 599)—for reasons

unrelated to its contrast with *watakushi shōsetsu*. For a critical appraisal of proletarian literature, see also Arima, 173–213.

32. But consider also the tenacity and sophistication of those that opposed such trends, as represented in Miriam Silverberg's *Changing Song: The Marxist Manifestos of Nakano Shigeharu*.

33. With only a few exceptions, such as Higuchi Ichiyō's association with the Romantic writers and their journal *Bungakkai*, or Sō Fusa's (b. 1907, nom de plume of Katayama Fusako) tie with Hori Tatsuo and the modernist school, women were rarely fostered in literary schools. For example, the White Birch Society, particularly active and influential in the 1910's, excluded women from the pages of its journal primarily because it relied on its own members, fellow students from the all-male Tokyo Imperial University, for contributions (Endō Yū).

34. The data used in this comparison were highly selective and cannot constitute a conclusive refutation of conventional wisdom. For example, Hayashi Fumiko's *Bangiku* (A late chrysanthemum) and Hirabayashi Taiko's *Watashi wa ikiru* (I will live) were the two works chosen as representative of women's literature.

35. A rare use of the term *joryū sakka* appears only in reference to the expectations of Yuriko's mother, a graduate of the Peers' Girls School, who saw her own literary ambitions in her daughter's future and wanted her to become a *joryū sakka* (Miyamoto Kenji, 17–18).

36. The essay was originally published under the title "Hayashi Fumiko ron" in *Fujin kōron* (June 1953).

37. Nakamura was not alone in such a judgment. Tamiya Torahiko characterized Hayashi as "the representative woman writer in our country" (221).

38. For a fuller discussion of her work and its relation to "women's literature" (as well as a translation of *Diary of a Vagabond*), see Ericson, "Hayashi Fumiko and Japanese Women's Literature."

39. As if to underscore this association in the 1939 revised edition, Hayashi added some sixty passages of classical grammar—or more appropriately, pseudo-classical grammar, since only the ending of each phrase or sentence was rendered into classical grammar, most often "nari." On one level, this may appear wholly as a literary affectation. However, it served to distance the actions or judgments that they were used to emphasize and conveyed a sense of the mundane as elevated, even transcendent.

40. For example, she confessed having aborted a child by an unnamed lover (identified as Okano Gun'ichi in *Hōrōki dai sanbu*—Part III—which was serialized from May 1947 to Oct. 1948 in *Nihon shōsetsu* and published as a book by Ryūjo shobō in 1949) in Onomichi by hitting her stomach repeatedly against a gravestone; later, she indicated that his family paid her to leave (Hayashi, *Hōrōki* II: 158–59, 161–64; III: 223, 224–25).

41. My entry "Hayashi Fumiko" in *Modern Japanese Novelists: Dictionary*

of Literary Biography, ed. Van C. Gessel, provides a partial bibliography of her writings, including 87 books and 63 of her best-known short stories.

42. Hayashi, "Chosha no kotoba," 249. On the distinctions between these two styles in the 1920's and 1930's, see Keene, *Dawn to the West*, 510–13.

43. Although Hayashi had first surfaced in the company of Anarchist and Proletarian writers, she never exhibited any political commitment to or interest in Marxist ideology. Soon after achieving prominence as a writer, she quickly distanced herself from leftist associations, despite her nine-day detention in the Nakano police station in Sept. 1933 for having purchased a subscription to a Communist Party newspaper. Even in 1929, Hayashi's work had been considered too *runpen* (lumpen) for subscribers to *Nyonin geijutsu*. Miyamoto quoted Hayashi's recollection of 1935: "Proletarian literature was on the rise [in 1929]. I was isolated, without support" (176).

44. See Ericson, "Hayashi Fumiko and the Transformation of Her Fiction."

45. Many of her ostensibly autobiographical works simply adopted the format of a diary or journal but were clearly fictional. Those explicitly about Hayashi, in effect a continuation of *Diary of a Vagabond*, were confessional in form but cannot be taken as an accurate reflection of her life. When scrutinized closely, there is enough of a discrepancy between these works and previous accounts of well-known incidents from her earlier work, both in tenor and detail, that one cannot help but view at least some of her later autobiographies as calculated to dissemble the details of her life. She had a tendency to reinvent herself to fit the times. Hayashi discussed her return to an autobiographical style in her "Atogaki," 245–46.

46. Hayashi left a massive body of work. Itagaki Naoko, her biographer, estimated that only a third of her published writings appeared in the 23-volume *Hayashi Fumiko zenshū* (Collected works of Hayashi Fumiko), produced by Shinchōsha from Oct. 1951 to Apr. 1953.

47. For a discussion of Hayashi's postwar novel *Drifting Clouds* (*Ukigumo*), see Chapter 10, by Noriko Mizuta, in this volume, pp. 329–51.

48. The small sweatshop that operated below my apartment during a year in Delhi in the mid-1980's was entirely male, and each step in the production process, from master cutter to overseer to sewer to embroiderer was occupied by a separate religion or caste.

49. Tsushima Yūko, personal interview, June 1991.

Works Cited

Akiyama Shun. "Ima joryū bungaku to wa nani ka: sengo shi to no kanren de." *Kokubungaku: kaishaku to kyōzai no kenkyū* 25, no. 15 (Dec. 1980): 124–27.

Arima, Tatsuo. *The Failure of Freedom: A Portrait of Modern Japanese Intellectuals.* Cambridge, Mass.: Harvard University Press, 1969.

Bernstein, Gail Lee, ed. *Recreating Japanese Women, 1600–1945.* Berkeley: University of California Press, 1991.

Bowring, Richard. "The Female Hand in Heian Japan: A First Reading." In *The Female Autograph: Theory and Practice of Autobiography from the Tenth to the Twentieth Century,* ed. Domna C. Stanton. Chicago: University of Chicago Press, 1987, 49–56.

Brownstein, Michael C. "*Jogaku Zasshi* and the Founding of *Bungakkai.*" *Monumenta Nipponica* 35, no. 3 (1980): 319–36.

Bundy, Roselee. "Japan's First Woman Diarist and the Beginnings of Prose Writing by Women in Japan." *Women's Studies* 19 (1991): 79–91.

Chabot, Jeanette A. Taudin. "A View of Tokugawa Women and Literature." *Women in Japanese Literature* (Netherlands Association for Japanese Studies) 1981: 55–66.

Chiba Kameo. "Bungaku no ichinen." *Kaizō,* Dec. 1921, 183–89.

Copeland, Rebecca L. *The Sound of the Wind: The Life and Works of Uno Chiyo.* Honolulu: University of Hawaii Press, 1992.

Danly, Robert Lyons. *In the Shade of Spring Leaves: The Life and Writings of Higuchi Ichiyō, a Woman of Letters in Meiji Japan.* New Haven: Yale University Press, 1981.

"'Dansei' to iu seido." *Nihon bungaku,* special issue, Nov. 1992.

Egusa Mitsuko and Urushida Kazuyo, eds. *Onna ga yomu Nihon kindai bungaku: feminizumu hihyō no kokoromi.* Tokyo: Shin'yōsha, 1992.

Endō Orie. "Kotoba to josei." *Kokubungaku: kaishaku to kyōzai no kenkyū,* special issue: "Feminizumu no kotoba: josei bungaku," 37, no. 13 (Nov. 1992): 28–37.

Endō Yū. "Shirakaba ha to joryū bungaku." *Kokubungaku: kaishaku to kanshō* 37, no. 3 (Mar. 1972): 28–33.

Ericson, Joan E. "Hayashi Fumiko and Japanese Women's Literature." Ph.D. diss., Columbia University, 1993.

———. "Hayashi Fumiko and the Transformation of Her Fiction." In *Translations and Transitions: Essays in Honor of Donald Keene,* ed. Amy Heinrich. Columbia University Press, forthcoming.

"Feminizumu no kotoba: josei bungaku." *Kokubungaku: kaishaku to kyōzai no kenkyū,* special issue, 37, no. 13 (Nov. 1992).

"Feminizumu no shinpuku." *Gunzō,* special issue, Oct. 1992, 264–345.

Field, Norma. *The Splendor of Longing in "The Tale of Genji."* Princeton: Princeton University Press, 1987.

Fowler, Edward. *The Rhetoric of Confession: Shishōsetsu in Early Twentieth-Century Japanese Fiction.* Berkeley: University of California Press, 1988.

Fujii Sadakazu. "Tsukurimono no jukusei." *Kokubungaku: kaishaku to kyōzai no kenkyū* 26, no. 12 (Sept. 1981): 82–89.

Fukuda Hirotoshi. "Hayashi Fumiko." *Kokubungaku: kaishaku to kanshō,* special issue: "Gendai joryū sakka no himitsu," 27, no. 9 (Sept. 1962): 43–48.

Fukuda Kiyoto and Endō Mitsuhiko. *Hayashi Fumiko: hito to sakuhin.* Tokyo: Shimizu shoin, 1966.

Furuya Tomoyoshi, ed. *Joryū bungaku zenshū.* 4 vols. Tokyo: Bungei shoin, 1918–19.

Garon, Sheldon. "Women's Groups and the Japanese State: Contending Approaches to Political Integration, 1890–1945." *Journal of Japanese Studies* 19, no. 1 (1993): 5–41.

Gates, Henry Louis. "'Authenticity' or the Lesson of Little Tree." *New York Times Book Review*, Nov. 24, 1991, 1, 26–30.

Gilbert, Sandra M., and Susan Gubar. *No Man's Land: The Place of the Woman Writer in the Twentieth Century*, vol. 1, *The War of the Words.* New Haven: Yale University Press, 1988.

Gilbert, Sandra M., and Susan Gubar, eds. *The Norton Anthology of Literature by Women: The Tradition in English.* New York: Norton, 1985.

Hayashi Fumiko. "Atogaki" (1949). In *Hayashi Fumiko zenshū*, 8: 245–46.

———. "Chosha no kotoba" (1936). In *Hayashi Fumiko zenshū*, 6: 249–51.

———. *Hayashi Fumiko zenshū.* 23 vols. Tokyo: Shinchōsha, 1951–53.

———. *Hōrōki.* Tokyo: Shinchōsha, 1979. Part I, trans. Joan E. Ericson, in Ericson, "Hayashi Fumiko and Japanese Women's Literature," 231–368.

Hirabayashi Taiko. "Self-Mockery." In *To Live and To Write*, ed. Yukiko Tanaka. Seattle: Seal Press, 1987, 75–96.

Ikari Akira. "Nihon no koten bungaku to kindai joryū no bungaku." *Kokubungaku: kaishaku to kanshō* 37, no. 3 (Mar. 1972): 53–57.

Inoue Yuriko. "Hiratsuka Raichō." *Kokubungaku: kaishaku to kyōzai no kenkyū* 24, no. 4 (1979): 182–83.

Itagaki Naoko. "Genkon Nihon no joryū bundan." *Bungaku* 1, no. 9 (Sept. 1931): 31–45.

———. *Meiji, Taishō, Shōwa no joryū bungaku.* Tokyo: Ōfūsha, 1967.

———. "Shōwa no joryū sakka." *Kokubungaku: kaishaku to kanshō* 26, no. 9 (Sept. 1962): 29–33.

Joryū bungakusha kai, ed. *Nyonin geijutsu*, no. 1 (Jan. 1, 1949).

"Kaku fujin zasshi no henshūsha ni kiku: kaku yo no hōfu to risō, hinan ni taishite no ben." *Yomiuri shinbun*, Dec. 29, 1930, 5.

Kanai Shigefumi. *Heian joryū sakka no shinzō.* Tokyo: Izumi sensho, 1987.

Kaneko Sachiko. "Taishō ki *Shufu no tomo* to Ishikawa Takemi no shisō." *Rekishi hyōron*, no. 42 (July 1984): 43–59.

Karatani Kōjin. *Origins of Modern Japanese Literature.* Trans. ed. Brett de Bary. Durham, N.C.: Duke University Press, 1993.

Katō, Shūichi. *A History of Japanese Literature*, vol. 1. Tokyo: Kodansha International, 1983.

Keene, Donald. *Dawn to the West: Japanese Literature in the Modern Era*, vol. 1, *Fiction.* New York: Holt, Rinehart & Winston, 1984.

———. *Travelers of a Hundred Ages.* New York: Henry Holt, 1989.

———. *World Within Walls: Japanese Literature of the Pre-modern Era, 1600–1867.* Tokyo: Tuttle, 1976.

Keene, Donald, ed. and comp. *Anthology of Japanese Literature.* New York: Grove Press, 1955.

Kikuta Shigeo. "Nihon no koten bungaku to kindai joryū no bungaku." *Kokubungaku: kaishaku to kanshō* 37, no. 3 (Mar. 1972): 73–78.

Kobayashi Hideo. "Watakushi shōsetsu ron" (1935). In *Kindai bungaku hyōron taikei*, vol. 7, *Shōwa ki II*, ed. Takahashi Haruo and Yasumasa Masao. Kadokawa shoten, 1972, 181–202.

Konishi, Jin'ichi. *A History of Japanese Literature*, vol. 2, *The Early Middle Ages*. Trans. Aileen Gatten. Ed. Earl Miner. Princeton: Princeton University Press, 1984.

Kōno Toshirō. "*Nyonin geijutsu:* sono tenkai to shiteki igi." Preface to the table of contents and index of the reprinted *Nyonin geijutsu*. Ed. Kitamura Masamitsu. Tokyo: Ryūkei shosha, 1981, 5–16.

Kōra Rumiko. "Jiko to tō no shinwa ka: Miyamoto Yuriko." In *Onna no sentaku*. Tokyo: Rōdō sentā, 1984, 95–111.

Kumasaka Atsuko. " 'Onnen to shite no joryū bungaku': Hayashi Fumiko to Okamoto Kanoko." *Kokubungaku: kaishaku to kyōzai no kenkyū*, special issue: "Joryū no zensen: Higuchi Ichiyō kara hachijūnen dai no sakka made," 25, no. 15 (Dec. 1980): 79–83.

Kume Masao. " 'Watakushi' shōsetsu to 'shinkyō' shōsetsu" (1925). In *Kindai bungaku hyōron taikei*, vol. 6, *Taishō ki III/Shōwa ki I*, ed. Miyoshi Yukio and Sofue Shōji. Tokyo: Kadokawa shoten, 1973, 50–57.

Lippit, Noriko Mizuta, and Kyoko Iriye Selden, trans. and eds. *Stories by Contemporary Japanese Women Writers*. Armonk, N.Y.: M. E. Sharpe, 1982.

Maeda Ai. "Taishō kōki tsūzoku shōsetsu no tenkai: fujin zasshi no dokusha sō." 2 parts. *Bungaku* 36, nos. 6– 7 (June–July 1968): 649–62, 808–22.

"Masei to bosei: onna no me de bungaku o yominaosu." *Shin Nihon bungaku*, special issue, 47, no. 1 (Winter 1992).

Mass, Jeffrey P. *Lordship and Inheritance in Early Medieval Japan: A Study of the Kamakura Sōryō System*. Stanford: Stanford University Press, 1989.

Mawatari Kenzaburō. "Joryū bungei kenkyū." In *Kindai joryū bungaku ron*, ed. idem. Tokyo: Nansōsha, 1973, 29–51.

Minemura Toshio. "Kigyō fujin zasshi keitai ron." In *Sōgō jaanarizumu kōza*. Tokyo: Naigaisha, 1931, 9: 63–87.

Miyake, Lynne K. "Women's Voice in Japanese Literature: Expanding the Feminine." *Women's Studies* 17 (1989): 87–100.

Miyamoto Kenji. *Miyamoto Yuriko no sekai*. Tokyo: Shin Nihon shuppansha, 1963.

Miyamoto Yuriko. *Fujin to bungaku: kindai Nihon no fujin sakka*. Tokyo: Jitsugyō no Nihonsha, 1947.

Miyoshi Yukio and Sofue Shōji, eds. *Kindai bungaku hyōron taikei*, vol. 6, *Taishō ki III/Shōwa ki I*. Tokyo: Kadokawa shoten, 1973.

Morris, Ivan. *The World of the Shining Prince*. New York: Penguin, 1964.

Muramatsu Sadataka. "Hayashi Fumiko no dansei henreki." In idem, *Sakka no kakei to kankyō*. Tokyo: Shibundō, 1964, 202–17.

———. *Kindai joryū sakka no shōzō*. Tokyo: Tokyo shoseki, 1980.

———. " 'Onna de aru koto' ron." In *Kawabata Yasunari kenkyū sōsho*, vol. 3, *'Jitsuzon no kazō,'* ed. Kawabata bungaku kenkyū kai et al. Tokyo: Kyōiku shuppan sentā, 1977, 168–82.

Muramatsu Sadataka and Watanabe Sumiko, eds. *Gendai josei bungaku jiten.* Tokyo: Tokyodō shuppan, 1990.

Murasaki Shikibu. *Murasaki Shikibu, Her Diary and Poetic Memoirs*, trans. Richard Bowring. Princeton: Princeton University Press, 1982.

Murō Saisei. *Ōgon no hari.* Tokyo: Chūō kōronsha, 1961.

Nagy, Margit. "Middle-Class Working Women During the Interwar Years." In Bernstein, 199–218.

Nakamura Mitsuo. "Hayashi Fumiko nyūmon." *Bungei* 14, no. 7 (June 1953): 20–27.

———. "Hayashi Fumiko ron." In *Gendai sakka ron sōsho: Shōwa no sakkatachi, II*, ed. Nakajima Kenzō et al. Tokyo: Eiōsha, 1955, 95–112.

Negoro Tsukasa. *Ōchō joryū bungaku no kotoba to buntai.* Tokyo: Yūseidō, 1988.

Nihon kindai kyōiku shi jiten. Tokyo: Heibonsha, 1971.

Nolte, Sharon, and Sally Ann Hastings. "The Meiji State Policy Toward Women." In Bernstein, 151–74.

Odagiri Hideo. "Sata Ineko: hito to sakuhin." In idem, *Gendai no sakka: sono imi to ichi.* Tokyo: Tōjusha, 1972, 170–79.

Ogata Akiko. *"Nyonin geijutsu" no hitobito.* Tokyo: Domesu shuppan, 1982.

———. *"Nyonin geijitsu" no sekai: Hasegawa Shigure to sono shūhen.* Tokyo: Domesu shuppan, 1980.

Okada, H. Richard. *Figures of Resistance: Language, Poetry, and Narrating in "The Tale of Genji" and Other Mid-Heian Texts.* Durham, N.C.: Duke University Press, 1991.

Okazaki Yoshie. *Japanese Literature in the Meiji Era.* Trans. V. H. Viglielmo. Tokyo: Tōyō bunko, 1955.

Okuno Takeo. *Joryū sakka ron: shōsetsu wa honshitsu-teki ni josei no mono ka.* Tokyo: Daisan bunmeisha, 1974.

Okuno Takeo et al., eds. *Josei sakka jūsannin ten.* Tokyo: Nihon kindai bungakkan, 1988.

Ōya Sōichi. "Bundan girudo no kaitai ki." *Shinchō* 23, no. 12 (Dec. 1926): 78–83.

Rimer, J. Thomas, ed. *Culture and Identity: Japanese Intellectuals During the Interwar Years.* Princeton: Princeton University Press, 1990.

Rodd, Laurel Rasplica. "Yosano Akiko and the Taishō Debate of the 'New Woman.' " In Bernstein, 175–98.

Roden, Donald. "Taishō Culture and the Problem of Gender Ambivalence." In Rimer, 37–55.

Saegusa Kazuko. *Ren'ai shōsetsu no kansei.* Tokyo: Seidōsha, 1991.

Satō Haruo. "Bungeika no seikatsu o ronzu." *Shinchō* 23, no. 9 (Sept. 1926): 2–18.

Seidensticker, E. G. "Hayashi Fumiko." *Jiyū* 5 (1963): 122–31.

Seki Reiko. *Higuchi Ichiyō o yomu*. Iwanami bukkuretto, no. 259. Tokyo: Iwanami, 1992.

Sen, Amartya. "More Than 100 Million

Shibaki Nobuo and Shōno Masanori, eds. *Orijinaru genban ni* Women Are Missing." *New York Review of Books*, Dec. 20, 1990, 61–66.*yoru Nihon no ryūkōka shi (senzen hen)*. Tokyo: Bikutā ongaku, 1977.

Shibaki Yoshiko. "Kaisetsu." In *Meshi*, by Hayashi Fumiko. Tokyo: Kadokawa shoten, 1962, 217–21.

Shiga Naoya. *A Dark Night's Passing (An'ya kōro)*. Trans. Edwin McClellan. New York: Kodansha International, 1976.

Shintō Junko. "Hirabayashi Taiko: joryū de aru koto ni genkai wa nai." *Kokubungaku: kaishaku to kanshō* 27, no. 10 (Sept. 1962): 48–52.

Shioda Ryōhei. *Meiji joryū sakka ron*. Tokyo: Nara shobō, 1965.

Shirane, Haruo. *The Bridge of Dreams: A Poetics of "The Tale of Genji."* Stanford: Stanford University Press, 1987.

Sievers, Sharon L. *Flowers in Salt: The Beginnings of Feminist Consciousness in Modern Japan*. Stanford: Stanford University Press, 1983.

Silverberg, Miriam. *Changing Song: The Marxist Manifestos of Nakano Shigeharu*. Princeton: Princeton University Press, 1990.

———. "The Modern Girl as Militant." In Bernstein, 239–66.

———. "Remembering Pearl Harbor, Forgetting Charlie Chaplin, and the Case of the Disappearing Western Woman: A Picture Story." *positions: east asia cultures critique* 1, no. 1 (1993): 24–76.

Tamiya Torahiko. "Kaisetsu" (1954). In *Meshi*, by Hayashi Fumiko. Tokyo: Shinchōsha, 1982, 217–21.

Tayama Katai. *The Quilt and Other Stories*. Trans. Kenneth G. Henshall. Tokyo: University of Tokyo Press, 1981.

Tokura Giichi. "Fujin katei tosho no shuppan kan." In *Sōgō jānarizumu kōza*. Tokyo: Nagaisha, 1931, 9: 19–33.

Tōkyō shi shakai kyoku. *Shokugyō fujin ni kan suru chōsa*. Tokyo, 1923.

Tomioka Taeko. *Fuji no koromo ni asa no fusuma*. Tokyo: Chūō kōronsha, 1984

Tsukada Mitsue. "Joryū bungaku ko josetsu: Hayashi Fumiko o chūshin ni." *Joshidai kokubun* 64 (Jan. 1972): 31–42.

Ueno Chizuko, Ogura Chikako, and Tomioka Taeko. *Danryū bungaku ron*. Tokyo: Chikuma shobō, 1992.

Uno Chiyo. *Confessions of Love (Iro zange)*. Trans. Phyllis Birnbaum. Honolulu: University of Hawaii Press, 1989.

———. "This Powder Box" ("Kono oshiroi ire"). Trans. Rebecca L. Copeland. In Copeland, 208–36.

Vernon, Victoria V. *Daughters of the Moon: Wish, Will and Social Constraint in Fiction by Modern Japanese Women*. Berkeley: University of California, Institute of East Asian Studies, 1988.

Wada Yoshie. "Hayashi Fumiko." *Shūkan dokushojin*, June 22, 1964, 3.

Wittgenstein, Ludwig. *Tractatus Logico-Philosophicus*. Trans. D. F. Pears and B. F. McGinnis. London: Routledge & Kegan Paul, 1961.

Yabu Teiko. *Tōkoku, Tōson, Ichiyō*. Tokyo: Meiji shoin, 1991.
Yamashita Etsuko. *Mazākon bungaku ron*. Tokyo: Shin'yōsha, 1991.
Yosano Akiko. *Tokugawa jidai joryū bungaku: Reiko shōsetsu shū*. Tokyo: Fuzanbō, 1916.
Yoshida Seiichi. "Kindai joryū no bungaku." *Kokubungaku: kaishaku to kanshō* 37, no. 3 (Mar. 1972): 10–17.
Yuri Sachiko. "Josei sakka no genzai." *Kokubungaku: kaishaku to kanshō*, special issue: "Josei sakka no shinryū," May 1991, 71–81.

Part II

Narrating the Body

4

The Body in Contemporary
Japanese Women's Fiction

SHARALYN ORBAUGH

> No wonder the really powerful men in our society, whether politi-
> cians or scientists, hold writers and poets in contempt. They do it
> because they get no evidence from modern literature that anybody
> is thinking about any significant question. — Saul Bellow

Saul Bellow probably intended no explicit message about gender
when he made the statement that appears as the epigraph to this
chapter. The "powerful men in our society" — politicians and scientists — are assumed by definition to be men, even if the politician or
scientist in question happens to be female. Although the phrasing of
Bellow's statement does therefore contain interesting implications
about gender, it seems to have been intended as a general assertion
about power and modern literature. This essay, too, is about power
and literature, but I intend in it explicitly to introduce the issue of
gender. The discussion will center on the gendered body in the work
of some contemporary Japanese women writers, particularly the use
of the body as a site of political expression in fiction.

I begin with a basic question, one that underlies any discussion of
the gendered body: What do we mean when we use the words *male*
and *female*? Are we referring to differences of gender identity, differences of anatomy, or a combination of both? Are we talking about reproductive behavior, and if so, how do we define those human beings
who do not perform reproductive sex — homosexual men and women,
or heterosexuals who prefer non-reproductive sex? Are we talking
about a political or power orientation to the world, in the style of Julia

Kristeva, wherein to be "female" is to resist the patriarchy, whatever the anatomy of the body that performs that resistance? The words *male* and *female* clearly are meant to demarcate some boundary between essentially different categories, but what are the parameters of those categories, and where do they come from? Do they change from one moment to another or from one place to another, or are they stable and fixed, somehow "natural" and "given"?

One could not begin to enumerate all the recent theories about the nature of sex or gender. Whereas scientists and medical researchers may be able to differentiate "conclusively" between a person with two X-chromosomes and a person with one X and one Y chromosome, and although human reproduction has most likely always and everywhere followed a two-sex model based on "obvious" anatomical differences, the work of Freud, Lacan, Nancy Chodorow, Judith Butler, Julia Kristeva, Thomas Laqueur, Hélène Cixous (to name but a few) shows that the parameters of what "counts" as male and what "counts" as female are constantly shifting, constantly contested.[1]

Luce Irigaray has said, "The body is not matter, but metaphor," but surely it is *both*. In our individual lives we might be said to oscillate between an experience of the body that is physical, private, bounded, and concrete and one that is cultural, linguistic, conceptual, abstract, and metaphorical. Many recent literary and cultural theoretical models have downplayed the importance of the physical and private, relegating such concerns to the refuse heap of "essentialist fantasy" and, worse, to the realm of the "apolitical."[2] But writers and readers are not necessarily theorists, and each of them lives in a body that constantly recalls itself to their attention through its needs to eat, drink, excrete, sleep, have sex, remain within a certain temperature range, and so on. I will not attempt the task (which I believe impossible) of untangling those elements of "body" experience—particularly the experience of the gendered body—that are culturally constructed, from those that are based on "real" biological or physiological differences. I do not think that necessary for writers or readers in order to *use* these various discourses of the body.

How, then, does literature, how do specific writers, appropriate and use all these "discourses of the body": the abstract, the physical and experiential, the linguistic, the psychoanalytic, the cultural, the erotic, and so on? It seems to me that writers seize on specific pieces of this wild conglomeration because of their own particular social and political circumstances, and because of their desire to answer the particular strategic needs of their time and place.

Our thinking about and experience of the body is mediated by all these various discourses – the ones that are current in our particular cultural/historical place and time. The body is, in fact, configured by these discourses. It is also possible, however, to look at these discourses as available for appropriation and re-presentation in fiction (or elsewhere), and this act of appropriation may have political ramifications. Mary Wollstonecraft Shelley's *Frankenstein, the Modern Prometheus* (1818) is a good example of a writer's use of the available discourses of the body (and its relationship to the mind or soul) to make an allegorical political statement.

Despite our difficulties in specifying what is meant by gender categories and despite the fact that the parameters of those categories differ according to specific cultural and historical circumstances, it is clear that encodings of gender are constantly superimposed on patterns of power and dominance, resulting in specific kinds of gender-determined relationships of power. Feminist (as well as postcolonial)[3] critical discourse in the United States and Europe has been configured by a set of dichotomous questions that reveal relationships of power. As critics from feminist film theorist Laura Mulvey (in "Visual Pleasure"; 1975)[4] to John Berger (in *Ways of Seeing*; 1972) have noted, one of the key indicators of power is revealed by the question: Who is doing the looking, and who is the object of that gaze? They point out that in the scopic economy it is men who gaze, and women who are the object of that vision.[5] Other critics have posed similar questions, all of which are related: Who speaks and who is spoken about? Who sets the definitions and who is defined? Who judges, and who must abide by those judgments? Who has the right to beat or kill with impunity and who is beaten or killed? I will call these and related paradigms "economies of power."

When posed in the context of gender-based relationships of power, these questions may seem simple, and the answers obvious: men do, and women get done to. But I want to emphasize a point not often addressed in these discussions: each of these questions does not set up a simple binary. Each question, in fact, encodes at least two axes of power: subject vs. object, and active vs. passive. In the form "Who gazes, and who is the object of that gaze," the question encodes the subject-object paradigm, with heterosexual men as gazing subjects and women as visual objects. But the question can be restated as "Who gazes and who is blind (or voluntarily unseeing)?" In this case, the active-passive configuration is encoded, with men performing the act of looking and women passively "failing" to look or see. In a painting of a classic European nude, the naked woman may have her eyes open, but not for the purpose of usurping or even meeting the male gaze.

Again, these apparently straightforward dichotomies are not as simple as they may appear. When we talk about the experience of "self," it is most common to think in terms of experiencing oneself as "subject." But it is also possible to experience oneself as "object," for example as the permanent object of the gaze of the dominant other. Women in a patriarchal social economy constantly experience themselves as objects of the gaze, the speech, the judgments, the violence of men. In the same way, although it is most common to think in terms of performing an act, it *is* possible to "perform" passivity. Rather than gazing, women can perform blindness; rather than speaking, women can perform silence; rather than judging, women can perform non-discrimination; rather than killing, women can commit suicide. The significance of this point will be addressed in a moment.[6]

Also important in many of these dichotomous scenarios are the differences in the body's function and emphasis between the active and the passive members. While the dominant side, the "male" in this case, uses its physical and sensory powers of speech, vision, rational judgment, and brute strength to perform its role in the various economies, it is not physically changed or affected by the role. Women, however, experience their roles in many of these economies directly through the body. Certainly a woman who is beaten or killed undergoes an obvious physical change, but even as the object of the male gaze a woman experiences her physical surface, delimited by the parameters of her body, as the determinant of her meaning in the scopic economy. How she fares in that economy depends solely on her ability to "perform" the required physical appearance.

Much early Anglo-European feminist writing, both critical and literary, was devoted to revealing the unequal nature of the roles in these performative economies of power.[7] The function of such writing was to *expose* and *indict* patriarchal paradigms. This is a crucial first step in coming to terms with power inequities, whether based on differences of gender, as in this case, or on differences of ethnicity, socio-economic status, or anything else. Since one of the strategies effective in maintaining exclusive power is to obscure the nature of the systems that sustain that power, it is vital that such patterns be exposed. But this is only a first step.

Thereafter, women had several choices, both in their lives and their writing, in dealing strategically with the reality they could now see. For the purposes of this discussion, I will concentrate on the strategies women employed in their writing, primarily the writing of fiction.[8] I will also confine the discussion to women writing *against* the prevailing economies of power. I think it could be argued that this, in fact, includes all writing by women who live in a patriarchal society. Even those women who claim to accept their roles in the economy of power would be implicitly challenging it by the very act of writing. "To speak" is not the woman's role, even if what she speaks is the language of the patriarchy. In my terms, to write *against a background of* patriarchal control, even if one is not writing "contra," is still an act of "writing against."[9]

The first option of women writing fiction against the dominant economies of power is the one delimited above for early feminist critics: that is, to maintain and *describe* the current configurations of power, exposing the harm done through them. Such fiction might concentrate on the harm done to women and those classed with them, such as children and other dependents, or it might go further to show how these fixed configurations of power ultimately do harm to society as a whole.[10]

A second strategy women might employ is to maintain and describe the current configurations of power, but to *invert the hierarchy of value,* to valorize the object/passive side of the equation. In this strategy a writer might show how women have used their received roles to their own advantage, how women have managed to find a positive value in their performance of passivity, their identification as object rather than subject of cultural performance.[11]

Finally, women writers might choose to maintain the current binary configurations of power, but to *reverse the gender coding* of the hierarchical power roles. Instead of being silent, women can speak; instead of being the objects of others' gaze, they can use their eyes; instead of being killed, they can kill; instead of being dominated, they can dominate. Women who choose this strategy in writing *realist* fiction must show their protagonists overturning the power hierarchies in a world still configured by those hierarchies. Such reversals are always temporary and end in tragedy.[12] A more systematic use of this strategy would place the story outside the bounds of the "real world," in a complete, fully articulated world of fantasy, or in a space contiguous to, but dislocated from, the world as we know it. In such a space it is possible to explore freely the implications of overturning the dominant hierarchies of power.[13]

It is also possible, of course, to mix elements of the three strategies in one work, or for one writer to use different strategies in different stories. All these possibilities rely, however, on the original set of binary or dichotomous paradigms, and none of these strategies ultimately alters those paradigms. None, not even the third, questions the validity of the original defining characteristics of power. None arises from a pre-patriarchal, somehow "purified" place where woman is equal or central, or where the obsessively binary nature of the oppositions is called into question. A work of fiction that employs these strategies is at best a raid against the fortress of patriarchal power; it may be momentarily shaken, but eventually it will fall back into the same configurations.

If women propose to construct (or reconstruct) a space in which their own experience is somehow primary, it would seem that the body, the physical body inside which we live, would be the "touchstone" that could keep us centered. Besides the essentially physical nature of the way women experience the effects of the passive, female role in the power paradigms mentioned above, women are constantly reminded of their bodies by the way society makes of them a legal and moral abstraction. I am referring not only to the literary, erotic, or religious abstractions of the female body, which reduce it (some would say elevate it) to the status of Woman—a cultural sign that can be activated by any one of various physical elements: breasts, hips, thighs, buttocks, a dainty foot, the nape of the neck, a maternal countenance. I am referring more specifically to the way a legal and moral abstraction is made out of the body in which a woman lives and walks around—this specific amalgam of muscle, blood, bone, fat, and so on that types these words. This body I inhabit and experience as real is the physical receiver/performer of all the abstract policies made by patriarchal institutions. The political and the ideological for women often boil down to the physical and the personal. As the late Audre Lord, among others, has pointed out: for women, far more than for men, the body *is* the political battleground; the personal is the political.[14]

It is not surprising, then, that fiction by women constantly returns to the female body as a source of metaphor, a locus of structural analogy. In works such as Enchi Fumiko's *Onna men* (Masks, 1958; English trans., 1983) or "Yō" (Enchantment, 1956) images of blood, of cyclic recurrence, of womb-like enclosures from which the protagonist emerges into new life, and the like are used to structure fiction according to tropes based on female physiology and anatomy. Other writers use the female body as a trope for the act of writing, such as Kurahashi Yumiko's self-conscious use of the image of the womb to center her literary structures around what she calls a fertile emptiness (Sakaki, 11).

Unfortunately, however, to privilege the experience of the female body without taking into account the social, political, and cultural codes that determine our *reading* of gendered bodies is naive, since, as discussed above, both gender and the body are "constructed," determined by historical forces. It is not possible, even for those of us who walk around in these bodies, to gain access to some hermetically "pure," unmediated, essential experience of what it is to be female. As psychoanalytic theorists such as Nancy Chodorow have shown, early experiences of identifying similarity with and difference from our mothers and fathers teach us what it is to be gendered human beings, and these lessons occur in a specific historical and cultural context. The codes that govern the specific social definition of femaleness play a large role in the way we interpret even physiological behavior.[15] It is thus probably impossible to identify which elements of one's own gender identity are culturally determined, and which are based on some fundamental physical, biological, or psychological difference.

For a woman writer who is aware of the constructed nature of an individual's experience even of her own body and yet recognizes that living inside such a body gives her a perspective different from that of a man, the search for a fictional strategy to encompass both the relativist and essentialist ends of the spectrum is extremely daunting. Those who have kept up with the current debates in French and Anglo-American feminist theory are aware that critics and theorists have as much trouble resolving this issue as do writers of fiction. The advantage that writers have is that they are rarely called upon to create policy; unlike cultural critics, they are not expected to invent strategies that can be actively used and institutionalized. Writers (and readers) of fiction are more free to explore the parameters of the social and physical body without explicitly engaging in a discourse of emancipatory praxis.

In this paper I will discuss discourses of the body as they relate to the work of major Japanese female literary figures from the early 1960's to the mid-1970's. The examples will come primarily from the work of one writer, Kanai Mieko (1947–), but to the extent space allows I will relate her writing of the body to that of other women writers of the period.

The decision to mark off this fifteen-year period is clearly a conveniently arbitrary one on my part, since no obvious social or political upheavals here neatly demarcate this as "a period." This is unlike, for example, designations such as "Shōwa" or "the Pacific War" or "the Occupation Period," whose "political" and "historical" boundaries are apparent. These commonly used period designations are of course arbitrary in the sense that they highlight only certain kinds of activity in the marking of boundaries. Between 1960 and 1975 Japan was well into the astonishing explosion of economic growth that followed the withdrawal of the Allied Occupation forces in 1952, the rebuilding of the industrial base during the 1950's, and the government's reconceptualization of the country's long-term economic strategy. Japan's return to a certain degree of economic and political autonomy in the world led to the questioning of national choices and relationships; many writers problematized the emperor system, Japan's continued dependence on and complicity with its former "big brother," the United States, and so on. These are among the issues most often raised in discussions of Japan's postwar history. Many male writers — Ōe Kenzaburō springs immediately to mind — actively engaged these issues in their fiction, making the political nature of their literary activity abundantly clear. Less clear is the relationship of women's writing to the prominent elements of the sociopolitical milieu. I would suggest that this is because the designation of which issues were of importance at the time as well as in the subsequent historical assessments of the period is an essentially male-centered view of what constitutes "politics" and "history." Women were writing, as always, "against" this background, not necessarily actively opposing it, but writing about the "physical" and "private" areas of life, which for them constituted the "politics" and "history" of the time.

I have chosen to focus on the early 1960's to mid-1970's because of activities I choose to highlight: a stage in the sociopolitical lives and writing careers of specific women. I am not prepared to identify here the issues and movements that might designate this a coherent "epoch"; such definitions, if necessary at all, should come after much more critical attention has been paid to women's postwar history. There is, however, evidence to suggest that for women writers this period represented a significant cultural moment in which they could explore through fiction the various discourses and power relationships of postwar Japan.

For example, during this period there was a sudden boom in women's writing. Kōno Taeko (1926–), Ōba Minako (1930–), Ariyoshi Sawako (1931–84), Takahashi Takako (1932–), Kurahashi Yumiko (1935–), Tomioka Taeko (1935–), Tsushima Yūko (1947–), and Kanai Mieko, among others, were all writing actively in the late 1960's and early 1970's. Women of a generation earlier, such as Amino Kiku (1900–1978), Uno Chiyo (1897–1996), Sata Ineko (1904–), Enchi Fumiko (1905–86), and Hirabayashi Taiko (1905–72) — women whose careers were already well established — were still active in this period.

Again, an element that strikes the reader forcibly on first encountering fiction by women from this time is an overlapping of themes and imagery — themes and images that many readers find disturbing or offensive. The reason for this strong reaction lies in the relationships, explored in these stories, between the body and the linguistic or cultural or psychosocial representations of it. Common themes include incest, explicit sado-masochism, amnesia, infanticide, cannibalism, murder, dismemberment, disfiguration, and so on. All of these except amnesia involve the body directly, and violently. And yet, another immediately striking thing about these stories considered as a whole is the fact that they are oddly lacking in any overt dichotomization of "victim" and "victimizer." These are not simple descriptions of men hurting or killing or otherwise victimizing women, stories with a simple moral thesis.[16] On the contrary, much of the violence or socially disruptive behavior in these stories is performed by (or at least fantasized by) women on the bodies of family members (their own mothers and fathers, or sons and daughters), on the bodies of husbands or lovers (both male and female), or on themselves. Neither do these stories enact a simple inversion of the male = victimizer, female = victim dichotomy; these are not simple revenge fantasies. Some of the violence is performed by men on the bodies of women, but with the active and joyous cooperation of the women involved (as in the sado-masochist stories).

What is the function of these disturbing themes, and how do they relate to the categories of writing against the patriarchy sketched above? Each writer uses these themes in slightly different ways. Kurahashi Yumiko, for example, uses both incest and sado-masochistic sex to challenge the binary nature of self and other, deconstructing the presupposition of unitary, bounded selfhood.[17] Kōno Taeko, on the other hand, uses sado-masochistic sex to explore female self-expression and socially determined female self-loathing. Takahashi Takako uses fantasies of murder and dismemberment to challenge the social ideal of motherhood, while Ōba Minako explores a woman's experience of motherhood using the topos of the *yamauba* — the demon woman who devours men.[18] Clearly it is not appropriate to construct one thematic analysis that will "explain" the appropriations of the discourses of the body in the diverse work of these various writers; each should be discussed separately. In this paper I propose to look closely at a set of very short stories by Kanai Mieko that foreground many of these themes and manipulate them in various ways. I will conclude with some remarks about the ways that these rather shocking appropriations of violent elements of the discourse of the body work as political expressions.

ॐ

These four extremely short stories are the first in a set of nine, each of which forms a discrete narrative but is linked to the others through numerous similarities.[19] In fact, the stories seem to form a sort of chain, working out a few central ideas in various scenarios through the playful appropriation, inversion, manipulation, discarding, and recovery of themes and roles. The first, "Kikan" (The homecoming), was written in 1970 and consists of 127 lines. The second story is "Funiku" (Rotting meat), written in 1972. It is slightly longer, 154 lines. The third story, "Boshizō" (Portrait of mother and child), also written in 1972, is about the same length, 144 lines. The fourth is "Usagi" (Rabbits), written likewise in 1972 but, at approximately 500 lines, quite a bit longer.

One of the consistent elements among all the stories is that none provides a name for any of the characters. They are referred to as *kanojo* (she), *wakai otoko* (the young man), *ano hito* (he or that person), *shōjo* (the girl), *chichi oya* (father), or by occupation, such as *fudōsan'ya* (the real estate agent).[20] The characters in each story are so few that this does not cause confusion, but the strategy certainly creates a heightened sense of the stories' taking place outside a specific mimetic realm. In addition, there are no physical descriptions of the characters. The few references to physical appearance are so vague as to be nearly universal. This, combined with the ambiguity of place —

there are virtually no clues to a story's location; they might not even take place in Japan—lends the stories an air of the fairy tale, folk tale, or fantasy. Although nothing that happens in them is strictly outside the bounds of normal physical possibility, the sense of fantasy challenges the surface realism in the stories, leaving the reader at first unsure of the conceptual location from which to interpret them. These stories do not stress a scopic economy. As just mentioned, visual description of the physical setting or of the appearance of the characters is minimal, and generally ambiguous. Other senses, particularly hearing and smell, are far more prominent. In addition these four stories seem related in that they draw freely from other texts, from folk literature, and from other religious and philosophical discourses, both Japanese and Anglo-European, for image and structure.[21]

Japanese critics writing about Kanai's work frequently cite her childhood exposure to film, the early death of her father, and her reading of postwar experimentalist Ishikawa Jun, "decadent" writer Sakaguchi Ango, and postwar poetry as some of the clearest influences on her writing, both poetry and prose. In her essays Kanai herself cites Lacan, Barthes, Blanchot, and other French philosophers and writers, as well as American and Canadian women writers of fiction. Like most postwar Japanese writers, her exposure to and knowledge of both Anglo-European and Japanese cultural sources is eclectic and undifferentiated. She is as comfortable in drawing from *Alice in Wonderland* as from Tanizaki or *The Tale of Genji*.

The first story, "Kikan," is unique among the four in having a third-person, completely undramatized narrator. The story opens like this:

> When she returned from a long trip, a young man spoke to her saying he had come to the station to meet her. She was very surprised, and said to the young man, isn't there some mistake.—No, absolutely not. I know all about you. Since your husband is sick and couldn't come to meet you himself, I've come along in his place. Your husband was terribly worried about you. So saying, the man took a crimson silk handkerchief out of his pocket with an elegant gesture like a conjurer's and wiped the sweat from his forehead. (147)[22]

The reader notices immediately that there is no demarcation between narrative and quoted speech, which are normally differentiated by quotation marks. It is difficult to distinguish direct and indirect discourse. The location of the narrator, and the identity of the two characters is ambiguous. This continues throughout the story, and although there is no unresolvable question as to who is speaking at what point, the rapid and unmarked changes from one speaker to another are extremely disorienting on first reading.

In response to the young man's explanation of his presence, the woman (*kanojo*) insists that there must be some mistake. It is true that the young man had called her correctly by name, but he couldn't have meant her; she has no husband, and no one even knew that she was returning that day.

To this the young man reacts as though she were joking with him, and gestures to her to hand over her luggage. He repeats the information that her husband is ill and is waiting for her, adding that he himself had sent her a telegram from her husband the night before, asking her to come home. He repeats to her the words of the telegram, as well as the reply he received from her:

Sugu kaereaishiteiru [sic] *itsumade mo eien ni otto* (147)

Come home immediately/I love you for ever always your husband.

Her reply had stated that she would return on the seventh at 2 P.M. and was signed, "your love." Since this was 2 P.M. on the seventh and here she was getting off the train, the young man asserts that he must be correct. As additional evidence, he cites the fact that he had recognized her right away from her husband's description:

Kuroi kami, kuroi me, umi no taiyō de yakareta hazu no hada (147)

Black hair, black eyes, skin that must be tanned from the sun at the seashore.

The woman, in consternation, asserts once again that she doesn't know what he's talking about; she neither received nor sent any telegram; she is single; she has no husband.

At this, the young man finally begins to catch on to the fact that something unusual is going on. He asks if she lives at N-chō 446. Hearing her correct address, the woman flies into a rage, convinced that someone is playing an elaborate joke on her. He, in turn, accuses her of playing a cruel joke, and is furious on behalf of her husband, who is waiting for her at N-chō 446, dying, he now informs her, of an incurable illness.

By this point, the woman is completely at a loss. Far from being married, she has never even been engaged, and yet the young man continues to insist that a dying husband who professes love for her is waiting in her home. "Her head hurt and she wondered if she had gone crazy, or if perhaps she had lost her memory. She felt sick, shivering as if lost in a bad dream" (148).

Since she is on her way home anyway, she agrees to accompany the young man there, declaring that everything will be made clear when they arrive, since she certainly does not have a husband. When they reach the house, the door is opened from the inside by someone who seems to be a nurse (*kangofu rashii hito*). The house is filled with a strange, unpleasant odor, and there is an unfamiliar picture in a silver frame on the table; everything else is as she remembers it. The picture shows a couple sitting on a terrace against a background of evening sea and clouds. The man is looking into the camera, the woman's face is hidden under the brim of a large white hat. The man has his arm around the woman's shoulders; she has her hand resting on his leg. The woman knows without asking that "they" (whoever "they" are) will tell her that this is a picture of her own honeymoon. And, indeed, the young man says exactly that.

She bursts out in anger: How can they claim this is a picture of her? True, the woman in the picture resembles her, but hiding the woman's face behind the brim of the hat is a crude trick. "You're mistaken if you think you can fool me that way." Burning with frustration, because it is clear to her that "they" have gone to a lot of trouble to manufacture evidence to bolster their story, whereas she has nothing but her own assertion that they are lying, she insists on being shown the man who claims to be her husband. She wants to confront this mysterious "husband" in order finally to resolve the issue.

When the young man leads her to her own bedroom, her fury mounts even higher; she can't believe they've dared to use her own room. The room is filled with an offensive odor, and there is a man lying in her bed.[23] He raises his head with difficulty, looks at her, and smiles.

> —You've come home. I knew you'd come back. You couldn't betray our love. Let's forgive everything. I love you.
>
> Trembling with nausea, and somewhat choked by the unpleasant odor that seemed to be produced by the man's disease-wracked body, she gasped out. —Who are you? Who are you? —Your lover forever.
>
> He answered in a voice so hushed it threatened to vanish away, yet was strangely audible to her. With the smile still on his lips, he slowly closed his eyes. Those were the man's last words. Still smiling, the man had died. (149)

And that is how the story ends.

A woman goes on a long trip and comes "home," that is, she returns to the place where, one would assume, her identity is most stably grounded. She is confronted instead with an alternative reality, based on the standards of normalcy of an anonymous young man. Perhaps because women often find themselves faced with a version of reality that bears little relation to their own experiences in the world, this woman behaves throughout the story as if the situation were normal. She is frustrated and angry at the incongruous reality presented by the young man, but she continues to assume that the situation is susceptible to explanation. The young man, too, treats the situation as "normal" but frustrating. He, too, looks for an explanation that will rationalize the woman's odd behavior. At first she believes that the "misunderstanding" can be resolved reasonably and equitably, but she is dismayed as she realizes the weight of "objective" evidence that has been assembled in support of the other, false version of reality. Even though some of this evidence is open to question—such as the ludicrously vague "description" of her provided by the husband or the photograph in which the woman's face is hidden—still, the fact that the young man can adduce any evidence at all, and she cannot, puts her at a tremendous epistemological disadvantage. All she can do is to assert her claims to self-knowledge, which are countered at every point by the young man, who, like the conjurer he is compared to early in the story, swiftly produces another piece of evidence.

She reacts as women often do. Overwhelmed by the sheer weight of "their" evidence, and by the arrogance of their claims to know her better than she knows herself, she wonders if *she* has gone crazy or if *she* has lost her memory. Although she rallies her courage in the end to fight for her own version of reality, confronting this "husband" in her own bedroom, she is finally defeated by the man's repeated assertions that he loves her and by his insensibility to her fury. And then he dies, removing all possibility of her successfully breaking through his adamant version of reality.

ø

In this story, the woman is confronted with two representations of herself produced by other people: the description and the photograph. In both cases she is essentially invisible and peripheral, while her husband is central. He is the one who defines her by producing the description, and in the photograph he is seen full-face, but she is hidden. After they have arrived at the woman's house, the narrator reports that the young man "seemed to have resolved not to pay any attention to her assertions [*shuchō*]." In the original the passage reads: "kanojo no shuchō ni mimi o kasanai kesshin o shita yō datta." The word *shuchō* is made up of the characters *haru* (to extend, put forward) and *nushi* or *shu* (owner, master, self, i.e., the one who is in control). The young man has resolved to ignore not just her verbal protests but all attempts on her part to assert her *self*. The woman's inability to control the representations made of her, her inability successfully to put forward her own claims to self-knowledge, are elements that link this very short, rather simple story to many others of the period.[24]

In "Kikan" there is little direct reference to the body, apart from the illness and malevolent odor of the purported husband. As it happens, this odor is the element that forms the most direct link with the next story, "Funiku" (Rotting meat).

∅

"Funiku," like the two stories that follow it, has two first-person narrators. Each of the three stories opens with a "frame narrator" telling us about a strange encounter with another person. This other person, the "internal narrator," enters the story at some point and then continues the narrative in her own voice. In each case, the story returns to the frame narrator at the end. The frame narrator is clearly situated in the world as we know it; the internal narrator inhabits a world removed from reality in one way or another. Like the *waki* in a *mugen* Noh play, these frame narrators seem to negotiate between the everyday world of the audience/reader and the extraordinary one inhabited by the internal narrator.[25] The frame narrator explores gender and the body in the realm of epistemology, whereas the internal narrator is concerned with gender and the body in an ontological sense.

In "Funiku," the frame narrator is a man. Here is the opening of the story:

> The fact that I went to her room is certain, but now, it would be difficult even to find it. When I left that room I knew it. I already knew that, once I left there, it would be impossible ever to return. I already knew that even if I tried, I probably wouldn't be able to find the real estate agent who had taken me there. But the instant that I saw that blood-covered rotting meat, all I could think about was getting out of that room and breathing the outside air as quickly as possible. (150)

The story opens with a man stressing his secure epistemological relationship with "the situation" (whatever that is; the reader does not know at this point). He emphasizes what he knows, what he is sure about. He *knows* he went to her room. He *knew* immediately that once he left, he could never go back. He *knows* he can find neither the room nor the real estate agent again. He is emphatic in his certainty. The reader is carried along by the weight of his conviction about these things. And then he casually mentions the lump of rotting meat that drove him from the room, and the reader is suddenly catapulted into another dimension of realism? fantasy? horror? At this point, we do not know.

The short second paragraph is again in the voice of the frame narrator: "This is what she told me."

Then the next several paragraphs are in the voice of *kanojo*, the internal narrator. Her story opens like this:

> Men came to this room every night, sometimes staying till morning, sometimes going home in the middle of the night, but invariably, after the men had left, there would be some new beautiful luxurious item in the room. Pretty lace underclothes, jewels, chocolate, silk, perfume, face powder, butter, coffee—anything you can think of. (150)

She goes on to say that sometimes men left things behind inadvertently—gold watches, jeweled lighters, and so on. She would keep them as mementos of each man, remembering, as she puts it, "what his preferences were, how he had loved me, how I had loved him—I would remember every detail."

The internal narrator, we realize, is or was a prostitute. We still know nothing of who she is, or when and where she told this story to the frame narrator. But as she continues, we learn more about her former livelihood. She says that, of course, not all the men brought gifts; some brought cash. She rather preferred gifts, since cash was a little awkward; neither she nor the man wanted to be too explicit about the nature of the transaction. But cash was useful for paying the rent and for buying food and other necessities. It was not that she didn't like cash, it was just socially delicate. But then, as if suddenly reminded of it, she tells us about one of her visitors who brought her something far more socially awkward:

> Once there was a man who brought me the meat of a whole, freshly butchered piglet (this man was a pigsticker and always smelled of

the blood of freshly killed animals, which is not surprising since before he came to see me, he would always toss back a glass or two of the warm blood of the freshly killed pigs. The day after the blood-spattered butcher visited me every joint in my body would ache, and I couldn't possibly see any other visitors), and so anyway about this piglet I couldn't eat it all myself and just didn't know what to do. After all, giving a slice to each man to take home as a sample of the local produce would be kind of awkward, and it seemed like a lot of trouble to offer the men a meat dish (since after all it would mean I'd have to cook), and on top of that, supposing I did cook something, I mean, when should I cook it, and when should we eat it? — I just didn't know what to do. The more I thought about it the more confused I got. (150–51)

She also feels a certain indelicacy about the fact that there is such a close connection between the resonances of the word "meat" and her chosen profession. She says it would be like selling slices of her own flesh, one at a time.

The whole piglet that the nicely built, hairy, vulgar butcher brought me was a lump of soft pink flesh, and rather than meat it would be more correct to call it an animal's corpse; and of course in this world there are corpses or live bodies it would be more correct to call meat — especially in the case of a prostitute people often call her body "meat" — but the thing the butcher brought, no matter how you looked at it, was the flayed corpse of a piglet he had killed. I wrapped the piglet's corpse in plastic wrap and newspaper, and shoved it under the bed. I mean, I just didn't know what to do with it. (151)

Because of the butcher's vigorous use of her body, the day after his visits she had to turn all customers away from her door. But already the number of men who came to see her was dropping off. In the old days, she tells us, men had had to make a reservation a month in advance just to get in.

At this point the frame narrator returns to tell the woman's story, this time in indirect discourse. He begins to relate how she became a prostitute (since, after all, nobody is born one), but then breaks off suddenly to explain how he came to meet her and why he did not ask her more about the rotting meat. He reasonably assumes that the reader must be curious about these questions.

He tells us that he had been looking for an apartment. He is a writer, but, far from wanting a quiet place to pursue his writing, he wanted a space in which to escape to the farthest degree of not writing, to do nothing at all until the "incomparably beautiful maiden of death" came for him. He was shown a small, furnished apartment by a real estate agent with horrifyingly bad breath and moved in right away. There was an offensive odor in the room, which he attributed to the lingering effects of the real estate agent's breath. But by nighttime that smell had dissipated, and he noticed another horrible odor that had been masked by the first — the smell of rotting meat. He traced the smell to a built-in wardrobe in the room. Inside he found a double bed with a woman lying in it. He was astonished; the real estate agent hadn't said anything about a bed and a woman in the wardrobe! Maybe she was the previous tenant, but she had no business being there. He tried to explain this to her, but she seemed oblivious to his logic. She told him that the man who had brought him there must have been her pimp. He continued to try to explain, but she remained serene in her own version of the situation, continuing to talk despite his evident confusion.

As he listened, the smell of rotting meat became more and more terrible, until he could stand it no longer and asked her if something smelled bad. She replied, "If something stinks, it must be the meat. It's beginning to rot." It was at this point, the frame narrator tells us, that she told him the whole story about the butcher and the piglet. He then asked:

> "In that case, this smell must be the meat from the pig the butcher brought, right?"
> "No, . . . he ate the pig, the butcher did. A long time ago."
> "Well then, what meat is it that's rotting?"
> "It's the meat of the butcher who killed the pigs. Look." (152, suspension points in original)

She lifts up the covers so that he can see under the bed. She explains that the butcher had been jealous and had not wanted her to see other men. He had wanted to marry her and set her up in a nice household.

> *"Sonna gehinna mane, dekiru mon desu ka. Atashi wa, ano hito o hontō ni ai shite itan desu mono. Dakara, korosarete tōzen na no yo."* (152–53)

> "How could I do something so vulgar? After all, I really loved that man. So it's only natural that he would be killed."

Looking at the lump of bloody, discolored, oozing meat under the bed, the man can't tell if it is the butcher but is inclined to believe her story. Overwhelmed, he runs out of the room.

And now, he tells us, he is looking for her again. He wants to find that malodorous room, find the woman, propose marriage, turn into a lump of rotting meat himself, and be swallowed up into her internal organs. As he thinks of this he is filled with a sad, warm feeling. Recently, he says, he has the impression that his own body has been rotting away little by little from the inside out and that his own breath has become nauseating like that of the real estate agent. This is where the story ends.

୫

As I mentioned above, the stench of a rotting body is the first link between this story and "Kikan." In comparison to "Kikan," however, the male and female roles are reversed as far as "home" is concerned. In "Kikan" the woman goes home, only to find it utterly changed and in the possession of a strange man. In "Funiku," the man goes to his new home, only to discover that it is not what he expected. His view of the world is challenged by the woman he finds "embedded" in his home. In a similar way, the male and female codings of epistemological centrality are reversed. The prostitute completely ignores his attempts to advance his version of the situation, leaving him no choice but to accept hers.

Unlike the first story, in "Funiku" the body is primary, particularly the differing ontological status of male and female bodies. All the discussion about what determines the distinction between a corpse—clearly a dead human body that demands to be treated with respect—and meat—the flesh of a dead animal that, far from being respected, is consumed—is directed toward this difference.

One of the binary power paradigms is: Who kills and who is killed? Or, considered a little bit differently: Who has the right to kill with impunity, and who is "killable"? In this story we have a man who kills pigs for a living. Clearly no one challenges his right to do so; it is a socially sanctioned violence. No one attempts to defend the right of pigs not to be killed. The power relationship here is obvious. Humans may kill animals with impunity, and once those animals are dead, their flesh becomes human food: meat.

This same man visits the prostitute and treats her so roughly that she is unable to work the following day. He not only has the "right" to sleep with her (because she is a prostitute) but also the "right" to consume her by exhausting her, thereby depriving her of her livelihood. Since he is a paying customer (even though his payments may take the unorthodox form of raw meat), his actions remain within the rules of the sexual and social economy of prostitution.

In addition, this story introduces a new binary paradigm that configures male-female (and other) relationships of power: Who eats, and who gets eaten? Or, who eats, as opposed to who is edible? Normally, meat—the flesh of a dead animal—is edible, and a corpse—the flesh of a dead human—is not. Both the frame narrator and internal narrator stress this distinction. But as the internal narrator, the woman, points out, it is often hard to distinguish meat and a corpse clearly. In her eyes, the dead piglet is closer to a corpse than it is to meat. Her identification of the piglet with the ontological status normally accorded only dead humans may be related to her remark that, after all, prostitutes are considered "meat." Since she, a prostitute, is usually called meat and yet her dead body would presumably be a corpse, she "elevates" the piglet to the same status.

The frame narrator, too, blurs the distinction between a corpse and meat when he points out (evidently paraphrasing the woman) that all meat starts out as a corpse, a dead body; it becomes meat— that is, it becomes edible—depending on the maner in which it is handled after death. The "corpse" of the piglet would unequivocally become "meat" if it were bled, skinned, gutted, and chopped into serving pieces. Because it is brought to the woman skinned but whole, its status is somewhat obscured. She cannot tell if it is *niku* (meat) or a *shitai* (corpse), and so she shoves it under the bed.

Normally, one would think, a woman (particularly a prostitute) equals meat equals edible. A man (particularly a butcher), on the other hand, equals killer/consumer equals inedible. The male butcher is the one who kills and eats; the female piece of meat is what gets "killed" and consumed. Males are human and become corpses; females and animals are, or become, meat.

In this story, of course, that paradigm is inverted. The butcher who killed the pig and consumes the prostitute ends up replacing the corpse of the pig and becoming meat himself. Although the prostitute does not actually eat this meat, it is implied that she brought about his death when she says, "After all, I really loved that man. So, it's natural that he should be killed." (We may find another inverted paradigm when we consider that he must die not because he threatens to abandon her, but precisely because he offers "to make a respectable woman of her.")

The frame narrator desires both to die and rot, like the butcher, and to be consumed by the woman, to pass through her internal organs. Although she does not consume any of the meat in the story (it is the butcher who eventually finished off the piglet) and in fact takes the opposite strategy, elevating what is usually considered meat to the ontological level of corpse, the male frame narrator imagines her as not only the killer of the butcher but also a cannibal, consuming the meat he has become. Initially the male frame narrator felt such terror at the realization that the normal paradigms had been overturned that he ran out of the room, even though he knew he would never be able to return. Later, perhaps because he is safely trapped back in the normal world, he begins to fantasize about the desirability of the overturning of the power relationships, so that he, too, could be "meat." Bear in mind that this frame narrator is a writer, but one who has decided that he no longer wants to write; he wants to go to the farthest pole of not writing. He is, therefore, a speaker, a subject, an agent, who has renounced his agency and, in fact, is simply waiting passively for death. After meeting the woman, he longs not simply to wait but to *perform* that passivity, to give himself over to be killed and consumed, to have his ontological status as human compromised. But it is too late; by the time he reaches that decision, he can no longer return to the magical woman who can invert his status. His only comfort is that he begins to detect internal signs of rot in himself. (Which just shows what happens to those who come into contact with women who are inverting paradigms.)

℘

In the third story in the chain, "Boshizō" (A portrait of mother and child), the narrative structure once again consists of a frame narrator in the "real world" and an internal narrator who tells her story to the frame narrator. In this case, both narrators are female. And, once again, odor is one of the first elements that link this story to the previous two. This is the way the story opens:

> "My falling in love with him," a voice said, "was of course because there was nothing else for me to do." All I could hear was the woman's voice; I couldn't even tell where she was. (153)

The frame narrator here is a woman lying in her bed in the darkness of her bedroom. The darkness is soft and humid; the room is so well curtained it is impossible to know if it is day or night. She tells us that the voice pauses after this opening statement, as if thinking of what to say next. During the silence, the frame narrator becomes aware of a presence in the darkness, a cold presence that chokes her. The room smells like her own perfume—Nuit de Noël—but there is an undercurrent of an unfamiliar odor. It is raw and bestial; she describes it as the smell that emanates from an animal's dampness and stickiness; it is definitely not the scent of her own sweat. The odor is coming from another person, and that person is standing still somewhere in the room, looking at her and talking to her. After the brief pause, the voice again speaks. The frame narrator realizes that the voice and the smell are inextricable: either the smell had taken on a voice, or the voice had turned to odor, but the two are definitely one entity.

At this point we return to the internal narrator. There are no quotation marks this time, just a long dash to show that she is speaking. She continues her earlier statement, and the narrative voice is hers until the penultimate paragraph of the story:

> The reason there was nothing else for me to do is because I loved him. Or rather, since for me, from the beginning, there was no distinction between my love for him and my being alive, my life was nothing other than my love, and love was my life. After all, in order to know everything about him, or rather to know his most secret place, I couldn't imagine anything but to gaze at him all the time, and to sacrifice myself for him. (154)

She can't remember when she met him (*ano hito*) because it was so long ago. But they've always been together. She never looked at other men. When she reached the age to have boyfriends, all she ever talked about was him, and all the boys around her thought her strange. They mocked her childishness. She explains the reasons for her interest in *ano hito* rather than these boys: "After all, he and I could look steadily at the same things, we could hold within ourselves the same absence, and, besides, I was completely absorbed in gazing at him" (154). The beautiful bodies and handsome, emotionally charged faces of young men held no interest for her. However, because she was so beautiful herself, she tells us, young attractive men — "with that special mixture of arrogance and conceit peculiar to them" — would try to make free with her body (*nikutai*). Unattractive men also pursued her. All of this was important to her and made her happy. She explains that such attention was necessary to her because she was a woman, but her satisfaction with herself as a woman depended on her promise to herself not to give in to their desire for her body.

She explains that she was also able to appreciate her happiness to the full because she was certain that "he" (*ano hito*) was always inside her; even within her darkest, most dubious places, even farther into the darkness, he was always there. Her one dream was to remain eternally a virgin for his sake, resisting the lustful desires that her beautiful body incited in other men. Her love for "him" was heightened by this sense of glorious purpose.

But to resist other men required that there be something to resist; it was not sufficient that they be indifferent to her. As she says, "The gaze of men was the sunlight and water necessary to ripen the peach that was my body. I hoped always for yet another man to become obsessed with me" (155). For that reason, she was constantly working hard to attract men, "just like a nymphomaniac, or a prostitute fishing for customers." Reigning as a virgin in the midst of these men, she maintained the integrity of her body for the sake of "him," as an eternal live sacrifice at the festival over which "he" presided.

Then, suddenly, she gives us further information about her situation:

> The reason I had to do this is because "he" was my father. I never once thought that it would have been better if he weren't my father. On the contrary, supposing he hadn't been my father, to whom I am bound by blood (that's a strange supposition to make), I probably wouldn't have loved him. The fact that in him flowed the same blood as in me, the fact that we shared several identical physical characteristics, the fact that we resembled each other closely, all of these things were important. The fact that he was my father, the fact that I was his daughter, was more important than anything else. (155)

After a page break, the story resumes. She tells us that precisely because she could not love anyone but her own father, she was a virgin who needed the blood-engorged gaze of numerous men. But all this time her father pretended to be unaware of the situation. She knew it must be a pretense—he could not be unaware of her constant gaze. On the contrary, since they were father and daughter alone in the house, she knew that with every conversation, every movement, "the sweet dangerous pain between [them] swelled like a balloon whose tautly stretched skin was about to burst." Nonetheless, as she points out, "My loving him was because he was my father, and his prohibiting of this was also because he was my father" (155).

At this point she introduces a new twist to the story. Something did happen in her life that was not mediated by her absorption in him: a serious automobile accident. The car in which the two were riding hit a guardrail in the rain, and although it would have been better, she says, if they had died together as a love suicide, both had somehow survived. She lost a leg and was left with a large, ugly scar on her face. Her father had no bodily injuries but lost his memory from a blow to the head. After this, all the men who had been attracted to her and all the women who had been attracted to her father disappeared from their life; the two of them moved to a new place where no one knew that they were father and child and lived quietly and happily like invalids in the darkness of their house.

> From that time on, we lost our names. As in the Wood Where Things Have No Names, in which Alice lost her way, at that point we completely forgot that we were father and child, and like Alice and the fawn, who normally could not have approached each other, we were closer than ever before. (156)[26]

It was better not to remember anything, she says. She spent all her time gazing at "him" as he sat silent in his chair, beautiful and ageless as a boy doll. At night they shared a bed as lovers, but with, for her, a strange simultaneous feeling of happiness and unease. She could become his lover because there was no longer any need for her to remain virginal for his sake. But, she adds, "In order for that to happen it may have been necessary to lose my beautiful face and my left leg and for my father to lose his speech and his memory" (156).

After they had lived this way for one year, suddenly her father, while embracing her, said his first words since the accident. Looking at her, as if calling to her, he uttered the word *okaasan* (mother). "When I heard that word, I resolved to become the thing my father had newly named me. Therefore, I do not question that I am his mother; however, the son who is in front of me is at the same time my father" (156).

This is the end of the internal narrator's story. After a page break, we return to the voice of the frame narrator. She tells us that she is still in her bed, but the other voice has fallen silent. The room is enveloped in the same humid darkness as before, but she can smell her own perfume, and all trace of any other presence has vanished.

ℬ

Four elements link this story to the two preceding it. First, all utilize the double-narrator structure. Second, the internal narrator intrudes in the frame narrator's most private space, the bedroom. In the place where one would expect to be most "at home," most stable, an extraordinary, ambiguous presence somehow, inexplicably, gains entry and relates a long story. The third element is smell. In the first two stories, the odor is that of rotting or diseased flesh, a sign of the process of human decay. In the third story the smell is described as raw and bestial, the odor of bodily secretions. As in the previous stories, it is contrasted with the smell of the "normal" world. In this case, in particular, there is a strong contrast between the scent of the frame narrator — the perfume Nuit de Noël, representing culture — and that of the internal narrator, representing the animalistic natural world.

And finally, this story is related to the first through the motif of amnesia. In "Kikan" the woman wonders if the discrepancy between her view of the world and that of the young man could possibly be her fault, the result of madness or amnesia. In "Boshizō" the internal narrator's worldview, her deepest desires, and most profound source of identity come to an unusual surface fruition through the onset of her father's amnesia. She is in love with her father. His worldview, his prohibition of incest, prevents her from realizing this love in any concrete sense. She waits, an eternal virgin, for the prohibition to be lifted. In the meantime it is precisely this state of tension between desire and the impossibility of its fulfillment that gives her her identity. When that tension is released because of the removal of the prohibition, she loses her name and eventually even the stability of her identity as daughter; she becomes the simultaneous mother, lover, and daughter to her son, lover, father. It is significant that this loss of stable identity results partly from the loss of her bodily integrity: having lost her left leg and received a large scar on her face, she is free to give up the body boundary of her virginity as well.

There is tension, and therefore identity, too, in the relationship between the body and the gaze in this story. In order for her love for her father to support her identity, this love must have some value in the larger economy of desire. She must be desired by others so that, in refusing them for her father's sake, she demonstrates her devotion to him. In order to be desired by others, she must be beautiful and flirtatious. Her body (*nikutai*) must be the object of the lustful gaze of men. All the while she is soliciting this gaze, she herself concentrates her own gaze on her father.[27] She needs the gaze of the men in order for her body to ripen, but its fruits are to be saved for the father, who himself prohibits the enjoyment of them.

Her father does not, of course, prohibit her *love* for him or her dependence on his presence as the element that defines her existence. What he prohibits is a physical relationship; it is the body that is susceptible of transgression, not the desiring mind or psyche. It is the father who prohibits, through judgment and voice; it is the actions of the woman's body that are prohibited, actions provoked by her beauty. For the prohibition to be removed, not only does the father have to lose his memory and speech, but the daughter must lose her beauty. Since it is as much the father's source of identity to be the one who prohibits as it is the daughter's to be the one who desires the father in vain, *both* lose their identities and their names when the prohibition is removed.

However, when the father does speak again, because the daughter has not lost *her* memory, because she still lives according to the law of the father, she must become what he designates her: his mother. She is still subject to his power of definition. She "performs" passive acquiescence, and *becomes* his mother, while remaining his daughter and his lover. The fact that he calls her this while they are embracing suggests that he had desired his own mother, just as she had desired her father—a chain of incestuous desire stretching back through generations of fathers and daughters, mothers and sons.

In The Wood Where Things Have No Names (somehow outside the symbolic realm, outside the realm of language and of the law of the father), it is possible even for creatures whose feelings toward each other should be fear and revulsion to come together freely. It is the definitions represented by names that cause prohibition. A man and a woman may have sex freely unless their relationship is defined by the names *father* and *daughter*, or son and mother (or brother and sister). Both in and out of the woods, Alice desires the company of the fawn, but when it remembers what it is, the fawn recovers its normal fear of humans. In "Boshizō," whether inside or outside The Wood Where Things Have No Names, the daughter desires her father; but if her father were to remember his "name," he would almost certainly return to his normal state of revulsion toward, or at least prohibition of, incest. Since the father in this story is still in the forest of amnesia, when he does come up with a name for his daughter—calling her "mother"—it is no more accurate than Alice's struggles to remember her own name ("L, I *know* it begins with L").[28]

♄

The epigraph to "Usagi" (Rabbits),[29] the final story to be analyzed here, is a quotation from *Alice's Adventures in Wonderland*: "When suddenly a White Rabbit with pink eyes ran close by her" (2). This is the first link to the previous story. Once again, we are in wonderland with a young, confused Alice.

This story, too, has a frame and an internal narrator; in this case both are female. Like the one in "Funiku," the frame narrator of this story is a writer. The "Funiku" narrator opened his story with assertions of epistemological stability; he told us what he knew. This narrator opens with her relationship to writing. The "Funiku" narrator told us that he wanted to escape the act of writing forever; this narrator emphasizes her inability to escape:

> "Writing (also not writing, since that is a part of the whole process) means putting pen to paper and this I can no longer escape. To write would seem to be my fate . . . "
> I wrote those words in my diary the day I pretty much forced myself to go out for a walk near my new house. (2)

Despite her opening assertion that she cannot escape writing, she immediately does, leaving her new home to take a walk. The weather is gray, and she is in a bad mood. She likens her mood to an elusive smell, linked to nausea, arising at intervals from somewhere inside herself. Here, once again, we have the motif of a bodily odor, and once again it is disturbing.

The woman becomes lost and finds herself in a woods she has never seen before. Suddenly a human-size white rabbit runs in front of her. She chases it, and, just like Alice, she falls into a hole and loses consciousness. She awakens to find the huge rabbit sitting nearby watching her. They begin to talk, and the frame narrator realizes that the rabbit is actually a young woman dressed in a suit of sewn-together rabbit skins with pink glass over the eyeholes. Sensing the frame narrator's curiosity about her outfit, the rabbit-woman invites the frame narrator to her nearby house (which is permeated by a strange animal odor) and voluntarily tells her story.

> "I have been wracking my brains for some time. There must be a logical reason why I have ended up like this. But I never could quite figure it out. The first inkling of what would happen to me occurred, I think, on that morning," she said slowly, as if trying to get her recollections in order. (4)

The internal narrator's story continues uninterrupted for most of the remainder of the text. She tells the frame narrator that on "that morning" she had awakened to discover that her mother and siblings had inexplicably disappeared; she and her father were thereafter alone together in the house. Even before her family's disappearance, she and her father had shared a special sensual bond:

To the family, my father was a ruddy-faced pig who did nothing but stuff himself and sleep. But I was different. Of them all, I loved my father best, his panting after the sweet, lovely pleasures of overeating and sleep, and the undulating of his fat stomach. At dinner, I sometimes kept my father company eating dishes which the other members of my family would not touch until I was full and could hardly keep my eyes open. We would both burp unashamedly afterwards. When we were so full that we could not eat any more, we did not stick our fingers down our throats in the barbaric manner of the Roman aristocrats, but drank a laxative made from special medicinal plants. Then, totally refreshed, we would commence eating again. (6)

One of their favorite shared meals was rabbit. Her father raised his own rabbits in a shed near the house. On the first and fifteenth of each month, he would get up early, select a fat rabbit, strangle it, and then cut its throat to drain it of blood. The daughter had often watched this with pleasure from her bedroom window. After breakfast the father would cut the rabbit open, remove its internal organs, and peel off the skin. The neatly peeled corpse would be hung in the shed, and the skin nailed to the wall in the shape of an X. That evening the father would prepare a special meal of stuffed rabbit, using not only the meat but also the rabbit's stomach, liver, and kidneys.

These preparations took place in the shed, which had been adapted for cooking after the rest of the family refused to witness the revolting process. As the mother says: " 'No decent household I know of reeks of animal blood and mine certainly won't be the first' " (7). In contrast, the young woman loves the odors of the meal: "The shed was permeated with the voluptuous odors of cooking vapors, spices, and rabbit's blood, and the jovial air was like that at a banquet of knights in the feudal age" (8). While eating, her father would question her about her interest in boys, saying that she was sure to abandon him someday. The young woman repeatedly assured him that she would never do so. After gorging themselves, father and daughter would fall asleep.

The day that her mother and siblings had disappeared was the fifteenth of the month, the day of the rabbit feast. She was unconcerned about their departure; she and her father had been waiting for a long time for this to happen. Her father had immediately suggested that she quit school, and thereafter the two of them lived together in perfect happiness, gorging on a different rich meal every night, and then falling into a sweet sleep. Given this unhealthy lifestyle, it is no surprise to the reader to hear that her father became increasingly obese, began to experience heart problems, and became bedridden. The job of killing and preparing the rabbits thereafter fell to her.

> At first I was a bit disgusted by the job, but soon I came to understand that even killing was one of the pleasures of life and I was happy when I stuck my hand into the still-warm belly of the rabbit and drew out the insides. So absorbed was I in my work that I felt I was plunging my hand into sweet roses of flesh. When the palpitations of the beating little heart were transmitted through the tips of my fingers, my heart also beat wildly. Of course, when I held the rabbit and squeezed its neck, I felt a pleasure that differed from that when I plunged my hand into its innards. To intensify the moment, I squeezed the neck trying various techniques. The rabbit was submissive as I held it up by its ears, and I felt the cruelty of killing this chubby soft white creature with my own hands. But I discovered that, by degrees, my reluctance had changed into a sensuous pleasure replete with a sweet rapture. Because the struggling rabbit would kick and hit me in the stomach when I slowly tightened my grip around its neck, my excitement rose to a fever pitch. Soon my fingers could sense that they had broken the rabbit's neck. At the same time, I would feel against my stomach the violent spasm that wracked the rabbit's body from one end to the other. (10–11)

In case anyone has missed the sexual nature of this encounter, the young woman goes on to tell us that, after some experimentation, she found that the best technique for holding the rabbit still while she strangled it was to clasp its struggling body between her bare thighs. Soon she began doing the whole thing completely naked.[30] She also began killing rabbits every day, just for the pleasure of it. She liked to stand under the dripping corpse and bathe herself in the animal's blood, using it, she tells us, to arrange her pubic hair in neat patterns. She also enjoyed licking the blood from whatever parts of her body she could reach.

Her identification with the rabbits eventually reached the point that she made herself a suit of their skins and practiced moving exactly as they did. She was so pleased with the effect of the performance that she decided to make a gift of it to her father. Carrying a sign on which she had written, "Stuff me and eat me please," and with a pink ribbon around her neck, she hopped into her father's bedroom on his birthday. Her plan had been to enjoy her father's surprise, but then to enjoy even more his mock strangling of her, during which:

I would thrash about a little, and at the end, I would send my whole body into a spasm, finally going absolutely rigid and playing dead. After that would come the climax of the skinning ritual. Before putting my fur on, I had bathed my whole body in blood to make it look as if I were really a rabbit with its fur stripped off. It thrilled me to think of the moment when I would feel my father's hand groping around inside me. (13)

Unfortunately for the young rabbit-woman, however, her father was not on the same wavelength, and had a fatal heart attack at the sight of a huge rabbit hopping into his room. Just before dying, he threw something at the rabbit, knocking the young woman out, and causing the pink glass of the eyepiece to pierce her real eye. When she recovered consciousness, she took off her rabbit hood and looked with her remaining eye at her own bloody, disfigured face in the mirror. She realized she had been responsible for her father's death.

After that, she tells the frame narrator, she knew she could never return to the world of humans. Since that time she has given herself over completely to being a rabbit. She is haunted by the face of her father in his dying terror, and this face prevents her from finding pleasure in the act of strangling rabbits. She is also haunted by the sight of her own disfigured face and gouged-out eye. Although terrible, she says, it was also the most beautiful sight she had ever seen. She has gouged out the eyes of all the rabbits in order to replicate it.

This is where the internal narrator ends her story and the frame narrator's voice returns. The frame narrator does not comment on this remarkable story, nor on how she had parted from the rabbit-woman and made her way back home. Instead, she tells us that she encountered the woman again much later. After searching for the woods and house again without success, one day she knew the way there instinctively, as an animal smells its way home. She found the dead body of the rabbit-woman on the floor, a piece of pink glass stuck in her remaining eye. With no explanation of her motives, the frame narrator tells us that she stripped the rabbit fur suit off the body, took off her own clothes, and put on the suit. Then she just crouched there, unmoving and silent, surrounded by the dead body and a bunch of blind rabbits.

⚄

"Usagi" depicts the logical conclusion of the *complete* performance of the passive elements of the dichotomous paradigms of the power economies discussed above. The internal narrator joins her father in killing but, in her identification with the rabbits, is also killed. She takes pleasure in both ends of the equation. And, of course, in the end, she literally kills herself. The internal narrator joins her father in eating, but again, in her identification with the rabbits, she sees herself as edible and takes enormous pleasure in the thought. The sexual nature of her bond with her father is clear; having shared the acceptable sensual pleasures of killing and eating, quintessentially "male" activities, she also wants to experience the "female" role of being the *object* of his physical pleasure. Once the obstacle of her mother has conveniently disappeared (like the conveniently nonexistent mother in "Boshizō"), all the daughter has to do is to disguise the nature of her desire for her father's use of her. It is not sanctioned for men to have sex with their daughters, but it is sanctioned for them to kill and pierce the bodies of animals, eventually consuming them. Unfortunately for her, her father, rendered helpless by years of overindulgence in this prerogative, perceives her as the nightmare inversion of that particular power paradigm: he believes that the rabbits he has killed are out for revenge, failing to recognize his daughter's attempts at absolute ultimate compliance with the power structure she learned from him.

This story presents an interesting manipulation of the scopic economy. The newly disfigured narrator, having failed to be the desired object of her father's gaze, looks at herself in a mirror, and is both horrified and entranced by what she sees. The entrancing part is precisely that newly blinded eye, the eye that is now quite clearly "performing blindness," as befits the female role in this paradigm. To enhance the performance of that passive role, that blindness, the young woman removes the eyes of her closest companions, the rabbits, and finally her own remaining eye. (It is difficult to refrain from thinking of Oedipus here.) Her identification with the subject/active roles played by her father, while remaining female and wanting to experience the object/passive "female" roles as well, may have led to her demise, which some might even view as her "punishment." It is interesting to note that, once again, the frame narrator has been seduced by the internal narrative. Here a writer, a woman in a subject/active role, abandons her humanity to put on the ultimate object/passive guise of the woman inside the rabbit suit.

⌀

That which is most physical in the world — the functions, activities, and processes of the body — is precisely that which is most often formulated in abstract and metaphorized terms. The body's sexual development, its assumption of a specific gender identity during early childhood and its lifelong sexual orientation, has been framed in psychoanalytic metaphors and analogies drawn from myth. The specific nature of the body's sexual activity is often framed in terms of moral or legal abstractions of prohibition or sanction. (This is especially true for women and homosexual men.) The body's reproductive activity is framed by social and legal metaphors of prohibition and sanction, as well as being metaphorized through visions drawn from post-romantic, post-Enlightenment capitalism. (Again, most of these metaphorized narratives refer to the reproductive activity of women rather than men.) Violence performed by or experienced by the body is legislated through legal, moral, and medical abstractions. History records the body only as it can be implicated in mass movements, or as it metaphorically replicates some pre-existing icon of power. Even science makes an abstraction of the body, reducing its individual characteristics to a statistically reproducible schema. Since women often experience the power economies of modern society directly through the body, this separation of actual physical experience from the abstract narratives used to mediate and legislate that experience serves to prevent women from controlling or narrativizing their own lives.

In this sense, it seems to me that Kanai's stories in this sequence, as well as much of the writing by Japanese women in the 1960's and 1970's, are insistently, although not explicitly, political. In Kanai's stories the rhetorical move is consistently to re-embody the theoretical, conceptual, abstract narratives that usually configure women's physical experience. Rather than retaining the metaphorized narrative of the sexual desire between child and parent, as in the Freudian / Lacanian models of Oedipal relations, Kanai has a daughter and father physically consummate this desire in "Boshizō." Oedipus literally kills his same-sex parent and has sex with his opposite-sex parent (who commits suicide—erases herself—when she realizes what she has done). This "literal" behavior has been mythologized and metaphorized in our narratives of child sexual development. Kanai returns these narrative elements to the "literal," physical level: the daughter in "Usagi" wants to have sex with and does kill her opposite-sex parent (after the voluntary disappearance of the wife/mother). And, like the original Oedipus, her blinding is self-inflicted and occurs at the "literal" level of the story (rather than being fantasized, for example).[31]

Rather than drawing a metaphorical comparison between women and food, as in some Western narratives of anorexia and shamanism,[32] Kanai makes the equivalency explicit in both "Funiku" and "Usagi." As in a fairy tale, the terror or desire in these stories is not directed toward some metaphorized death of the soul or of subjectivity; these stories exploit the fundamental human terror or desire of being literally eaten—a real "edible complex."[33]

The integrity of the body and its boundaries is, for both men and women, a powerful metaphor for the integrity of personal identity. As Nick Fiddes, among others, has pointed out, in normal everyday life, the only activities that involve the breaching of the body's apparent boundaries are eating and sexual intercourse (144).[34] One reason for the profound uneasiness surrounding explicit discussions of both eating (especially meat eating) and sex is precisely this conceptual connection between the boundaries of the body and those of the identity. Eating and sex may be the activities most stringently bound by taboos and prohibitions (such as those against cannibalism and incest), all arising from culture-specific narratives designed to obscure the brute physicality of the body. It is significant, therefore, that Kanai exploits these discourses of the body in all four of these stories. For the frame narrator in each story, the boundaries of the home are breached. And for at least one character in each story, the integrity of the body is compromised. The dying "husband" in "Kikan" gives off the stench of decaying flesh. In "Funiku" the prostitute's body is violated by the butcher, who is in turn reduced to a lump of putrefying meat, and, of course, at the end of the story the frame narrator welcomes in himself the signs of internal decay. In "Boshizō," the daughter's physical injuries contribute to her gaining her heart's desire, the loss of her virginity and access to her father's love. The rabbit-woman in "Usagi" first blurs the boundary between her human body and her rabbit guise by covering her skin with blood, then looks forward to the moment when she will feel "[her] father's hand groping around inside [her]," and finally pierces her own eyes. For each of these characters, the ambiguity of identity is a major issue, particularly in the slippage inherent in the sources of identity formation that are socially sanctioned in metaphor but absolutely prohibited in practice. The "cannibalism" in "Funiku" and the graphic scenes of preparing the rabbits for dinner in "Usagi" are reminders of the connection between anxiety over eating and body boundaries.[35]

Rather than depicting the typical abstract dislocation from epistemological reality felt by women as that reality is configured for them by male-centered definitions of truth or naturalness, Kanai's "Kikan" shows a woman who confronts a reality, complete with physical appurtenances, that defies what she knows to be the truth about herself. There have been many realistic stories about an epistemologically tyrannical husband who hides his despotic control over the power of definition by treating his wife with superficial tenderness. In "Kikan," however, the tyranny is expressed not metaphorically through instances of domestic dominance but rather through a woman's *literal* confrontation with a completely formed physical reality different from her own. Her so-called husband's physical death, far from freeing her, leaves her trapped in this unfamiliar embodiment of her own identity.

In each of these stories, the relentless direction of movement is away from the abstract and socially "universal" toward the realm of physical, graphic, temporal, *gendered* experience. And it is precisely this movement — back to the individual, the specific, the personal, the physical — that is, I would argue, one of the primary political strategies of feminist and postcolonial discourse.[36] In classical Marxist terms, economics *is* politics. This is just as true of the economies of power that configure any society or any arena of cultural production as it is for the more common use of the word *economy*. To overlook these economies of power as sites of important political struggle is to continue to deny the possibility of self-definition to those on the passive/object ends of the dichotomies. To overlook the body as an important site for political messages involving both physical and abstract issues is to continue to deny women in particular a significant voice in political or academic discourse.[37] In contrast, this focus on the discourses of the body in the writings of Kanai and other contemporary authors brings to the surface and makes visible the ways in which the body has been used in the production and maintenance of economies of power, even while its role in such production has been simultaneously denied or erased.

This aggressive return to the physical, to the body, is not an appeal to some pure source of gender identity for women. Kanai's stories do not propose a *model* for women's reclamation of a specifically female subjectivity and centrality; we are not being asked to empower ourselves by dressing up in rabbit suits and fantasizing about how daddy will kill and eat us. In fact, neither the frame narrators nor the internal narrators of these stories escape the received structures of power. The women in these stories do not fulfill some (Judeo-Christian) romantic ideal of escape and healing. But by appropriating aspects of the gender-based power economies and inverting them, collapsing them, twisting them, and particularly by *exaggerating* them through rendering them literal, Kanai (and with her Kurahashi, Ōba, Kōno, Tsushima, Takahashi, among others, in various ways) makes obvious the grotesqueries, absurdities, and actual dangers to women that are glossed over by abstract, intellectualized narratives of power. The move of returning these narratives to the body results in what readers perceive as violence, often horrifying violence. But that is the point. By taking the power paradigms that are abstract, and therefore difficult to see, and returning them to the physical plane implicit in all of them, writers can expose the violence to women's bodies and identities inherent in these paradigms.

In Kanai's case, at least, this is done through literary structures that reflect what might be considered a particularly female subjectivity. In these stories, characters are identified relationally by the roles they play in some economy. Rather than a stable central character whose experiences in the world progress in plotted, architectonic, *Bildungsroman* fashion, each of the women in these stories represents a different facet, a different role, a different embodiment, of women's experience in the world. The subjectivity (or rather subjectivities) we find here are contiguous and relational rather than central and monolithic. This is very different from the proactive, conquering paradigms of *male* agency that configure much of modernist fiction.

In all but the first story, a number of voices speak with almost equal centrality. The frame narrators, who normally would "control" the stories within the frame, have virtually no power over these internal narrators, who invade their homes and change their ways of thinking. But the internal narrators are dependent on the frame narrators for the dissemination of their stories into the larger world. The internal narrators are left in positions that are, at best, equivocal victories. In "Funiku" the prostitute has conquered the butcher and enticed the frame narrator, but she is alone in a wardrobe with a lump of rotting meat, unable to pursue her formerly thriving career. In "Boshizō" the daughter has achieved the desired union with her father, but at the cost of her beauty and physical integrity, and, finally, at the further cost of the stability of her identity as his daughter. The daughter in "Usagi" has found an ecstatic pleasure and beauty in her own identification with the rabbits and the violence they suffer, but by the end of the story she is dead, having gouged out her own eyes. To modern(ist) readers, especially Anglo-European ones, who prefer to entertain the possibility of escape, revolution, and cure, the equivocal nature of these "victories" may seem highly unsatisfactory and in fact anti-feminist. But, as Kurahashi Yumiko points out, an artist does not paint an apple because she wants to eat an apple.[38] These stories do not emplot physical violence to advocate physical violence. Rather, the graphic embody-ment of selected elements of various power structures is a way of revealing the gaps and absurdities that riddle those structures, even though men and women are still relentlessly trapped within them.

Finally, one of the most important aspects of these stories is their avoidance of simplistic dichotomies or monolithic indictments such as "men are victimizers and women are victims." The identification of women as victims is ultimately not useful, except insofar as it keeps us from forgetting specific instances of injustice (one wonders how far they ever are from the minds of women, no matter how rarely they may appear in official histories). The "discourse of indictment," which proposes to identify texts and writers as "complicit" (bad) or "subversive" (good), does little to change, or even further our under-standing of, the processes that still configure gender-based or other power relations. And as long as our conceptualization of "the politi-cal" remains based on male-centered paradigms, the kinds of "resist-ance" or "subversions" attempted by women may continue to be in-visible or politically empty to the eyes of critics.[39]

The very act of dichotomizing—of relentlessly dividing things into two with the inevitable concomitant privileging of one (Eastern-Western, gay-straight, female-male, complicit-subversive)—is coun-terproductive in terms of allowing women (or other dispossessed groups) any chance to change their situation. This is true even, or maybe especially, when a division is made between men and women, and it is women who are "privileged" through their identification as *victims*, the only role women have yet been accorded in ideological criticism in recent Japanese cultural studies. It seems much more use-ful to look at the ways women have behaved, or could be imagined to behave, in the power contexts in which they have found themselves, the ways they have manipulated the discursive elements they found imposed upon them, and the strategies they have used to survive and encode their own subjectivities in even the most restricted of circumstances. Given the horrifying limitations of some women's options, it is unlikely that we will often find these strategies "emancipating" women in any way that seems significant by normal (male-centered) standards of success. But it is only by exploring what actual gendered human beings — including writers and their characters — have done in specific contexts that we can come to any complex understanding of what gender is and the ways in which it affects our experience of the world.

Notes

The original idea for this essay grew out of a directed reading class with Andra Alvis and Yoko Clark at the University of California at Berkeley in spring 1991. I want to express my appreciation for the push toward reading women writers that Andra, Yoko, and my other female graduate students gave me. Three compelling talks on Japanese women writers given at Berkeley in 1992 and 1993 — Kathryn Sparling on Kōno Taeko, Maryellen Mori on Takahashi Takako, and Atsuko Sakaki on Kurahashi Yumiko — also spurred my interest in contemporary women writers. The paper written for presentation at the Rutgers Conference on Japanese Women Writers benefited from the comments and reading suggestions of Joseph Parker and Joshua Mostow. The revised version of the paper as it appears here was enriched by the useful and perceptive comments of Lucy North, the respondent to the original presentation. In addition, Joshua Mostow, Patricia Welch, and John Treat read various versions of this paper during the revision process and contributed both support and provocative criticism of some of the ideas here. Finally, I thank the editors of this volume for their invaluable help in turning an oral performance into a written text.

1. For examples of attempts to retheorize or recast theoretical constructions of gender, see: Chodorow, *The Reproduction of Mothering* and *Feminism and Psychoanalytic Theory*; Butler; Kristeva, *Polylogue* and *Desire in Language*; and Cixous and Clément. For examples of historical accounts of the way sex and gender have been differently constructed according to the needs of time and place, see Laqueur; and Schiebinger.

2. The issue of what "counts" as political in current academic discourse is one of the main concerns of this paper, but I will defer specific discussion of this issue to the Conclusion.

3. Although in this essay I concentrate on male-female power relations, these same questions are applied to other central-marginal configurations,

such as the relationship between Europe and "the Orient" in Said's *Oriental-ism*, between white Americans and Americans of color in the critical dis-course of race relations, and so on.

4. See also Mulvey, "Afterthoughts" (1989). Berger also discusses the gaze as it configures colonial and class relations in *Ways of Seeing*.

5. Recent work in the field of premodern Japanese literature on the motif of *kaimami* (peeking through the gap) invests the act of *kaimami* with the same power equation: the male act of viewing gives him power over the female object of the gaze. See, e.g., Field. For a different view of women's role in the scopic economy of Heian art and literature, see Mostow.

6. Irigaray (*This Sex Which Is Not One*, 23–26) suggests that when one considers women's self-expression and pleasure, the very distinction be-tween activity and passivity may not be particularly relevant; the distinction is important only in the dominant phallic economy.

7. I am thinking here of the classics of feminism, such as Simone de Beauvoir's *The Second Sex*.

8. The line between fiction and nonfiction is ambiguous in the work of many modern Japanese writers, both men and women. Caught up in the questions that preoccupied the intellectuals of the time — interrogation of the notion of the individual and of the boundaries of the self, the issue of what constituted literary authority or sincerity — women writing in the 1920's and 1930's were in some cases self-consciously experimenting with the bounda-ries of fiction and autobiography. See Joan E. Ericson's discussion of women writers' experimentation with the *shishōsetsu* (I-novel) form in Chapter 3 in this volume, pp. 74–115. The idea that fiction and autobiography are distin-guishable and mutually exclusive is in itself an Anglo-European assumption that may not apply to Japanese linguistic and literary structures. I might also add that such writing is not confined to women. Although I will not address examples of them here, men have also been involved in the production of lit-erary works that challenge the received gender-based configurations of power.

9. Lacan suggests that the child's entering of the realm of language is a matter of entering the realm of the symbolic, which is the realm of the "name of the father," configured by the phallic/non-phallic binary. Lacan argues that girls have a more complex, and potentially difficult, experience with this entry into the realm of language since a domain defined by such a binarism offers them no active, positive position with which to identify. Certainly a woman's use of language (and the specific linguistic codes of literature) as a tool of self-expression is a complicated gesture, given the phallocentrism La-can attributes to it.

Recently, many critics have attempted to define literary texts as "subversive" (good), or "complicit" (bad). Often the value of a text or writer is determined in such terms by ideological critics. These attempts to adjudi-cate the political "complicity" or "subversiveness" of a text have rested on implicit assumptions of what "counts" as political behavior or engagement, assumptions specific to a given ideological stance. Few ideological critics have yet considered the ways that gender-determined differences in sites and modes of political expression are overlooked in the assumptions that underpin their discussions. Certainly few ideological approaches have incorporated psychosocial elements—such as the phallocentrism of linguistic and other forms of cultural expression—into their discussions of power.

10. Gilman's "The Yellow Wallpaper" is an example of such a text.

11. In the often-cited story "A Jury of Her Peers" by Susan Glaspell, the painfully won skill of maintaining silence in the face of male speech and male judgment is used by the two women protagonists to protect the life of a third woman, who has murdered her husband for his silencing of her. One might argue that Agemaki/Ōigimi (in the "Uji chapters" of *The Tale of Genji*), in starving herself to death to resist forming a liaison with Kaoru, is another female protagonist who uses the only means she has to perform her own will: her "performance" of passive suicide.

In Takahashi Takako's story "Saihō no kuni" (The country to the west; 1973), the narrator explains how her performance of passivity enhances her life:

> I myself have no particular preferences. Adjusting myself to the preferences of my partner—you might say that was my preference. Now that I think about it, I was always a woman living the passive role. If I were strongly to put forward my own self with the various people I met in life, the scenario would be the same no matter whom I was with; there would be no more than a constant repetition of my own self. And as for my own self, I already knew it too well.

12. The film *Thelma and Louise* might be one recent example of this form.

13. This may be one of the reasons why so much women's fiction is written in what seems to be a fantasy or science fiction format. In order for real emancipation to be depicted—which is, after all, a lot more fun to read than tragedy—it is necessary to get completely outside the power relationships of the "real world."

14. As Audre Lord writes: "I urge each one of us here to reach down into that deep place of knowledge inside herself and touch that terror and loathing of any difference that lives there. See whose face it wears. Then the personal as the political can begin to illuminate all our choices" (113). I have recently seen the phrase "The personal is the political" cited as being so familiar as to be a cliché of feminism. But, as I will discuss at the end of this chapter, the phrase clearly has not yet been heard and understood by theorists of Japanese cultural politics. Until it has been, it would be unfortunate to forget the implications of this axiom, or to dismiss it as cliché.

15. For example, it is flattering and tempting for women to interpret female physiology and female reproductive power as being somehow more in tune with the rhythms of the natural world, with ecological balance; and some women claim to experience themselves as "close to nature." Many women's esteem-building movements, and many contemporary women

novelists in the United States and Canada (such as Margaret Atwood in *The Edible Woman*, or *Surfacing*), use an identification of women with the natural world to promote a positive image of "woman as shaman." But, as anthropologist Sherry Ortner has pointed out, this is a socially, conceptually constructed equation: Man = culture and Woman = nature, a construction that has often worked *against* the social and political advancement of women. Moreover, since all human beings evolved on the same earth, since the species has both male and female members and could not survive without both, it would be difficult to sustain an argument, no matter how appealing, that women — by virtue of their ability to bear children or by virtue of their cyclic menstrual rhythm — are somehow more "natural" than men.

For another example of the way cultural constraints influence our reading and even the experience of our own bodies, we might consider the effect of the wholesale acceptance, in both high and popular culture, of Freudian definitions of health. Given the primacy accorded by Freud and his followers to the role of male anatomy in normal childhood psychic development, it might be difficult to imagine how someone lacking a male body could possibly be psychically healthy. And, of course, in Freudian terms, women are not healthy; they suffer the permanent incurable ailment of not being male. The recent official designation by the American Psychiatric Association of PMS ("pre-menstrual syndrome") as a *mental* disorder rather than a recurrent endocrinological phenomenon is one sign of the psychiatric establishment's equation of "the female" with "the unwell." Such designations encourage women to identify themselves, and experience themselves, as "sick," simply by virtue of having normal female hormonal cycles.

16. These stories by Japanese women writing in the 1960's and 1970's are in marked contrast to the "women are good, men are bad" stories of, for example, Margaret Atwood, Maxine Hong Kingston, or Suzette Hadin Elgin, stories of the "type one" strategic choice mentioned above.

17. See Sakaki, for a complete discussion of Kurahashi's problematization of such binary structures.

18. See Kurahashi Yumiko, "Sasoritachi" (Scorpions; 1963), "Himawari no ie" (House of sunflowers; 1968), "Kamigami ga ita koro no hanashi" (A story from the time when gods existed; 1971), "Uchūjin" (The extraterrestrial; 1964), and "Seishōjo" (Divine maiden; 1965); Kōno Taeko, "Yōji-gari" (Toddler-hunting; 1961), "Ari takaku" (Ants swarm; 1964); Takahashi Takako, "Sōjikei" (Congruent figures; 1971); and Ōba Minako, "Yamauba no bishō" (The smile of a mountain witch; 1974).

19. These stories are from the *Chikuma gendai bungaku taikei*, vol. 93. The stories in this series are arranged chronologically, but otherwise the choice of the stories and the order in which they appear represent the decision of the Chikuma editors.

20. This phenomenon has been common since at least the late Meiji and early Taishō periods; one thinks immediately of Natsume Sōseki's K and Sensei in *Kokoro* (1914), or the "K"s and "S"s that pop up here and there in the

work of Shiga Naoya. In these stories by Kanai, however, it is striking that *none* of the characters has a more complete name or identification.

This technique is also common in the work of other women writing in the 1960's and 1970's. For example, Kurahashi's characters are often called L and K. The K seems almost a reference to the ubiquitous "K"s of earlier fiction, but if the L is to be taken as an initial (as were the abbreviations in earlier works), then it suggests a name no longer Japanese, since Japanese does not possess an "L" sound. Kurahashi also includes characters called *sakka* (the writer), and so on.

Ōba Minako's stories from this period are full of characters identified only through their resemblance to animals, birds, or plants. In "Aoi kitsune" (The pale fox; 1973), for example, the narrator's lovers are identified only as "the Pale Fox" and "the Praying Mantis" even though the story takes place in a "realistic" setting of modern urban hotels and telephones.

21. Some readers might see this as a postmodernist literary technique of playful pastiche. I leave that argument to be made by someone else. Instead, I prefer to consider the structural idiosyncrasies of these stories as more suggestive of a particularly female expression of "the subject." The absence of names could be seen as a strategy that helps to distance the characters from the "always already male" subjectivity discussed by Irigaray (*Speculum of the Other Woman*, 133–46), with its focus on the legitimacy and authority conferred by the name, especially the surname. Identifying characters only by role also keeps the focus on the relationship pertaining between characters, and the valence of that character within a network of social and family connections. This may be related to Irigaray's vision of a woman as having not one unitary "self," but rather "a multitude of 'selves' appropriated by them, for them, according to their needs or desires" ("The Looking Glass, from the Other Side," in *This Sex Which Is Not One*, 17). See also Gilbert and Gubar's citation from "In the End" by Laura Riding (*Chelsea* 35: 96): "And the lady of the house was seen only as she appeared in each room, according to the nature of the lord of the room. None saw the whole of her, none but herself. For the light which she was was both her mirror and her body. None could tell the whole of her, none but herself" (*Madwoman in the Attic*, epigraph, 3). This relates, too, to the extreme brevity of these stories, and the way in which similar themes may be played out in different ways in the different stories, each mirroring a particular aspect of a woman's experience, or mirroring the same aspect from a different point of view. The fact that three of these four stories avoid a scopic economy (and the fourth challenges it) can be seen as a strategy that distances the characters from the visual realm, which Irigaray identifies as consistent with the strict subject/object dichotomy that configures male desire, as opposed to female desire, which is multiple and based on senses other than the visual.

22. Unless otherwise noted, all translations are mine. I have made every effort to duplicate the punctuation and sentence and paragraph divisions of the original Japanese texts.

23. This is the first instance of a Three Bears motif that is repeated in two of the following stories, in which an alien presence is found to have invaded the narrator's bed or bedroom.

24. It is worth noting that one of the most common words for husband (the one used, in fact, by the young man) is *shujin*, which has the same first character as *shuchō* and *jin* (person) as the second character. The woman's inability to *shuchō suru* (assert herself) is *determined* by the existence of this husband, this "person in control."

25. *Mugen* Noh was a type of play originated by Zeami Motokiyo (1363?–1443?), the Noh theater's first great playwright and theorist. In *mugen* (phantasmal) Noh plays, the *waki* (the secondary character, or "side-man") usually meets the *shite* (the primary character, or "doer") inhabiting a "normal" identity in the first part of the play; in the second part the *shite*'s true identity as the ghost or incarnation of an important figure from history or legend is revealed. The *waki* remains, together with the audience, firmly within the bounds of "present-day reality," but the *shite* simultaneously inhabits the "present-day" and the "latter-day, fantastic" world.

26. The comment in the story about Alice and the fawn in The Wood Where Things Have No Names is a reference, of course, to Lewis Carroll's *Through the Looking Glass*, specifically the episode in which Alice has wandered into that very woods. Puzzled that she cannot recall her own name, she meets a fawn, although she cannot remember what it is called either. The fawn is similarly puzzled, but is confident that once they leave the woods, they will be able to recall who they are. They proceed through the forest in happy intimacy, but, once outside, the fawn recalls who and what it is, and perceives that Alice is human and therefore alien and threatening. To Alice's great disappointment, the fawn flees in terror.

27. It is interesting that the word for the gaze of the anonymous men is *shisen* (line of vision). Her gaze is *chūshi*, the act of watching intently, or focusing one's attention on something.

28. Although there is no space to pursue the point here, it is worth noting that many of the original adventures of Alice have to do with the issue of edibility and identity and the blurring of distinctions between the animal and the (female) human.

29. All quotations are from Birnbaum's translation; henceforth page numbers are cited in the text.

30. Note that both "male" and "female" sexual paradigms are involved in the young woman's killing of the rabbits: penetration of the rabbits' "sweet roses of flesh"; and squeezing the rabbits between her thighs until they are wracked by violent spasms against her stomach. As I argue below, this story shows a young woman identifying simultaneously with both "halves" of the gender paradigm set up by her father, and enjoying both. As she explains, "Of course, when I held the rabbit and squeezed its neck, I felt a pleasure that differed from that when I plunged my hand into its innards."

31. It is important to note that Kanai switches the gender roles of the

Oedipal story: instead of mother-son incest, she portrays father-daughter incest, narrated from the daughter's point of view. Kurahashi, too, in her stories of intergenerational incest, encodes a father-daughter pairing, again from the daughter's point of view (in *Sumiyakisuto Q no bōken*, [The adventures of Sumiyakist Q; 1969], for example). This might be viewed as the daughter's overcoming of the father's prohibition of incest, which cancels out his power to define her. Other contemporary women have written stories that present a mother-son incest bond, but from the mother's point of view; we hear Jocasta's story rather than Oedipus's. Both Takahashi and Kōno, for example, create adult female narrators who fantasize about or consummate sexual relationships with young sons or surrogate sons. In either case, it is significant that women writers explore the ramifications of the female roles in these incestuous paradigms, rather than focusing on the male roles deemed important in traditional psychoanalytic theory.

32. See, e.g., the discussion in Gilbert and Gubar's *The Madwoman in the Attic* of the heroine of Castle Rackrent, or Atwood's *The Edible Woman*.

33. This terror is commonly exploited in Japanese and Anglo-European folk and fairy tales, such as Hansel and Gretel or the *yamauba* stories, as well as modern narratives of horror, such as the *Jaws* movies.

34. It is worth pointing out that although men and women ingest food in an identical manner, the "violation" of body boundaries that occurs in heterosexual intercourse is confined to the woman's body. It is also significant that Fiddes does not mention pregnancy and childbirth among the "normal, everyday" violations of body boundaries, perhaps because these are normal only for female bodies.

35. The connection between body boundaries and identity is also explored in, for example, Kōno's "Yōji-gari," Kurahashi's *Sumiyakisuto Q no bōken*, and Takahashi's "Sōjikei."

36. Mani's essay on *sati*; the work of Radway, Penley, or Clover on the ways people use cultural products for their own purposes (and often with results contrary to the apparent political valences of those products); much of the critical writing of bell hooks; and Crimp's work on AIDS sufferers are examples of people using this political strategy in their critical writing.

37. In recent years the nature of subjectivity as represented in and through post–Meiji Restoration Japanese fiction has been addressed with increasing frequency, both in North America and in Japan. Scholars such as Karatani Kōjin, Noguchi Takehiko, Mizumura Minae, Suga Hidemi, and others in Japan, and Edward Fowler, James Fujii, Masao Miyoshi, Mary Layoun, and Alan Wolfe, among others, in the United States, have recently published interrogations of the nature of "the self" or subjectivity as seen in modern Japanese fiction. These studies explicitly challenge the underlying assumptions and hidden power relationships that have configured previous models of Japanese modernization, but none adequately addresses the role of women in modernization, thus perpetuating one of the most pernicious assumptions of previous studies; that is, the assumption that women *had* no

role of significance in Japanese modernization. If women, comprising half the population of Japan, have not been involved in the issues and movements that modernization scholars choose to interrogate, doesn't that indicate something about the painfully restricted nature of such interrogations? Doesn't that indicate something about the painfully restricted nature of the domain defined as political?

38. Kurahashi, "From the Author of *Blue Journey*"; quoted in Sakaki, 7.

39. This invisibility has not been without advantage in some circumstances. See Radner for ways in which women have managed "political" self-expression under the most oppressive of circumstances, using strategies and media that rendered the messages invisible or incomprehensible to the hegemonic group.

Works Cited

Berger, John. *Ways of Seeing*. London: British Broadcasting Corporation, 1972.

Butler, Judith. *Gender Trouble: Feminism and the Subversion of Identity*. New York: Routledge, 1990.

Carroll, Lewis. *Alice's Adventures in Wonderland* (1865).

———. *Through the Looking-Glass, and What Alice Found There* (1872).

Chodorow, Nancy. *Feminism and Psychoanalytic Theory*. New Haven: Yale University Press, 1989.

———. *The Reproduction of Mothering: Psychoanalysis and the Sociology of Gender*. Berkeley: University of California Press, 1978.

Cixous, Hélène, and Catherine Clément. *La Jeune née*. Paris: Union Générale d'Editions, 1975.

Clover, Carol. *Men, Women, and Chain Saws: Gender in the Modern Horror Film*. Princeton: Princeton University Press, 1992.

Crimp, Douglas. "Portraits of People with AIDS." In Grossberg et al., 117–33.

Enchi Fumiko. "Enchantress" ("Yō"; 1956). Trans. John Bester. *Japan Quarterly* 5, no. 3 (1958): 339–57.

———. *Masks (Onna men*; 1958). Trans. Juliet Winters Carpenter. New York: Aventura Books, 1983.

Fiddes, Nick. *Meat: A Natural Symbol*. London: Routledge, 1991.

Field, Norma. *The Splendor of Longing in "The Tale of Genji."* Princeton: Princeton University Press, 1987.

Gilbert, Sandra M., and Susan Gubar. *The Madwoman in the Attic: The Woman Writer and the Nineteenth-Century Literary Imagination*. New Haven: Yale University Press, 1979.

Gilman, Charlotte Perkins. "The Yellow Wallpaper" (1890).

Glaspell, Susan. "A Jury of Her Peers" (1917).

Grossberg, Lawrence, Cary Nelson, and Paula Treichler, eds. *Cultural Studies*. New York: Routledge, 1992.

Irigaray, Luce. *Speculum of the Other Woman*. Trans. Gillian C. Gill. Ithaca, N.Y.: Cornell University Press, 1985.

——. *This Sex Which Is Not One*. Trans. Catherine Porter with Carolyn Burke. Ithaca, N.Y.: Cornell University Press, 1985.

Kanai Mieko. "Boshizō" (1972). In *Chikuma bungaku taikei*, vol. 93. Tokyo: Chikuma shobō, n.d., 153–56.

——. "Funiku" (1972). In *Chikuma bungaku taikei*, vol. 93. Tokyo: Chikuma shobō, n.d., 150–53.

——."Kikan" (1970). In *Chikuma bungaku taikei*, vol. 93. Tokyo: Chikuma shobō, n.d., 147–49.

——. "Rabbits" ("Usagi"). Trans. Phyllis Birnbaum. In *Rabbits, Crabs, Etc.: Stories by Japanese Women*. Honolulu: University of Hawaii Press, 1982, 1–23.

——. "Usagi" [1972]. In *Chikuma bungaku taikei*, vol. 93. Tokyo: Chikuma shobō, n.d., 157–67.

Kōno Taeko. "Ants Swarm" ("Ari takaku"; 1964). Trans. Noriko Mizuta Lippit. In Lippit and Selden, *Stories by Contemporary Japanese Women Writers*, 105–19; reprinted in Lippit and Selden, *Japanese Women Writers*, 112–25.

——. "Toddler-hunting" ("Yōji-gari"; 1961). Trans. Lucy North. *Mānoa: A Pacific Journal of International Writing* 3, no. 2 (Fall 1991): 42–57.

Kristeva, Julia. *Desire in Language: A Semiotic Approach to Literature and Art*. Trans. Leon S. Roudiez, Alice Jardine, and Thomas Gora. New York: Columbia University Press, 1982.

——. *Polylogue*. Paris: Seuil, 1977.

Kurahashi Yumiko. "Himawari no ie" (1968).

——. "Kamigami ga ita koro no hanashi" (1971).

——. "Sasoritachi" (1963).

——. "Seishōjo" (1965).

——. *Sumiyakisuto Q no bōken* (1969).

——. "Uchūjin" (1964).

Laqueur, Thomas. *Making Sex: Body and Gender from the Greeks to Freud*. Cambridge, Mass.: Harvard University Press, 1990.

Lippit, Noriko Mizuta, and Kyoko Iriye Selden, trans. and eds. *Japanese Women Writers: Twentieth Century Short Fiction*. Armonk, N.Y.: M. E. Sharpe, 1991.

——. *Stories by Contemporary Japanese Women Writers*. Armonk, N.Y.: M. E. Sharpe, 1982.

Lord, Audre. "The Master's Tools Will Never Dismantle the Master's House." In idem, *Sister Outsider*. Freedom, Calif.: Crossing Press, 1984, 110–13.

Mani, Lata. "Cultural Theory, Colonial Texts: Reading Eyewitness Accounts of Widow Burning." In Grossberg et al., 392–408.

Mostow, Joshua S. "*E no gotoshi*: The Picture Simile and the Feminine Reguard in Japanese Illustrated Romances." *Word & Image: A Journal of Verbal/Visual Enquiry* 10, no. 1 (Apr.–June, 1994): 37–54.

Mulvey, Laura. "Afterthoughts." In idem, *Visual and Other Pleasures*. New York: Macmillan, 1989, 29–38.

———. "Visual Pleasure and Narrative Cinema." In idem, *Visual and Other Pleasures*. New York: Macmillan, 1989, 14–26.

Ōba Minako. "The Pale Fox" ("Aoi kitsune"; 1973). Trans. Stephen W. Kohl. In *The Shōwa Anthology: Modern Japanese Short Stories*, vol. 2, ed. Van Gessel and Tomone Matsumoto. Tokyo: Kōdansha, 1985, 337–47.

———. "The Smile of a Mountain Witch" ("Yamauba no bishō"; 1974). Trans. Noriko Mizuta Lippit, with Mariko Ochi. In Lippit and Selden, *Stories by Contemporary Japanese Women Writers*, 182–96; reprinted in Lippit and Selden, *Japanese Women Writers*, 194–206.

Ortner, Sherry. "Is Female to Male as Nature Is to Culture?" In *Women, Culture and Society*, ed. Michelle Zimbalist Rosaldo and Louise Lamphere. Stanford: Stanford University Press, 1974.

Penley, Constance. "Feminism, Psychoanalysis, and the Study of Popular Culture." In Grossberg et al., 479–500.

Radner, Joan Newlon, ed. *Feminist Messages: Coding in Women's Folk Culture*. Urbana: University of Illinois Press, 1993.

Radway, Janice. *Reading the Romance: Women, Patriarchy, and Popular Literature*. Chapel Hill: University of North Carolina Press, 1984.

Said, Edward W. *Orientalism*. New York: Random House, Vintage Books, 1979.

Sakaki, Atsuko. "The Intertextual Novel and the Interrelational Self: Kurahashi Yumiko, a Japanese Postmodernist." Ph.D. diss., University of British Columbia, 1992.

Schiebinger, Londa. *Nature's Body: Gender in the Making of Modern Science*. Boston: Beacon Press, 1993.

Takahashi Takako. "Congruent Figures" ("Sōjikei"; 1971). Trans. Noriko Mizuta Lippit. In Lippit and Selden, *Stories by Contemporary Japanese Women Writers*, 153–81; reprinted in Lippit and Selden, *Japanese Women Writers*, 168–93.

———. "Saihō no kuni" (1973).

5

Translation and Reproduction in Enchi Fumiko's "A Bond for Two Lifetimes—Gleanings"

DORIS G. BARGEN

Double Fiction

Ueda Akinari's (1734–1809) story "Nise no en" (The destiny that spanned two lifetimes; 1802)[1] is the text that Enchi Fumiko used as a ground (*shitajiki*) for her own story "Nise no en—shūi" (A bond for two lifetimes—gleanings; 1957).[2] It is not uncommon for authors to include, as part of their work, invented materials they claim to be authentic, but this literary convention of quoting from seemingly verifiable sources seems invariably to be a hoax.[3] Enchi, however, departs from literary convention and reproduces the entire story by Akinari— with one caesura, the colloquialization of its language, and some extensively embellished passages—in her work of fiction. The device might be Enchi's literary invention. It is quite different from the conventional "story within a story" by a single author; different, too, from the "allusive variation" (*honkadori*) familiar in all genres of Japanese literature; and different, still, from the use of historical documents within fiction. That Enchi's original literary contribution constitutes only half of "A Bond for Two Lifetimes—Gleanings" (hereafter, "Gleanings") is another indication of its uniqueness.[4]

In "Gleanings," Enchi experiments with an existing literary source in a direct, scholarly manner aimed at exploring the literary heritage of a late Edo period male author. By explicitly quoting Akinari's entire fictional text, Enchi manages both to demonstrate her recognition of gender difference in authorship and to deconstruct the difference. Furthermore, Enchi authorizes her fictional characters, by virtue of their professions as translator and copyist/editor, to process Akinari's text in order to make it accessible to an audience removed from the original by a century and a half. With this particular literary technique, in which a text of fiction is reproduced as translation and subjected to scholarly analysis, Enchi creates the illusion that her own fictional frame is ontologically different from a mere story. In contrast to Akinari's fiction, her frame seems historically "real."

Enchi has intentionally designed "her" story—conceptually and structurally—as a competition between male and female authorship. Her overt changes of Akinari's story, effected through the fictional medium of a male translator and a female copyist/editor (who also happens to be Enchi's narrator), are easy to document.[5] Less obvious is the semantic transformation of Akinari's text by its placement within the environment of Enchi's fictional con-text. Like particles exposed to an electromagnetic field, the meanings of his words are reconfigured by hers. In an analogy drawn from the puppet theater, Enchi imagines the male puppeteer who, half-forgotten by the audience, injects the "urgency of living flesh" (Tanizaki, 24) into a female doll whose textual autonomy exists on a different ontological plane. On the fictional plane of her story's last, climactic scene, Enchi's female protagonist challenges received notions about manipulator and manipulated, male puppeteer and female puppet. In the final analysis, gender itself is at issue.

"Gleanings" is unquestionably among Enchi's most complex works, not only in terms of literary technique but also in terms of the themes addressed. In fact, an unusual wedding of form and content is celebrated in this story, which Enchi considered her best work of short fiction.[6] Its immediate literary predecessor, "Yō" (Enchantment; also translated "Enchantress"; 1956), anticipates in direct and explicit fashion some of the profound mysteries more subtly developed in "Gleanings," published just four months later. The two works share an intense effort on the part of the female protagonists to challenge, if not overcome, stereotypes about women's secondary, subservient function in society. Concretely, Enchi presents this problematic by ingeniously combining women's roles in professional and sexual reproduction. The themes of literary production and reproduction are embedded in the themes of sexual insemination and reproduction. Professionally, the women in the two stories seem condemned to passivity as translators and copyists rather than creative artists; sexually, their reproductive capacity depends on male impregnation. Both women seek a uniquely feminine creativity that is not dependent on male input. Although the professional aspect of this goal seems realizable, self-engendered sexual reproduction is utopian.

"Enchantment," set in the 1940's, features an aging, unhappily married female protagonist whose personal mid-life crisis seems to parallel the hardships of postwar Japan. Chikako, desperately in need of money because of the selfishness of her husband, Keisaku, is forced to do a translation into English of a pornographic book, harmlessly entitled "Honeymoon."[7] Exploited and humiliated, Chikako, to her own astonishment, finds herself sexually reawakened:

> The forthright descriptions of sexual intercourse that had merely disgusted her then would now, as she did the translation, make her lay aside her pen from time to time and sit wrapped in a kind of ecstatic daydream. In real life, she had never known the moments of happiness that a woman could supposedly find through a man, yet her whole being now thrilled at the suggestion that they could be found through an intercourse of the flesh. (78)

Finishing one translation, she contracts to do another. As she advances from pornography to the Japanese classics, she simultaneously becomes an expert at masking the aging process. Assisted in her work by a young scholar physically aged by the war, she indulges in erotic fantasies. The two briefly discuss episode 63 of the *Ise monogatari* (Tales of Ise; ca. 950), about the archetypal lover Ariwara Narihira's (825–80) compassionate lovemaking to a lady with thinning hair. Chikako's alternately frustrating and stimulating encounters with the prematurely aging man and her reflections on Heian women cause her moods to oscillate from self-hatred to self-confidence, from despair to longing. To compensate for sexual unfulfillment, Chikako craves sensual experience: "Sometimes she would stand with her umbrella up in the rain" (90). At other times she channels her raging emotions into attempts at fiction. In the text, no more than a brief, interpretive summary is given of these autobiographical outpourings, which are admittedly influenced by her earlier translation of pornography.

Finally, the increasingly impassioned Chikako experiences a trance-like moment resembling sexual fulfillment. One rainy night, as she lies awake filled with dark romantic thoughts, she hears the persistent ringing of the doorbell. When she and her husband investigate, they see "two white things wriggling against each other. . . . The white mass twisted, then split in two and was off" (92). The initial mystery of the ringing bell is deflated by a trivial explanation: lovers seeking shelter from the rain had unwittingly been leaning against the door-bell, oblivious of the noise. Yet it is precisely their uncalculating inno-cence that triggers both Chikako's and Keisaku's awareness of re-newed sexual desire. Whether that desire is meant to be shared or pursued independently is an uneasy question to which there may not be a definite answer.

In "Enchantment," a story that critics have praised extravagant-ly,[8] Enchi prepared the way for "Gleanings." The earlier story com-pels through its frankness and fresh approach to the somewhat taboo topic of sexual desire among the no longer young. It does not, how-ever, elaborate on the connection between literary/sexual production and reproduction. Nor is it a technically innovative story. Although the female protagonist's translation projects revive her self-esteem as an intellectual and her sexual desire as a woman, Enchi seems not to have realized the metaphorical possibilities of a translation project for a feminist thesis.

More effectively in "Gleanings" than in "Enchantment," the translation project is transformed, through the adapted and embel-lished reproduction of the original, into an integral part of the male-female contest. Furthermore, the theme of gender and sexual desire is elevated to a metaphysical level through the topos of the bell ringing in the rain. There is, in fact, an important religious dimension to a major question addressed in the various texts referred to in Enchi's story: Do male ascetics have the power to circumvent death through Buddhist self-mummification (described as "entering into a state of suspended animation" [nyūjō])? In corresponding gender terms, what role do women play in this exclusively male process, and what self-transcending powers can they offer in place of nyūjō?

Akinari's legendary sources claim that men can indeed achieve Kūkai's (774–835) ideal of "attaining Buddhahood in this very body" (sokushin jōbutsu). These claims have been partially confirmed by modern field research,[9] which has provided scientific evidence that a form of self-mummification was indeed accomplished, if only by a very few ascetics. Akinari's sources, however, following popular lore, go further and claim that bodily resurrection also occurred. Akinari satirizes the nyūjō legends by featuring a humorously nicknamed as-cetic, Nyūjō no Jōsuke, who is completely unworthy of Buddhahood.

A weakness for women is the pitfall in Jōsuke's path to enlighten-ment.[10]

Enchi wrote her story at the timely intersection of two events. The relatively recent discovery of the manuscript and evaluation of Aki-nari's *Tales of the Spring Rain*[11] coincided with the sensational research then in progress on Buddhist mummies.[12] Like Akinari, who fre-quently borrowed from other literary works, Enchi favored an "aes-thetic of discord" (*hachō no bi*) (Kamei, "Onna to otoko," 154) gener-ated by a "two-layered fictional structure" (Birnbaum, "Introduc-tion," 25). In the case of "Gleanings," the discord occurs when the woman writer draws attention to the fact that her story encom-passes — and thus transforms — a male writer's narrative. Male-female tension, as expressed in the dialectic of production and reproduction, appears therefore not only thematically, within Akinari's tale and En-chi's, but also biographically, between the two authors.

Enchi's differences with Akinari concerning the legend of *nyūjō* and its meaning are transposed to a pair of fictional characters: the male translator of Akinari's work, Professor Nunokawa, and his for-mer student Mrs. Noritake, who acts as the aged professor's copy-ist/editor. Too infirm to write, Nunokawa dictates his colloquial ver-sion of the *Tales of the Spring Rain* to Noritake, whom he nicknames Tamakazura, in a reference to the strong-willed character in *Genji mo-nogatari* (The tale of Genji; ca. 1010) famous for her defense against Genji's seductive wiles, and for her insights into fictional discourse as an art that tells the truth obliquely. It is impossible to resist con-structing a series of parallel characters, beginning with the two authors themselves. Enchi's characters — who in turn are associated through literary nicknaming with still other fictional characters, such as Tamakazura — can be linked back to Akinari's characters.

In Enchi's double fiction, Nunokawa's literary interests suggest his close affiliation with Jōsuke, the revived ascetic of Akinari's story, and thus Enchi establishes a link among Akinari, Nunokawa, and Jō-suke. This male triangle is balanced by a female triangle. As a female author who copies a male author's work, Enchi is represented on the fictional level of her story by the copyist/editor, Mrs. Noritake, or, in technical terms, the first-person narrator "I" (*watakushi*). Moreover, it is hardly a coincidence that Enchi's female protagonist is a middle-aged widow. Her situation links her directly to Akinari's "widow," unhappily married to the disappointingly resurrected ascetic. In this way, it is possible to match the male triangle with a female triangle consisting of Enchi, Mrs. Noritake (alias Tamakazura/*watakushi*), and the widow.

The religious belief in *nyūjō* is, furthermore, complemented by a popular belief that marriage between a man and a woman constituted a "bond for two lifetimes" (*nise no en*).[13] For Enchi's and Akinari's fictional characters, attempts to embody the twin ideals of self-mummification in a trance-like state of suspended animation (*nyūjō*) and marriage as a human bond that survives death (*nise no en*) end in failure and disappointment. But it would appear that Enchi, the writer, succeeds where her fictional characters, or those adopted from Akinari, fail; for she boldly resurrects the male author's text and creates a literary liaison à la *nise no en* with Akinari. The theme of source adaptation occurs at two levels, as both the author and her characters translate/copyedit and interpret Akinari's text. Consequently, the borderlines between fiction and reality, production and reproduction, author and character, translator and critic, male and female, become perforated. At the end of her story, Enchi dramatizes this multilayered dialectic in one surreal scene. Although male-female tensions affect binary opposites to varying degrees, they are perhaps most deeply felt in sexual experiences. Just before the climactic scene, the female protagonist, Noritake, reaches the end of her intellectual capacities and indulges in carnal thoughts culminating in the scandalous remark: "My very womb cried out in longing" (44; *shikyū ga dokiri to natta*; 340). This emotional outburst triggers a fantastic sexual encounter that promises a resolution to gender differences, the lowest common denominator of irreconcilable opposites.

The Legend of Nyūjō

In order to examine the gender-related interactions among the thematic, meta-fictional, and biographical strands of Enchi's story, it will be helpful to explore the underlying legend of *nyūjō* (or *zenjō*). This complex legend is closely associated with Kūkai (774–835), also known by his posthumous name of Kōbō Daishi, the founder of the esoteric sect of Shingon Buddhism. Kūkai lurks behind Enchi's text because he is said to have achieved the state of *nyūjō* sought by Akinari's protagonist. In particular, Kūkai's male asceticism and his reputed patronage of "male love" (*nanshoku*)[14] and invention of the *kana* syllabary (or "woman's hand" [*onna-de*]) combine to make him a legendary figure capable of transcending the gender differences thematically central both to Akinari's story and to Enchi's.

The blind, lute-playing monks (*biwa hōshi*) who disseminated tales of the heroic feats of the Gempei wars (1156–85) have provided the most fascinating and dramatic account of Kūkai's achievement of enlightenment through the technique of suspended animation.[15] This strange religious phenomenon may have been included in a military epic (*gunki monogatari*) because the constant threat of death in battle intensified hopes for individual survival and for some assurance of the clan's immortality. At any rate, as the great saga of the *Heike monogatari* (The tale of the Heike; recorded in 1371) approaches its military climax, "The Book of Kōya" (X.9) interrupts the narrative sequence with the story of Kūkai's *nyūjō*.

For modern readers familiar with "orthodox" Buddhism, this path to enlightenment seems almost heretical, but adherents to the doctrines of Kūkai's Shingon sect accept this apparent anomaly.[16] Whereas mainstream Buddhist doctrine prescribes contemplating the decaying body at death as an aid to severing bodily attachments, the practice of self-mummification urges distancing oneself from the "festering corpse" and seeks instead its "transformation and purification." Believers in the Yudono branch of the syncretic Shugendō sect, heavily influenced by Shingon Buddhism, put special emphasis on *nyūjō*. Like the charismatic Ch'an (Zen) masters of medieval China, Yudono Shugendō ascetics did not share the "orthodox" view of the corpse "as a lifeless lump of fetid flesh to be disposed of posthaste [as] is attested throughout the Buddhist canon" (Sharf, 4, 3). In their view, the "flesh icon" (Sharf's term) achieved through mummification actually presented the worshiper with a living Buddha or Tathāgata. In contrast to the Chinese Ch'an abbot's mummification, which aimed at a "true-to-life effigy for the departed" (Sharf, 20), the Japanese practice did not, and could not, produce such a venerable lifelike portrait of the ascetic. Due to different techniques, the focus was placed differently. Instead of achieving physical verisimilitude, the rather gruesome-looking mortal shell of the Japanese ascetic bears indisputable witness to the extreme austerities leading to "self-mummification."[17] The mummified ascetic's religious charisma derives from his excruciating appearance. Chinese and Japanese practices share the view that the enormously difficult process of mummification proves the incorruptibility of the flesh and, by inference, the ascetic's enlightenment.

Despite the "normalization" of *nyūjō* through its acceptance by Kūkai's followers, an air of hubris lingers about this feat of extreme asceticism. After all, the historical Buddha had, after subjecting himself to severe austerities, come to advocate the moderation of the "middle path." The *Heike* bards, however, told the legend of Kūkai's *nyūjō* in tones of unadulterated veneration. There was no incredulity or irony in their accounts of the liminal state of suspended animation into which the Great Teacher of Shingon had passed. In the theater of war, the experience of liminality as the encroachment of death on life was omnipresent. It is not surprising that, under this extraordinary impact of mortality, the concept of *nyūjō* should have nourished the dream of life-in-death.

Women play no part in the *nyūjō* legend of Kūkai as it is told in this chapter of *The Tale of the Heike*. The prototypical legend is told in close conjunction with the stories of two men, Saitō Tokiyori and Taira Koremori, who have come to Mount Kōya to pay homage to Kūkai and to achieve a degree of ascetic sacrifice comparable to his liminal state of *nyūjō*. Their stories introduce an aspect of the practice crucial to Akinari's and Enchi's depiction of a failed *nyūjō* ascetic. Women, as the embodiment of beauty and passion, were believed to have the power to interfere with the successful completion of the process. It is precisely for this reason that Tokiyori and Koremori in the *Heike* intend to pursue their religious ambitions at a holy mountain forbidden to women.[18] Although neither attains *nyūjō*, both are firm in their resolve to resist the world of women and to sacrifice worldly ambitions to the otherworldly Buddhist ideal of enlightenment. Their stories are to Kūkai's, in the *Heike*, as Nunokawa's and Noritake's are to the revived monk's in Akinari's tale disseminated by Enchi. Although the *Heike* bards do not explore how women are affected by their persona-non-grata status, Akinari and Enchi spin the ascetic tale further and weave women into the fabric with bright, and sometimes garish, colors.

Kūkai's *nyūjō* seemed unreachable to ordinary mortals. Only the most austere of ascetics could even come close to the ideal. It may be an accident of history that Akinari and Enchi wrote their stories on the thresholds of new revelations concerning such attempts at emulating Kūkai. The anthropologist Carmen Blacker, who has unraveled the complex history of austerities in Japan, has discussed the practice of tree eating (*mokujiki*) that led directly to the six documented instances of self-mummification. The six[19] extant Buddhist mummies, dating to between the seventeenth and the nineteenth centuries, belonged to the now-extinct cult of the ascetic Shugendō sect based on Mount Yudono.[20] Blacker mentions neither Kūkai's exemplary *nyūjō* nor the *Heike* episode, but she does elaborate on the miserable failure of most attempts at "attaining Buddhahood in this very body" despite strict adherence to a rigorous diet consisting of little but nuts, berries, bark, and pine needles. The most famous of these tree-eating ascetics, a sculptor known as Mokujiki Shōnin, died in 1810, one year after Akinari, who, toward the end of his literary career, wrote a satirical story about the practice of *nyūjō*. Mokujiki Shōnin is not among those who are said to have accomplished the amazing feat of self-mummification. Those who did achieve this feat, according to a special ethnological research group, were not discovered until 1960, just after Enchi made Akinari's treatment of the legend the subject of her story. Whether Akinari or Enchi had any knowledge of these particular mummified *isse gyōnin*,[21] worshiped by locals before they achieved nationwide publicity through the activities of the research team, remains a matter of speculation. There can be little doubt, however, that they knew about Kūkai's ideal of "attaining Buddhahood in this very body," as transmitted through the *Konjaku monogatari* (Tales of times now past; ca. 1120), *The Tale of the Heike*, and numerous legends of the medieval period.[22]

The Rain Bell: Akinari's "The Destiny That Spanned Two Lifetimes"

That fiction writers with an interest in occult practices of the past as they relate to the present should be passionate about the *nyūjō* legend may not come as a surprise. After all, those ascetics who slowly starved themselves were, like Kafka's macabre *Hungerkünstler*,[23] artisans if not artists of the extreme. As they endured a more extreme form of austerity than shamanistic initiation sickness, they entranced and empowered themselves. While their bodies were literally withering away, their senses were to become sharper and their minds keener. Approaching religious ecstasy, these holy men imbued others with the glow of their charisma. How could literary artists like Akinari and Enchi, who, unlike many other artists, frequently found themselves in liminal, life-threatening situations,[24] not become interested in the aesthetics of asceticism? The legend of *nyūjō* might well have intrigued them in its most simplistic reading because it appeals

to a bizarre hope for surviving the death of the body through an esoteric religious technique. Moreover, Akinari's fascination with the supernatural and Enchi's with shamanism doubtlessly inspired their
searches for such techniques and their fascination with the topic. In
order to understand why Enchi chose Akinari as a kindred spirit to
discuss the boundary between life and death, contested by gender, it
is first necessary to examine the male writer's view of these issues. At
the same time, the symbolic imagery of *nyūjō*, placed in the context of
its literary evolution, serves as a key to this metaphysical experience
and provides a link between Akinari's classical and Enchi's modern
vocabulary and conceptualization.

In Akinari's story, the aesthetics of asceticism is gradually decon-
structed. That ascetics can fail miserably as well as ridiculously in
their claim to a unique, religious power is attributed to the distracting
attraction of the opposite sex. Although initially Akinari's exhumed
bell-ringing mummy is proclaimed a fake by sheer virtue of the fact
that it can be fully resuscitated to live again the full, that is, sexually
active, life of a man, *nyūjō* ultimately seems to have failed because of a
woman. Since women were excluded from the practice, they became
feared as a potential hindrance to its completion. Once female beauty
and carnal passion distracted the ascetic, he became subject to the folk
belief that attachment, as institutionalized in marriage, for better or
for worse constitutes a bond lasting for two lifetimes. Although *nyūjō*
and *nise no en* should by definition be mutually exclusive, they become entangled when the ascetic ideal of *nyūjō* is corrupted by sexual
desire,[25] which is exactly what happens in Akinari's "The Destiny
That Spanned Two Lifetimes." This male-centric value system may
have challenged Enchi to create a female protagonist who is not content with a peripheral, negative role.

Most likely, Akinari's principal source for "The Destiny That
Spanned Two Lifetimes" was "Sanshū amagane no koto" (About the
rain bell of Sanshū [Sanuki province]), from *Kingyoku neji-bukusa* (The
golden gemmed twisted wrapper; 1704).[26] By contrasting male
bonding in the narrative frame with male-female attachment in its
core, the legend raises questions about the degree of male versus female hindrance to male enlightenment. Yet neither the legend nor
Akinari's adaptation imagines the possibility of female enlightenment
through the ascetic or an alternative path. This conspicuous omission
may have stirred Enchi's literary response.

The rain-bell legend's surrealistic core tale is reflected in the narrative frame of Akinari's "The Destiny That Spanned Two Lifetimes," and it is important to Enchi's story in terms of its plot and symbolic imagery. It consists of an epiphany experienced by a certain Umeno- suke as a consequence of his pursuit of a mysterious prayer bell that he hears only in the rain. Tracing the sound to a grave, he exhumes a man who had died about three centuries earlier in a failed attempt to achieve *nyūjō*. Having entered a trance-like state of suspended ani- mation, the man had at the last moment been distracted by the sight of a beautiful woman, and his arousal had made it impossible for him to attain final enlightenment. The sound of the bell he continues ever after to ring is the symbol of his moral failure.

At this point Akinari introduces an element of satire while his source legend continues along grave and highly didactic lines. Thus, when Umenosuke reveals that the beloved woman died long ago, the would-be mummy crumbles before his very eyes. With the removal of the object of the ascetic's attachment, the attachment itself dies. When the mummy crumbles in the rain-bell legend, its disintegration sym- bolizes the attainment of *nirvana*. The ascetic *is* enlightened, but at the price of becoming a "flesh icon" as a result of *nyūjō* and its unortho- dox path to enlightenment.

The fact that Umenosuke not only hears the rain bell, as do others, but also responds to it links him to the ascetic. Both share a lingering attachment, in Umenosuke's case for a man and in the ascetic's for a woman, that obstructs enlightenment. Umenosuke's shock upon find- ing his friend Fujisuke dead is dramatically repeated in the case of the exhumed ascetic. Yet, since the dead have a powerful hold over the living, Umenosuke's attachment continues to ring in his ears like a rain bell even after he turns to the priesthood for solace. The bell con- nects the real and the surreal and facilitates the protagonist's vision of an attachment even more destructive than his own. In the bell-ringing mummy, Umenosuke is faced with a frightful mirror image of him- self. This new shock, of self-recognition, is enough to enlighten him about the vanity of human attachments.

If indeed Akinari adapted the rain-bell legend in his "The Destiny That Spanned Two Lifetimes," he did not retain the element of male bonding through blood brotherhood but instead emphasized the rain- bell epiphany of an ascetic arrested in the process of *nyūjō* by his at- tachment to a woman. Curiously, the realistic frame of "The Destiny That Spanned Two Lifetimes" explores male-female tensions not erotically but through two sets of mother-son relationships, one pair introduced at the beginning and one at the end of the story. Neither the mothers nor the sons meet. Both sons are faithful believers in the *nyūjō* legend, the first for scholarly and poetic reasons and the second for traditional religious motivations. Their mothers gradually become repulsive to them as they nag their sons about their allegedly naive faith in folk beliefs. Ignoring such complaints, the sons adhere to their faith in esoteric Buddhism. In a reversal of the usual stereotypes about devout parents and prodigal sons, one of the mothers turns hedonist and the other apostate.

The contrast between the steadfastness of the sons and their mothers' fall from moral discipline and religious faith is made clear in Akinari's surrealistic core tale. As in the rain-bell legend, the transition from one ontological plane to another occurs at night. While engaged in nocturnal study, a young scholar-poet hears a bell just as Umenosuke did, locates it, and exhumes an ascetic who has been in a trance for ten generations. However, this is where Akinari begins to satirize the legend. The wealthy scholar-poet is not endowed with the qualities of character that would assure the kind of epiphany experienced by Umenosuke. Akinari's anonymous male protagonist's leisurely pursuits expose him as an unfilial, useless sort of fellow. Indulging in shallow luxuries few can afford, he seems, in his response to the rain bell and to the ascetic, cold and unfeeling, even bookish, like some pretentious footnote in a dry treatise. He lectures to the gawking crowd: "This must be a case of what Buddhism calls *zenjō* [suspended animation]" (74).

When the young scholar allows his mother to take over the task of nourishing the mummy back to life, the *nyūjō* legend plummets into a world of farce.[27] Along with the other women of the village, the scholar's mother plays a grotesque version of woman's traditional role in giving birth to new life. The creature they revive is a frightful caricature that stands in sharp contrast not only to Kūkai, who requested that his remains be camouflaged in a brown robe for his mystic epiphany, but also to the general topos of the bell-ringing ascetic and even to the ghoulish abbot who achieves enlightenment through a hood in Akinari's "Aozukin" (The blue hood; 1776).[28] Jōsuke flies into tantrums, gobbles his meals (including fish, forbidden to ascetics), and indulges his insatiable sexual appetite. When the revived Jōsuke turns out to be stupidly lustful rather than religiously inspiring, the women are the first to mock him. Their lack of faith is unattractive.[29] By contrast, the men appear steadfast in their belief. Nevertheless, they also come to seem ridiculous because of their inability to control women, who, no longer interfering with the *nyūjō* ideal through their mere presence, now pervert the extreme spiritual goals of this particular form of asceticism — paradoxically realized through self-mummification — by turning the body into a fetish. The villagers' vulgar perceptions reflect as poorly on them as on the ascetic, who, distracted from *nyūjō*, becomes vulnerable to various forms of abuse.

Akinari's "The Destiny That Spanned Two Lifetimes" appears, then, thoroughly to satirize the *nyūjō* ideal introduced through Kūkai's Shingon doctrine of "attaining Buddhahood in this very body." The clumsy attempt of overzealous people to resuscitate a corpse is a mocking contrast to the revered religious practice. No serious mummy should be expected to tolerate the temptations of this world and its attachments without crumbling to dust in disgust. Jōsuke is not even granted this didactic twist but is forced to become part of the very corrupt world he presumably wanted to leave behind. In fact, Akinari seems to make sport of the moral tone prevalent in the *setsuwa* genre of short folk narratives, which frequently elaborated on the religious miracle of *nyūjō* while cautioning women against posing a hindrance to male enlightenment. It must be emphasized, however, that the buried bell ringer was a haunting religious figure until his trance was violated by those who not only exhumed but resuscitated him into a pathetically lustful failure.

Furthermore, "The Destiny That Spanned Two Lifetimes" is spun so much further into another realm incompatible with Kūkai's lofty ideal that *nyūjō* proper can hardly be regarded as the object of the author's satire. Rather, the satire seems to be directed at those who turn the ascetic into what he wanted to escape, namely, a living man desiring all the attachments that ultimately cause endless suffering, as predicted in Buddhist teaching. In the rain-bell prototype, a solemn bond is established between the bell-ringing ascetic and the profoundly troubled man who finds the ascetic. The former holds up a mirror to the latter, who recognizes himself in it. In Akinari's story, by contrast, the man who hears the bell fails to recognize its meaning, loses control over his find, and lets those unauthorized to be in the presence of the mummy do as they please with him. Unabashedly, they proceed to create their own mirror image — and it cannot be anything other than a hideous distortion of a living Buddha. Akinari paints in satiric strokes those who do not recognize themselves in their perverted creation.

The public perceives Jōsuke as a scandal whose failure as an ascetic was the result of his marriage before becoming a priest. Thus the idea of *nyūjō* is grotesquely coupled with that of *nise no en*. If a woman hindered Jōsuke on the path of enlightenment, then poetic justice — or is it poetic injustice? — requires that the scoundrel be "married off, as an adoptive husband, to an impoverished widow" (76). He must live the inferior carnal life with the reincarnation of the woman who originally spoiled his ambitious undertaking.

The widow to whom Jōsuke is coupled in unholy matrimony is herself a parody, simultaneously rejecting Jōsuke as the reincarnation of her husband while continually longing for that departed husband's return: "What a good-for-nothing husband I've got this time! I was better off living alone, picking up grain that the harvesters overlooked! Oh, how I wish my first husband would come back again, just once!" (78). Even richer gleanings[30] would be gathered by Enchi: in the same way that Akinari seems to have seized upon — and transformed — the rain-bell legend, Enchi picked up and reworked Akinari's satirical story. As scholars of both Enchi and Akinari have pointed out, the way both authors used source materials served, in the words of one critic, as "a corrective, if not subversive, gleaning."[31]

Under One Umbrella: Enchi's "A Bond for Two Lifetimes — Gleanings"

Aside from *nyūjō*, Enchi's story addresses *nise no en* through the classic ontological question concerning human experience as "dream or reality" (*yume ka utsutsu ka*).[32] Enchi introduces the dream-reality problematic by quoting Akinari's "Preface" to *Tales of the Spring Rain*.[33] Akinari claims to have nothing new to write about, and yet he does not want to be reduced to retelling traditional tales that no one can believe. He concludes, cheerfully if not gleefully, that deceiving his readers with fantasy is the only option for an author whose life has been so regretfully uneventful. Akinari commences with a shrug to tell his incredible tales. Who knows? Perhaps they are true after all. Or perhaps the objective truth does not excite, as do lies and deception, as integral aspects of the human condition. It is this latter "truth" that artists prefer to tell. One is reminded here of the attitude expressed in the "Fireflies" chapter of *The Tale of Genji*, where not only fiction but also the Buddha's parables are said to tell the truth obliquely.[34]

How exactly is the truth distorted by the art of fiction writing? A deceptive element enters into even the sort of harmless translation project undertaken by the male protagonist of Enchi's story, the aged, infirm Professor Nunokawa; with this fictional project Enchi screens herself from being perceived as the actual translator of Akinari. The problem of translation and its inevitable distortions must have occurred to Akinari as he adapted material like the rain-bell legend for "The Destiny That Spanned Two Lifetimes," just as they must have troubled Enchi when she committed herself to the arduous and lengthy task of modern translations of the classics,[35] eventually culminating in "her" *Tale of Genji*. To translate or otherwise reproduce means to take possession of original materials and inevitably to transform them. To the extent that the translator identifies with the original author, in an archaic sense, shamanistic transformative processes with the intent of resolving differences are involved. Last but not least, since "translation" means not only a linguistic transaction but also a cultural one, Akinari and Enchi share the boldness required to render not merely the words but also the beliefs of the past into a contemporary idiom. In this sense, the expression *nise no en*, homophonous with *nise no en* or "fake connection,"[36] may be seen to carry a novel connotation, as the intrepid translator erases the temporal gap and produces the illusion of cultural familiarity.

Enchi further complicates the meaning of *nise no en* by presenting us with the figure of the poverty-stricken, sickly professor-translator, who strikes the historically informed reader as a reincarnation of Akinari. Like Enchi's professor, the destitute Akinari, then nearly blind, was forced to dictate his last work.[37] In yet another reading of *nise no en* as intergenerational connection, this resemblance occurs to Noritake, the professor's amanuensis, whose job it is to take down the professor's dictated translation and reproduce it in her capacity as editor in a publishing house. Lastly, Enchi establishes a literary *nise no en* with Akinari by translating and reproducing his work as part of her own. At the same time, Enchi spins intertextual threads by shuttling back and forth between extra-textual and textual levels. Authors and fictional characters become so tightly linked through situational and character analogies that they raise the possibility of interchange-ability.

Weaving multilayered connections was Enchi's *modus scribendi* as much as it was Akinari's. What the rain-bell legend presumably was to Akinari's story, Akinari's story becomes to Enchi's. This core fiction by a male author, re-presented in two parts, is framed by a woman writer's fiction of a man's view, and a woman's re-view of the experi-ence of *nyūjō*. Like nesting boxes, old legends are thus enclosed by ever new versions, exploring and remapping gender territories.[38]

In the literal sense of translation, Enchi breaks her story into two parts, each containing one half of Nunokawa's "colloquial transla-tion" (28) of Akinari's "The Destiny That Spanned Two Lifetimes." At the turning point in Akinari's story, the male translator is forced by humiliating physical necessity to take another break from dictating to his female copyist/editor. In an act suggestive of both his diminished sexual energy and his creative impotence, he painfully urinates with the aid of a catheter provided by his maid and common-law wife, Mineko. Ironically, the break occurs just when, in Akinari's tale, the resuscitated ascetic has turned into such a monster that he threatens the entire community's faith in Buddhism.

During this interlude between the two halves of Akinari's tale, Nunokawa and Noritake discuss and reflect upon Akinari's story in terms of the male author's life and work. Enchi's two characters agree with the general scholarly opinion that, compared to Akinari's earlier supernatural tales collected in his popular *Ugetsu monogatari* (Tales of moonlight and rain; 1776), his *Tales of the Spring Rain* is a more politi-cally and morally challenging work.[39]

Before Nunokawa begins to dictate the second half of his collo-quial version of Akinari's story, he mentions another source for it: "Nyūjō no shūnen" (The attachment that plagued suspended anima-tion), from *Rōon chabanashi* (The old woman's teatime stories; early 1740's),[40] a tale in which an attractive woman prevents an ascetic named Keitatsu from completing his *nyūjō*. With this story as the im-petus, Nunokawa, a scholar of Edo literature, and Noritake, his for-mer student, proceed to debate whether, with increasing age, Akinari did well to decrease the erotic elements of his fiction in favor of a more philosophical and religious approach to the subject matter of *nyūjō*. Nunokawa complains that "The Attachment That Plagued Suspended Animation" does not dwell long enough on the beauty's agonizing temptation of the priest. As if to underline his own preference for full treatment of the erotic element, the professor mentions the *Kinsei retsuden-tai shōsetsu-shi* (A history of the novel: the lives of authors; 1897) by Tsubouchi Shōyō (1859–1935) and Mizutani Futō (1858–1943), in which Aeba Kōson (1855–1922) claims to have heard of a version of "The Destiny That Spanned Two Lifetimes" in which the erotic goes entirely unmentioned.[41] Instead, the story is said to end with a chaste religious discourse between the man who heard the bell and the ascetic he exhumed. Noritake agrees that such piety contradicts Akinari's extravagantly sensual style; she identifies the "more fulsome eeriness and deep pathos" of the erotic as being "more typical of Akinari" (37) and vital to the version of "The Destiny That Spanned Two Lifetimes" that Nunokawa is translating into modern Japanese. Almost unthinkingly, she slips from the literary critic's mode of discourse to the personal as she recalls that Nunokawa had once attempted to seduce her. Blending the scholarly and the biographical in her mind, she is thoroughly repulsed by Nunokawa's appetite for literary eroticism.

Although Noritake continues to see a resemblance between Nunokawa and Akinari as scholarly transmitters of legends, both of them plagued by illness and old age, she comes to see an even stronger resemblance between Nunokawa and Akinari's pathetic character Jōsuke, who, resuscitated from the brink of death, behaves like a lecher. These meditations on extra-textual and intra-textual resemblances leave Enchi's female protagonist with extremely ambivalent feelings toward her former teacher. Since her student days, when she was newly engaged to the man she was destined to lose after only one year of marriage, she has "sustained [her] contempt" (35) for the professor's amorous pursuit of her. It is clear from the beginning of the story that whatever "feelings of pity or compassion" Noritake might have had for Nunokawa's physical condition have turned into "an abhorrence of this wretchedness" (27). Her change of heart resembles the communal disillusionment with the resurrected Jōsuke in Akinari's story. Nunokawa's provocative actions in the past and his equally provocative comments on literature cause Noritake to reassess her relation not only to him but also to her dead husband.

What are Nunokawa's perceptions of the situation? The professor, it seems, has an incorrigible penchant for giving literary nicknames. During the break between the two parts of his modern translation of Akinari's story, Noritake withdraws to leave the management of the professor's urinary crisis to Mineko. The latter has been nicknamed "Usume no mikoto," a pun on Uzume no Mikoto, the archetypal shamaness (*miko*) who, according to the oldest Japanese chronicles, the *Kojiki* (Record of ancient matters; 712) and *Nihon shoki* or *Nihongi* (The records of Japan; 720), lured the aggrieved sun goddess Amaterasu Ōmikami out of her cave by exposing her genitals in a dance before the assembly of deities gathered outside the cave; their boisterous laughter led the curious sun goddess to emerge, thus returning light to a darkened world. Although Nunokawa may not be so pretentious as to see himself as a sun goddess, he certainly knows how it feels to be confined to darkness, particularly during his painful bouts with illness. In her imitation of a sexually powerful yet innocent *miko*, Mineko can restore a few rays of sunshine to his darkened world and figuratively replenish his sexual energy. As a result of these imagined shamanistic qualities, she can recall and impersonate dead spirits, such as Nunokawa's wife, thereby satisfying a surrogate connubial role as dictated by the fantasy of the dead spouse's return in the proverbial *nise no en*.

This surrogate role is very important. It is an intriguing feature of the Akinari story that a failed ascetic is presented as the reincarnation of a widow's *husband*. The reincarnation of a dead *wife*, as introduced in Enchi's contemporary plot, is another matter. There, *nise no en* cannot be achieved through *nyūjō* because that ascetic exercise is the exclusive domain of men. But if not through *nyūjō*, how then can a deceased female spouse be "returned" to her living husband? The professor's literary nicknames provide clues to the solution of this problem: Mineko, the replacement for his late wife, is imagined to be a *miko* who can summon and incorporate the spirits of the dead.

The second of Nunokawa's nicknames applies to the main female protagonist herself. Noritake, for whom he has been cherishing an unrequited, forbidden desire, introduces a fresh variation on the entranced shamaness's powers. As a literary connoisseur of women, Nunokawa had, since the early days of their student-teacher relationship, associated Noritake with Tamakazura.[42] In *The Tale of Genji*, the eponymous hero amorously pursues Tamakazura as a substitute for her mother, Yūgao, whom Genji had loved passionately even beyond her tragic death from spirit possession. Genji finds it difficult to accept Yūgao's death. Haunted by mysterious dream visions of Yūgao trailed by a twin-like beauty,[43] he conceives of her as both dead and alive. Eventually, Genji takes Tamakazura, who is, after all, a physical reproduction of her mother, to be the visionary double. He discovers, however, that she is a person with an identity and will of her own who vehemently resists acting as her mother's substitute or reincarnation. Nunokawa seeks, like Genji, to recover a lost woman, but he is no idealized hero. Although Genji intends to violate the taboo pertaining to foster and adoptive relationships,[44] which is a worse offense than the abuse of the student-teacher relationship, he remains an impressive figure and Tamakazura maintains her respect for him. Her modern counterpart Noritake, however, has no respect whatsoever for Nunokawa's ineffectual "lechery" (35).

As with Mineko's nickname, there are two aspects to the comparison: one entails a thematic (fictional) resemblance, and the other refers to technical (meta-fictional) matters. Not only does Tamakazura stand for dignified female resistance to unwanted sexual advances, but she also has gained a formidable reputation as an intellectual. In this latter capacity, she proves her independence from male-dominated discourse about the merits of chronicles (*ki*) versus tales (*monogatari*) by defining how fiction relates to truth and dream to reality. In this sense, Noritake, too, holds her own in the scholarly debates with the professor about this same fine line between fictional and nonfictional realms. How important is it for Enchi to redraw the line between fiction and truth or dream and reality that Akinari draws so casually? Or does Enchi become an even more radical advocate of an oblique fictional "truth" than the *Genji*'s author, Murasaki Shikibu, and Akinari?

Enchi's modern female protagonist, anxious to maintain Tamakazura's high ethical standards, is vaguely incited by the professor's nickname into combining meta-fictional aspirations from Murasaki Shikibu's *Tale of Genji* and metaphysical aspirations from Akinari's story. Enchi bridges these classical elements in the figure of Noritake, whose literary and religious sensibilities are activated in her resistance to the role of substitute lover—a form of *nise no en*—and her search for a hitherto undefined female *nyūjō* equivalent. If Murasaki Shikibu tipped the scales in favor of female power in her depiction of Tamakazura's debate with Genji, and if Akinari portrayed women as farcically undermining the exclusively male territory of religious asceticism, how can Enchi redress the balance? What can Enchi hold against the figure of the domineering male—most strikingly recalled in the ascetic archetype—if not a woman whose sovereignty can be traced to the ascetic's numinous counterpart, the ancient *miko*?

At this critical juncture, the belief in marriage as *nise no en*, which always seems to pale in comparison to the awe-inspiring attainment of *nyūjō*, assumes a new significance. *Nise no en* can be seen as a medieval translation of the classical literary topos of human substitution, frequently a relative for a lost lover (as, in *Genji*, Tamakazura for Yūgao).[45] Inasmuch as both classical and medieval variants of the topos require the recalling of a dead spirit who becomes reincarnated in a living person, the topos has roots in indigenous Shintō shamanism, a female practice. *Nyūjō*, by contrast, is a male practice that emerged from Kūkai's esoteric Shingon Buddhism. Enchi's female protagonist is trying to embrace both concepts as she senses her affinity to the religiously empowered figures of the ascetic and the shamaness. Sadly reflecting on her lonely life as a widow, Noritake suspects others of ridiculing her as "a woman as parched in body and soul as the dried-up salmon" (35) in Akinari's satiric imagery of the exhumed ascetic. As a practical matter, will she be able to sustain her *nyūjō*-like resistance to the professor or will she, according to *nise no en*, replace Mineko as his substitute wife?

The answers to these questions are complicated by the fact that Noritake must think not only of Nunokawa's needs as a widower but also of her own as a widow. Noritake's increasingly emotional response to Akinari's story and to Nunokawa can be traced in part to events that transpired after her student days but before the narrative present. She has been proud of her decision not to remarry; instead, she has remained single, a "war widow with a young boy to look after, living a marginal existence in the ten years since the end of the war" (35). Ironically, it is Nunokawa who, by assigning to her a literary role underlining female self-satisfaction and independence, fuels his "Tamakazura's" longing for the fulfillment of *nise no en* from her own female perspective. The professor finally accepts that Noritake, who has expressed her preference for the latter half of Akinari's story, which focuses on the widow's *nise no en* rather than the ascetic's *nyūjō*, would rather have her dead husband back than become a reincarnation of her former professor's dead wife. At least this is her current, still unsettled position; hence it is premature for Nunokawa to display jocular resignation over losing her to her dead husband: "'Ha, ha, ha,' the professor laughed weakly, his sharp Adam's apple twitching. 'You want that to happen to you, don't you? That's perfectly natural. You would like to have a bond that extends over two lifetimes'" (37).

At present, Noritake finds herself in a pivotal position between her own fantasies as a widow and those of the widower Nunokawa.

In the last fantastic scene of Enchi's story, Noritake's conflict soars to a level where logical contradictions become meaningless and gender roles interchangeable. Having finished the copying and discussion of Akinari's story, she leaves the professor in a state of complete exhaustion, suggestive of trance. On the way home, she herself experiences a deep trance brought about primarily by her reflections on their discussion of Akinari's work. Her conscious choice of the darker, narrower path to the bus stop, through liminal territory, so to speak, stimulates an altered state of consciousness. The atmospheric conditions of a twilight winter rain, pattering on her umbrella like a rain bell, add to her emotional turmoil. But is she hearing the rain bell or ringing it herself?

At this point in her continuing reflections about Akinari's story, Noritake is not aware of any specific source for the topic of the rain bell. Since Enchi wrote her story before Nakamura Yukihiko suggested the rain-bell legend as a source for Akinari (in the 1959 edition of *Tales of the Spring Rain*), Enchi was presumably also unaware of this possibility. Nonetheless, the powerful beginning of Akinari's "The Destiny That Spanned Two Lifetimes" — the bell ringing on a windless, moonlit night — cannot have failed to resound with her literary associations. Not knowing of this possible source for Akinari's tale, Enchi may instead have associated the bell imagery with the well-known Dōjōji legend.[46] Before we examine in detail the significance of this legend, it will be helpful to link Akinari's legendary bell with Enchi's "bell."

A significant bell, of whatever literary provenance, is sounded in Nunokawa's translation of Akinari's story. In Akinari's "The Destiny That Spanned Two Lifetimes," the wealthy scholar-poet identifies the sound as coming from a mummy after first hearing a bell mysteriously ringing in the absence of wind and apparently stirred by the moon suddenly breaking through the clouds; in Enchi's "Gleanings," the female copyist has a mystic encounter under a bell-equivalent — her umbrella — after transcribing Akinari's literary rendering of metaphysical bells into a contemporary idiom. Thus, the ancient religious icon of the bell is transformed into the secular commodity of an umbrella at the end of Enchi's story.

When Noritake, like Chikako in "Enchantment," feels compelled to open the umbrella in the light rain, the season is not spring, as in Akinari's depiction of his young male protagonist's mystic awakening. Rather, Enchi has chosen late autumn as the appropriate season for dramatizing her middle-aged female protagonist's approach to ecstatic experience. The bell-ringing Jōsuke preoccupies Noritake, so much so that she begins to confuse the literary and the extra-literary levels. While her mind is still operating in scholarly, analytic fashion, she rationalizes the depraved image of the failed ascetic by attributing his degeneration to Akinari's widowerhood, blindness, and depression. In her increasingly agitated state, she draws analogies not only between Akinari and Jōsuke but also between Nunokawa and Jōsuke, for both author and translator are widowers in dismal circumstances and their views of religion and sexuality are as ambivalent as the aspirations incorporated by the fictional Jōsuke. Finally, all these ambivalent men are subsumed under one umbrella.

Bell and umbrella constitute analogous images whose respective meanings can best be revealed through the Dōjōji legend — since this is the legend that implicitly echoes through Akinari's rain bell — and through the umbrella variations at the end of Enchi's story.[47] The "legend of Dōjōji was originally based on ancient rain-invoking rituals" (Skord, 129), a link that thereby enriches the metallic substance of its central religious icon with associations of fertility and sexuality: for its bell shape, in particular, suggests the female reproductive organ. As one scholar has noted, "Bells function metaphorically in Japanese esoteric Buddhism as symbolic wombs, particularly associated with the Womb (*Taizō*) Mandala, and the temple bell certainly retains those associations in *Kanemaki* [a Nō version of the Dōjōji legend] and [the Nō play] *Dōjōji*" (Klein, 310). Under normal circumstances, the bell remains dysfunctional until it is suspended from the bell tower and ready to be rung by thumping a wooden beam against it. Thus, through the extended social anthropology of the bell's apparatus, the male's sexual organ is implicated as well when the phallic wooden pole strikes the womb-shaped bell, symbolically sounding the moment of conception. Yet mysteriously, in the Dōjōji legend and in the rain-bell legend as transmitted through Akinari, the bell sounds without being struck by a phallic object. Instead it is struck, in a most puzzling poetic metaphor,[48] by the moon, a phenomenon traditionally linked to the menses and, as such, symbolic of female fertility. Is this self-fertilizing female mystery not as potent as the male privilege of *nyūjō*, which is in fact based on the ascetic premise of phallic arrest?

The female protagonist of Enchi's story approaches such a mystery immediately after recalling conventional marital intercourse. At this point in Noritake's reflections, halfway between the safety of the professor's house and the bus stop, she enters a psychic zone crowded with unconscious desires and fears. As she recalls her last sexual orgasm with her husband, she relives it as a surreal sensation: "My body and soul seemed to have vanished" (44). In the present moment of solitary ecstasy under her own umbrella, she repeats the experience of dissociation from herself by identifying her female essence with the reproductive part of her body: "My very womb cried out in longing" (44).[49] Much in the way that the moon striking the bell sounds an unorthodox, atonal poetic note, so Enchi's sentence is said to have sent shockwaves running through the reading public upon the story's publication.[50] Yet the statement contains more than a scandalously unabashed female affirmation of sexual lust. It constitutes no less than the female protagonist's trance-lation of *nyūjō* into a female idiom.

In the sense that here the female reproductive organ is understood synecdochically, the distinctly female potential of physical reproduction can be seen to correspond to male religious enlightenment as experienced in *nyūjō*. The womb signals fertility, just as the bell is resonant when struck by the moon, even without sexual intercourse. Yet the element of sexual desire—whether as reality, memory, or *nise no en* fantasy—hinders both sexes from achieving the completion of *nyūjō*. Just as the ascetic keeps ringing his bell, Noritake hears her womb cry out. In other words, although they are able to enter into a trance, neither can sustain it long enough to attain enlightenment: the release from all attachments.

Hence Noritake's trance experience complements that of the ascetic. In fact, her ecstatic cry triggers a surreal sexual encounter with a strange ghost-like man, not wholly unlike an incompletely mummified ascetic:

> Although I could not see his face clearly, from his voice and appearance he seemed rather old and shabby, yet the hand he put on top of my gloved one was soft like a woman's. . . . My body was completely encircled within his arms. We had to walk along entangled in this way.
>
> In the darkness I staggered frequently and each time he adjusted his hold on me, like a puppeteer manipulating a puppet. (45)

Within the context of Akinari's story about a male ascetic, in this joint trance Enchi succeeds in skillfully coordinating male *nyūjō* and her conception of its female equivalent. The scene is described in terms suggestive of Bunraku, where the magical movements of the puppet are manipulated by the invariably male puppeteer. Indeed,

this form of theater openly acknowledges the fact that the male puppeteer controls the fictional character embodied by the puppet. Yet, at
the same time, Enchi undermines the male Bunraku tradition by
drawing attention to the distinctly feminine feature of her puppeteer's
soft hand. Although as an artist the puppeteer is peripheral to the plot
of the puppet play, he becomes implicated in it through his visibility
as the puppet's shadow. As if to underline this point, the puppet is
manipulated by two additional male puppeteers who wear hoods to
suggest that they are operating anonymously as part of a collective
male force. The male puppeteer must conceal his identity in order to
assume the gender of the play's frequently female main character.
Ideally in Bunraku, puppet and puppeteer(s) become nearly indistinguishable as their identities merge—until the play is over. Noritake
and the ghost-like man become similarly intertwined.

Noritake's ecstatic sensations seem no longer merely derived
from cultural traditions exemplified by Akinari's satirical transmission of women's interference with men's pursuit of Buddhist enlightenment. Instead, they assume a meaning of their own, as they sharply
reflect back on other traditional patterns. Enchi's Bunraku analogy is
a reminder of the fact that in this, as in other major forms of Japanese
theater, women are entirely a male creation.[51] They are excluded from
the roles of creators, craftsmen, producers, and actors. In mainstream
Japanese theater, women are, in other words, a male fiction. If the
umbrella trance does not completely reverse this traditional pattern, it
does at least attempt to strike a balance. Therefore, it is no exaggera-
tion to say that in the liminal space of that scene, the entranced
woman wholly invents, evokes, and thereby controls the stereotypically manipulative man. His sexual advances can be relished in a
mood of detached astonishment: "Touching me on my breasts, my
sides, and other parts of my body, he would laugh, but whether out of
joy or sadness, I could not tell. I suddenly had the idea that he might
be crazy, but that did not diminish the strange pleasure I took in his
embrace" (45). Whether there is indeed a lecherous man or whether
he is a figment of Noritake's trance experience is irrelevant. What is
indisputable is that, in the perception of the female protagonist, the
unidentifiable man serves as a projection of her own ambivalent lust.
Enchi thus modifies the ordinary pattern of the male puppeteers'
skillful manipulation of the female doll, who, in the deluded eyes of
the audience, seems to have a life of her own.

However, gender differences cannot be entirely eliminated by means of Enchi's quasi-acrobatic literary balancing act in which her female protagonist suspends her sexual identity in a trance, just as the male puppeteer suspends his, as a performer in the woman writer's dramatic scene. There is, nevertheless, evidence that casts the perception of any remaining divisive gender difference in severe doubt. Thus, Noritake, who first entered this trance because of her unrestrained longing for her dead husband, finds herself uncertain whether it is his hand touching her or her own hand. Is she an independently active agent, or is she merely the recipient of "a bond for two lifetimes" through the return of her husband? Although she associates some of the mysterious man's physical features with those of her husband, this feeling of familiarity becomes repulsively distorted by the superimposition of Jōsuke, who returns from a failed attempt at *nyūjō*.

While struggling to maintain a sense of her own identity, Noritake is possessed by conflicting male images whose distinctions break down in her trance and assume her own gender's qualities. She wavers back and forth between thinking that the hand touching her is and is not her husband's. Although she notes emphatically and repeatedly that it is "fleshy and soft as a woman's" (46), she does not conclude that this hand might be her own. She stops just shy of proclaiming the heretical notion that *nise no en* might be achieved not because of traditionally male *nyūjō* but because of female *nyūjō*. In Akinari's story, the ascetic fails because of his supposed attachment to his wife. Enchi endows her female protagonist with the capacity of a modern shamaness who, in a trance, not only recalls her husband's dead spirit as a collective male spirit but also controls male sexual power by infusing it with femininity. Thus the modern female author rewrites a classical male author's story about an ascetic from the perspective of the ascetic's counterpart, the shamaness.

In her dream-like state, Noritake permits herself neither openly revolutionary nor unambiguous conclusions about the strange sexual encounter. Yet her attitude has narrowed the gap between male and female. In her sexual trance-action, the distinction between gender roles is so blurred as to become irrelevant. The result is an unleashing of raw power, making Noritake's "body [spring] up convulsively like some stray dog" (46).[52] As in Akinari's story and the Dōjōji legend, a poetic climax has been reached where the moon can strike the bell and a sound be heard. The startling image is reminiscent of Hakuin's (1686–1769) Zen kōan about the "sound of one hand" (*sekishu no on-*

jō).[53] If it is possible in a deep trance to transcend gender differences and to create the paradox of sex-indifferent sexual desire, what creature emerges? In the case of the male, it may be a bell-ringing mummy. In the case of the female, the appearance of the creature herself is as yet undefined except for the bell-equivalent of the umbrella or detached womb. What transformation analogous to the ascetic-turned-mummy must the female undergo?

Women excluded from male domains are bound to appear, sometimes in unfamiliar guises, to claim a powerful role. In the religious sphere, undisguised female beauty has been recognized as challenging the male prerogative of *nyūjō*. On the semi-religious and semi-secular stage of Japanese traditional theater, women's roles are conceived and acted by men. On the secular plane, women are denied access to male privileges in numerous areas, most conspicuously — in Enchi's contemporary story — the transmission of the literary tradition and military participation in war. In her professional life, the female copyist is subservient to the male translator. In her private life, she is continuing to combat her late husband's secular asceticism and the exclusionary male attitude toward "compliance with the military" (a translation of the characters [*kanji*] used to write her husband's surname, Noritake). Even in a demilitarized Japan at peace, years after Mr. Noritake's death from a bomb rather than in combat, his war widow still bitterly resents having been spurned as a woman: "My husband loved me, but being a soldier, he made a distinction in his mind between loving and dying alone" (46).

In legends and folk tales, the motif of the woman spurned because of religiously or secularly defined restrictions inspired female metamorphoses into phallic serpents and compelled female dancers (*shirabyōshi*) to wear male attire. Once again, the Dōjōji legend is instructive in its presentation of conflicting male-female perspectives: it begins with a monk (usually named Anchin) who first flaunts his charms to an attractive young woman, who is, significantly, in many versions, a widow.[54] In the early twelfth-century *setsuwa* collection *Tales of Times Now Past*, this final moral lesson is drawn from the popular belief associated with her marital status: "That evil woman's passion for the young monk must also have come from a bond formed in a previous life" (Ury, 96). Second, the monk, having encouraged her amorous expectations, then spurns her by using the religious excuse of his pilgrimage, that is, a quasi-*nyūjō* argument. Third, after the successful completion of his pilgrimage, he flees from her wrath into

Kiyohime, her spurned passion for the monk Anchin having turned her into a serpent, coils around the temple bell of Dōjōji and stares at the terrified monk hiding inside. Wood and ivory *netsuke*, carved by Minkō of Tsu (fl. late 18th century). (Copyright British Museum)

sacred territory forbidden to women. At Dōjōji he hides, ironically, under the temple bell. Since the bell is a symbol of religious enlightenment through chastity, the monk believes he is cleverly seeking pious refuge from carnal pursuit. But the dialectic of the bell not only calls for chastity; in ancient fertility cults, the bell emits reproductive signals. The monk has therefore failed to consider this primeval aspect of the bell—which turns into a trap. His fate resembles Jōsuke's, who also falls into a trap set by females at the instigation of other men who have heard bells ringing in the rain. Chastity and fertility, Buddhist asceticism and Shintō shamanism, male and female, all clash within the symbolism of the bell.

In the *Dōjōji monogatari* (Tales of Dōjōji), the medieval *otogi-zōshi* synthesis of the legend's variants, the woman is first shown to turn into a serpent that coils itself around the bell to destroy the man hiding inside.[55] Then, she is shown gaining access to the forbidden space wearing the white clothing of a man typical of *shirabyōshi* dancers.[56] In the latter alternative, the woman claims to be no ordinary woman. She appears as a dancer who expresses her hatred of the bell and then leaps after the man inside the bell[57] in an attempt to bypass the five female hindrances (*goshō*) and achieve enlightenment. This strategy may seem more noble than the sheer destructiveness commonly interpreted as female wrath and vengefulness, but since it is a female pretending to male religious aspirations, it cannot be allowed to succeed. Thus, the bell grows hot, and the woman, changed into a serpent, emerges from the bell and slithers, unenlightened, into the Hidaka River.

In Enchi's story, the Dōjōji paradigm is complicated by the fact that the female protagonist has been spurning men ever since she herself was spurned because of her own husband's military commitment. In this sense, her experience with the opposite sex cuts both ways, which enables her to assume the roles of both male and female: those who spurn and those who are spurned. In terms of the paradigm, she bears an affinity both to the monk Anchin and to the nameless widow of the Dōjōji legend. Within the immediate context of Enchi's story, she can, on the one hand, identify with Akinari's ascetic even in his most degenerate form of Jōsuke, as is evident from Noritake's self-images, which range from the parched salmon to the stray dog. On the other hand, she can also identify with Akinari's widow as she aggressively pursues her longing.

The carnal desires of Enchi's widow have remained dormant during a long period of sexual abstention and even disgust with men. They are suddenly reawakened when she copies a male writer's provocative tale and critically discusses it with a male scholar. Within the male-dominant hierarchical structure of her culture, the female protagonist is caught in an inferior, subservient position, whether in her role as copyist to translator, former student to retired professor, or wife to husband. This occupational and domestic gender inequality is reinforced ethically by the apparent misogyny conveyed through the *nyūjō* rain-bell legend and, by extension, the Dōjōji legend. Noritake rebels against such discrimination and seeks moral reconciliation and religious transcendence of the conflict. In this she resembles those female figures who transform their single-sex identity into phallic serpents — as in theriomorphic tales[58] — or into the ambiguous gender role of the *shirabyōshi* — as in the Nō play *Dōjōji*.[59] Yet Noritake is their literary descendant with a difference: she does not reflect a man's vision of a woman but a woman's. She, too, is no ordinary woman.

Enchi's presentation of her female protagonist's view of men illuminates that difference. As the story progresses, Noritake's emotions change, and in the climactic scene she appears to embrace the very men who had oppressed, repelled, and disappointed her. What makes this remarkable new attitude not only tolerable but exciting? In her earlier reflections during the break in dictation, she had intimated that she had "recently begun to view the inevitable sexual aggressions of men with a sympathetic eye" (35). At that time she had also envisioned herself as a female mummy, still attached to the world by longing for her husband and his mirror image: "Deep within my being, I sometimes embrace my husband's visage quite vividly in the face of my small son" (35). Whereas the male ascetic aspires to become a "flesh icon" in a formidable mummification process testifying to his aloofness from sexual desire and to his enlightenment, the female counterpart creates her own "flesh icon" not through denial but through recognition of sexual desire.[60] Thus, in her self-engendered trance, the female protagonist as modern shamaness relives the process of physical reproduction rather than mummification. On a metafictional level, the author as shamaness summons the spirit of Akinari by translating and reproducing his newly exhumed, parched manuscript.

When the outside world begins to threaten her trance, Noritake's initial elation rapidly degenerates, and her desire for her husband is threatened by re-emerging fears of pursuit by the Jōsukes and the Nunokawas of this world. Ironically, the man she still longs for is the one who spurned her, while she in turn had been spurning the men who desired her. The trance experience does, however, allow her to realize an abstract form of sexual desire.[61] Only in the liminal state of her trance can the female protagonist play all the parts herself, as if attempting to deconstruct gender binarism. When she awakens from this illusory effort, she is frightened of losing her identity to that of a "stray dog." Nonetheless, she has opened up an alternative to the male-dominated tradition, as here defined by Kūkai's *nyūjō*, Akinari's "The Destiny That Spanned Two Lifetimes," Japan's traditional theater, and the contemporary male power structure.[62]

Her trance finally enables Noritake to break loose from men's concept of sexual desire, power, and control, whether that concept is formulated by Akinari or Nunokawa or Noritake's husband. Ultimately it is she who subsumes the men, whoever they are, under her umbrella. Their collective Jōsuke identity falls so much under her influence that it appears vaguely female. After all, she, too, knows what it is to be a Jōsuke. In her trance, Noritake has developed a view of both men and women shaped by herself rather than by men. Yet once the outside world again impinges on her consciousness, this trance vision fades again into an ambiguous mode, reflecting the social and political reality of male dominance.

Thus, in the end she is left with the gleanings — the "flesh icon" — of her love for her deceased husband, as reproduced in their son, much as Genji is left with a Tamakazura who will never be anything more — or less — to him than her mother's daughter. And like a veritable Tamakazura, Noritake has designed her own key to gender relations. She notes with decisiveness that she has found herself, as she basks in the afterglow of her ecstasy: "an unsettling agitation that warmed my heart" (47).

Notes

1. "Nise no en" is from Ueda Akinari's collection of stories, *Harusame monogatari* (Tales of the spring rain; 1802–9). A complete version of the text did not become available in print until 1950, when Urushiyama Sōshirō edited the *Urushiyama-bon Harusame monogatari*, based on a copy made by Takeuchi Yazaemon in 1843. Text editions consulted are Nakamura, 170–75; Nakamura et al., 511–17 (Nakamura Hiroyasu, text and notes). Page numbers for Barry Jackman's English translation, "The Destiny That Spanned Two Lifetimes," are cited in parentheses.

2. For the text of "Nise no en — shūi," see *Enchi Fumiko zenshū*, 2: 329–42. There are two English translations: "A Bond for Two Lifetimes — Gleanings," in Birnbaum, 27–47; and "Love in Two Lives: The Remnant," in Lippit and Selden, 97–111. Hereafter, all quotations are from Birnbaum's translation.

3. Enchi exploited the literary convention of the literary hoax in later works, most spectacularly in the *Namamiko monogatari* (A tale of fake mediums; 1959–65). This work is purportedly based on the *Namamiko monogatari — Eiga monogatari shūi*, a work of fiction claimed by the narrator to have actually existed. In fact, the invented work is based on the existing historical work, *Eiga monogatari* (A tale of flowering fortunes; ca. 1092). In *Saimu* (The mist in Karuizawa; 1975–76), Enchi's plot revolves around an invented picture scroll, the "Picture Scroll of the Kamo High Priestess" ("Kamo saiin e-kotoba"). See Sodekawa, chaps. 2 and 4, for an extensive examination of Enchi's literary borrowing technique.

4. It is impossible to believe that there is no previous example of this literary technique. Perhaps Enchi was inspired by Ueda Akinari's unconventional literary technique, for example, in his "Uta no homare" (The glory of poetry) from the *Harusame monogatari*. In that brief piece, undefinable in

terms of genre, Akinari quotes four actual eighth-century *tanka*, almost identical in subject matter and ending in the same seven syllables. The author's prose commentary is intended to exonerate the poets from the charge of plagiarism and instead applaud them for the unabashed liberty each took with the texts of others. Moreover, Enchi uses Akinari's text by carefully acknowledging her technique, and she therefore cannot be accused of plagiarism. There is, however, a tradition of borrowing without acknowledgment derived from China; see Borgen, 68. For the evolution of allusive variation (*honkadori*) as a rhetorical trope, see Bialock, 225, *et passim*.

5. For a meticulous study of Enchi's changes of and additions to Akinari's "Nise no en," see Kamei, "Koten shakkei," 115–22.

6. Pers. comm., Ōba Minako, Rutgers University, Apr. 10, 1993, based on memories of a conversation with Enchi. This evaluation of "Nise no en—shūi" as a masterpiece is supported by Mishima, "Gendai no bungaku."

7. John Bester's English translation, "Enchantress," renders the name as Chigako. The page numbers cited refer to this translation.

8. For the critics' appraisal of "Enchantment," see Rieger, 101–2.

9. See Andō; Sakurai and Ogata; and Hori.

10. The paradigm of the ascetic prevented from complete *nyūjō* by a beautiful woman complements, without mirroring, the paradigm recently exposed as the "sacralization" or "deification" of courtesans; for detailed discussions of the latter paradigm, see Marra; and Terasaki.

11. The text of *Tales of the Spring Rain* was not known until 1907, when Fujioka Sakutarō published five of its ten stories, based on an autograph manuscript discovered in Tomioka Tessai's collection. In the 1940's Nakamura Yukihiko found the five missing works, including an incomplete version of "Nise no en," in the library of Tenri-kyō in Tenri, Nara prefecture; he published this incomplete edition in 1947. The *Urushiyama-bon Harusame monogatari* of 1950, cited above, constituted the first complete text version of "Nise no en." For a detailed textual history, see Nakamura, 16–19; and Jackman.

12. "The Japanese term *miira* (mummy) seems to have come from the Portuguese *mirra*, or myrrh, one of the spices used in mummification, a word and substance brought to Japan in the sixteenth century by the Portuguese" (Maraini, 276). In most cases, however, the term *miira* designates the mummies themselves, or a powdery substance made from them. Egyptian mummies were appreciated for their medicinal properties and were ground to a powder and exported to Europe from the sixteenth to the eighteenth centuries; see D'Auria et al., 14. The Portuguese were the first to bring this exotic powder to Japan in the sixteenth century, and the Dutch later imported whole mummies to Japan from about 1700; see Pekarik, 23–24. The precious medicinal *miira* powder was placed in medicine boxes (*inrō*) and attached to a man's sash with toggles (*netsuke*) carved from ivory or wood. See p. 191.

13. In Jackman's translation, *nise no en* is "a bond that unite[s] two souls for the duration of two consecutive reincarnations as human beings" (Ueda,

Tales of the Spring Rain, 79n13). In addition to the belief that the bond of marriage lasted for two lifetimes, it was thought that the bond between parent and child lasted a single lifetime, and that between lord and retainer three lifetimes.

14. See Schalow, 7; see also 318n19, as well as numerous references in Saikaku's stories.

15. The same episode appears in *Konjaku monogatari* 11.25, but the *setsuwa* is not embedded in the larger fictional or historical context that makes the *Heike* episode so much more relevant for an understanding of the narrative techniques employed by Akinari and Enchi.

16. See Sharf. What Sharf points out for the Chinese practice of mummification also applies in part to Japan. At first sight the bizarre practice may seem to violate Buddhist canonical teachings that interpret as attachment "any attempt to resist the inevitability of death and the impermanence of the body." Yet it is important to recognize that in the context of the economic difficulties many monastic centers faced, mummification ensured institutional survival through the iconic charisma of a mummified master. Moreover, the mummified master incorporated the dialectic tension between form and emptiness in the Buddhist goal of *nirvana*: "A dead abbot . . . serves as well as a living one to give form to the formless — provided, that is, that he can be kept from rotting away" (Sharf, 26–27).

17. Sharf judges this term to be "somewhat of a misnomer: even in Japan the full mummification of a monk who fasted to death required the postmortem treatment of the corpse" (14n37). See also Hori, 224; Sakurai and Ogata, 214–23.

18. The Shingon temple complex on Mount Kōya was originally off-limits to women, who could proceed up the mountain only as far as the *nyonin-dō*, a worship hall where women prayed just outside the sacred precincts. The restriction was lifted only in the late nineteenth century.

19. In passing, Hori mentions four twelfth-century mummies of members of the Fujiwara clan and two others, Kōchi Hōin (d. 1363) and Jun-kai Shōnin (d. ca. 1630) (Hori, 223, 226).

20. For detailed information on the six *miira* and their austerity practices, see Hori, 223–26; and Blacker, 87–90.

21. The *isse gyōnin* were the highest order of ascetics in the Yudono sect of Shugendō. Hori (228, 234, and 235) points out the interesting fact that all six mummified *isse gyōnin* received the "*kai*-suffix" (for Kūkai) and were under the control of Mount Kōya's main temple, Kongōbu-ji. Hori also notes that in pre-Tokugawa times the eclectic Shugendō practices included celibacy, whereas later their ascetic training was "voluntary" and presupposed "abandoning wife and children" (235, 237).

22. For references to these works, see Hori, 227; Ueda, *Tales of the Spring Rain,* 69.

23. See Kafka. Kafka's story resembles Ueda Akinari's in the sense that the Hungerkünstler's sensational feat is increasingly ridiculed and exposed

as a pointless fad. Kafka seems to satirize not only the behavior of the public but also, in the end, that of the Hungerkünstler, who, when questioned about his motivation, claims that there was never any food that he had especially liked. Is he, like Akinari's Jōsuke, finally permitted to laugh at those who have denigrated his achievement and grown used to laughing at him? Unlike Jōsuke, the Hungerkünstler must pay a greater price, for he breathes his last along with his triumphant last laugh.

24. Ueda Akinari's medical history includes smallpox, deformities of both hands, and eventually almost total blindness; see Young. Zolbrod speculates that Akinari may have been "sterile by heredity" (24). For Enchi's medical history, which included uterine cancer, extensive dental reconstruction, and detached retinas, see Carpenter, 348–55.

25. It is no coincidence that Kūkai's *nyūjō* ideal was pursued exclusively by ascetics of the eclectic Shugendō Yudono mountain sect, which continued to insist on celibacy when other sects, beginning with the Jōdo Shin sect of Shinran (1173–1263), permitted monks to marry. The image of the celibate monk thus began to fade in the early medieval period and was largely replaced by the image of the lustful monk. Typically powerless against the passionate wiles of female beauty, the lustful monk inspired numerous didactic tales. These *setsuwa* preached misogyny in order to preserve male chastity and reassert the male prerogative of enlightenment, a privilege that was challenged by the increasingly popular Pure Land belief of enlightenment for all. By the late Edo period, Buddhist monasticism generally could claim neither coherence nor discipline and came under fire from advocates of Confucianism and Shintō. By contrast, the single-minded intensity of Shugendō ascetics must have appeared to be a curious, awe-inspiring relic from the past.

26. Nakamura made this suggestion in his 1959 edition of Ueda Akinari's works (20, 171n48, 393n49), and it is not an unlikely one since "Aozukin" (The blue hood) follows a similar plot line. Enchi does not mention this possibility in her story because it was published two years before Nakamura's 1959 commentary. For a lengthy summary of the rain-bell legend, see Ueda, *Tales of the Spring Rain*, 69–71.

27. The question of whether Ueda Akinari meant to satirize orthodox Buddhism is too complex to discuss here. For some views on this difficult issue, see Ueda, *Tales of the Spring Rain*, 72; Young, 132.

28. Published in Ueda Akinari's *Ugetsu monogatari* (Tales of moonlight and rain; written in 1768; published in 1776), "The Blue Hood" is based on the historic figure of a fifteenth-century Sōtō Zen priest named Kaian (d. 1493), who saved an entire community from one crazed abbot's ghoulish visitations of homes and graves. Kaian offers his own flesh to the necrophagous abbot and thereby awakens him from his blind attachment to his dead boy lover. Kaian's sacrificial offering of his living body converts the abbot's carnal passion to a religiously oriented male bond that, through the catalyst of the hood, leads to enlightenment.

29. It has been pointed out that in her adaptation of Ueda Akinari's text,

Enchi shifted pessimistic sentiments from mother to son; see Kamei, "Koten shakkei," 118.

30. For "gleanings," both Akinari and Enchi use the term *ochibo* (fallen ears of rice). Widows were traditionally allowed to pick up fallen ears after the reapers; see Ueda, "Nise no en," in Nakamura, 175*n*28; and in Nakamura et al., 517*n*14. For Enchi's use of the term, see "Nise no en—shūi," 338.

31. Gessel, "The 'Medium' of Fiction," 380. Gessel's remark is specifically directed at Enchi's *Namamiko monogatari* (1965), itself literary "gleanings" from *A Tale of Flowering Fortunes*. For a similar point, see Hulvey, 4–5. In specific reference to Enchi's "Gleanings," Pounds has stated that "Enchi's frame story alters Akinari's social satire to a satire of the patriarchal literary tradition, and it assimilates the sexual imagery of Akinari's story to the thematics of creativity" (178). For Ueda Akinari's transformation of sources, see Jackman's "Introduction" to "The Destiny That Spanned Two Lifetimes," in Ueda, *Tales of the Spring Rain*; and Washburn, 47.

32. See, e.g., episode 69 in *Tales of Ise*.

33. See Jackman, trans., "Akinari's Preface, 'Jo,'" in Ueda, *Tales of the Spring Rain*, 3.

34. See Murasaki Shikibu, *The Tale of Genji*, 438.

35. See Enchi et al., *Ugetsu Monogatari*.

36. Young has pointed out that "phonetically . . . the same words may be interpreted to mean 'fake destiny,' and the pun was probably intentional, since the Buddhist teachings on the relationship of cause and effect are made to appear false" (132).

37. In Nunokawa, Enchi created a character who anticipated her own failing eyesight at the end of her life. While translating the *Genji monogatari* into modern Japanese (1967–72), Enchi twice had eye surgery for detached retinas, but continued her work by means of dictation. See Carpenter, 355.

38. Enchi's technique of weaving actual or invented texts from classical literature into a contemporary plot is conspicuous in *Onna men* (Masks; 1958); *Namamiko monogatari*; "Otoko no hone" (Skeletons of men; 1956); and "Yō." For explications of this technique in the *Namamiko monogatari*, see Gessel, "The 'Medium' of Fiction." For an analysis in similar terms of the narrative technique of Tanizaki Jun'ichirō, a writer Enchi greatly admired, see Chambers, 370–74.

39. See Jackman, xiv–xvii.

40. At the end of the story, Noritake does not verify this source and instead suggests that "The Destiny That Spanned Two Lifetimes" may have been "an imaginative creation of Akinari's later years" (43). Concerning this possible source, Enchi follows Urushiyama Tendō's suggestion as put forward in the Iwanami-bon annotations available at the time she wrote her story; see Shigematsu and Miyazaki, 101.

41. For this rumored version, "Amayo monogatari" (The rainy night tale), as a possible source, Enchi again follows Urushiyama Tendō; see Shigematsu and Miyazaki, 101.

42. Enchi links Harume to Tamakazura in her novel *Onna men*. For an analysis of this work, see Bargen, "Twin Blossoms," especially, 152–54.

43. Murasaki Shikibu, *The Tale of Genji*, 83. See also the passage that echoes Genji's dream-like hallucination in the nightmares suffered by Yūgao's women in charge of raising Tamakazura (388; Seidensticker's translation of *The Tale of Genji* renders Yūgao as "Evening Faces").

44. For a discussion of Genji's incestuous attraction to Tamakazura, see Bargen, "The Problem of Incest," 119–20.

45. Tamakazura is named after a jeweled wreath, which, according to Gary L. Ebersole, "seems to have served as a *katami*, a ritual object used to recall the spirit of a deceased individual" (174; see also 165).

46. That the literary association of the ascetic and the rain bell with the Dōjōji legend virtually suggests itself is further substantiated by Kōno Taeko's explicit connection in *Miira tori ryōki-tan* (The bizarre seizure of *miira*; 1990). In this prize-winning novel, an ascetic physician asks his lustful wife to torture him in a World War II bomb shelter under a darkened lamp shade strongly resembling the Dōjōji bell.

47. The umbrella imagery is also prominent in "Jasei no in" (The lust of the white serpent; 1776) from Ueda Akinari's *Ugetsu monogatari*; see Zolbrod, 161–84. For a detailed summary of the Dōjōji legend, see pp. 190–92.

48. For an alternative view, see Klein, 315–16.

49. Enchi herself experienced, as a medical trauma, the loss of her womb when she had a hysterectomy in 1946; see Carpenter, 348.

50. See Birnbaum, "Introduction," 26. Mishima recognized the famous womb imagery in his 1964 appreciation of "A Bond for Two Lifetimes — Gleanings," but he himself was more intrigued by the canine teeth Noritake feels on her tongue and senses to be her husband's. This, to Mishima, suggests Enchi's mastery of a ghastliness surpassing even that of Akutagawa Ryūnosuke; see Mishima, cited in *Enchi Fumiko zenshū*, 2: 391.

51. It is noteworthy that Enchi succeeded in establishing herself first as a modern playwright, and only later came to feel that working as a prose writer and translator was more rewarding.

52. The imagery of the dog as an indicator of carnal desire is also used at the end of Enchi's "Enchantment": "From the foot of the hill came the shrill yelping of a dog" (92).

53. For Hakuin's exposition of this kōan in his *Yabukōji* (1753; printed 1792), see Yampolsky, 163–69.

54. One of the few notable exceptions to the motif of the passionate widow can be found in the *Dōjōji engi emaki* (Picture scroll of the founding of Dōjōji), traditionally attributed to the emperor Go-Komatsu (r. 1382–92; 1393–1412), in which the widow is replaced with the local innkeeper's innocent daughter. The Nō play *Dōjōji*, attributed to Kanze Kojirō Nobumitsu (1435–1516), also features a sexually inexperienced girl who is cruelly encouraged by her own father to wait for the untrustworthy priest; see Keene, 237–52.

55. The story of Priest Chingen, "An Evil Woman of the Muro District of Kii Province," in the *Dainihonkoku hokekyōkenki* (or *Hokkegenki*, ca. 1040–43) is the earliest surviving version of the Dōjōji legend; see Dykstra, 145–46. In the version in *Tales of Times Now Past*, the widow must first die before being transformed into a snake. In this guise she pursues the monk, who escapes into the bell. She then wraps herself around the bell and reduces him to ashes (Ury, 94–95).

56. In Mishima's modern Nō play *Dōjōji*, an aggressive female dancer enters the bell-equivalent of a wardrobe in pursuit of the lover who spurned her and in search of her sexual identity.

57. In the classic Nō play *Dōjōji*, the dancer, between striking the bell with her fan and leaping inside, strikes off her court hat (*eboshi*) with the fan, thereby shedding her male disguise.

58. For an analysis of female transformations into serpents, with special attention to the Dōjōji legend, see Lillywhite and Yamamoto, 142–51. The authors note not only the phallic shape of serpents but also their symbolic capacity for rebirth, as implied in the shedding of their skin (149).

59. It is no accident that *shirabyōshi* are prominent in Nō plays about women who have not been treated as men's equals; see, e.g., the plays *Yoshino Shizuka*, *Futari Shizuka*, and *Giō*.

60. Yoko McClain interprets the end of Enchi's story as meaning that "the spirit of the dead man" lives in both men and women: "Watching these men, *watashi* feels a tremor within her from the fresh consciousness that her long-lost sexual impulse is still alive in her body even after years of dry widowhood" (37).

61. Van C. Gessel has noted that "one of Enchi's greatest virtues is her ability to portray women who are trapped within the social structures created by men but who are able to dig down within themselves and find resources of great vitality, strength, passion, revenge—a flowing river of potential that has resisted and overcome whatever restrictions may have been placed upon them in the external world" ("Echoes of Feminine Sensibility," 412).

62. Masao Miyoshi passes harsh judgment on Enchi when he argues that she is "not an articulate strategist for feminism, nor is she an intellectual speculator on social history. She is thus finally incomplete, inasmuch as she refuses to confront the material historicity of contemporary Japan, taking refuge instead in erotic daydreaming and unresolved discomfiture located in a transcendental personalism and aesthetic culturalism" (209–10). Various Enchi studies, however, have shown Enchi to be a supremely skilled writer who not only works within a tradition created by both male and female writers, but also creates new literary forms that engage contemporary gender issues.

Works Cited

Andō Kōsei. *Nippon no miira.* Tokyo: Mainichi shinbunsha, 1961.

Bargen, Doris G. "The Problem of Incest in *The Tale of Genji.*" In *Approaches to Teaching Murasaki Shikibu's "The Tale of Genji,"* ed. Edward Kamens. New York: MLA, 1993, 115–23.

———. "Twin Blossoms on a Single Branch: The Cycle of Retribution in *Onnamen.*" *Monumenta Nipponica* 46, no. 2 (Summer 1991): 147–71.

Bialock, David T. "Voice, Text, and the Question of Poetic Borrowing in Late Classical Japanese Poetry." *Harvard Journal of Asiatic Studies* 54, no. 1 (June 1994): 181–231.

Birnbaum, Phyllis. "Introduction" to "A Bond for Two Lifetimes—Gleanings," by Enchi Fumiko. In Birnbaum, *Rabbits, Crabs, Etc.,* 25–26.

Birnbaum, Phyllis, trans. *Rabbits, Crabs, Etc.* Honolulu: University of Hawaii Press, 1982.

Blacker, Carmen. *The Catalpa Bow: A Study of Shamanistic Practices in Japan.* 1975; reprinted—London: Allen & Unwin, 1986.

Borgen, Robert. "The Case of the Plagiaristic Journal: A Curious Passage from Jōjin's Diary." In *New Leaves: Studies and Translations of Japanese Literature in Honor of Edward Seidensticker,* ed. Aileen Gatten and Anthony Hood Chambers. Ann Arbor: University of Michigan, Center for Japanese Studies, 1993, 63–88.

Carpenter, Juliet Winters. "Enchi Fumiko: 'A Writer of Tales.'" *Japan Quarterly* 37, no. 3 (July–Sept. 1990): 343–55.

Chambers, Anthony H. "A Study of Tanizaki's *Shōshō Shigemoto no haha.*" *Harvard Journal of Asiatic Studies* 38, no. 2 (Dec. 1978): 357–79.

D'Auria, Sue, Peter Lacovara, Catharine H. Roehrig, eds. *Mummies & Magic: The Funerary Arts of Ancient Egypt.* Boston: Museum of Fine Arts, 1988.

Dōjōji. In Keene, 237–52.

Dykstra, Yoshiko Kurata. *Miraculous Tales of the Lotus Sutra from Ancient Japan: The "Dainihonkoku hokekyōkenki" of Priest Chingen.* Hirakata: Kansai University of Foreign Studies, 1983.

Ebersole, Gary L. *Ritual Poetry and the Politics of Death in Early Japan.* Princeton: Princeton University Press, 1989.

Enchi Fumiko. "A Bond for Two Lifetimes—Gleanings" ("Nise no en—shūi"). In Birnbaum, *Rabbits, Crabs, Etc.,* 25–47.

———. "Enchantress" ("Yō"). Trans. John Bester. In *Modern Japanese Short Stories,* trans. and ed. Edward G. Seidensticker, John Bester, and Ivan Morris. 1961; rev. ed.—Tokyo: Japan Publications, 1970, 72–93.

———. *Enchi Fumiko zenshū.* 14 vols. Tokyo: Shinchōsha, 1977–78.

———. "Love in Two Lives: The Remnant" ("Nise no en—shūi"). In *Japanese Women Writers: Twentieth-Century Short Fiction,* trans. and ed. Noriko Mizuta Lippit and Kyoko Iriye Selden. Armonk, N.Y.: M. E. Sharpe, 1991, 97–111.

————. *Masks* ("Onna men"). Trans. Juliet Winters Carpenter. New York: Alfred A. Knopf, 1983.

————. *Namamiko monogatari*. In *Enchi Fumiko zenshū*, 13: 115–214.

————. "Nise no en—shūi." In *Enchi Fumiko zenshū*, 2: 329–42.

————. "Otoko no hone." In *Enchi Fumiko zenshū*, 2: 278–86.

————. "Saimu." In *Enchi Fumiko zenshū*, 13: 215–414.

————. "Skeletons of Men" ("Otoko no hone"). Trans. Susan Matisoff. *Japan Quarterly* 35, no. 4 (Oct.–Dec. 1988): 417–26.

————. "Yō." In *Enchi Fumiko zenshū*, 2: 287–302.

Enchi Fumiko, Kubota Mantarō, Funabashi Seiichi, trans. *Ugetsu monogatari, Ukiyodoko, Harusame monogatari, Shunshoku umegoyomi*. Nihon koten bunko 20. Kawade shobō shinsha, 1988.

Gessel, Van C. "Echoes of Feminine Sensibility in Literature." *Japan Quarterly* 35, no. 4 (Oct.–Dec. 1988): 410–16.

————. "The 'Medium' of Fiction: Fumiko Enchi as Narrator." *World Literature Today: A Literary Quarterly* 62, no. 3 (Summer 1988): 380–85.

Hori Ichirō. "Self-Mummified Buddhas in Japan: An Aspect of the Shugen-dō ('Mountain Asceticism') Sect." *History of Religions* 1, no. 2 (Winter 1962): 222–42.

Hulvey, S. Yumiko. "Conjuring up the Past: The Enigmatic Oeuvre of Enchi Fumiko (1905–1986)." Unpublished paper, presented at the Convention of the Modern Language Association, New York, Dec. 30, 1992.

Jackman, Barry. "The Manuscripts of *Harusame Monogatari*." In Ueda, *Tales of the Spring Rain*, xix–xxiii.

Kafka, Franz. "Ein Hungerkünstler" (1922). In *Erzählungen*, ed. Max Brod. 1935; reprinted—New York: Schocken Books, 1946, 255–68.

Kamei Hideo. "Koten shakkei: *Nise no en—shūi* no baai." In Kamei and Ogasawara, 113–34.

————. "Onna to otoko aruiwa sei to kenryoku no kyokuchi." In Kamei and Ogasawara, 134–57.

Kamei Hideo and Ogasawara Yoshiko. *Enchi Fumiko no sekai*. Tokyo: Sōrinsha, 1981.

Keene, Donald, ed. *20 Plays of the Nō Theatre*. New York: Columbia University Press, 1970.

Klein, Susan Blakeley. "When the Moon Strikes the Bell: Desire and Enlightenment in the Noh Play *Dōjōji*." *Journal of Japanese Studies* 17, no. 2 (Summer 1991): 291–321.

Kōno Taeko. *Miira tori ryōki-tan*. Tokyo: Shinchōsha, 1990.

Lillywhite, Jamie, and Akira Y. Yamamoto. "Snakes, Serpents, and Humans." In *Japanese Ghosts & Demons: Art of the Supernatural*, ed. Stephen Addiss. New York: George Braziller in association with the Spencer Museum of Art, University of Kansas, 1985, 139–53.

Maraini, Fosco. Review of *Il corpo e il paradiso: esperienze ascetiche in Asia Orientale*, by Massimo Raveri. *Monumenta Nipponica* 48, no. 2 (Summer 1993): 276–78.

Marra, Michele. "The Buddhist Mythmaking of Defilement: Sacred Courtesans in Medieval Japan." *Journal of Asian Studies* 52, no. 1 (Feb. 1993): 49–65.

McClain, Yoko. "Eroticism and the Writings of Enchi Fumiko." *Journal of the Association of Teachers of Japanese* 15, no. 1 (Apr. 1980): 32–46.

McCullough, Helen Craig, trans. *The Tale of the Heike*. Stanford: Stanford University Press, 1988.

Mishima Yukio. *Dōjōji*. In idem, *Death in Midsummer and Other Stories*. New York: New Directions, 1966, 119–38.

———. "Gendai no bungaku" (Apr. 1964). Cited in Enchi, *Enchi Fumiko zenshū*, 2: 391.

Miyoshi, Masao. *Off Center: Power and Culture Between Japan and the United States*. Cambridge, Mass.: Harvard University Press, 1991.

Murasaki Shikibu. *The Tale of Genji*. Trans. Edward G. Seidensticker. New York: Knopf, 1976.

Nakamura Yukihiko, ed. *Ueda Akinari shū*. Nihon koten bungaku taikei 56. Tokyo: Iwanami shoten, 1959.

Nakamura Yukihiko, Takada Mamoru, Nakamura Hiroyasu, eds. *Hanabusa sōshi, Nishiyama monogatari, Ugetsu monogatari, Harusame monogatari*. Nihon koten bungaku zenshū 48. Tokyo: Shōgakkan, 1973.

Nihon miira kenkyū gurūpu, comp. *Nihon miira no kenkyū*. 1969.

Pekarik, Andrew J. *Japanese Lacquer, 1600–1900: Selections from the Charles A. Greenfield Collection*. New York: Metropolitan Museum of Art, 1980.

Pounds, Wayne. "Enchi Fumiko and the Hidden Energy of the Supernatural." *Journal of the Association of Teachers of Japanese* 24, no. 2 (Nov. 1990): 167–83.

Rieger, Naoko Alisa. *Enchi Fumiko's Literature: The Portrait of Women in Enchi Fumiko's Selected Works*. Mitteilungen der Gesellschaft für Natur- und Völkerkunde Ostasiens, vol. 103. Hamburg: MOAG, 1986.

Sakurai Kiyohiko and Ogata Tamotsu. "Japanese Mummies." Trans. R. Freeman. In *Mummies, Disease, and Ancient Cultures*, ed. Aidan Cockburn and Eve Cockburn. 1980; abridged ed.— Cambridge, Eng.: Cambridge University Press, 1983, 211–23.

Schalow, Paul Gordon. "Introduction" to *The Great Mirror of Male Love*, by Ihara Saikaku. Stanford: Stanford University Press, 1990, 1–46.

Sharf, Robert H. "The Idolization of Enlightenment: On the Mummification of Ch'an Masters in Medieval China." *History of Religions* 32, no. 1 (1992): 1–31.

Shigematsu Yasuo and Miyazaki Takahiro. " 'Nise no en—shūi' o megutte." *Kokubungaku: kaishaku to kanshō* 32 (Feb. 1967): 97–102.

Skord, Virginia. "Introduction" to "The Tale of Dōjōji." *Tales of Tears and Laughter: Short Fiction of Medieval Japan*. Trans. Virginia Skord. Honolulu: University of Hawaii Press, 1991, 129–30.

Sodekawa, Hiromi. "Enchi Fumiko: A Study in the Self-expression of Women." M.A. thesis, University of British Columbia, 1988.

Tanizaki Jun'ichirō. *Some Prefer Nettles*. Trans. Edward G. Seidensticker. 1955; reprinted—New York: Putnam's Perigee, 1981.

Terasaki, Etsuko. "Is the Courtesan of Eguchi a Buddhist Metaphorical Woman? A Feminist Reading of a Nō Play in the Japanese Medieval Theater." *Women's Studies* 21 (1992): 431–56.

Ueda Akinari. "Aozukin." In Nakamura, 122–31; in Nakamura et al., 441–53.

———. "The Blue Hood" ("Aozukin"). In idem, *Ugetsu monogatari: Tales of Moonlight and Rain*, 185–94.

———. "The Destiny That Spanned Two Lifetimes" ("Nise no en"). In idem, *Tales of the Spring Rain*, 73–79.

———. "Nise no en." In Nakamura, 170–75; in Nakamura et al., 511–17.

———. *Tales of the Spring Rain: Harusame Monogatari*. Trans. Barry Jackman. Tokyo: University of Tokyo Press, 1975.

———. *Ugetsu monogatari: Tales of Moonlight and Rain*. Trans. Leon Zolbrod. Vancouver: University of British Columbia Press, 1974.

Ury, Marian, trans. *Tales of Times Now Past: Sixty-Two Stories from a Medieval Japanese Collection*. Berkeley: University of California Press, 1979.

Washburn, Dennis. "Ghostwriters and Literary Haunts: Subordinating Ethics to Art in *Ugetsu Monogatari*." *Monumenta Nipponica* 45, no. 1 (Spring 1990): 39–74.

Yampolsky, Philip B. trans. *The Zen Master Hakuin: Selected Writings*. New York: Columbia University Press, 1971.

Young, Blake Morgan. *Ueda Akinari*. Vancouver: University of British Columbia Press, 1982.

6

The Quest for *Jouissance*
in Takahashi Takako's Texts

MARYELLEN TOMAN MORI

When Takahashi Takako's surrealistic tales first began appearing in Japanese literary magazines in the late 1960's, they captured attention for their shocking subject matter as well as for their stylistic elegance. By the 1970's Takahashi was enjoying a successful career as a fiction writer; in the mid-1980's she abandoned such worldly pursuits to lead a contemplative life. This shift in direction is not surprising in view of the spiritual sensibility that informs her fiction, for a mystical vein runs through even her most macabre stories.[1]

The influence of Western literature and culture on Takahashi's writing can hardly be overestimated. As a student at Kyoto University, she majored in French literature, writing her senior thesis on Charles Baudelaire. She went on to complete a master's degree with a thesis on the novelist François Mauriac. During this time, she became intrigued by psychoanalytical theories of the subconscious, Christian concepts of the supernatural, and literary theories of the fantastic; naturally, she was attracted to aesthetic representations of intrusions of the irrational or "demonic" into everyday life. In numerous essays she has revealed how her study of French literature nurtured her taste for the uncanny and perverse and led her to infuse elements from such diverse literary currents as *fin de siècle* decadence, Christianity, and surrealism into her own fiction. In "Furansu bungaku to watakushi" (French literature and myself; 1980), she writes:

I became acquainted with Christianity through Baudelaire's diaboli-
cal world. . . . What attracted me to Christian literature was its vivid
depictions of demonic things rather than its evocations of divinity.
Because human beings dwell amid the former.

I liked the Marquis de Sade for the same reason. The more lurid,
grotesque, or frightening something was, the more powerfully it
drew me. . . .

After immersing myself in Christian literature for some time, I
became sick of it and set it aside. I then became keenly interested in
surrealism. . . . There is another reality that is different but not separate from our so-called reality and that is constantly invading it and
mingling with it; as I read André Breton's works, I came to experience this, not just accept it as a theory. . . .

After studying surrealism thoroughly, when I again turned to
Christianity, what had baffled me before made perfect sense. The
two had fused within me. . . . I have recently realized that what I had
been seeking all along was release into an "inner world." (90–93)

While an undergraduate Takako met her future husband, Takahashi Kazumi (1931–71), a student of Chinese literature who later became a highly reputed writer of philosophical novels. She was captivated by Kazumi's ascetic good looks, in which she perceived an
exquisite blend of genius, fragility, and otherworldliness; this constellation of traits is discernible in the ethereal, "divine boy" archetype on which many of her male fictional characters are modeled. The
couple was married in 1954, the year of Takako's university graduation.

In her memoir of their life together, Takako depicts her husband
as hypersensitive, self-absorbed, and inept at handling practical affairs. Ironically, such qualities must have contributed to the transcendent aura that she found so appealing about him. Moreover, Kazumi's reclusiveness and passivity seem to have fostered Takako's
assertiveness and her self-image as a dominant woman. She remarks,
"My husband had an extremely feminine nature; I, on the other hand,
have a masculine disposition" (*Takahashi Kazumi no omoide*, 51).[2]

Takahashi's literature, although not written from an explicitly
feminist perspective, shares considerable common ground with feminist literature written in the 1970's and 1980's, both in Japan and the
West. Like most feminist fiction, her stories usually revolve around
alienated female protagonists who oppose patriarchal society's values
and its prescriptions for women's lives. These protagonists resent or
reject marriage, reproduction, and child rearing, because they entail

women's subordination to men and their confinement within the domestic sphere. They envision alternative selves through dreams, fantasies, and madness, or they create alternative worlds by adopting countercultural lifestyles.

However, Takahashi's fiction resists classification with feminist literature of its era that reflects the essentialist, moralistic, and anti-male tendencies within the feminist movement. Much feminist literature glorifies female solidarity, female sexuality, and feminine values and virtues, and thereby naively reifies the "eternal feminine" and the autonomous female self. Its heroines often reject heterosexual relationships altogether as stifling or destructive, and they turn to alliances with women or solitary creative or spiritual practices for personal growth and fulfillment. They denounce hierarchical relationships and violence in all forms. Takahashi's literature challenges this polarized outlook. Rather than celebrating femininity, her stories deconstruct stereotypes of female nature and desire, and thereby unsettle gender categories themselves. They debunk myths of women's innate disposition to such traditional feminine virtues as maternal feeling, empathy, sexual passivity, and nonviolence. Many of Takahashi's heroines are prevented from developing a sense of affinity with other women by their contempt for most women's uncritical acceptance of social norms. Far from rejecting men, they mine the emancipatory potential of unconventional heterosexual relationships. They view eros and death as inextricable, and violent or transgressive acts as means of inducing illumination.

Much of Takahashi's fiction portrays a woman's obsessive pursuit of ecstatic experience; even the most nihilistic of Takahashi's antiheroines seems to harbor a dim vision of a transfigured world. In this respect, Takahashi's literature resonates with that of Kōno Taeko (1926–), whose stories about freethinking, sexually adventurous women similarly defy categorization; Kōno's typical female characters, like Takahashi's, totally reject conventional domestic life and the traditional feminine ideal, yet deviate from feminist values in their revulsion toward girls, the female body, and motherhood, their glorification of the charms and revitalizing power of boys, or their taste for sadomasochistic sexual practices.[3] The common thread in both women's fiction, which produces remarkable similarities in their plots and their characters' predilections, is the search for sexual transport and spiritual rejuvenation. Both Takahashi's and Kōno's stories record women's quest for *jouissance*, often through sadistic violence or masochistic self-shattering.

♋

This essay explores several representations of *jouissance* in Taka-hashi Takako's fiction. By *jouissance* I mean to suggest a rapturous, disorienting sensation of self-dissolution.[4] Takahashi's fiction prob-lematizes myths of the individual self and stable gender identity, and challenges socially constructed binary categories of all kinds, by de-picting women who experience a collapse of boundaries between self and other, or between male and female gender roles, an inversion or merging of other normally separate roles, or an overturuning of value hierarchies. The theme of violating social codes of meaning and iden-tity is reinforced on the texts' structural level by such narrative devices as logical contradiction, temporal distortion, mirroring, metamorpho-sis, the splitting of supposedly single identities, and the conflation of supposedly separate identities. Takahashi's stories make extensive use of paradox, oxymoron, and ambiguity, and they shift between re-alistic and surrealistic modes of narration. The essay discusses the techniques used in two of Takahashi's stories to dissolve gender and individual identity and thereby to convey the exhilarating experience of self-rupture that French theorist Julia Kristeva describes as an influx of "semiotic energy," or *jouissance*, into the symbolic order.[5]

Kristeva's theory of the interaction between the semiotic and the symbolic processes in the psyche, language, and society provides a useful paradigm for unveiling and interpreting the deconstructive dynamic at work in much of Takahashi's literature. According to Kristeva's complex theory, the semiotic and the symbolic are two in-terrelated psychic registers, somewhat analogous to Freud's distinc-tions between id and ego, or unconscious and conscious processes. The semiotic refers to the chaotic flow of drives experienced by the infant, to whom self and other are not yet distinguishable; this psychic stage is characterized by prelinguistic consciousness, polymorphous sexuality, and perception of the mother as bisexual and omnipotent. As this diffuse drive energy becomes organized, the child becomes conscious of its separateness, acquires language, represses the semi-otic, and functions as a unified, gendered subject.

The domination of the semiotic mode by the symbolic order is tenuous, however; the individual's coherent identity is a thin veneer. In moments of "madness, holiness, and poetry" (Kristeva, "Pratique signifiante et mode de production," 12), the semiotic transgresses its boundaries, causing a breakdown of individual or sexual identity, logical meaning, or social order. The flow of the semiotic into the symbolic order may be experienced by the subject as *jouissance*, a diffuse sense of bliss produced by an explosion of meaning and identity. Because *jouissance* exposes the "abject"—what has been repressed from consciousness and excluded from cultural or linguistic representation—and subverts the unified subject or the cultural order, it is linked with the death drive rather than the pleasure principle. Whereas pleasure reinforces the subject's culturally constructed identity, *jouissance* threatens to unravel that identity.[6]

In Takahashi's writings, the *jouissance* of dissolving the autonomous self is often depicted as resulting from a collapse of traditional gender distinctions. According to Kristeva's theory, only men are capable of directly transgressing the symbolic order, since one must be securely positioned within that order to be able to transgress it.[7] Consistent with this view, women in Takahashi's stories often rely upon a "self-sacrificing" male to mediate their experience of *jouissance*. Such stories revolve around a complete reversal of gender roles. They portray a woman who usurps the male role in her relationship with a man and assists in his symbolic castration, or "phallic divestiture": the renunciation of male social status and sexual role, and alignment with the traditional female subject position.[8] Phallic divestiture is a strategy the woman deploys to bring about the temporary submersion of the patriarchal symbolic order in the maternal semiotic. The remainder of this essay will examine the role of the male intermediary in "the *jouissance* of the woman"[9] in two works by Takahashi. It will elucidate the pattern of phallic divestiture in three different passages from these stories and show how the transgression of gender identity facilitates "self-divestiture," the dissolution of individual identity.

Takahashi's novella "Higi" (Secret rituals; 1978) and the novel *Yomigaeri no ie* (The house of rebirth; 1980) are two of many works by the author in which phallic divestiture is a prominent motif.[10] Both reveal Takahashi's fascination with the idea of a dominant older woman's multifaceted liaison with a beautiful adolescent boy.[11] The relationship does not conform to any one socially sanctioned paradigm, but cuts across the borders of several relationship models designated as mutually exclusive; it is a taboo hybrid that makes visible the culturally nameless or abject. The pair are twins of a sort; they mirror each other in various respects, and they enjoy a wordless emotional rapport. The woman serves as both mother surrogate and erotic

partner to the youth, and thus their relationship takes on an incestuous coloring. Not only does the woman breach the sacrosanct boundary between the roles of consort and mother, but she shifts easily between benign and malefic manifestations of these roles; she is both
affectionate companion and dominatrix, castrator and nurturer, sor-
ceress and goddess of wisdom. The woman acts as the youth's erotic
and spiritual guide to "a *jouissance* beyond the phallus,"[12] leading him
on a dark descent through an underworld of deviant behavior and
bizarre occult practices in quest of sexual and spiritual liberation. She
encourages him to refuse the power and status to which his male sex
entitles him. She nurtures his feminine tendencies and antisocial impulses on the grounds that renouncing normative masculinity and
bourgeois respectability is a prerequisite and means to ecstatic experience.

The doll-like youth in each of these stories (who is cast in the
same mold as Tamao in Takahashi's best-known story, "Ningyō ai,"
Doll love; 1976),[13] is physically delicate and mentally malleable, a
tabula rasa on which the woman can inscribe her designs and perform
her experiments. His effeminacy gives their relationship a vaguely
homoerotic cast, and at the same time it encourages a gender role reversal. With the compliant male as partner, the woman can explore
the masculine role and indulge her considerable appetite for power.
Each person enables the other's cross-gender qualities to emerge
fully.

Both "Secret Rituals" and *The House of Rebirth* are parable-like
tales that thematize the pursuit of *jouissance* by mysterious middle-
aged women whose passive young lovers serve as mediums and sacrificial victims in esoteric rituals created and conducted by the
women-priests. These rituals form the nucleus of dramatic scenarios
that fuse mysticism with sadomasochistic eroticism. The rites incorporate various sexual and occult techniques intended to induce in the
youths, and through them in their tender dominatrixes, an exuberant
sense of self-loss and expanded consciousness. In "Secret Rituals," a
ceremony that evokes dismemberment and death yokes the horror of
castration with the ecstasy of escape from the prison of gender codes.
In *The House of Rebirth*, cross-dressing, hypnotic regression to infancy,
and immersion in water are highlights of a ritual that symbolically
enacts the rupture of the symbolic order, the reversal of the socialization process, and rejuvenation through a plunge into the semiotic. In
"Osanai otoko" (A young man), a short story within the novel *The*

House of Rebirth, a rite revolving around an unusual autoerotic act produces first nirvana-like bliss, then physical disintegration.

In each story the youth's surrender to the woman's will brings about his own release from the burdens of masculinity, adult sexuality, and individual selfhood, and at the same time it enables the woman to experience, through the boy's mediation, the bliss of self-surrender. During these ceremonies the participants in a sense reverse positions, the victim-initiate emerging from his ordeal as an emancipated "savior" who temporarily liberates the priest from her isolated position of mastery. The woman's loving identification with her male victim reconciles her yearning for the *jouissance* of self-loss with her refusal of the traditional feminine-masochistic role.

In "Secret Rituals," the female protagonist and first-person narrator is a reclusive woman in her late thirties, and her lover and soul mate, Sumiyo, is an androgynous young adolescent of "pale, wax-like" beauty, with an uncanny physical resemblance to her. Several years before the events of the story occur, the woman suffered a mental breakdown that led to her awareness of a luminous inner world of dreams. Since then, she has adopted the theosophical view that the everyday world is a pale reflection of a rich subconscious reality. She and the boy devote themselves to developing bizarre and sometimes risky techniques of temporarily stripping off the "false" physical or social self in order to gain access to this inner world.

One day the woman is inspired to have life-size wax replicas of Sumiyo's various body parts made in the form of candles. She and the boy visit a wax-doll maker's shop. When she makes her request, the man pointedly inquires, "So you want to dismember him?" The woman replies, "Our purpose is deliverance, not dismemberment."

The vivid account of the couple's eerie nocturnal experiment is a focal point of the narrative. The woman places the candles here and there around the room, turns off the lights, and lights the candles. Then she begins a hypnotic incantation, lulling Sumiyo into a trance:

> "See, there's a flame coming out of your head. Become one with that head. Become one with the flaming arms, legs, torso . . . . Once you've done that, feel your entire body in flames. Can you feel the fire entering your body from some deep, distant place?"
>
> "Mmmm." Sumiyo's reply was like a sigh.
>
> "What we're doing has set your body on fire. Abandon your body to the fire. It's just like the last time. Our purpose is to abandon our bodies. . . ."

Sumiyo's head, his two arms, his two legs, his torso, were all burning in the darkness. His face was unusually radiant; it glowed with the rapture inside him. But his arms, legs, and torso were even eerier. I took up his right leg and said, "Here is the leg you shed."

Even after Sumiyo had shed it, his leg burned more and more vigorously and was scorching to the touch. The thick knee bone protruded from the meager flesh. I slid my hand up. The thigh was very tender. The leg was cut off there, so my hand slid down again. I stroked the shin; for a man it had very little hair. When I reached the foot, I nestled the lean, smooth instep in the palm of my hand and squeezed the small toes, lined up like white teeth.

"Here is the torso you shed," I said and took up the torso. The chest, stomach, and shoulders were all so smooth that it nearly slipped from my grasp. The navel was deeply recessed and its flesh coiled around tightly; something about it resembled Sumiyo's face. Apparently the wax craftsman had felt reticent; the male organ was missing. The girlishly smooth place was all the more deeply erotic. I caressed that hollow, and I stroked the cleft in the buttocks over and over, as if I were examining it. Even the anus was there.

"Sumiyo, where are you?" I asked.

Sumiyo's head, right arm, left arm, right leg, left leg, torso, each had a large flame spurting up from its wick. The gleam at the center of that light was especially intense; there the cusp of the other world was visible. Actually, we had already entered deep into that world.

"I'm here," replied Sumiyo.

"I shed my body when you did," I said.

"Where are you?" Sumiyo asked this time.

"Our bodies are still together. But I've penetrated deep inside."

"We're making love!" declared Sumiyo.

"That's not the point. That's what our bodies are doing."

"I get it! Now I get it!" Sumiyo cried.

"Well, here we part company."

"Why?"

"I told you once, didn't I? It's like diving into water. To penetrate the boundary of the body and plunge down into it is something one does alone. But way down below we can meet. We're separated by the boundaries of our bodies, but down below we can meet each other directly. Because we've shed our bodies. . . . Well, be brave, Sumiyo." My voice faded into the distance.

The next day all that remained of Sumiyo's head, arms, legs and torso were grossly distorted shapes. Their original forms were beyond recognition. ("Higi," 129–33)

Like "Secret Rituals," *The House of Rebirth* depicts the strange relationship between a morbidly intense middle-aged woman and her moody, ethereal teenage lover. The protagonist, again the first-person narrator, describes her purpose in life as "scooping up" the "lush darkness swirling inside me." (The image evokes Kristeva's notion of the revolutionary subject as one who risks psychosis to release the flow of *jouissance* into conscious life.) The boy, whom she calls Yukiyo, is her disciple and accomplice in this perilous undertaking; in fact, she regards his medium-like receptivity as essential to her experiments in altering consciousness.

Whenever the youth visits her, the woman's home becomes a numinous enclave, a separate world where social codes and scientific laws are suspended. In accordance with her role as surrogate mother, the woman gives the youth a new name, which she insists he use when visiting her: Yukiyo, "snow creature." She calls her house "the house of scorpions," suggesting of course her potentially lethal nature.

The woman fosters the youth's interest in occult practices and instills in him her views on the worthlessness of conventional life and intellectual understanding. She persuades him that recovering one's "archetypal self" requires shedding one's social persona and systematically exploring forbidden territory. She nurtures his deviant inclinations so as to undo the repressive effects of cultural conditioning. One evening she attempts what she calls an "unusually elaborate ritual":

> I brought out some of my accessories. I removed Yukiyo's pajamas and began adorning his naked body. I remained fully dressed. Yukiyo yielded without a bit of resistance. He was always like that.
>
> First I fastened a bracelet on Yukiyo's left arm. . . . It clinched the slender white limb like a manacle. Next I wound a blood-red coral necklace around his neck. His long fine hair became entangled in it. The prickly coral thorns seemed to torment the soft skin around his neck. . . . Finally, I wrapped a belt woven from navy and crimson silks around his wasp-like waist. One might say I had taken Yukiyo captive.
>
> Yukiyo himself did not utter a word; his breath was still; he had become like a warm doll. The more aroused he was, the more inert he became. And he became receptive.
>
> I continued to murmur. "You feel life's darkness, don't you? You must become completely naked. Not physically naked, but naked in your whole being. Life's darkness is opening its maw. There's no longer anything to hold on to. Letting go feels delightful. Nothing else feels so delightful. A woman like your mother is beckoning, beckoning the real Yukiyo to emerge from deep inside you. You feel

that happening, don't you? That Yukiyo will become one with you. You'll become the self you've forgotten. I'll become the self I've forgotten too. That's the kind of relationship we have. I'll take off my 'self' and you'll take off your 'self,' just as if we were shedding our clothing. And we'll remember that this is who we were long ago. Once you realize that, you'll be able to be Yukiyo in your ordinary life. . . . The things people tell you at home and at school will begin to seem meaningless. . . ."

I turned on the bath water. As I stood watching the water fill the tub, a scene took shape in my mind. Guided by that vision, I led in the dozing Yukiyo. . . . I immersed him in the water. . . .

I knelt down on the bathroom floor, rested my left elbow on the edge of the tub and stretched out my right arm. Then I began slowly stroking the bare white shoulders and neck beneath the water. Yukiyo's eyes were open wide but his breathing was shallow, and he was completely still. Serenity suffused the room, mingling with Yukiyo's silence. As perfectly passive as ever, Yukiyo surrendered to my caresses. . . .

"You're the epitome of Yukiyo," I said.

"This is bliss," murmured Yukiyo in a languid voice, more to himself than to me.

My hand slipped over the transparent water, Yukiyo's skin, the various accessories. Inside and outside had grown perfectly silent, and in the fullness of the moment, the world around us seemed to have vanished. Since evening I had felt released from human identity; I couldn't even remember who I was. . . .

"I'll leave you alone now," I said and left the bathroom.

There was a voice behind me. I hurried back to the bathroom to find Yukiyo crying in a loud voice, tears streaming down. . . . I stood dumbfounded at the threshold. It seemed as though his wailing was coming from within me, awakening more and more of my memories. That voice was bringing something inside me into vivid focus. But what that was, I could not say.

"This is bliss," I murmured to myself. Those were the words that best expressed my mood at that moment.

Yukiyo had become so attached to those accessories that he insisted on sleeping in them.

The next morning when he awoke there were red marks on his left arm, around his neck, his middle finger, his ankle, his waist. Since his skin was far softer and more sensitive than the average person's, the imprints were as vivid as if they had been stamped on indelibly. I was pleased with those marks. (*Yomigaeri no ie*, 58–63)

"Secret Rituals" and *The House of Rebirth* are based on their female protagonists' fantasy of assuming status as a full-fledged subject within the symbolic order and then escaping that order and re-entering the primal flow of the semiotic. The scenes cited above may be read as attempts to represent the *jouissance* that is released by the subversion of gender identity and self-identity.

In both stories, a major device for unsettling gender categories is the characters' reversal of conventional gender and sexual roles; in every aspect of their relationship, the woman is dominant, the man submissive. The ritual scenes focus the reader's attention on this pattern of reversal, because the rituals themselves symbolically enact the disruption of gender codes and the blurring of sexual difference, and they valorize these transgressions as means for inducing ecstatic states.

As the older, more experienced, and more aggressive partner, the woman assumes the authoritative position usually occupied by the male. She plays the roles of priest and spiritual guide, and the boy is her disciple, initiate, medium, and sacrificial victim. The woman instigates all their experiments in "deviant" behavior, and she creates and conducts the rites. Throughout much of them she supervises, assists, and observes the youth's "disintegration" while she herself remains "intact" and in control. In both stories, the boy is stripped nude by the woman while she remains fully clothed (signifying not only his sexual objectification and subordination, but his abjection from the social order). In "Secret Rituals" it is the boy's body that is ritually dismembered and "sacrificed." When Sumiyo mildly protests that only icons of his body parts will be used in the ceremony, the woman reminds him of the difference in their respective statuses: "*I* am the one who will conduct the rite."

Sexually and aesthetically the woman is coded as "masculine," the youth as "feminine." Expectations created by conventional gender-based norms of characterization are thwarted in these texts by the attention given to the boy's physical attributes and the elision of information about the woman's body. Moreover, throughout the stories, the boy's body is described in terms ordinarily applied to women: soft, smooth, white, wax-like, luminous, delicate, slender, doll-like. His physical attributes are central to the woman's interest in him; she values him primarily for his beauty and his "feminine" character traits. The passionate woman is consistently positioned as sexual aggressor; the boy, who is virtually without desire, passively submits to her advances. During the ritual scenes, the woman caresses and stimulates the boy, while he simply offers no resistance. The woman

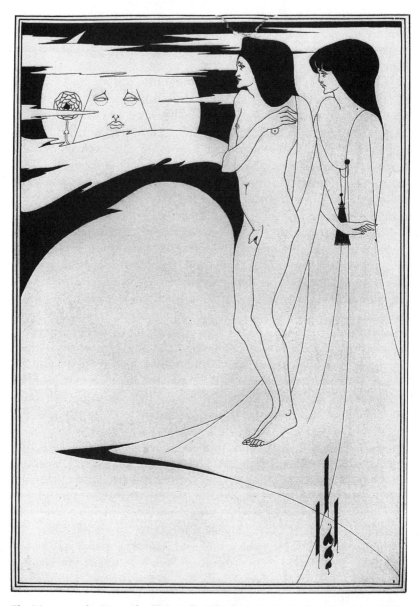

The Woman in the Moon (for "Salome"), 1894. Drawing by Audrey Beardsley (1872–1898). Reproduced by permission of the Harvard University Art Musuem, Bequest of Grenville L. Winthrop.

occupies a subject position—admiring, seducing, violating the male, who is cast as object of the female gaze and female desire; conventional erotic modes, including the dynamics of the gaze, are reversed.[14] During the rites, the boy's process of psychic transformation is correlated with his physical appearance and responses, and these are described in loving, sensual detail from the perspective of the female narrator; she records her own actions and feelings in abstract language. The texts proffer the male body to the reader's gaze, as it were, while shielding the woman's body from similar aesthetic and erotic objectification.

Cross-dressing is a feature of the gender reversal inscribed into the ritual cited from *The House of Rebirth*. Wearing the woman's accessories accentuates the boy's physical and psychological "femininity." This aspect of the ritual has sadomasochistic overtones; the woman perceives the ornaments as being painful and restrictive and compares them to torture implements, thereby emphasizing her perceptions of the boy as victim and herself as persecutor. The common association of the female with masochism and the male with sadism is thus inverted.

The woman's fantasy of abolishing gender difference by first ritualistically rectifying the traditional power imbalance between male and female is manifested in the all-pervasive theme of castration. (Castration itself is a metaphor for both the boy's psychological reversion to a state of sexual indeterminacy and his refusal of phallic authority within the social scheme.) Images of literal castration are supplemented with such obvious metonymies for castration as mutilation, dismemberment, disrobing, and disembodiment. The castration motif is overtly present in "Secret Rituals": the youth is symbolically dismembered and destroyed in the form of his wax "double." As if this symbolism were not explicit enough, the wax image lacks male genitalia, a deviation from realism that perversely heightens the doll's erotic appeal for the woman. In both stories, the woman seductively urges the youth to "shed" his body, echoing the dark romantic theme of a man's emasculation by a Delilah-like *femme fatale*.

A simple reversal of traditional gender roles that elevates the woman and relegates the man to the status of victim or slave hardly constitutes a vision of gender deconstruction; it merely substitutes one binary scheme for another. These stories, however, succeed in affirming gender fluidity because of the couple's shifting power positions. Since the stories posit self-subversion as a condition for *jouis-*

sance, during the course of the ritual performance of self-divestiture, the boy-victim subtly replaces the woman as leader and liberator, thereby undermining her authority and de-centering her role in the rite. By ritually undergoing mutilation (refusing the phallus) and relinquishing power to the woman, he enables her to inscribe herself as male within the ritual's symbolic order. Only from this position of power can she go beyond the phallic pleasure of mastery. It is the masculinized woman's masochistic identification with the castrated male that allows her to transgress the symbolic order and experience *jouissance*. This reversal is a crucial subtext of the rite described in each story. In "Secret Rituals," after joining the male in self-renunciation ("I shed my body at the same time you did"), the woman is able to "dive into the water" — to transgress the boundary between symbolic and semiotic. In *The House of Rebirth*, too, the man's "surrender" (symbolized by his gradual regression to infancy) catalyzes the woman's self-dissolution: "Since evening, I had felt released from human identity; I couldn't even remember who I was."

⌀

The subversion of gender identity in these stories is situated within the broader context of dismantling the unified self. The stories present the man's phallic divestiture and the woman's acquisition of phallic power as prerequisites for their respective experiences of the *jouissance* of self-divestiture: the collapse of individual selfhood. "Self-divestiture" resonates with both psychological and spiritual nuances. From a Kristevan perspective, it signifies the *jouissance* of boundlessness experienced by the infant or psychotic; transgressing the symbolic order means escaping the prison of isolated identity, language, gender, and genital sexuality and recovering the polymorphous eroticism of infancy. As a religious concept, it connotes "self"-renunciation, or the enlightened state of recognizing the independent self as illusory. In Takahashi's stories, the woman's quest for *jouissance* suggests the narcissistic yearning for an original condition of continuity and libidinal fluidity, as well as the mystical impulse to withdraw from the mundane world into a nirvana-like state in which desire and the personal self have been extinguished. As in the case of phallic divestiture, the symbolic unraveling of the male self is central to the ritual; the woman's experience of self-divestiture depends on the male's self-annihilation.

In "Secret Rituals" and *The House of Rebirth*, numerous narrative strategies contribute to evoking the quest for de-individuation. One is the thematization of self-deconstruction by the use of certain conventions from visionary literature. The archetypal quest pattern traces a character's process of self-divestiture through an inner or underworld journey whose "grail" is the recovery of a prior state of void or plenitude, in which distinctions between self and other do not exist. In "Secret Rituals" and *The House of Rebirth*, images of and allusions to "shedding" the false social self, regression to infancy, recollection of a mythic past, the emergence of a hitherto repressed mode of subjectivity, and descent into a netherworld where one can "encounter others directly" seem intended to evoke the atmosphere of quest-romance. The protagonists of both stories may be viewed as a female quest-hero who, in search of mystical vision, abandons conventional life, secludes herself from the world, and rejects rational thought and contemporary discourse. In Rimbaud-like fashion, she experiments with various techniques to facilitate the "dérèglement de tous les sens," including sensory deprivation, meditation, hypnotic trance, psychological regression, torture, symbolic mutilation and dismemberment, erotic stimulation, and transgressive sexual practices. During "rituals" of her creation that incorporate these practices, she experiences sensations traditionally associated with the attainment of higher states of consciousness, including loss of personal identity, a feeling of merging with others, transcendence of dualistic thinking, catharsis, and bliss.

The rituals conducted by the woman enact and celebrate the collapse of the autonomous self by inducing in their participants feelings of fusion or confusion of self with other, as well as feelings of self-destruction. In "Secret Rituals" the woman hypnotizes the boy into experiencing the wax images around him as his own dismembered body parts: "Become one with the flaming arms, legs, torso." Here, self-loss is also expressed in terms of self-destruction. The "other" with which Sumiyo is urged to identify is an object undergoing immolation. The woman tells him, "Feel your entire body in flames. . . . Abandon your body to the fire."

Imagery of euphoric self-loss also pervades the ritual incantation intoned by the woman-priest in *The House of Rebirth*. She guides Yukiyo in visualizing a dark void opening up before him and in hearing a seductive, motherly woman beckoning him to fall rapturously into that abyss. The scene evokes the *jouissance* of relinquishing one's individuality for the voluptuous darkness of the maternal womb. The woman also draws a connection between self-loss and the expansion of consciousness; she assures Yukiyo that "shedding" his "self" will give him access to a mode of being that is "far richer than your ordinary self."

In both stories, the mystical quest for release from the delusion of selfhood is represented by fantasies of physical and psychological regression. Spiritual rapture and infantile erotic pleasure are conflated. Allusions to dark rooms, inner darkness, hollows, and abysses are supplemented by other metonymies for the womb; water imagery, suggesting amniotic fluid, is used extensively. Images of immersion in a watery underworld clearly express a fantasy of re-entering the womb, one that is reinforced by the incestuous aspects of the couple's relationship.

In "Secret Rituals," ritualistic disembodiment gives the couple access to a subterranean realm where they "can encounter each other directly." The woman urges the boy to "plunge down" into his body and says it is "like diving into water." The boy's disintegration and "plunging down" into a watery environment suggest reunion with the phallic mother of infancy. In *The House of Rebirth*, the woman submerges the boy in the bathtub as part of their ritual. Caressed by the water and the priest-woman (phallic mother), Yukiyo, passive as an infant, experiences the omnipotent woman as both erotic and maternal and his own body as polymorphously perverse. In the end, the boy's weeping indicates his complete withdrawal from the symbolic order. The woman's sensation that the boy's crying is coming from within her confirms his devolution into a fetus. The pair's symbiotic fusion is represented by the woman's experience of complete tranquillity, silence, and timelessness. The borders between self and other, inner and outer, mother and lover, past and present, all collapse.

The sense of confusion or convergence of self and other, inside and outside, that the characters in these stories are said to experience is conveyed to the reader through various textual ambiguities. For example, when the woman in "Secret Rituals" strokes Sumiyo, it is not clear whether she is stroking the boy or his wax double. In both stories, the characters of the woman and the youth are not fully distinguishable from each other. The boy's thoughts and feelings are often conveyed to the reader not through dialogue but in the words of the female narrator, who claims to experience the boundary between her psyche and the boy's as permeable. In *The House of Rebirth*, the woman speaks in a nearly uninterrupted monologue. When she does ask Yukiyo about his feelings, either he remains silent and she answers for him ("I wonder if you understand. You do understand, don't you? You must understand. See how much you've understood!") or he responds but she dismisses his perception in favor of her own interpretation of it. Sometimes the woman and the boy express the same feelings in the same words. Patterns of mirroring, doubling, and echoing link the words, actions, feelings, and appearance of the two characters, causing the reader to constantly wonder whether Sumiyo and Yukiyo are intended to be independent characters or projections of the woman's imagination.

The confusion of the characters' identities is paralleled by the subversion of narrative meaning through the ambiguous use of words. Words with both literal and figurative meanings, for example, are used in a way that makes it impossible to know in which sense they are intended. The contradictory nuances of the word "fire," for instance, come into play when the woman in "Secret Rituals" speaks of "feeling the fire," "abandoning the body to the fire," and the body being "on fire." These expressions have connotations of both orgasmic bliss and the extinction of desire. Whether the woman is using them to ignite the boy's sexual desire or to assist him in extinguishing carnal passion (by conjuring up the image of his body's destruction) is left unclear. (Although the words of the rite link emancipation with "disembodiment," the woman's amorous behavior during the rite contradicts her speech, affirming the inseparability of erotic and spiritual ecstasy.) On the whole, language is used in these passages to subvert logic and unequivocal meanings and to create ambiguity and confusion. This is especially true of the woman's mantra-like incantations, whose predominantly imagistic, rhythmic, hypnotically repetitious language is intended to rupture discursive thought; such language mimics the enchanting but "meaningless" sound patterns of the semiotic register by seducing the reader away from rational discourse and into its sensual, nonsensical flow.

✄

The preceding discussion has explored the relationship between male "phallic divestiture" and male and female "self-divestiture" in the stories "Secret Rituals" and *The House of Rebirth*. This section will consider how the conflation of maternal love and erotic love and the inversion of the socially acceptable manifestations of these drives function as techniques of facilitating both phallic divestiture and the dissolution of the self–other distinction.

"A Young Man" is a self-contained short story embedded in *The House of Rebirth*. The novel's protagonist is inspired to write this story in tribute to her young lover, Yukiyo, and in recognition of their relationship's transformative effect on both their lives. This story within a story is one of the most powerful and revealing scenes not only of this novel but of Takahashi's entire oeuvre. The following is an abridged version of the tale:

A woman was living with a young man. The young man was very docile. Except in one respect. He said he disliked bodies. He himself had an unusually beautiful body, but he was quite indifferent to it, and he loathed other people's bodies, especially women's. Yet he responded to female nudes portrayed in paintings with the discerning eye of a connoisseur. In short, he despised raw flesh and he loathed physical contact. . . .

One day the woman said, "You can't settle the matter simply by saying you have no desire. You're still young, but there's your future to consider. So let me teach you a good method." Without further ado, the woman told the young man to take off all his clothes. The young man immediately did as he was told, as if he were perfectly used to being nude. The woman was always amazed at his compliance. . . .

When the young man was completely naked and lying face up on the bed, light seemed to radiate from the whiteness of his skin. . . . The creature who lay before her had a sexless translucence that made his body seem neither quite male nor female.

That day the woman taught the young man a technique that did not require a woman's involvement. It was not something described in any book. It was the woman's invention.

At first it was rather difficult. Although the young man had remarkably supple limbs, he could not yet curl himself up until his spine formed an arc. The woman stood by the bed and did her best to help the youth raise his head and feet and bring his mouth to his groin. "Do you see? You'll be able to do it with your own mouth. Then throughout your life, even if you're alone, you'll be able to satisfy yourself."

Since the young man was intelligent, he completely understood what the woman had in mind. And he began to enjoy this practice. But he never enjoyed himself to the point of abandon. . . .

The woman, on the other hand, was utterly rapt. A young man who lacked desire seemed like a perfect match for a woman of limitless desire. Because a game made it possible for her to slip through a crack in everyday reality and deeply penetrate the infinite. . . .

The woman would chant, "Become round, become round," and stroke the youth's spine until it formed an arc. She did this over and over and finally, just like the acrobat who curls up into a ball and rolls along the ground, the young man was able to lithely lift his feet over his head and back so that his whole body formed a circle. Then he became able to thrust his head into the center of the circle and grasp the axis with his mouth. In other words, his two most vital parts came together.

When this happened, the youth became a more vigorous creature than he had been before. Because he had become a circle. Because he had become continuous, something like vitality or ardor started flowing through his body. It was as if the life force itself began circulating within him, and not a bit of it seeped outside.

The youth's white body glowed all the more radiantly and became delicately moist. But there was not a trace of lewdness in it; if anything, a plant-like sensuousness suffused that graceful circular shape. The woman wished that this circle were eternal, but alas, like all humans, it was ephemeral.

Perhaps because he had discovered a way of satisfying himself, the young man became increasingly indifferent to other people. But he needed the woman's help to become a circle. Because each time she stroked him while silently intoning the ritualistic words, the youth became more perfect. It was through this rite that their relationship became vital to both of them.

One day, as usual, the youth's white body formed a circle. The woman stepped back a bit and gazed at it. There was an object there, as well as a life. . . . She had a sudden impulse to roll it like a large ball. She summoned all her strength and lifted it up. . . .

The woman went out into the garden and walked over to the thicket of wild roses that grew at one side. . . . Holding the young man between her hands, she tossed him gently toward the thicket. He rolled slowly along and entered the flowers. But suddenly the white circle of flesh was mottled with blood. . . . The woman let out a cry. Already the circle was more like a mass of blood than a young man. But the shape of the sharply arched spine and the head curled inward was still faintly visible in the bloody mass.

There was a tap on her shoulder and the woman looked around. Her husband was standing there.

"Are you thinking about that again?" he asked gently.

"What do you mean?" She stared intently at him.

"Our son who died." He spoke very gingerly.

"Died, you say?" The woman continued to stare at him. . . . "You're very sweet. But eighteen years ago . . . who knows if that was a boy . . . that lump of blood. It was just the fourth month when I miscarried," the woman said. (100–107)

This story in its own right is a hauntingly lyrical tale whose tone is at once mythic and quintessentially decadent. In the context of the novel, it is a poetic rendering of the relationship between the novel's protagonist and Yukiyo. The tale enriches one's understanding of the frame story because it distills the essence of Yukiyo's and the woman's personalities and clarifies the dynamics of their relationship. By literalizing certain aspects of their relationship, such as incest and violence, that are treated symbolically or ambiguously in the frame story, it brings these into focus.

In the novel it is clear that Yukiyo and the woman are not biologically related, for the youth visits her and returns to his parents' home, and the woman is single and lives alone. There is no mention of her ever being married or pregnant. Thus, the tale seems primarily to express its author's incestuous and murderous fantasies toward her young lover, whom she regards as a surrogate son, rather than a mother's grief over miscarriage. (The tale also serves an important deconstructive function in the novel, by intensifying the reader's suspicion that Yukiyo exists only in the woman's mind. Since the boy in "A Young Man" turns out to exist only in the imagination of the tale's female protagonist, the character Yukiyo, on whom that boy is modeled, is perhaps a figment of the heroine's imagination.)

The tale may also be interpreted independently of the context of the novel, as I shall do here. The reader is stunned by the ending of the tale for two reasons: it reveals the erotic partners to be mother and son, and at the same time it reveals the events of the tale to be the female character's fantasy. A married woman who suffered a miscarriage is daydreaming about what their relationship might have been like had her child been a boy. Even if we consider the story as the wish-fulfilling fantasy of a childless woman, the relationship that woman imagines having with her child is highly aberrant; the story voices female desires that would be labeled pathological or perverse by conventional standards.

The fantasy elaborated in the tale challenges and radically reshapes dominant psychosocial and literary paradigms of both the erotic relationship and the mother-child bond. It inverts male and female gender roles and psychological traits; it conflates maternal and erotic love and then reverses the normal direction of these impulses. The story presents a woman resisting assimilation into mainstream discourses on love and desire and guiding her child to do likewise.

The quasi-incestuous relationship between mother and son reinforces the motifs of phallic divestiture and self-divestiture in the tale. When a woman uses her position as mother primarily as a vehicle for expressing her erotic and destructive desires toward her child, then motherhood, an institution normally aligned with society, is transformed into an anticultural force; it becomes a means of subverting social order and thereby releasing *jouissance*.

The incest taboo is commonly viewed as the foundation of culture at large as well as the basis of the individual, gendered subject. From the child's perspective, to violate the mother-child incest taboo is literally to reclaim the maternal body and to return symbolically to psychological infancy. The incest fantasy is hence a rejection of culture in all its manifestations, including the gender hierarchy and gendered identity.[15] As a metaphor for returning to the pre-symbolic phase, mother-child incest signifies the refusal to recognize a distinction not only between legitimate and illegitimate sexual acts and alliances, but between all binary categories. Besides expressing a rejection of procreative sex and socially sanctioned sexual relationships, the incest motif is used in Takahashi's stories to convey the utopian desire to recover the infantile domain of multiple sexual possibilities. Mother-child incest represents a reversion to a sexuality preceding patriarchal law, a polymorphous state of *jouissance*.

After transgressing the border between maternal and erotic love, this mother performs an inverted version of society's definition of the "good mother": she undermines her son's socialization process by fostering his antisocial behavior, and she nurtures his psychological regression and physical disintegration rather than his growth. She defies her social mandate to develop her son's masculine assertiveness, object-love, and non-incestuous heterosexuality; instead she encourages his passivity, his distaste for all relationships, and his autoeroticism.

As in the other passages discussed, the male and female in this tale reverse gender roles. Although various features of each character's psychology, appearance, and behavior link them with the opposite gender or sex, the aspect of gender inversion highlighted here involves the characters' relative degrees of desire. The boy's lack of desire and the woman's "limitless desire" code the two as feminine and masculine, respectively. The woman assists the youth's phallic divestiture by deflecting the "faint stirrings of desire" that he feels for her and rechanneling them toward himself. She returns the boy to a state of "self-sufficiency," symbolically enacting his regression to the primary narcissistic psychic stage through a solemn ritual of shaping his body into a circle, a pose resembling the fetal position.

To be without desire is to be infantile, autoerotic, whole, "circular." Desire arises when a subject perceives itself as separate from others. To "mature," according to dominant paradigms of psychosexual normalcy, means to become trapped in an economy of futile desire. Desire is phallic; *jouissance* is pre-phallic. In this tale, phallic divestiture leads to the eradication of desire itself.

At the beginning of the tale, the boy is in a liminal zone, between the state preceding desire (the semiotic) and the realm of desire (the symbolic order). The feebleness of his desire indicates that he has not yet become fully individuated or phallic. He has not yet fully emerged from the pre-gendered contentment of infancy to assume masculine status and to experience desire for others. By refusing not only heterosexual desire but any object love, the boy is spared the torment of desire and reclaims his own body as love object; he recovers the *jouissance* that precedes desire.

Unlike the "good mother," this woman does not assist her son in assuming his rightful position in the symbolic order. Instead, she helps re-immerse him in the semiotic. She prevents him from developing desire by teaching him how to satisfy himself, to reincorporate "other" into "self." By subverting the normal developmental process, she brings about the triumph of self-love over object-love and thus destroys the hegemony of the symbolic over the semiotic. Reversing the boy's meager flow of sexual desire has a perversely invigorating effect on him; he experiences the re-eroticization of his entire body: ("Because he had become continuous, something like vitality or ardor started flowing through his body. . . . The youth's white body glowed all the more radiantly and became delicately moist.")

The woman, on the other hand, is a person of voracious desire. As the boy is gradually de-phallicized through their ritual "game" of turning him into a circle, the woman becomes increasingly phallic. (The circle, as a "hole," represents the female organ, an obvious symbol of phallic divestiture. By transforming the boy into a "circle" the woman can become a "penetrator.") Ironically, by occupying the male position vis-à-vis her partner, the woman is liberated from female subordination and marginality, but is trapped in the self–other split, consigned to futile desiring. Yet she relishes desire itself; the presence of the passive, "feminized," complacent male reaffirms her status as the dominant, desiring partner, a status she savors. ("Helping him attain a state in which he would no longer want her was a joy for a woman of intense desire. The woman's desire was only stirred up by a sense of futility, and the surging of desire itself surpassed satisfaction.") Moreover, she cannot relinquish her phallic position without losing her power to transgress the symbolic order she has created. By helping the youth "become a circle" — return to a pre-phallic state — the woman acquires phallic power and uses her phallus to "slip through a crack in ordinary reality and penetrate the infinite." In other words, the ritual she performs with the boy enables her momentarily to rupture the symbolic order ("slip through the crack"), plunge into the semiotic ("penetrate the infinite"), and then resume her position of phallic mastery.

In the other passages discussed, the bliss of self-divestiture is conveyed predominantly (though not exclusively) through images of violence and loss (stripping, dismembering, burning up, letting go, falling, weeping, branding); throughout most of "A Young Man," however, release from selfhood is represented in positive terms, with images of self-sufficiency, contentment, and completeness. The boy, who has renounced his phallic status and his other-directed erotic desire, dwells for a while in nirvana-like (w)holeness and harmony, symbolized by the circle. He is a world unto himself, "indifferent to others," like an infant or a psychotic. Or one might say that his self has expanded to encompass the other: he makes love to himself. The circle represents intrauterine bliss, the nonlinear continuity of the semiotic modality. Psychologically, the mother has assisted her son in negotiating his way back to the semiotic dimension; in religious terms, the mother, as spiritual guide, has helped awaken her disciple to original, desireless mind.

Again we are confronted with the intersection of deviant sexuality and mystical ecstasy. The circle that is created by the boy's autoerotic pose is the key image in the story; it evokes both spiritual and carnal spheres through its diverse associations. The circle is a traditional symbol of Buddhist enlightenment, but it also suggests, by its shape, the fetus's symbiotic union with its mother and perverse sexual pleasure. Transcending desire is a universal goal of spiritual practices. Once purged of desire or ego, the self–other distinction appears illusory. The woman transforms the boy into a circle through a ritualistic act. Ritual suggests both religious rite and erotic game; the formulaic quality of the couple's game infuses the act and its regen-

erative effects with religious significance. Thus, the woman-priest repeatedly murmurs a mystical incantation ("Become round") intended
to induce the boy to relinquish all traces of desire for others, including
herself. The boy's "sacrifice" of desire, his phallic divestiture, has an
empowering effect on the woman; it enables her to temporarily
"penetrate the infinite."

The rite centers around an antisocial sexual practice. The boy literally "becomes a circle" by performing self-fellatio. "His two most
vital parts came together"; his head and penis are joined. Head represents the spiritual realm, and penis the sexual. The boy's physical
pose stands for the fusion of mystical and erotic. The youth embodies
both deviant sexuality and divinity. The woman marvels at his aloofness, calling him a "freak of nature." ("A man with no desire was like
a freak of nature.") His "freakishness," or marginality, marks him as a
"divine boy." The story refers to his lack of carnality ("he detested
raw flesh, and he loathed physical contact"), his highly developed
aesthetic sense ("he had the eye of a connoisseur"), his "plant-like
sensuousness," his "sexless translucence," and his luminosity ("light
seemed to radiate from the whiteness of his skin"); all these traits
connote spirituality, even divinity, and inspire the woman's reverent
attitude toward the youth. She gazes at the circle-boy with wonder,
like a meditator contemplating a mandala.

This tale dramatically juxtaposes images that convey the positive
and negative connotations of self-divestiture. Whereas the image of
the boy as circle represents self-loss as blissful self-expansion, the
boy's ghastly degeneration in the tale's violent finale treats self-
divestiture in terms of self-extinction and thus exposes the fundamentally thanatopic nature of *jouissance*. After blocking her child's
entrance into the symbolic order and returning him to a womb-like
existence, the mother in the tale takes her child out to the garden and
hurls him into a thorny bed of roses that mutilates him beyond recognition. The woman's final interaction with her child is a macabre parody and inversion of birth and motherhood. Instead of delivering her
fetus into the world of the living and nurturing his growth, this
mother tosses her fetus-like adolescent into a deathbed and watches
him decompose. The boy's devolution into a bloody mass resembling
an embryo represents his return to origins; it is a grisly metaphor for
the disintegration of gender identity and individual identity. This
story itself has a circular structure. The end of the fantasy supplies the
link that completes the circle of meaning, by superimposing the image

of the woman's unborn child onto the formless flesh into which her violent act has transformed her erotic partner. In this image, past and present, sexual and maternal, eros and death, converge.

The boy who undergoes phallic divestiture in Takahashi's stories is always a sacrificial victim. All the rituals of phallic divestiture discussed in this essay end in their victims' destruction, through literal or symbolic mutilation or death. In "Secret Rituals" the candle replicas of the boy's body are burned and distorted beyond recognition; in the cross-dressing scene of *The House of Rebirth*, Yukiyo is reduced to helpless, wailing infancy, and the next day evidence of his physical abuse remains in the form of red marks on his skin. In "A Young Man," the boy is reduced to a lump of fetal tissue, and the woman is left reflecting on the loss of her child. "A Young Man" follows the same pattern as the other passages that describe rituals ending in a male victim's annihilation: phallic divestiture, self-divestiture, death. In this tale the mother strips her son first of his gender identity, next his individual identity (as one term of a self–other dyad), then his humanity (she turns him into an "object"), and finally his life. Paradoxically, the boy's spiritual evolution and physical devolution coincide; his adeptness at transforming himself into a perfect circle marks an intermediate stage in his regression to an original state of undifferentiation. The ritual enacts the sacrifice of a "divine child" and his return to the spirit realm.

All of Takahashi's stories involving a woman's thirst to "penetrate the infinite" include motifs of death and destruction. Her fiction is informed by a vision of the inseparability of the erotic instinct and the death drive, of pleasure and pain. Sexual and religious motifs intersect in her stories, because both sexual ecstasy and mystical rapture are means of temporarily extinguishing the isolated, individual self.[16] Fantasies of murder and suicide abound in her works; her eroticized violent fantasies, reminiscent of Mishima's orgasmic death scenes, suggest a wish for total fusion that has both nostalgic and apocalyptic nuances. According to Roland Barthes's classification, Takahashi's stories are primarily "texts of bliss" rather than "texts of pleasure," since they provoke feelings of disturbance and loss in the reader.[17]

In Takahashi's writings, the woman who empowers herself through a man's phallic divestiture manifests traits of both feminist and *femme fatale*, yet cannot be reduced to any "type." Her female characters are complex, introspective, enigmatic women whose motivations and desires remain inscrutable even to themselves. As the antiheroine of the short story, "Harema" (A fine interval; 1975) muses while contemplating the murder of her "radiant" young lover: "Why murder and beautiful youths seemed to go together Kyōko could not say. Was it because she thought that beauty was perfected by murder? Was it because she felt she could possess a man completely by murdering him? Or did Kyōko prey on youthful beauty because she had a taste for unequal power relationships?" ("Harema," 231).

∅

The stories discussed here depict women who reject the traditional female role of self-sacrifice and submissiveness to men as oppressive and create personal "countercultures" in which they seize phallic power and assert their authority over men. Paradoxically, by creating an alternative symbolic order in which they define themselves as central and men as Other, the women position themselves to transgress this order and thereby experience the *jouissance* of self-dissolution. In these works Takahashi re-visions self-loss and claims its ecstatic and emancipatory potential for women.

Takahashi's feminization of the visionary quest to divest oneself of "false" social selves hinges on a reversal of male and female roles. Woman is removed from the auxiliary position of helpmate, muse, or grail (object of desire) and placed in the central position of hero-quester. Man is assigned a subordinate, self-sacrificing role as a catalyst for woman's integration of her "masculine" and "feminine" aspirations. Only after assuming phallic authority and assisting a man in divesting himself of conventional masculinity can the woman follow the man in "phallic renunciation." The man's symbolic castration opens an abyss into which the male-identified woman can plunge and lose herself, temporarily renouncing the false distinctions required to maintain both gender identity and individual autonomy.

On one level, then, these stories are a feminist critique of male power and female subordination. But they surpass and undermine the binary dynamic itself. Because of her love for and identification with the feminine male who is son, lover, and twin, the heroine cannot be assimilated to any single cultural model: mother, wife/consort, traditional masochistic woman, sadistic *femme fatale*. Nor is the couple's relationship signifiable in terms of existing categories: Is it filial, marital, heterosexual, homosexual, mutually autoerotic? The stories attempt to represent the abject of culture—that which crosses borders, resists attempts to classify and confine. They express a utopian vision of men's and women's release from the arbitrary limits imposed by the socialization process through fantasies of transgressing culture's dominant cognitive, psychological, and erotic paradigms. By subverting the notions of fixed gender and individual identity and claiming for women both the transgressive exhilaration of seizing phallic power and the *jouissance* of self-surrender, Takahashi's stories enunciate a social and spiritual vision that surpasses and subverts the binary patterns ingrained in both traditional femininity and feminism.

Notes

1. Takahashi (Okamoto) Takako, born in 1932, converted to Catholicism in 1975 and frequently traveled to France to participate in religious life there. Following the publication of *Ikari no ko* (Child of rage) in 1985, she became a Catholic nun in France, where she lived until 1988. In 1989 she entered a Catholic convent of a different religious order in Japan. During this period her published writing was limited to essays on religious topics. In a Nov. 1993 conversation with Haniya Yutaka in Japan (published as "Tamashii no katsubō" [Spiritual thirst] in *Gunzō* in Jan. 1994), Takahashi stated that she had left formal religious life in 1990 but continued to devote herself to spiritual practice; she also spoke of the possibility of resuming her career as a fiction writer. Perhaps as a transitional step, in 1994 she published a four-volume collection of some of her previous fiction, entitled *Takahashi Takako jisen shōsetsu shū* (Takahashi Takako's selected literary works).

2. The book is Takako's account of her seventeen-year marriage to a man who was both a source of exasperation and an object of adoration to her. Kazumi died of cancer in 1971 at the age of 40.

3. For a discussion of one of Kōno's stories, "Yōji-gari" (Toddler-hunting), see Chieko M. Ariga's chapter in this volume, pp. 352–81.

4. Lacan, Kristeva, and Barthes use the word *jouissance* to connote an anarchic joy that subverts ego stability, intellectual assumptions, and cultural norms, in contrast to *plaisir*, which fortifies the ego, confirms assumptions, and helps conserve the social order. Most English translators of these writers' works retain the French word, on the grounds that English has no word that adequately conveys the oxymoronic nuances of the original.

5. The brief synopsis that follows is a vast oversimplification of an intricate and at times abstruse theory. For a complete exposition of her theory, see Kristeva, *Revolution in Poetic Language*, especially chap. 1, "The Semiotic and the Symbolic," 19–106. For lucid commentaries on Kristeva's work, see Grosz; and Moi.

6. Kristeva writes: "*Jouissance* alone causes the abject to exist as such. One does not know it, one does not desire it, one joys in it [*on en jouit*]. Vio-

lently and painfully. . . . We may call it a border; abjection is above all ambiguity. Because, while releasing a hold, it does not radically cut off the subject from what threatens it—on the contrary, abjection acknowledges it to be in perpetual danger" (*Powers of Horror*, 9).

7. Elizabeth Grosz elucidates Kristeva's perspective as follows: "If women are subjects in the symbolic at all (and not simply objects for other subjects), they are not subjects in the same ways as masculine subjects. If transgression implies a position from which transgression is possible, this may explain why Kristeva does not accord the feminine, or women, the subversive position of the avant-garde. Only men can transgress the symbolic because only they are subjects with a position to subvert" (67–68).

8. I borrow this term from film theorist Kaja Silverman, who uses it in *The Acoustic Mirror* to denote the process of symbolic "self-castration" undertaken by male film characters "who renounce power and privilege—who sever their relationship to the phallus" (219). In chap. 6 of this work, Silverman analyzes the behavior of the male characters portrayed in several films by the Italian director Liliana Cavani in terms of this concept. She observes that the chief function of women in these films is to assist men in accomplishing phallic divestiture. My interpretations of the male-female dynamic described in Takahashi's "Secret Rituals" and *The House of Rebirth* have benefited much from Silverman's discussions.

Silverman echoes Kristeva in conceding transgressive power to men. Speculating on why Cavani's films consistently feature marginal men to represent the *jouissance* of rejecting social norms of identity and social status, she states: "Cavani is obliged to rely upon male characters to express this dream because they alone occupy a position from which divestiture is possible. Her constant return to male subjectivity speaks to the desire to participate in a renunciation which is not yet possible for the female subject (which indeed can only be seen as a dangerous lure at this moment in her history)—the renunciation of power in all its many social, cultural, political, and economic guises" (*The Acoustic Mirror*, 231). See also Silverman's recent *Male Subjectivity at the Margins*, especially the section "Masochism," 185–296.

9. I refer to Lacan's famous essay, "God and the *Jouissance* of The Woman."

10. *The House of Rebirth* is divided into three individually titled parts. In this essay I deal with only Part II, "Sasori no ie" (The house of scorpions). Within Part II is a complete short story entitled "Osanai otoko" (A young man); the story is the third passage that I discuss in this essay.

11. The idea of gender role reversal in a relationship between an older woman and a boy or young man has provided the author with a seemingly limitless source of literary inspiration. Other stories of hers informed by this theme include "Rasen kaidan" (The spiral staircase; 1972), "Harema" (A fine interval; 1975), "Ten no mizuumi" (Lake of heaven; 1977), "Ningyō ai" (Doll love; 1976), "Araware" (Revelation; 1979), and "Byōshin" (Invalid; 1978). For a discussion of "The Spiral Staircase," see Mori.

It is interesting to note that Takahashi co-translated the 1889 French novel *Monsieur Vénus* by Rachilde (Marguerite E. Vallette) into Japanese. This sensational decadent tale (whose subversions have received less critical attention than its perversions) concerns an aristocratic woman who "keeps" a male consort, gradually transforming both of them, down to their dress, into the opposite gender. After her lover's death, the woman preserves relics from his corpse in a life-sized wax replica of him, to which she pays nocturnal homage. (In her essay "Muishiki o horu" [Plumbing the unconscious; 1980], Takahashi expresses her astonishment at the similarity between her fantasies and those of Rachilde's. She was introduced to the French author's works only after she had published her own eerie tales of women who amuse themselves with wax doll "doubles" of their beautiful young lovers.)

12. The phrase is from Lacan's essay "God and the *Jouissance* of ~~The~~ Woman," 145; here Lacan draws a connection between female sexual pleasure and mystical rapture, identifying these with *jouissance* and contrasting them to male sexual gratification.

13. "Doll Love" appears in English translation in the anthology *This Kind of Woman*, edited by Tanaka and Hanson. The Japanese text can be found in Takahashi's short-story collection, *Ningyō ai* (1978).

14. Lacan, for example, distinguishes the visual, mastering, desiring nature of male sexuality from the diffuse, "primitive" ineffable quality of female sexuality, which he equates with *jouissance*. See Gallop, 22–32, for an astute and irreverent commentary on this binary paradigm of Lacan's.

15. Accepting Lévi-Strauss's premise that culture originates with the incest taboo, Gayle Rubin argues in "The Traffic in Women" that the end of both female subordination and gender-based sexual restrictions would require the overthrow of culture itself. This would allow individuals to recover the genderless state of multiple libidinal possibilities that they enjoy before entering the cultural order. For a recent illuminating discussion of Rubin's thesis and its implications, see Butler, 72–78.

16. Takahashi's paradoxical view of eroticism is consistent with the theory expounded by Georges Bataille in his classic study, *Death and Sensuality*. Bataille defines eroticism as "assenting to life up to the point of death" (5) and argues that "our obsession with a primal continuity linking us with everything that is" (9) underlies the connection between erotic and destructive impulses. The striking similarity between Bataille's and Takahashi's sensibilities may be attributable to the involvement of both writers with surrealism. The surrealists were dedicated to liberating the "authentic" heterogeneous self repressed within the unified bourgeois subject; their main strategies for dissolving the "false" social persona were criminal and sexual deviance and transgressive aesthetic practices (such as automatic writing). Takahashi makes frequent reference to surrealism in her essays. She claims to have studied its literature extensively and been greatly influenced by its philosophy. She seems to associate the surrealist goal of unraveling the self with both sadomasochistic erotic pleasure and the experience of mystical

states within a Christian contemplative tradition. Bataille was a member of the surrealist movement in France until 1929, when his criticism of its leader, André Breton, led to his expulsion. Bataille saw Breton's personal ambitions as undermining the movement's revolutionary impact, both socially and artistically. Surrealist philosophy is certainly the point of departure for Bataille's thinking; Bataille's originality lies in associating the erotic pleasure of self-loss with both religious ecstasy and political revolution. For a lucid account of the surrealist movement and Bataille's relationship to it, see Dean.

17. Barthes defines the "text of pleasure" (*plaisir*) as "the text that contents, fills, grants euphoria; the text that comes from culture and does not break with it, is linked to a comfortable practice of reading." Conversely, the "text of bliss" (*jouissance*) is "the text that imposes a state of loss, the text that discomforts . . . , unsettles the reader's historical, cultural, psychological assumptions, the consistency of his tastes, values, memories, brings to a crisis his relation with language" (14).

Works Cited

Barthes, Roland. *The Pleasure of the Text*. Trans. Richard Miller. New York: Hill & Wang, 1975.

Bataille, Georges. *Death and Sensuality: A Study of Eroticism and the Taboo*. New York: Ballantine Books, 1962.

Butler, Judith. *Gender Trouble*. New York: Routledge, 1990.

Dean, Carolyn J. *The Self and Its Pleasures: Bataille, Lacan, and the History of the Decentered Subject*. Ithaca, N.Y.: Cornell University Press, 1992.

Gallop, Jane. *The Daughter's Seduction: Feminism and Psychoanalysis*. Ithaca, N.Y.: Cornell University Press, 1982.

Grosz, Elizabeth. *Sexual Subversions: Three French Feminists*. Sydney: Allen & Unwin, 1989.

Haniya Yutaka and Takahashi Takako. "Tamashii no katsubō." *Gunzō* 49, no. 1 (1994): 290–335.

Kristeva, Julia. *Powers of Horror: An Essay on Abjection*. Trans. Leon S. Roudiez. New York: Columbia University Press, 1982.

———. "Pratique signifiante et mode de production." In *La traversée des signes*, ed. Julia Kristeva et al. Paris: Seuil, 1975, 11–29.

———. *Revolution in Poetic Language*. Trans. Margaret Waller. New York: Columbia University Press, 1984.

Lacan, Jacques. "God and the Jouissance of The Woman." In *Feminine Sexuality: Jacques Lacan and the école freudienne*, ed. Jacqueline Rose and Juliet Mitchell. New York: W. W. Norton, 1982, 137–48.

Moi, Toril. *Sexual/Textual Politics: Feminist Literary Theory*. London: Methuen, 1985.

Mori, Maryellen Toman. "The Subversive Role of Fantasy in the Fiction of Takahashi Takako." *Journal of the Association of Teachers of Japanese* 28, no. 1 (1994): 29–56.

Rubin, Gayle. "The Traffic in Women: Notes on the 'Political Economy' of Sex." In *Toward an Anthropology of Women*, ed. Rayna R. Reiter. New York: Monthly Review Press, 1975, 157–210.

Silverman, Kaja. *The Acoustic Mirror: The Female Voice in Psychoanalysis and Cinema*. Bloomington: Indiana University Press, 1988.

———. *Male Subjectivity at the Margins*. New York: Routledge, 1992.

Takahashi Takako. "Araware." In idem, *Ayashimi*, 97–145.

———. *Ayashimi*. Tokyo: Shinchōsha, 1981.

———. "Byōshin." In idem, *Tōku, kutsū no tani o aruite iru toki*, 161–83.

———. "Doll Love" ("Ningyō ai"). Trans. Mona Nagai and Yukiko Tanaka. In *This Kind of Woman: Ten Stories by Japanese Women Writers, 1960–1976*, trans. and ed. Yukiko Tanaka and Elizabeth Hanson. Stanford: Stanford University Press, 1982, 197–223.

———. "Furansu bungaku to watakushi." In idem, *Odoroita hana*, 90–93.

———. *Hanayagu hi*. Tokyo: Kōdansha, 1975.

———. "Harema." In idem, *Hanayagu hi*, 195–267.

———. "Higi." In idem, *Ningyō ai*, 59–137.

———. "Invalid" ("Byōshin"). Trans. Van C. Gessel. *Mānoa* 3, no. 2 (1991): 132–40.

———. *Kyōsei kūkan*. Tokyo: Shinchōsha, 1973.

———. "Muishiki o horu." In idem, *Odoroita hana*, 94–98.

———. "Ningyō ai." In idem, *Ningyō ai*, 5–57.

———. *Ningyō ai*. Tokyo: Kōdansha, 1978.

———. *Odoroita hana*. Tokyo: Jimbun shoin, 1980.

———. "Rasen kaidan." In idem, *Kyōsei kūkan*, 179–226.

———. *Takahashi Kazumi no omoide*. Tokyo: Kōsōsha, 1977.

———. *Takahashi Takako jisen shōsetsu shū*. 4 vols. Tokyo: Kōdansha, 1994.

———. *Ten no mizuumi*. Tokyo: Shinchōsha, 1977.

———. *Tōku, kutsū no tani o aruite iru toki*. Tokyo: Kōdansha, 1983.

———. "Yomigaeri no ie." In idem, *Tōku, kutsū no tani o aruite iru toki*, 5–159.

Part III

Defining the Female Voice

7

In Pursuit of the Yamamba:
The Question of Female Resistance

MEERA VISWANATHAN

> When, however one reads of a witch . . . , of a woman possessed by
> devils, of a wise woman selling herbs . . . who dashed her brains
> out on the moor or mopped and mowed about the highways
> crazed with the torture that her gift had put her to . . . any woman
> born with a great gift in the sixteenth century would certainly have
> gone crazy, shot herself or ended her days in some lonely cottage
> outside the village, half witch, half wizard, feared and mocked at.
>
> —Virginia Woolf, *A Room of One's Own*, 50–51

In contemporary Japanese literary studies in the West, there has
been a marked interest of late among translators and critics in representations of "female resistance." Western readers long accustomed
to a pabulum of benign images of passive and pleasing Japanese
womanhood are now assaulted by numerous translations of texts featuring powerful, rebellious, adamant, and often unrepentantly violent
female characters, ranging from Tanizaki Jun'ichirō's (1886–1965) *Naomi* (*Chijin no ai*; 1924) to the mother-in-law, Mieko, in Enchi Fumiko's
(1905-86) *Masks* (*Onna men*; 1958) to the protagonists in the anthology
of short stories entitled *To Live and to Write*, edited by Yukiko Tanaka.
Critical attention as well reflects this new focus: Norma Field, Victoria
V. Vernon, H. Richard Okada, and others have put forward persua-
sive arguments for new interpretations of canonical texts that highlight female resistance or for inclusion of neglected works into the
canon that may feature aberrant or recalcitrant female characters.

Yet the identification of aberration with resistance poses difficulties: although resistance may affect an aberrant posture, aberration, for example, in the case of fetishism, need not always be the site of resistance, as Tanizaki's notion of a *feminisuto* (feminist) as a man who worships women suggests. Understanding resistance itself proves to be problematic, since it can be comprehended only in opposition to complicity and hence invariably embodies an irresolvable dialectical impulse between order and anarchy, between restoration and creation, between return and exile—between the moral poles, however situated, of good and evil. Further, the dominant ideology, by discounting resistance as mere aberration and hence blurring the distinction between the two, may itself denature or co-opt any threat to itself. The paradigmatic *maquisarde* who infiltrates the enemy, seduces him into a false sense of well-being, and then proceeds in subversive fashion to undermine and overpower him in order to express a heretofore suppressed authentic self both parallels and stands in opposition to the lesbian "ball-busting" Nazi storm trooper *à la* Marlene Dietrich, whose subversion of male dominance may in itself constitute a manifestation of authentic self. As with other subaltern pairings, from the classical mythical figures of Procne and Circe to the Judaeo-Christian Judith and Lilith to the Hindu Draupadi and Kali, we see a tension between the subversive activities of the virtuous woman anxious to restore order and meaning by resisting or opposing the advances of those males who seek to violate her very wifeliness and the more general resistance connoted by the unfettered power of the witch or demonic figure, whose nature is necessarily uncontrolled and anarchic. The tension in the dialectic of the *maquisarde* / storm trooper mirrors the dualism we face in reading female aberration as resistance: whether to read aberration pathologically in terms of the marginalization and suppression of women by social instruments and institutions or to valorize aberration as authentic female Being.[1]

The issue of resistance is further problematized when we consider the implications of what Alicia Ostriker refers to as "revisionist mythmaking": "Whenever a poet . . . is using myth, . . . the potential is always present that the use will be revisionist: that is, the figure or tale will be appropriated for altered ends, the old vessel filled with new wine, initially satisfying the thirst of the individual poet but ultimately making cultural change possible" (72). Revisionism may indeed be the intent, but, as with the adage that cautions against putting new wine in old skins, the results of such mythic appropriation may well stretch beyond the intended limits or "altered ends."

One such mythic figure of resistance that was repeatedly revised and reappropriated in the course of Japanese literary history is the topos of the *yamamba* (or *yamauba*), the legendary female demon of the mountains. Although literally scores of folk tales and oral narratives from various parts of Japan attest to its ubiquity throughout Japanese history, much of its impact in literary history derives from the representation of the yamamba in the fifteenth-century eponymous Nō play alluded to a number of times by Zeami Motokiyo (1363–1443) in his critical work *Sarugaku dangi* (An account of Zeami's reflections on art). For example, in the Edo period (1600–1868), Jion-ni Kenka, a female student of the founder of the Shingaku (heart/mind learning) movement, Ishida Baigan (1685–1744), was accustomed to hear him lecture regularly in the evenings on the Nō play *Yamamba* (Robertson, 102); given the sharply defined gender distinctions advocated by him in his other disquisitions, it would be of great interest to know how his audience, both male and female, interpreted his reading of the play.

In modern literature as well, the topos of the yamamba crops up with surprising frequency. Margaret Mitsutani, in a recent essay entitled "Renaissance in Women's Literature," detects the presence of the yamamba in the work of Tsushima Yūko (1947–): "The *yamamba*, or mountain witch, who provides a metaphor for Odaka Takiko, the heroine of *Woman Running in the Mountains* [*Yama o hashiru onna*; 1980], is an embodiment of passions that surpass rational understanding and threaten the harmony of village life" (316). Although Tsushima Yūko's novel never directly develops the idea of the yamamba, the title of the novel, as well as the bleak, exhausting, and alienated existence of the main character, who refuses to remake herself into a "normal" being following society's dicta, reminds us of the predicament of the yamamba in the Nō play, whose wearying *yama-meguri* (making the rounds of the mountains) seems never ending.

✄

But what exactly is a yamamba?[2] The characters used in writing the term connote only an old woman of the mountains, but because of the frequency with which demons in folklore become old women and vice versa (Mabuchi et al., 60), the notion of a crone living in the mountains immediately conjures up the notion of a female demon.

Along the same lines, the standard dictionary *Kōjien* variously defines the yamauba as "a legendary female dwelling deep within the mountains who is thought to manifest superhuman strength," "a mountain woman," and "a female demon." Monica Bethe and Karen Brazell, summarizing the ideas of Baba Akiko, assert that "she is an enigma—a god, a demon, an entertainer, a mother; enlightened, tormented, helpful, and harmful" (8). Yet the yamamba is never all these things simultaneously; instead, as the figure of the yamamba intervenes in a number of texts, her character becomes reformulated, fragmented, and disjointed in its accommodation of revisionist views. In each literary manifestation, the question of her definition or provenance becomes highlighted against a new field of opposition.

Normally, the pronunciation "yamauba" seems to be used in conjunction with the mythical figure of folklore, who remains ahistorical and unreclaimed, whereas the nasalized form "yamamba" is reserved for the literary accretions surrounding the figure in the wake of the fifteenth-century Nō play.[3] In this essay, "yamamba" will be used for all literary/textualized treatments of the figure, including those predating or contemporaneous with the Nō play.

In folkloric versions of yamauba stories,[4] we see her as a terrifying old woman with long gray hair, possessing superhuman strength and prescience, dwelling in the mountains. Preying on stray male travelers who intrude on her as she occupies herself with the task of spinning, she is capable of extraordinary transformations, ranging from animal to beautiful maiden. Should her prey attempt to escape, she chases it down in the mountains and devours it with uncanny delight. Yet, interestingly, this figure of dread also appears in alternative guise in folk tales: as a comical dupe, a fool, a greedy and selfish creature, who is ultimately punished for her unnatural ways. Here the threat posed by the figure of the yamauba becomes doubly contained in these narratives, first, by her failure to realize her desires, and, second, by the denaturing of her character through her representation as an object of ridicule. The figure of a man-eating female demon is peculiar neither to Japan nor to premodern narratives; we see, for example, in the myths of the New World people known as the Tainos, a similar female demon graphically described as "la vagina dentada" (the vagina with teeth), reminding us as well of D. H. Lawrence's character Bertha Coutts in *Lady Chatterley's Lover*, with her dreaded "beak" down there that shreds and tears at men, not unlike the yamamba in Ōba Minako's story "Rōsoku-uo" (Candlefish; 1980). The delineation of these ravenous figures suggests an overarching preoccupation with the danger posed by female consumption as well as the need to defuse the threat, leading us to question whether the provenance of such man-eaters, ironically, is rather in the realm of male anxieties about castration than simply in female notions of resistance.

In his 1927 essay "Fetishism," Freud noted: "Probably no male human being is spared the fright of castration at the sight of a female genital" (154). He argued that a "disavowal" (*Verleugnung*) takes place, in which the male represses the sight of the "penis-less" mother, substituting in its place a fetish, a magically imbued object that invites the same kind of interest, as a kind of defense. "But this interest suffers an extraordinary increase as well, because the horror of castration has set up a memorial to itself in the creation of this substitute. Furthermore, an aversion, which is never absent in any fetishist, to the real female genitals remains a *stigma indelebile* of the repression that has taken place. . . . [The fetish] remains a token of triumph over the threat of castration and a protection against it" (154).

As we consider Freud's description of the fetishizing process in conjunction with an examination of the yamamba figure, numerous questions arise. If we accept the notion that the yamamba represents just such a fetishized figure, what then does it mean to appropriate and recast it as a figure of resistance? Does such a figure ultimately resist resistance? Is there such a thing as a female fetish into which it can be transformed? If male fetishism is ultimately about castration anxiety, what does the female fetish signify?

Although literary representations of the yamamba figure abound, we can isolate a few crucial works in which the role of the yamamba is significantly altered and rewritten. From the mountain-dwelling female demons in *Konjaku monogatari* (Tales of times now past; ca. 1120) to the fifteenth-century Nō play *Yamamba* to Chikamatsu Monzaemon's (1653–1724) puppet play *Komochi yamamba* (The yamamba with child; 1712) to Ōba Minako's story "Yamauba no bishō" (The smile of the mountain witch; 1976), the trajectory of the yamamba may be described as one of naturalization and domestication, moving from the demonic to the demotic.

The eleventh- or twelfth-century anthology of prose narratives known as *Konjaku monogatari*, a repository of tales gleaned from numerous sources, Indian and Chinese as well as indigenous, alludes numerous times to female demons living in the mountains, especially in section 27, which is dominated by stories of demonic apparitions.

Many episodes are virtually indistinguishable from folkloric versions, but in episode 15 in section 27, the legendary version of yamauba is startlingly recast.[5] Whereas in almost all folkloric versions,[6] it is a male lowlander or lowlanders (whether traveler, hunter, stepson, and so on) who confront the yamauba, this story depicts a meeting between two females, a young pregnant woman, who lives in the capital without spouse, parents, or acquaintances to help her, and the old woman of the mountains, who befriends her and offers her shelter for her lying-in. Similarly, in folk-tale versions, the outcome is generally violent: either the yamauba triumphs and the hapless victim is crunched with gusto, or the male protagonists manage to escape and either wound or kill the yamauba, or some such combination involving the outpouring of healthy doses of blood results. In this story, however, neither the yamamba nor the young woman and her party are harmed. We are told of the young woman that she is a bright person, who, fully cognizant of her predicament and its implications, forms a plan to go somewhere deep in the mountains and give birth under a tree. Although the mountains are far more remote than she initially realizes, eventually, when her time approaches, she propels herself into the mountain fastness and finds herself an abandoned hut. There she decides, betraying little maternal solicitude, that "after giving birth here, I will set off alone" (62), content to abandon the child to its fate, which is no doubt to be devoured by wild beasts in the wilderness.

At this point she meets up with the old woman, who, sympathizing with her condition, takes her in and treats her with such great tenderness that the young woman feels that Buddha himself has interceded with help. It is only after the delivery of a male child that conflict emerges. First, we witness a startling change in the mother's attitude: now we are told she feels delighted about her situation. Since he is a handsome baby boy, she finds it impossible to think of abandoning him. Some time later, the new mother, while dozing in the afternoon, overhears the old woman mutter, "How yummy, just that one bite's worth" (63) as she stares at the little boy. Aghast, the mother deduces that the old woman must be a demon (oni), and determines to try to escape. Once again she calls on Buddha to intercede for her and, while the old woman naps, flees her hut and returns to the capital. The story concludes without further reference to the demon, whose fate remains unknown; we are informed that even the young woman did not speak of the story until she was quite old.

Though the appellation "yamamba" is never used in this story, clearly this tale belongs to the category of yamamba narratives, with the image of the demonic man-eating old woman dwelling in the mountains. It is interesting that neither the young woman nor her maid is at risk of being eaten by the yamamba. One wonders what the outcome might have been had the baby been female. Would the mother have stayed with her original plan and abandoned it? Would the yamamba have found it to be such a toothsome morsel? Equally, it is significant that the demonic side of the old woman is manifested only after the mother betrays a properly "maternal" consciousness.

Unlike the folk narratives, a carefully balanced structure of reversals governs this entire tale. We begin with a difficult ascent into the mountains and conclude with a rather hasty descent. The inhumane aspect of the pregnant woman's character, which is evident in her ready willingness to abandon her child to the whim of mountain beasts at the beginning of the story, is countered at the end by the old woman's unnatural penchant for young male flesh. The old woman initially is understood to be an instrument of Buddha's benevolence, but later the mother finds herself exhorting the Buddha for his help in escaping the demon. The young woman discovers the yamamba's nature while she is napping, and she manages to devise an escape while the old woman herself is sleeping. The callous young woman is revealed to be a good and caring mother, and the kindly and helpful old woman is uncovered as a man-eater. At the end of the story, the mountain witch has disappeared, and the narrative is related by the young woman only when she herself is old, having in a sense displaced the old woman. In reading this tale of multiple transformations, it is difficult not to read the old woman of the mountains as a mirror, albeit distorted, of the young woman of the capital, the two of whom become adversaries only after the arrival of the male child, whereupon they contest its possession. They represent the dialectic of female resistance, in which we see not so much an opposition between female characters as an internal struggle between production and consumption, between the sacrifice of self and the assertion of self, between order and anarchy.

In the fifteenth-century Nō play *Yamamba*,[7] whose authorship is unknown, we see a similar scenario ensue between two women, one young, one old; one from the capital, one from the mountains. In this narrative, the issue of mirroring becomes more critical in an encounter between Yamamba, famed for her dance performance, and a court dancer from the capital, named Hyakuma Yamamba, who imperson-ates her. As in the earlier *Konjaku* story, no violence intrudes in this play, despite the fact that the yamamba, now formally christened as such, has become an object of dread and loathing. The most signifi-cant section of the play is the *kusemai*, or dance, performed by the ya-mamba herself, which Zeami in his *Sarugaku dangi* described as one of the most noteworthy (Rimer and Yamazaki, 198). Ironically, the im-pulse for her performance initially emerges in the yamamba's desire to see how well the performer Hyakuma imitates her. As Monica Bethe and Karen Brazell comment, the play "highlights the questions of appearance, reality, and art by introducing an entertainer who im-personates Yamamba to the real Yamamba who in turn entertains her impersonator" (8).

The play opens with the dancer Hyakuma and her entourage set-ting forth on a pilgrimage to a temple, Zenkō-ji. Strangely, the day wanes suddenly, and in their search for lodging they meet an old woman living in a rude mountain hut who welcomes them in. As she bids Hyakuma to sing and dance for her, she questions whether Hyakuma's party has considered what sort of being a true yamamba is. The *waki*, or side character, answers glibly that "the yamamba is a female demon living in the mountains" (508). At the heart of this play is this question about the identity of the yamamba, and fittingly the yamamba responds that that term indeed describes her: one is a ya-mamba "whether a demon or whether a human, if one is a woman who lives in the mountains" (508). Just as the line between the de-monic and the human seemed somewhat permeable in the encounter between the two women in the *Konjaku* story, so, too, in this play do we see the complete denial of polarities. The yamamba, in keeping with the nondualism of Zen, quotes, shortly before the *kusemai*, the Buddhist epigram *zen'aku funi*—there is no distinction between good and evil.

Ultimately, the play having conveyed the delusion implicit in the dualistic idea of the true and false yamambas, the collapsed character of Hyakuma is elided, and only the yamamba performs during the climactic *kusemai*. Rather than projecting a chilling revelation of de-monic impulses, the yamamba's mournful litany assails us with its desolation: "Scaling the foot-wearying slope, hauling the weight of good and evil behind her, the yamamba painfully makes her rounds from mountain to mountain" (517). In contrast to the folklore ver-sions, or even the *Konjaku* story, for the first time we are allowed access into the feelings of the yamamba herself. Far from being inhuman or depraved, she is represented here as pitiful and pathetic. And, whereas our sympathy in the *Konjaku* story was for the young woman who lacked parents and friends, here we commiserate with this aged mountain woman who knows no place of origin and possesses no home. It is this, she points out, that renders her something other than human. Not only does she deny the opposition between good and evil, but she unequivocally rejects the oppositions between falsehood and truth, between the phenomenal and the void.

Nowhere does the contradictory nature of the yamamba appear so clearly as in the passage in the *kusemai* where, instead of terrorizing the human inhabitants around her, she describes her attempts to join and aid them:

> Then, amusing myself with humanity . . . sometimes as mountain dwellers traversing the woodman's trail take rest in the shade of blossoms, I help shoulder their burden, accompanying them as they make their way down the mountain just as the moon rises, sometimes as far as their village. Again, at other times, like the warbler on the willow branch I reel thread, entering in at the window where scores of looms of weaver maids stand, placing myself in the spinning hut simply for the purpose of helping people; unseen by the eyes of these humble women, they wonder, Must it not be some sort of phantom? (518–19)

Whereas in the legendary accounts of the yamauba she appears always as a culpable figure, whose deceptions serve only to mask her violent and cannibalistic nature, in this account she relates how in her benevolence, using her vaunted strength and preternatural insight, she renders service to all the rustic folk of the mountain, the very individuals who presumably give rise to the legends slandering her. Far from reveling in her solitary state, the yamamba in the play derives great satisfaction from the society of human beings and craves their acceptance. What distinguishes her from others is not her demonic nature but her extraordinary powers. Just as the polarities of good and evil, truth and falsity, the void and the phenomenal, are illusory, so, paradoxically, the true nature of the yamamba, defined as a female demon (as by the *waki* at the beginning), encompasses, in fact, humane compassion. Ironically, in effacing herself, literally rendering herself invisible, in the midst of human beings, she has assumed in their minds the contours of a demon. Hence, her last words are a plea not only for relief, in the form of Buddhist enlightenment, but also a plea for recognition: "Round and round, unable to escape the wheel of rebirth, the dust clouds of deep-seated delusion piled high have made me a yamamba. Look, look at the form of this female demon!" (521). Having seen her as anything but demonic in the course of the play, what we recognize at the end is the limitation of human understanding, in which the volatile and unstable nature of the female demon must necessarily be recuperated and normalized. In one sense, the denial of good and evil obviates the possibility of female resistance, and hence her cry for acknowledgment becomes proof simultaneously not only of her own deluded nature but also of that of humanity at large.

The Edo period witnessed something of a boom in what has come to be called *yamamba mono* (yamamba pieces),[8] which, strictly speaking, are performance pieces deriving from the kabuki theater. But in addition to Chikamatsu's *jōruri* (puppet theater of the Edo period) and other kabuki plays and the *tokiwazu, tomimoto,* and *kiyomoto* ballads (such as the well-known *nagauta,* or "long song," entitled "Shiki yamamba" [The four seasons of the yamamba]), and so forth, in which the yamamba is featured, a number of narrative works mention the yamamba, including *kana-zōshi* (prose fiction written in syllabic script) such as *Nise monogatari* (Tales of nise, or False tales; ca. 1639), and *ukiyo-zōshi* (prose fiction of the 'floating world') such as Ihara Saikaku's (1642–93) *Budō denraiki* (The transmission of the martial arts; 1687), suggesting that the topos of the yamamba was more popular than ever. For example, whenever the "world" of pre-fourteenth century Japan was evoked in Edo period *kaomise jidaimono* (debut historical plays), it was virtually a rule that the climactic *kusemai* in the last scene would feature the yamamba. Despite its direct reliance on the Nō play, however, Chikamatsu's *jōruri* play *The Yamamba with Child* represents an extraordinary shift from the perspectives of both the *Konjaku* story and the Nō play. The yamamba is no longer a shadowy figure without a past, a figure unconnected to society; instead, the yamamba now appears as a historical figure whose principal role emerges as mother of the legendary Kintarō, who in his adulthood is known as the supernaturally strong and heroic Sakata Kintoki, one of the retainers of Minamoto no Yorimitsu (948–1021).[9] Although Sakata Kintoki appears in earlier accounts, including *Konjaku monogatari,* he was not connected with the yamamba narratives until the Edo period.

In these Edo period plots, a warrior, Sakata Kurando, having fallen into disgrace at court, leaves the capital and ends up becoming an itinerant peddler in the distant mountains. His lover, Yaegiri, pregnant with their child, follows him and eventually meets up with him shortly before he dies. She remains in the hills, with her child, known as Kaidōmaru, raising him among the wolves and bears in the area around Mount Ashigara, a way of life that earns her the appellation "yamamba." One day the retainers of Yorimitsu are amazed to discover Kaidōmaru, now a powerful young warrior, in the forest. They give him the name Kintoki, and he leaves the mountains for the capital, where he joins the retinue of Yorimitsu. The climax of the play occurs as the yamamba, Yaegiri, bids farewell to Kintoki and then returns to her endless wandering through the mountains.

Apart from these literary references to the yamamba figure, woodblock prints frequently represent the yamamba, again usually deriving her significance from her position as the mother of Kintoki. Kitagawa Utamaro (1753–1806), for example, in a number of prints, depicts the adorable round and ruddy little boy, engaged in mischievous tasks, lovingly watched by his mother, the yamamba. No longer does she summon up fear, gone are the long gray hair and the haggard and aged countenance; instead, we are presented with a voluptuous woman in the prime of her life (one is reminded of the expression *onna-zakari*, or the appeal of a mature woman in the fullness of her blossoming), her hair becomingly uncombed and wild, and her scanty and disarrayed clothing suggesting a certain *iki*-like dishabille (*iki*, or "chic," disarray became an influential aesthetic ideal for women in the latter part of the Edo period). She was also frequently seen suckling her toddler as he fondles her breasts. In an intriguing shift from the demonic to the erotic, the topos of the yamamba seems to have become conflated with another topos, that of the lonely woman in an improbable place, of classical *monogatari* (the tale genre), who awaits presumably the voyeuristic notice of the male gaze.

Chikamatsu's *The Yamamba with Child*,[10] a historical play, consists of five loosely connected acts. Only the second act, which foreshadows Yaegiri's transformation into a demon, and the fourth act, which is the *michiyuki* (lovers' flight), deal directly with the yamamba. The first act consists of a rather complicated plot involving young lovers who have sought refuge with Yorimitsu, and their vendetta against their common enemy, Mononobe Heita; the third act involves a famous "exchange" scene centering around the lamentations of Kojijū, the wife of a retainer, who has killed her own son in place of Yori-

Yamamba, playfully teasing Kintoki with a chestnut. Untitled woodblock print by Kitagawa Utamaro (1753–1806). Art Institute of Chicago, Clarence Buckingham Collection of Japanese Prints, 1952.394. (Photograph © 1994. The Art Institue of Chicago. All Rights Reserved)

mitsu; and the fifth act is a lighthearted story narrating the adventures of the three-foot-tall, sake-guzzling child Kintoki in overcoming spirits, demons, and enemies.

The second act, which is commonly known as "the loquacious yamamba" (*shaberi yamamba*), introduces us to Sakata Kurando, now in the guise of the *chōnin* (townsman) Genshichi, and Yaegiri of the Oginoya, one of the leading courtesans of the day. Through various complications of love and loyalty, Genshichi at the end of the act resorts to ritual self-disembowelment (*seppuku*), but only after impregnating Yaegiri in order to ensure that his heir will one day destroy the enemy. What is of interest to us is that Yaegiri, prostrate after the death of her lover, is described as becoming a veritable female demon (*kijo*) as the spirit of her lover comes to abide in her. This, then, is the genesis of Yaegiri's transformation into a yamamba—a righteous indignation and a need to avenge her lover's death through her as yet unborn son. Having been directed by Genshichi to abandon her ordinary life in the world as a woman, she presumably betakes herself to the mountains.

Act IV is known as the *michiyuki* of Minamoto Yorimitsu, but in fact the poignancy of the travel portion is provided by the movements of the yamamba living deep in seclusion in the mountains. Thinking they have stumbled on mountain brigands, Yorimitsu and his party encounter the strange mother and son. Therein begins the yamamba's lament, much of which is appropriated directly from the Nō drama: "Scaling the foot-wearying slope, hauling the weight of good and evil behind her, the yamamba painfully makes her rounds from mountain to mountain"; "the yamamba is a female demon living in the mountains"; one is a yamamba "whether a demon or whether a human, if as a woman one lives in the mountains"; "the yamamba who knows no place of origin and possesses no home" (215–16). Her account of how she came to be a yamamba differs from that of the yamamba in the Nō version, however: "Having separated oneself from humanity and secluded oneself in the mountains, before you know it, the result of having been obsessed in your heart about a single thing is that you begin to sprout horns amidst your mountain wanderings" (218). What has obsessed her, of course, is her husband's wishes for a vendetta, and her role in that scheme. The yamamba then begins a mournful dirge, recollecting in a kind of *mono-zukushi* (literary catalogue), as is common in *michiyuki*, the various peaks she has crossed, according to their seasonal associations—for example, she alludes to Mounts Yoshino, Hatsuse, and Takama, all of which are famed for springtime beauty. Apart from the sonority provided by the list of *utamakura* (poetic place-names), the inclusion of Mount Sarashina in autumn is especially significant. "The hue of the clear sky in autumn. Ah, the unchanging light of the moon at Sarashina. The mountain of the deserted crone. Famed for its moon viewing" (218). Suddenly, through the brilliant imagination of Chikamatsu, we witness a strange conflation of two equally old legends, both concerning old women in the mountains: the female demon yamamba who preys on hapless human males, and the *obasute*, the old woman deserted by her son and left to starve on top of a mountain. As we envision the yamamba completing her mountain rounds, we are asked to imagine her atop Mount Sarashina gazing at the moon, just as the deserted crone does, according to legend. The figure of the old woman as predator comes face to face with that of the old woman as victim, the two becoming fused in their dichotomous predicament.

In *The Yamamba with Child*, the yamamba metamorphoses into an entirely different being, one lacking the awesomeness and alien nature of earlier avatars. Instead, she is first and foremost mother and wife, loving, loyal, and somewhat pathetic. Her demonic nature is not intrinsic to her, but merely an unfortunate outcome of her appropriation of male concerns. She must be sacrificed so that the larger issues of politics and moral justice may be played out. Her role, being subsidiary, results in her being forgotten at the end, left to roam the mountains, her heart perturbed and her spirit unassuaged. She is simultaneously yamamba and *obasute*, ever at the mercy of the men around her.

Appropriately, given the trajectory we have traced, Ōba Minako's story "The Smile of the Mountain Witch" in some ways recapitulates all these disparate versions of the yamamba legend. In this story, Ōba probes the margins of the yamamba topos, not only asking the by now familiar question of what constitutes a yamamba, but also posing the even more engaging problem of the yamamba's provenance. She begins by rehearsing the classical yamamba narrative: the story opens with a nervous young man who seeks lodging at the yamamba's mountain dwelling; the hideous hag smiles at him as she reveals to him her power to read his thoughts. As he begins to imagine escaping, she exposes his thoughts, and just when it seems his hour has come, the narrator of the story intervenes and explains that this is the traditional tale of the yamamba as told from time immemorial. Then, the narrator begins to subvert received opinion about yamamba by raising hitherto unasked questions about their origins and motivations.

With respect to definition, she ruminates on the problem of what yamamba were before they were old and lived in the mountains:

> But, although they're called yamamba, it cannot be that they were withered crones from the time of their birth. . . . Though, for some reason, stories of young yamamba are not circulated. Probably, the young yamamba couldn't bear to be cooped up in the mountains, and it's as though the tales were refashioned so that dwelling as various beasts, for example, cranes or foxes or herons, and so forth, they became transformed into beautiful wives and dwelt in villages. (338–39)

She notes that their destinies are bleak and that perhaps the reason they become yamamba is because of "the bitterness and pain they harbor" (339). After spending their lives among humans "unstintingly serving males" (339), and angry and downtrodden, they often decide to return to the mountains. What we see is a veritable vindication of the yamamba figure; even the man-eating tendencies of the terrifying demon are explained. In a passage that is almost a direct translation of the old woman's comment in *Konjaku*, the narrator points out the parallel between the yamamba and the mother whose loving feelings for her baby prompt her to say, "You're so cute I could just eat you up" (339). In this provocative redaction of the yamamba motif, Ōba rationalizes the actions and behavior of the allegedly irrational, alien, and threatening female demon, but as the story progresses we realize, more significantly, that the fundamental crux of Ōba's story involves the awareness that, far from an opposition between yamamba and normative womanhood, perhaps all women are yamamba at heart.

The narrator, after the preamble alluding to the traditional yamamba tale, begins her story afresh, asserting that "Now, she was an honest-to-god yamamba," as if to suggest that much of the accepted lore has presented only spurious articles. The suggestion reminds us of the question, engendered by the presence of Hyakuma Yamamba in the Nō play, regarding what is real and what is constructed. The plot that follows recounts the life of a yamamba who died at the age of 62, from her formative years as a small girl who quickly comes to recognize her own preternatural intuition, as manifested in her ability to read people's thoughts, to her adult years as a devoted mother and wife—what Virginia Woolf once called "the Angel in the House"[11] phenomenon. Having suppressed her true nature, feelings, and desires, she ends by dying alone, though surrounded by family.

As the young girl grows up, she realizes that people, including her own mother, resent her ability to penetrate their thoughts, and from then on she becomes increasingly more reticent. When she reaches young womanhood, she marries an ordinary man who demands that his wife embody the entire spectrum of possibilities from mother to demon, as his caprice requires. Alternately feeling gratitude toward him and overpowering rage at his solipsism and suppression of her feelings, she assumes a persona, which, as he himself admits, serves to camouflage his own hardly reasonable desires, thereby safeguarding him; having little recourse, she escapes into her imagination: "Listening to his voice, she saw her own face reflected in a spring. Thereupon, a loving mother's smile passed over half of her face while the other half of her face boiled over with the rage of an evil demon" (345). In this passage, which is a rewriting both of the Narcissus myth and of the conventional trope of the woman examining her loveliness in a mirror, the reflected visage does not serve to confirm or deny the intrinsic beauty of the yamamba; rather, it functions to mirror her own fractured being necessitated by the pressures of a society dominated by male desire. She imagines simultaneously devouring the man, even as she suckles him at her breast. And yet, throughout the story, she suppresses the demonic urges, manifesting only the benevolent, good, kind mother image sanctioned by society. The most poignant section of the story is when the yamamba envisions what it would be like to be in the mountains, in what some might term a kind of feminist utopia, liberated from the confining shackles enforced by years of education and domestication learned living among humans. Again, in a passage reminiscent of *The Yamamba with Child*, she describes the sprouting of horns on her head, though this time as a signal of release and the emergence of authentic being.

At the end of the story, we are confronted by the terrible irony of her daughter reading the expression on her dead face as beatific and murmuring "How lovely her face looks even in death! Mother, you really were blessed, weren't you" (351). The grotesqueness of the daughter's extraordinarily inappropriate comment is offset by the yamamba's own belated recognition, shortly before she dies, that "probably, even her own dead mother had also been an honest-to-god yamamba" (351). Just as her own daughter misunderstands her, so, too, we are reminded, she may have misinterpreted her own mother, thereby perpetuating the cycle of alienation and frustration. Each mother, repressing her own nature, raises her daughter without acknowledging their true commonality and thereby teaches her to conform by disguising her true emotions. It is a bleak legacy, and one that makes the yamamba's smile all the more ironic and wretched.

In each of these yamamba narratives, we witness a tension about women's nature and its relation to society, as represented in the dynamic between women, whether it be between the old woman and the young woman of the *Konjaku* story; between the true Yamamba and her impersonator Hyakuma Yamamba in the Nō play; between the yamamba who was once Yaegiri and the *obasute* she becomes; or between the mother and daughter in Ōba Minako's story. In each case, a type of mirroring occurs in which the resistance of unregenerate womanhood is transmuted into complicity; in other words, we witness a process of domestication through the evocation of victimization, one in which the foremother is vilified, ignored, or misunderstood.

Just a year before Ōba's "Smile of the Mountain Witch" appeared in 1976 in the periodical *Shinchō*, the French feminist critic Hélène Cixous published an essay decrying the suppression of women's being, with the curiously resonant title "Le rire de la méduse" (The laugh of the Medusa),[12] in which, through the evocation of another mythic, demonic figure, she exhorts women to seek out their own natures, to explore their inner, dark, labyrinthine structures, to delight in their hidden aspects. In many ways, it projects an inverse image from that of the yamamba topos, suggesting possible solutions to the bleak questions posed by Ōba in her earlier story. Women, Cixous argues, have been silenced by society and have been unable to give voice to their dreams and desires. In a passage that sounds uncannily like Ōba writing of the yamamba, she states,

> Time and again I, too, have felt so full of luminous torrents that I could burst—burst with forms much more beautiful than those which are put up in frames and sold for a stinking fortune. And I, too, said nothing, showed nothing: I didn't open my mouth. . . . I was afraid and I swallowed my shame and my fear. I said to myself: You are mad! What's the meaning of these waves, these floods, these outbursts? Where is the ebullient, infinite woman who, immersed as she was in her naivete, kept in the dark about herself, led into self-disdain by the great arm of parental-conjugal phallocentrism, hasn't been ashamed of her strength? Who surprised and horrified by the

fantastic tumult of her drives (for she was made to believe that a
well-adjusted normal woman has a . . . divine composure), hasn't accused herself of being a monster? ("The Laugh of the Medusa," 876)

If the yamamba represents, in some respects, a fetishizing of men's
fears of castration in her role as man-eater, then the Medusa may signify another kind of fetish in which the fear of male paralysis (that is,
the Medusa dares men to gaze on her countenance and then turns
them to stone) necessitates the transfixing of women. Cixous's answer
to Ōba's obliquely posed question of how women can recover their
authentic selves appears in the first paragraph: "Woman must write
her self. . . . Woman must put herself into the text—as into the world
and into history—by her own movement" (875). The tone of the essay
significantly emerges as triumphant and certain. Cixous jubilantly
exhorts:

> Write! and your self-seeking text will know itself better than flesh
> and blood, rising, insurrectionary dough kneading itself, with sono-
> rous, perfumed ingredients, a lively combination of flying colors,
> leaves, and rivers plunging into the sea we feed. . . . But look, our
> seas are what we make of them, full of fish or not, opaque or trans-
> parent, red or black, high or smooth, narrow or bankless; and we are
> ourselves sea, sand, coral, seaweed, beaches, tides, swimmers, chil-
> dren, waves. . . . More or less wavily sea, earth, sky—what matter
> would rebuff us? We know how to speak them all. (889)

Yet the imaginary dialogue between Cixous and Ōba does not
end here. In Ōba's 1986 story "Candlefish," she returns to the yamamba topos, invoking many of the same images and ideas, involving the sea, the association of women with yeast and bread, and the
issue of women's language and voice, that Cixous does. In various
ways, this work mediates the gap between the bleak prospect facing
women in Ōba's earlier story of the yamamba and Cixous's clarion
call to women in "The Laugh of the Medusa," neither denying the ef-
ficacy of women's actions nor asserting the liberation of women
through a disavowal of the legacy of the past.

In this story, the narrator describes a figure who visits her at night
or just before dawn, when she lies awake in bed thinking. This unreal,
chameleon-figure of a woman, whom she variously designates as
Tsukiko or Olga, mirrors the narrator's own transformation into a
yamamba who devours men. As the yamamba-narrator crunches
with gusto the skeleton of the man, as well as his small, shriveled pe-

nis, which she pejoratively refers to as a dead candlefish, Tsu-kiko/Olga comes to her, transforms herself into a large, luminous candlefish, and speaks in what Ōba describes as "candlefish language."

> This candlefish language, which sprang up between Tsukiko and me without our realizing it, is one that does not acknowledge the names, nationalities, or languages affixed to us from our birth; because we speak in such a language, those people who cling to nationality or native tongue will never really understand. Candlefish, living in the sea, after all can swim to the shores of every country. (308)

No longer are women men without penises, as Freud would have it, but, now, in an about-face, it is men who lack "candlefish-ness," their very penises attesting to that fact. The candlefish symbol evokes women's archetypal associations with the fluidity and fertility of the sea as well as the mystical illumination emerging from the depths. The candlefish, associated with the night and the moon, seems to hark back to a fundamental commonality in which all women are conjoined.

Much of the story centers around the past, when the narrator knew a woman named Olga, whose struggles to survive are recounted in some detail. Having been abused by her husband, Olga seeks to establish a life for herself and her children free from the trammels of marriage and subservience. It is Olga who chooses to wear old and torn underwear, reserving what little money she has for buying Bach recordings. It is Olga who assiduously bakes fresh bread for all the children, nourishing them both literally and spiritually. It is Olga transformed into Tsukiko, daughter of the moon,[13] who appears to console the narrator through long, sleepless nights. The narrator remarks early on, "People always dream of things that they can never realize. Dreams are things that do not exist in reality" (311). Hence, though Olga leaves her abusive husband, and our narrator continues her artistic quest despite the burdens of husband and family, neat solutions for women in the manner outlined by Cixous are not forthcoming.

The atmosphere of the story is hazy, like the early dawn, and we, as readers, intuit the significance of these imaginings of the narrator rather than lay bare their meaning. The narrative hints at the power of imagination that links women and allows them to dream. And yet, in contradistinction to Cixous's confident pronouncements, women's powers to dream and create do not entirely alter the world around them. Whereas the narrator possesses the imaginative powers of the artist, Olga, after her marriage to a wastrel musician, remains suspicious of artistic tendencies. We are told she marks those persons with the label "useless person." The narrator comments that perhaps resisting this label is precisely what will enable her to pursue her work. This is the struggle of the woman artist, whose work invariably becomes the site of contention over its worth and its utility, both by men and by other women. Interestingly, at the end, the narrator once again dreams of Olga, who seems more luminous than ever, and who, in her final words in the story, states that she has completely forsworn all her labels.

Both Ōba and Cixous acknowledge the distinctiveness of women and the way in which society condemns that difference as pathological, but in contrast to Cixous's feminist prescription for the future in the form of *jouissance*, an orgasmic vitality and delight in those pleasures proscribed by society, as a mode of authentic being, we find in the yamamba a description of the constraints of the past, in which progressively through the centuries, the figure of the yamamba becomes more and more vitiated, eager to be reclaimed and domesticated. We return once again to the dialectic of resistance and aberration, in which the topos of the yamamba can be read as a kind of palimpsest of women's quest throughout the ages for a place of authentic being, a quest both volatile and indeterminate.

Notes

1. For another view on victimization, see Marcus, 81–82.

2. According to Origuchi Shinobu (*Nihon kokugo daijiten*, 544), the term originally designated shrine maidens living in the mountains who would perform ritual purification rites (*misogi*) and keep watch over the waters of sacred mountains. See also the provocative chapter on the yamamba and the Japanese psyche by Kawai: "The Woman Who Eats Nothing."

3. See, e.g., the parallel entries in *Kōjien*; *Nihon kokugo daijiten*; and *Encyclopedia Japonica* (*Dai Nihon hyakka jiten*), vol. 17.

4. See, e.g., the three stories in Araki et al., 7: 155–70; or Ikeda, 32. See also the fascinating speculation by Ōba Minako, in a dialogue with Mizuta Noriko, that yamamba have always existed in the Japanese cultural imagination—for example, in the myth of Izanami and Izanagi, in which, in Orpheus-and Eurydice-like fashion, Izanagi goes to the underworld after his spouse has died to entreat her to return with him to the world of the living. Seeing

her maggot-infested corpse, he flees back to the upper world. For Ōba this is another early prototype of the yamamba motif. See Ōba and Mizuta, 123–56.

5. All page references in the text to the *Konjaku* story are to Mabuchi et al., 60–64. Translations are mine, but there is an excellent English translation, "How a Woman Who Was Bearing a Child Went to South Yamashina, Encountered an Oni, and Escaped," by Marian Ury, in *Tales of Times Now Past*, 161–63.

6. By contrast, cf., e.g., the rather happy outcome in the yamauba's interaction with a young girl in Mayer, 6–8.

7. All references in the text to the Nō play *Yamamba* are to Koyama et al., 502–21. There are several translations of *Yamamba* into English, including one of the *kuse* scene in Bethe and Brazell, 21–23, 92–123; one by Royall Tyler, "Granny Mountains," in *Granny Mountains*, 155–75; and, most recently, a new translation by Royall Tyler, "Yamamba: The Mountain Crone," in *Japanese Nō Dramas*, 309–28.

8. See, e.g., the entry *yamamba mono*, in *Encyclopedia Japonica*, 17: 674–75; and in *Nihon kokugo daijiten*, 19: 544.

9. See the entry for "Kintarō," in *Kodansha Encyclopedia of Japan*, 4: 218.

10. All references in the text to the play *Komochi yamamba* are to Chikamatsu, 177–226.

11. The phrase derives from a poem of the same name by Coventry Patmore whose heroine epitomized the virtuous woman prized by the Victorians: pliable, gentle, self-sacrificing, eager to please. Woolf notes in an essay entitled "Professions for Women" that this is the mythic legacy that women must struggle to resist if they seek to express their true selves: "Killing the Angel in the House was part of the occupation of the woman writer" (286).

12. *L'arc*, 39–54; the quotations are from a translation by Keith Cohen and Paula Cohen of a revised version published in *Signs* (Summer 1976), which was subsequently published as part of a collection edited by Elaine Marks and Isabelle de Courtivron entitled *New French Feminism*, and again in *The Signs Reader* edited by Elizabeth Abel and Emily K. Abel.

13. This appellation seems to hark back to the motto of the feminist journal *Seitō* (Bluestocking), published in the early decades of the twentieth century: "In the beginning, woman was the sun. / An authentic person. / Today she is the moon. / Living through others. Reflecting the brilliance of others . . ." (cited in Sievers, 163). See also Vernon, epigraph to title page.

Works Cited

Abel, Elizabeth, and Emily K. Abel, eds. *The Signs Reader: Women, Gender, and Scholarship*. Chicago: University of Chicago Press, 1983.

Araki Hiroyuki et al. *Nihon densetsu taikei*. Tokyo: Mizuumi shobō, 1982– .

Benstock, Shari, ed. *Feminist Issues in Literary Scholarship*. Bloomington: Indiana University Press, 1987.

Bernstein, Gail Lee, ed. *Recreating Japanese Women, 1600–1945.* Berkeley: University of California Press, 1991.

Bethe, Monica, and Karen Brazell. *Nō as Performance.* Ithaca, N.Y.: Cornell University Press, 1978.

Chikamatsu Monzaemon. *Komochi yamamba.* In *Chikamatsu jōruri shū (ge)*, ed. Shuzui Kenji and Ōkubo Tadakuni. Nihon koten bungaku taikei 50. Tokyo: Iwanami shoten, 177–226.

Cixous, Hélène. "The Laugh of the Medusa." Trans. Keith Cohen and Paula Cohen. *Signs: Journal of Women in Culture and Society* 1, no. 4 (1976): 875–93; reprinted — Marks and de Courtivron, *New French Feminism*, 247–64; and Abel and Abel, *The Signs Reader*, 279–97.

———. "Le rire de la méduse." *L'arc* (1975), 39–54.

Enchi Fumiko. *Masks (Onna men).* Trans. Juliet Winters Carpenter. New York: Knopf, 1983.

Field, Norma. *The Splendor of Longing in "The Tale of Genji."* Princeton: Princeton University Press, 1987.

Freud, Sigmund. "Fetishism." In *The Standard Edition of the Complete Psychological Works of Sigmund Freud*, trans. and ed. James Strachey. London: Hogarth Press, 1961, 21: 152–57.

Ikeda Hiroko, ed. *A Type and Motif Index of Japanese Folk-Literature.* Helsinki: Suomalainen Tiedeakatemia, 1971.

Kawai Hayao. *The Japanese Psyche: Major Motifs in the Fairy Tales of Japan.* Dallas: Spring Publications, 1988.

———. "The Woman Who Eats Nothing." In idem, *The Japanese Psyche*, 27–45.

Koyama Hiroshi, Satō Kikuo, and Satō Ken'ichirō, eds. *Yamamba, Yōkyoku shū.* Nihon koten bungaku zenshū 34. Tokyo: Shōgakukan, 1975, 502–21.

Lippit, Noriko Mizuta, and Kyoko Iriye Selden, eds. *Japanese Women Writers: Twentieth Century Short Fiction.* Armonk, N.Y.: M. E. Sharpe, 1991.

Mabuchi Kazuo, Kunisaki Fumimaro, and Konno Tōru, eds. *Konjaku monogatari shū.* Nihon koten bungaku zenshū 24. Tokyo: Shōgakukan, 1976.

Marcus, Jane, "Still Practice, A/Wrested Alphabet." In Benstock, 79–97.

Marks, Elaine, and Isabelle de Courtivron, eds. *New French Feminism.* Amherst: University of Massachusetts Press, 1980.

Mayer, Fanny Hagin. *Ancient Tales in Modern Japan.* Bloomington: Indiana University Press, 1984.

Mitsutani, Margaret. "Renaissance in Women's Literature." *Japan Quarterly* 33, no. 3 (1986): 313–19.

Ōba Minako. "Candle Fish" ("Rōsoku-uo"). In Tanaka, *Unmapped Territories*, 18–38.

———. *Ōba Minako zenshū.* 10 vols. Tokyo: Kōdansha, 1991.

———. "Rōsoku-uo." In *Umi ni yuragu ito. Ōba Minako zenshū*, 9: 306–26.

———. "The Smile of the Mountain Witch." ("Yamamba no bishō"). In Lippit and Selden, 194–206.

———. "Yamamba no bishō." In *Ōba Minako zenshū*, 3: 335–51.

Ōba Minako and Mizuta Noriko. "'Yamauba' naru mono o megutte." In *Yamauba no iru fūkei*. Tokyo: Tabata shoten, 1995.

Okada, H. Richard. *Figures of Resistance: Language, Poetry, and Narrating in "The Tale of Genji" and Other Mid-Heian Texts*. Durham, N.C.: Duke University Press, 1991.

Ostriker, Alicia. "The Thieves of Language: Women Poets and Revisionist Mythmaking." *Signs* 8, no. 1 (Autumn 1982): 68–90.

Rimer, J. Thomas, and Yamazaki Masakazu, trans. *On the Art of the Nō Drama*. Princeton: Princeton University Press, 1984.

Robertson, Jennifer. "The Shingaku Woman: Straight from the Heart." In Bernstein, 88–107.

Sievers, Sharon. *Flowers in Salt: The Beginnings of Feminist Consciousness in Modern Japan*. Stanford: Stanford University Press, 1983.

Tanaka, Yukiko, ed. *To Live and to Write: Selections by Japanese Women Writers, 1913–1938*. Seattle: Seal Press, 1987.

———. *Unmapped Territories*. Seattle: Women in Translation, 1991.

Tanizaki Jun'ichirō. *Naomi (Chijin no ai)*. Trans. Anthony Hood Chambers. San Francisco: North Point Press, 1990.

Tyler, Royall. *Granny Mountains: A Second Cycle of Nō Plays*. Ithaca, N.Y.: Cornell University East Asian Papers, 1978.

———. *Japanese Nō Dramas*. New York: Penguin, 1992.

Ury, Marian. *Tales of Times Now Past*. Berkeley: University of California Press, 1979.

Vernon, Victoria V. *Daughters of the Moon: Wish, Will, and Social Constraint in Fiction by Modern Japanese Women*. Berkeley: University of California Press, 1988.

Woolf, Virginia. "Professions for Women." In *Collected Essays*, ed. Leonard Woolf. London: Hogarth Press, 1966, 2: 284–89.

———. *A Room of One's Own*. New York: Harcourt, Brace & World, 1929.

8

Hayashi Kyōko and the Gender of Ground Zero

JOHN WHITTIER TREAT

> A-bomb victim: the contradiction of what "man" did to "man."
> —Hayashi Kyōko, "Shanghai and August Ninth"

In 1982 Hayashi Kyōko (1930–), a survivor of the atomic bombing of Nagasaki, published a story entitled "Buji" (Safe) in an important literary journal. In it she recounts a visit made the previous year to Hiroshima, Japan's other A-bomb city but a city to which she had never traveled. Hayashi tells of going to Hiroshima with memories of her native Nagasaki fresh in her mind, revived by the recent death of a favorite high school teacher from bomb-related causes. As her plane approaches the airport, she is haunted by the delusion that she is aboard the American bomber *Enola Gay*, a plane that 36 years earlier had delivered its fateful payload. Once on the ground, however, Hayashi is struck by how beautifully rebuilt Hiroshima is, and soon she takes note of other striking differences between this city and her own Nagasaki.

Most prominent of these differences is one that unexpectedly limits Hayashi's qualifications to report on Hiroshima, despite her reputation as Japan's most prominent atomic-bomb writer alive today.[1] When she visits the Atomic Dome memorial, she is humbled to discover, despite her presumption of a congruence of the experiences of Hiroshima and Nagasaki *hibakusha* (A-bomb survivors), that August Sixth belongs in fact to Hiroshima and Hiroshima alone:

Until today I had never regarded August Sixth and the Atomic Dome with such poignant emotion. I had forgotten that the Dome existed until, walking through Peace Park, I recognized it towering above the verdant leaves of the laurel trees. "Forgotten" is not quite the right word: I had come here thinking that our commonality as hibakusha meant that August Sixth belonged to all of us. But the Dome made such camaraderie utterly impossible. (41)

Hayashi's brief trip to Hiroshima made her question her assumption that she knew what the bombings, in their plural senses, had meant. But the visit also reaffirmed her knowledge of the continuing crisis initiated by the advent of nuclear weapons. The single word "safe" that makes up the title of the story refers to what was scribbled on a roster next to the names of Hayashi's classmates who had survived the blast on August Ninth, 1945. But it is a word that can only sound ironic, after not only decades of the cancers and other bomb-related illnesses that have killed those classmates who thought themselves spared, but also after the Bikini Atoll tests, Three Mile Island, Chernobyl, and most of all the global arms race. "What can 'safe' possibly mean today," asks Hayashi, "for any of us living in the present of the nuclear age?" (55).

But Hayashi's insistence on the universal nature of a nuclear terror contrasts with her equally resolute assertion that, just as a knowledge of August Sixth is epistemically confined to Hiroshima's survivors, of which she is not one, so the greatest familiarity with the import of the double events that commenced this terror remains the preserve of those who were their targets. Hayashi's realization in "Safe" of how the dimensions of Hiroshima's tragedy are not entirely graspable even by a Nagasaki hibakusha implies a wider, even unbridgeable, chasm that must separate the non-hibakusha from what is frankly proposed as the privileged, post-Hiroshima insight granted to survivors of these atrocities. "If I hadn't been bombed," Hayashi was once quoted, "I would not write" (Nakayama, 239): and, conversely, she seems to imply, those of us who were not, should not.

In this reservation of a special view into the human future by virtue of attendance at either of its two rehearsals, Hayashi is not alone among hibakusha. Indeed, she is acutely aware of how her own relative fortune as a survivor must condition what she knows and constrain what she writes. The narrator of her short autobiographical story "Tomo yo" (Friend; 1977), a woman who herself lost no relatives in the bombing of Hiroshima, guiltily notes the difference that exists between herself and a friend who has seen six members of her family die (185–89). Hayashi's recurring theme of the historical and psychological isolation of atomic-bomb survivors often seems to imply the incommunicability of what it meant to be in Hiroshima and Nagasaki: an implication that challenges the feasibility of ever successfully writing for a larger, non-hibakusha audience.

But this insistence upon incommunicability is, in another irony, precisely what is communicated again and again in atomic-bomb literature, and perhaps in Hayashi's especially. Readers may understandably react with impatience to the insinuation that they will never understand but should nonetheless listen attentively. It is the arrogance perceived in such claims of privilege, ethical as well as experiential, that has periodically fueled bitter public attacks on Hayashi Kyōko and her writing. In a joint review of "Safe" by the critics Karatani Kōjin and Kawamura Jirō and the late novelist Nakagami Kenji published shortly after the work's appearance, Nakagami exploded in a complaint that revealed signs of a long-standing frustration, not just with Hayashi but with the theme of the bombing of Hiroshima and Nagasaki in literature overall:

> I have never, even once, recognized as fiction anything that Hayashi has written. . . . Basically she believes that merely writing about atomic bombings achieves something literary, but . . . her work is neither essay nor fiction. . . . I felt her piece "Safe" somewhat pathetic when I read it—pathetic in that Hayashi should have thought that just writing so artlessly about the atomic bomb could be literature, or that she thought it could be publishable in a literary magazine. . . . If she thinks the atomic bomb is automatically literature by making a text out of it, then I guess we've got to conclude that the A-bomb has finally shown us how literature is to be done, don't we? (Karatani et al., 288)

This sarcastic rejection of atomic-bomb literature as literature echoes a history of similar charges leveled against survivor-writers for nearly half a century. Ōta Yōko,[2] the most prominent woman atomic-bomb writer before Hayashi, had her work demeaned in the early 1950's when, for example, the Hiroshima poet Shijō Miyoko rejected the genre in toto for its inartistic "utilitarianism."[3] Just as Nakagami resisted the equation of the writing of personal experience— when that experience is an atomic bombing—with the aesthetic category of the literary, a generation of inhospitable critics before him had similarly shielded literature against incursions by themes and points of view derived from the atrocities committed in Hiroshima and Nagasaki. At the same time, however, it must be said that hibakusha writers have a history of erecting their own insurmountable barricades: as one character in an atomic-bomb novel declares, no one not there "has any chance at all of entering in from the outside to empathize" (Iida, 388). From the inception of atomic-bomb literature, then, the impasse has been between writers who insist that others cannot know what they themselves know, and critics who insist that such knowledge is not automatically literary. The long life of such incompatible positions was demonstrated again when Kawamura Jirō applauded Nakagami's testy dismissal of Hayashi. Since her first works, Kawamura observed, she has written "out of an absolute need to write of her experience, but that has come to be replaced in her works with a sense of 'mission.' In my view this sense of mission—the sense that this experience must not be allowed to fade from memory—is itself a manifestation of the fact that it is fading" (289).

Encouraged perhaps by Kawamura's concurrence, Nakagami raised the rhetorical stakes of his verbal assault on Hayashi to new heights when he accused her of being an "atomic fascist" for insisting that whatever she wrote—wrote of the bombing, that is—was immediately literary. To this political charge was added a psychoanalytical one, when Nakagami and Karatani agreed that the nuclear issue had in fact become something of a "fetish" in literary circles (290).[4] The use of such powerfully censorious language as "fascist" and "fetish" derives in part from an exasperation with the unrelenting attention paid the atomic bombings by hibakusha writers. Hayashi Kyōko annoys her critics on at least two scores: her single-minded dedication to a politically suspect theme—suspicious because it reproduces what Maruyama Masao described as the modern Japanese predilection for assuming the posture of the aggrieved victim—and her concomitant refusal to trade that dedication for other, more cogent literary or historical issues.

In 1978, Nakagami bluntly expressed his resentment toward Hayashi in the following summary judgment of her then recently published short-story collection, *Giyaman — biidoro* (Cut glass, blown glass; 1978):

> It is ironic that the more one realizes that, among all Japanese fiction, there is none more poisonous than atomic-bomb literature, the more one realizes that there is no more perfect fiction for those Japanese

who mourn the war. "This is how badly I was bombed," etc. But what really happened back then isn't in any of this fiction, is it. And that's why it can't be literature. . . . In Hayashi Kyōko's *Cut Glass, Blown Glass* readers are easily moved to tears just because it's about hibakusha. This is fiction put together through tricks. And nothing could be better suited for those old folks who made the war and committed crimes and yet want to feign innocence and wallow in regrets. (Nakagami et al., 109–10).

Nakagami gives angry vent to the collective impatience of a number of younger critics who have resisted what they perceive as the self-indulgent, manipulative, and ultimately self-serving literature of a wartime victimhood that not only fails to analyze the legacy of Japanese victimizing but ignores it altogether.[5] In light of the attempts to rewrite modern Japanese history, or to forget it altogether, Nakagami's complaints are motivated by a legitimate suspicion of the consequences, if not the intentions, of a literature that seems myopically and miserably focused on the individual measure of suffering in World War II, rather than on its international origins and import. This is a type of writing with which Hayashi, a survivor-writer, has come to be identified, but which Nakagami's postwar generation would prefer to subordinate to a more contemporary, and more basic agenda of what it sees as the issues of Japan's socially, politically, and economically distorted modernity.

One cannot easily absolve Hayashi Kyōko of the charges that her work is, in fact, often monotonously autobiographical, relentlessly morose, and petulantly indignant. But what Nakagami does not acknowledge, and what must make these traits in her writings understandable, if not more welcome, is that Hayashi Kyōko—unlike us—has witnessed a nuclear war. The result of this bifurcation, if it is as fundamental as claimed by many hibakusha writers, is that our respective registers of what may seem appropriate or acceptable to say are now permanently askew. Novelist Abe Tomoji once stated that literature has had to deal with epochal events before, but the problem of writing and nuclear weapons nonetheless marks a "rupture" (*rui o zesshite*) in culture, a rupture that earlier cultural expressions faced with simply assimilating social and technological change did not experience (80). "There is no explanation whatsoever for me of August Ninth, or August Sixth," writes Hayashi, as if to spurn Nakagami's demand for the same. "No ideology, no claim, no history, no era, has anything to do with August Sixth or Ninth" ("Shanhai to hachigatsu

kokonoka" [Shanghai and August Ninth], 114). One will be patient
with Hayashi's obsession with herself and that day, once one accepts
the double truth of Nagasaki's unprecedented, but now normal, lesson—once one accepts that she writes to us from a place we should
hesitate to judge because, after all, it does mean something not to have
been there. It was perhaps with Nakagami in mind that Hayashi
wrote this apology for her work:

> We hibakusha shall unfortunately never take one step beyond the ex-
> traordinary. For the most part those who read what I write are peo-
> ple who have had nothing to do with August Sixth or Ninth; they are
> people who are physically normal. The work of communicating the
> extraordinary faithfully and from within the interior of the extraor-
> dinary to people who are normal is difficult. I often end up letting
> my sense of being a victim take over and complain. August Sixth and
> Ninth, never exclusively a personal event, do conclude with a private
> rancor. This pain should never be only personal, but he who feels the
> pain is, one by one, the solitary individual "I." That is why those of
> you who are normal may be so sensitive to the whining complaints
> of hibakusha. Maybe those of you sensitive to our whining feel some
> unwarranted sense of being a victimizer yourselves. I do indeed
> think it difficult, this work of conveying, as some common theme,
> what only some possess to others who do not. ("Shanhai to hachi-
> gatsu kokonoka," 117)

Here it is history, rather than nationality, or race, or gender, that
stands between our ken of our experience and that of those whom we
would read, or to whom we would write. The irascibility, and possibly the incomprehensibility, of Hayashi Kyōko for a fellow writer as
astute as Nakagami Kenji—whose own identity as a member of Japan's disadvantaged burakumin caste surely might have made him
sympathetic to Hayashi's claims of a social marginality—should
sound a cautionary note for all of us who might fail to see the atomic-
bomb writer's frustration as one part of that same writer's earnest
mimesis: the representation of the unrepresentable is, as Hayashi says
in a studied understatement, "difficult." Perhaps it is just that one
word, and the constellation of conflicting memories and emotions it
represses, that constitutes the most powerful representation of what it
means to have survived a nuclear attack—however much the aesthetics of those opposed to such alternately baffled and hostile writing demur; or their politics protest.

When Hayashi returned to Nagasaki in 1945 after a childhood

spent in Shanghai, where her father worked for Mitsui Industries, it was because the home islands were thought the safer places to be as the war pressed closer. Her mother and three sisters took up residence in the old castle town of Isahaya outside of Nagasaki, but Kyō-ko, in order to attend higher school, boarded in the city proper. Subsequently, she was conscripted with her schoolmates to work at a Mitsubishi munitions works near the bomb's epicenter; as a consequence, "99 percent" of Hayashi's class "became Nagasaki hibaku-sha" ("Dōkikai," 66). August 9, 1945, was only days before Hayashi's fifteenth birthday: the bombing made her seriously ill for several months, and Hayashi claims she has never enjoyed full health since. "I was bombed in Nagasaki when a junior at the Girls High School, while mobilized as a worker. I was 1.4 kilometers from ground zero, within the 'special zone' where all forms of life both above and below the earth were said to have been exterminated" ("Arumi no yōki," 10).

Like many hibakusha, Hayashi recalls her experience of the bombing in only partial and discontinuous impressions that fail to constitute any simple and simply reiteratible narrative. "There was the deafening sound of something in a nosedive, and then darkness. I have written of this any number of times, but all that I know of that instant when the atomic bomb exploded was the buzz of something plummeting to earth. I have no memory of a flash, or a fiery blast, or an explosive force. Was it only a second between that sound and darkness? Or a minute?" ("Hibaku," 55). The fragmentary and finally irreconcilable pieces of Hayashi's memory are what may have condemned her to rehearse that "instant" over and over again in her works, the same repetition that antagonizes some critics. She began writing in the early 1960's after a young adulthood that was complicated, first, by the relative poverty caused by the Occupation's dissolution of the conglomerate that had employed her father, and then by the breakup of a marriage made singularly unsuccessful, at least in part and by her own admission, by her bomb-related neuroses.

Critical praise and a wide readership did not come until 1975, when her story "Matsuri no ba" (The site of rituals) won first the New Writer's Prize from the literary journal *Gunzō* and then, in a more prestigious honor, one of that year's two Akutagawa Prizes. "The Site of Rituals" stands both chronologically and thematically at the head of her long list of works concerned with the theme of physical degeneration and psychological demoralization in the hibakusha subculture. Adopting the same narrative format found in nearly all her later stories, Hayashi has a first-person narrator relate the accounts of herself and her fellow Nagasaki victims over a period of years, but focuses specifically on the days and weeks immediately following the bombing. This narrator—a fourteen-year-old schoolgirl ordered, as was Hayashi herself, to work in a Mitsubishi munitions factory—describes in exact detail, supplemented with much objective scientific and journalistic data, the fates of her classmates, teachers, family, and relatives.

The "site" of the story's title refers to a concrete courtyard at the factory, the "rituals" to the send-off dance that the high school boys, also mobilized as munitions workers, would perform whenever one of their number was sent to the front. "By that time, students were sent to battle everyday," Hayashi writes. "That concrete, brutal factory courtyard had become their site of rituals" (38). More than forty of them would be enacting their "sad, pantomime-like dance" when the bomb exploded overhead:

> The students who were dancing their farewell dance in the courtyard died instantly, or were so seriously burned that they survived only an hour or two. One was thrown to the concrete by the pressure of the blast and had his intestines squeezed out of him; so young, his screams were horrible. A friend who had heard those screams while fleeing himself must even now cover his ears when speaking of it. (40–41)

Most of "The Site of Rituals," however, is concerned with Hayashi's own female classmates and family. Like Hayashi, the story's narrator was the only member of her immediate family in the city proper that morning. Her father was still abroad, and her mother and sisters safely evacuated to Isahaya. "Not one of them imagined that Nagasaki, 25 kilometers away, had been bombed and was now aflame" (33). Later on the ninth, as bits and scraps of clothing—pieces, literally, of Nagasaki—fall from the sky, as does an odd black rain, rumors gradually reach Isahaya that, indeed, Nagasaki had been the target of an air strike. But surely, reasons the narrator's mother, the whole city could not have been bombed; surely her daughter is safe.

The next day, with the added information that, in fact, most of Nagasaki had sustained damage, the narrator's mother just as easily believes her daughter must be dead. Yet she has survived, miraculously, if only for the time being. Thirty years later, the narrator notes of her friends that "fragments of glass remain in their bodies" (37). Her survival is certainly extraordinary. For others, the majority of her classmates working on that factory floor, death was quick and presumably without comprehension. For them, the narrator reflects, "there was neither light nor sound" (38). She recalls the horrible fires that swept through the factory and notes that "in an atomic attack, the best thing is to die immediately" (42). The narrator continues to be amazed at her survival: "Living and dying were separated by less than a thin sheet of paper" (43).

After the initial explosion, she crawls out of the factory and makes her way, with difficulty, to a neighborhood closer still to ground zero. She sees disfigured victims whom she describes in detail so complete as certainly to repel some readers. Moreover, she does so in the local Nagasaki dialect, rendering the written description oral, testimonial, and thus all the more rhetorically, immediately real. She is grateful whenever she spots someone who has managed to retain any semblance of their humanity, be it an eye, a nose or any recognizable feature. Many have not. Hayashi, like other survivor-writers but with a uniquely sardonic touch, intersperses dry statistics and scientific reports on the mass impact of the bomb with wrenching, anecdotal details, such as those of her own vomiting, which commenced approximately two hours after the blast. In her ill condition, she acutely feels not only the degradation of her surroundings but also their absurdity. After noting how her nausea was soon compounded with diarrhea, she goes on to observe how both destruction and a strangely detached calmness can coexist.

It is this coexistence that makes "The Site of Rituals" a successful combination of the two scales of destruction that the bombings wrought, for they were at once both a historical crisis and an individual ordeal. For instance, next to a report on the statistical death rate for those victims suffering from diarrhea, Hayashi juxtaposes her private memories of the unnerving silence that settled over her leveled high school. A descriptive and narrative rhythm is established in the story through the alternation of public information with subjective first-person accounts. Hayashi assembles a representation of "Nagasaki, August Ninth" through diverse data, the exercise of memory, and a carefully deployed literary pathos. Within the "site" in "The Site of Rituals" the narrator steadily descends into the typical "death-in-life," compromised existence of the hibakusha. "Amid the countless dead of Urakami, I had become as indifferent as a robot" (58).

Eventually the narrator is found in Nagasaki and brought to Isa-haya on foot, where many other refugees have come, only to fall ill. Many have already died. Some—one of the narrator's former teach-ers, for example—go insane just before death. It is fear, she thinks to herself, that does that, and it is fear that wracks her own body once she notices her hair has begun to fall out. So distraught is she by the onset of the symptoms of radiation disease that her mother takes her comb away. This first sign is soon followed by others, and her family can do nothing but stand by helplessly. Lethargy renders the narrator immobile. As her blood count reaches critical levels, uncomfortable tensions rack the house. She begins to think of herself as a burden to others, and even concludes that it is her duty to die quickly rather than prolong the inevitable. But somehow her condition stabilizes a month later, and she even becomes capable of humor, albeit a cynical one. When she receives a check for eighteen yen for her last two months' work at the munitions factory, for instance, she wryly jokes that the money might best be spent on flowers for her funeral.

Her mother tries various folk remedies to help her, but it is only after special attention from an American doctor that the inflammation recedes and her wounds begin to heal. Still, other survivors, some of whom are the narrator's friends, continue to die. When school re-sumes in October, and she attends the opening ceremony despite her doctor's advice, the eulogies delivered in memory of the deceased classmates make her feel acutely guilty for surviving. Indeed, some of the schoolgirls who were alive in early autumn died soon afterward, and others are still dying. The seemingly endless menace of radiation disease and its complications ironically undermines the last sentence of "The Site of Rituals"—a quote from an American film on the bombing that optimistically concludes, "Thus the destruction came to an end" (68). "What conceivable destruction having come 'to an end' could they be talking about?" Hayashi angrily asked in an essay written some years later. "What 'ended' was the destruction of buildings: for the bodies of us hibakusha, August Ninth marks the beginning of the destruction" ("Shanhai to hachigatsu kokonoka," 115).

In fact, the thematic thrust of Hayashi Kyōko's atomic-bomb lit-erature has been to show how the damage associated with the bomb-ings has not and cannot so easily, if ever, conclude. This is the theme throughout "The Site of Rituals," a first-person memoir unusual within the history of atomic-bomb literature in that it declines to dispose of the events of August 1945 as a nightmarish incident now firmly behind us. Rather than reiterate what other Nagasaki survivor-writers, such as Nagai Takashi, had already amply demonstrated to have been terror on an unprecedented scale, Hayashi endeavors to make the bombing a present-day problem for a world that only looks as if it is at peace. As a character in one of Hayashi's later novels puts it, "A nation at peace does not mean an individual person is at peace" (*Naki ga gotoki*, 141). Perhaps more than any other atomic-bomb writer, Hayashi Kyōko has considered the problem of the hidden wounds that continue to torment in spite of whatever outward healing might have taken place. It is for this reason that Nakano Kōji, a sympathetic critic who was also singled out for Nakagami's scorn, considers Hayashi the writer who "best carries on the legitimate line of atomic-bomb literature" (Nakano and Nagaoka, 14).[6]

This responsibility, however, has placed a special burden on Hayashi. The jurors of the 1975 Akutagawa Prize praised "The Site of Rituals" effusively, noting in particular "the weight of its facts" (Inoue Mitsuharu), "the vividness of the experience" (Haniya Yutaka), and "the power of its material" (Ōoka Shōhei),[7] but they also expressed doubts over the work's literary style. They posed questions long familiar to atomic-bomb writers: Is this fiction? Reportage? Or criticism? Like the work of Ōta Yōko, of whom other critics had asked the same questions more than twenty years earlier, "The Site of Rituals" is not a unified narrative. Several perspectives compete for our empathy: it is a work in which it is impossible for readers to identify with a hero or to submerge themselves in a fictional premise. In her attempt to represent Nagasaki as both a point in time and a continuing state of being, Hayashi's work can become difficult to read. The chronology of events is shuffled, and several people's stories are dealt with at the same time. This is, of course, part of the power of "The Site of Rituals." It reaches for inclusiveness when it describes August Ninth not just from Hayashi's point of view, but with information she later learned about "that day." "Nagasaki" refuses to be contained as an individual experience in any of Hayashi's work, but argues instead an entire history. Yet that history, however many times Hayashi returns to detail it more, always seems to fall short of some impossible mark for her. "When I began writing 'The Site of Rituals,'" Hayashi herself has admitted, "I rejected every vestige of fictional themes. I vowed to put down in words, as much as possible, just what happened. I also planned to end my career with its completion. But in fact the results were just the opposite" (quoted in Kōuchi, 50).

In other words, the story that was meant to tell "just what happened" did not. Hayashi's rejection of the fictional failed to be sufficiently full and exhaustive. The penalty has been Hayashi's Sisyphean return to Nagasaki and August Ninth in many of her subsequent writings. For example, most of the stories in *Cut Glass, Blown Glass* deal with her complex personal feelings about the special thirty-third anniversary of the bombing and the thirtieth class reunion of fellow schoolgirls—both of which took place in 1977. In "Akikan" (The empty can; 1977), the best-known story in the collection, she writes of revisiting her former high school and being overwhelmed by memories of the hundreds who perished there. The story examines the guilt intertwined with those memories: it is a guilt incumbent upon survivors and points to the gap not only between those "exposed" and "not exposed," but between those "exposed fatally" and those simply "exposed"; those "exposed" versus those "exposed more." Each human point in this cruel hibakusha topology is ignorant and at the same time guilty of the suffering of every nearer human point; "position" and "identity," words that in our contemporary, Western critical context typically refer to our indices of race, class, and gender, in Nagasaki can mean only the literal "standpoint" of hibakusha at two minutes before eleven that workday morning. Part of Hayashi's project as an atomic-bomb writer has been to demonstrate and contemplate the range of both the injury and the survival of injury, the complex net of often contradictory feelings that a hibakusha has toward herself and toward other hibakusha either living or dead— feelings that are perpetually linked to that unique place one stood, or sat, or—if one were in "the site of rituals"—danced.

In 1981 Hayashi published a full-length novel entitled *Naki ga gotoki* (As if not). It is the story of four hibakusha women who were classmates in 1945 Nagasaki, but two of whom, thirty years later, are now dead of bomb-related causes. *As If Not* discusses a wide range of historical incidents, political issues, and ongoing hibakusha concerns. Of special import to both the surviving women—an unnamed narrator and her old friend Haruko, married to an American who deserted the military during the Korean War—are the fears and hopes associated with their decisions to bear children. What emerges as a unique problem for the narrator alone—a narrator evenly split between an

"I" who recounts the events of the past and another noted simply as "the woman" (*onna*), who inhabits the narrative present — is additionally the act of narration itself: "Since suffering the atomic attack on August 9, 1945, my life has not moved one step forward from that point in time. However, I bear the responsibility to pass on my experience to the next generation. I write fiction in the attempt to be the ritual reciter of August Ninth" (quoted in Kuroko, "Genbaku bungaku," 262).

Hayashi's narrator's desire to be a "ritual reciter," or *kataribe*, is an ambition to serve as a communal memory of a people's most important narratives. It is a term that apparently reaches back before the advent of literacy in Japan, when designated official or hereditary clans (*be*) were charged with certain functions, among them the role of performing the recitation (*katari*) of key genealogies and cosmologies. The most famous of the historical kataribe was Hieda no Are, a woman who was commanded by Emperor Temmu to "recite . . . the 'royal genealogy' and 'the legends of antiquity'" for the compiler of the eighth-century *Kojiki* (Record of ancient matters; 712) because — presumably due to a growing number of contending versions — "they had reached a perilous state" (Konishi, 254–56). In this context, to serve as the kataribe of Nagasaki means to speak for it with a special authority and special responsibility; to speak of it for the future, and to protect the true record of events from the otherwise inevitable entropy that the passage of time promises.

Indeed, Hayashi Kyōko has worked hard to earn that authority and carry out that responsibility. Her experiences have been recorded in her stories and novels in a piecemeal and fragmented, but consistent, way over the past two decades. Together, her works take an unmistakably clear stand on the broader implications of nuclear war as well as of Nagasaki. The monotony of her work that discourages and even alienates some of her critics arises in some measure from the kataribe-like, ritual recitation of August Ninth that Hayashi performs in order to preserve, as if through sheer repetition, the veracity of what she had not to memorize but simply to recall. This is a project, however, riddled with questions, doubts, and even self-recriminations. In one sense, the ambition to serve as Nagasaki's kataribe is a plea for the rest of us to listen, and it is that plea, its constant refrain heard so frequently in Hayashi's writings, which, perhaps predictably, produces an antipathy to her work among more restless readers.

At the same time, however, Hayashi does not easily believe in our ability to understand what we are asked to listen to, a doubt that does more to undermine her ability to serve as a kataribe than does any objection from her audience. Her dilemma is whether a kataribe would speak of Nagasaki to change the world or to change Nagasaki itself. "The woman resolved to become the kataribe," Hayashi writes in *As If Not*, "because she wanted to prevent, if only by a little, Nagasaki from becoming routine. But, ironically, her very speaking of August Ninth was beginning that same process" (77). At the conclusion of the novel, the narrator suddenly sees her dilemma clearly. She understands the principal contradiction of her life over the thirty years that have passed since the bombing. To the world, she looks like nothing other than what she is, a hibakusha. But she herself has always wanted to be a "normal person." When her husband of twenty years finally left her, he told her that his entire marriage had been a marriage to a hibakusha. If you truly want to be a kataribe, he admonished, then all you need do is describe your own everyday life. This advice startles her: all these years of fearing the label "hibakusha," of repressing her identity, is ironically exactly what a hibakusha's life is all about. "It was precisely because I am a hibakusha, that I wanted to be a normal person. . . . Could anything have been more precious a waste?" (216).

Like that of Hayashi herself, this forever abnormal character's desire to be normal is inextricably linked with the longing to give birth to a child and the fear of what might happen when she does. One of the most successful stories in *Cut Glass, Blown Glass*, "Seinen-tachi" (Young men; 1977), is about the deep and unconfessed fears shared by both Hayashi and her son that, despite his good health, he will one day develop a fatal ailment whose cause was inherited from his hibakusha mother. Of the stories in the collection, nine more elaborate similar sets of desires and their countermanding fears. "The Empty Can" introduces the reader to the former Nagasaki Girls High School, as well as to Hayashi's private feelings of guilt at surviving what few of her classmates had; "Kompira yama" (Mount Kompira; 1977) leads us further into the company of the small group of women friends with whom Hayashi had grown up, attended school, and worked in the same wartime munitions plant. All are hibakusha. But most of them suffered more than Hayashi herself, who in fact neither lost close relatives nor retained any visible physical scars. These women will turn 46 in the year in which this story is set, and they express a sad relief at being — finally — beyond their childbearing years. Their complex and conflicting apprehensions are focused especially upon the special risks for hibakusha associated with childbirth, namely the inordinate loss of blood, stillbirths, genetic defects, and, most of all, a lifetime of concern over whether their children will be inherently susceptible to bomb-related cancers. The women blame the bomb for the high incidence of uterine myoma in Nagasaki's female population, as well as for other problems that seem to afflict hibakusha in unexpected numbers. These women, the reader soon learns, have spent the decades since the bombing waiting uneasily for something terrible to happen, a "something" whose exact details remain a frightening mystery.

This is the theme that dominates *Cut Glass, Blown Glass*. In the title story Hayashi, while visiting Nagasaki, accompanies a friend on her fruitless search for a piece of antique Nagasaki glass, a famous craft of the city. Each piece they examine conceals somewhere an imperfection, a hairline crack perhaps, that suggests it too was damaged internally, nearly invisibly, by the force of the atomic blast over thirty years ago. As Hayashi looks at one sample of glass fused by the heat—a piece that had been further away from the epicenter than she herself was—she feels the "truth" of Nagasaki all over again. As she writes in "Kiroku" (Document; 1977), another of the collection's stories, August Ninth looms over Hayashi's and, by implication, all hibakushas' lives, however much time may pass. "Even when we think we have moved one step forward, when sense returns, we are standing on August Ninth" (166). This ever-present realization—described by Hayashi's son in "Young Men" as "like being condemned to an innocent death" (84)—has a permanent effect on these women. Some have refused to marry, others to bear children. But Hayashi, who has done both, feels she has somehow inadvertently betrayed the others, and thus inflicts upon herself more reasons for guilt. The impact of these stories is one of a dire and inescapable oppression. The characters of *Cut Glass, Blown Glass* comprise a community of women for whom the terror of Nagasaki has not only never ended, it has not even measurably lessened. Hayashi portrays this terror with a sensitivity made complex by her relief at having been spared the absolute worst, and by her insight that it is a terror perhaps infinite in its ability to persist through time into succeeding generations. The survivors of Nagasaki Girls High School are understandably concerned with what effects of their exposure to the bomb, whether physiological or psychological, might be passed on to their offspring. The issue is a consequential one, taken seriously by science. "Whole body irradiation injured the nuclei of the cells and . . . may lead . . . to alteration of genes," states one study. "One should never forget that such momentary injurious action of an atomic bomb can have aftereffects for years and generations to come."[8] It is the psychological repercussions of this issue that are explored in Hayashi's work more deeply than anywhere else in Japanese atomic-bomb literature.

For Hayashi, the crux of the problem is the relationship between nuclear weapons and the biological survival of the species. The first focus of this concern is Hayashi's own physical health, and then the health of other women survivors. "In any era, war is a tragedy for young men," she writes, but the nature of weaponry in World War II means that in Hiroshima and Nagasaki women were "also subjected to physical ordeals. The signs of what affects us may appear much later in life, given that women tend on the average to live longer than men" ("Shanhai to hachigatsu kokonoka," 103). Most troubling for Hayashi, however, is the concern that, even once direct hibakusha like herself have died, the indirect hibakusha — including the nisei hibakusha or "second-generation survivors" — might themselves face some part, if not most, of the unsettling health problems that their parents had worried about. In her work "Zanshō" (Afterglow; 1985), a long meditation on her relationship with her son, Hayashi explains:

> As a hibakusha I fear the recurrence of August Ninth; I also fear the aftereffects I may have passed on to my son. . . . I worried that every nosebleed he had was a sign of leukemia, and I would go around and ask his classmates if they had nosebleeds, too. Every natural growing pain he had brought the ninth back to me. It all comes from a private concern, the one that, independent of ideology or politics, is found in all countries north or south, east or west: that parent and child be allowed to live free from danger. (239)

This concern of parent for child is described as being as "universal" as the nuclear age itself; unfortunately, that means that no mother can ever or anywhere raise a child without fear of his or her destruction. This brutal coincidence of women's desire with man's terrorism parallels Hayashi's private dread of a collective consequence: that the species will never wholly repair itself of the insidious damage inflicted in August 1945. "I raised my son worrying of nothing but whether he would be attacked by radiation disease," Hayashi wrote. "Now I have the same apprehension for his own child" (Kāki-iro kara kon-iro sedai e," 58).

"No ni" (In the fields; 1978), the concluding story of *Cut Glass, Blown Glass,* describes Hayashi's return to Tokyo and her review of the events of her busy week in Nagasaki attending both the school reunion and the memorial services. Recalling how some of her classmates had died instantly, she guiltily marvels anew at her own fair health. Her provisional survival, however, in no way lessens her obsession with the bombing and its perversion of life. A character in *As If Not* asserts that "all people alive today, throughout the world, may quite properly be called hibakusha" (205), and Hayashi concludes in "In the Fields" that everyone, hibakusha and non-hibakusha alike, is caught up in the events of Hiroshima and Nagasaki: "Everyone alive today feels terror toward the nuclear age, and not just on the days of August Sixth and Ninth. Just to think of it is to bring on anxiety" (243). For Hayashi, that anxiety is a broad and omnipresent one, rendering every moment of her adult life as mortally critical as those months immediately following August Ninth. Moreover, that critical moment does not belong to her alone, but to her generation and, indeed, the human race as a whole. "These are wounds inflicted by human beings," Hayashi writes at the end of "In the Fields." "These are deliberate wounds precisely calculated and inflicted by human beings. On account of these calculations, the very life that we would pass on to our children and grandchildren has sustained injury" (243).

☙

These comments succinctly express both Hayashi's anger and her fear: her sense of a crime having been perpetrated against her and the rest of her immediate world, and her frightening intuition that the crime may also have been perpetrated against future generations not yet conceived. For those who would like Hiroshima and Nagasaki to be, if a tragedy, then a tragedy now safely ensconced in history, "a lesson learned," or "a mistake never to be repeated," Hayashi's writings are disturbing, unnerving, and potentially even immobilizing. One could conclude, however, that the dismal future predicted by Hayashi's fears is little worse than the daily anguish her stories and essays report. In "Young Men" Hayashi finds herself trying to deny the possibility that what has happened to other children of hibakusha—death from cancer—could ever happen to her own son. Maybe one day he will indeed fall ill, she finally forces herself to admit. Her fear has long prevented her from contemplating such possibilities. But they are there, and they are possibilities conspicuously highlighted in the literature by Nagasaki writers, perhaps because, in recent decades, they have been largely women, the gender that has paid special attention to the long-term disruption of biology, and to those cultural and social values linked to biology: fertility, marriage, child-bearing—in other words, to the very survival of the race. "A woman gives birth," Hayashi once wrote. "And what of a man? His wife's baby is surely his own, but he has no history of having carried the child in his womb" ("Yobun na omoi," 73–74)—words that suggest Hayashi would not object to the notion of an *écriture féminine* guaranteed by biology.

Unlike some critics in the West, however, Hayashi finds little to celebrate in the possibility of a sexual difference that governs a literary one. Whether Hayashi's assertion that "women, to one degree or another, all have the maternal instinct" ("Yobun na omoi," 74) is true or not, her stories of women who never give birth out of fear, and of women who do, only to have that fear realized, are unbearably forlorn and bleak: their bodies, if not their souls, are permanently compromised in ways that challenge their very right to be women. Hayashi's work thus lacks any of the hope that others might see in a female alternative to masculine culture. In much Western feminist literary criticism, the woman's body is also a body that in its "bloodiness"—be it the literal menstrual blood that writes creatively upon a "blank page," or the figural blood of the Freudian castration that is woman's enabling stigma as well as the mark of her victimization—represents the genesis of a sexual difference that, in turn, accounts for what is purportedly different about women's writing. The effect of an anthropological feminist criticism, which took the body as both the source as well as the sign of an *écriture féminine*, has been profound and long-lasting. "I write woman: woman must write woman," declared Hélène Cixous in "The Laugh of Medusa" (877). "If there is a 'propriety of woman,' it is paradoxically her capacity to depropriate unselfishly, body without end, without appendage, without principal 'parts'" (889). "'She' is indefinitely other in herself," theorized Luce Irigaray in "This Sex Which Is Not One," likewise drawing upon female anatomy. "This is doubtless why she is said to be whimsical, incomprehensible, agitated, capricious . . . not to mention her language, in which 'she' sets off in all directions leaving 'him' unable to discern the coherence of any meaning" (28–29).

But woman's body for Hayashi Kyōko, and so too its language that leaves others "unable to discern the coherence of any meaning," is hardly the natural body: it is the irradiated, post-nuclear and destroyed body, a biological body betrayed by physics. It is neither "body without end" nor "indefinitely other." It is not indefinitely anything, except perhaps a permanent repository for those shards of glass shot into it like deadly arrows. Once, woman's body was meant for uniquely female things: the conception and bearing of children, and, with that, the promise of a human future. But after August Ninth, that same body risks being the sterile, and thus reproductively genderless, hibakusha body. Even if she manages to carry her baby successfully to term, as indeed Hayashi did, the woman hibakusha cannot trust that new body she has brought forth to survive; and that contingency makes her own body singular in ways unexplored in those feminist theories unconcerned with the one difference — not so much sexual as historical and atomic — that obsesses Hayashi, and rightly so: the difference between those of us with limbs and eyes and wombs that are intact and those of us for whom the very idea of such health, and with it the certain possibility of progeny, is an absurd and hopelessly nostalgic memory. No less than a Cixous or an Irigaray, Hayashi writes from her "different" body, a body that makes her speak, accordingly, words that are "different." But that difference is Nagasaki's curse, not women's promise; and it is a difference that Hayashi would prefer to have been spared.

⌀

The deep nihilism that informs every Hayashi Kyōko story, memoir, and essay has culminated in the most cynical pose and writing style of any major atomic-bomb writer. When Hayashi speaks of "human dignity," for instance, it is always within brackets. She frankly does not believe that such terms, after Nagasaki, retain any identifiably meaningful referent. For her, such anachronistic notions can now apply only ironically. Equally useless to her are such concepts as "humanity" or "modernity," ideas implying an ameliorable, civilized condition, and that is an implication that she regards as void in the wake of the barbarity of nuclear weapons.

Hayashi's bitter cynicism is illustrated in this passage from "The Site of Rituals":

> At present, were I to die, I would receive money for my funeral from the state. The amount would be 16,000 yen. This is the amount designated for "special hibakusha." However, it is not enough simply to die. Certification of a bomb-related cause of death is required.
>
> A "special hibakusha" is one who carries a special hibakusha health record. One who qualifies in Categories I through V of the

Atomic Bomb Medical Treatment Law Enforcement Ordinance Clause Six.

I am a Category I Special Hibakusha. This is limited to those hibakusha and their interuterine children who were directly hit within three kilometers of the blast. It also includes those who were in other special areas, such as where the black rain fell. Isahaya apparently does not qualify.

In order to receive the 16,000 yen, one must submit the following: a Funeral Expense Allowance Application Form, a death certificate, one's Residence Card canceled for reason of death, one's Special Hibakusha health record, and one's legal seal.

I intend to leave instructions that my 16,000 yen be used to purchase flowers. That should buy 80 tulips even at winter prices. That should make for a gorgeous funeral. If that is not acceptable, giant radishes will do fine. You could buy 80 of those. Their price is going up even as I write this: 53 giant radishes. (90–91)

It is easy to sympathize with Hayashi's sarcasm at how non-hibakusha culture seemingly discharges its guilt and moral responsibility through pathetic and patronizing gestures. The most scathing of the survivor-writers, Hayashi is unable to countenance the ersatz nurturance that distant authorities legislate for her, and so she rejects it with skepticism and even contempt.

At the same time, however, Hayashi rejects something else as well. She jettisons, along with the outside world's meager sympathy, the readers who inhabit that outside world and who must feel themselves equally the target of Hayashi's accusations. At the root of Hayashi's cynicism is the thought behind her character Wakako's rhetorical question in the short story "Two grave markers" ("Futari no bohyō"; 1975): "How could anyone who had not been there understand?" (26). Surely this is Hayashi's own sentiment, and so just as surely she shares the view of earlier atomic-bomb writers, such as Ōta Yōko and Hara Tamiki, that their common experience in Hiroshima and Nagasaki is in fact not common in all regards, but radically singular. Moreover, Hayashi would appear to deploy her proprietorship of that experience as a preemptive weapon: her insistence on the incommensurability of our respective lives leads to her defensive denunciation of the non-hibakusha world as inevitably cruel in its helpless ignorance. One might argue that the sheer number of Hayashi's stories and novels contradicts these sentiments, and that, quite to the contrary, they announce her steadfast belief in the communicability of her experience, or at the least the worth of trying. Yet the impression a reader takes away from Hayashi's work, such as "The Site of Rituals," is that Hayashi is at pains to tell us not the experience of Nagasaki per se, but rather the empty void which that experience occupies, paradoxically, in history. In other words, the insistence that "understanding" is limited works as a foil in her fiction, a manipulation meant to direct our attentions toward other issues, issues of the continuing states of victimization decades—perhaps even generations—later. For some critics, Hayashi's often arrogant cynicism defeats her as a writer insofar as she discourages readers from sympathizing with her. Perhaps this is what Nakagami Kenji meant when he histrionically accused Hayashi of "atomic fascism." For Nakagami, Hayashi's cynicism was so total as to curb any sympathetic encounter with her work; readers end up confronting a door-less wall denying them the right to proceed, or even perceive, past it.

But the stories of *Cut Glass, Blown Glass* suggest that it is not absolutely accurate to call Hayashi's style cynical, and that Nakagami's charge reveals a certain blindness in not recognizing the value of work by an author perhaps purposely melancholy and obsessive. Hayashi does not so much hold the reader in contempt as irritably insist that we admit, under the pressure of her bitterness, that her world is different from ours. This is a fact that she would force us to accept, and it is not surprising that some of us resist. What strikes some critics as indulgent arrogance is, perhaps, more compassionately described as a pathetic chasm between the separate experiences of writers and readers that fiction finally does not bridge.

"The very life that we would pass on to our children and grandchildren," wrote Hayashi, "has sustained injury": but just as her ambition to be the kataribe of Nagasaki was complicated, contradicted, and frustrated by her conviction that those not in Nagasaki could never understand it as she does, the "very life" that she would will her children and her children's children is similarly complicated, contradicted, and frustrated. She fears not only that her offspring will inherit her own fragile health but also that that offspring, while a continuation of her own life, is also the same affront to it that all non-hibakusha are. There is, in other words, a deep and undecidable ambivalence common to both Hayashi as kataribe and Hayashi as mother. Both roles potentially link the past with the future, both are broadly social (as opposed to individual) functions, and both possess lineages that reach back far into Japanese and human history—but both are also roles that the modern fact of a nuclear war has rescripted, perhaps permanently and in ways that question our trust in stories and even our love for our children.

In *As If Not,* that Hayashi work most concerned with the work of the kataribe, several characters are discussed but never appear in person: the sons of the Nagasaki survivors who promised to attend the dinner party at Haruko's but never do. Young men who are presumably out in the city enjoying themselves, they would probably want to avoid the depressed atmosphere of the older people's gathering. Hayashi implies here, as well as elsewhere in her works, a certain envy of the good health that Hayashi's and her characters' children enjoy; she also seems to resent that the experience of August Ninth is of much less consequence to those children than it is to their mothers. Hayashi is aware that part of her worry over her son's health is a projection of her own apprehension of mortality, but she seems somewhat less aware of the degree to which that worry is also her desire for her son to join her in the melancholy loneliness of her victimhood. Just as a kataribe's testimony of August Ninth must entail speaking the limits of that knowledge, "passing on" life to a child must also signal the end of the parent, the negation of her own experience.

In her story "Omowaku" (Anticipation; 1981) Hayashi reveals how complicated and poignant the distance between hibakusha parent and child can be:

> Hata looked at her daughter's face. The daughter looked at her mother's face. Their lines of vision seemed to casually, accidentally, meet: both then just as casually averted their eyes from each other. The August Ninth that the mother had experienced now seemed to have created uncomfortable feelings in a daughter who had grown in good health. The daughter's August Ninth was not one she directly possessed, as was that of hibakusha such as Hata and the rest of us. That had to have meant that knowledge of it came to her via many refractions, and with complicated reactions on her part toward her mother's August Ninth. I can say the same is true of my own son. (130–31)

The hibakusha desire to be a parent, to circumvent the mortality made palpable by August Ninth, can—when realized in the form of adult children whose lives seem impossibly remote from their own— ironically remind hibakusha of how truly uninheritable their isolation is, although surely none would wish upon their progeny the trauma responsible for that private quarantine. Similarly, the desire to be an

A-bomb writer or kataribe would seem, frustratingly, to guarantee the inevitable lesson that such an ambition must fail, since presumably to make readers really understand what Hiroshima or Nagasaki is would mean inflicting the same original pain. Either way, whether as writer or parent, hibakusha experience cannot be translated or reproduced for reasons ontological, epistemic, and ethical in equal measure—and therein lies whatever "representation" of that experience we would inherit.

Kurihara Sadako, the well-known Hiroshima survivor, writer, and political activist, wrote a poem shortly after the bombings that has become her most famous. In "Umashimen ka na" (Let us be midwives!; 1946), a young mother gives birth to her baby amid the squalor of a basement room packed with dying bomb victims and at the cost of the life of the midwife who delivers it. It is a poem that, despite its tragedy, suggests that that tragedy is transient and finite. "New life was born," Kurihara wrote in its last lines, "even at the cost of our own lives." It is a poem whose theme, according to the poet herself, is "the recovery of our humanity from amid the most extreme inhumanness" (quoted in Masuoka, 171). Kurihara, writing in the immediate aftermath of the bombing, had no knowledge of the tenacious aftereffects of radiation or any expectation that in all likelihood this "new life" too would soon die. The irony in "Let Us Be Midwives!" absent when Kurihara composed these lines was paramount by the time Nagasaki women writers such as Hayashi Kyōko emerged in the 1970's.[9] Later writers know better: as if to reverse the terms of Kurihara's poem, in novels such as *As If Not* it is relatively healthy women who fear for their real or prospective children's well-being.

Perhaps it would have to be women writers, culturally if not biologically more sensitive to issues of intergenerational survival, who would create that branch of atomic-bomb literature most dedicated to pursuing the widest implications of nuclear weapons and their institutions, namely, the deleterious effect of even a limited nuclear war on the human species and on the history our own bodies inscribe within it. Perhaps, too, it would have to be Nagasaki writers, writers from the "second" A-bomb city, a place whose fullest historical significance is seldom recognized, who would produce writings with an uncomfortable warning seldom heeded—perhaps because we do not know how. This is a literature of things that, its authors fear, have only begun to happen.

"These are wounds inflicted by human beings," wrote Hayashi

Kyōko. "These are deliberate wounds precisely calculated and inflicted by human beings": in Hayashi's analysis the advent of nuclear weapons is first expressed as a human act, and second as one that augurs a possibly permanent, certainly long-lived, distortion of life as it was known before in aspects simultaneously physiological and psychological. This is why Nagasaki atomic-bomb literature, only a small part of such literature in general, may imply the genre's most disturbing conclusion. To suggest that the fundamental assumptions we grasp in the world—that we are part of a human continuum—are changed, and changed in ways graphically or invisibly etched into human flesh and sentiment that no volume of concrete, no groves of newly planted trees, no institutionalized memorial observances, can quite efface, is to undermine much of the ground we, as readers, might wish to stand upon. The agony of Hayashi's portrait of a mother worrying over the health of her son, and of similar moments in other works of atomic-bomb literature written by women, but not only women, is a fear writ large throughout life now. It is a fear that does not pass briefly, but rather is one marking an era in which warfare and its technology leaves no part of the ken of human existence whole or intact. The contribution of Nagasaki atomic-bomb writers and their works is to guarantee that the unbelievable stories initiated in Hiroshima do not end in Nagasaki but continue as long as does the threat of annihilation, either in the past or future, by weapons whose insidious effects still remain imaginatively estranged from us yet are still too near to view in their terrible entirety.

ℒ

In 1975, the first year of her notorious fame, Hayashi Kyōko traveled to the museum that displays the famous Hiroshima murals of painters Maruki Toshi and Maruki Iri. Her essay describing this trip dwells on one mural in particular. Entitled "Mizu" (Water) in a reference to the thirst of the burn victims, the painting portrays a mixed crowd of hibakusha. But Hayashi, who elsewhere has declared the bond between mother and child "the origin of love" ("Ai no genten," 79), is drawn among the many to that one, most pathetic, depiction which bears the caption: "The twentieth-century image of madonna and child: an injured mother cradling her dead infant."[10] Hayashi interprets this detail for us: "What the dead infant signifies must surely be the lack of any future awaiting us" ("Mizu—karasu—shōnen shōjo," 33–34). She might just as well as have been addressing the meaning of her own art.

The twentieth-century image of madonna and child: an injured mother cradling her dead infant, 1950. Detail of Hiroshima mural entitled "Water" ("Mizu"), by Maruki Iri (1901–95) and Maruki Toshi (1912–).

I want to place this painting—and Hayashi's impossibly pessimistic reading of it—next to those remarks made by critics a decade ago who saw no reason to take her seriously. Nakagami, for one, would have preferred that Hayashi stop writing, if writing means rehearsing that day yet another time. It is indeed a problem for all of us to decide what to do to the messenger who brings us bad news. Do we kill her? Have we then done away with the message, too? Or do we heed the message and retreat into the useless cynicism that is undeniably there in Hayashi's work? The problem is the same for Hayashi herself, as Holocaust novelist Elie Wiesel knows well even if Nakagami did not:

> Therein lies the dilemma of the storyteller who sees himself essentially as witness, the drama of the messenger unable to deliver his message: how is one to speak of it, how is one not to speak of it? Certainly there can be no other theme for him: all situations, all conflicts, all obsessions will, by comparison, seem pallid and futile. And yet, how is one to approach this universe of darkness without turning into a peddler of night and agony? (Wiesel 16)

I would suggest that the only real choice we have in the face of Wiesel's quandary is to recognize both the twentieth-century madonna and child and the twentieth-century writings of Hayashi and her fellow hibakusha as the truth that our victims experienced to depict: a truth that is theirs, not our own, but is nonetheless profoundly linked to the ways in which we now have to read, and live, post-Hiroshima. I am the same age as Hayashi's son, but so are we all in one sense: we are all "second-generation" survivors of a nuclear war that some, myself included, believe began with Hiroshima and Nagasaki but has yet to be declared over. And as her children, our relationship to her writings has to be a struggle to understand them and separate ourselves from them, just as we would both acknowledge our lineage and demand our independence from it. Perhaps the anger of Nakagami Kenji is that of a son against a parent, locked in that old struggle to recognize one's ancestry while insisting upon the right to be free of it. But none of that is, finally, Hayashi Kyōko's fault or even her necessary concern. If, however, as she told us, "August Ninth is nothing but the present," then it is our own: not as an experience, or as a memory, but still our sad bequest.

Notes

1. A few of Hayashi's stories have been translated into English. "The Empty Can" can be found in the anthology of atomic-bomb literature edited by Ōe Kenzaburō, *The Crazy Iris*; "The Site of Rituals," under the title "Ritual of Death," is included in *Nuke Rebuke*, edited by Morty Sklar; "Two Grave Markers" has been translated by Kyoko Selden and can be found in the *Bulletin of Concerned Asian Scholars* 18, no. 1 (1986). Though not discussed in this essay, one of the *Cut Glass, Blown Glass* stories—"Yellow Sand" ("Kōsa"; 1977)—appears in Noriko Mizuta Lippit and Kyoko Selden, trans. and eds., *Japanese Women Writers: Twentieth Century Short Fiction*. The most recent addition to the body of Hayashi's work in English is Kashiwagi Hirosuke's translation of "Kumoribi no kōshin" (1967; in *Matsuri no ba*, 163–207), "Procession on a Cloudy Day," in *Bulletin of Concerned Asian Scholars* 25, no. 1 (1993).

For the most complete discussion of Hayashi, her works and her critical status among other survivor-writers and contemporary Japanese writers in general, see Kuroko, "Hayashi Kyōko ron." In English, see Bhowmik. For an overview of the entire genre of Japanese atomic-bomb literature, see my recent study, *Writing Ground Zero*.

2. For the principal works of Ōta Yōko, see Treat, "Hiroshima and the Place of the Narrator." There are English translations of several of her works, including "Fireflies" ("Hotaru"; 1953) in Ōe; and *City of Corpses* (*Shikabane no machi*; 1948) in Minear.

3. For an account of this and other critical attacks on the literary worth of atomic-bomb literature in the 1950's and 1960's, see Kurihara, "Gembaku bungaku ronsō shi"; in English, see Treat, "The Three Debates," in *Writing Ground Zero*, 83–120.

4. Both Hayashi's "Safe" and the critical review of it appeared in print at a time when the "Writers' Appeal Against the Dangers of Nuclear War," a petition calling for nuclear disarmament eventually signed by hundreds of prominent Japanese writers, was being circulated amid public controversy over its political motives and naiveté. For a history of the Writers' Appeal and its critique, see Horupu shuppan henshūbu; and Yoshimoto.

5. Nakagami et al. regrettably omit any mention of Hayashi's considerable body of work that deals not with the atomic bombing of Nagasaki but with her childhood spent in wartime Shanghai—work that explores Japanese imperialism and colonialism from the perspective of a child innocent of their implementation but acutely cognizant of their local consequences. In places, her memories of both Shanghai and Nagasaki overlap in ways that implicitly point to the sort of global and historical analysis of the war that Nakagami demands. In "Hibiki" (Echo; 1977), for example, Hayashi writes the following about Nagasaki victims fleeing the city after the ninth:

"The same as the Chinese, like refugees," my mother said. . . . My mother had watched her compatriots fleeing and recalled the sight of Chinese who had once been driven from Shanghai by the war. But we were not "like refugees," we were refugees. My mother could not believe the fact that Japanese, herself included, could be fleeing with our own pots and pans. She had lived in Shanghai as the citizen of the victor nation. If even our evacuation from Shanghai in March had been a sorry sight, the Japanese could still think of themselves as the victor nation. When the war started, those that fled with pots and pans had always been the Chinese and never the foreign Japanese. While living in someone else's country, Japanese mothers—citizens of the victor nation—could watch the Chinese flee from the sidelines. That is why "Chinese" and "refugees" were the same thing for my mother. Nothing could have seemed more natural for my mother, who had never had to run for her own life. (115–16)

6. For the details of Nakagami Kenji's displeasure with Nakano's leading role in the organization of the "Writers' Appeal Against the Dangers of Nuclear War," see Nakagami, "Karasu."

7. See Ōsato, 98.

8. Committee for the Compilation of Materials on Damage Caused by the Atomic Bombs in Hiroshima and Nagasaki, 115–16. The Committee also reports that

> from the theoretical aspects of radiation genetics, Y. Tajima (1972) estimated the number of children born to the exposed, between 1946 and 1980, to be 63,000 in Hiroshima and 42,000 in Nagasaki. Based on individual radiation doses and relative biological effectiveness (RBE) of neutron to gamma ray, the estimated number of affected offspring of the exposed would be increased by 11 percent to 16 percent in Hiroshima and by 5 percent to 7 percent in Nagasaki, when compared with the rate of abnormal offspring born to non-exposed controls. Tajima also pointed out the possibility of spreading recessive traits in the heterozygous condition in subsequent generations. Further studies are obviously needed to test his hypothesis. (327)

9. In my study of the history of Japanese atomic-bomb literature, I discuss several of these Nagasaki women writers—Sata Ineko and Gotō Minako as well as Hayashi Kyōko—collectively. My reasons are not based solely on these writers' common gender, but additionally on their shared concern with the issue of human reproduction in the wake of the atomic bombings—a concern one hopes is not restricted to women. I refer readers to the chapter "Nagasaki and the Human Future" in my *Writing Ground Zero*.

10. The English translation of the caption to the painting is taken from Dower and Junkerman, 39.

Works Cited

Abe Tomoji. "Gembaku to bungaku." In *Kaku-sensō no kiken o uttaeru bun-gakusha*, 15: 80–88.

Bhowmik, Davinder. "Temporal Discontinuity in the Atomic Bomb Writings of Hayashi Kyōko." M.A. thesis, University of Washington, 1993.

Cixous, Hélène. "The Laugh of Medusa." Trans. Keith Cohen and Paula Cohen. *Signs: Journal of Women in Culture and Society* 1, no. 4 (1976): 875–93.

Committee for the Compilation of Materials on Damage Caused by the Atomic Bombs in Hiroshima and Nagasaki, ed. *Hiroshima and Nagasaki: The Physical, Medical, and Social Effects of the Atomic Bombings.* Trans. Eisei Ishikawa and David L. Swain. New York: Basic Books, 1987.

Dower, John, and John Junkerman, eds. *The Hiroshima Murals: The Art of Iri Maruki and Toshi Maruki.* Tokyo: Kodansha International, 1985.

Hayashi Kyōko. "Ai no genten." In *Shizen o kou,* 76–84.

———. "Akikan." In *Giyaman – biidoro,* 7–26.

———. "Arumi no yōki." In *Shizen o kou,* 9–22.

———. "Buji." *Gunzō* 27, no. 1 (1982): 32–57.

———. "Dōkikai." In *Michi,* 63–90.

———. "The Empty Can" ("Akikan"). Trans. Margaret Mitsutani. In Ōe, 127–43.

———. *Giyaman – biidoro.* Tokyo: Kōdansha, 1978.

———. "Giyaman – biidoro." In *Giyaman – biidoro,* 47–65.

———. "Hibaku." In *Shōwa jidai o ikiru: sorezore no sengo,* ed. Uchiyama Hideo and Kurihara Akira. Tokyo: Yūhikaku, 1980, 46–63.

———. "Hibiki." In *Giyaman – biidoro,* 109–27.

———. "Kāki-iro kara kon-iro sedai e." In *Shizen o kou,* 52–62.

———. "Kiroku." In *Giyaman – biidoro,* 151–67.

———. "Kompira yama." In *Giyaman – biidoro,* 27–45.

———. *Matsuri no ba.* Tokyo: Kōdansha, 1975.

———. "Matsuri no ba." In *Kaku-sensō no kiken o uttaeru bungakusha,* 3: 29–68.

———. *Michi.* Tokyo: Bungei shunjū, 1985.

———. "Mizu – karasu – shōnen shōjo." In *Shizen o kou,* 33–43.

———. *Naki ga gotoki.* Tokyo: Kōdansha, 1989.

———. "No ni." In *Giyaman – biidoro,* 229–47.

———. "Omowaku." In *Michi,* 123–40.

———. "Procession on a Cloudy Day" ("Kumoribi no kōshin"). Trans. Kashiwagi Hirosuke. *Bulletin of Concerned Asian Scholars* 25, no. 1 (1993): 58–69.

———. "Ritual of Death" ("Matsuri no ba"). Trans. Kyoko Selden. In Sklar, 21–57.

———. "Seinen-tachi." In *Giyaman – biidoro,* 67–86.

———. "Shanhai to haichigatsu kokonoka." In *Sōsho bunka no genzai 4: chūshin to shūen,* ed. Ōe Kenzaburō, Nakamura Yūjirō, Yamaguchi Masao et al. Tokyo: Iwanami shoten, 1981, 101–21.

———. *Shizen o kou.* Tokyo: Chūō kōronsha, 1981.

———. "Tomo yo." In *Giyaman – biidoro,* 169–88.

———. "Two Grave Markers" ("Futari no bohyō"). Trans. Kyoko Selden. *Bulletin of Concerned Asian Scholars* 18, no. 1 (1986): 23–35.

————. "Yellow Sand" ("Kōsa"). Trans. Kyoko Selden. In Noriko Mizuta Lippit and Kyoko Selden, trans. and eds., *Japanese Women Writers: Twentieth Century Short Fiction*. Armonk, N.Y.: M. E. Sharpe, 1991, 207–16.
————. "Yobun no omoi." In *Shizen o kou*, 69–75.
————. "Zanshō." In *Michi*, 233–61.
Horupu shuppan henshūbu, ed. *Hankaku: bungakusha wa uttaeru*. Tokyo: Horupu shuppan, 1984.
Iida Momo. *Amerika no eiyū*. Tokyo: Kawade shobō shinsha, 1977.
Irigaray, Luce. "This Sex Which Is Not One." Trans. Claudia Reeder. In idem, *This Sex Which Is Not One*, trans. Catherine Porter with Carolyn Burke. Ithaca, N.Y.: Cornell University Press, 1985, 23–33.
Kako-sensō no kiken o uttaeru bungakusha, ed. *Nihon no genbaku bungaku*. 15 vols. Tokyo: Horupu shuppan, 1984.
Karatani Kōjin, Kawamura Jirō, and Nakagami Kenji. "Sōsaku gōhyō." *Gunzō* 37, no. 2 (1982): 274–94.
Konishi Jin'ichi. *A History of Japanese Literature*, vol. 1, *The Archaic and Ancient Ages*. Trans. Aileen Gatten and Nicholas Teele; ed. Earl Miner. Princeton: Princeton University Press, 1984.
Kōuchi Nobuko. "Hayashi Kyōko ron." *Kokubungaku: kaishaku to kanshō* 50, no. 9 (1985): 47–52.
Kurihara Sadako. "Genbaku bungaku ronsō shi (shō) — Ōta Yōko o jiku ni." In Kaku-sensō no kiken o uttaeru bungakusha, 15: 269–300.
————. " 'Let Us Be Midwives': Four Poems (1941–45) by the Hiroshima Poet Kurihara Sadako." Trans. and introduced Richard H. Minear. *Bulletin of Concerned Asian Scholars* 21, no. 1 (1989): 47.
Kuroko Kazuo. "Genbaku bungaku o nokoshita hitobito." In Horupu shuppan henshūbu, 249–93.
————. "Hayashi Kyōko ron." In idem, *Genbaku to kotoba: Hara Tamiki kara Hayashi Kyōko made*. Tokyo: San'ichi shobō, 1983, 55–68.
Masuoka Toshikazu. *Hiroshima no shijin-tachi*. Tokyo: Shin Nihon shuppansha, 1980.
Minear, Richard H., trans. and ed. *Hiroshima: Three Witnesses*. Princeton: Princeton University Press, 1990.
Nakagami Kenji. "Karasu." *Gunzō* 37, no. 3 (1982): 82–92.
Nakagami Kenji et al. "Warera no bungaku tachiba — sedai ron o koete." *Bungakkai* 32, no. 10 (1978): 98–117.
Nakano Kōji and Nagaoka Hiroyoshi. "Genbaku bungaku o megutte." *Kokubungaku: kaishaku to kanshō* 50, no. 9 (1985): 10–23.
Nakayama Kazuko. "Sakka annai." In Hayashi, *Naki ga gotoki*, 234–44.
Ōe Kenzaburō, ed. *The Crazy Iris and Other Stories of the Atomic Aftermath*. New York: Grove Press, 1985.
Ōsato Kyōzaburō. " 'Matsuri no ba.' " *Kokubungaku: kaishaku to kanshō* 50, no. 9 (1985): 98–102.
Sklar, Morty, ed. *Nuke Rebuke: Writers and Artists Against Nuclear Energy and Weapons*. Iowa City: The Sprit That Moves Us Press, 1984.

Treat, John Whittier. "Hiroshima and the Place of the Narrator." *Journal of Asian Studies* 48, no. 1 (1989): 29–49.

———. *Writing Ground Zero: Japanese Literature and the Atomic Bomb.* Chicago: University of Chicago Press, 1995.

Wiesel, Elie. *One Generation After.* Trans. Marion Wiesel. New York: Pocket Books, 1970.

Yoshimoto Takaaki. *"Hankaku" iron.* Tokyo: Shin'ya sōshosha, 1982.

9

Becoming, or (Un)Becoming:
The Female Destiny Reconsidered in
Ōba Minako's Narratives

MICHIKO NIIKUNI WILSON

Ōba Minako (1930–), a major force in the resurgence of Japanese women's writing, combines her artistry with the subversive spirit of a sociocultural critic. This spirit gives her work a distinctive voice and, in tandem with her sense of playfulness, creates a style that is invariably tongue-in-cheek, with a tone that is witty, wise, sarcastic, and merciless yet forgiving. Her literary imagination was sharpened by the fairy tales she read as a young woman, but it is the Heian female tradition that she identifies as the direct source of her creative energy as a novelist and as a literary critic.[1] In a 1990 roundtable discussion of *The Tale of Genji* with the noted Genji scholar Akiyama Ken, Ōba emphasized the subversive qualities of Murasaki Shikibu's writing:

> *The Tale of Genji* gives me the kind of pleasure I get when I am reading a contemporary novel. . . . It is said that Hikaru Genji is the ideal male, but Murasaki's portrayal of him seems to say otherwise. I think she describes him in such a way that he is not meant to be the ideal male at all. . . . She certainly observes things with great care — particularly those things that tend to jar the reader — and coats them with lovely descriptions. . . . *Genji* is a dangerous novel — No, I should say that literature in general is inevitably dangerous because it contains an element of rebellion against what has been established [by the ruling class]. . . . The author [Murasaki] never narrates in a combative voice, but as you read along, you begin to feel like attacking [Murasaki's male characters for their actions]. (Ōba and Akiyama, 13, 15)[2]

These remarks, which left Akiyama almost speechless, indicate a position for which Ōba has been criticized: in her own words, "What I am asserting [in my writings] is what those male critics want to deny, that is to say, my refusal to embrace the patriarchal way of thinking" (Ōba, "Onna no hyōgen," 10).[3] Male critics point out the "inconsistency" of her self-assertions, her leaps of logic, and the episodic movement of plots linked by association, but Ōba is neither embittered by the criticism nor apologetic or repentant for her stance. Her sense of equality with male writers and her secure identity as a female writer are absolute. In this respect, Ōba, it seems to me, is a breed apart from contemporary Japanese women writers. Whether she is conscious of it or not, Ōba's perspective is a feminist one, as she inevitably plays with the role of an outsider, a nonconformist, and a breaker of taboos.

In one of the many humorous passages in her autobiographical fiction, in the work *Oregon yume jūya* (Ten nights of Oregon dreams; 1981), the diarist Ōba, about to depart for the United States, goes through a ritual leave-taking at Narita Airport that seems to last interminably. Against her wishes, her husband accompanies her to the airport. Her friends and acquaintances dutifully gather around her, and the ritual exchange of farewells begins:

> "Abandoning your husband for three months!"
> "What will he do while you're gone?"
> "He'll be so lonely."
> All sorts of people fired questions at me, things that I found totally meaningless. How did I reply?
> "He's used to it."
> "What do you mean by, What will he do all alone? He's no child. He'll manage by himself, I'm sure. You can't be serious. Would you put the same question to a wife when her husband stays away from home for a long time?" (9)[4]

The typical response in such a social context would be: "I know I'm totally selfish to take off by myself, leaving my husband in the lurch. Please be nice to him and take care of him, if you can. I'd be forever indebted to you. I'll be counting on your goodwill." The brief abortive exchange that I have quoted contains the core of Ōba's literary imagination, one that introduces a female hero who is "autonomous, intellectual, unwomanly, and ultimately, lovable" (Heilbrun, *Hamlet's Mother*, 308). Women writers do not have to limit themselves to delineating the pain and suffering of woman as married, widowed, kept, or single; they can also describe the relationship of man and woman in its wholeness, a relationship in which "love and work" do not conflict. In fact, Ōba's representative female protagonist is neither the suffering nor the loving woman, but the thinking woman, the subversive woman, the absolutely unrepentant and unapologetic woman.

Yukie in *Urashima-sō* (The Urashimaso plant; 1977—trans. as *Urashimaso*; 1995), Yurie in *Kiri no tabi* (A journey through the mist; 1980), Yurie in *Naku tori no* (Birds crying; 1985), or Keiko in *Ōjo no namida* (The princess's tears; 1987), are a breath of fresh air, clear, innovative alternatives to what Carolyn G. Heilbrun calls the "failure of imagination"—a trap into which Western women writers themselves have also fallen:

> Yet women writers (and women politicians, academics, psychoanalysts) have been unable to imagine for other women, fictional or real, the self they have in fact achieved. . . . Women writers, in short, have articulated their pain. But they cannot, or for the most part have not, imagined characters moving, as the authors themselves have moved, beyond that pain. Woman's most persistent problem has been to discover for herself an identity not limited by custom or defined by attachment to some man. Remarkably, her search for identity has been even less successful within the world of fiction than outside it, leaving us until very recently with a situation largely unchanged for more than two millennia. (*Reinventing Womanhood*, 72–73)

Feminists in the United States, England, and France have repeatedly pointed out the pernicious identification that patriarchy has imposed upon women: she exists only in her relationship to a man, whether father, husband, or son.[5] How can women free themselves from this predetermined definition, from a male view of women, from imagining only "a constricted destiny for themselves, allowing the imagination of possibility to be appropriated for the exclusive use of men"? (Heilbrun, *Reinventing Womanhood*, 34).

Throughout her work Ōba, directly and indirectly, responds to these and other related issues raised by Heilbrun: Why cannot we imagine ourselves "as selves, as at once striving and female"? Why not look to literature "not only for the articulation of female despair and constriction, but also for the proclamation of the possibilities of life"? Why not ask women writers to "give us, finally, female characters who are complex, whole, and independent—fully human"? (*Reinventing Womanhood*, 34). In Ōba's literary world we see abundant examples of such female characters. What is so refreshing and empowering about Ōba is that, equipped with the subversive spirit of Murasaki Shikibu, she goes one step further and creates not only female but also male characters who are unacceptable, indeed impossible, from the patriarchy's perspective.

Furthermore, perfectly aware that the modern Japanese literary tradition has been dominated by confessional male authors, who flaunted their egos, woes, and flaws in painstaking detail,[6] Ōba categorizes many of their male protagonists as *darashi no nai otoko* ("Onna no hyōgen," 18). The adjective *darashi no nai*, translatable as "pathetic," "slipshod," "out of line," and "unkempt," refers by extension to undisciplined, lax, or immoral behavior. What Ōba means by *darashi no nai otoko* is a man whose irresponsible behavior is deemed outrageous but is nevertheless tolerated, and even sanctioned, by male-centered society. The almost universal intolerance of loose behavior among women is an issue that Ōba the literary woman finds pointless even to contest, so deeply is this double standard ingrained in the social system. In a response to critics who find her female characters morally lax, she raises an eyebrow: "It wasn't long ago, was it, that men themselves began to write about *darashi no nai* men. Of course, if female writers do that, male writers get upset. But they still give positive reviews of those written by men. Look at Dan Kazuo [1912–76] and Shimao Toshio [1917–86]. . . . They must find [the subject of *darashi no nai otoko*] very realistic" ("Onna no hyōgen," 13).[7]

In a similar way, when it comes to depicting "immoral" female characters, Western male writers are masters, Ōba continues. How about Flaubert's *Madame Bovary*, or Tolstoi's *Anna Karenina*? Again, Ōba's comment reminds us that neither Dan Kazuo's trickster-like hero nor Shimao Toshio's pathetic one comes to a tragic ending; they continue living a good life, whereas Madame Bovary and Anna Karenina must kill themselves to end their misery and to atone for their "sins." If the reading public and scholars can accept a man writing about a woman or a man who rebels against the established moral codes, surely it is equally acceptable for a woman to write about a man or a woman who is, according to conventional cultural constructs, "immoral."

Ōba defends a literary woman's right to imagine a female character in her own way. A literary man, by contrast, has never had to defend his right to imagine a male character any way he sees fit. The "literary patrilineage"[8] regards, for example, the notion of the anti-hero (and an amorous hero) with a particular sense of adoration. A tradition in itself in Western literature, it started with the picaresque narrative in Europe, emigrated to England, and has been more recently revived by Norman Mailer and Henry Miller, among others.[9] The powerful image of what Sandra M. Gilbert and Susan Gubar call "male intellectual struggle" among strong equals ultimately enables the "male writer to explain his rebelliousness, his 'swerving,' and his 'originality' both to himself and to the world, no matter how many readers think him 'not quite right' " (*Madwoman*, 74). In other words, society would look upon him as a "dissenter," which is not at all a dishonorable term.

Suppose a Japanese woman writer portrayed an antihero or antiheroine of great magnitude, then what would happen? "I can already foresee, though," Ōba acknowledges facetiously; "that a work like this by a woman would be panned by male critics" ("Onna no hyō-gen," 13). In fact, this happened in 1956 when Harada Yasuko (1928–) introduced a new Japanese female character, Reiko, in *Banka* (Elegy), a work that won the Women's Literature Award and was enthusiastically received by the public but dumbfounded male critics. Harada depicted a 23-year-old woman, a whimsical seducer who wraps a well-established middle-aged man around her little finger. That was unheard of. No female writer had ever dared to create such a *darashi no nai* heroine. Reiko broke taboos on all fronts. The sensational debut of the unknown writer almost succeeded in making a clean break with the stereotypical image of the self-sacrificing Japanese woman. But within less than a year, the majority of male critics had caught on to Harada's rebellious intent and unleashed their harshest criticism. In their eyes, Reiko became simply a prankster and a spoiled girl, incapable of loving a decent man. Worse yet, she had no principles or morality, and was an egotist to the core.[10] (Of course, Naomi, the *femme fatale* in Tanizaki Jun'ichirō's *Chijin no ai* [A fool's love, trans. as *Naomi*; 1924] did not count as a taboo-breaking heroine. Not only did the male protagonist want her to be that way, but she was the creation of a male author.)

Unfortunately, although Japan has left the postwar period behind and has undergone enormous social and economic changes, the tradition of patriarchal literary criticism is still very much intact.[11] Ōba's ambitious *A Journey Through the Mist*, which is loosely based on her own life, became the target of unhappy male critics. The main criticism was directed at an extramarital affair that the female protagonist, Yurie, has with a Swedish man while living in Sweden with her husband. Peter, the boyfriend of a colleague of Yurie's husband, is an aspiring writer of mediocre talent, who tutors the couple in Swedish. Eventually Peter seduces Yurie, and the sexual affair continues for a while. One morning he invites the heroine to a lakeside house, and on impulse she accepts; the experience does not sit well with her, however, and late that night she returns home by train. Her husband accepts her with no questions asked. Neither the reader nor Yurie is sure at this point whether he has the knowledge of his wife's ongoing affair with Peter. "I was wondering what would happen after it [the excursion]," one critic says, "but what a miserable guy! [meaning the husband]." Another critic responds in disbelief: "This is in no way a realistic portrayal of a man . . . even if he actually exists, I cannot think of him as real" (Miki, 279; quoted. in Ōba, "Onna no hyōgen," 12). What they dare not mention but are really saying is that Ōba should not have written about this kind of relationship, for to do so is too unwomanly. A wife enduring her husband's love affairs in silence (such as Tomo in Enchi Fumiko's *Onna-zaka* [The woman's slope, 1957; trans. as *The Waiting Years*]) is normative, but the reverse is not. I have a distinct feeling that these same critics would never for a moment doubt the "sincerity" of the egotist Shimamura, who does not think twice about making a plaything of an intelligent, sensitive, and imaginative geisha, Komako, in Kawabata's *Snow Country*.[12]

These reviewers of *A Journey Though the Mist* employ the same age-old methods as Western male critics to, in Joanna Russ's words, "bury [women's] art, to explain it away, ignore it, downgrade it, in short, make it vanish" (17):

> She didn't write it.
> She wrote it, but she shouldn't have.
> She wrote it, but look what she wrote about.
> She wrote it, but "she" isn't really an artist and "it" isn't really serious, of the right genre — i.e., really art.
> She wrote it, but she wrote only one of it.
> She wrote it, but it's only interesting/included in the canon for one, limited reason.
> She wrote it, but there are very few of her. (Russ, 76)

Whether Western or Japanese, the male critics seem to agree on the strategy of denying women's achievements. These "logically fallacious" (Russ, 17) and silly denigrations are a clear indication that, despite their past glory, Japanese women writers also have a long way to go in gaining the respect of the male critical establishment.

Yamamoto Michiko (1936–), a recipient of the Akutagawa Prize for "Betty-san no niwa" (Betty's garden, 1972; trans. as "Betty-san"), was labeled a "housewife novelist" (*shufu sakka*) by the media, which trivialized her art by way of false categorization.[13] In addition to applying a double standard in terms of content, the abovementioned critics reviewing *A Journey Through the Mist* also use the false-categorization ploy. One of them refers to Ōba as a "mere woman writer," meaning that she is not to be taken seriously; if she would only break out of her non-patriarchal mold and realize that pain and frustration are *human* issues, then they could accept her as a "novelist," not a woman writer. That is to say, for these critics, as long as a literary woman writes from a woman's perspective, she is not a true artist.[14]

Ōba's counterattack is always the same: not to respond in an emotional exchange of words, but to continue writing what male critics do not want to read, what they want to deny, ignore, and downgrade.[15] "Half of the human population is female, isn't it?" Ōba flatly states. "It is just a law of nature that women and men be given a fifty-fifty chance [in every area] to live out their lives" ("Onna no hyōgen," 15). This comment expresses a feminist sentiment and truth in its most logical fairness, one that is cogently articulated by the historian Gerda Lerner: "Women's experience encompasses all that is human; they share—and always have shared—the world equally with men. Equally in the sense that half, at least, of all the world's experience of women has been theirs, half of the world's work and much of its products. In one sense, then, to document the experience of women would mean documenting all of history: they have always been of it, in it, and making it."[16]

Ōba has a story to tell, a story of the all-encompassing female experience. The new ground Ōba is pioneering is a story of woman's free choice, of how woman decides, in Carolyn G. Heilbrun's words, to "manage her own destiny when she has no plot, no narrative, no tale [of quest] to guide her." This is a very significant and relevant point because, according to Heilbrun, "in literature and out, through all recorded history, women have lived by a script they did not write. Their destiny was to be married, circulated; to be given by one man, the father, to another, the husband; to become the mothers of men. Theirs has been the marriage plot, the erotic plot, the courtship plot, but never, as for men, the quest plot" (*Hamlet's Mother*, 126). Ōba's literary sisters, the Heian women who wrote the *Kagerō nikki* (The Kagerō diary, ca. 974; trans. as *The Gossamer Years*), the *Izumi Shikibu nikki*

(*The Diary of Izumi Shikibu*; ca. 1008), or the *Sarashina nikki* (The Sarashina diary, ca. 1060; trans. as *As I Crossed a Bridge of Dreams*) — to paraphrase Heilbrun's words — had to live by a script they had no choice but to write themselves, in which they were forever waiting for a man to appear, be it a husband or a lover. We might call the plot of the script they adopted that of the "visited" and the "read."[17] Heilbrun's comment refers to the fact that women writers in the West have not created a story in which a woman and a man are on equal terms, affecting each other and adjusting to each other, where a man grows along with the woman he cares for, and allows her to undertake her quest, the "perilous journey to self-development" (Heilbrun, *Hamlet's Mother*, 307), at her own pace.

In this regard Ōba seems to be a pioneer. She has created a pair that fits the bill quite nicely. Yurie and Shōzō in *Birds Crying* are probably the most compatible, equal, independent-minded yet inseparable, and fully human married couple portrayed in modern literature. Ōba introduced Yurie and Shōzō for the first time in *A Journey Through the Mist*, covering Yurie's encounter with Shōzō at the age of eleven; her contact with the notorious cousin Fu, the "bad woman"; and her college life, marriage, and move to Sweden because of Shōzō's job. This traditional move of Yurie, in which a wife follows her husband, is balanced by a role reversal between husband and wife in the sequel, *Birds Crying*. As every film director knows, the creation of a sequel poses a great risk, for it often falls short of the original. But *A Journey Through the Mist* and *Birds Crying* are true equals; they offer a reading as one continuous intertext or as two separate, independent, permeable texts. Ōba establishes here a pattern that is often repeated in subsequent works; that of making her texts resonate with each other, relate to each other, and speak with each other.

We might call *A Journey Through the Mist* the narrative of a perilous journey of a young woman to self-development and female self-assertion through words. At this point in her life, Yurie is still in a foggy state of mind, unable to assert her growing self-identity effectively. The metaphor of mist (*kiri*), as she journeys through it, is most appropriate for this novel of development. The young Yurie gropes her way to find her identity as a woman who wants to write but is held back, not by marriage but by her own ambivalent self. To use a female metaphor, the narrative is about the process of labor pains before the emergence of Yurie the literary woman. Mizuta Noriko views *A Journey Through the Mist* as a *kyōyō-shōsetsu* (a novel of self-development, the Japanese translation of *Bildungsróman*), a "spiritual history of a woman" (427), but argues that it goes beyond the classic genre as it explores a symbolic cosmic space and the birth of a myth.[18]

When the sequel opens, Mama Yurie (the unusual surname Mama is surely meant as a pun) is a free-spirited, spacey novelist, and Shōzō is a former salaryman who has retired early from his company in order to enjoy life as a househusband, secretary, cook, and dependent all in one. Their daughter, Chie, an only child, left the nest long ago. Although their intellectual interests do not always mesh — one of them is a writer, the other a trained scientist — they reluctantly admit to each other how the difference keeps boredom at bay, how much they learn from each other. Presenting a woman's view of the world, society, and human relationships, Ōba is, of course, also writing for men, who have "very little understanding of what women really are" (Ōba, "Onna no hyōgen," 15). Therefore, she creates the character of Shōzō, a man who articulates a woman's perspective, openly incorporating a feminist experience of the world into his own.

What especially interests me in *A Journey Through the Mist* and *Birds Crying* is Ōba's emerging sense of self as a woman and a writer, the way she addresses female sexuality,[19] and how she expresses her awakening to new possibilities in middle age. For many women, middle age offers opportunities never before anticipated. At 56 Virginia Woolf mustered enough courage to publish *Three Guineas* (1938), on which she had worked for six years, an outspoken indictment of patriarchy that finally unleashed her feminist anger. Nine years earlier, at 47, she had written *A Room of One's Own* (1929) with a more gentle, patient, indirect voice, still hesitant about showing her anger at patriarchy.

Adrienne Rich, a poet and critic, has not missed this "sense of effort, of pains taken, of dogged tentativeness, in the tone of [*A Room of One's Own*]." She understands it perfectly:

> I had heard it often enough, in myself and in other women. It is the tone of a woman almost in touch with her anger, who is determined not to appear angry, who is *willing* herself to be calm, detached, and even charming in a roomful of men where things have been said which are attacks on her very integrity. Virginia Woolf is addressing an audience of women, but she is acutely conscious — as she always was — of being overheard by men. . . . She was trying to sound as cool as Jane Austen, as Olympian as Shakespeare, because that is the way the men of the culture thought a writer should sound. (37)

Do male writers have a similar concern? Rich answers in the emphatic negative: "No male writer has written primarily or even largely for women, or with the sense of women's criticism as a consideration when he chooses his materials, his theme, his language. But to a lesser or greater extent, every woman writer has written for men even when, like Virginia Woolf, she was supposed to be addressing women." Rich looks forward to the day when women writers feel secure: "If we have come to the point when this balance might begin to change, when women can stop being haunted, not only by 'convention and propriety' but by internalized fears of being and saying themselves, then it is an extraordinary moment for the woman writer—and reader" (37–38). Ōba is not only unconcerned about being overheard by men in Japan but openly challenges what she calls their "potted plant" nature through the character of Shōzō.

☙

Ōba serialized Part I of *A Journey Through the Mist* in the literary magazine *Gunzō* in 1976–77, Part II in 1979–80. She had begun the novel at 46, and completed it at 50. Five years later, at 55, she published the sequel, *Birds Crying*. Aging, for her, is never a regression but a blessing, a chance for a second life and empowerment. "To allow oneself at fifty the expression of one's feminism," Carolyn G. Heilbrun notes in describing Woolf's courage in deciding to write *Three Guineas*, distinguishes women fundamentally from men because it "is an experience for which there is no male counterpart, at least for white men in the Western world. If a man is to break into revolt against the system he has, perhaps for his parents' sake, pretended to honor, he will do so at a much younger age. The pattern of men's lives suggests that at fifty they are likelier to reveal their egoism than their hidden ideals or revolutionary hopes" (*Writing a Woman's Life*, 124).

A Journey Through the Mist begins with a fourteen-page prologue in which Ōba brings the reader into the heart and mind of the middle-aged Yurie, Ōba's fictional alter ego, who reveals all the signs of feminist inclinations that are still unformed and unidentified. Even at the end of the novel, the young Chie is shown trying in vain to wake Yurie from her "hibernation":

> In the dream Chie was gently tugging at me.
> "Mommy sleeps all the time."
> "I can't open my eyes. Can't see a thing. I'll wake up when the mist clears." I mumbled in my sleep. (424)[20]

We learn from the prologue almost everything we need to know about Yurie's "doubled view of women as agents as well as victims" (Fraiman, 124). The prologue states that "given the same circumstances as men, women can be as cautious, crafty, and romantic as men ordinarily are; those traits are not particularly masculine" (12). Women and men are described as being like the opposite poles of a magnet (or a *yin* and *yang* dyad): "If both poles, the male and female sexes, successfully come into contact, we get a quiet stability, but if they do not meet and stay parallel to one another, the situation remains unstable and frustrating, and one begins to hate the other. But, even if these opposites fail to come into contact, the situation won't be as bad as when there is unipolarity. It will not create any energy, everything will be suspended in midair" (10). In other words, what interests Yurie is "how *yin* and *yang* accommodate each other rather than how different they are" (13). It is important to keep in mind that she sees the *yin-yang* dyad as a fusion of complementarity *and* that she considers *yin* and *yang* interchangeable between genders. In her dyadic world, which is in continual flux, the traditional dichotomy of femininity (*yin*) versus masculinity (*yang*) does not dictate the lives of men and women. This gender flexibility leads to her innocent openness about men: "I have always liked men. I get disappointed by them but I'm never weary of dreaming the impossible about them. This is the way I have survived" (10).

It is clear from Yurie's dramatic monologues that Ōba's subversive intent as a writer is to avoid a direct frontal assault on patriarchy such as a denunciation of the entire male sex for all the injustices and crimes committed against women in history. Another, and more difficult approach, and the one that Ōba prefers, is to form an "alliance" with men. This poses a more troublesome situation for men because, whereas a direct attack might provide hardened men with an excuse to maintain the status quo at any cost, this indirect approach poses no clear-cut threat, leaving them with no excuse not to join with women in their struggle for the betterment of women's and men's lives. As noted by Gerda Lerner, everything women have done and experienced has also involved men, and thus, a change for equality must come from both women and men; it cannot be accomplished without the contributions of both. Ōba refuses to "segregate" men from the female experience: she holds men equally accountable for every step women take in life.

The subversive intent of Ōba's art is reflected in the plot and in the portrayal of the heroine of *A Journey Through the Mist*, which show distinct similarities to those of the classic *Bildungsroman* genre. Defined in its pure form as a "novel of all-around development" (Nobbe, 6) that is "unremittingly concerned with the *Werden* [becoming] of an individual hero" (Swales, 29), this genre found its first major example in Goethe's *Wilhelm Meister's Apprenticeship*. The prototype of the *Bildungsroman* hero "is in many respects a weak and indecisive hero," but he "does have an active mind, and he speaks it often and at length" (Buckley, 10).[21] (As we shall see, Ōba's heroine is herself quite garrulous, at least in private.) Defined "in terms of works by, about, and appealing to men" (Fraiman, 3), this classic genre has largely ignored the possibility of a *Bildungsroman* heroine.

> A crude picture of the genre shows an especially rugged or especially sensitive young man, at leisure to mull over some life choices, not so much connected to people or the landscape as encountering or passing through them as "options" or "experiences" en route to a better place. Travel, . . . is key, for though the story pulls toward settling the youth—its telos is repose—what it actually recounts is his relentless advance. (Fraiman, 125–26)

The "resisting reader"[22] cannot help but think what a formidable risk a woman writer might have to take to create a female *Bildungsroman* without inviting ridicule from patriarchal critics. After all, simply changing the gender of the hero would not improve the status of literary women and would instead encourage a more scathing accusation from male critics: that all literary women can do is copy the masculine plot. If George Eliot's solution to this dilemma was to "resist[s] it [the *Bildungsroman*] with special vehemence" (Fraiman, 126) and parody it, Ōba has happily reappropriated it and put it to her own parodic use. *A Journey Through the Mist*, for all its outward resemblance to the classic *Bildungsroman* form, is uniquely female, making neither an apology nor grand claims for the legitimacy of telling a story of a female artist growing up. Therefore, the main concern of the narrative discourse of *A Journey Through the Mist* is not for Yurie to "become" but for her "not to become" the woman required by conventional female destiny. It is not a story of *Werden*, but of unlearning and undoing, of "unbecoming" a woman, and thereby becoming an "unbecoming" woman.[23]

Mobility and individualism, which Susan Fraiman names the two key concepts in the quest/adventure plot of the *Bildungsroman*, play important roles in Yurie's growing-up tale. However, the author's inclusion of options and experiences that do not particularly serve Yurie's self-development can be seen as an intentional, and continual, parody of the genre of the *Bildungsroman*, while simultaneously playing on the picaresque genre. Yurie, seemingly indecisive and unfocused, does not excel in academic matters, but she is active in the drama club at college. In Japanese society, she would be called a "juvenile delinquent," for during college she has affairs with two men, gets pregnant by one, and almost ruins her health by having an abortion. The man she is really after is Shigeru, but her overtures meet with rejection because he is sexually involved with his older brother's wife, Fu. Her sexual conquests stalled at two, Yurie has only one option: to take Shigeru's advice and go to Shōzō, who has somehow never stirred her interest. Rejected by Shigeru, she is relentless in her verbal assault. Her parting words to Shigeru, which take male egoism to task, reveal an independent-minded woman who is willing to take risks and is prepared to begin a long quest of self-development:

> "I thought you were more courageous than that. You are really a coward. You think you're safe by rejecting me, but you've given up what you could have grabbed with your own hands. You're thinking to yourself, 'I've had enough mess in my life. No more.' I'm sure you'll play safe for the rest of your life, but never find what you wish you could. But I'm going to find it.
>   . . . .
> "Nothing scares me. I'll find out in any way I can what men's true colors are. I won't stop watching until my face turns blue. Then I may learn how wonderful men are, or how insignificant, whether there's something I really want from them, or nothing." (123)

In Sweden, where Shōzō has a one-year contract with a forestry research center, Yurie has an affair with Peter, a live-in boyfriend of Monica, Shōzō's colleague. Yurie expresses her need for Peter in the following way: "I've been able to survive so far because men have once in a while cleared away the mist that blocked my way . . . and the mist was also men themselves" (11). Yurie's statement reflects Ōba's feminist presentation of a "doubled view of women as agents as well as victims" (Fraiman, 124). Here, Ōba stays away from the notion of a woman as only the victimized heroine, passively sacrificing her own story to allow a man to tell his. Men in *A Journey Through the Mist* are victims as well as victimizers, symbolizing simultaneously the mist that blocks the path of women to self-development and the agent who clears away that mist for women.

There are two things to consider here as we deal with Ōba's heroine. First, Yurie is living in a postwar Japan that has been simultaneously crushed and liberated by the United States, its self-esteem and self-identity almost nonexistent. Second, Yurie attends the most liberal and liberated college in the country, a college based on Ōba's alma mater, Tsuda Women's College. These two historical conditions are reflected in the character of Yurie: she desires to be free from what convention and propriety dictated to women up to the end of the war, to apply the spirit of liberal education in her own life, but she is held back by an unawakened, unformed sense of herself as a woman. As a further impediment to Yurie's awakening, the Japanese patriarchal force continues to run, unchanged and unchanging, beneath the current of political and social liberation by a Western power.

So thick is the mist of her ambiguity that Yurie realizes she needs a "complementary, equal relationship" (113) with a man if she is to find her way through it. But to find such a man in postwar Japan seems next to impossible, and the idea of a conventional marriage as defined by patriarchy never enters her mind. That marriage is not a goal in her life is symbolic of her larger rejection of the female destiny laid out for women by society. Her mother, herself a rather free-spirited soul, nevertheless starts searching for a husband for her daughter in college by sending her photographs of prospective candidates. This is how Yurie aborts one of those marriage proposals, from the son of the owner of a well-known private hospital:

> I never bothered to respond to the young doctor's request for a *miai* [a formal meeting between prospective bride and groom preceding an arranged marriage]. In the meantime, unable to wait any longer, he showed up alone one Sunday morning at the visitors' lounge of my dormitory, where he met a young woman with uncombed hair, no makeup, wearing a sweater inside out and a skirt with holes, and her feet dragging worn-out slippers. He was so flabbergasted that all he could do was to make small talk before he hastily took his leave. (156)

What is intriguing about *A Journey Through the Mist* is how small a role Shōzō *seems* to play in the process of Yurie's sexual and intellectual awakening. Shōzō, Yurie's future husband, is as unassuming as all other male characters created by early feminist women writers.

Like Dorothy Sayers's Lord Peter Wimsey, Lucy Maud Montgomery's Gilbert, and Louisa May Alcott's Professor Bhaer,[24] Shōzō gives Yurie what a man in a romanticized courtship fails to recognize—a woman's need of time and breathing space. Shōzō waits until Yurie knows what to do with the free choice given to her, until she makes a decision on her own terms. Another way to look at Shōzō's importance is as the only person who lets Yurie speak her mind. In public, Yurie plays the role of listener. "I always listened, never had a chance to talk about myself" (20). As a writer in the making, she "collects" all kinds of stories people share with her: confessions, made-up stories, complaints.

Does this mean that Yurie does not like to talk? On the contrary, she has opinions on everything under the sun, and this is one of the reasons why she needs Shōzō. A self-proclaimed misanthrope, he would rather listen to or look at trees, plants, and animals. Or, to put it differently, Yurie is the only person he enjoys talking with and listening to. In *A Journey Through the Mist*, his lines are few and far between, but the couple's humorous, tongue-in-cheek verbal exchanges represent key moments in the story. For example, here is a "love-scene" that turns into a marriage proposal:

> When we stood up, the beach was shrouded deep in the darkness of dusk.
> It so happened we were facing each other as we stood up. He suddenly bit hard into my lips.
> I cannot describe it in any other way but to say he bit my lips. They began to swell.
> Afraid that they were cut, I gently touched them while he looked at me as if filtering his gaze through a shadow among thick leaves.
> "I don't know how to kiss properly. Show me," he said and held me close.
> . . . .
> "Stay with me tonight."
> He took me to his grandfather's house.
> "We may have the same ancestors," he said. I remembered that he had left behind a bouquet of *hamanasu* flowers. "Shall we go back and look for it?"
> He shook his head. "I may have to go to a place much farther away, farther even than Hokkaidō." He suddenly said this in front of his grandfather's house.
> "Where?"
> "A forestry research center in Sweden."
> "For a long time?"

"I don't know. I don't know about the future. Will you come?"
. . . .
"So, who will keep the house key?" I asked.
"Let's get two. One for each of us." He looked up and laughed.
(187–89)

Yurie's married life turns out to be rather ordinary, and she suffers from the female anxiety of not being able to speak her mind.[25] Words fill her brain, but she cannot find an outlet for them. As briefly mentioned above, the pivotal episode in the novel involves Peter, the Swedish-language tutor of both Shōzō and Yurie. Shōzō eventually drops the lessons, but Yurie continues them because Peter unknowingly selects as a textbook a book of fairy tales, her favorite type of literature. The routine of the language lesson is for him to read a story in Swedish, and for her to retell it in her own words. One day, when her husband is away, Peter bangs on the window at Yurie's house, and she lets him in. Thus begins Yurie's "fairy tale" affair with Peter.

His clandestine visits continue for a while, and in the meantime the sexual relationship with Peter enhances Yurie's domestic lovemaking as well. However, she does not consider her relationship with Peter to be an affair of love; rather, it is like two animals sniffing at each other. Besides, she loses something precious in this relationship: "The sexual fantasy I had about Peter [before I slept with him] lost its luster, and I had to make every effort to keep it alive" (292). At Peter's urging, the two take off on an impromptu excursion to a lakeside house that belongs to his grandfather. Although she accepts Peter's invitation, she has no intention of leaving Shōzō for good and calls Shōzō up to give him an alibi. When she calls him a second time, Shōzō is clearly upset and says, "You can't even explain to me what's going on. You say you can't come home tonight. And you expect to have a place to come home to tomorrow?" (316). After they spend one full day together, Peter assumes that Yurie wants to have a more permanent relationship with him.[26] But then something really baffling happens. When she insists on returning home that night and tries to start the car engine, she begins to cry "like an animal" (338), her face against the steering wheel.

Yurie tells us, the baffled reader, part of the reason she is crying: "I was not crying to put the blame on Peter. I was struggling with my own incomprehensibility" (338). This sentence does not explain the sense of hopelessness, confusion, wretchedness, and pain all rolled into one that seems to grip her. Is she ashamed of her adultery or of her own sexual desire? Is she full of remorse for having considered eloping with Peter? One thing we know from male-inflected texts: if Yurie were a man, she would not experience such a desperate feeling. In the end, Yurie goes back to her husband that night by train and says to him, "I'm sorry" (343). The female text in *A Journey Through the Mist* asserts that Yurie cries for some other reason.

The outing with Peter makes explicit what Yurie has been vaguely aware of but also fears: the discovery of an "as-yet-unwritten story" (Heilbrun, *Hamlet's Mother*, 126), a female destiny that she has to manage on her own. However brief it may be, she thinks to herself, it would be fun to be part of the destiny of a man; if he has the same aspirations as she does, all the better. In this she shows her perhaps unintended complicity with a male-gendered script for women. But Yurie quickly begins to see Peter as he is: a stereotypically well-meaning male for whom she has to play the role of a typical female, pretending to be captivated by his boyish romantic charm and suppressing her own ego and creativity. She is sick of the lies and pretensions that social decorum forces upon her—how could she possibly think of a life with Peter? After all, up to this point, Yurie seems to be nothing but a contented housewife, but in reality she is slowly killing herself by not being able to say what is really on her mind. It is this pain, a pain she is inflicting upon herself, as well as her willingness to hazard the distasteful, that is incomprehensible to her. This is probably what Yurie means by her "own incomprehensibility."

At the end of the novel, we learn that Yurie has become the mother of a young girl. Thus, her "labor" in creating her own story coincides with a real pregnancy.[27] But Ōba's depiction of Yurie goes against the stereotype of female contentment in motherhood; Yurie does not become a motherly figure, and her reproductive power is not used to support the Freudian myth that motherhood is the attainment of the ultimate female desire. Instead, Yurie persists in striving to write her own story. This fact forces her husband, Shōzō, to undergo a transformation. It is Yurie's relationship with Peter that makes Shōzō redefine himself as a man who understands manhood not in his separation from the *feminine* or the *womanly* but in equal partnership with a woman. With Peter as the catalyst, Shōzō emerges as a rare male character in modern literature: a man who allows a woman to have her own destiny apart from his.

Seen in another way, Yurie's affair with Peter is more than a sexual seduction; it is a literary seduction as well, an initiation into fiction, for involvement with Peter opens up a new world of fantasy, lies, and secrecy: "We didn't stop seeing each other [even though I had to make every effort to keep the sexual fantasy alive]. We were having lots of fun being frightened of our secret, and lying to each other" (292). Finding herself tangled in a web of fabrication and seduced by the power of her "lies" and imagination, Yurie finds herself moving closer to her ultimate goal, fiction writing.

To complicate matters, Ōba's heroine, even though she has been carrying an embryonic literary woman inside her for some time, seems to wish for a stillbirth in spite of herself. In this, she is experiencing what every female writer has gone through: the dilemma of being "forced to choose between the life of a woman or the life of the mind" (Lerner, *The Creation of Feminist Consciousness*, 30). Yurie instinctively knows that there is no one with whom she can share the knowledge of this dilemma, and that is why she conceals her literary ambition from Peter and from everyone else except Shōzō, who early on sees in Yurie the gifts of a writer. In the end, she realizes that he alone is capable of letting her nurture her literary self at her own pace.

⚘

That Yurie's fit of tears in *A Journey Through the Mist* represents a turning point in the *Bildungsroman* is made vividly clear in the sequel, *Birds Crying*. Yurie's perilous journey to self-development continues in *Birds Crying*, but now she is a well-established woman writer, older, more aggressive, and more confident in her self-assertion. She is also changing and aging in an equal partnership with Shōzō. The middle-aged Yurie has settled comfortably into the role of an "unbecoming," unrepentant woman writer, sharing her life with a husband who does not agree with the stereotypical view that "men can be men only if women are unambiguously women" (Cameron, 209).

Just as we would expect from Ōba, the narrative voice in *Birds Crying* often shifts. Individual chapters are contiguous yet independent, in a way reminiscent of the traditional genre of linked verse (*renga*) and of the loose, open-ended structure of *The Tale of Genji* or *Tales of Ise*. The title of the narrative literally means "of crying birds" (*naku tori no*), and is itself open-ended. Here the grammatical particle *no* is the classical Japanese subject marker, which survives in modern Japanese, and it indicates more to come. The particle frequently ends a phrase in a haiku, inviting another line. Ōba has given this explanation of the symbolic meaning of the carefully chosen title: "A fictional world is basically a human world, and in a larger sense it is a universe, within which exists every conceivable kind of space and time. There is no such thing as a state of completion, as the fictional world expands to infinity, yet it exists at this very moment" (Takeda, 314).

If *Birds Crying* lacks a stereotypically exciting plot and is structured "without beginning, without ending," then what is it that Ōba is offering? She offers us human life as it is — in Ōba's words, *shizen sono mama* (things just as they are) — not life in an idealized, romanticized, or sanitized form. The author's presentation of Yurie and Shōzō's life offers an unconventional alternative for all married couples and a broad cross-cultural perspective to challenge the insular Japanese mind. And — for the jaded reader — it provides a delightful, humorous exchange of opinions and ideas on things that are considered outrageous by Japanese society. Japanese women have finally found a voice in the character of Yurie, a voice that is unapologetic and uninhibited, full of what Japanese call *honne* (one's true feelings, in contrast to what one is supposed to feel or say). It is Yurie's voice that fills the major part of the dialogues in *Birds Crying* with Shōzō and with her second cousin, Mizuki.

Despite Ōba's claims that she does not rely on a conscious modus operandi and that her best works are the result of some subconscious force, or of the "living spirit" of her Heian sisters prodding her forward, *Birds Crying* has a carefully structured narrative movement. The story covers a half-year time span, beginning in winter, on Mount Hiei near Kyoto, and ending with the rainy season, in early summer. During these months, different people appear before Yurie and Shōzō, and with each of these visits the reader is entertained anew. We are first introduced to Mizuki, the daughter of Yurie's "notorious" cousin Fu; the young Yurie had had a crush on Fu's lover, Shigeru, who is the younger brother of Fu's husband. Then, Fukiko, Shigeru's wife, visits, and the reader learns the scandalous story of her husband. But before we can engage ourselves in Fukiko's story, Yurie's old friend, Lynn Ann, a Chinese American, appears with her second husband, Henry. Through this couple, we retrieve the thread of memory all the way back to Yurie's affair with Peter in *A Journey Through the Mist*. Next comes Shigeru's son, Tōichirō, and we then meet for the first time the grown-up Chie, Yurie's daughter. The novel closes, for the moment (as Ōba might say), with Shigeru's final visit and sudden death and with the news of Lynn Ann's and Henry's deaths in a car accident. To tell the complex story of these human relationships and interactions, Ōba adopts a complex technique: two narrative voices, one that of

Mizuki, the other the omniscient narrator, as well as the dramatic monologues and the dialogues of the characters.

In other words, *Birds Crying* tells the story of different kinds of "birds," singing and crying out, who visit Yurie and Shōzō, then "fly away," sometimes to return, sometimes never to return. Using birds as a metaphor for humanity, in this case represented by a pair of "rare birds," Yurie and Shōzō, Ōba intentionally blurs the line between the human habitat and the animal kingdom. Birds in the wild sing when they feel like singing; they cry out when there is danger. The spontaneity of the act, the naturalness of it, is what moves Ōba. In contrast to being the "caged bird," one of the metaphors Western women writers have most frequently used to describe a woman's emotional and physical confinement,[28] Yurie is a bird flying freely in the wild.

Two spheres usually seen in conflict, the human habitat and nature, are blended in the dialogues and dramatic monologues of Yurie and Shōzō. And the poeticality of the narrative in *Birds Crying* is woven together in an intricate pattern with critiques on sociocultural issues such as the environment, motherhood, parenthood, mother-daughter relationships, the institutions of family and marriage, and meditations on humankind. In this sense, Yurie is a poet, sometimes a poet with a social message, sometimes a poet of unspoiled nature. For example, retrieving the thread of memories all the way back to Alaska, where Yurie and Shōzō once lived, Yurie the nature poet hypnotizes Mizuki and the reader with a description of an ocean kingdom:

> Yurie also began to describe the Sea of Alaska with dreamy eyes: the way gigantic sea anemone in full bloom on the ocean bottom flip their tentacles; sea cucumbers resembling monster leeches; intimidating sea urchins; and how abalone, legless and finless, can quickly hop from one rock to another in the water. Yurie, whose arms were now out of the sleeping bag, made flapping movements with her fingers. For a moment, Mizuki had the illusion that Yurie was one of the strange sea creatures in her story.
>
> The dark green of their sleeping bags resembled the color of the ocean, and their body movements underneath, undulations.
>
> There were more. The yellow waves swollen by a large school of herring headed for shore; beaches carpeted by roe; the cries of flapping gulls clamoring after the fish trapped between rocks after spawning, bloodied and dying.
>
> When they spoke of those sea creatures, they ceased to be human. Sometimes they were crabs, other times abalone or herring.

One could hear the sound of waves, see the seaweed swaying, the insides of an abalone's suckers, the scintillating white underbelly of a herring. (31)

The shift from a description of nature back to the human habitat, or vice versa, is often swift, effectively keeping the reader "hooked." Ōba depicts human beings as an integral part of nature, which is not something to be subdued or subjugated according to human whim, existing for human convenience. Her view is Taoist-Buddhist rather than Judeo-Christian. She does not romanticize nature, because she recognizes the fierce struggle for life that goes on in the wilderness. In Ōba's view, if women and men are to share a sense of equality in society, humanity and nature must also be placed on an equal footing.

Whether concerned with humanity or nature, Ōba structures her cultural critiques carefully. For example, she places Mizuki as the foil in the dyad Yurie and Shōzō in order to unfold a battle of wits over the unconventional and "un-Japanese" couple. Like other characters who appear before Yurie and Shōzō, Mizuki has an unusual tale to share: her mother, Fu, has hinted time and again that her uncle, Shigeru, may be her real father. As if to get rid of her, Fu sent her to the United States at the age of fourteen, where she continued her education. While there, Mizuki had married Carl, a German, and become the mother of two adopted children, one half-Chicano and half-Chinese, the other a blue-eyed Scot. She and her family normally reside in the United States, but Mizuki is staying in Japan on a sabbatical leave. Since Mizuki's understanding of non-Japanese culture is substantial, Ōba is perhaps offering her as the best foil to Yurie and Shōzō, whose decade-long residence abroad had made them quite cosmopolitan.

Mizuki works successfully as a foil because, in spite of her extensive experience abroad, she tends to be rigid and conventional in her views when dealing with her own culture. The interesting twist here is that the voice expressing disapproval of Yurie and Shōzō's unconventionality comes not from a typical Japanese who has never left Japan but from the well-traveled and serious-minded Mizuki. To use a Japanese euphemism, she is extremely "worried" about them. Mizuki is ambivalent in her response to Yurie and Shōzō, for as much as she wants to criticize them frankly, she also feels the need for diplomacy. As it becomes clearer and clearer that the poker-faced taboo-breaking couple is simply beyond Mizuki's conventional imagination, the reader begins to lose patience with Mizuki. She is simply no match for them. Hers is the collective voice of anxious Japanese, who have difficulty with anyone being "ambiguously" woman (or man) or being an "unbecoming" woman, as illustrated in the following exchange between Mizuki and Shōzō:

> "Shōzō, Yurie writes anything she damn pleases, doesn't she?"
> "It seems what she writes really infuriates men out there. I wonder why. It doesn't upset me at all and I'm her husband."
> "They're probably furious about you, too. Like husband, like wife, they'd say." Mizuki tried baiting him. She wanted to see him riled up a bit, but he merely nodded his agreement, completely unruffled.
> "I guess so. You might be right. Seiichirō was also like that," he said, changing the subject to Mizuki's father.
> "In her novels, Yurie lets her female protagonists do what they damn please with men."
> "It looks like my counterparts in her stories are either cuckolded or bovine, or sometimes quack doctors, incompetent scholars, or retirement-age businessmen who have been kicked upstairs."
> "Oh, dear, you mean you really enjoy reading that stuff?"
> "That may be the case. You never have a dull moment hanging around a woman like Yurie."
> Mizuki was silenced. She could think of no response.
> "It must have been the same with Seiichirō," said Shōzō.
> The subject bounced right back to Mizuki's father.
> "Don't you agree with me?" he continued. "He was crazy about Fu. Rumor has it, though, he hit her from time to time."
> "All right, all right," Mizuki conceded. (10–11)

Mizuki's reactions and thought patterns reveal deep-seated Japanese cultural biases. Besides being disturbed about the unrepentant, unapologetic female characters Yurie creates, Mizuki finds several facts about the couple difficult to accept: they share a double bed, sleeping naked together; they go everywhere and do everything together; and Shōzō retired early to help his wife's career. All these things are virtually unheard of between a wife and husband in their early fifties in Japan. It is as though the reader were observing an initiation ritual that Mizuki must undergo: she must first accept the "outrageous" lifestyle of Yurie and Shōzō and then learn how to be as articulate and self-assertive as they are. In fact, it is Yurie's youngest sister, Momoe, who gives Mizuki the best advice:

> "Yurie has lost a marble or two, you know. Be aware of that when you deal with her. It's gotten to Shōzō as well. They're no longer

young lovebirds, but the way they're glued to each other all year around—I call them goldfish dung. Shōzō just listens with a straight face, enthralled by his wife's selfish ramblings.

. . . .

"When she's upfront, you've got to be the same." (7–8)

Mizuki's sojourn in Japan turns out to be a time of unlearning traditional feminine behavior, of coming to terms with her own past. Another good example of how she copes with her own conventionality with regard to Japanese society comes from a chance encounter with Shōzō as he shops for fish:

> Every Tuesday morning, a fish vendor came up the mountain. Mizuki ran into Shōzō this morning. Apparently it was his job to buy fish, and he was eyeing them with great affection. He was able to tell the freshness of each fish by just looking and began to show Mizuki which one to choose. "Horse mackerel is in season," he said. He wanted to know where the mackerel came from, and checked the van's license plate number. . . . When he found out that the vendor was from Karasu-chō, he said, "That's good. Close enough to the sea."
>
> After he left with a purchase of eels, the vendor asked Mizuki, "Is he a college professor?"
>
> It must have been very rare for a man to come to buy fish during the day. Finding it a lot of bother to answer, Mizuki just nodded, "Uhm, hum."
>
> He tried again.
>
> "Does he teach or work in an office?"
>
> "Probably both." Mizuki's vague reply did not seem to satisfy him. "I think he's doing some research on Mount Hiei. Working on a book, I gather," she added.
>
> Residents in this area often held university-related jobs or were self-employed, among them potters and painters. Mizuki's answer seemed to have satisfied him, and he no longer questioned her. A few housewives nearby pricked up their ears.
>
> A man in his prime who hangs around at home really sticks out and invites suspicion, Mizuki realized. Loafing around was not accepted by society. (103–4)

Mizuki represents the stereotypical Japanese whose life abroad, and whose direct contact with non-Japanese culture, has had hardly any impact upon her intellectual development. According to Mizuki, Shōzō's indirect contribution to Yurie's career (in this case, doing the shopping) has little social value, a sign that she regards so-called women's work as unimportant. But the prejudice works against men as well: women doing the shopping and other domestic tasks are simply fulfilling their duties, but men engaged in household jobs are seen as "loafing around." As Carolyn G. Heilbrun says, "The hardest thing in the life of women to learn is to say: Whatever I am is woman" (*Reinventing Womanhood*, 140). Afraid of affronting a man's and society's sensibilities about gender roles, Mizuki is also fearful of expanding her definition of woman for what it might require of her regarding her own identity as a woman. She is not prepared to face the vendor or the eavesdropping neighborhood wives if she tells him the truth. Nor does she possess the mischievousness to tease and shock them with the truth by saying, "He's a househusband!"

Ōba lets Shōzō, rather than the anxious, humorless Mizuki, affirm his status as a househusband and articulate his view of the female experience. After Carl, Mizuki's husband, finishes comparing the Western diet to the Japanese diet, Shōzō, a man of few words, suddenly opens his mouth:

> "I've been stitching scrub cloths all day today. . . . I used to think, how ridiculous to do anything like that. But now I know it's not really a dumb thing at all. It's a very simple task, not requiring much mental work. That means you can really get into the world of imagination while you stitch. Your mind is completely on something else. The only time you come back to reality is when you have to pay attention to how you're stitching." (70)

A typical, good-natured patriarchal male, Carl does not know how to respond to this re-examination of the female experience articulated by a man. Right after Shōzō's comment, Yurie comes up with a truly revolutionary possibility: "I've read somewhere that in the animal kingdom, in every other generation, a male turns into a female, and a female turns into a male. I wonder what that means" (71). This is the kind of satiric and subversive spirit that lurks in Yurie's imagination.

Henry, Lynn Ann's husband, is an older man who shares some of Carl's prejudices. He ridicules Shōzō, but with a certain amount of envy and chagrin.

> "But you are male, aren't you?" Henry said.
> "Huh?"
> "You are a man, but you don't let masculine reason dictate your life. You're still in your prime but you quit your job, and now you sit back and absentmindedly watch what your wife is doing. You certainly are self-secure. I could never do that."

"I may look that way, I may be all bewildered inside, you know. Yurie doesn't like noise, so I watch television with earphones. If I don't, she moves to another room. . . ."

". . . So you watch television right next to your wife even if you have to use clumsy earphones. What egos! Both of you."

"These days she says the screen bothers her eyes, so she does reading sitting away from the television set."

"I see. I must take my hat off to you. You refuse to turn off the television, still watch what you want to watch."

"I don't know whether I deserve your praise; a person is the same as a stone in the wilderness. One human being cannot tell another what to do if he or she doesn't want to do it."

"Maybe so, but I would think about smashing the whole earth to get my way. Of course, that's ridiculous. I guess it's a bit like dreaming that I've become the center of the universe, the sun." (174–75)

Henry is a mouthpiece for Western culture, reflecting the Western concept of rugged individualism and "relentless advance" to conquer the universe, although he at least shows some self-awareness in this regard.

Ironically, the most patriarchal and stereotypically male character in *Birds Crying* is Shigeru, a man with whom Yurie once thought she wanted to share her life. In hindsight, we could say that Yurie narrowly escaped the tragedy of pursuing the conventional female destiny, because this was the man who had detected in Yurie a budding "unbecoming woman" even before she was completely aware of it and had rejected her as an unsuitable partner with whom to fulfill his male destiny. As if to highlight Shigeru's own intransigent defense of the masculine plot, Ōba brings in his Western counterpart, Carl, and again inserts Mizuki between the two men as a foil:

"I'm younger than you, Shigeru. That's why I still find women pitiable. I also find women who say things off-the-wall cute." Carl shook his head as he turned toward Mizuki. "But I'll never let Mizuki climb up a utility pole and work."

"But you certainly have fun watching me pick ginkgo nuts, don't you?" Mizuki said.

"I just let you do it because you seem to enjoy it so much, that's all. One of the very few things I don't mind doing is putting frozen fried chicken into the oven."

"Even if there's food already prepared in the fridge, if I have to serve it myself, I'd eat out," Shigeru answered curtly. (195–96)

Shigeru's sudden death from a heart attack toward the end of the novel reinforces his image as a stereotypical Japanese male who has lived out the Japanese version of a masculine plot, fulfilling the male destiny as the institution of patriarchy in Japan has prescribed it for him: a loveless marriage but a highly successful climb up the career ladder. The premature ending of his career by death from overwork (*karōshi*),[29] a social phenomenon increasing at an alarming rate among white-collar workers, suggests Ōba's criticism of the Japanese masculine plot.

The combined narrative of *A Journey Through the Mist* and *Birds Crying* re-examines the institution of patriarchy, ultimately rejecting conventional male destiny. Central to Ōba's look at the masculine plot and manipulation of the *Bildungsroman* is her depiction of Shōzō's growing awareness of Yurie's desire to write, an ironic twist on men's stereotypical view of women as manipulative and lying:

> When the situation became intolerable — she had found no one to speak her mind to — the idea of submitting something to a literary magazine in Japan began to take shape [while in Sweden].
> She talked off the top of her head about things that didn't really interest her, lying to herself day in and day out. To make matters worse, people could never sense what she really wanted to say; her duplicity didn't seem to bother them at all. It almost drove her nuts. (135)

Realizing how necessary writing is to Yurie's well-being, Shōzō reshapes his life to accommodate her needs. This puts him in the unconventional position of the man who makes sacrifices for the sake of his wife's professional and personal fulfillment. Shōzō reflects on his role as nurturer of Yurie's talents at the end of the novel:

> He began to feel that what he had been doing for forty years since he met that smart-alecky little kid was indeed the stuff of heroism.
> All he wanted was to let her live. He convinced himself that if he could not let her say what was really on her mind, she would die. Why does a parent take care of a crying baby? (311)

Shōzō's unconventionality is further expressed in his capacity to recognize and value the kind of work that a woman deserves credit for doing but rarely gets: the endless labor of serving as family cook. Shōzō's appreciation of the effort it takes to make meals on a regular basis is sharpened when he decides to prepare an elaborate dish. In the scene, we see Shōzō trying to dress a rather unyielding fish and having a hard time of it: "Yurie immediately picked up the knife, and with a few deft strokes, the fish was prepared" (43). Admiration and compliments immediately follow from Shōzō, the novice: "Boy, you're good at that. Well, I shouldn't be surprised, after thirty years of cooking" (43). Shōzō later reflects on how his accommodating stance sets him apart from other Japanese men.

> Those men who didn't do what I did and were highly critical of me — with looks of contempt that said, "What a nuisance to let a wife like that have her own way"—must have taken it for granted that a breakfast of miso soup, grilled fish, eggs, and fresh green tea would be served to them and enjoyed by them every morning. Even this simple breakfast wasn't available to me until I began to assume the role of cook, after Yurie finally switched to the daily routine of getting up early in the morning to write. (312)

Shōzō's true feelings (*honne*) about the Japanese male role are presented by Ōba to counter Shigeru's crudely misogynistic remark: "Even if there's food already prepared [by my wife] in the fridge, if I have to serve it myself, I'd eat out."

What makes *Birds Crying* radically different from *A Journey Through the Mist*, and at the same time defines the sequel clearly as a feminist work, is Yurie and Shōzō's reversal of roles, which is heightened by Ōba's success in achieving the "reversal of emotions or symbolic value" that rarely accompanies a role reversal in male literature (Fetterley, 72). This she accomplishes through the mutuality and complementarity of the relationship between Yurie and Shōzō, with all their foibles, rough edges, and contradictions. Finally freed from the masculine view of the female destiny, *Birds Crying* is a pioneering work in which unconventional male and female plots coexist, each one affecting the other in equal measure. It is this choice of "both/and" over "either/or," the examination of both sides of the delicate gender issues Ōba explores in the novel, that is so endearing and empowering to the reader.

In Yurie, Ōba has created a woman character who, though middle-aged and married, is freed from being stereotyped or idealized and is "autonomous, intellectual, unwomanly and, ultimately, lovable" (Heilbrun, *Hamlet's Mother*, 308). Here is a woman writer who has imagined for other women the self that she has in fact achieved, a female self that has moved, without apology or false modesty, beyond internalized pain and anger.[30] Yurie's long apprenticeship, which offers possibilities of life often denied to women, provides a model for a continuing process of unlearning, of unbecoming the woman prescribed by men, and of forging a female destiny imagined and constructed by women.

Notes

I thank Fujimoto Kazumi for providing me with many journal articles and other relevant information on Ōba Minako. My heartfelt thanks also go to Janet A. Walker, Paul G. Schalow, Susan Fraiman, Becky Thomas, and Mike Wilson for their valuable comments and suggestions.

1. See Chapter 1, by Ōba, pp. 19–40, in this volume.

2. A year after Ōba expressed this skepticism about Genji's character, Komashaku Kimi, in her study *Murasaki Shikibu no messēji*, challenged the canonical reading of the masterpiece and reclaimed it for female readers as a narrative of women's experience. Her contention was that the main theme of the *Tale of Genji* is Heian women's refusal to marry, which translates into an indictment of the marriage institution.

3. Miki Taku, a critic who attacked Ōba for "inconsistency" and "lack of logic" in *A Journey Through the Mist*, has also reluctantly admitted: "I've never heard a voice this candid from any other [Japanese] woman writer" (Miki, 285).

4. Unless indicated otherwise, all translations from Ōba's works are my own.

5. In Tokugawa Japan (1600–1868), the role of women in society was formalized along Confucian lines—the lifelong duty of a woman was obedience to parents (usually the father), parents-in-law, husband, and male children. The most representative work of this misogynistic teaching is Kaibara Ekken's *Onna daigaku* (Great learning for women; 1672). For a discussion of the work, see Robertson, 91–94.

6. See also Saegusa Kazuko's essay, "Onna ga shi-shōsetsu o kaku toki" (When women write an "I-novel"), in her *Sayonara otoko no jidai*. She argues that the confessional "I-novel" (*shi-shōsetsu*) is written by men for men, and its central strategy is for the male protagonist to "dig up" or expose his inner self as the victimizer, not as the victimized (129).

7. In his 1975 autobiographical fiction *Kataku no hito* (The sufferer), which won the Japanese Literature Grand Award and the Yomiuri Literary Award, Dan Kazuo portrays a slipshod writer who, though the father of several children, is happily (or pathetically) in search of the romantic bohemian life, unable to overcome a taste for booze and women. Shimao Toshio's best novel, *Shi no toge* (The sting of death; 1977), a work of autobiographical fiction that describes the madness of Miho, his wife, between 1954 and 1955, was the recipient of the same two major awards. In the face of Miho's "madness," Toshio, the husband, is helpless, incapable of taking any action,

and seems to drive her into madness because he needs an accomplice in a charade of going mad himself. For a feminist reading of the novel, see Ueno et al., 65–132 (I thank Chieko Ariga for bringing this work to my attention). For an extensive discussion in English of Shimao Toshio and *The Sting of Death*, see "The Eternal War: Shimao Toshio," in Gessel, 125–80.

8. The term is borrowed from Gilbert and Gubar, *The War of Words*, 146.

9. See Wilson, particularly chap. 4, "The Image of Embattled Cultural Hero and Picaresque Narrative," 33–47.

10. See Ozaki, 37.

11. See Chapter 11, by Chieko M. Ariga, pp. 352–81, in this volume.

12. It comes as no surprise that *Snow Country* is probably the favorite novel among Japanese businessmen and male scholars to take with them abroad (Tsuruta, 49). In a feminist reading of the novel, Tajima Yōko calls it a "sanitarium for male self-recovery" and finds Komako "a sexually liberated, unpaid nurse"; Tajima shows the protagonist, Shimamura, far from being an "example of the meaninglessness, isolation, and futile love of modern man" who brings himself closer to "modern enlightenment" (as patriarchal critiques of the novel would have it), to be nothing more than an immature man who is totally incapable of developing an equal relationship with a woman. Tajima's article originally appeared in Egusa and Urushida, 149–80. Here, when I think of how long it has taken Japanese female scholars to challenge the male-dominated world of criticism, I am as helpless as Ellen Moers to resist the temptation of borrowing a famous line: "I cannot quite, though I should, resist the temptation to quote 'You've come a long way, baby' from that ad which sells cigarettes to the liberated women" (129).

13. In a formal discussion (*taidan*) with Nakayama Chinatsu, Yamamoto Michiko describes how the label of "housewife novelist," coined by the male-dominated media, has made her feel denounced by society, as if a married woman's writing were harmful to the maintenance of family life. She once told a male journalist, "If you insist on calling me a 'housewife novelist,' then why not call a male writer a 'husband novelist' [*teishu sakka*]?" Later, she again spoke of the unfairness of the situation between literary men and women: "A male writer can work all day, while his wife looks after all his needs. I really envy them" (Yamamoto and Nakayama, 58–62).

14. See Miki, 283; quoted in Ōba, "Onna no hyōgen," 11. The most outspoken Japanese woman writer to deplore the frustrating situation of literary assessments, a situation that also affects male writers in Japan, is Kōno Taeko; see Ōba and Kōno, 142–43. Carolyn G. Heilbrun also questions the unchallenged usage of the word "human," which excludes women: "Isn't it natural and even desirable that a successful woman should move from involvement with the female condition to involvement with the human condition? To agree, however, is to overlook the unhappy fact that in all aspects of our culture, the feminine element has been so long ignored that movement toward apparently 'human' concerns is in fact movement back into a cultural tradition still dominated by male-centered values" (*Reinventing Womanhood*, 86).

15. In this regard, Kōno Taeko admires Ōba's undaunted spirit, which gives her "the ability not to let such negative responses bother you. You have a wonderful talent, a career firmly in hand, and a clear sense of your self." She implies that no one else could be as unfazed as Ōba is under the same circumstances: "You were never crushed but steadily went on to produce *Katachi mo naku* [Amorphous] and *Naku tori no* [Birds crying], which have given us hours of pleasure." Ōba at one point responds: "Oh, yes, terrible abuse they [the critics and reviewers] heaped on me. People have often told me to respond to those nasty remarks, but I have always replied, 'I'd rather do so in my novels.' . . . I wonder whether I should counterattack [in person]? . . . Well, [I can't.] I guess it's my personality" (Ōba and Kōno, 150, 152).

16. Lerner, *The Female Experience,* "Introduction," xix. See also Lerner, *The Majority Finds Its Past,* 160.

17. The quotation is from Bowring, 54. Richard Okada takes a much more positive view of the Heian women writers' sociopolitical position in relation to writing: "They were enabled, through their linguistic medium and by their politicocultural space, to speak for themselves and for their men, the latter often existing to be 'read' and 'written' by women, in a 'feminine hand'" (163).

18. Mizuta Noriko is sometimes known in her English writings as Noriko Mizuta Lippit.

19. In his discussion of Japanese women writers, Masao Miyoshi complains of the absence of serious discussion of sex and gender on the part of Japanese intellectuals: "Whether Confucian or bourgeois in genesis, taciturnity about sexuality—male, female, heterosexual, homosexual, or autoerotic—in intellectual discourse is still prevalent. Its existence is as disturbing as it is puzzling" (205–6).

20. Page numbers following excerpts from *A Journey Through the Mist* refer to the text of *Kiri no tabi* in Ōba, *Ōba Minako zenshū,* vol. 6.

21. The *Bildungsroman* hero's close relative, the picaresque hero, is helpful to our appreciation of the bumbling heroine in Ōba's story. The former, by choice, undergoes a series of rites of passage to attain maturity; the latter is forced by circumstance to fight for his survival by using the only resource available to him, his wits. For further discussion of the picaresque narrative, see Heilman; Frohock; Wicks; and Dooley. One recent work finally focuses on a female version of the *picaro*: Kaler, *The Picara.*

22. The term is from the title of a book by Judith Fetterley, *The Resisting Reader: A Feminist Approach to American Fiction.*

23. I am indebted to Fraiman's study, *Unbecoming Women,* which prompted me to apply the concept of "unbecoming" to the female *Bildungsroman.* The focus in Fraiman's discussion is how a conventional female destiny eventually harms women, undoing their authority. I use "unbecoming" in two ways: first, in the sense that Yurie must "unlearn" the conventions of what it is to be a woman; and second, in the sense that her refusal to become a conventional woman is inappropriate or "unbecoming." For Yurie, as for the

heroines created by the British Georgian and Victorian women writers that Fraiman discusses, "the way to womanhood" can be seen "not as a single path to a clear destination but as the endless negotiation of a crossroads. . . . Thus, becoming a woman," in Yurie's case—becoming an unbecoming woman—"may be thought of as . . . 'an incessant project, a daily act of reconstruction and interpretation. . . .' It is a lifelong act continuing well past any discrete season of youth" (x). Yurie also shares with the British *Bildungsroman* heroines the struggle "unbecoming" women in any culture must face: "a loss of authority" and, although a temporary one, "an abandonment of goals." The story they tell, Fraiman continues, challenges "the myth of courtship as education, railing against the belittlement of women, [and shows them to be] willing to hazard the distasteful and the indecorous" (xi).

24. For the popularity among women readers of these writers and their creations of male and female characters, see Showalter: "Alcott's heroine Jo March has become the most influential figure of the independent and creative American woman" (42). See also Heilbrun, "Sayers, Lord Peter, and Harriet Vane at Oxford" in *Hamlet's Mother*, 301–10; and Patner.

25. The act of speaking one's mind is not as easy as it seems, especially in Japanese culture where stating one's views and position on a certain subject is the equivalent of asserting one's individuality, something to be avoided even by men. It is doubly challenging for women brought up in that society to articulate their thoughts and opinions. The anxiety of Japanese women in such a situation is not quite comparable to that of men because Japanese society allows men to have many other outlets for the assertion of their individuality and gender identity.

26. We see a role reversal here because it is traditionally a woman who assumes that a love affair will lead to marriage; cf. Anna Karenina and Madame Bovary, both of whom are disappointed in this expectation.

27. Mizuta Noriko, viewing Yurie as a *yamauba* (or *yamamba*, mountain witch), connects the creation of a myth with her procreative power; in the mythical forest of Sweden, Shōzō becomes the gatekeeper who lets Yurie back in regardless of her sexual escapades and protects her. Saegusa Kazuko, on the other hand, in a short review of *A Journey Through the Mist*, sees the reversal of male and female roles as a sign of female domination (*Sayonara otoko no jidai*, 177–80), but clearly it is Ōba's intention to avoid a situation in which one gender dominates the other; the relationship between genders should be a dynamic in which the power of each is respected.

28. See Moers, 244–51.

29. For an excellent discussion of this phenomenon, see Lummis et al.

30. In the final scene of *Birds Crying,* we see Ōba's subversive intent clearly at work in her refusal to idealize Yurie. At the news of the deaths of Lynn Ann and Henry, the unidealized heroine Yurie blows her nose as she cries: "Yurie was busy crumpling the tissues [Carl handed out to her] and began to toss them into the wastebasket" (312).

Works Cited

Bernstein, Gail Lee, ed. *Recreating Japanese Women, 1600–1945*. Berkeley: University of California Press, 1991.

Bowring, Richard. "The Female Hand in Heian Japan: A First Reading." In *The Female Autograph: Theory and Practice of Autobiography from the Tenth to the Twentieth Century*, ed. Domna C. Stanton. Chicago: University of Chicago Press, 1987, 49–56.

Buckley, Jerome Hamilton. *Season of Youth: The Bildungsroman from Dickens to Golding*. Cambridge, Mass.: Harvard University Press, 1974.

Cameron, Deborah. *Feminism and Linguistic Theory*. 2d ed. New York: St. Martin's Press, 1992.

Dan Kazuo. *Kataku no hito*. Tokyo: Shinchōsha, 1975.

Dooley, D. J. "Some Uses and Mutations of the Picaresque." *Dalhousie Review* 37 (1957–58): 363–77.

Egusa Mitsuko and Urushida Kazuyo, eds. *Onna ga yomu Nihon kindai bungaku: feminizumu no kokoromi*. Tokyo: Shin'yōsha, 1992.

Fetterley, Judith. *The Resisting Reader: A Feminist Approach to American Fiction*. Bloomington: Indiana University Press, 1978.

Fraiman, Susan. *"Unbecoming" Women: British Women Writers and the Novel of Development*. New York: Columbia University Press, 1993.

Frohock, W. M. "The Idea of the Picaresque." *Yearbook of Comparative and General Literature* 16 (1967): 43–52.

Gessel, Van C. *The Sting of Life: Four Contemporary Japanese Novelists*. New York: Columbia University Press, 1989.

Gilbert, Sandra M., and Susan Gubar. *The Madwoman in the Attic: The Woman Writer and the Nineteenth-Century Literary Imagination*. New Haven: Yale University Press, 1979.

———. *No Man's Land: The Place of the Woman Writer in the Twentieth Century*, vol. 1, *The War of the Words*. New Haven: Yale University Press, 1988.

Heilbrun, Carolyn G. *Hamlet's Mother and Other Women*. New York: Ballantine Books, 1990.

———. *Reinventing Womanhood*. New York: W. W. Norton, 1979.

———. *Writing a Woman's Life*. New York: W. W. Norton, 1988.

Heilman, Robert B. "Variations on the Picaresque (Felix Krull)." *Sewanee Review* 66 (1958): 547–77.

Kaler, Anne K. *The Picara: From Hera to Fantasy Heroine*. Bowling Green, Ohio: Bowling Green State University Popular Press, 1991.

Kolb, Elene. "When Women Finally Got the Word." *New York Times Book Review*, July 9, 1989.

Komashaku Kimi. *Murasaki Shikibu no messēji*. Tokyo: Asahi shinbunsha, 1991.

Lerner, Gerda. *The Creation of Feminist Consciousness*. London: Oxford University Press, 1993.

Lerner, Gerda, ed. *The Female Experience: An American Documentary*. New York: Oxford University Press, 1977.

————. *The Majority Finds Its Past: Placing Women in History.* New York: Oxford University Press, 1979.

Lummis, Charles Douglas, and Satomi Nakajima with Kumiko Fujimura-Fanselow and Atsuko Kameda. "The Changing Portrait of Japanese Men." In *Japanese Women: New Feminist Perspectives on the Past, Present, and Future,* ed. Kumiko Fujimura-Fanselow and Atsuko Kameda. New York: Feminist Press, 1995, 229–46.

Miki Taku. "Dokusho teidan." *Bungei,* Mar. 1981, 272–86.

Miner, Earl. *Japanese Poetic Diaries.* Berkeley: University of California, 1969.

Miyoshi, Masao. "Gathering Voices: Japanese Women and Women Writers." *Off-center: Power and Culture Relations Between Japan and the United States.* Cambridge, Mass.: Harvard University Press, 1991, 189–216.

Mizuta, Noriko. "Mori no sekai: Ōba Minako ni okeru monogatari no genkei." In *Ōba Minako zenshū.* Tokyo: Kōdansha, 1991, 6: 427–36.

Moers, Ellen. *Literary Women: The Great Writers.* New York: Oxford University Press, 1985.

Nobbe, Susanne Howe. *Wilhelm Meister and His English Kinsmen.* New York: Columbia University Press, 1930.

Ōba Minako. *Birds Crying,* chap. 1. Trans. Michiko Niikuni Wilson and Michael K. Wilson. *Chicago Review* 39 (1993): 186–95.

————. *Kiri no tabi.* Tokyo: Kōdansha, 1980.

————. *Naku tori no.* Tokyo: Kōdansha, 1985.

————. *Ōba Minako zenshū.* 10 vols. Tokyo: Kōdansha, 1991.

————. *Ōjo no namida.* Tokyo: Shinchōsha, 1987.

————. "Onna no hyōgen, otoko no hyōgen." *Waseda bungaku,* Nov. 1985, 8–18.

————. *Oregon yume jūya.* Tokyo: Shueisha, 1984.

————. *Urashima-sō.* Tokyo: Kōdansha, 1977. Trans. Ōba Yu. Sakada-shi, Saitama: Josai University, Center for Inter-Cultural Studies and Education, 1995.

Ōba Minako and Akiyama Ken. "Monogatari e—*Genji monogatari* to no ōkan." *Kokubungaku: kaishaku to kanshō,* Jan. 1990, 6–27.

Ōba Minako and Kōno Taeko. "Bungaku o gaisuru mono." *Bungakukai,* July 1987, 138–58.

Okada, H. Richard. *Figures of Resistance: Language, Poetry and Narrating in "The Tale of Genji" and Other Mid-Heian Texts.* Durham, N.C.: Duke University Press, 1991.

Ozaki Hideki. "Sengo besuto serā monogatari." *Shūkan jānaru,* Aug. 7, 1966, 35–39.

Patner, Myra Mensh. "Still Crazy About Anne: The Green Gables Novel Going Strong at 83." *Washington Post,* Sept. 12, 1992, C4.

Rich, Adrienne. "When We Dead Awaken: Writing as Re-Vision." In idem, *On Lies, Secrets, and Silence: Selected Prose, 1966–1978.* New York: W. W. Norton, 1979, 33–50.

Robertson, Jennifer. "The *Shingaku* Woman: Straight from the Heart." In Bernstein, 88–107.

Russ, Joanna. *How to Suppress Women's Writing.* Austin: University of Texas Press, 1983.

Saegusa Kazuko. "Onna ga shishōsetsu o kaku toki." In idem, *Sayōnara otoko no jidai,* 128–32.

———. *Sayōnara otoko no jidai.* Kyoto: Jinmon shoin, 1984.

Shimao Toshio. *Shi no toge.* Tokyo: Shinchōsha, 1977.

Showalter, Elaine. "Little Women: The American Female Myth." In idem, *Sister's Choice: Tradition and Change in American Women's Writing.* New York: Oxford University Press, 1991, 42–64.

Swales, Martin. *The German Bildungsroman from Wieland to Hesse.* Princeton: Princeton University Press, 1978.

Tajima Yōko. "A Rereading of *Snow Country* from Komako's Point of View." *U.S.-Japan Women's Journal* 4 (Jan. 1993): 26–48.

Takeda Katsuhiko. "Yojō bungaku towazugatari." *Chishiki* 52 (Apr. 1986): 314–21.

Tsuruta, Kinya. *Kawabata Yasunari no geijutsu: junsui to kyūsai.* Tokyo: Meiji shoin, 1981.

Ueno Chizuko, Ogura Chikako, and Tomioka Taeko. *Danryū bungaku-ron.* Chikuma shobō, 1992.

Wicks, Ulrich. "The Nature of Picaresque Narrative: A Modal Approach." *PMLA* 89 (1974): 240–49.

Wilson, Michiko N. *The Marginal World of Ōe Kenzaburo: A Study in Themes and Techniques.* Armonk, N.Y.: M. E. Sharpe, 1986 (reprinted 1995).

Yamamoto Michiko and Nakayama Chinatsu. "Kuyashisa no naka kara umareta 'Betty-san no niwa.'" *Sandē Mainichi,* Mar. 18, 1973, 58–92.

Part IV

Locating 'Woman' in Culture

10

In Search of a Lost Paradise:
The Wandering Woman in
Hayashi Fumiko's *Drifting Clouds*

NORIKO MIZUTA

Wandering and Sexual Difference

Not only is *Ukigumo* (Drifting clouds; 1949–50) Hayashi Fumiko's
(1903–51) most important work, but it is also considered a masterpiece of postwar literature for its depiction of men and women living
in the devastation following the war.[1] The novel, alternatingly narrated through the male and the female protagonists' points of view,
effectively gives shape to the heroine, Yukiko, as a woman who is destroyed even as she tries to survive the chaos of the defeat; it also successfully depicts the internal landscape of the male protagonist, Tomioka, who is filled with a sense of emptiness and desolation as he returns to a Tokyo that has been reduced to rubble.[2]

The breakdown of order caused by the defeat, however, holds
different meanings for Yukiko and Tomioka. Tomioka's sense of emptiness and desolation is situated within the history of Japan's defeat in
the war, which I will examine in more detail below. He goes abroad as
a result of Japan's victories in war and its colonial policies and returns
with the country's defeat. Tomioka's idle lifestyle in French Indochina
and his decadence in Tokyo, as well as the ultimate destruction of his
spirit, parallel the events of Japanese history.

For Yukiko, in contrast, the collapse of Japanese political and social structures and the ensuing chaos signify the possibility of freedom and escape from the constriction of the sociopolitical system,
much like her earlier escape to Japan's colonies before and during the

war. Amid the ruins of Tokyo, Yukiko in fact feels a strong sense of relief:

> Yukiko bought a bag of mandarin oranges for twenty yen and climbed a mountain of rubble where she sat down and, peeling the oranges, began to eat them. She was comforted in her loneliness by a certain feeling of being refreshed, as if all the antiquated, troublesome things had been destroyed in some sort of revolution. She felt more comfortable here than anywhere, and she spit out the sour skins of the oranges all around her. (76)[3]

Even in the rubble of burned-out Tokyo or on the dirty tatami mats of a cheap, rundown hotel, Yukiko's skin shines with a glow that impresses even herself. Although *Drifting Clouds* depicts postwar Japan, it also represents the topos of Tokyo and is, like Hayashi's debut work *Hōrōki* (Vagabond's song; 1927),[4] a city novel. The world of *Drifting Clouds* develops toward degeneration and ruin within the chaotic and free space of Tokyo immediately after the war, a space full of immorality, crime, internal collapse, and death.[5] Tomioka and Yukiko's wandering takes the pattern of movement toward the city, within the city, and away from the city. Their final escape from Tokyo is a quest for liberation, but it also leads to their ruin because of the ambiguity of Tokyo itself, which contains the duality of freedom and degeneration. But the ambiguity of this urban space in the immediate postwar era becomes explicit only in relation to Yukiko's wandering.

Yukiko's wandering clearly holds a different significance from Tomioka's. This gendered difference is precisely what reveals several dualities in the novel: of the prewar system and its collapse, of the colonies and the withdrawal from them after the defeat, and of the topos of Tokyo, which is in a state of transition from ruin to renewal. Yukiko separates herself from the Japanese social system that forces women to stay at home and departs for an external space; although this is a journey in search of freedom, it also leads to her descent to the margins of society. The dual nature of a woman's movement to escape the social system not only affects Hayashi's depiction of the postwar era and the topos of Tokyo but also renders ambiguous the meaning of the colonies, the defeat, the family, and the body. Although *Drifting Clouds* depicts a world supported by a seemingly unshakable structure of gender dichotomy, the woman's wandering outside the social system is shown as gradually destructive of the system's values and meanings.

The gendered difference in wandering, which Hayashi Fumiko

understood as an asymmetrical dualism, is the theme of *Drifting Clouds*. Through Yukiko's wandering, *Drifting Clouds* depicts the differences between men's and women's lives, which are constructed by the social system to coexist but never to intersect. This essay focuses on these differences, through which Hayashi Fumiko reveals the dualistic implications of the order and chaos of both prewar and postwar Japanese social and political systems for men and women and expresses her pessimistic views of the inherent asymmetry of men and women and the consequent impossibility of romantic love.

The Ideologies of Wandering and Stability

With the exception of the unfinished *Meshi* (Meal; 1951), *Drifting Clouds* was Hayashi Fumiko's last work, and, along with her first novel, *Vagabond's Song*, is a masterpiece in Hayashi's corpus of work. Hayashi serialized *Drifting Clouds* in a journal and intended it to be only about 300 pages long, but as she continued writing, it grew to a length of over 700 pages. During its serialization it was advertised as a work that would stand alongside *Vagabond's Song*, and in that spirit Hayashi Fumiko herself put great effort into it.

Both the wandering of a vagabond and drifting clouds are explicit images antithetical to stability and domestication, and it is clear from the titles alone that both *Vagabond's Song* and *Drifting Clouds* depict women who reject the idea, or are denied the chance, of settling down. *Drifting Clouds* is thus a work that continues the theme of a woman's wandering that Hayashi initiated with *Vagabond's Song*, and in this sense it makes clear the ultimate destination of the wandering woman. Yukiko in *Drifting Clouds* does not necessarily represent the future of the narrator/heroine of *Vagabond's Song*, yet *Drifting Clouds* is nevertheless a text that should be appreciated in terms of the literary task that Hayashi first undertook with *Vagabond's Song*.

The heroines of both *Vagabond's Song* and *Drifting Clouds* are dislocated women, and their drifting signifies that they do not follow the publicly acknowledged roles of women — as wife and mother — within the socially and legally guaranteed space of women: the home. The women of *Vagabond's Song* and *Drifting Clouds* have no homes; they exist outside the framework established for women, who typically moved from being sheltered daughters to being sheltered wives, from one home to another, and they thus fall outside what might be called the institution of womanhood.

Many Japanese writers, within the process of modernization that treated them as marginal to society, made themselves the main subjects of their works through the genre of "I-fiction" (*watakushi shōsetsu*), the dominant form of fiction in the early twentieth century. Rejected by society, these writers rejected society in turn and adopted an ideology of wandering. Nagai Kafū (1879–1959), for example, wandered in foreign countries in his youth, never had a stable family life, and ultimately died alone; Kaneko Mitsuharu (1895–1975) wandered abroad with his wife; Dazai Osamu (1909–48) lived a life of self-destruction without a thought for his wife and children, in the belief that domestic happiness was the root of all evil; Shiga Naoya (1883–1971) moved often, first to Onomichi and then to Nara, and throughout his life distanced himself from Tokyo literary circles, throwing himself into an individualistic, almost hermetic life. Many of these authors made the spirit of being outside the system the basis of the act of writing. Of course, compared to the heroes of popular literature such as homeless drifters and masterless samurai who had lost their stipends, the wandering of the writers of high literature, who enjoyed the privilege of writing, was often nothing more than a change of residence.

The theme of wandering in modern Japanese literature, however, clearly has a gendered difference. For women, wandering presupposes living outside the institution of marriage, and while this presents economic problems, it is, above all, the result of a problem in relations between men and women. In a culture where the Meiji Constitution of 1889 deprived women of basic human rights and decreed that the very existence of a woman was to be determined by her relationships with men, exclusion from marriage touched upon the very essence of what it meant to be a woman. A woman's wandering thus signified her separation from the culture's definition of "woman."[6] Among the women writers who left Japan and wandered in Japan's wartime colonies are Tamura Toshiko (1884–1945) and Hirabayashi Taiko (1905–72); their wanderings, which shared an anarchic sensibility with Hayashi Fumiko's, began with the rejection of a conventional marriage and an escape with men of their own choosing.

Hayashi Fumiko's *Vagabond's Song* had such an impact because the heroines depart in every respect from the prewar stereotype of the decent woman. Not only do the mother and daughter live at the bottom levels of society, but they transgress behavioral norms in a number of other ways. The mother, who leaves her husband after he takes a mistress, runs off with a man twenty years younger than herself and travels from place to place as a peddler; the daughter works with her mother and never stays in one place long enough to go to school and receive a proper education.

The daughter, who narrates the novel, appeals as a protagonist for two reasons. First, rather than rebelling against or feeling bitter about her upbringing and the environment of adversity in which she grew up, she in fact develops into a spirited woman with a unique personality; the young heroine's perspective on society differs from that of a daughter in a "good" home, and she matures quickly into a strong young woman without a trace of naiveté. Second, she is transformed from a girl raised outside a normal home into a successful author. Her mobility in the end works as a positive asset in nurturing in her the creative imagination and sensibility of a writer.

Vagabond's Song is a text of the narrator/heroine's self-creation as an author; its appeal and freshness come from the unprecedented depiction of a woman's wandering as providing a path for the writer's self-development. A woman's wandering subverts not only the system of gendered dualism, which deprived women of self-development in the wider realm outside the home, but also the established concept of the writer in prewar Japan, since the mainstream of modern Japanese literature was male. Through *Vagabond's Song*, Hayashi Fumiko presented a new story, a distinctive narrative of a woman's maturation into a modern writer. It is the subversive nature of the protagonist's path toward maturity and the resultant birth of the female writer that made *Vagabond's Song* a truly groundbreaking work.

Development and Decline

Vagabond's Song was originally entitled "Uta nikki" (Poetic diary), and in fact, the work is based on Hayashi Fumiko's own diary. Before its publication, she edited it considerably, adding many fictional elements that differed from the events she had experienced; nevertheless, it is undeniable that *Vagabond's Song* draws on the classical "poetic diary" (*nikki*), a genre of literary autobiography that flourished in the Heian period (794–1185) in which the seemingly uninhibited expression of the author's private feelings received literary license.[7] Hayashi combined the tendency toward emotional expression inherent in the traditional form with generic elements of the *Bildungsroman* (novel of development) to create a self-begetting narrative of a woman-writer-to-be.[8]

Wandering and poverty were not necessarily new themes for

modern male writers, but Hayashi Fumiko's depiction of a woman's wandering as leading to the birth of the woman writer was new, even shocking, especially since it presented a woman's experience of poverty, hunger, and social dislocation. Other contemporary women writers came from urban middle-class backgrounds. The heroines of these works, such as Nobuko in Miyamoto Yuriko's *Nobuko* (1926) and Machiko in Nogami Yaeko's *Machiko* (1930), unlike the narrator of *Vagabond's Song*, aim to realize the bourgeois ideal of individualism; they strive to become modern individuals valuing the subjectivity and humanity of others. The resolutions of their struggles with men and with the patriarchal familial relations that obstruct their desire for modern selfhood include, as in *Machiko*, marriage to a "good" man who understands the desires of the "new" woman and who aids her; or, as in *Nobuko*, divorce from the "bad" man who has frustrated the woman's aspirations. Readers who sympathized with this drama belonged to the same intellectual environment as the heroines, or aspired to it, and the men who understood them were progressive intellectuals.

In contrast, the heroine of *Vagabond's Song* learns of sexuality and of relations between herself and men, and between herself and others, instinctively, as a condition of life within a daily existence where obtaining food and a place to sleep are urgent problems. The heroine reaches womanhood, thanks to her anarchic energy for self-development, while drifting through poverty-stricken and chaotic urban labyrinths, outside the cultured environment of the urban middle class. *Vagabond's Song* depicts a woman's freedom of a sort visible only outside the middle-class home. Nevertheless, *Vagabond's Song* shares with *Nobuko* and *Machiko* the positive and even romantic atmosphere of a woman's novel of development, for it depicts a woman on the path of self-formation as an artist. In fact, Hayashi Fumiko became an author by completing this work.

Drifting Clouds, written some twenty years after *Vagabond's Song*, continues the theme of wandering but abandons the notion of a woman's development. The protagonist of *Drifting Clouds* is, like that of *Vagabond's Song*, a marginal woman separated from the mainstream, but she has lost her self-esteem and any desire to develop into something. She simply continues to wander, in a process that ends with her complete ruin and death.

Drifting Clouds, like *Vagabond's Song*, depicts the heroine's downfall as an urban phenomenon, and the story of the drifting woman develops within the overwhelming visual and literary images of urban devastation, chaos, and disorder. However, the postwar disorder in Japan holds a different meaning for women than the prewar urban disorder, when the social system itself was moving toward collapse and thus allowed a space for women to escape from it; in the postwar situation, women were excluded from a vital role in the construction of a new system. Although Yukiko in *Drifting Clouds* feels free and strong in the devastated Tokyo urban landscape and displays her strength by surviving there, her wandering within that landscape, far from paving the way for a new life or a chance to escape from the old social system, works instead to confine her within the devastation of the system, thus contributing only to her ruin. *Drifting Clouds*, lacking the elements of self-development or escape from the urban labyrinths, thus presents itself as a realistic work that unfolds the heroine's story of ruin within the dark setting of a wasted, destitute landscape of postwar Japan.

In contrast to *Vagabond's Song*, *Drifting Clouds* is a narrative of a woman's self-destruction and depicts the condition and fate of modern women. There are no illusions about a woman's potential for love or development in *Drifting Clouds*. It is an anti–love story that from the beginning destroys and negates the pattern of the Bildungsroman. It is the impossibility of development and of love as the inevitable condition of contemporary women that Hayashi Fumiko presents through her depiction of Yukiko's wandering amid the emptiness and desolation of the defeat that marked the end of modernity in Japan.[9]

The wandering in *Vagabond's Song* takes place toward Tokyo, toward the center. In contrast, the wandering in *Drifting Clouds* moves from Tokyo to the countryside and beyond that to the areas colonized by Japan, the so-called outer territories (*gaichi*). This movement is a search for escape from Tokyo, but it is also clearly not just a movement from the center to the margins, but a movement toward the bottom. Whereas *Vagabond's Song* is a tale of a woman's successful movement from the countryside to Tokyo as society moved toward collapse on the eve of protracted war, *Drifting Clouds* is the narrative of a woman's downfall as she leaves behind a Tokyo in which society is about to experience rebirth.

Although the issue of Japan's colonies in Asia is highly problematic, they did provide prewar Japanese women an escape route from a rigid social system that confined them to marriage and home. Some women tried, like Yukiko, to discover freedom of self-expression there. But although women may have gone to the colonies to escape the poverty and restrictions within Japan, they did not necessarily succeed in finding freedom and independence. In many cases, they were as exploited as the native women of the colonies, or they participated in the exploitation as agents of colonization.

Since for prewar women the opportunity to pursue self-development through study abroad was virtually nonexistent, it is clear that, for many, even the opportunity of working in the colonies inspired a desire for independence from which they drew the anarchic energy to make themselves free. It is not surprising that in the prewar period of historic upheaval, the escape to the outer territories strongly stimulated women to believe in the possibility, however illusory, of both manifesting their modern selfhood as women and escaping the confines of the institution of womanhood.

In the postwar period, on the other hand, the defeat and subsequent American occupation made it virtually impossible for women to leave Japan. In the postwar process of moving from renewal to rapid economic growth, women were pushed back into the home and a domestic role, which defined them as full-time housewives in a nuclear family. Women who worked in the labor market bore the double burden of household work and employment in the workplace. The legal structures of the new constitution and postwar democracy made it even more difficult for women to escape from their domestic roles.

In *Drifting Clouds*, Yukiko, who had gone to French Indochina during the war, is repatriated to Japan at the war's end. Through Yukiko, Hayashi Fumiko made it clear that the situation of postwar women was even more constricting than it had been before or during the war, for although the new civil law established during the Occupation created the illusion of a better position for women within the family, the near-disappearance of socially legitimate justifications for women to travel abroad meant the loss of any possibility of attaining freedom by escaping the system as "wanderers." Wandering in this context came to mean dislocation from the family, which symbolized woman's downfall within the social system.

After Yukiko's forced repatriation, she fantasizes about returning to her lost paradise, the village of Dalat in the outer territories where she had lived,[10] but her wandering amounts to nothing more than aimless drifting within Japan. Below I consider whether Yukiko's final destination of Yakushima, a primitive island off the southernmost main island of Japan, should be considered Yukiko's paradise regained or her graveyard, and whether her drifting to Yakushima represents a successful escape or simply her ruin; but it is clear that Yukiko's wandering in *Drifting Clouds* takes her only as far as Yakushima, and this fact seems to signify the condition of postwar women, in which the possibility of anarchic wandering has disappeared and stability in the nuclear family within a democratic social system has become the ruling concept.

Order and Chaos

Drifting Clouds depicts a world of chaos in which defeat has caused all previous order to collapse. There is gendered difference in this chaos, however, just as there was in order. Just as the prewar order held a different meaning for men and for women, so does the postwar chaos.

During the war, Yukiko leaves her family home in the country outside Shizuoka and travels to Tokyo to become a typist, living at her relatives' house while attending typing school. This movement has a positive implication, at least in the beginning. Yukiko, in her attempt to become a working woman, represents a modern woman aspiring to independence and is already at this point leading a different life from that of the typical housewife. Her home in Shizuoka is not a pastoral arcadia; rather, her parents' home and the countryside represent confinement, and she must escape them for Tokyo, where the modern, urban environment supplies women with new opportunities for self-development. Her move to the city in search of work was thus inspired and encouraged by the modernizing society and culture of prewar Japan. The number of women working in industry was increasing rapidly at the time, for society needed working women as substitute labor for men drafted into the wartime military.[11]

Yukiko's rape by her uncle Iba, however, shows that even in her relatives' house she is not treated with the respect usually accorded an unmarried young woman. A woman who left her parents' home to work in Tokyo was treated differently from the daughter of a "good" family, in that her sexuality and chastity were held in low esteem. Yukiko lives in a small maid's room at the entrance to her uncle's house and helps with the housework, but because she becomes a sexual object for her uncle, she serves not only as a maid but as a prostitute as well. Yukiko is no longer qualified to live within the social system as a respectable woman, and she decides to go to Indochina to work as a typist in order to escape from the sexual relations forced on her by her uncle for the past three years.

For Iba, the prewar order is a social system in which a married man is allowed to have a mistress and relations with prostitutes. For Yukiko, this means an order that supports only two choices for a woman in relation to a man: she can either marry or become a prostitute. As someone aspiring to be a single, working woman, Yukiko has no place in this male-centered order. Neither Yukiko nor Iba's wife can change the humiliating position Iba puts her in. Yukiko's move to Japanese-occupied Indochina is an escape from this personal morass and a flight in search of freedom from the Japanese social system that privileges men.

Yukiko discovers this freedom in Dalat, a mountain village in Indochina where she finds not only economic independence but freedom from the Japanese institution of womanhood. Yukiko is following her own desires when she starts a relationship with Tomioka, and although she has sexual relations with him, it is not as a prostitute. Yukiko realizes that she is in love with a man for the first time, and as she becomes aware that her passion is unmediated and unconstrained by social institutions, Yukiko feels for the first time her strength as a woman. The primeval forests of Indochina where Yukiko and Tomioka fall in love are a dreamland located outside the institutions of Japan. For Yukiko, it is a place that returns men and women to a primitive state, and a place in which Yukiko's youth, sexual appeal, and vitality show their true strength. The chaos of wartime Japan, where the social system is moving toward destruction, makes possible Yukiko's escape, and her anarchic existence outside society gives birth to the possibility, however illusory, of woman's freedom.

For Tomioka, however, the situation is different. He has been sent by the Japanese government; he is married, and he accepts the work assignment only in order to support his family in Japan. Before Yukiko's arrival, he had already taken a local woman, Niu, as his mistress, even while he writes to his wife, Kuniko, almost daily. There is no change in the fact that his wife and family form the basis of his existence. Although he takes a lover as soon as he arrives and even has relations with Yukiko, Tomioka's family in Japan nevertheless remains the source of his identity; he thus never leaves the institutions of Japan, even while residing in the outer territories.

For Tomioka, an agricultural engineer, the forests of Indochina are nothing more than a workplace; he is under the protection of the

Japanese military and is an invader of the forest rather than its protector. He ignores the plea of a Frenchman who studies forestry to preserve the primitive forest, and he exploits the local men and women as well as the forest. Dalat for Tomioka is neither a pastoral setting nor a dreamland in contrast to the urban disorder of Tokyo, as it is for Yukiko, but rather an undesirable workplace that finally causes his moral destruction. Indeed, Tomioka in Dalat is a decadent colonist, who takes a native woman as his mistress and then, when she becomes pregnant, sends her home with some money. Tomioka, who self-deprecatingly describes himself as an "old rotting Japanese cedar transplanted to the fields of Dalat" (264),[12] has lost interest in everything, having been, in his view, banished to the forest outside Japan. Only Yukiko's sexuality and life force provide him with a chance for rebirth.

In contrast, Yukiko, alone and vulnerable after her escape from the unhappy situation in Tokyo, has placed herself in the primeval forest of this other world, and her presence does not act as a force to invade or exploit the forest. Now that Yukiko has isolated herself from the Japanese social system, she can display her intrinsic sexuality and vitality toward men and be on an equal footing with them. As it turns out, the sexual vitality and power Yukiko displays in the primeval forests of a foreign land are the only power that Yukiko is able to realize in her entire life. Only here in the forests of Indochina, where she first becomes aware of the power of her sexuality, does Yukiko feel free and alive.

The basis for Tomioka's identity, however, lies in the communal order of Japan, even while he lives outside it. Although he wishes to recharge his life energy through Yukiko's youthful sexuality, he is unable to achieve any new self-consciousness because he remains integrated into the Japanese social order. Within this context, Yukiko is nothing more than a replacement for his Vietnamese lover. After their repatriation to Japan, Tomioka supports Yukiko financially only to avoid trouble; later, when he loses his job, it is only natural that he breaks with her. For Yukiko, the memory of the time spent with Tomioka in Dalat is like a dream, but for Tomioka, when Yukiko comes to him seeking money and a reconciliation on the basis of that memory, it is a nightmare that he would like to forget.

Both Dalat and Yukiko's sexual power are ambivalent and problematic. For Yukiko, both represent personal freedom, but as they are taken over by Tomioka and by the opposing implications that the primeval forest and women's sexuality suggest for him, Dalat recedes into the background of the narrative as an illusory dreamscape, and Yukiko's sexuality quickly loses its fresh vitality, turning instead into something futile and meaningless.

Wandering and Topography

In *Vagabond's Song*, wandering has aspects of both freedom and destruction, but this dual significance disappears in *Drifting Clouds*, where wandering leads Yukiko only to destruction. The process of her decline is represented by the places to which Yukiko drifts, each of which is a metaphor that reveals the ongoing internal drama between Yukiko and Tomioka and the significance of her wandering at that point.

Yukiko's first physical move, from Shizuoka to Tokyo, signifies not only a move from the country to the city but also a move from her family home to the maid's room in her relatives' house. In that maid's room Yukiko is raped by Iba, her uncle and supposed guardian. Yukiko's move to Tokyo thus coincides with her development from girl to woman, but the sexual development comes with a loss of innocence; she experiences the fall from unblemished virgin to household maid and finally to prostitute. Yukiko's first sexual experience determines her outlook on men and plays an important role in her later life. Yukiko's rite of passage from girlhood to womanhood contains a sense not of human development but only of social and personal decline.

Yukiko escapes from the maid's room by finding work in Indochina, now a Japanese colony, but there she lives only in temporary residences, such as hotels or boarding houses. After fleeing Iba's house, the only time that she lives in a real house is when she is kept as a mistress.

Tomioka's move to Dalat, however, is not a personal escape from Japan but part of a national movement to colonize Asia. Tomioka does, for a time, consider forsaking his job and family to live with Yukiko, but separating himself from family and nation would mean becoming a rootless person, and he does not have the will or courage to do so. His affair with the native woman, his relations with Yukiko, and his elegant and decadent lifestyle as a colonist in Dalat are the fruit of Japan's colonial invasion of foreign territory; none of Tomioka's experiences would have been possible without the national power and protection of Japan. In the same way, Tomioka's return home after the war is not personal but national and occurs because of historical necessity as part of the national process of repatriation. Yukiko's return, in contrast, is an unwilling return to the place from which she had escaped and signifies a forcible expulsion from the timeless dreamscape of Dalat back into temporality and Japanese history.

Thus, there is an unbridgeable difference between Tomioka's return to Tokyo and Yukiko's. Tomioka returns home to his wife and mother, but his colonial experiences have created a deep abyss separating him from his family. As his wife complains, he has changed. Being a colonizer during the war has devastated him mentally; the defeat of Japan in the war is his personal defeat, and Japan's postwar devastation is his own devastation.

Yukiko, by contrast, returns to Tokyo as a homeless person. She is naturally unable to go to the married Tomioka's home, and she does not wish to go to the home of Iba, although he wants to restore their relations. Yukiko thus settles into a room in a dirty, rundown hotel in Ikebukuro, from which she sets out daily to make a living. In order to survive, she steals goods from Iba's home, and she rents a small storage space in a hardware store in a back alley. She also becomes a prostitute to an American soldier. Although she falls into decadence, her decadence, unlike that of Tomioka, suggests her vitality and capacity for survival. In fact, the wasted landscape of Tokyo and the ruins of the prewar social order bring her a sense of relief.

As a prostitute catering to an American soldier in Ikebukuro, Yukiko is still free and independent. The American treats her kindly and humanely, and above all, Yukiko has her own room. Yukiko says that her rundown room, which has "only a single skylight and no electricity or water" and "two old tatami mats," is "like a palace to me" (306). Yukiko's downfall in Tokyo does not arise from the fact that she becomes a prostitute; rather, it begins with Tomioka's and Iba's reappearance in her life, at her "palace." The place she had guarded for herself is invaded by men from her past.

Despite her resistance to linking herself once again to Tomioka, Yukiko is unable to leave him because of her attachment to the memory of their love in Dalat and even wants to have a child by him. Tomioka has found that he is unable to bridge the psychological gap with his wife resulting from his absence. He also no longer wishes to return to his life as a government official but wants to start a black-market business instead. Spending time with Yukiko in a rundown hotel room depresses Tomioka, due largely to his guilt over his earlier treatment of her. But, almost in spite of himself, he is pleasantly overwhelmed by her vitality and even envious of her resilience in surviving in the wasted city. Tomioka wishes to kill himself with Yukiko in a double love-suicide and, with this in mind, takes her to an inn at Ikaho, a mountain hot spring. The movement from devastated Tokyo to an inn at the antiquated hot springs in the mountains is a step toward death, but there is no romantic aspect to it. Confined by rain to their room, the two are in different states of mind. For Tomioka, who is disgusted with the world and in despair, death promises salvation. But then, his desire for life is unexpectedly rekindled by a young married woman, Osei, whom he happens to meet at the inn, just as it was earlier by Yukiko. He decides he would rather not die with Yukiko, but keep both his life and Osei. Yukiko, meanwhile, no longer has any intention of dying with Tomioka and wants to get back to Tokyo as soon as possible:

> Last night they had talked so much about dying together, but now they didn't give a thought to dying. She felt it would be stupid to die in such a place. She didn't believe Tomioka was sincere in what he said, and she only wanted to sell off her watch and return to her house in Ikebukuro that day. The memory of French Indochina was a tie binding their hearts together, but as they lay there side by side, it may have been that their dreams went in different directions. (156)

Toward a Lost Paradise

The retreat to the mountain hot springs at Ikaho does nothing to revive relations between Tomioka and Yukiko; instead, it destroys the memory of their love in Dalat and brings about the deaths of several people. The two of them return to Tokyo with ruined spirits, like two dead people. Tomioka tries to live through the force of young Osei's sexuality and moves in with her, but because of this Osei is murdered by her crazed husband, Mukai. Yukiko, who discovers herself pregnant with the child of Tomioka's she had once longed for, decides to have an abortion. In desperation, she turns to Kano, Tomioka's rival for her love in Dalat, but he dies soon after Yukiko visits him. In addition, Tomioka's wife dies of an illness. Tomioka seems to have become a plague god, bringing death to everything he touches.

Meanwhile, Iba, the other invader of Yukiko's two-mat palace, has become a priest in a new Buddhist religious cult that makes a business of salvation. He entices Yukiko to become his mistress by offering her a house and thus takes her out of her small but independent space in the Ikebukuro alley. It is Iba who induces Yukiko's true fall: kept as a mistress by the dubious, lecherous priest, Yukiko steals money from his temple organization and leaves with Tomioka, who has sold off his house and belongings, on what is finally a true escape.

Yakushima, where the two end up, was at the time the novel was written a remote territory that all but marked the border between Japan and the outside world. Covered by ancient forests, Yakushima suggested the primeval forests of Indochina. The dense mountain rainforests are, like the forests of Indochina, a place where a proper Japanese woman would rarely set foot, but for Yukiko, now a thief, they are a suitable and proper place to hide. There, Tomioka and Yukiko should be able to make a life together. For Yukiko, Yakushima is a location with a dual significance: it is the final destination in her downfall, but it is also a place with the potential to revive her dreams. On this island, Yukiko clings both to her memories of Dalat and to the possibility of her rebirth.

For Tomioka, the move to Yakushima is not so much an escape as a return to his former position as government official in Indochina. The forests are his place of employment, and the move to Yakushima is a first step toward his return to society. Because Yakushima holds an opposite metaphorical significance for Tomioka and because for him Yukiko has lost her sexual attractiveness, Yakushima cannot become the site of Yukiko's emancipation, nor can she revive her dreams there; instead, it becomes the site of her ultimate ruin and death. When Tomioka leaves the sick Yukiko lying in bed in their hut to climb the mountain, he encounters a young local woman. Her soft skin reminds him of Osei, and he is enchanted by the same life force. Tomioka turns to this young woman, whose sexual vitality he feels will renew his life force and help him regain his desire for life, as a replacement for Yukiko, whose energy has been sapped by illness. It seems only a matter of time before he abandons Yukiko on this remote island and returns to Tokyo to re-establish his life.

Yakushima is the final stop in Yukiko's wandering and represents the last possibility for her renewal, but it is too ambiguous a location in the narrative to allow her to achieve her dreams. Its dense forests and steep mountains are metaphors for the emotional obstacles that prevent the sick and weakened woman from approaching her goal, and the heavy rains confine her to a shabby cottage. Indeed, the awe-inspiring atmosphere of the island is explicitly masculine, rejecting the intrusion of women and underlining the ultimate impossibility of female sexuality exercising its power. In its gloom, primitive heaviness, and rushing rains, Yakushima seems antithetical to an idyllic view of nature that embraces female sexuality, and it becomes instead Yukiko's graveyard, wiping out whatever innocence, youthful exuberance, and sexual vitality had remained within her.

The destructive potential of the rains on Yakushima, appropriately called "Noah's flood" (465),[13] points toward the complete annihilation of the old social order, but the rains instead destroy only Yukiko's health, as well as her dreams. Yukiko becomes a sacrificial lamb, offered to the sacred masculine spirits of the island to make possible Tomioka's return to the society of postwar Japan.

Yet Yukiko's pathetic death in a forest hut during a heavy rain squall nevertheless contains an element of rest and salvation, as though she is returning home at last to the ancient earth. In contrast, there seems no hope for Tomioka's salvation or peace of mind. As he sits drinking sake next to Yukiko's corpse and feels the life returning to his flesh, he suffers from a terrible sense of guilt. The novel ends with a depiction of Tomioka, as he takes a week's vacation in the city of Kagoshima on the southernmost main island of Japan. His thoughts are drawn to the island of Yakushima, not far off the coast. He has no desire to return, yet he feels that he cannot leave Yukiko's remains there. In the end he gets drunk, buys a prostitute, and abandons himself to his feelings of loneliness, like an uncertain, drifting cloud.

Wandering Toward Liberation or Destruction

Yukiko's life of wandering includes several changes of residence in Tokyo after she leaves the hotel room in Ikebukuro, but these moves signify not so much a decline as a tenacious determination to survive, to seek shelter and a place of her own. The time when she is dragged to Ikaho by Tomioka and the time when she follows Tomioka to Yakushima are the only two moves that threaten Yukiko with destruction.

The vector of liberation and freedom in Yukiko's wandering is constantly obstructed by Tomioka's movement toward destruction. Yukiko's wandering intersects with Tomioka's, and she is dragged down by him to her destruction. The moves to Ikaho, the ancient mountain hot springs cordoned off from the desolation of Tokyo, and to Yakushima, the faraway island covered in deep primeval forests, should have been journeys for Yukiko to recapture her lost paradise. Instead, for Tomioka, they are nothing more than occasions to discover new women, and for Yukiko steps toward her final ruin and death.

The wandering depicted in *Drifting Clouds* is one in which the path of Yukiko's dream, from Dalat to Yakushima, intersects with the path of ruination, from Tokyo to Yakushima. However, Tomioka's journey follows a different trajectory: for Tomioka, Dalat is simply an extension of Tokyo, and Tokyo in turn an extension of Dalat. In the same way, the trip to Yakushima is a way to get rid of Yukiko, and after Tomioka buries Yukiko, he finally and truly returns to "Japan." The degeneration of the war, the desolation of the defeat, and the imminent postwar reconstruction parallel the path of Tomioka's personal wandering.

In contrast to Yukiko, for whom there is no hope of salvation within Japanese society, Tomioka's recovery is ultimately possible only when he returns to it. Yukiko has wandered from place to place—from her birthplace to a maid's room to hotels to cheap inns to a storage room—without ever having a physical or psychological resting place; indeed, she has no hope of finding one in Japan or in her relations with men. As long as she wanders within Japan, drifting from one man to another, Yukiko has nowhere to go but down. Just as there was no place for Yukiko in prewar Japan, Hayashi Fumiko saw no place for her in the postwar reconstruction. The space outside the "institution of womanhood" that Yukiko desires to attain is an uncertain illusion that may or may not exist, yet the imagination that yearns to escape the institution is nevertheless a strong motivation for both Yukiko and the narrative.

Tomioka's abandonment of his family and wife mirrors the war's destruction of the old social order; his personal fate as a wanderer is linked to the nation's postwar devastation. But it is clearly suggested that as the nation returns to order, he will also successfully return to Japan, taking part in the postwar reconstruction and recovering from the physical and psychological wounds of war. His wandering is always internal to Japan, and is, furthermore, directed toward its center, Tokyo. It was only because of the war that he went along with his country to "faraway Indochina" (319), where he met Yukiko "and lost her, just as his country lost the war" (330). Tomioka's personal history coexists with the history of Japan through its prewar, wartime, and postwar periods. Yukiko remains to the end, in contrast to Tomioka, outside Japanese history.

The Asymmetry of Men and Women

Drifting Clouds captures the spirit of Japan after its defeat, and it is a masterpiece of postwar literature, but it is above all the narrative of a woman and a man, an anti–love story. As we have seen, Hayashi Fumiko presented the internal desolation created by defeat as well as the spectacle of devastation in terms of an explicit gender-based difference.

In the world of *Drifting Clouds*, men and women experience dissatisfaction with marriage and home life in different ways. Both Iba and Tomioka seek women outside their marriages, and both eventually leave home to wander. Ironically, however, they find that the only place they can coexist with women is within a household, where the roles are clearly defined. The men do not know how to face women outside the home, for such women are filled with a strange dual significance: they either evoke illusions in the men of life, vitality, and salvation, or else they drag them into ruin.

Once a woman's body becomes separated from reproduction, as defined in the institution of marriage, her body becomes a symbol for men of sexuality and vitality, yet at the same time it threatens and disgusts men. For Tomioka, Yukiko in Dalat is a symbol of vitality calling forth his passion, but when they meet again in postwar Tokyo, the dirty tatami mats in Yukiko's rundown hotel room contrast so strongly with those in the tearoom in his own home, where his wife prepares tea for him, that he cannot at first rekindle his former passion. Yukiko presses Tomioka to take responsibility, threatening to "hound him just like a moneylender to make him pay for his former passion" (329); to him, she has become nothing more than an annoyance whom he wants only to discard. In contrast to Yukiko, who tries to survive in devastated Tokyo even to the extent of using her own body as an asset, Tomioka has no internal resources.

When Yukiko aborts Tomioka's child, she is acting autonomously. Tomioka has been unable to integrate her into his life as wife, lover, or prostitute; he could neither bring her into his home nor keep her as a mistress outside his home. She has simply resisted all sanctioned modes of relation between women and men. His only chance for survival is to find another woman who can provide him with the sexual energy he needs. He fails in this, however. Exhausted at the end of his wandering, Tomioka thinks only, "I don't need a wife or a woman any longer" (426).

Tomioka and Yukiko were able to meet because of the extraordinary circumstances of the war, which created a moment of connection in an "other" world far removed from their previous lives. Yet their memory of that time becomes fainter and fainter as the narrative progresses, and they begin to doubt whether it even existed; in fact, the more they try to recapture the past, the more their passion dissipates. Tomioka's actions in Tokyo merely confirm Yukiko's view that men see women only as sexual objects, and she is disappointed in him. Thus, Yukiko's return to Tokyo means a return to the system that separates men and women in an ideology of asymmetry; ultimately, Tokyo comes to represent for her the impossibility of love beyond the established gender roles. The fact that women are nothing but sexual objects for men in this order reconfirms for Yukiko the conclusion she reached through her wanderings: that to escape becoming a pawn of men, she must use men for her own purposes — seduce them, press them to take responsibility, and somehow survive. For her, too, the freedom and vitality she experienced with Tomioka in Dalat finally become only a distant, evanescent dream.

Yukiko, nevertheless, does not leave Tomioka, for the only way their momentary dream can be revived in her is through a revival of her former relations with him. Just as Tomioka clings to the illusory hope that he will be saved by women's sexuality, Yukiko is unable to discard her illusion that she will be saved by a man. The relationship between Tomioka and Yukiko is truly a fatal bond, but only, the narrative seems to say, because all relationships between men and women are hopeless.

After writing *Drifting Clouds*, Hayashi Fumiko began *Meal*, but it was left unfinished by her sudden death in 1951. In this last work, one again finds Hayashi's devastatingly cynical and nihilistic view of romantic love and the relations between men and women. In *Meal*, women are unfulfilled and unhappy even while having their own home and settling down in a family; this, in fact, is the source of their unhappiness. In such works as *Meal* and "Bangiku" (A late chrysanthemum; 1949), a short story that deals with a geisha in her old age, Hayashi Fumiko depicted women trying to survive within the roles of housewife and prostitute — the two publicly acknowledged roles for women within the established social order. Even while remaining within the system, these women nurture a dream of escaping. Hayashi's narratives, by embracing the illusory dream of escape as a central symbol in the female protagonists' internal landscape, reveal women to be drawing their tenacity to survive from the contradictions of the system itself.

Drifting Clouds depicts a woman who has acted upon her dream. Yukiko's wandering, however, is more than a depiction of her personal escape from confinement within the family; it is also Hayashi's implicit criticism of women's unrealistic expectations of a successful escape from the system and of their fantasies of finding salvation and happiness through romantic relations with men. Hayashi accomplishes this criticism by setting up Yukiko's illusory paradise in the outer territory of Indochina and then destroying the memory of that paradise in the course of her subsequent wandering.

Yukiko rejects the family, but because she is unable ultimately to reject love relations with a man — in other words, because she clings to the dream of loving a man — she is unable to survive and ends up a destroyed woman. If for Tomioka Dalat is simultaneously made possible and destroyed by the war, Dalat is more poignantly made possible and destroyed for Yukiko by her continued belief in men. Although the novel *Drifting Clouds* starts as a concrete narrative of Yukiko's escape from and return to Japan, the unreality of her move outside Japan and the paradise she felt she found there becomes progressively emphasized. Yukiko's innocent belief in her own sexuality and even her intense nostalgia for Dalat fade away in the course of her moral decline in the city. The downward movement is the expression of Hayashi's message: female attempts at growth and maturation through linkage with men and national history are doomed to failure, for women's actual experience of them always leads to disillusionment. Moreover, in *Drifting Clouds* Hayashi negated the concepts of personal growth and fulfillment, treating them as illusory and pathetic, not even tragic. Through Hayashi's narrative of the asymmetrical wanderings of man and woman, the postwar urban landscape of chaos, moral desolation, and despair becomes the site of gendered conflict, a battleground between men and women.

Hayashi Fumiko did not give the women in her works a chance at salvation, nor did she allow the men redemption; both salvation and redemption are merely hinted at as metaphors within the topos of wandering and drifting. Only in regard to Osei's murder at the hands of her husband does Tomioka wish to make atonement. Tomioka ends up destroying all his women — Kuniko, Niu, Osei, and Yukiko —

and has neither the will nor the ability to save them. To the end, men and women in *Drifting Clouds* move in different directions without crossing paths. Hayashi Fumiko, who in *Vagabond's Song* depicted within the social and political chaos of prewar Japan a woman's wandering with the potential for self-development, demonstrated in *Drifting Clouds* that in the chaos of the postwar period, where the social system was revealing its capacity for self-renewal, a woman's attempt to defy history through wandering must end in failure. It is correct to see a direct line of development and maturation in Hayashi Fumiko's works, from the poetic diary-like self-expression of *Vagabond's Song* to a realism that negates lyrical self-exploration in *Drifting Clouds*. Yet *Drifting Clouds* is not merely a realistic portrayal of postwar Japan, but is, as Hayashi mentioned in her afterword to the novel, a "novel outside the novel" that imagines the illusory possibility of a life for women outside the institution of womanhood.

Notes

1. For the high regard in which *Drifting Clouds* is held, see Nakamura; Hirabayashi; and Ōkubo.

2. Many critics have analyzed Hayashi's skillful characterization of Tomioka, and there are many who view both Tomioka and Yukiko as representations of the author. See, e.g., Takenishi; and Mori. At the same time, there are those who contrast Tomioka with Yukiko, critiquing Tomioka as a quintessential male character. For this approach, see Itagaki.

3. The page number here refers to the 1953 Shinchō bunko edition of Hayashi's *Ukigumo*. An English translation by Koitabashi Yoshiyuki, originally titled *Floating Cloud* and published in 1957, was subsequently revised with Martin C. Collcutt and republished as *The Floating Clouds* in 1965; it is not widely available.

4. Several excerpts from *Hōrōki* appear in an English translation by Elizabeth Hanson titled "Vagabond's Song," in Tanaka, *To Live and to Write*. For more on *Hōrōki*, see Chapter 3, by Joan E. Ericson, in this volume. Ericson's unpublished dissertation contains a translation of Part I of *Hōrōki*; she translates the title as *Diary of a Vagabond*.

5. The two centers that Hayashi chose to depict in Tokyo's vast cityscape were Shinjuku and Ikebukuro. On the representation of Tokyo in *Vagabond's Song*, see Unno.

6. For a discussion in Japanese of the dual themes of wandering and escape from womanhood in a wide range of modern Japanese women's writing, see Mizuta. The essay was originally presented in English as the keynote address for the Rutgers Conference on Japanese Women's Writing in Apr. 1993.

7. On the topic of literary autobiography in Japan, see Walker; and Miller.

8. See Chapter 9, by Michiko Niikuni Wilson, in this volume for a discussion of the genre of the *Bildungsroman* in relation to Ōba's fiction.

9. For a conflicting view of the impact of defeat on the Japanese project of modernity, see Koschmann.

10. Dalat serves as the dreamscape to which Yukiko tries to return through her postwar wandering. Similar uses of a non-Japanese dreamscape as a subversive device to reveal the confining situation of women in prewar Japan can be seen in Hayashi's other works and in works of many women writers, such as Okamoto Kanoko's (1889–1939) "Kawa akari" (River light; 1939), in which Malaysia is figured as a territory of freedom and love.

11. On the expansion of female employment from the end of Taishō to early Shōwa and its impact on literature, see Maeda.

12. This and subsequent references are to the 1969 Chūō kōronsha edition of *Drifting Clouds* in vol. 47 of the series *Nihon no bungaku*.

13. During the war, Hayashi resided in French Indochina as a member of the army's press corps. She also visited Yakushima before writing *Drifting Clouds*, experiencing its rains firsthand. See Isokai. On the symbolic meaning of rain in *Drifting Clouds*, see Imamura.

Works Cited

Hayashi Fumiko. *Floating Cloud (Ukigumo)*. Trans. Y. Koitabashi. Tokyo: Information Publishing, 1957. Rev. ed. — *The Floating Clouds*. Trans. Koitabashi Yoshiyuki and Martin C. Collcutt. Tokyo: Hara shobō, 1965.

———. *Hōrōki, Part I*. Trans. Joan E. Ericson. In idem, "Hayashi Fumiko and Japanese Women's Literature." Ph.D. diss., Columbia University, 1993.

———. *Ukigumo*. Tokyo: Rokkō shuppansha, 1951. Reprinted — Tokyo: Shinchō bunko, 1953. Reprinted — *Nihon no bungaku 47: Hayashi Fumiko*. Chūō kōronsha, 1969.

———. *Vagabond's Song (Hōrōki* [excerpts]). Trans. Elizabeth Hanson. In *To Live and to Write: Selections by Japanese Women Writers, 1913–1938*, ed. Yukiko Tanaka. Seattle: Seal Press, 1987, 105–25.

Hirabayashi Taiko. "Kaisetsu." In *Nihon no bungaku 47: Hayashi Fumiko*. Tokyo: Chūō Kōronsha, 1969, 486–96.

Imamura Junko. "Ame no hyōgen ni miru kanjō in'yu ni tsuite: *Ukigumo* o chūshin ni." In *Kindai joryū bungaku*, ed. Nihon bungaku kenkyū shiryō kankōkai. Tokyo: Yūseidō, 1983, 123–30.

Isokai Hideo. "Hyōden." In *Shinchō Nihon bungaku arubamu 34: Hayashi Fumiko*. Tokyo: Shinchōsha, 1986, 2–96.

Itagaki Naoko. *Hayashi Fumiko no shōgai*. Tokyo: Yamato shobō, 1965.

Koschmann, J. Victor. "Maruyama Masao and the Incomplete Project of Modernity." In *Postmodernism and Japan*, ed. Masao Miyoshi and H. D. Harootunian. Durham, N.C.: Duke University Press, 1989, 123–41.

Maeda Ai. "Taishō kōki tsūzoku shōsetsu no tenkai." *Bungaku*, June–July 1968. Reprinted in *Kindai dokusha no seiritsu*. Tokyo: Iwanami shoten, 1993, 211–83.

Miller, Marilyn Jeanne. *The Poetics of "Nikki Bungaku": A Comparison of the Traditions, Conventions, and Structure of Heian Japan's Literary Diaries with Western Autobiographical Writings*. New York: Garland, 1985.

Mizuta Noriko. " 'Irui' toshite no jiko ninshiki: Nihon kindai josei bungaku ni okeru dasshutsu to hōrō." In idem, *Monogatari to han-monogatari no fūkei: bungaku to josei no sōzōryoku*. Tokyo: Tabata shoten, 1993, 87–114.

Mori Eiichi. *Hayashi Fumiko no keisei: sono sei to hyōgen*. Tokyo: Yūseidō, 1992.

Nakamura Mitsuo. "*Ukigumo shohyō*." *Yomiuri shinbun*, May 7, 1951.

Ōkubo Norio. "Sengo bungakushi no naka no joryū bungaku: Hayashi Fumiko *Ukigumo* no ichi." *Kokubungaku: kaishaku to kanshō* 37, no. 3 (1972): 47–52.

Takenishi Hiroko. "Kaisetsu." In *Kawade Nihon bungaku zenshū 20: Hayashi Fumiko*. Tokyo: Kawade shobō shinsha, 1966, 430–41.

Unno Hiroshi. "Hayashi Fumiko *Hōrōki*: toshi to bungaku." *Umi* (Aug. 1982): 172–83. Reprinted in *Modan toshi Tokyo: Nihon no nijū nendai*. Tokyo: Chūō kōronsha, 1988. 151-71.

Walker, Janet A. "Reading Genres Across Cultures: The Example of Autobiography." In *Reading World Literature: Theory, History, Practice*, ed. Sarah Lawall. Austin: University of Texas Press, 1994, 203-35.

11

Text Versus Commentary: Struggles over the Cultural Meanings of "Woman"

CHIEKO M. ARIGA

Bringing "different" positions of woman into the Japanese cultural network is a crucial agenda for contemporary Japanese feminism, which aims at changing the subordinate position of women and transforming the unequal relations of power between the sexes in Japanese society. One of the most important sites of this operation is mass-produced literature, such as paperback books, that sells in large numbers and at low prices. The goal of bringing new positions for women to the fore in such literature is undermined, however, by a culturally legitimated dominant discourse that, consciously or not, serves to erase literary representations of "different" women and smooth out the disruptions they may cause. The mechanism of control at this site is the practice of writing commentaries (*kaisetsu*) in which only the "women" who can be naturalized and domesticated into the existing subordinate gender position are reconstructed and circulated.

In Japanese publishing, it is standard practice to engage a writer or a critic to compose an afterword evaluating a work of fiction. These commentaries are generally not found at the end of hardcover editions, but are customarily included at the end of almost all paperback editions as a service to the general reader.[1] They include detailed information on the author and an analysis of the work. For the reader who has just finished the book, they put into words the thoughts, feelings, and impressions that the reader might otherwise be unable to formulate. Thus, commentaries serve a valuable role in the overall process of establishing the meaning of the work for the reader. In fact, it is not unusual for readers who want to know in advance what the book is about to read the commentary first.

What is immediately noticeable about commentaries is that those on works by women writers are written almost entirely by male critics (*hihyōka* or *hyōronka*). Out of 100 randomly selected paperback books by women I surveyed, 95 percent of the commentaries were written by male critics, 20 percent of whom were male writers; 3 percent had an author's postface instead of a commentary, many of these in addition to a commentary; and only 2 percent were written by women other than the author. All the women in the last category are writers; not one is a critic. A survey of commentaries in a paperback series of the works of modern writers published by Shinchōsha revealed that none of the commentaries had been written by a woman, and this in a series that publishes such major writers as Abe Kōbō, Dazai Osamu, Mori Ōgai, Murakami Ryū, Nagai Kafū, Natsume Sōseki, Shiga Naoya, Shiina Mokoto, Shimada Masahiko, Shimazaki Tōson, and Yasuoka Shōtarō.[2] This reflects the fact that even though women critics have gradually been increasing in numbers in recent years, male critics have traditionally been the ones who write the commentaries.[3]

A close look at the contents of these commentaries reveals that the influence of the primarily male *bundan* (literary establishment) in Japanese criticism is impeding the development and influence of women's literature.[4] In the process of commentary criticism, women's works often become framed in patriarchal discourses and appropriated for their purposes. Since it is usually only after a book comes out in paperback that it becomes widely circulated, these commentaries are likely to be seen by a large number of readers. The fact that any work that enters mass circulation comes under the lens of *bundan* critics has a huge impact on how works written by women are assimilated into social culture.[5] Of course, the problem of the lack of feminist perspective and the exclusion of women is not limited to the commentaries published in paperback editions. As all feminist literary critics in Japan have pointed out, the problem occurs in every phase of mainstream literary criticism and in literary institutions in Japan today. In fact, this has been the basic premise of Japanese feminist literary criticism since it started in the early 1980's, and it can be found in the critical writings of Komashaku Kimi, Mizuta Noriko, Kurosawa Ariko, Ueno Chizuko, Ogura Chikako, Tomioka Taeko, Egusa Mitsuko, and Urushida Kazuyo.[6] In the words of Ueno Chizuko, "There is only a handful of female critics, leaving men to virtually monopolize the field as well as the screening committees for the major literary prizes given to works considered 'superior'" ("The Rise of Feminist Criticism," 5). The lack of attention to feminist concerns is readily observable in the "literary criticism" sections of publications like *Bungei nenkan* (Yearbook on literature), a yearly summary of literary and cultural productions in Japan. Although not a few feminist writings are published every year,[7] they are rarely included in this section. Thus, feminist criticism has not gained its citizenship in the world of literary criticism.

It is, of course, not necessarily the case that all *bundan* male critics ignore the issues of women in textual analysis, nor are their positions singular or homogeneous. There are certainly male readings that do not erase women, and that are not trapped within the stereotypical male/female dichotomy, even though they may not be avowedly feminist. However, it is possible to point out in many instances a shared patriarchal gender assumption regarding "woman." I am here calling into question an often unconscious tendency toward the appropriation of woman in the *bundan* institution as a whole.

Under the influence of postmodern theories, there has recently been a shift in Western academic feminism away from general categories, including terms as basic as "patriarchy," "women," and "men." These categories are labeled "totalizing," "essentializing," or even "imperialistic."[8] Even though postmodern criticism has contributed greatly to our understanding of the linguistic nature of our existence, a blanket application of this approach to all feminisms can be unnecessarily limiting and lead to unproductive results. If feminism is a collective political movement to emancipate women who are situated differently but are relationally oppressed nonetheless, general categories are necessary. I join with Tania Modleski in asking the question "why women, much more so than any other oppressed group of people, have been so willing to yield the ground on which to make a stand against their oppression" (Modleski, 15).[9] We certainly need to be aware of the totalizing traps of any general categories, but generalizing, establishing categories, or essentializing is a necessary "strategy" for any collective and transformative politics against oppression.[10]

The purpose of this paper is to question and problematize the cultural placement of woman in one important site of signification: mass-produced paperback literature, where "different" women are proposed by women writers, but are often, in the authoritative discourse of commentaries, subsumed back into the positions prescribed for women in patriarchal social relations. The paper will highlight and politicize those textual moments of erasure and displacement, while focusing on the position of women.

In my analysis, therefore, I will not lose sight of feminism's political commitment to the cultural resistance to, and transformation of, the material conditions of women's lives. It is particularly crucial to keep this perspective when dealing with Japanese literary criticism, where women are seriously underrepresented. I owe my insight into the dialectical relationship between textual women and "real-life" women to materialist feminist criticism, which tries to re-theorize and re-situate postmodernism in the political context.[11]

This chapter is part of an emerging feminist discourse in Japan on the critique of patriarchal assumptions in male literature and the literary establishment. Even though challenging the existing *bundan* has been the basic premise of Japanese feminist literary criticism, until recently the emphasis of research was on the analysis of women's literature. The situation in America is just the opposite of that in Japan. American feminist literary criticism started with the critique of masculine assumptions regarding male literature, as observed in the fierce criticism by feminists of Norman Mailer's works, and evolved into the study of women's literature. In what follows, I will analyze the commentaries by four *bundan* critics, but it is again my intention here to critique the gender assumptions encoded in the discourse of Japanese commentaries as a whole.

Before I begin my analysis, a few words on the term "patriarchy" are in order. There are many different definitions of patriarchy,[12] but for my present purposes, I shall observe the following strategic definition: "the organization and division of all practices and signification in culture in terms of gender and the privileging of one gender over the other, giving males control over female sexuality, fertility, and labor" (Ebert, "The Romance of Patriarchy," 19). Although many feminists accept that the hegemony of patriarchy exists transhistorically and globally, patriarchy is not one universalizing system; rather, it takes diverse forms and manifestations across time and location. For example, patriarchy in the present-day industrial world, including

Japan, is intricately intertwined with the development of capitalism.[13] In Japan, maternalism has traditionally been accorded a higher status than in the industrialized West, but the labor market has been attracting more and more women to work outside the home, especially since the 1970's, thus creating a large number of economically independent women. And after the Equal Employment Opportunity law was passed in 1985, managerial positions also became accessible to women.

Although some claim that capitalism has contributed to the collapse of gender differences in the face of labor demands (see Illich), Japanese corporate-centered society has remained strongly patriarchal, permitting few women access to the career ladder. Moreover, capitalism in Japan has been using women to its advantage as a convenient variable.[14] A sizable number of women are hired as part-time workers who are paid very low wages and can be laid off at any time. Many women, too, voluntarily choose this option because they need to take care of children and/or the elderly, the primary cause for the continuing low economic status of women in Japanese society. Japanese capitalism, then, instead of erasing gender differences, has been reinforcing the division between two kinds of women: one for equal (masculine) positions, the other for subordinate (feminine) positions, thereby strengthening the existing gender differences. In an era of postmodern consumerism and multinational and transnational capitalism, the interaction between patriarchy and capitalism will necessarily be more complex and involve more variables such as aging workers, foreign laborers, and immigrants. At a time of complex socioeconomic change such as the present, a critique of patriarchal ideology is required to be all the more rigorous and all the more forceful, if it is to locate both the visible and the invisible mechanisms of hegemonic patriarchal ideology in Japan's cultural institutions, an ideology that tries to keep women in a secondary status.[15] It is against this backdrop that paperback commentaries are examined in the present study.

Commentaries on Works by Women Authors

I will illustrate the problems of gender politics in commentaries, using four examples of works that attempt to construct "different" women. In order to show that this is an ongoing occurrence, I have chosen a range of books that appeared in the 1960's, 1970's, and 1980's: Kōno Taeko's short story "Yōjigari" (Toddler-hunting; 1961) and Takahashi Takako's collection *Ronrii ūman* (The lonely woman; 1977), books on women's identity crises and hatred of womanhood and/or motherhood; and Nakazawa Kei's *Umi o kanjiru toki* (When you feel the sea; 1978) and Matsumoto Yūko's *Kyoshokushō no akenai yoake* (The excessive overeater: a day without dawning; 1988), which focus on the meaning of female sexuality and beauty in society.[16] The following discussion will not touch upon the possible contributions of each critic toward a better understanding of the texts but will be limited to the portions of the commentary that involve moments of erasure and displacement of the "different" women.

We begin with an analysis of Kōno Taeko's (1926–) works, many of which deal with the theme of aversion to children. "Toddler-hunting," published in 1961, brought Kōno fame when it was awarded the Shinchōsa Dōjin Zasshi Award.[17] The book's heroine, Hayashi Akiko, a former chorus girl in a theater group but now almost thirty and economically independent, has no desire to marry. She is in an uncommitted relationship with a man by the name of Sasaki, who is two years her junior.

Three years earlier, Akiko contracted pulmonary tuberculosis and was told by her doctor that she should not bear children. She feels not quite fit to be a mother and is somewhat relieved at the thought that she cannot have children. In fact, her dislike for girls is so powerful that it is a physiological aversion. They remind her of her own miserable childhood, when she felt as if she lived under a curse.

> The more typical a little girl of this age group was, the more unsettling Akiko found it to be near her. The sickly, white flesh, the etiolated body, the bobbed hairstyle exposing the yellowish neck, the unnaturally high, insipid manner of speaking—even the cut and color of the girl's clothes: for Akiko, these characteristics were all linked with the closeness and filth that she had glimpsed in the pupa.[18]

On the other hand, Akiko has a curiosity about and an interest in boy children that could be called "abnormal." Even though she has no children of her own, she goes so far as to impulsively buy boys clothes. But in her secret ecstatic fantasies, the boys, the objects of her sadistic sexual urges, are chastised by their fathers. These fantasies eventually move beyond simple punishment into tyrannizing violence, including such acts of cruelty as burning and disemboweling.

The world described by Kōno is a complex blend of the ordinary and uncommon, of daily incidents, subconscious memories, uncon-

scious desires, curiosity, and sadomasochism—all mixed together
into a complex female psychology of obsession, love, and aversion.
The common thread throughout her works is that they are about
middle-aged women with no children who have obsessive levels of
interest in boys but who do not yet have the capacity to be as dominant and forceful as men. Both the aversion toward girls and the excessive pedophiliac interest in boys do their part to turn the myth of
motherhood on its head.

What is problematized here also is the issue of female sexuality,
for Akiko is actively engaged in sadomasochistic sex with her love
partner, Sasaki. Her pursuit of this passion was once so extreme that
Akiko almost lost her pulse. After spending a couple of nights this
way, she always develops a strong longing for a small boy. The ending of "Toddler-hunting" is a scene in which Akiko sees a little boy on
her way back from a public bath and asks for a bite of the watermelon
he is eating. In the sexual game of sadomasochism, the heroine's position is the masochist, the position of a person who completely submits to a sadist. Akiko actively seeks to be a masochist and revels, to
the extreme, in the role of the subordinate position. Her active seeking
of masochistic pleasures can be characterized as assertive or aggressive, signifying a strong claim for her own subjectivity and a desire
for the autonomous identity she has won to be equal to that of men.[19]

But the commentary on this book treats women's issues as though
they are a problem that can be experienced by people of either sex.[20]

> The kidnapping of infants, spouse-swapping, and lifestyles of sadis-
> tic love between men and women are seen everywhere. What can
> this degree of obsession with suspicious-looking dreams mean? In a
> word, the author's intent is to cast into doubt the very foundations of
> that which provides order to *our* daily existence by removing all the
> givens in life and causing *us* to re-examine the exposed structure of
> *human* interaction.
>
> Starting with those things that have names given to them in the
> ordinary world, such as evil, immorality, and perversion, she re-
> moves the garments that ordinarily veil them to allow a clear view of
> the way things have been. That is what she specifically intends to un-
> cover. (293, my italics)[21]

In other words, Kōno's works are a total and candid disclosure of
the most secret parts of "human" existence.[22] Here, "woman" is being
equated with "human beings." By this displacement, the conflicts of
"women" are universalized as the timeless predicaments of "human

beings," which dangerously implies that they are devoid of history and, therefore, are neither correctable nor changeable.

What underlies this kind of commentary is the Japanese variety of modern criticism (*kindai hihyō*), modeled after Western criticism, in which a work is valued solely by how well it addresses the universal truth of "human beings." As the recent critique of the founding principles of "modern" has made clear, however, the notion of universal "human beings" is a fabrication of the "modern" era, which has suppressed such historical and cultural "differences" as gender, race, and sexuality; according to this critique of the "modern," "human beings" are shown to be synonymous with "heterosexual middle-class (Japanese) men."[23]

What keeps reappearing in Kōno's text is the psychology of "woman" and the subversion of motherhood and female sexuality as defined as "good mother" and "submissive/passive sex." The fact that the central concern of the text is about unsettling *female* issues is disregarded in the commentary, and thus the problematic nature of the system within which men and women are gendered is ignored.

ॐ

Next we will look at Takahashi Takako's (1932–) collection of stories *The Lonely Woman*, published in 1977.[24] Not surprisingly, this collection has as uneasy a relationship with its commentary as does "Toddler-hunting." In addition to the title story, the collection includes "Otsuge" (The revelation), "Kitsunebi" (Fox fire), "Tsurihashi" (The suspension bridge), and "Fushigi na en" (A strange coincidence), a total of five short stories. The heroines of all these stories are interconnected. For example, the old woman who lives next to Yamakawa Sakiko, the heroine of the first story, "The Lonely Woman," is the mother-in-law of Yōko, the heroine of the next story, "The Revelation." And the heroine of the third story, "Fox Fire," whose name is Nozawa Ichiko, is the department store clerk in "The Revelation." Aside from these seemingly arbitrary connections, however, the heroines also have in common a lack of commitment to men and/or family in their lives.

Yamakawa Sakiko, the heroine of "The Lonely Woman," has been employed in an office for the past six years, since graduation from college. At first she was interested in her job, but now she is in a state of inertia. One night while the landlord from whom she is renting a room is away, there is a big uproar in the neighborhood over a fire set by an arsonist in the auditorium of a nearby elementary school. Initially imagining that this must have been the doing of some woman like herself in search of an outlet for her loneliness, Sakiko, in her world of one, gradually starts feeling that she is the arsonist. Frequently in her secret imagination, she envisions that all the schoolchildren burn to death, screaming. The ending suggests that the arsonist is an old lady in the neighborhood.

The second story, "The Revelation," is about the dreams of a young widow named Yōko, whose husband, Gōkichi, died some time ago in a traffic accident. He had worked for a large trading company and was, as she remembers, a good husband. She had no complaints about him. One morning, in a dream, Yōko sees her late husband walk away from her as though he is rejecting her and stand beside a pool at a hotel. There, she sees him displaying a more than normal intimacy with his older sister, Haruyo. In an effort to find out what this dream means, she visits Haruyo, who, it turns out, is away visiting her mother (Yōko's mother-in-law). After a while, she has a similar dream. This time, she sees in her dream a woman and child in a family circle with Gōkichi. Yōko, realizing that the woman is Nozawa Ichiko, a clerk, at a department store she had once visited with her husband, visits the department store in search of Ichiko, although she knows such a visit is futile.

In a third dream, Yōko sees a girlfriend from college, Makimura Mitsue, riding on a camel with Gōkichi. The pair disappears into the desert. Strangely enough, when Yōko goes to visit Mitsue, she finds out that Mitsue has just died and her funeral is in progress. Greatly disturbed by these dreams, Yōko recalls, from the deepest reaches of her memory, the serious wound caused by an old boyfriend's betrayal.

The third story is "Fox Fire," which here refers to the waves of heat the heroine sees in her hometown. The fox fire (kitsunebi) is a phosphorus fire seen burning at night. In folk tradition, it is believed that a fox exhales this fire. The heroine of this story, Nozawa Ichiko, sees a heat haze in a field, which, for some reason, reminds her of the word "fox fire." Ichiko, the woman in the second dream in "The Revelation," is 28 years old and works at the accessories counter of a department store. She is living a tired, purposeless life. One day she witnesses a girl shoplifting a turquoise pendant and a wig. The girl, while being taken to the security office, cries out loudly in tears, saying that she has a stomach ache. And yet when a doctor comes to check her, she behaves differently, as if flirting with the doctor. Ichiko takes the girl home. Ichiko dislikes children, especially girls; they evoke in her the same kind of fear she feels toward a slug or a wall lizard. Ichiko later wants to meet the parents of this girl. When she gets to the place that the girl says is her home, Ichiko finds Yoshimura Ruriko, an old woman living alone, who has nothing whatsoever in common with the girl.

The fourth story is "The Suspension Bridge." The heroine is Haruyo, the older sister of Yōko's husband in "The Revelation." When Haruyo was a child, she had often walked to the center of a suspension bridge and experienced the sensation of dissolving into thin air. Then one day, thirteen years after her graduation from college, one of her college friends informs Haruyo that her old lover, Ikawa Toshiaki, has returned from America. He is an elite member of the government bureaucracy in the Foreign Ministry.

Haruyo now has a trustworthy and reliable husband, Eizō. Although she and Eizō have children, Haruyo now realizes that she still feels some passion for her old lover. When she thinks of him, even her own children become a nuisance. This old boyfriend is hard-to-please, cold-hearted, and proud, and an inveterate womanizer; but when she knew him, there had been something powerful about him that caused Haruyo to lose control of herself. During that period in her life, she had often felt as if she were turning into a demon out of jealousy over him. His return causes her to feel so shaky that she does not know what to do with herself. One day, during this period of instability, she learns that Ikawa has jumped off a building and killed himself, and even though she is shocked, she feels a great sense of relief.

The last story, "A Strange Coincidence," is about Yoshimura Ruriko, the old lady in "Fox Fire." Ruriko was a refugee from Manchuria, and both her husband and her son died in the war. She also lost her younger sister, and she is now all alone in the world. For some reason, she often encounters people's deaths or suicides. For example, on the way to visit a sick friend in the hospital, she sees a man kill himself by jumping off a building. This man is Ikawa Toshiaki, from "The Suspension Bridge." Ruriko also recalls that, long before, when she was about 48 and was crossing the Seto Inland Sea on a ferryboat, she had witnessed a young man jump into the sea from the boat. She also recollects an incident that had occurred about ten years before: while walking through a neighborhood in a large subdivision, she had encountered a dazed-looking infant walking out of one of the houses. Upon entering the house, Ruriko found the child's father near death after having tried to asphyxiate himself.

One day, the same girl who gave Ruriko's address as her own in "Fox Fire" comes calling to tell her that a housewife in the housing complex has gone insane and is burning up a summer orange (*natsumikan*) tree. Ruriko, while watching the burning tree, gives herself over to the wild fantasy that each orange is a baby and that they are all burning up. Ruriko suspects that the woman's insanity probably has something to do with babies. Finally, Ruriko, who is visiting her friend in the hospital again, sees another person who has committed suicide being delivered in an ambulance. The name of the person is Yamakawa Sakiko, the heroine of the first story ("The Lonely Woman").

The common thread linking these stories is the loneliness of women or women who, having been deceived by men, have been forced to live in a desperation and an insanity that has become for them a kind of hell. They find no meaning in their lives; each of them, fully aware that she does not fit anywhere in society, goes on living in despair. This is as true of Yōko and Haruyo, who are housewives, as it is of Sakiko and Ichiko, who work for a living.

But the commentary on *The Lonely Woman*, as clearly shown in the following excerpt, treats the issue of women as if it were no different from that of "human beings" in general:

> They are absolutely isolated. And, therefore, these women never learn to cope successfully with their loneliness. They are continually threatened with feelings of instability, and the more threatened they feel, the further they move in the direction of more instability and into the danger zone created by their loneliness and isolation. They are not pushed by outside influences, but rather push themselves in this direction. The old woman, Yoshimura Ruriko, complains that "the inside of a person is like a haunted house," but *people* go on living under the weight of not knowing what is going to emerge from their inner selves. As they become more isolated and lonely, however, they peel off their outer layers one at a time.
>
> All these lonely women have left is their inner realities, which they have totally exposed. And they no longer have any choice but to behave in accordance with those same inner selves. What is described by these stories is the terrifying direction this can lead in, and the astonishingly fertile world that opens up therein. (214, my italics)

The reason that Ms. Takahashi ceaselessly takes herself into this condition of extreme loneliness and isolation is that this is where she becomes creative. She strips off her external self and exposes her innermost self. And there, for the first time, she can expose the dangerous fertility hidden within *human* existence. From this fertility, her works are developed. At this point, however, the distinction between imagination and fact, dream and reality, and oneself and others disappears; the bounds of fertility vanish and threaten the author. (216–17, my italics)[25]

Here, the critic uses words such as "people," "inner selves," and "human existence," but the theme throughout the book is the condition of *women*.

Sakiko, from the first story, has been out of college for several years, but she is not trying to establish herself as a working woman through her job, nor is she planning to marry. She does not know what she wants to do with her life. She makes loneliness and isolation her friends and seems to be getting on with her life (though, in the last story, "A Strange Coincidence," the reader is informed that she has committed suicide). In the next story, Yōko loses her husband when she is still young. During his lifetime, he had secretly had many affairs, and after his death these affairs intrude on Yōko's dreams. And then there is Ichiko, in story three, for whom it has been a long time since she graduated from school and started working at the department store. She does not have a real purpose in life either. It is insinuated that she was one of the partners in the love affairs of Yōko's husband, from the previous story. The fourth heroine, Haruyo, is a woman caught between her insane passion for her cold-hearted lover from college, and her peacefully secluded life with her husband and children. And the last heroine, Yoshimura Ruriko, has been left behind by all her dead family and relatives and, again, is an old woman living alone with no real purpose for living.

The predicament of these characters is not, as the commentary asserts, a quantity that can be labeled "the loneliness and isolation of people living in modern society." Rather, it clearly is born of a situation specific to *women* who are betrayed by men. And the real tragedy is that they can find no way to escape from their predicament. The one choice remaining to them is to give up, avoid men, and abandon themselves to a loneliness and isolation that gives rise to insanity and suicidal desires. By clearly laying out the psychological state of nearly crazed women living on the fringes of society, who have no way to establish their own identities or live independently, the short stories in *The Lonely Woman* are a vehement protest against that society. To the critics for whom such women's issues are invisible, however, the various phases of insanity of the women in these stories become simply "the astonishingly fertile world that opens up therein" (214). To such critics, these women who have fallen into an abyss of destruction merely "become more and more animated" (216).

But what the critic sees as "animation" is rather an insanity expressed in related states of delusion: Sakiko's delusion of schoolchildren getting burned in "The Lonely Woman"; Yōko's mother-in-law naming birds after the women her husband has had affairs with and then killing the birds one after another; Yōko, imitating her mother-in-law, also killing birds in "The Revelation"; the demon face of Haruyo in "The Suspension Bridge"; and, finally, Ruriko's fantasy of children being burned in "A Strange Coincidence." The violent insanity and jealousy that cause them to kill living things literally (the birds) or in fantasy (small children) are an explosion of the anger that has been welling up inside these female characters, who have been unable to express their anger, rage, and frustration toward men and the society that centers around them. In addition, the aversion toward young children that keeps reappearing throughout this book is an aversion toward motherhood on the part of women who are bound by their biological role as the birth-giving sex.[26] But all these, to the commentary writer, express nothing more than the terror of lonely and isolated "human beings" or "a dangerous overabundance."

As recognized in feminist writings on Japanese women's literature, the works of Kōno and Takahashi, published in the 1960's and 1970's, respectively, display strong doubts about and hatred toward motherhood and womanhood.[27] But none of these themes emerges in the commentaries. All the angry and deranged women of Takahashi and the subversive women of Kōno are subsumed under the rubric "human beings" or the "human race" in modern society.

∞

A woman's discovery of her own sexuality is the focus of Nakazawa Kei's (1959–) *When You Feel the Sea*, which the author wrote when she was 18 and published in 1978.[28] The work is about a high school girl named Nakazawa Emiko, the narrator and heroine, and her uncommitted boyfriend, Takano Hiroshi, who used to be in the school's Newspaper Club and who is now working. It is also about the antagonism between Emiko and her mother, whose husband (Emiko's father) died some time ago.

Although Hiroshi and Emiko are sleeping together, Hiroshi is not in love with her; his only interest is her body. But he thinks that this is not quite right and feels guilty about it. Even for the heroine of the story, the affair began as just an adolescent physical interest. Her own sense of guilt tells her, however, that she should justify the affair in the name of romance. And in order to prove to herself that the affair is right, she aggressively pursues Hiroshi. At first, he gives her the cold shoulder, but the more he tries to get away from her, the more she pursues him. Since her mother had always told her that to do nothing else with her life but raise a child was stupid, Emiko has decided to become a professional woman. Yet, even though she had had a definite plan to become a social worker and marry a supportive husband, she now feels that she would like to be a "professional" wife: knitting, taking care of her husband, and having his child. At one point, she can think of nothing but him, she is so obsessed. Finally, Hiroshi, not knowing how to get rid of her and with no intention of marrying her, says they can try living together for a while. She, however, is hesitant and does not want to go through with it.

The conflict we see here is caused by the heroine's discovery of her sexuality, her attachment to the man with whom she had her first physical experience, and the pressure she is under to justify this sexual encounter as socially acceptable "love." She feels that her sexuality is surrounded and confined by social rules controlling women's sexuality. Even though both Emiko and Hiroshi know that their mutual physical interest is not "love," still they remain together because doing so provides them with acceptable social roles. The larger the gap between them, the greater and more desperate are Emiko's attempts to fill it.

When her mother, who has lived only to care for her daughter, finds out that Emiko and Hiroshi have had sex, she has a fit of anger. For a period of months, the mother complains bitterly about it in a deranged manner. One night, Emiko and her mother quarrel, and while watching her mother run out to the seashore, Emiko feels physiologically that the same female blood, like dark, filthy seawater, is running in both her mother's and her own veins. Emiko, all this time, had thought her mother to be a different category of woman, an authority figure who told her what to do; now she realizes that they are, after all, the same sex, stuck and struggling in their collective predicament as women. The ending is the source of the book's title. Emiko says,

> In my mother, and in me as well, there is a deep sea.
> My mother is surprised . . . that I am a woman. I was also surprised to realize that my mother is a woman too.

The critic who wrote the commentary quotes this last part and then continues:

> From these expressions of honesty and straightforwardness, the central beauty of this story throws off rays of light as from a diamond in the rough. "My mother is a woman and I am a woman." We know that from the start.
> Nevertheless, even while there is nothing surprising about this statement, in looking back with a heart consumed in grief, you feel a sense of wonder that gives cause for surprise deep inside.
> This sense of wonder may not seem a particular oddity when compared to something like a mountain suddenly crashing down into the sea or the mysterious things born of diligent cultivation in a strange world. It may seem more like the scenery of gently rolling hills, but if you just realize that the wind blowing through the clusters of hills, the rays of sunlight falling gently on the hills, and the waves coming in from the sea are all breezes and light and waves born of nature, you can no longer say that they are in any way inferior to more dramatic scenes.
> Through the expressions found in this story, we take it to mean that the author is just obediently conforming to her body, but I would like to just add that through this obedience she entrusts her body to the care of nature, and this is reflected in her sensitivity and tranquillity, which are embraced in it. (168)[29]

Significant here are the words "body," "obedience," "entrusting her body to the care of nature," "embraced," and "tranquillity." The person making these comments is, through the use of these words, trying to equate the sexuality of women, as described in this book, with nature, which he describes as gentle and something to be worshiped. Another part of the commentary says this: "The area where she naturally equates the light of her body with the light of nature is where the real strength of her work lies." To the commentary writer, this book is about the natural sexuality of women; to him, women's sexuality is comparable to beautiful scenery in nature, in which every feature gently blends in with everything else. It is not difficult to see here that the female character is being made to conform to a typical stereotype of woman, for the commentary reflects the yearning for the nostalgic fantasy of the mythic "natural" woman.

As pointed out by a variety of feminists,[30] such a view of woman as close to "nature" is often a dangerous fabrication of the patriarchal ideology. In this equation, women are associated with nature/emotion/heart, as opposed to culture/reason/head, and the former is considered to be inferior. Since culture means the control of nature, this equation has contributed to the objectification of women. For this reason, we are justifiably suspicious when "women," "the sea," and "gentle nature" are all equated in the commentary.

When You Feel the Sea describes the feelings of a woman who has discovered her sexual body: her first menstruation, her enlarging breasts, her bodily fluids, and her bodily hair. The eyes of the author, which are observing this changing body of a woman, are, indeed, fresh and straightforward. But the commentary only focuses on this part, equates it with a description of scenery and the last part about the sea, and concludes that the book is about the natural and mysterious quality of woman's body. What is interesting here is that, contrary to what the commentary says, the text makes the sea a symbol of woman's abject body, and certainly not something beautiful. In the passage preceding the section quoted earlier, Nakazawa writes: "Mother found the 'sea' in me, the filthy . . . obscene . . . sea. You will need to collect the menstrual blood of all the women in the world to make this dark sea. The waves will make the sounds of a curse. . . . The sea is dark and deep, filled with women's blood" (94).

If anything, the sea signifies women's predicament, the "bloody" meaning of female sexuality in society, but this escapes the attention of the commentary writer. Accordingly, no attention is given to other gender issues: the problematic nature of the relationship between Emiko and Hiroshi, in which the double standard of society always pushes a woman to find meaning in relationships. What is also pushed out of sight is the tense relationship between mother and daughter, who constantly fight, disagree, hurt one another, and yet somehow cling to each other in the mother/daughter home. The commentary goes no further than a mythical romanticism toward the female body, and this romanticized sexuality tends to become immediately the object of adoration. The commentary displaces the meaning of "woman" in the text in order to perpetuate the stereotype of the "pure and natural woman" in the very areas where she is fundamentally different from men.[31]

∅

Finally, let us take a look at *The Excessive Overeater: A Day Without Dawning* by Matsumoto Yūko (1963–), which deals with the sufferings of a college woman with an eating disorder.[32] The heroine is a 21-year-old woman named Sawada Tokiko who is never satisfied no matter how much she eats. This work is written in a colloquial style, somewhat reminiscent of the works of Dazai Osamu (1909–48). It is a first-person narrative, with the heroine confessing, as if in a diary, the events and feelings of her daily life. Tokiko is majoring in economics at college. Her present problem is with overeating, but it used to be a refusal to eat, which started while she was in junior high school. When she entered college, she weighed 47 kilograms, but reduced her weight to 40 kilograms. However, following a breakup with her boyfriend, she began to eat out of desperation and now weighs 60 kilograms. Extremely self-conscious, she is too embarrassed to step outside and loses all interest in school. Her daily life has deteriorated to the point where she sleeps all day and therefore cannot sleep at night. She is clearly self-destructive.

As Tokiko's problem with overeating developed, she gradually became more knowledgeable about the issue through magazines and television, as well as through friends and associates. Ironically, this information only increased her desire to eat. The more she realized that what she was doing was not good for her, the less she could stop herself. Before she realized it, she had become a full-blown obsessive overeater. When she says, at the end of the first chapter, "I wish I had never been born," we know that Tokiko's extreme dependence on food has caused her to loathe the source and origin of her own existence. Compared with album pictures from just one year before, her whole face now looks puffed up; the eyelids are unflatteringly swollen, even hiding part of her eyes; the cheeks are puffy; the skin is oily with a glistening shine; and she has acquired a double chin, making her nose look flat.

All she has to do to be happy is lose weight, she thinks; then, she will be pretty and confident, find a new boyfriend, and have a wonderful life. If she does not lose weight, she will remain buried in hopelessness and continue to just sputter along. In Tokiko's mind, being thin symbolizes everything that is good and wonderful in life. "To be thin is to be delicate, cute, graceful, supple-limbed, clean, sexy, intellectual, fast, modern, sophisticated, urban, smart, eccentric, sickly (of the contemporary kind that has a strange beauty to it), polished, high-strung, nervous, androgynous, tragic, skeletal, beautified death, Sharon Tate, passing, fleeting, gloomy, ennui, beautiful girls, fairies, Mia Farrow" (68).[33]

Tokiko decides to seek therapy, is given tranquilizers and some sleeping pills, and is referred to a counselor named Sasaki. But Sasaki turns out to be a blunt and overly scrupulous person, a type Tokiko cannot stand, and she is unable to bring herself to open up and pour her heart out to him. One other important reason for her reticence is that Sasaki is a man. Even the decor of the counseling room, which she is convinced was designed by an insensitive male, makes her uneasy:

> The small counseling room had one wall that was covered with a paneling with monotonous uniformly drilled holes for absorbing sound. The walls of the small room somehow left me feeling as though they were closing in on me, this room with a man I didn't even know. I continued to feel the need to protect myself. The idea to cover the walls with soundproofing had to have come from an insensitive man. And I'll bet that same man is selfishly proud that he's kind and sensitive. (24)

Adding to her self-consciousness and discomfort, Tokiko felt as though he was about to start pushing his body up against hers; from start to finish, there wasn't a second when she felt that she could let down her guard with him. Even when she finally succeeded in opening up and talking about how much she ate, something she had never told anyone, he showed no sympathy or warmth as he methodically proceeded to compare her to his other patients. Tokiko descended deep into a pit of personal regret, hopelessness, and despair as she learned the true extent of her foolishness. That night, after leaving the counseling session, she tried for the first time to throw up after her eating binge.

No matter how much she eats, it is never enough. She eats to excess and suffers, yet in her mind her belly is empty. Her stomach, it seems to Tokiko, is connected to a never-satisfied vagina. She keeps going to see Sasaki every week, and Sasaki gradually starts asking about her old boyfriend and her periods, among other personal issues. Tokiko does see her breakup as the starting point of her problem, but at the same time knows it is not the cause. She believes the real cause is her mother, who, when she was only one year old, laid her to sleep in the closet and then abandoned her family. Her mother later married another man. But the helplessness and despair that she felt there in the darkness as an infant remains, just as if it had happened yesterday. She used her boyfriend to try to heal her loneliness, but the intensity of her feeling was far too great for her to feel fulfilled in her love. Her very neediness made her seek out the love of a man, but she really needed a more basic kind of love. Now, as an adult, she wants to return to a universe of order and control. She feels now, more than ever, a desire to be enveloped in her mother's tender and protective embrace.

In the last chapter, this whole story about her mother is turned on its head. We are told that what Tokiko wrote is only a fiction. Her mother did in fact walk out on the family when Tokiko was one year old; but when she was five, her mother came back and rejoined her father in raising the family. When Tokiko discovers that her mother has secretly read this story, a fight ensues. Her mother takes off and does not return, even late into the night. The story then concludes, leaving the audience hanging as to whether Tokiko has resolved any feelings toward her mother.

The reason the title of this book uses the term "excessive" overeater, rather than the more common "overeater," is carefully explained in the book. The in thing among young people in Japan is to use exaggerated terms when describing themselves, especially terms that no one else uses. One of those terms is "excessive," which is used to describe "excessively" large civilizations and "excessively" large corporations. Thus, the word "overeater" has a dated ring to it, whereas "excessive overeater" fits in well with the culture of modern young people "Super-overeater" might work, but that term carries connotations of the 1960's, when everyone naively believed in the creation of a utopia where all the world's problems would be solved by science (55–56).

Literary works dealing with eating disorders have become more and more common recently. Feminist research has already shown that the problems of anorexia and bulimia are one of the distortions caused by the patriarchal order under which women live.[34] In developed nations, where hunger and starvation are no longer considered major problems, the expected standard for female beauty has become the slim body. Society puts heavy pressure on modern women, unlike men, to be both slim and beautiful, a doubly oppressive burden. The result is that even when it comes to something as basic as eating, disorders caused by oppression take place in the form of women starving their bodies of necessary nutrition, binge eating, and then purging what they eat. Matsumoto remarks in a postscript:

> If this disorder came from purely physical causes, there would also be men who suffer from it. So why are the victims almost always women? I have come to believe that there are social factors at work. I believe that the way motherhood and female sexuality have been historically and culturally controlled, the political exploitation of female beauty, the lack of female self-esteem and self-importance in the sociopolitical arena, and the commercialization of female sexuality – all these realities permeate the environment, wherein these eating disorders can fester and flourish. (172–73)

Many readers have reportedly written to Matsumoto since this book was published, about their suffering from these maladies. On the page following the author's postscript, in the commentary, the critic begins with gossip he heard in his literary circles:

> Well, this is how I first learned the name of Matsumoto Yūko. It was shortly after the recipient of the Eleventh Subaru Literary Award had been announced. A literary friend started this conversation with me:
> "I hear that the recipient of the Subaru Literary Award, Matsumoto Yūko, is an intimidating beauty, even more than Takagi Nobuko."
> "If that's true, then she's got to be at the top of the literary world."
> "That's right. That's what I hear." (175–76)

The fact that the commentary writer felt it appropriate to engage in gossip about the physical appearance of a female author is, I must say, clear evidence of the general insensitivity to gender issues in the *bundan*. Even more disturbing is the commentary writer's discussion of her work on the eating disorders of anorexia and bulimia. Here again we see, just as in the commentaries on the works of Takahashi and Kōno, that issues relating specifically to women are treated as a product of the loneliness and isolation prevalent in "modern people":

> Within these words, we see in graphic clarity the insecurity, loneliness, and isolation that *modern people* live with in this world of excessively large civilizations, businesses, and industries. This isolation, loneliness, and insecurity is pervasive and common to *all people*. . . . However, it is this very world of emptiness that is the living environment of *modern people* which provides the background for *The Excessive Overeater*. "I" know intuitively that the establishment of one's

own identity and being as something truly independent is a delusion. "I" don't want to establish an identity for "myself" nor do "I" want one established for "me," because "I" want to remain soft, pliable and forever evolving. This clarifies the vision of a *modern human being*. (180–81, my italics)

The commentary concludes by saying:

It appears that the individual, in trying to escape from this expanse wherein she has become totally exposed to the elements, projects her frustration onto her mother. This has nothing to do with alienation from mother earth. Nor does it have to do with the loss of a sense of community. It is just the simple fact that the refrigerator in the kitchen of her apartment has become the one place where she can get relief. In that space, *modern people* have become like clowns on a stage performing only for themselves. This realization is the core element of the story. With this realization comes the death of this old self. Without passing through this circuit of darkness, the day certainly will never dawn for them. (183, my italics)

Here we see another commentary that relegates work about women to the heap of those written about "modern people (men)," "the modern individual," or "all people." But it is more than obvious that Matsumoto's work deals with a problem that is virtually unique to young "women." The problems of anorexia and bulimia among women today cannot rationally be discussed or understood without relating them to the patriarchal values under which women live.

♋

When we observe what happens when the works of women are subjected to the *bundan* discourse, it becomes quite clear just how easily the "differences" become naturalized. The gynocidal commentaries exclude and silence the heterogeneous "other" by repeating what Irigaray calls "the logic of the same," which means positing the feminine as other only in relation to masculine sameness and not as a different mode of signification (Irigaray, 221). The first two and the last discussions presented examples in which the commentary avoids acknowledging *female* anger, rage, madness, protest, and resistance and posits these instead as conditions common to all "human beings." And in the two last examples, the commentary writers glorified the authors and their works for presenting women as symbols of "nature" and beauty, thereby completely displacing the issue of the problematic nature of woman's body and sexuality in society.

The mechanisms of avoidance and idealization of women that we see in these commentaries parallel Mizuta Noriko's description of the position of women inscribed in the works of modern Japanese (male) literature:

> The mystification of women in modern literature can be called a reflection of [1] a desire to provide relief and support to modern individuals (men) and eliminate the stress and suffering due to their identity crisis, by creating an image of women that says women are pure and innocent, without these sorts of problems, and by creating a yearning for women as an element of nature; and [2] an intention to escape from equal engagement with women through symbolizing "woman" as an entity outside the realm of society and history. (*Hiroin kara hiirō e*, 30)

The commentaries on Matsumoto and Nakazawa belong in group (1); those on Takahashi and Kōno (and part of Matsumoto's) belong to group (2). These four examples demonstrate how "different" women, put under surveillance by *bundan* voices of authority, are all turned into easy-to-comprehend "readerly" women as opposed to resisting "writerly" women (Barthes). Thus, the representation of problematic or subversive woman in women's texts may not directly enter the symbolic network. There will always be a danger, therefore, of "different" women being reconstructed to conform to the prescribed position given to women. The end result will then be only to strengthen the existing patriarchal gender definition of men and women.

As Volosinov (Bakhtin) and A. J. Greimas claim, the sign is an arena of social conflict; thus, the text and its commentary are sites of political struggle where the cultural meanings of woman are contested. In modern-day Japan, there are a great number of women authors, and these authors do and will make various attempts at new ways of representing women. But no matter how much female authors increase in number, as long as those who exercise control over literary knowledge and signification make feminist questions and gender issues invisible, the "different" women will never be successfully inscribed in our cultural network.[35] This is why there is a pressing need for a feminist intervention in the discourse of paperback commentaries in Japan.

Notes

Earlier versions of this essay were presented at the Rutgers Conference on Japanese Women Writers, April 9–10, 1993, and at a workshop at UCLA on

"Cultural Constructs, Social Representations in Japan," Part II of "The Cultural and Political Construction of Norms: Late Imperial China and Japan," May 28–30, 1993. I thank all the participants for their helpful feedback, in particular the audience at the Rutgers conference, whose enthusiasm was a motivation behind my renewed commitment to this project. I also thank Kawashima Yōko and Kōno Taeko for their valuable information and materials as well as for their encouragement of this project. I am indebted to Miriam Silverberg for her careful reading and constructive comments and suggestions.

1. Japanese literature is customarily divided into two major categories: *jun bungaku* (pure literature), often associated with "I-fiction" [*shi-shōsetsu*], and *taishū bungaku* (popular literature), written as entertainment for the masses. Although in paperback editions most works of "pure literature" have a full-fledged commentary, there is a tendency for "popular literature" and essay collections to carry more casual and impressionistic comments, or none at all. But the distinction between "pure" and "popular" literature has increasingly been collapsing, and the works of some younger writers, such as Murakami Haruki (1949–) are less likely to have a commentary. In general, however, paperback commentaries of the sort discussed in this essay are not intended to be full-fledged scholarly critiques.

2. These data were collected at the Kinokuniya Bookstore in San Francisco on Dec. 21, 1995.

3. At the Rutgers Conference on Japanese Women Writers, Ōba Minako and Kōno Taeko noted that as writers they generally leave it up to the publisher to decide who will write the commentary for paperback editions of their works, but they retain veto power over the publisher's choice.

4. For the term "bundan," which originally referred to the exclusive Tokyo coterie made up of male writers and critics of the Meiji (1868–1912) and Taishō (1912–26) periods, see Ariga, "Dephallicizing Women." I use the term in a broad sense to include established writers and critics, some free-lancers, and others belonging to academic institutions. These people write in newspapers and magazines for general readers, as well as in specialized academic publications.

5. The arguments are sometimes raised that not all women writers raise gender issues, and that not all women critics necessarily give a feminist reading of texts. This is true, but if one extends these arguments and claims that feminist writing and reading can be done by either sex, the monopoly by male critics that has excluded women from Japanese critical discourse for decades, even centuries, will most likely never change. Here, then, is a pitfall of postmodern criticism: since "woman" is a cultural construct, a man can therefore position himself as "woman," too. Certainly, men can participate in feminism, since feminism is for the benefit of both men and women. But the postmodern emphasis on categories as constructs often ignores the fact that women continue to experience daily a collective discrimination in the material world based on their gender classification. For a full discussion of the

male position as well as the pros and cons of male participation in feminism, see Jardine and Smith.

6. See Komashaku, *Majoteki bungaku ron* and *Murasaki Shikibu no messeeji*; Mizuta, *Hiroin kara hiirō e*; Tomioka; Kurosawa; Ueno, Ogura, and Tomioka; and Egusa and Urushida.

7. See Kitada, 162–71.

8. See Maureen Mullarkey, "Hard Cop, Soft Cop," May 30, 1987, cited in Ebert, "Postmodernism's Infinite Variety," 24.

9. Another apt question to ask might be the one addressed by Nancy Hartsock: Why has the postmodern claim to divorce verbal constructs from reality arisen "precisely when women and non-Western peoples have begun to speak for themselves and, indeed, to speak about global systems of power differentials?" (Mascia-Lees et al., 15).

10. For varied arguments in favor of essentialism vis-à-vis or by way of postmodernism in feminism on political and practical grounds, see, e.g., Miller; Schor; Spivak, "Can the Subaltern Speak?" and "In a Word"; Alcoff; Fuss; de Lauretis; Mascia-Lees et al.; Ōgoshi; Hartsock; and Modleski. See also the essays in Nicholson; and Barrett and Phillips.

11. The expression "real life" refers to the fact that although our experience is dictated by cultural categories, we also experience the consequences of the contradictions between theory and praxis in our material lives. For the position of materialist feminism, see Newton and Rosenfelt; Ebert, "The Romance of Patriarchy," and "Postmodernism's Infinite Variety"; Fraser; Rooney; and Belsey, 259.

12. See, e.g., Rubin, 167–69; Barrett, 10–19; Omvedt; Lerner; and Walby.

13. See Kuhn and Wolpe; Barrett; Eisenstein; Walby; and Ueno, *Kafuchō-sei to shihonsei*. The analysis of women's oppression in terms of patriarchy and capitalism is the so-called dual-system theory. For the pros and cons of this analytical framework, see Sergent. See Fraser for an approach informed by postmodern theory.

14. For a discussion of the female labor force in Japan, see Kawashima-Horne; Takenaka, *Sengo joshi rōdōshi ron*, and "Restructuring of the Female Labor Force"; Hirota; Ueno, *Kafuchōsei to shihonsei*, 295–308; and Ōsawa, "Corporate-Centered Society" and *Kigyō chūshin shakai o koete*.

15. For an analysis of Japan's multinational and transnational capitalism, see Miyoshi.

16. The problem with paperback commentaries can be observed in many other works by women. A listing of them would be endless, but see, e.g., Tsumura Setsuko, *Gangu* (Shūeisha bunko, 1978); Mori Yōko, *Onna-zakari* (Kadokawa bunko, 1989); Hiraiwa Yumie, *Onna to misoshiru* (Shūeisha bunko, 1989); and Yamada Eimi, *Hāremu wārudo* (Kōdansha bunko, 1990).

17. Kōno Taeko was graduated in economics from what is now known as Osaka Women's College. In 1945, the year the war ended, she decided she wanted to become an author and became a member of the literary journal *Dō-jinsha* under the sponsorship of the "I-fiction" writer Niwa Fumio (1904–).

Her training period was very long, and she was in her thirties before she began her career as a professional author. In 1963 she was awarded the Akutagawa Award for her short story "Kani" (The crab).

18. Trans. Lucy North, "Toddler-hunting," 43.

19. For a similar view of Kōno's works, see Yonaha, "Onna no sekushuariti," 75; and Mizuta, *Hiroin kara hiirō e*, 190, and *Feminizumu no kanata*, 241. For a thorough psychoanalytic reading of "Toddler-hunting" and the meaning of masochism in it, see Yonaha, *Gendai joryū sakka ron*, 9–29. According to Kōno (at the Rutgers Conference on Japanese Women Writers, April 9–10, 1993), she intended both positions (masochism and sadism) to be interchangeable and equal; a man can be masochistic and a woman can be sadistic. For Kōno's view of masochism, see Kōno, *Tanizaki bungaku to kōtei no yokubō*.

20. This commentary was written by the critic Kawamura Jirō, who also wrote the one for *When You Feel the Sea*. The two other critics whom I discuss in this paper are Matsumoto Tōru (*The Lonely Woman*), and Kawanishi Masaaki (*The Excessive Overeater*). It is only a coincidence that Kawamura is the author of two of the commentaries analyzed in this essay.

21. Page numbers refer to the 1973 Shinchō bunko edition of Kōno's "Yōjigari."

22. In this excerpt, as well as in the subsequent excerpts, the reference to "human beings" may be less overt in Japanese, in which the subject of a sentence is often omitted.

23. See Lyotard; and Foucault. At the UCLA workshop mentioned in the headnote, this paper, along with another feminist paper, was excluded from the summary discussion on Japanese cultural norms at the concluding session. "Women" were erased under the name of "human" culture—the very thing I am warning in this paper that we should not do!

24. Takahashi Takako won the the Woman of Letters Award for *The Lonely Woman*. For more on Takahashi, see Chapter 6, by Maryellen Toman Mori, in this volume.

25. Page numbers refer to those in the 1982 Shūeisha bunko edition of *Ronrii ūman*.

26. Concerning Takahashi's aversion toward motherhood, see Mizuta, *Hiroin kara hiirō e*, 185–87; and Yonaha, *Gendai joryū sakkaron*, 30–63, and "Onna no sekushuariti," 73–75.

27. See Yonaha, *Gendai joryū sakkaron* and "Onna no sekushuariti," regarding the question of female sexuality and motherhood as expressed in women's literature since the 1960's and 1970's. *Gendai joryū sakka ron* also has a comprehensive bibliography of essays in Japanese on Kōno Taeko (231–35) and Takahashi Takako (235–40).

28. Nakazawa Kei was awarded the *Gunzō* New Author Award for *When You Feel the Sea*, and it remained on the best-seller list for an extended period.

29. Page numbers refer to the 1984 Kōdansha bunko edition of *Umi o kanjiru toki*.

30. See Ortner; Dinnerstein, 208–9; Cixous; and Keller.

31. Many of Nakazawa's other works also treat the topic of female sexuality. So far, it has been predominantly male critics who have discussed her works. See, e.g., Suzuki; and Okude. What to me is most problematic is a group discussion of her works solely by male critics, such as one in *Gunzō* (Takahashi Hideo et al.). Although the content of the discussion dwells on the literary values of Nakazawa's *Suiheisenjō nite* (On the horizon; 1984), the format itself reminds me of expressions such as "a woman's body in exchange" or "a woman's body in circulation" among men.

32. Matsumoto Yūko won the Subaru Award for *The Excessive Overeater* in 1988. Since then, she has been writing full-time. Her other works are *Itsuwari no Maririn Monrō* (1990; The false Marilyn Monroe; 1990); *Wakare no bigaku* (The art of breaking up; 1991); and two collections of essays, *Sakka izen* (Before I became an author; 1991); and *Budōshu to bara no hibi* (Days of wine and roses; 1993).

33. Page numbers refer to the 1991 Shūeisha bunko edition of *Kyoshokushō no akenai yoake*.

34. See, e.g., Orbach; Chernin; Seid; Wolf; and Ikuno.

35. At the same time, it is possible that women authors might either wittingly or unwittingly allow such criticism to affect their work in the belief that their writing must be done with an eye to obtaining approval from *bundan* critics. Thus, the writer Tomioka Taeko (1935–) says:

> What women write is, consequently and for the most part, determined by the criticism and evaluations of men in "men's words." Therefore, without our even being aware of it, female expression has been created to please men. The phrase "to please men," more than "men's words," means that even things made by women are in effect being made by men. Whether intentionally or not, women use "the words of men" in order to "curry the favor of the male critics." Female poets who write poetry in the "feminine" style and female authors who write works in the "feminine" style do not invite the hostility of men because they do not go against "the words of men." Words of praise from men, such as, "You can't compete with women," or, "Men are going to have to work hard to keep ahead," are usually said about the type of thing written in the appropriate "feminine" style, and not about the philosophy manifested therein. (118)

Women's literature, therefore, is likely to remain in a dilemma. Whether women writers unknowingly write their work to appeal to the *bundan* male critics, or whether they try to shout loud enough to challenge the system oppressing women, the critics will go ahead and attach their critique to women's words. An added difficulty may be the fact that Japanese society is run by intricately woven human relationships, built on associations between individuals that are established over a long period of time. Since writers are not represented by agents, as they are in the United States, once they are networked with certain critics, editors, and publishers, they tend to form close professional ties that are difficult to break.

Works Cited

Alcoff, Linda. "Cultural Feminism Versus Post-Structuralism: The Identity Crisis in Feminist Theory." *Signs* 13, no. 3 (1988): 405–36.

Ariga Chieko. "Dephallicizing Women in *Ryūkyō shinshi*: A Critique of Gender Ideology in Japanese Literature." *Journal of Asian Studies* 51, no. 3 (1992): 565–86.

———. "Politicizing Gender: Amino Kiku and the Literary Canon in Japanese Literature." In *Japanese Women: New Feminist Perspectives on Past, Present, and Future*, ed. Kumiko Fujimura-Fanselow and Atsuko Kameda. New York: Feminist Press, 1995, 43-60.

Barrett, Michèle. *Women's Oppression Today: Problems in Marxist Feminist Analysis.* London: Verso, 1980.

Barrett, Michèle, and Anne Phillips. *Destabilizing Theory: Contemporary Feminist Debates.* Stanford: Stanford University Press, 1992.

Barthes, Rolland. *S/Z.* Trans. Richard Miller. New York: Hill & Wang, 1974.

Belsey, Catherine. "Afterword: A Future for Materialist Feminist Criticism?" In *The Matter of Difference: Materialist Feminist Criticism of Shakespeare*, ed. Valerie Wayne. Ithaca, N.Y.: Cornell University Press, 1991, 257-70.

Chernin, Kim. *The Hungry Self: Women, Eating, and Identity.* London: Virgo Press, 1986.

Cixous, Hélène. "Sorties." In *New French Feminisms*, ed. Elaine Marks and Isabelle de Courtivron. New York: Schocken Books, 1981, 90–98.

de Lauretis, Teresa. "The Essence of the Triangle or, Taking the Risk of Essentialism Seriously: Feminist Theory in Italy, the U.S., and Britain." *differences: A Journal of Feminist Cultural Studies* 1, no. 2 (1989): 3–37.

Dinnerstein, Dorothy. *The Mermaid and the Minotaur: Sexual Arrangements and Human Malaise.* New York: Harper & Row, 1977.

Ebert, Teresa L. "Postmodernism's Infinite Variety." *Women's Review of Books* 8, no. 4 (Jan. 1991): 24–25.

———. "The Romance of Patriarchy: Ideology, Subjectivity, and Postmodern Feminist Cultural Theory." *Cultural Critique* 10 (1988): 19–57.

Egusa Mitsuko and Urushida Kazuyo, eds. *Onna ga yomu kindai bungaku.* Tokyo: Shin'yōsha, 1992.

Eisenstein, Zillah R. *The Radical Future of Liberal Feminism.* Boston: Northeastern University Press, 1981.

Felman, Shoshana. "Women and Madness: The Critical Phallacy." *Diacritics* 5 (1975): 2–10.

Foucault, Michel. *The Order of Things.* New York: Random House, 1970.

Fraser, Nancy. *Unruly Practices.* Minneapolis: University of Minnesota Press, 1989.

Fuss, Diana. *Essentially Speaking: Feminism, Nature and Difference*. New York: Routledge, 1989.

Greimas, A. J. *On Meaning: Selected Writings in Semiotic Theory*. Trans. Paul J. Perron and Frank H. Collins. Minneapolis: University of Minnesota Press, 1987.

Hartsock, Nancy. "Foucault on Power: A Theory for Women?" In *Feminism/Postmodernism*, ed. Linda J. Nicholson. New York: Routledge, 1987, 157–75.

Hirota Hisako. *Zoku: Gendai joshi rōdō no kenkyū*. Tokyo: Rōdōkyōiku sentā, 1990.

Ikuno Teruko. *Kyoshokushō, kashokushō to wa*. Tokyo: Mebaesha, 1993.

Illich, Ivan. *Shadow Work*. London: Marion Boyers, 1981.

Irigaray, Luce. *This Sex Which Is Not One*. Trans. Catherine Porter. Ithaca, N.Y.: Cornell University Press, 1985.

Jardine, Alice, and Paul Smith, eds. *Men in Feminism*. New York: Methuen, 1987.

Johnson, Barbara. *The Critical Difference*. Baltimore: Johns Hopkins University Press, 1980.

Kawashima-Horne, Yōko. *Joshi rōdō to rōdō shijō kōzō no bunseki*. Tokyo: Nihon keizai hyōronsha, 1985.

Keller, Evelyn Fox. *Reflections on Gender and Science*. New Haven: Yale University Press, 1985.

Kitada Sachie. "Feminizumu bungaku hihyō no genzai: Nihon hen." In Mizuta, *Nyū feminizumu rebyū*, 162–71.

Komashaku Kimi. *Majoteki bungaku ron*. Tokyo: San'ichi shobō, 1982.

———. *Murasaki Shikibu no messeeji*. Tokyo: Asahi shinbunsha, 1991.

Kōno Taeko. *Tanizaki bungaku to kōtei no yokubō*. Tokyo: Bungei shunjū, 1976.

———. "Toddler-hunting." Trans. Lucy North. *Mānoa* 3 (1991): 42–57.

———. *Yōjigari, kani*. Tokyo: Shinchō bunko, 1973.

Kuhn, Annette, and AnnMarie Wolpe, eds. *Feminism and Materialism: Women and Modes of Production*. London: Routledge & Kegan Paul, 1978.

Kurosawa Ariko. *Onna no kubi: gyakkō no Chiekoshō*. Tokyo: Domesu shuppan, 1985.

Lerner, Gerda. *The Creation of Patriarchy*. Oxford: Oxford University Press, 1986.

Lyotard, Jean-François. *The Postmodern Condition*. Trans. Geoff Bennington and Brian Massumi. Minneapolis: University of Minnesota Press, 1984.

Mascia-Lees, Frances E.; Patricia Sharpe; and Colleen Ballerino Cohen. "The Postmodernist Turn in Anthropology: Cautions from a Feminist Perspective." *Signs* 15, no. 1 (1989): 7–33.

Matsumoto Yūko. *Kyoshokushō no akenai yoake*. Tokyo: Shūeisha bunko, 1991.

Miller, Nancy K. "Changing the Subject: Authorship, Writing, and the Reader." In *Feminist Studies, Critical Studies*, ed. Teresa de Lauretis. Bloomington: Indiana University Press, 1986, 102–20.

Miyoshi Masao. "A Borderless World? From Colonialism to Transnationalism and the Decline of the Nation-State." *Critical Inquiry* 19 (1993): 726–51

Mizuta Noriko. *Feminizumu no kanata*. Tokyo: Kōdansha, 1991.

———. *Hiroin kara hiirō e*. Tokyo: Tahata shoten, 1982.

Mizuta Noriko, ed. *Nyū feminizumu rebyū 2: onna to hyōgen*. Tokyo: Gakuyō shobō, 1991.

Modleski, Tania. *Feminism Without Women: Culture and Criticism in a "Postfeminist" Age*. New York: Routledge, 1991.

Nakazawa Kei. *Umi o kanjiru toki*. Tokyo: Kōdansha bunko, 1984.

Newton, Judith, and Deborah Rosenfelt, eds. *Feminist Criticism and Social Change*. New York: Methuen, 1985.

Nicholson, Linda J., ed. *Feminism/Postmodernism*. New York: Routledge, 1987.

Oda Motoko. *Shisutemu ron to feminizumu*. Tokyo: Keisō shobō, 1990.

Ōgoshi Aiko. "Nihon shugi feminizumu o koete." *Femirōgu* (1990): 179–204.

Okude Ken. "Nakazawa Kei ron: sei kara buntai made." *Kokubungaku: kaishaku to kanshō*, special issue: "Josei sakka no shinryū 5 (1991): 98–105.

Omvedt, Gail. "'Patriarchy': The Analysis of Women's Oppression." *Insurgent Sociologist* (1986): 30–50.

Orbach, Susie. *Fat Is a Feminist Issue*. London: Hamlyn, 1979.

Ortner, Sherry. "Is Female to Male as Nature Is to Culture?" In *Women, Culture and Society*, ed. Michelle Zimbalist Rosaldo and Louise Lamphere. Stanford: Stanford University Press, 1974, 67–87.

Osawa Mari. "Corporate-Centered Society and Women's Labor in Japan Today." *U.S.-Japan Women's Journal: English Supplement* 3 (1992): 3–35.

———. *Kigyō chūshin shakai o koete*. Tokyo: Jijitsūshinsha, 1993.

Rooney, Ellen. *Seductive Reasoning*. Ithaca, N.Y.: Cornell University Press, 1989.

Rubin, Gayle. "The Traffic in Women: Notes on the 'Political Economy' of Sex." In *Toward an Anthropology of Women*, ed. Rayna R. Reiter. New York: Monthly Review Press, 1975, 157–210.

Sakurai Hiroko. "Ekorojikaru-feminizumu ronsō wa owatta ka." In *Feminizumu ronsō: nanajūnendai kara kyūjūnendai e*, ed. Ehara Yumiko. Tokyo: Keisō shobō, 1990, 119–46.

Schor, Naomi. "Dreaming Dissymmetry: Barthes, Foucault, and Sexual Difference." In Jardine and Smith, 98–110.

Seid, Roberta Pollack. *Never Too Thin: Why Women Are at War with Their Bodies*. New York: Prentice-Hall, 1989.

Sergent, Lydia, ed. *Women and Revolution*. London: Pluto Press, 1981.

Spivak, Gayatri Chakravorty. "Can the Subaltern Speak?" In *Marxism and the Interpretation of Culture*, ed. Cary Nelson et al. Chicago: University of Chicago Press, 1988, 271–313.

———. "In a Word." *differences: A Journal of Feminist Cultural Studies* 1 (1989): 124–56.

Suzuki Sadami. "Nakazawa Kei ron: bungaku suru koto." *Bungei* 25 (1986): 334-37.

Takahashi Hideo, Takubo Hideo, and Kawamura Jirō. "Sōsaku gōhyō." *Gunzō* 40 (1985): 273-92.

Takahashi Takako. *Ronrii ūman.* Tokyo: Shūeisha bunko, 1982.

Takenaka Emiko. "The Restructuring of the Female Labor Force in Japan in the 1980s." *U.S.-Japan Women's Journal* 2 (1992): 3-15.

———. *Sengo joshi rōdōshi ron.* Tokyo: Yūhikaku, 1989.

Tomioka Taeko. *Tō no koromo ni asa no fusuma.* Tokyo: Chūō kōronsha, 1984.

Ueno Chizuko. *Kafuchōsei to shihonsei: Marukusu shugi feminizumu no chihei.* Tokyo: Iwanami shoten, 1990.

———. "The Rise of Feminist Criticism." *Japanese Book News* 2 (1993): 5, 20.

Ueno Chizuko, Ogura Chikako, and Tomioka Taeko. *Danryū bungaku ron.* Tokyo: Chikuma shobō, 1992.

Volosinov, V. N. (Mikhail Bakhtin). *Marxism and the Philosophy of Language.* Trans. Ladislav Matejka and I. R. Titunik. Cambridge, Mass.: Harvard University Press, 1986.

Walby, Sylvia. *Theorizing Patriarchy.* Oxford: Basil Blackwell, 1990.

Wolf, Naomi. *The Beauty Myth.* New York: Doubleday, Anchor Books, 1991.

Yonaha Keiko. *Gendai joryū sakkaron.* Tokyo: Shinbisha, 1988.

———. "Onna no sekushuariti: gendai shōsetsu ni hyōgen sareta onna no sei." In Mizuta, *Nyū feminizumu rebyū,* 72-80.

12

Connaissance délicieuse, or the Science of Jealousy: Tsushima Yūko's "The Chrysanthemum Beetle"

LIVIA MONNET

There seems to be a consensus in the by no means substantial critical literature on the noted woman writer of fiction Tsushima Yūko (1947–)[1] that her writings dramatize a limited number of "themes" and "motifs," such as the meaninglessness and absurdity of family ties / blood relationships; the struggle of lonely, defiant women against the oppressive patriarchal institutions of marriage and the family and the regulative ideologies/fictions that support them; the revision of traditional (Japanese) definitions of motherhood and female sexuality; and the unusual, Faulknerian configuration of brother-sister incest, in which the brother is almost always mentally retarded and totally subjugated by a protective but authoritarian sister.[2] Japanese critics also agree that Tsushima's predilection for these topics reflects the writer's unusual life story and experience as a divorcee and single mother, and that many of her short fictions are autobiographical,[3] employing narrative techniques close to those of the confessional *shishōsetsu* (I-fiction). None of the critical essays on Tsushima's work that I have examined, however, attempts to construct feminist readings of her fiction[4] or to position her texts in broader sociocultural, political, and critical contexts.

The readings of the story "Kikumushi" (The chrysanthemum beetle; 1983) that I will construct in this essay are aimed both at exposing the inadequacy of the traditional methodologies of *kokubungaku kenkyū* (Japanese scholarship of the indigenous literature) and of journalistic literary criticism (*bungei hihyō*) in dealing with women's texts[5] and at countering the prevailing critical view of Tsushima's fiction as narrowly focused depictions of typically feminine experiences. My readings also dramatize, I think, a recognition that our habitual politics of reading—even the most "subversive," most staunchly feminist or most committedly "politically correct"[6]—often fail us in the face of irreverent, fantastic texts such as the one presented here, texts that resist discursive closure, as well as the critic's imperial positioning of herself at the center of the interpretive act. I hope the following pages will make clear that we need to remain alert not only to the historicity of our politics of reading—that is, the fact that familiar theories, critical strategies, and discourses arise in response to specific historico-cultural needs—but also to the fictional, ultimately mythical character of the readings we produce.

The Story "The Chrysanthemum Beetle"

"The Chrysanthemum Beetle" is included in *Ōma monogatari* (Spooky tales), a short story collection published in 1984. The protagonist of the story is Izumi, a single woman in her mid-thirties living with her mother in an apartment building on a busy Tokyo thoroughfare. In another apartment building fifteen minutes away lives her former schoolmate, Kazuko. Kazuko is also single but has a six-year-old daughter from a relationship with a married man. The story opens with a scene in Kazuko's apartment: while gazing at the white plastic cover over the fluorescent light tubes in Kazuko's living room, Izumi and Kazuko reminisce about their schooldays.

Izumi is involved with Takashi, the younger brother of the real estate agent whose family occupies the first floor in Izumi's apartment building. Takashi, who lives alone in an apartment nearby, helps his brother and sister-in-law with the cleaning and maintenance of the building. Both Izumi and Takashi seem content with a pleasant sexual intimacy, carefully avoiding a deeper emotional commitment to each other. Gradually Izumi discovers traces of another woman in Takashi's apartment. She becomes increasingly jealous but attempts to conceal her feelings from Takashi. When she discovers not only that Takashi is involved with another woman but that he has deliberately left things belonging to that woman lying around for her to notice, Izumi can no longer contain her jealousy and anger and, after a dramatic confrontation with her lover, temporarily breaks with him.

Three weeks later, Izumi meets Takashi's other girlfriend, a younger woman named Nobuko. Nobuko tells Izumi the story of her six-year relationship with Takashi, describing at length his timid, jealous nature, his immaturity and emotional instability. She also relates an incident from Takashi's schooldays that she heard from his mother and that seems to have left a deep imprint on her lover: when Takashi was in junior high, a girl in his class attempted suicide by gassing herself but was saved and sent to another school. The girl sent Takashi a postcard, saying that she wanted to die because of him and that she would come back as a ghost and curse him to death.

Not long after hearing Nobuko's story, Izumi resumes her relationship with Takashi. One day she goes to her friend Kazuko's apartment to help her clean the plastic case over the fluorescent light tubes in the latter's living room. The case is full of dead insects, from among which Kazuko's daughter retrieves a black beetle with a white pattern on its back. That evening the little girl wants to show her father the beetle, which she had wrapped in tissue paper, but the insect is no longer there. The father, astonished, tells the little girl the insect may have been a chrysanthemum beetle (*kikumushi*), which became a white butterfly and flew off into the sky. After the little girl goes to bed, the father tells Kazuko the story of Okiku, the servant who was shoved down a well as punishment for allegedly having placed a needle in her master's (who was also her lover's) plate, and whose desire for vengeance lives on in the form of the chrysanthemum beetle bearing her name (*kiku* = chrysanthemum). Later, in a conversation with Takashi while they are lying in bed together, Izumi revises the version of the Okiku legend she heard from Kazuko: not Okiku, but the jealous wife who put a needle in her husband's plate and who wrongly accused Okiku of this mischief should be regarded as the tragic heroine of the story.

Still under the spell of the legend of the unfortunate Okiku, Izumi has a vision of Takashi's transformation into countless black beetles, which subsequently turn into butterflies. The butterflies, each of which is a blissful Takashi, are borne by the wind toward heaven.

Beyond the Ending: The "Sarayashiki" (Manor of the Dishes) Tradition and the Postmodern Turn

The *sarayashiki* (Manor of the Dishes) tradition—the corpus of folk tales and legends featuring the unfortunate servant Okiku, as well as the kabuki and puppet plays based on these legends — plays a crucial role in the construction of the discursive space of "The Chrysanthemum Beetle." Before I turn to an analysis of the function of this tradition in Tsushima's story, let me anticipate one of the main motifs of the readings that follow by stating that "The Chrysanthemum Beetle" is a fantastic text which theorizes on fantasy and subverts not only the readings it engenders but also its own resistance to appropriation and renewed fantasizing by the reader. Fantasy will serve as a testing ground for my readings. In order to facilitate the interpretive activity I will conduct (and hope to seduce the reader to participate in), I will assume that three levels of discourse/narration may be distinguished in "The Chrysanthemum Beetle": a dominant/hegemonic, a residual, and an emergent level. This division is based on Raymond Williams's distinction between residual, dominant, and emergent cultures.[7]

Viewed from the perspective of Williams's tripartite division, "The Chrysanthemum Beetle" presents an interesting configuration. The Manor of the Dishes, or Okiku, tradition clearly occupies the dominant level of narration in the story. The legend recounted in Tsushima's text is a lesser known variant of this tradition: accused by the jealous wife of her master and lover to have deliberately put a needle in one of his dishes, Okiku is shoved down a well with her hands tied behind her back. To show her indignation and despair at Okiku's gruesome death, her mother throws herself into the same well and dies. Okiku's desire for vengeance lives on in the form of the chrysanthemum beetle, which has a white pattern on its back supposedly representing Okiku as she is about to be pushed down the well. It is said that this beetle eventually turns into a white butterfly and flies up to heaven.

The best-known, and most frequently dramatized, version of the Okiku legend is the one in which Okiku is put to death for having broken a precious dish belonging to the samurai household she serves. In this version Okiku's ghost appears at night and patiently counts the dishes in her charge until she reaches the missing dish, a process she repeats endlessly because the broken dish cannot be replaced. The earliest extant dramatization of this legend is the puppet play *Banshū sarayashiki* by Tamenaga Tarōbei and Asada Itchō (1741).[8] The most popular kabuki versions of the Okiku legend, most of which are adaptations/interpretations of *Banshū sarayashiki*, are Kawatake Mokuami's *Shin sarayashiki tsuki no amagasa* (1883), and Okamoto Kidō's *Banchō sarayashiki* (1916).[9]

On the residual level of the narrative in "The Chrysanthemum Beetle," we find a conflation of modern interpretations/adaptations of various versions of the legend of the Manor of the Dishes, including the versions mentioned above. If we recall the incident of the aborted suicide of Takashi's classmate in junior high and the fact that Takashi had befriended, not the girl who tried to commit suicide, but her boyfriend and, in addition, the fact that Takashi was, and continues to be, haunted by this incident, we can easily perceive the way Tsushima's story manipulates the *sarayashiki* tradition: the girl who tried to gas herself may be regarded as a conflation of Okiku and the jealous wife in the version of the legend narrated by Kazuko's lover. From the girl's perspective, Takashi, interestingly enough, would be the counterpart of Okiku, since the girl was jealous of Takashi, who claimed for himself part of the affection of the girl's boyfriend, and since the girl is, at least in part, the modern equivalent of the jealous wife of Okiku's master. But he is also the counterpart of Aoyama Tetsuzan from the puppet play *Banshū sarayashiki*: the girl = Okiku promised to come back as a ghost and torment Takashi = Tetsuzan to his death.

From the perspective of the *sarayashiki* tradition, the girl who tried to gas herself and Takashi thus appear as both victims and victimizers. The "residual" triangle girl-who-tried-to-gas-herself + her boyfriend + Takashi is replicated in the "dominant," or narrational present, triangle Izumi + Nobuko + Takashi. Both triads are re-creations of triangular relationships that appear in various versions of the Manor of the Dishes legend, which thus becomes the "residual subtext" for both the residual narrative of Takashi and his two classmates from junior high school, and the dominant narrative of Takashi, Izumi, and Nobuko. Before I comment on the implications of this discursive configuration, let me quote the passage from Nobuko's narrative on the incident of the failed suicide attempt of Takashi's classmate, as well as Izumi's visualization of the curious triangular relationship between Takashi, the girl who tried to gas herself, and her boyfriend:

> "I don't pretend to understand much about it, but it seems something happened in his early teens. I don't know how significant it might be. . . . When I'd just started living with him, we went out for a drink with a man he'd been to school with in Tokyo—in your part of town. . . .
>
> "Well, we went out together and he chatted about me and where we were living, and they reminisced, and then at some point their

conversation went like this: 'Come to the reunion!' 'Not on your life!'
Then the other man said, 'It's all right, you-know-who is in the
States, and won't give a damn about what happened all those years
ago, anyway.' When he heard that he turned pale and knocked the
man over, sending his chair crashing, then walked out and left him
lying there. The next day he still looked so fierce I didn't like to ask
what had happened with 'you-know-who.'

"Quite a time later—it would have been about four months after
that—his mother came to see how we were getting on. He wasn't in
at the time and she only stayed half an hour, but she brought up the
same subject.

"She told me that when he was at junior high a girl in his class
had transferred to another school after attempting suicide. If it hadn't
been for that unfortunate business, she said, he'd have gone on to a
good university and a job in Tokyo. 'But I suppose he's standing on
his own feet,' she said, 'and I can't ask better than that.' I wanted to
know more about the 'business' at school, because it had me worried
by this time. And his own mother admitted she couldn't make head
nor tail of it.

"The girl who attempted suicide had sent him a postcard. The
writing was so big it jumped right out at you, she said, and without
meaning to she read it. 'My life is not worth living and it's your fault.
I'll come back and curse you to your death.' The family was stunned.
They couldn't get any explanation out of him. They hoped it might
be some sort of chain letter, since kids of that age are still children
when you get down to it. But his mother was worried enough to go
to his school and make inquiries.

"She learned the girl had tried to gas herself but was saved and
afterwards sent to another school. This really horrified his mother.
She told his teacher about the postcard and asked, 'Was my boy the
cause?' The teacher answered flatly that he couldn't have been. . . .

"His mother later got hold of some of his classmates and managed indirectly to find out about his connection with the girl who'd
changed schools. The story seemed reassuring. It was actually the
girl's boyfriend he'd been friendly with from the start, and he'd had
nothing to do with the girl. . . .

"Then he chose a college even farther away and left home,
which started her thinking that perhaps she *had* seen some sort of
change come over him after what had happened. Not that she could
have asked him about it though. It had been too long ago, she said,
and he wouldn't have told her the truth. . . . What do you think,
Izumi ? . . ."

Izumi couldn't answer at once, and before she did they came to
the subway entrance, where Nobuko said simply, "Well, this is my
station." As Izumi automatically gave a slight bow of her head,

Nobuko put on a smile and went bouncily down the stairs. She didn't glance back though Izumi waited, so with a sigh Izumi started walking. At the back of her mind were the dim figures of three thirteen-year-olds: Takashi and the other boy had their arms round each other's shoulders, while on the opposite side the boy held hands with the girl as they looked happily into each other's faces. (71–73)

In view of the parallels and convergences between "The Chrysanthemum Beetle" and the *sarayashiki* tradition described above, Tsushima's text may be said to be structured by a spatiotemporal dimension that is strikingly reminiscent of Ernst Bloch's concept of non-synchronicity/non-synchronism. Bloch argues that we live in several different times and spaces at once, and that this phenomenon, which he calls non-synchronism, may be found both in real life and in the fictions we ceaselessly produce. "Not all people exist in the same Now. They do so only externally, by virtue of the fact that they may all be seen today. But that does not mean that they are living at the same time with others" (22). Takashi, Izumi, and Nobuko thus appear to live simultaneously in several times and spaces both with respect to the Manor of the Dishes tradition and with respect to the incident of the aborted suicide of Takashi's former classmate.

Another dimension of non-synchronicity may be found in the structure of the narratives of the lives of Izumi, Takashi, and Nobuko as presented to us by Tsushima's text. The stories these characters tell each other about each other's lives (the narrativization/textualization of lived experience is foregrounded in "The Chrysanthemum Beetle," and Nobuko, Izumi, and Takashi become each other's biographers/psychoanalysts) and, in addition, the narrative that frames all these stories and links them to one another — the text of "The Chrysanthemum Beetle" as a whole — combines premodern, modern, and postmodern features that are attuned to residual/traditional, dominant/hegemonic, and emergent forms of culture. This phenomenon points to the ambiguity of the present historical moment as described by Steven Best and Douglas Kellner: "We might want to speak of postmodern phenomena as only emergent tendencies within a still dominant modernity that is haunted as well by various forms of residual, traditional cultures, or which intensify key dynamics of modernity, such as innovation and fragmentation. Our present moment, in this view, is thus a contradictory transitional situation which does not yet allow any unambiguous affirmations concerning an alleged leap into full-blown postmodernity" (279–80).

Two discourses in "The Chrysanthemum Beetle" best illustrate not only the non-synchronism and the working of fantasy and irony but also the construction of theory (theory-as-fiction / fiction-as-theory) and the coexistence of the three forms of culture described above in this text. These are, first, what I would call the entomological discourse and, second, the "theme" of jealousy.

The Entomological Discourse

"The Chrysanthemum Beetle" is a story teeming with insects. We are figuratively assailed by insects at almost every step in our exploration of this text. Two instances discussed above are the dead insects in the florescent light fixture in Kazuko's room, from which Kazuko's daughter selects a beetle with a white pattern, and the legend of the *kikumushi*. But numerous other narrative moments feature insects. For example, Izumi reminisces about her curious habit, in her last year in high school, of killing winged ants attracted by the desk lamp in her room, piling up their dead bodies in little mounds, and counting them every night (417). Kazuko tells Izumi that her six-year-old daughter is "awfully keen on insects" (75). In his discussion with Izumi about the legend of Okiku, Takashi remarks that the end of this folk tale, as related by the father of Kazuko's daughter, is a little farfetched (i.e., scientifically untenable) (77).[10] Izumi's fantasy of Takashi as countless *kikumushi* that turn into white butterflies is, of course, the most impressive instance of "entomological discourse" in this story:

> She glanced at Takashi's head. His stiff hair was slightly wavy. She pictured scores of tiny black insects turning one by one to white butterflies and wavering into the air. Was Takashi conjuring up the same scene and watching enraptured? Izumi stood up distractedly.
>
> Each of the chrysanthemum beetles is Takashi, and when its body becomes vaguely restive and itchy it begins gradually changing shape, growing softer, till it exhales deeply and wafts upward like a petal. Hey, he says, exhilarated, this feels great! The same thing is happening over here, and there too. And every one of them is Takashi himself. Glancing around he sees a great many fluttering white butterflies, like a shower of blossoms. I thought I was in big trouble when I first turned into an insect, but if this is what happens it's not so bad, Takashi thinks with a blissful smile. Though now that his body is a butterfly's, being lighter, it works differently from a black beetle's and he can't move the way he wants at all. Wafting gently on the breeze is comfortable, though he supposes it's an uncertain kind of comfort. . . .

Takashi sat up and looked at her. Izumi smiled, with a touch of embarrassment. (79)

The *sarayashiki* tradition, which determines to a great extent as we have seen, the configuration of the dominant and the residual levels of narration in "The Chrysanthemum Beetle," not only testifies to the continued vitality and significance of traditional, residual cultures in the "dominant modernity" lived by the characters in the text (the fact that the social and cultural landscape—Japan in the first half of the 1980's—in which the characters in Tsushima's story move is hardly one of "full-blown postmodernity"[11] is attested to by a number of textual instances I will discuss in the following sections) but also gives rise to conscious/unconscious identifications, as well as a variety of complicated emotions in one more triangular relationship: that of Kazuko, her lover, and her lover's wife. In this relationship, Kazuko may be equated with Okiku, her longtime lover is the counterpart of Okiku's master, and his wife is, of course, the counterpart of the jealous wife in the Okiku/*kikumushi* legend. Ironically Kazuko = Okiku both longs for and dreads the vengeance of her lover's wife. The wife, however, not only is not jealous but has never shown the slightest inclination to meet her husband's longtime mistress.

The text also suggests, with even more devastating irony, that Kazuko not only wishes to be killed, out of jealousy, by her lover's wife, but that she *may* have been killed, that is, she is a living ghost who has to go on living in order to incite the other woman's jealousy! In other words, in terms of the tradition of the Manor of the Dishes, Kazuko may be said to lead a double existence, as both living being and ghost, on the one hand—since she is the one who carries through her "vengeance" against her lover's wife by having a child with him—and as both Okiku and the jealous wife of the original legend, on the other hand. The supreme irony in this view is, of course, that Kazuko = Okiku is, so to speak, forced to avenge herself against herself, to be a double victim, before she can obtain full membership in a community living in the present. Significantly, Kazuko has such an ambiguous status that she is almost never granted full membership in any community: not only is she barred from enjoying the same rights as her lover's wife but also, in terms of the Okiku legend that she unconsciously stages in her life, she paradoxically plays a subordinate role. She cannot become a tragic heroine like Okiku unless she dies, and she obviously cannot die because her rival is determined to ignore her existence. Moreover, from the perspective of the story as a whole, Kazuko is a marginal character, not only because she appears mostly as a character in a story, told either by herself (45-48) or by other characters about her (76-77) but also because she plays the part of ushering in Izumi and her story while serving as a foil to bring the latter character into clearer focus.

Let us now listen to Kazuko, as she describes her relationship with her daughter's father and presents her views on jealousy before she hears the story of Okiku:

> "But I wasn't intending to have a baby from the start," Kazuko replied, staring at the palm of her hand.
>
> "Something made you get more deeply involved, didn't it ? Not the baby, and not him either. . . ."
>
> Kazuko didn't answer at once.
>
> "Well, that's one way of looking at it," she said at length. "Since his wife wasn't the type to lose her head, I may have wanted to know how she *would* take it. If she hadn't been so tolerant of her husband's affair, perhaps I wouldn't have had the baby. . . . It's hard work making someone jealous."
>
> "I'd have thought it was easy."
>
> "As long as it's not important, yes. But when you brace yourself for a showdown, nothing happens. I longed for a scene, for his wife to burst in here on the rampage with a knife in her hand. . . . I'd sigh over those stories when I saw them in the papers. When you think about it, though, she may have been longing for me to do the same. Not longing, exactly, but clinging to a hope. . . ."
>
> Izumi shifted her gaze beyond the glass doors of the balcony as she said, "What it comes down to, in fact, is that no one wants to be killed out of jealousy. Or there'd be murder everywhere."
>
> Kazuko was also gazing out at the trees. ". . . True, but there comes a time when—without knowing how you reached that point—you're convinced that's really the only thing left. Not that you want to be killed, but the time comes when you suddenly know you *have* been. . . . You can't drop your guard." (48)

When told the story of Okiku by her lover, Kazuko is struck by the uncanny similarities between her experience and the legend of Okiku. Her reaction, at this recognition, is one of fear and instinctive rejection of the invisible bond that ties her to Okiku: "'She [Kazuko] says she can't believe it was really such a remarkable insect,' Izumi told Takashi, 'but the thought of it woke her up in the night with the shivers'" (76-77).

As for the connection between Izumi, Kazuko, and Nobuko and the tradition of the Manor of the Dishes, I think we can say that Izumi and Kazuko activate a "premodern sensibility" in their identification with Okiku and the jealous wife in the version of the Okiku legend known to them (as well as in the various other versions that may have influenced Tsushima's text). Nobuko, by contrast, may be said to identify with Takashi's classmate in junior high school who attempted suicide—that is, she also identifies with Okiku and the jealous wife since the girl who attempted suicide is, as we have seen, a conflation of these two characters. Unlike Izumi and Kazuko, however, who participate in the transmission and conservation of the *sarayashiki* tradition (as well as the residual culture in which this tradition is embedded) by narrating and commenting on it and, in the case of Izumi, even revising it, Nobuko is allowed only an indirect participation in / identification with this tradition, a participation/identification that is, of course, unconscious. For Nobuko is not aware of the correspondences between the experience of the girl who committed suicide and the legend of Okiku.

In other words, Izumi and Kazuko consciously allow premodern ethics, attitudes, and frames of mind to intervene in their "modern" lives, whereas Nobuko allows a threatening residual culture to overshadow her relationship with Takashi through a move of unconscious identification that I have called, in an essay on Tsushima's story "Fusehime" (1984), a meta-textual, karmic discursive operation.[12] That is to say, the relationship between Nobuko and Takashi is influenced by Okiku's premodern karma for reasons that not only are independent of Nobuko's will but also are never revealed to her. This karmic influence, moreover, occurs unbeknownst to Nobuko, although, as readers, we are aware of the fact that the karmic interference in Nobuko's experience is the outcome of the compositional design of the story, which, as I showed above, is structured to a great extent by the *sarayashiki* tradition. Both the narrative Nobuko tells Izumi about the suicide attempt of Takashi's classmate and the continuation of this narrative after the two women leave the Italian restaurant in which they had dinner attest to Nobuko's continuing preoccupation with the suicide incident (71–72).

If we place these observations in the context of Bloch's theory of non-synchronism, we can easily see that Izumi, Kazuko, and Nobuko not only live in several different times and spaces at once but also share at least some of these other times and spaces without knowing it. Since one of these times and spaces of difference is an entomologic one—the version of the Okiku legend presented in this text is, after all, the story of an *insect*—it follows that Izumi, Nobuko, and Kazuko share a *different order of being* without necessarily being aware of this commonality. The three women have been, are, and will and can become insects at any time. We find evidence of the "entomological identity" of these characters scattered throughout the text: Izumi and Nobuko are attracted to Takashi like moths flying blindly, and in Izumi's fantasy Takashi is the chrysanthemum beetle that turns into a white butterfly—that is, he is Okiku. Since Izumi, Nobuko, and Kazuko identify, either consciously or unconsciously, with Okiku, it follows that they can become (*o*)*kikumushi* and, subsequently, white butterflies as effortlessly as Takashi does in Izumi's fantasy.

Izumi relates how she and her family used to kill hawk moths with wet newspapers (46) and how she swatted winged ants that landed on her desk (47). For her part, Kazuko is so frightened by the dead insects piling up in the case of the fluorescent tubes in her living room that she endlessly postpones cleaning it (46, 73). These instances suggest the equally fantastic possibility that Izumi and Kazuko act cruelly toward insects because they fear that their "real" insect nature might be betrayed by their kind. Although this would seem to link "The Chrysanthemum Beetle" with the nightmarish, dystopian world of Kafka's "Metamorphosis," the lovely vision conjured by Izumi of Takashi as a chrysanthemum beetle suggests a critique of modern anthropocentric theories and discourses, including that of evolution, as well as the imperative to view our interaction with the environment from the margins, from outside ourselves.

Rosemary Jackson has argued that all manifestations of the fantastic imagination attempt "to compensate for a lack resulting from cultural constraints" and seek "that which is perceived as absence or loss" (3). The different aspects of the entomological discourse in "The Chrysanthemum Beetle," especially the fantasy of a social order of human insects, certainly express such a lack or loss and the desire to overcome it. None of the main characters in the story is happy with her/his present circumstances; all of them appear to be longing for a change. Takashi, whose job consists in helping his sister-in-law with the cleaning and maintenance of the apartment building where Izumi lives, not only looks just as fed up with this work as the principal caretaker but vehemently protests Izumi's insinuation that he eats at his brother's house and states that he agreed to help his brother and his wife only because he wanted to use them to his advantage:

> Glimpsed from the side, his features wore the sulky look of a child forced to do as he is told, helping his parents with hated chores. . . . Perhaps Takashi caught the hint of sarcasm in her inquiry, for he answered with a rancor that startled her, "I don't go to their goddamn place, why the hell should I? . . . I simply thought I could use them. That's all they're good for, the lot of them," Takashi muttered, this time without expression. (50–51)

There is little enthusiasm, either, in Izumi's attitude toward her job: "She described the job she'd been doing as a buyer of imported sheet music since leaving college ten years earlier. Though not without complaints, she added that it was too late to think of doing anything else" (53).

All the female characters in "The Chrysanthemum Beetle" express various degrees of discomfort with or resistance to the assignment of gender-specific roles, as well as the discursive construction, the socialization, and the repression of sexuality by the powerful patriarchal order in which they live. Izumi, for instance, is ashamed of her situation as an unmarried woman in her thirties who still lives with her mother and of her unfulfilled and unexpressed sexual desires, which seem to her unsuitable for a woman of her age: "She didn't want to believe that what had prompted Takashi toward a sexual relationship was his seeing the hunger deep down in her body and, moreover, recognizing her limitation: that at this late stage she wasn't going to be able to leave her mother's side" (58). The passage also seems to point to the anomalous subject position of unmarried working women in their thirties (women past the generally accepted marriageable age) in contemporary Japanese society, an impression confirmed by available studies and statistics. Sociologist Ueno Chizuko (1), for instance, points out that, despite the dramatic changes in Japanese women's labor in the past two decades and the image of the liberated "career woman" presented by the mass media, in the 1980's full-time working women in their thirties made up only 20 percent of this age group—this figure includes unmarried, divorced, and widowed women as well as those without children.[13]

Despite the text's undeniably critical perspective on the reality of Japanese society in the 1980's, the entomological speculations and fantasies in "The Chrysanthemum Beetle" clearly do not aim at formulating either a post-Marxist critique of mass culture in contemporary Japan or a Marxist-feminist analysis of changing patterns in women's labor and/or of the unequal treatment of women in the workplace. Its fantastic configuration notwithstanding, the entomological discourse in this text also cannot be said to articulate "a fantasy of power that would revise the social grammar in which women are never defined as subjects" and that "disdains a sexual exchange in which women participate only as objects of circulation" — a discursive practice that Nancy K. Miller (41) identifies as one of the major characteristics of modern and contemporary women's fiction. Rather than placing women in a position of power, the variations on the legend of Okiku, as well as the intricate network of visible and invisible relations they create between the characters in Tsushima's story, reveal alternative economies of desire that are like magic-filled hologram projections of the present transitional moment. One might argue that Izumi's vision of Takashi as a chrysanthemum beetle does indeed place Izumi in a position of superiority and advantage over her lover, but this position reveals itself on closer examination as quite precarious: not only is Izumi, as a potential human insect, subject to a sudden transformation like Takashi's, but this fantasy remains, after all, a mere fantasy, which will affect neither the configuration of Izumi's relationship with Takashi nor the "social grammar" in which the two interact.

That is to say, these fantastic alternative economies can be evoked not only because individuals in late capitalist, informational societies such as Japan's have more leisure and easier access to knowledge than inhabitants of other social orders but also because the mass of available information is manipulated in such a way as to create a sense of continuity with the past and the future alike, as well as the illusion of an unlimited ability of the individual to intervene in and alter these histories. At the same time, these economies of desire, as suggested above, have a critical potential that transcends the moment in time in which they originate. Izumi's fantasy in the final scene of the story is also indicative, not of an "impulse to power" (Miller, 41) or of a desire to colonize the future, but of a utopian impulse, which may not be able to resolve present contradictions and problems and prevent future disasters but can at least create a dream space of *jouissance*, a lightness of being, and an uninhibited freedom, seemingly free of gender, class, racial, and other inequities.

The Discourse of Jealousy

The discourse of jealousy in "The Chrysanthemum Beetle" offers fertile ground for speculation on the positionality of this text, that is, on the question of whether it straddles modernity and postmodernity or whether it may be regarded as an emergent literary product pointing to new possibilities in the cultural landscape of present-day Japan. Jealousy may certainly be viewed as the central "theme" of the story: the text is framed by two conversations centering on jealousy, and in between these conversations are several narratives in which jealousy plays a prominent role. In the opening conversation between Kazuko and Izumi (quoted above), the former describes her efforts to make the wife of her lover jealous, going even so far as to state that she (Kazuko) would not have given birth if it had not been for the keen competition with her rival for the affections of the man the two women are obliged to "share" (48). In the closing scene, Izumi and Takashi discuss the version of the Okiku legend recounted by Kazuko's lover. As mentioned above, Izumi revises this legend by assigning to the jealous wife a position of tragic heroine at least as important as Okiku's and by interpreting Okiku as an ambiguous character, rather remote from the figure of the innocent victim haunting the numerous variants of the *sarayashiki* tradition, and by emphasizing the role of the audience in the construction of this tradition.

Thus, Izumi sees Okiku as an insensitive, conceited young woman who let her master's infatuation with her "go to her head" and forgot her status as a mere servant. In Izumi's interpretation of the aftermath of Okiku's gruesome death, the unfortunate maid owes her transformation into an insect — her "immortality" — not to her own desire to remind the world of her thirst for vengeance but to the reluctance of the audience of this legend (readers, spectators, actors, storytellers) to release Okiku from her consuming grudge against the employers who put her to death and to let her be reborn in paradise. This reluctance to "save" Okiku stems, in Izumi's view, from the audience's jealousy/envy of the unfortunate young woman, who was able to inspire such strong sentiments that popular imagination has enshrined her as a legendary figure. Here is Izumi's disrespectful reinterpretation of the legend.

"But if Okiku really existed, I wonder what became of the jealous wife, who must have existed too?"

"After the truth got out she was probably investigated, but she hadn't committed murder directly. . . . I don't know. In those days, maybe she'd have had to kill herself, and they'd have told her to get on with it."

"I guess the husband would be beheaded, since he was the direct culprit. But when you think about it, wouldn't the wife's spirit have more reason than Okiku's to come back from the grave? It all started with her husband falling for a maid, which was mortifying enough, but she didn't have the right to dismiss her. So she'd have tried to drive her out. But maybe Okiku wasn't a very sensitive girl. If she had been, you'd think she'd have found some way of getting round the wife, getting into her good books. Or maybe, knowing the master loved her, Okiku let it go to her head. Anyway, the wife's bitterness escalates till she puts a needle in the husband's dinner. It would never have killed him. It was surely no more than a silly piece of mischief. But the husband flies into a rage and has Okiku killed—though his wife may have encouraged that—and then even Okiku's mother throws herself accusingly down the same well. They can't hush it up any longer, and the wife finally has to commit suicide. The husband curses her on the way to his execution. It must have been a nightmare for her from beginning to end. And all because her husband couldn't keep his hands off the servants. There'd be no rest for her soul. What comfort could there be for a grievance like that? So her ghost still comes out at night. You know, I begin to feel sorry for her, somehow. . . ."

"No one knows what really happened. And her story and Okiku's aren't the same—class would have entered into it, too. No, you can say what you like but Okiku's the heroine," Takashi said, watching Izumi's face.

Izumi nodded. "And anybody will tell you that Okiku was a beauty, and the jealous wife was ugly. . . . No, you're right, I suppose. The story of the jealous wife doesn't give people a thrill. With a woman like Okiku, now, in a position of weakness, the plaything of destiny bewailing her fate as she goes to a tragic death—a woman like that doesn't actually mean much to us, so we can afford to be fascinated by her and think 'how lovely.' How lovely it must feel to inspire such jealousy. I'm sure that's why Okiku's story has become so famous. We can forget ourselves and share just a little of Okiku's pleasure . . . That's not such a bad thing, you know, because meanwhile we're spared being jealous of anybody at all. . . .

". . . But we won't allow Okiku eyes and a mouth like ours. Or arms that she could move freely. If she so much as opened her mouth or took a look out of her eyes we'd want to beat the daylights out of her—the shameless hussy. We're as jealous as that. And Okiku's ghost knows it, so all she ever shows is her back view as she falls into the old well. . . . Perhaps her spirit still roams not because she can't rest but because we won't let her. For a woman as enviable as Okiku, wanting paradise would be too greedy altogether." (77–79)

In between the opening and ending conversations, we witness the main narrative of the growing intimacy between Takashi and Izumi, on the one hand, and of the drama of mystery and suspense Takashi deliberately stages, by placing "suggestive feminine items" (63) in his apartment in such a way as to incite Izumi's jealousy, on the other. In this main narrative are embedded two more narratives that dramatize jealousy: the story of Nobuko's relationship with Takashi; and the story, related by Nobuko, of the suicide attempt of Takashi's classmate. Through Nobuko's narrative about her six-year involvement with Takashi, we learn that Takashi is "timid and extremely jealous" (69), and that he, though fully aware of his own weaknesses, nevertheless "doesn't believe he'd be capable of it [i.e., jealousy] himself," dismissing the "very idea" as "ridiculous" (71). We learn also that Nobuko, like Izumi a victim of Takashi's "tricks" to make her "aware of this three-way arrangement by the most concrete means he could think of" (70), is just as jealous of her rival Izumi as Izumi is of her: "'Izumi, what do you think of jealousy? I've got jealousy on the brain — he's had that effect on me'" (70).

There are several instances of theorizing on jealousy in "The Chrysanthemum Beetle." Apart from Izumi's and Kazuko's brief meditations in the opening conversation ("'What it comes down to, in fact, is that no one wants to be killed out of jealousy. Or there'd be murders everywhere.' . . . 'True, but there comes a time when — without knowing how you reached that point — you're convinced that's really the only thing left'" [48]), we encounter, for instance, Izumi's definition of jealousy in response to Nobuko's query about this peculiar state of mind: "'Well . . . the usual answer is possessiveness, isn't it? But it strikes me that's not quite it. . . . Could it be pride? A state where no matter what you do you can't have confidence in yourself — that might be more like it'" (70).

The central narrative about the relationship between Izumi and Takashi contains stunning descriptions of Izumi's elaborate speculations and imaginative detective work to construct, on the basis of the evidence provided by the various "women's things" scattered in Takashi's apartment — a women's magazine, two matching coffee mugs, several long hairs on the bathroom floor, a gold chain, a stocking—a coherent story—namely, the narrative of Takashi's involvement with another woman. Here is a sample of such convoluted speculating, hypothesizing and imagining, operations that are, of course, activated by Izumi's jealousy and suspicions that there is "something fishy going on" (64).

> It was then that Izumi was first struck by something different, something she couldn't accept. In front of Takashi she kept her displeasure well hidden, but after returning home she choked and began to tremble. What was he up to ? Those mugs were an exceedingly theatrical prop, no matter how she looked at it. Being Takashi, he was hardly likely to have checked carefully around his rooms in case there was anything Izumi shouldn't see. And yet he did have a fastidious streak: his sharp eyes noticed things dropped in the street, right down to ten yen coins and rubber bands. He must have been aware of those mugs whether he liked it or not. And the mugs weren't all: even if he hadn't been consciously checking, shouldn't his eyes have taken in the women's magazine, the bag of biscuits, the hairs on the bathroom tiles? She could see Takashi glance at the bathroom floor, notice the hairs, and stare at them for several seconds before laughing grimly and leaving. But that might not be the worst of it: she could also see Takashi inspect the bathroom floor, take a closer look in the waste-paper basket and under the mat where hairs tended to catch, pick out two or three which by their length were clearly a woman's and, with a grin, carefully position them in the middle of the floor. On the point of throwing out the woman's forgotten magazine with a bunch of old newspapers, he might have remembered that it was the day Izumi came and put the pile back in the kitchen, leaving the magazine on top where she couldn't miss it. What if he hadn't actually been using the mugs with the woman, either, but had deliberately taken them from the shelf and placed them in the draining rack, then gone over to the bed and surveyed the kitchen, smiling faintly? "Yes," he'd say, "that'll do nicely for today." (59–60)

The numerous instances of theorizing and fantasizing on, or because of, jealousy in "The Chrysanthemum Beetle" allow us, it seems to me, to argue that this text is deliberately attempting to construct not only a theory of knowledge, an epistemology or science of jealousy, but also a new radical theory of fantasy. Although Izumi's speculations on the "suggestive feminine items" in Takashi's apartment do not display the nearly ostentatious familiarity with modern scientific knowledge that we find in the endless questionings and hypotheses of the jealous narrator in Proust's *La prisonnière*,[14] they certainly present what Mal-

colm Bowie, referring to the discourse of jealousy in this celebrated
novel, describes as a "dynamics of knowing, a portrait of the mind in
process" (58). Izumi wants to know to whom the various feminine
objects in Takashi's apartment belong, what Takashi's intention was
in staging this puzzle for her to solve, what he thinks about her and
their relationship (60–61). Even after she discovers Takashi's "nasty
scheme" — "making deliberate use of women's things all this time in
order to test Izumi's reaction" (64–65) — after she meets Nobuko, listens to her story, and resumes her relationship with Takashi, Izumi
must still admit that "I don't know you very well yet. Really, you're
full of things I don't know yet" (79). When Izumi bursts into a fit of
rage, acknowledging her jealousy, Takashi admits that he had left
"women's things" for Izumi to see because he did not know what she
was "really thinking" (65). Like Izumi, Takashi also becomes absorbed in endless hypothesizing and fantasizing about the women
with whom he is involved, trying to determine whether they are jealous, what they think of him, and the like. As Nobuko perceptively describes him:

> "He goes through life dreading his own jealous nature, so that as
> soon as he finds a relationship that takes some of the pressure off — as
> I did, and you did — he can't rest until he's satisfied himself that the
> other person is jealous too. And while he's at it he seems to lose his
> own balance. It's both a disappointment and a relief when it turns
> out that we are jealous, and then he starts brooding over what makes
> us that way, which leads him into very deep water." (71)

The goal of "The Chrysanthemum Beetle," then, appears to be to
seduce us into subscribing to a set of axioms that are strikingly similar
to those programatically inscribed in the politics of interpretation
proposed by Proust's *La prisonnière* and *Du côté de chez Swann* (in a
certain sense the whole opus of *A la recherche du temps perdu* may be
described as a monument of hermeneutics as well as an equally
monumental exegesis of its own hermeneutic practices): jealousy as
"a quest for knowledge" (Bowie, 58). Knowledge is truth (to know is
to have access to truth); all the characters in Tsushima's text (and by
extension, all individuals) experience various phases and aspects of a
"jealous inquiry," for which they activate "inductive and hypothetico-
deductive methods" (Bowie, 55). Not content with merely constructing an epistemology of jealousy, however, "The Chrysanthemum
Beetle" suggests that jealousy is the obligatory premise of all scientific

inquiry, that all science is based on jealousy. In an even grander and more totalizing fashion, the text also seems to claim that all human relations are motivated by / based on jealousy and that love is sustained solely by jealousy. Jealousy is a primary impulse, as basic and unavoidable as sexual desire, and can become indistinguishable from sexual desire. This is attested by passages such as the following: "Whenever she went to Takashi's room she was made to feel the presence of another woman, but she reprimanded herself—just because she was sexually involved, did she have to instantly turn on the silly suspicions?—and decided to take no notice" (59).

In *La prisonnière* and *Du côté de chez Swann*, however, "the idea that the lover may become an honorary scientist or scholar by virtue of his jealous calculations and hypotheses is present as an insistent refrain" (Bowie, 50). Moreover, the pathological curiosity motivating the jealous inquiry is celebrated as a "passion for truth" and its methods of investigation are defended time and again as "methods of scientific investigation with a genuine intellectual value and legitimately employable in the search for truth" (Proust, *Du côté de chez Swann*, 274). "The Chrysanthemum Beetle," by contrast, emphasizes the *visual aspect*, the role of the *gaze* and of *fantasy* in the practice of the jealous inquiry / science of jealousy and the epistemology it proposes. Thus, not only does Takashi incite Izumi's curiosity and "passion for truth" by placing "suggestive feminine items" in conspicuous places for her to *see*, but several passages in the text suggest that there can be no epistemology / poetics / metaphysics of jealousy without a preliminary, thoroughly visual investigation. The speculative, philosophical-epistemological work of the "jealous intellect" (Bowie, 59) is preceded and sustained by the work of the ravenous, inquisitive gaze. Three passages from "The Chrysanthemum Beetle" admirably describe how the inquisitive gaze feeds the jealous intellect, providing it with the foundation on which it then erects its fantastic imaginary architecture.

> What had been in Izumi's eyes as she watched Takashi laughing? For he'd been aware of her gaze. And that wouldn't have been the only time; he'd been aware all along. Aware of Izumi's eyes slipping furtively away and yet always pursuing, never letting him escape her attention, watching avidly for her chance. Had he muttered, smiling tightly to himself, "Oh, her"? The idea made Izumi stiffen with shame. At the same time she felt the man had shown himself in a sinister light. How could he have noticed a woman's covert gaze? Or had her eyes begun to pursue him so openly? (55)

Yet no matter how sternly she warned herself, her eyes went about their work as acutely as before. After a number of visits she could tell it wasn't her imagination. There was a women's magazine which Takashi couldn't possibly want to read on top of the stack of old newspapers in the kitchen. Two or three long hairs lay on the bathroom floor. They weren't Takashi's and Izumi's own hair was short. A bag of raisin biscuits had been stuffed into the china cabinet. (59)

Izumi reminded herself that she couldn't call Takashi to account, whatever he might be doing or thinking when she wasn't there, because her own eyes were roving restlessly over Takashi's head in hopes of a man who would come if she asked him to her mother's apartment, or, failing that, at least let her complain in peace about her mother—but the next thing that those eyes fell on was two coffee mugs left upside down in the dish rack in Takashi's kitchen. (59)

The function of the jealous gaze in "The Chrysanthemum Beetle" substantiates Teresa de Lauretis's contention that spectatorship (viewing) is a "site of productive relations" (51). It is certainly Izumi's intent to watch over Takashi, like that of a spectator following the movements of the actors on the screen, that causes him to respond, thus causing a "productive relation" to emerge between the two of them. The consequent relationship between Izumi and Takashi is productive in the various senses examined above: it manipulates traditional gender hierarchies, participates in the transmission and conservation of residual cultures and traditions even while questioning and revising them, and constructs its own narratives, myths, and hermeneutic practices. Moreover, the representation of the female jealous subject in Tsushima's text is characterized by identifications that de Lauretis locates in the position of the female spectator in cinema. And I think the reader will agree that Izumi, Nobuko, and Kazuko are cast in the position of the spectator often, if not throughout most of the text; each of them watches not only Takashi and other people but also one another, as well as herself.[15] The identifications de Lauretis mentions are (1) "the masculine, active identification with the gaze (the looks of the camera and of the male characters) and the passive, feminine identification with the image (body, landscape)" (144); and (2) a figural, double identification with "the figure of narrative movement, the mythical subject, and with the figure of narrative closure, the narrative image" (144). De Lauretis describes the functioning of the second figural identification as follows:

Were it not for the possibility of this second, figural identification, the woman spectator would be stranded between two incommensurable entities, the gaze and the image. Identification, that is, would be either impossible, split beyond any act of suture, or entirely masculine. The figural narrative identification, on the country, is double; both figures can and in fact must be identified with at once, for they are inherent in narrativity itself. It is this narrative identification that assures "the hold of the image," the anchoring of the subject in the flow of the film's movement. (144)

"The Chrysanthemum Beetle" presents female jealous subjects/spectators who enact double figural identifications in the flow of narrativity—for example, Izumi and Nobuko identify both with Okiku = the figure of narrative movement or the mythical subject and with Takashi = the figure of narrative closure or the narrative image. It also presents at least one male jealous subject, Takashi, who is, interestingly enough, cast in a position of "to-be-looked-at-ness"—to use Laura Mulvey's apt term (314)—a position that is traditionally identified as feminine in the patriarchal social order. As if to make matters worse for Takashi's gender identity, the text writes off his masculinity altogether and unhesitatingly transforms him, through Izumi's fantasy, into an (o)kikumushi, that is, into a reincarnation of Okiku, which puts poor Takashi in the shoes of the quintessential female victim. (Okiku is described by Izumi as "the plaything of destiny bewailing her fate as she goes to a tragic death" [78].)

Because of these wry, ironic textual moves and manipulations and the convergences of Tsushima's text with recent feminist film theory, I would venture a few more interpretations. First, the narrative space inhabited by the jealous subjects in this story is a space of "femininity," or rather what Rey Chow calls "image-as-feminized space" (*Woman and Chinese Modernity*, 18).[16] Second, the dynamic of the jealous inquiry in "The Chrysanthemum Beetle" is not only voyeuristic and "scientific," but also cinematic, for Izumi's remarkably vivid visualization, quoted above, of the way Takashi arranged "women's things" to incite her jealousy, clearly consists of "filmic images." Third, the epistemology/metaphysics/poetics of jealousy, as well as the mode of jealous inquiry posited by Tsushima's text, is feminine not in the arrogant masculinist sense advertised by Takashi ("women want you to be jealous, that's all they ever think about" [71]) but in the sense of a feminine potential for subversion, deconstruc-

tion, revision, or replacement of existing paradigms. Thus, the epistemology of jealousy proposed by "The Chrysanthemum Beetle" is
both a metaphysics and a poetics: it is a metaphysics because it has all
the traits of the science of jealousy constructed by the narrator in
Proust's *La prisonnière* in the course of his interminable mental calculations and hypotheses. This is how Malcolm Bowie describes the
metaphysical dimension of the epistemology of jealousy in *La prisonnière* and *Du côté de chez Swann*:

> But over and against these emotional and moral penalties the jealous
> lover hears, and heeds, an imperious call to know. His privilege is to
> be summoned to the limits of what is thinkable, and to risk every-
> thing for a glimpse of what lies beyond. Overshadowing the promise
> of sexual satisfaction another, improbable, order of pleasure is seen:
> that of a mind suddenly confronted by, and able to grasp, "une
> étroite section lumineuse pratiquée à même l'inconnu" (a luminous
> section cut out of the unknown). (Bowie, 45)[17]

The discourse of jealousy in Tsushima's text may be regarded as a poetics because jealousy in this story, as in Proust's novels, functions as
a semiotic model for the making of fictions.[18]

Another possibility suggested by the epistemology of jealousy
projected by "The Chrysanthemum Beetle" is that of the narrative
space / sociocultural landscape that frames this epistemology — namely, contemporary, affluent Japan (or, more precisely, Japan in the
1980's) — as a feminized discursive space controlled by a feminine
symbolic order of jealousy. Although this may seem an overly generalizing statement that erases the various strategies of resistance/
affirmation of difference articulated by the text, it is nevertheless
substantiated by the latter: Izumi uses the plural pronoun "we" to
lend additional weight to her resistant reading of the legend of the
Manor of the Dishes (78–79). And the theorizations of jealousy scattered throughout the story also allow us to ascribe to it a "representative" status, that is, to assume that "The Chrysanthemum Beetle" reproduces the state of affairs in Japan in the particular historical moment when it was created.

The representation of the female jealous subject as spectator and
the cinematic structure of the narrative in "The Chrysanthemum Beetle" enable us to locate two sets of identifications in the position of
Izumi, Nobuko, and Kazuko — namely, a masculine, active identification with the gaze and a feminine, passive one with the image, on the
one hand, and a double, figural identification with the mythical sub-

ject and the narrative image, on the other. But we should bear in mind that the mode of jealous inquiry as described in this story and in other texts in which jealousy figures prominently, such as the two novels by Proust mentioned above, Enchi Fumiko's novel *Onna men* (Masks; 1958), and Robbe-Grillet's novel *La jalousie* (1957), is also constituted by identification. If we consider that any identification, as Judith Butler has demonstrated, is a fantasy within a fantasy, "a double imagining that produces the effect of the empirical other fixed in an interior topos," and that gender not only is constituted by identification but also is at the same time "the disciplinary production of the figures of gender fantasy through the play of presence and absence in the body's surface, the construction of the gendered body through a series of exclusions and denials, signifying absences" (334–35), two more ironic plays of signification enacted by "The Chrysanthemum Beetle" become apparent. The epistemology/science of jealousy posited by this text is a science of fantasy, literally a *science fiction*, and the feminized discursive space of contemporary Japan that is equally projected by this story and that is controlled by the Symbolic Law of Jealousy (as much as by the Law of the Father) is a fantasy.

However, fantasy is also reality, not only because it is constructed by "real" characters as an alternative economy of desire, as a paradise for jealous subjects (which is what Izumi has in mind when she points out to Takashi that "for a woman as enviable as Okiku, wanting paradise would be too greedy altogether" and mockingly declares to him that "nobody would be fascinated by you, so you could probably go straight to paradise" [79]), but also because this fantasy is historical, that is, it is embedded in a certain historical time and place—Japan of the 1980's—as well as in the feelings, thoughts, and knowledge created by the dynamics of jealousy. It follows, then, that the fantasy of contemporary Japanese society as a feminized discursive space governed by jealousy is a fantasy of a transitional reality that cannot—will never—quite be free of contradictions, constraints, and oppression. This reading not only contradicts the readings produced above, which argue for a paradise for jealous subjects, a utopian space of uninhibited freedom devoid of inequities and cultural constraints, and a powerful, transcendental epistemology of jealousy, but also points to the fact that the production of fantasies and fictions is ultimately self-defeating rather than liberating and that the series of fantasies spun by "The Chrysanthemum Beetle" does not quite succeed in disguising a bleak social reality, which is, however, sparingly and fragmentarily revealed. Tsushima's vision of contemporary Japan's feminized, jealous discursive space matches the holographic vision that, as we saw above, is projected by the entomological fantasies in the story.

In light of the various lines of interpretation suggested above, "The Chrysanthemum Beetle" appears to fit comfortably neither in the early modern Tokugawa culture from which the legend of Okiku stems nor in the "dominant modernity" of contemporary Japanese late/techno-capitalist society nor in the world of postmodern/postindustrial phenomena such as the information explosion, computerization, and new media technologies.[19] In fact, "The Chrysanthemum Beetle," like most texts by Tsushima, is thoroughly indifferent to such technologies. The use of a "realist" mode of storytelling and standard colloquial Japanese in the dialogues and the presentation of an epistemology/metaphysics/poetics of jealousy in this text seem to indicate that it is located, simultaneously, in three modern "traditions" (if we go by the canon of orthodox literary history) — namely, realist-naturalist literature (the "mainstream" of modern Japanese literature since at least Shimazaki Tōson and Natsume Sōseki);[20] the mimetic-representational "school" of women writers (*joryū bungaku*) from Nogami Yaeko (1885–1985) and proletarian/anarchist authors such as Sata Ineko (1904–) and Hayashi Fumiko (1903–51) onward; and literature marked by modernist narrative practices and cultural styles.[21] But an important body of textual evidence in "The Chrysanthemum Beetle" suggests that it is closely related to postmodernist meta-fictions and that it articulates a postmodern sensibility. Such evidence is found, for instance, in the triangular love relationships that are endlessly reproduced in this story as in a play of mirrors. These relationships, like similar arrangements in other texts by Tsushima such as the novels *Chōji* (Child of fortune; 1978), *Hi no kawa no hotori de* (On the banks of the river of fire; 1983), and the short fiction "Mitsume" (The third eye, included in *Ōma monogatari*; 1984) suggest not only that the ideal of the modern nuclear family is obsolete, but that such arrangements, as well as other forms of unorthodox communal living such as single-parent households and gay/lesbian or "incestuous" partnerships are gradually replacing earlier family institutions and challenging the regulative fictions that have historically sustained the latter.[22]

Another example of "postmodern sensibility" in the story is the relationship between Izumi and Takashi, which is undoubtedly characterized by what Umberto Eco calls the "lost innocence" of post-modernism. In a delightful essay entitled "Postmodernism, Irony, the Enjoyable," Eco imagines the typical "postmodern attitude" as that of a man who cannot say to a woman "I love you madly" because "he knows that she knows (and that she knows that he knows) that these words have already been written by Barbara Cartland." The solution proposed by Eco is to incorporate fantasy into the (impoverished) love utterance by saying, "As Barbara Cartland would put it, I love you madly." If "postmodern" lovers will thus "consciously and with pleasure play the game of irony," their relationship may at least partly regain the richness and depth of which it has been deprived by history (Eco, 67–68).

Not only do Izumi and Takashi "consciously and with pleasure play the game of irony" that is the supposed postmodern equivalent of a genuine romance,[23] but the exaggerated importance that jealousy assumes in their relationship — as in the relationship between Nobuko and Takashi — suggests that this intense, highly theatrical mode of expression is indeed, as Kazuko asserts at the beginning of the story, "the only thing left" of long-defunct discourses, gestures, and feelings of romantic love. Here is one instance of the ironic love games played by Izumi and Takashi to disguise their reluctance, and/or fear of committing themselves to a lasting relationship.[24]

> When the autumn colors were out they had strolled in Hibiya Park, near the band shell. That was the one time that Izumi had been in unconditionally high spirits, scampering after the pigeons or bursting operatically into song among the trees. As if this too were playfulness she clung to Takashi's arm and said sweetly, "I'd love some popcorn," and Takashi, who seemed not to mind as long as Izumi was having fun, bought her some with a wry smile. As she took handfuls from the bag, she added the final touch by resting her head archly against his shoulder and saying in a confiding whisper:
> "We could be on a real date like this, couldn't we? I've always wanted to try a typical date."
> Takashi laughed and played along by stroking her head till, self-consciousness returning, he quickly shoved Izumi away.
> "Behave yourself! What's 'a typical date' supposed to mean?"
> "Walking like lovers in the movies." Izumi laughed uproariously. (58)

Finally, to the extent that "The Chrysanthemum Beetle" is governed by fantasy and irony and by a symbolic of jealousy that is in itself a fantasy, and to the extent that fantasy and irony, as Brian Attebery, Nancy A. Walker, Linda Hutcheon, and others argue, are the dominant discursive modes in postmodern literature and art,[25] Tsushima's text may be said to display features of both fantastic and postmodern fiction. In spite of its apparent postmodernist allegiance, however, "The Chrysanthemum Beetle" certainly does not celebrate but articulates discomfort with the current transitional cultural moment, the "postmodern" irony, playfulness and loss of innocence it enacts, and even with the fantasies it engenders.[26] Perhaps the emergent culture anticipated by this story, as I suggested above in the discussion of the fantastic feminized discursive space projected by this text, is one of dystopia, or at least one in which dystopias loom large. Even if this were so, it would not be a surprising conclusion, for the present moment, of which "The Chrysanthemum Beetle" is undeniably a product, "contains both utopian and dystopian aspects which open toward conflicting futures" (Best and Kellner, 302). The ambiguous way this story reaches beyond its ending is in itself an indication of the indeterminacy of, as well as of the dangers inherent in, the present moment.

So far we have examined the various ways in which "The Chrysanthemum Beetle" rewrites the *sarayashiki* tradition as well as the strategies of fantasy and irony, including utopian and dystopian aspects, dramatized by the epistemology of jealousy projected by the story. Although all these discourses articulate, implicitly or explicitly, the various critiques that I have discussed, my concern was to delineate the configuration of such discourses and the way it structures the narrative, rather than the content of the critiques or the sociocultural constraints that they target. Since "The Chrysanthemum Beetle" is as preoccupied with epistemological questions and the construction of knowledge as it is with the construction and role of gender, in the next section I explore the stance adopted by Tsushima's story toward the relation between gender and knowledge, whether or not it formulates a feminist critique of that relationship or a critique of feminist critiques of traditional epistemological/philosophical inquiry.

"The Chrysanthemum Beetle" and the Construction of Knowledge

In recent years Western feminist philosophers have engaged in a systematic critique and deconstruction of all branches of mainstream academic philosophy. As Lorraine Code points out in her recent *What*

Can She Know? Feminist Theory and the Construction of Knowledge, feminists have shown not only that the sex of the knower is epistemologically significant but that traditional philosophical concepts such as objectivity, impartiality, universality, and the separation of knower from the object of knowledge are rooted in culturally constituted male experiences (xi). In addition, feminist epistemologists argue that knowledge is a cultural construct "that bears the mark of its constructor" (Code, 55), that the "sex/gender system"[27] structures significantly the construction and dissemination of knowledge in Western societies, and that knowledge does not transcend but is rooted in "specific interests and social arrangements" (Code, 68). At the same time, they take issue with traditional dichotomies such as mind/body, abstract/concrete, objective/subjective, universal/particular, and with the equating of the second terms in these dichotomies with femininity. Warning against the utopian project of a feminist epistemology in which masculine modes of inquiry would be "simply displaced by feminine ones" (Code, 322), Code and other feminist philosophers/epistemologists advocate a middle-ground position on the "ecologically mapped" epistemic terrain for feminist epistemological analyses, a position that would be characterized by epistemological relativism, resistance to closure, and a commitment to a politics of difference and to ecological and emancipatory projects—one that would leave room for debate and a productive ambiguity (Code, 321-24). Although I disagree with the middle-ground position advocated by Code,[28] I note here that feminist critiques of Japanese philosophy and epistemology are still scarce.[29]

If we scrutinize the representation/construction of knowledge in "The Chrysanthemum Beetle," we can see that the various kinds of knowledge that appear in this text—knowledge about people, networks, and communities and about affective relations such as dates and love affairs; professional specialized knowledge; awareness/recognition of various emotions/affects and their impact on the subject-knower—as well as the language serving to express these knowledges—are subject to and structured by gender politics. Thus, Izumi plays, with great conviction, the role of the enamored girl in a glamorous "typical date" like those shown in the movies, because, despite her awareness of the "game of irony," the farce she and Takashi are consciously enacting, she is expected to act like a typical lover (58). Nobuko is present at the conversation between Takashi and his former classmate from junior high school, in which the old affair of the girl who had attempted suicide surfaces, but she is not invited to participate in it (71). Takashi expects Nobuko to do all the domestic chores in his apartment and even brazenly suggests having an extra key made for her so that she would be able to go on with the housework while he makes love to Izumi (69–70). In her interpretation of the *sarayashiki* legend, Izumi seeks to correct the stereotypical view of the ugly, jealous wife versus the beautiful, unjustly treated Okiku (78). All knowledge possessed and put to use by the female characters in "The Chrysanthemum Beetle" works against them by virtue of their status as products of an oppressive, patriarchal social order. On the other hand, the very attempt in Tsushima's story to construct jealousy both as fundamental knowledge and as a theory of knowledge (epistemology) may be construed as a critique of (Western) androcentrically derived philosophical/epistemological ideals such as pure objectivity, impartiality, and the value-free / value-neutral nature of knowledge.

There is, however, no one-to-one relationship between "The Chrysanthemum Beetle" and Western (or Japanese) epistemology: Tsushima's story, interestingly enough, articulates a dissent, and/or a resistance to the dominant epistemic and capitalist social systems that is ambiguous and equivocal, perhaps even subversive of its own subversive intent. "The Chrysanthemum Beetle" suggests that in certain situations questions such as "Whose knowledge are we talking about?" as well as "Is the sex of the knower epistemologically significant?" —questions central to the project of "feminist philosophy in general, and epistemological inquiry in particular" (Code, 322) — become irrelevant. In the face of the complex dynamic of jealous inquiry enacted by the Izumi-Takashi-Nobuko triad, notions such as gender inequality, the epistemic oppression of women, or philosophical binaries that subjugate women collapse. Takashi, Izumi, and Nobuko are equally jealous of each other, and their knowledge of each other's jealousy and of each other's minds will always remain incomplete;[30] they refuse to try to know more about each other, draw lines between themselves, and manipulate each other. In Izumi's fantasy of Takashi as countless chrysanthemum beetles that turn into white butterflies, Takashi becomes the paradigmatic tragic heroine, the helpless victim of an oppressive feudal order, while remaining Takashi himself. Not only do gender distinctions disappear altogether in this fantasy, but Takashi is cast in a hermaphroditic role that seems an ironic transposition, into an even bolder realm of fantasy, of Vir-

ginia Woolf's Orlando and Joanna Russ's Janet in *The Female Man* —
characters that are in themselves outrageous, fantastic parodies of
patriarchal discourses on femininity.[31] There is no hint in Izumi's
fantasy of Takashi as a chrysanthemum beetle that he knows why he
has turned into a butterfly, where the wind is taking him, whether he
will be reborn in paradise. Knowledge of the reasons for his transformation into an insect, as well as about his past, present, and future
condition, is withheld from Takashi, which encourages us to construe
this fantasy as a form of imaginary revenge taken by Izumi on Takashi not only for his inciting her jealousy and for compelling her to
participate in a three-way arrangement with Nobuko as her rival, but
also for his refusing to reveal complete and reliable information about
himself. The traditional epistemic oppression of women is here ironically reversed.

"The Chrysanthemum Beetle" also disagrees with other tenets of
recent feminist critiques of mainstream, androcentrically biased philosophy and epistemology: namely, the notion that knowledge is a
cultural construct that bears the (gendered) mark of its constructor,
and the proposal for the adoption of a middle-ground position on the
"ecologically mapped epistemic terrain" as an ideal position for feminist epistemological/philosophical inquiries that oppose the classic
"adversarial paradigm." With respect to the notion of knowledge as
gender-specific cultural construct,[32] "The Chrysanthemum Beetle"
suggests that non-anthropocentric, non-gendered knowledge whose
"constructedness" is so ancient that it displays, so to speak, the mark
of erasure and of instinct (i.e., "genetically transmitted" knowledge),
has no place in that proposition. Butterflies, for instance, possess sophisticated knowledge about flying, pollination, and the like that is
neither culturally constructed nor necessarily reflective of the complex operations of the sex/gender system. As far as the middle-
ground position on the epistemic terrain is concerned, Tsushima's text
shows that subject-knowers, regardless of gender, are always already
captive to a middle-ground epistemic position, which is always already ambiguous and as open-ended and inclusive as it is exclusive
and self-contained. Thus, all three participants in the triangular relationship Izumi-Takashi-Nobuko agree to be inclusive and tolerant,
but each one of them would at the same time like to revert to the traditional couple arrangement. Many bodies of knowledge, acquired
skills, discursive practices, and fantasies are excluded from the tacit
"contract" among these three subject-knowers, none of whom seems

able to give up her/his middle-ground position. Izumi's revision of the Manor of the Dishes legend not only does not put forward a "feminist explanatory diagnostic analysis" of the epistemic oppression[33] of Okiku and the jealous wife in the *sarayashiki* lore in the context of Tokugawa culture and society but even mocks the undeniable reality of the social oppression of the women. For example, there is a brief mention of the class issue — the fact that Okiku and her master's wife belonged to different "classes" — but no attempt whatsoever to develop a Marxist feminist critique of the condition of women during that period (77–79).

The role of fantasy, *jouissance*, and sexual desire is another important area of disagreement between "The Chrysanthemum Beetle" and traditional epistemology/philosophy, as well as feminist critiques of them. Tsushima's story indicates that fantasy plays a much more important role in the construction of knowledge, epistemologies, and philosophies in general than either Western or Japanese modern philosophers, including feminists, have been willing to admit. Although Lorraine Code discusses the role of creativity and of cultural location in the construction and production of knowledge and endorses Kant's view that knowledge is the product "of a creative synthesis of the imagination," and of the "cooperation of perception and thought" (Code, 56), her analysis and critique concentrate on the "objective," pragmatic knowledge that can be put to use in situations of everyday life, as well as on the equally "objective," abstract-intellectual knowledge discussed by Kant (cf. *The Critique of Pure Reason*) and other Western philosophers. "The Chrysanthemum Beetle" suggests both that knowledge is shot through with fantasy and that fantasy is the backbone of epistemological inquiry. Izumi's knowledge as well as non-knowledge about Takashi is based as much on conversations with Takashi and Nobuko and on hearsay as on Izumi's speculations and fantasy. The speculative streak in Izumi's knowledge of Takashi, for example, may be seen in the scene in which she imagines him deliberately arranging "suggestive feminine items" in his apartment to incite Izumi's jealousy. Kazuko's knowledge about her lover's wife is also based to a great extent on fantasy. And Takashi and Izumi play at / fantasize about being lovers in the movies (58) or being children playing with puppets (63). The desire for knowledge and the power it brings with it is motivated in "The Chrysanthemum Beetle" to a great extent by jealousy, and jealousy, as we have seen, is a mode of fantasy, or fiction making.

In regard to the relations between knowledge and pleasure/*jouissance*, and knowledge and sexual desire, "The Chrysanthemum Beetle" may be said to propose several arguments. First, knowledge is *jouissance*, the "connaissance délicieuse" (delightful knowledge) envisioned by Roland Barthes in *Le plaisir du texte*.[34] The mode of jealous inquiry posited by Tsushima's story—which, as we have seen, is the only mode of epistemological investigation endorsed by all characters in the text—certainly fits Malcolm Bowie's apt description of the mode of jealous inquiry developed by the narrator in *La prisonnière* and other Proustian novels as "knowing-in-delight" (64). Such knowing-in-delight, the joy and pleasure (which may be painful, but a pleasure nonetheless), is described by Izumi as follows :

> With a woman like Okiku, now, in a position of weakness, the plaything of destiny bewailing her fate as she goes to a tragic death—a woman like that doesn't actually mean much to us, so we can afford to be fascinated by her and think "how lovely." How lovely it must feel to inspire such jealousy. I'm sure that's why Okiku's story has become so famous. We can forget ourselves and share just a little of Okiku's pleasure. (78)

The knowledge, shared by Takashi and Izumi, about the neighborhood in which they lived during their schooldays also brings them pleasure (60–61). Izumi's fantasy of Takashi as a chrysanthemum beetle is also—to Izumi and the human insect Takashi—a kind of knowing-in-delight, what Baudelaire calls "an ecstasy made of pleasure and knowledge" (785). (This rapturous mood however, is also disquieting because it entails "non-connaissance," non-knowledge as well.)

"The Chrysanthemum Beetle" also posits that sexual desire plays just as important a part in the construction/production of knowledge as fantasy and reason and the intellect. From the perspective of this story, psychoanalysis may be redefined as the epistemology of sex(ual desire), and epistemology may be redescribed as the psychoanalysis of knowledge. It is undoubtedly sexual desire that incites Izumi's curiosity about Takashi, and that constitutes the primary motif, as well as the basis of her jealousy, of her theorizing about love, jealousy, and woman's gaze and of her revision of the Manor of the Dishes lore.

What "The Chrysanthemum Beetle" proposes, then, is the construction of a new epistemology that would be alert not only to the politics of gender and to other culturally specific factors but also to the various ways in which sexual desire, sensual cognizance, and fantasy—the polar opposites of the classic philosophical mind, or "pure" reason—affect the production and dissemination of knowledge.

The Work of Fantasy

The operations of fantasy in "The Chrysanthemum Beetle" are, as the foregoing discussion has shown, political in the broad sense of proposing and enacting a politics of resistance to hegemonic patriarchal discourse and institutions and in highlighting the experience of a woman that, though intensely personal, "radiates outward into the common, shared hopes and goals" (Walker, 5) of other women or into a critique of such aspirations. The fantastic discourse in this story is also political in the sense that it calls for certain readings that challenge existing epistemic and social structures.

In terms of the dual typology of the mode of fantasy theorized by critics such as Lynette Hunter,[35] "The Chrysanthemum Beetle" clearly dramatizes fantasies, both of desire and of games. The rhetorical stance underlying these fantasies, however, unlike that posited by many Western theories of fantasy, is not as ambitious and imperialistic as to want to control the world. The "pure" fantasies in Tsushima's story, such as Izumi's butterfly fantasy, are deconstructive, non-anthropocentric, anti-humanist, and irrational, expressing a desire not so much to control the environment and the other as to make this world a better, more tolerant, and more joyful place for all species. (The ambiguity in Izumi's vision of Takashi as a chrysanthemum beetle/butterfly is such as to allow this more "optimistic" reading, in addition to the more somber readings I have suggested.) The "reality-bound" fantasies in this text—Izumi's imaginings of Takashi's elaborate arrangement of women's things to incite her jealousy, the love games between Izumi and Takashi—are subversive, ironic, and demystifying (Takashi, the self-declared sexist who claims that women think of nothing but jealousy is shown to be inordinately jealous, suspicious, weak, and spineless)—but privately, modestly so. In other words, "The Chrysanthemum Beetle" does not articulate an apocalyptic revolutionary rhetoric or a grand feminist critique; rather, it suggests that important social changes begin at the local (micro) level and can be achieved only by recognizing the significance of micropolitics.

Although the not-worlds in this story (the Manor of the Dishes lore, Izumi's butterfly fantasy, and her vision of the love triangle of

Takashi, his classmate who tried to commit suicide, and her boy-friend) seem immediately within reach, "a country that lies just beyond or alongside, or within the landscape" that the characters "can see and touch,"[36] their relationship with the world is ambiguous, unsettling, untamable—both firmly within, alongside Japanese cultural landscapes and reaching beyond, challenging, reshaping, these dimensions. Fantasy in this text resists its own politics of resistance and does not allow it to congeal and become dogmatic. Its irreverent, highly self-reflexive, ambiguous rhetoric cautions against "definitive" readings and the stance of the master critic. The play of fantasy in "The Chrysanthemum Beetle" alerts us to the complex materiality of the text, to the fact that literary fictions are structured not only by language and various "axes of identity" such as gender, race, ethnicity, and class but also by "histories" and "traditions" we have not made and cannot easily undo: the life cycle and social organization of insects, the work of time, what may be called the memory, or unconscious, of the planet we inhabit. To do justice to visions such as those projected by Tsushima's story, political criticism has to reconsider—as well as constantly redefine—the ethics, philosophy, ecology, and sensual appeal of the activity of interpretation.

Notes

A different version of this essay appeared in *Japan Review* 4 (1993): 199–239.

1. Tsushima's reputation as one of the foremost contemporary Japanese women writers rests mainly on her short fiction. Notable among her short stories are: "Mugura no haha" (The mother in the house of grass; 1975), "Kusa no fushido" (A bed of grass; 1977), "Hyōgen" (Ice field; 1979), "Danmari ichi" (1982; The silent traders; 1982); and the short-story collections *Ōma monogatari* (Spooky tales; 1984), *Mahiru e* (Toward midnoon; 1988) and *Yume no kiroku* (A record of dreams; 1988). Of the novels she has published so far, *Chōji* (Child of fortune; 1978), *Yama o hashiru onna* (Woman running in the mountains; 1980), *Hi na kawa no hotori de* (On the banks of the river of fire; 1984) and *Yoru no hikari ni ōwarete* (Driven by the light of the night; 1986) have received critical acclaim. Her most recent novel is *Kaze yo sora kakeru kaze yo* (Wind, O wind blowing high in the sky; 1995). Tsushima is also a prolific essayist and the recipient of several important literary awards, including the Women's Literature, Tamura Toshiko, Izumi Kyōka, Kawabata Yasunari, and Yomiuri Literature prizes. Two of Tsushima's novels have appeared in English translation so far, both by Geraldine Harcourt: *Child of Fortune* and *Woman Running in the Mountains*. Geraldine Harcourt is also the translator and compiler of a collection of Tsushima's short stories, *The Shooting Gallery*,

which includes a translation of "Kikumushi" (The chrysanthemum beetle); all quotations from this story appearing in this chapter are from Harcourt's excellent translation. Page numbers are indicated in the text.

2. For fairly exhaustive bibliographies on Tsushima's work, see Negishi, 129; and Yonaha, "Sakka annai," *Ōma* 352. I have placed the words "themes" and "motifs" in quotation marks not so much because the pursuit of these issues is currently discredited, but because to my mind a focus on thematic concerns prevents the critic from engaging with the larger discursive socio-political and cultural horizons that are addressed by the text / cultural product that she studies. There are to my knowledge no critical assessments of "The Chrysanthemum Beetle."

3. Tsushima's father, the celebrated writer Dazai Osamu (1909–48), was found dead when Tsushima was barely one year old. Her elder brother had Down's syndrome and died in 1960 at the age of fifteen. Married in 1970, Tsushima gave birth to a daughter in 1972. Tsushima divorced in 1976 and gave birth to a son out of wedlock the same year. Subsequently, she assumed sole responsibility for the education of her children. Her son, Daimu, died suddenly in 1985 before reaching the age of nine.

For discussions that emphasize the autobiographical orientation of Tsushima's fiction, see especially Komori; Sengoku; Yonaha, "Tsushima Yūko ron, II" and "Yoru no hikari ni ōwarete." Masao Miyoshi (212–16) also endorses this view in his brief discussion of Tsushima's novels *Child of Fortune* and *Woman Running in the Mountains.*

4. Even a critic like Yonaha Keiko, who perceptively argues that Tsushima's explorations of female sexuality, childbirth and motherhood, and family/heterosexual relations have a powerful critical potential that is at the same time mythical and visionary, all but overlooks the function of gender, as well as the play of irony, ambiguity, and humor in Tsushima's texts. See Yonaha, "Sakka annai"; and *Gendai joryū sakka ron*, 122–27, 139–43.

5. Takeda Seiji, for instance, points out that Tsushima's stories avoid the favorite themes of modern Japanese literature — namely, existential traumas and the struggle for acceptance and recognition of isolated individuals in a hostile modern world — in favor of a portrayal of "something lurking behind the free self that governs the (modern) individual as an unknown power" (*jiyū na "naimen" no haigō ni hisomi, "watashi no shiranai" chikara toshite ningen o kitei shiteiru nanimono ka*) (84). I do not see how such vague, unfocused assertions can help us grasp the complexity of Tsushima's fiction and what it tries to accomplish, challenge, or change.

6. I am reacting here against the current proliferation of "politically correct" interpretive strategies, theories, and methodologies in American literary and cultural studies, discourses that are so passionately committed to the glorification of the subaltern subject / the Other, emergent / Third World literatures and so on that they tend to overlook the fact that the practice of "speaking for others" also effectively covers their voices, once again silencing or misrepresenting them. For a critique of "politically correct" discursive

practices, especially of their tendency to "other" the Other / the Third World, see Rey Chow's essays " 'It's you, and not me' "; and "Violence in the Other Country."

7. In *Marxism and Culture*, Williams calls attention to the internal dynamic of any actual process/culture, suggesting that, rather than speaking of stages or variations within a certain culture, we should recognize the characteristics of the residual, dominant, and emergent phenomena, as well as the way the latter interrelate, in that culture:

> We have certainly still to speak of the "dominant" and the "effective," and in these senses of the hegemonic. But we find that we have also to speak, and indeed with further differentiation of each, of the "residual" and the "emergent," which in any real process, and at any moment in the process are significant both in themselves and in what they reveal of the characteristics of the "dominant." (121–22)

8. In this play, Okiku, a lady-in-waiting in the household of Lord Hosokawa Masamoto, overhears the plans of Aoyama Tetsuzan and others to poison the master and take his place. Tetsuzan conceals a valuable plate belonging to the Hosokawa family and blames the loss of the artifact on Okiku. He then kills her and throws her body into a well. Okiku reappears as a ghost and begins to count the precious dishes, of which one is missing. Tetsuzan's plot is eventually discovered, and he is forced to flee, but he is relentlessly pursued by Okiku's ghost. Unable to endure this confrontation, Tetsuzan kills himself.

9. Okamoto's play focuses on Okiku's love for Aoyama Harima, a *hatamoto* (member of the shogun's guards), rather than on her slaying or her reappearance as a vengeful ghost. Worried by rumors that Harima is about to marry another woman, Okiku decides to test his feelings toward her and smashes a plate that is a treasured heirloom of his family. Thinking that this was an accident, Harima is inclined to forgive Okiku but changes his mind when he learns of her true motives. Then, angered by Okiku's unfounded suspicions, Harima smashes all the other dishes that formed a set with the one broken by Okiku, cuts her throat with his sword, and orders his men to throw her body into the well of the mansion.

10. The "chrysanthemum beetle" (*kikumushi*, or *okikumushi*) mentioned by the father of the little girl in this story is actually the pupa (chrysalis) of the butterfly *Atrophaneura alcinous* (*jako ageha*, which translates roughly as "musk swallowtail"), family *Papilionidae*. The larva of this butterfly is brownish red with transverse white bands and several rows of fleshy tentacles. The pupa is creamy yellow and has a waxy appearance. It also has orange spots on the mesothorax and dorsal projections. The adult has a long body, with the swallowtail-like rear part showing yellow or red patches of color, and white-yellowish wings. The description in the text ("Just a beetle with a white pattern in the centre" ["The Chrysanthemum Beetle," 75]; in the Japanese original, *nimai hane no marui mushi de, shiroi moyō ga mannaka ni aru dake de* [a

winged round insect with just a white pattern in the centre], "Kikumushi" in *Ōma monogatari*, 191) is not an exact description of the pupa, the larva, or of the adult of the *jako ageha* of the swallowtail family. The hypothesis of Kazuko's lover that the specimen selected by his daughter from the pile of dead insects in the case of the fluorescent light tubes was a *kikumushi* is thus not so much scientifically untenable as simply erroneous.

11. The phrase is from Best and Kellner's (279–80) definition of the present historical moment, quoted earlier. The contextualization of "The Chrysanthemum Beetle" in a modern cultural landscape may be seen, among other things, in the particulars of the daily life, family relations, and careers of the characters in the story. Except perhaps for the fact that Nobuko and Izumi (and probably Kazuko as well) are skilled white-collar workers with full-time jobs, their lifestyles, like that of Takashi and his family, are not very different from that of the urban middle class in prewar Japan.

12. See my essay "The Politics of Miscegenation."

13. For a Japanese version of this essay, see Mizuta, 17–29.

14. Consider, for instance, the following passage in Proust's *Remembrance of Things Past*:

> I had in the course of my life followed a progression which was the opposite of that adopted by peoples who make use of phonetic writing only after having considered the characters as a set of symbols; having, for so many years, looked for the real life and thought of other people only in the direct statements about them which they supplied me with of their own free will, in the absence of these I had come to attach importance, on the contrary, only to disclosures that are not a rational and analytical expression of the truth; the words themselves did not enlighten me unless they were interpreted in the same way as a rush of blood to the cheeks of a person who is embarrassed, or as a sudden silence. Such and such an adverb . . . bursting into flames through the involuntary, sometimes perilous contact of two ideas which the speaker has not expressed but which, by applying the appropriate methods of analysis or electrolysis, I was able to extract from it, told me more than a long speech. Albertine sometimes let fall in her conversation one or other of these precious amalgams which I made haste to "treat" so as to transform them into lucid ideas. (trans. Moncrieff and Kilmartin 1: 83)

15. Consider, for instance, the following passage: "Nobuko broke off, and studied Izumi's face at length. All Izumi could do was wait blankly for Nobuko's next words. After a sip of water, she continued" (68).

16. According to Chow, image-as-feminized space can be occupied both by men and by women, and once this is done, " 'femininity' as a category is freed up to include fictional constructs that may not be 'women,' but that occupy a passive position in regard to the controlling symbolic" (*Woman and Chinese Modernity*, 18).

17. The quote is from Proust's *Du côté de chez Swann*, 1: 283; *Remembrance*, 309. The translation is Bowie's.

18. Malcolm Bowie describes the function of the discourse of jealousy in Proust's *Remembrance of Things Past* as epistemology, poetics, and metaphys-

ics at the same time: "Jealousy is an alertness of eye and ear and intellect; it is an experience of manifold potentiality; it is a stimulus to the making of fictions; it is a comprehensive way of inhabiting space and time. When these things are produced by pain and absence they may be called jealousy. But the same things, rediscovered in joy, and by joy transformed, may as fittingly be called *knowledge*" (64).

19. These are, according to Steven Best and Douglas Kellner (302), the most salient characteristics of the current configuration of techno-capitalist societies.

20. I am thinking here, of course, of textbook or academic literary history, in which one "school" succeeds another and all writers are neatly categorized. The *joryū sakka*, or female school of writers, have traditionally occupied the periphery of the academic canon, in which the "mainstream" (*shu-ryū*) is constituted by the succession and/or simultaneous coexistence of "naturalism" (*shizen shugi*, which has its own mainstream, identified with the "I-fiction" [*shishōsetsu*], or confessional novel); *shirakaba ha*, proletarian literature, modernism, wartime literature; *sengo ha* (postwar or *après-guerre* school); and so on. In spite of various attempts (the most influential of which is probably Karatani Kōjin's *Nihon kindai bungaku no kigen*, 1980; trans. *Origins of Modern Japanese Literature*, 1994), to deconstruct the master narrative of modern Japanese literary history, this myth still wields great authority. See Suzuki for a recent critique of the ideology at work in the construction of the canon of contemporary Japanese literature.

21. A similar mode of inquiry into jealousy, though less obsessive and intense than that described in "The Chrysanthemum Beetle," may be found in Kawabata Yasunari's modernist-surrealist experiment *Suisō genshō* (Crystal fantasies; 1934).

22. For recent explorations/critiques of family ideology, especially of the role of the mother in this discourse, and of the latter's integration in nationalist discourses and state policies concerning women from the latter part of the Meiji period onward, see Ochiai Emiko, "The Modern Family and Japanese Culture" (Japanese version in Mizuta, 45–66); and *Kindai kazoku to feminizumu*. See also Nolte and Hastings; and Miyake. For a discussion of contemporary partnerships and family-like arrangements, see also the transcript of the symposium "Women and the Family: Postfamily Alternatives."

23. Nancy A. Walker points out that, although irony and fantasy are ancient literary devices, the combination of the two may be regarded as "closely related to some definitions of the postmodern spirit or temperament" (29).

24. The representation of love as an ironic game is a common characteristic of texts by Murakami Haruki, Yoshimoto Banana, Shimada Masahiko, and other contemporary Japanese writers of the so-called new wave or new generation.

25. See Attebery, 1–17, 36–50; Walker, 14–37; and Hutcheon, 1–23.

26. Apart from Izumi's fantasy of Takashi as a chrysanthemum beetle, the following passage clearly displays uneasiness with the "game of irony"

(soon to be replaced by the "game of jealousy") in which Izumi and Takashi engage in the first few months of their relationship:

> As the time they spent together grew more intimate, she couldn't help wishing she could spend every weekend at Takashi's. Takashi said nothing when she closed her eyes and whispered, "I'm so sleepy. If I go to sleep now, I wonder if I can wake up before morning?" He said neither "Get some rest," nor "Don't you dare." Only when she'd reluctantly climbed out of bed and begun dressing would Takashi say with an air of relief, "Look at the time. We'll be half asleep tomorrow," as he also got up. Takashi had never said out loud, "Don't come any closer." Izumi had never said in so many words, "I want to come a little closer." She was convinced that they'd been able to preserve the sense of intimacy they'd had till now because she'd drawn her own line and made sure to back away when she reached it. Though she didn't draw the line gladly. (61)

27. The label "sex/gender system" originated with Gayle Rubin in "The Traffic in Women."

28. A middle-ground position on the epistemic terrain that commits itself to "epistemological relativism" and "a productive ambiguity" could easily accommodate ethnocentric, racist, or fascist epistemological/philosophical claims.

29. For a recent example of a feminist critique of the phallogocentric discourse in Western (not Japanese!) philosophy, see Ōgoshi.

30. Not only does Izumi declare to Takashi "I don't know you very well yet. Really, you're full of things I don't know yet" (79), but the "conversation" between Izumi and Nobuko the one time they meet is for the most part a confessional monologue on Nobuko's part, to which Izumi hardly has a chance to add anything. Nobuko evidently does not know a lot about Izumi, for Takashi has not revealed more than was necessary about his relationship with the latter:

> He started playing tricks on you, too, didn't he? . . . He did the same to me. That is, I don't know if the tricks were the same, but . . . It's one of his peculiar theories that people don't take things in when they're merely told. So he seems to have convinced himself that we had to be made aware of this three-way arrangement by the most concrete means he could think of. . . . I won't go into the details of what he did to me, but I can tell you I had a very rough time, too. I expect that neither of us came off any better than the other, you know. (70)

31. Joanna Russ's *The Female Man* presents a fantastic vision in which four different female characters, each of whom is actually a different aspect of the same personality and each of whom inhabits a different universe, come together and engage in a lively discussion about the condition of women in their respective worlds/societies. The unifying consciousness is that of Janet, who comes from an all-female utopia called Whileaway. Rejecting the concepts of the culturally determined self and of the equally culturally constructed gender, Janet declares herself to be a man: "For years I have been saying *Let me in, Love me, Approve me, Define me, Regulate me, Validate me, Sup-*

port me. Now I say *Move over.* If we are all Mankind, it follows to my interested and righteous and right-now very bright and beady little eyes, that I too am a Man and not at all a Woman" (140).

32. The notion of knowledge as cultural construct originated with Kant, although Kant of course did not concern himself with the role of gender in the construction of knowledge.

33. Seyla Benhabib notes that feminist scholarship in all disciplines is committed to developing an *explanatory diagnostic analysis* of women's oppression across history, culture, and society and to articulating an *anticipatory-utopian critique* of current social, cultural, and political norms and values.

34. Noting that the notion of pleasure has come to be regarded as politically and intellectually suspect, Barthes wonders: "Et pourtant, si la connaissance elle-meme était délicieuse?" (39).

35. According to Hunter, twentieth-century Western theories of fantasy posit a dual typology for this mode: namely, fantasies of desire and of games. The rhetorical stance underlying both modes of fantasy is that of an activity of control, which assumes that human beings have the right to, and can, impose their authority on the environment, and that language can represent the world as it is. This rhetoric is negative, "a stance that tries to hide its own stance." The stance in women's writings about alternative worlds is somewhat more complex, although still tied to the epistemology and ideology of the "rationalist humanism" that has dominated Western thought since the Enlightenment. Rationalist humanism aside, the double structure of fantasy as desire and game certainly applies to the modern Japanese literature of fantasy, which is usually described with the term *gensō bungaku.* Although it may comprise tantalizing distinctions between *gensō junbungaku* (literature of pure, or high-brow, fantasy) and the rest of fantasy, as well as alternative definitions such as *fantaji, kaiki,* and *misuterii,* the term refers to a vast mass of writings that have been traditionally assigned to the even vaster realm of entertainment and popular culture. For critical assessments and theoretical discussions, see journals such as *Gensō bungaku,* which is published by Gensō bungaku shuppankyoku.

36. The phrase is from Doris Lessing's novel *The Four-Gated City,* 355.

Works Cited

Attebery, Brian. *Strategies of Fantasy.* Bloomington: Indiana University Press, 1992.

Barthes, Roland. *Le plaisir du texte.* Paris: Seuil, 1973.

Baudelaire, Charles. "Richard Wagner et Tannhäuser à Paris." In *Oeuvres complètes,* ed. Claude Pichois. Bibliothèque de la Pléiade. Paris: Gallimard, 1976, 2: 785–88.

Benhabib, Seyla. "Generalized and Concrete Other." In *Feminism as Critique: On the Politics of Gender,* ed. idem and Drucilla Cornell. Minneapolis: University of Minnesota Press, 1987, 77–95.

Bernstein, Gail Lee, ed. *Recreating Japanese Women, 1600–1945*. Berkeley: University of California Press, 1991.

Best, Steven, and Douglas Kellner. *Postmodern Theory: Critical Interrogations*. New York: Guilford Press, 1990.

Bloch, Ernst. "Nonsynchronism and the Obligation to Its Dialectics." *New German Critique* 11 (1977): 22–38.

Bowie, Malcolm. *Freud, Proust and Lacan: Theory as Fiction*. Cambridge, Eng.: Cambridge University Press, 1988.

Butler, Judith. "Gender Trouble: Feminist Theory and Psychoanalytic Discourse." In *Feminism/Postmodernism*, ed. Linda Nicholson. New York: Routledge, 1990, 324–40.

Chow, Rey. " 'It's You, and Not Me': Domination and 'Othering' in Theorizing the 'Third World.' " In *Coming to Terms: Feminism, Theory, Politics*, ed. Elizabeth Weed. New York: Routledge, 1989, 152–61.

———. "Violence in the Other Country: China as Crisis, Spectacle and Woman." In *Third World Women and the Politics of Feminism*, ed. Chandra Talpade Mohanty, Ann Russo, and Lourdes Torres. Bloomington: Indiana University Press, 1991, 81–100.

———. *Woman and Chinese Modernity: The Politics of Reading Between West and East*. Minnesota: University of Minnesota Press, 1991.

Code, Lorraine. *What Can She Know? Feminist Theory and the Construction of Knowledge*. Ithaca, N.Y.: Cornell University Press, 1991.

de Lauretis, Teresa. *Alice Doesn't: Feminism, Semiotics, Cinema*. Bloomington: Indiana University Press, 1984.

Eco, Umberto. *Postscript to "The Name of the Rose."* Trans. William Weaver. New York: Harcourt Brace Jovanovich, 1984.

Hunter, Lynette. *Modern Allegory and Fantasy: Rhetorical Stances in Contemporary Writing*. New York: St. Martin's Press, 1989.

Hutcheon, Linda. *The Politics of Postmodernism*. New York: Routledge, 1989.

Jackson, Rosemary. *Fantasy: The Literature of Subversion*. London: Methuen, 1981.

Karatani Kōjin. *Nihon kindai bungaku no kigen*. Tokyo: Kōdansha bungei bunko, 1988 (1980).

———. *The Origins of Modern Japanese Literature*. Trans. ed. Brett de Bary. Durham, N.C.: Duke University Press, 1993.

Kawabata Yasunari. *Suisō genshō*. Tokyo: Kaizōsha, 1934.

Komori Yōichi. "Tsushima Yūko ron: haramikomu kotoba." *Kokubungaku: kaishaku to kanshō* 33, no. 10 (Aug. 1988): 87–93.

Lessing, Doris. *The Four-Gated City*. 1969; reprinted—New York: Bantam, 1970.

Miller, Nancy K. "Emphasis Added: Plots and Plausibilities in Women's Fiction." *PMLA* 96, no. 1 (Jan. 1981): 36–48.

Miyake Yoshiko. "Doubling Expectations: Motherhood and Women's Factory Work Under State Management in Japan in the 1930's and 1940's." In Bernstein, 267–95.

Miyoshi, Masao. *Off Center: Power and Culture Relations Between Japan and the United States.* Cambridge, Mass.: Harvard University Press, 1991.

Mizuta, Noriko, ed. *Josei to kazoku no hen'yō: posuto famirii e mukete.* Tokyo: Gakuyō shobō, 1990.

Monnet, Livia. "The Politics of Miscegenation: Fantasy in 'Fusehime' by Tsushima Yūko." *Japan Forum* 5, no. 1 (Apr. 1993): 53–73.

Mulvey, Laura. *Visual and Other Pleasures.* Bloomington: Indiana University Press, 1989.

Negishi Yasuko. "Tsushima Yūko." *Kokubungaku: kaishaku to kanshō* 35, no. 6 (Nov. 1990): 128–29.

Nolte, Sharon, and Sally Ann Hastings. "The Meiji State's Policy Toward Women, 1890–1910." In Bernstein, 151–74.

Ochiai Emiko. *Kindai kazoku to feminizumu.* Tokyo: Keisō shobō, 1988.

———. "The Modern Family and Japanese Culture: Exploring the Japanese Mother-Child Relationship." *Review of Japanese Culture and Society* 3, no. 1 (Dec. 1989): 7–14.

Ōgoshi Aiko. "Feminizumu riron to tetsugaku." In *Feminizumu riron: Nihon no feminizumu,* ed. Inoue Teruko et al. Tokyo: Iwanami shoten, 1994, 100–117.

Proust, Marcel. *A la recherche du temps perdu.* 3 vols. Ed. Pierre Clarac and André Ferré. Bibliothèque de la Pléiade. Paris: Gallimard, 1954.

———. *Du côté de chez Swann.* In *A la recherche du temps perdu,* vol. 1.

———. *La prisonnière.* Ed. Jean Milly. Paris: Flammarion, 1984.

———. *Remembrance of Things Past.* Trans. C. K. Scott Moncrieff and Terence Kilmartin. 3 vols. London: Chatto & Windus, 1981.

Rubin, Gayle. "The Traffic in Women: Notes on the 'Political Economy' of Sex." In *Toward an Anthropology of Women,* ed. Rayna R. Reiter. New York: Monthly Review Press, 1975, 157–210.

Russ, Joanna. *The Female Man.* 1975; reprinted — London: Women's Press, 1985.

Sengoku Hideyo. "Kazoku no yume: Tsushima Yūko no tanpen no sekai," *Gunzō* 39, no. 9 (Sept. 1984): 86–103.

Suzuki Sadami. *Nihon no "bungaku" o kangaeru.* Tokyo: Kadokawa shoten, 1994.

Takeda Seiji. *"Sekai" no rinkaku.* Tokyo: Kokubunsha, 1987.

Tsushima Yūko. *Child of Fortune (Chōji).* Trans. Geraldine Harcourt. Tokyo: Kōdansha International, 1983.

———. *Chōji.* Tokyo: Kawade shobō shinsha, 1978.

———. "The Chrysanthemum Beetle" ("Kikumushi"). Trans. Geraldine Harcourt. In Tsushima, *The Shooting Gallery,* 45–79.

———. *Danmari ichi.* Tokyo: Shinchōsha, 1984.

———. *Hi no kawa no hotori de.* Tokyo: Kōdansha, 1983.

———. "Hyōgen." Tokyo: Sakuhinsha, 1979.

———. "Kikumushi" (1984). In Tsushima, *Ōma monogatari,* 137–99.

———. *Kusa no fushido.* Tokyo: Kōdansha, 1977.

————. *Mahiru e.* Tokyo: Shinchōsha, 1988.

————. *Mugura no haha.* Tokyo: Kawade shobō shinsha, 1975.

————. *Ōma monogatari.* Tokyo: Kōdansha bungei bunko, 1989.

————. *The Shooting Gallery.* London: Women's Press; New York: Pantheon Books, 1988.

————. *Woman Running in the Mountains (Yama o hashiru onna).* Trans. Geraldine Harcourt. New York: Pantheon, 1991.

————. *Yama o hashiru onna.* Tokyo: Kōdansha, 1980.

————. *Yoru no hikari ni ōwarete.* Tokyo: Kōdansha, 1986.

————. *Yume no kiroku.* Tokyo: Bungei shunju, 1988.

Ueno Chizuko. "Women's Labor Under Patriarchal Capitalism in the Eighties." *Review of Japanese Culture and Society* 3, no. 1 (Dec. 1989): 1–6.

Walker, Nancy A. *Feminist Alternatives: Irony and Fantasy in the Contemporary Novel by Women.* Jackson: University Press of Mississippi, 1980.

Williams, Raymond. *Marxism and Culture.* New York: Oxford University Press, 1977.

"Women and the Family: Postfamily Alternatives." *Review of Japanese Culture and Society* 3, no. 1 (Dec. 1989): 79–95 (Japanese version in Mizuta, 171–214).

Yonaha Keiko. *Gendai joryū sakka ron.* Tokyo: Shinbisha, 1986.

————. "Sakka annai." In Tsushima, *Ōma monogatari.* 341–52.

————. "Tsushima Yūko ron, II." In Yonaha, *Gendai joryū sakka ron,* 144–64.

13

Power and Gender in the Narratives of Yamada Eimi

NINA CORNYETZ

This essay is concerned with the production of gender, the eroticization of African-American men, and the related inscription of
power relations in the narrative texts by the Japanese female author
Yamada Eimi (1959– ; sometimes written Yamada Amy). My reading
originates in a belief that power is invested in discourse and that, in
the words of the collective authors of *Changing the Subject*: "Discursive
practices produce, maintain, or play out power relations. But power is
not one-sided or monolithic, even when we can and do speak of dominance, subjugation or oppression. Power is always exercised in relation to a resistance. The 'system' we describe is riddled with sites of
resistance and conflict" (Henriques et al., 115). Accordingly, the
questions I pose of Yamada's texts are: How do resistance to and collusion with dominant Japanese sex/gender and racial power relations
and ideologies manifest themselves in Yamada's texts? What is the
relationship between Yamada's treatments of gender and race in narrative text? Because I believe that Yamada's racialism is partly dependent upon her conceptualization of gender, I have placed the issue
of gender first.

Gender

"Always the same metaphor: we follow it, it carries us, beneath
all its figures, wherever discourse is organized. If we read or speak,
the same thread or double braid is leading us throughout literature,

philosophy, criticism, centuries of representation and reflection. Thought has always worked through opposition" (Cixous and Clément, 63). The critical frames of reference for this essay are a reading of Western culture as a patriarchal system that locates the white, European male as the normative center of the universe, against whom all others obtain meaning only relatively, and my belief that modern Japanese patriarchy is similarly structured despite disparities in the specifics of the two "systems." Hélène Cixous begins her essay "Sorties: Out and Out: Attacks/Ways Out/Forays" in *The Newly Born Woman*, by listing pairs of binaries that she claims frame all discourse in Western patriarchal systems and by which women are conceptualized only as a negative mirror to the male norm (63). This essay will show how similar binaries inform and produce gender ideology in Yamada's work.

The ideology of gender within any nation, with its attendant separation of roles and valuation of these roles, relates to the economic and political system by which that nation is organized and functions. I use "ideology" here as defined by Judith Newton and Deborah Rosenfelt as "not a set of deliberate distortions imposed on us from above, but a complex and contradictory system of representations (discourse, images, myths) through which we experience ourselves in relation to each other and to the social structures in which we live" (xvii). For both the West and Japan, different as they are, contemporary gender ideology is thus inextricable from (changing) capitalist modes of production in a patriarchy. For both nations, male centrality is produced through all the varied social discourses (philosophy, religion, science, politics, among others) that originate in and continue to reproduce validation of economic and political privilege based on exclusion and inclusion. In Japan, the continued dominance of the "Yamato" Japanese male, who is perceived as "pure," is posed in opposition to others within the nation-state such as the *burakumin* (outcaste), Ainu, and Korean-Japanese. In Japan, as in the United States and Europe, women are also other, distinguished as such by both bodily and additional (assumedly natural) marks of difference from the male norm. Assumedly natural marks of difference are generally encoded within gender performance, by which discursively and culturally constructed behavior may be unproblematically read as biological, genetic, or, more simply, "natural" (see Butler, *Bodies That Matter*).

Actual physical differences notwithstanding, the manner in

which these differences are interpreted is inseparable from other epistemologies. Moreover, although ideology (including that which produces discourses of gender) may further the economic interests of the dominant classes, as ideologies circulate, the process of reproduction becomes to an extent autonomous from both economic and political functions (Newton and Rosenfelt, xix). Representations (be they legal, scientific, or literary) of "engendered" human beings thus tend to serve to reproduce, under the mantle of the natural, the dominant teleology of phallocentrism, which is based on an antipodal hegemonic structure.

As a feminist critic, I am interested in the inscription in texts of power (im)balances between men and women. In political terms, male-centric discourse is both produced by and reproduces relationships of power and control between men and women. How women and men see their own and each other's selves as "engendered" thus interacts with other discourses. The existing sex/gender system whereby difference between men and women is both inscribed and produced is no more independent of its historicity than any other discourse and, in both Japan and the West, makes use of the same binaries of dominance/submission, culture/nature, victimizer/victim. But inevitably something "else" must leak through to constitute arenas of resistance.

The focus of many feminists has been not simply to describe how woman is absent in such a system (absent because representations of women are never more than distorted mirrors of man) but to celebrate women's body (and sexuality) as a potential site of resistance. For Cixous and other feminists, women's desire constitutes an uncolonized space (one of many gaps inherent in the system) wherein woman can write herself. Writing-the-body (primarily the sexual body) through a language that deconstructs such bilaterals and replaces unitary meaning with multiplicity and diffusion becomes for Cixous an act of personal and political liberation (Cixous and Clément, 63–132).

The actual political and economic subordination of women to men in modern Japanese society is also a premise of this chapter. Such subordination was demanded by premodern Neo-Confucian ideology, as evident in Article 19 of the Edo period (1600–1868) text *Onna daigaku takarabako* (A treasure chest of greater learning for women; 1716), which bluntly states: "Women are inferior to men. Since women are ignorant, they should remain humble, obeying their husbands' orders at all times."[1] Although provocative studies indicate that Japan's premodern divisions of labor did not mirror those of the West, the gender-specific separation of spheres of labor in postwar Japan and the West have grown increasingly similar, thereby narrowing the gap between Western and Japanese patriarchies.[2] The essay does not, however, seek to compare political, economic, social, and other systems of Western and Japanese patriarchy (which are similar in some aspects and different in others) and focuses instead on the organization of power in relationships between men and women (most notably sexual relations) as written in Yamada's narratives.[3]

Specific differences between women's subordination in the West and Japan today notwithstanding, in both nations a dominant discourse links men with culture and dominance and marks women as the passive other, inversely subsumed within the natural.[4] This chapter will show that this ideology repeatedly informs how Yamada writes women in text.

Yamada's texts blaze with erotic descriptions of women pursuing sexual fulfillment with a blatant disregard for anything or anyone or any morality that might interfere with that pursuit. Repeatedly, the narrators of Yamada's modern tales of love write their pleasure through the medium of the body, experiencing the world from an entirely sensual vantage point. In entering Yamada's narrative topography, spatial and temporal guideposts grow vague, rendered inconsequential in a world described in purely sexual/sensual terms. Desire propels the narratives directly, with little or no attention to plot. Although her longer fictions offer sketchy storylines and general information about their protagonists, her short works abandon even such minimalist pretensions to structure. *Beddotaimu aizu* (Bedtime eyes; 1987; hereafter *Bedtime*) tells of a love affair between Kim, a Japanese cabaret singer, and Spoon, an American soldier who is selling military secrets. The circumstances of their lives are mentioned only in passing, but attention is lavished on the steamy details of their affair. Yamada's much shorter "Seijin-muki mōfu," (X-rated blanket; hereafter "X-Rated"),[5] included in the anthology *Boku wa biito* (I am beat; 1988), is a single-consciousness, detailed narrative soliloquy upon the unnamed heroine's rapturous sexual intercourse with her lover, George:

> My body weakly collapses into a shape mirroring the space between his arms. Like mine, his body caves and coils. When my skin makes a depression, his skin touching that spot rises to fill it in. When my

nipples are erect they are buried by his body. We love each other exactly like liquids.

This is loving. My artless mind thinks so: the grinding of naked
bodies against each other, leaking, sparking, blending, all of this. Is
there any finer way to love? Crying, yelling, laughing. These things
all happen at once; is there anything else so preposterous? ("X-
Rated," 51, 53)

Yamada's narratives of pleasure have no room for more mundane
concerns. Readers spiral through repeating patterns of desire (absence) and fulfillment (presence), as lovers meet, gaze, touch, kiss,
make love, eat, drink, smoke, and part. In Yamada's work, an underlying instinctual (libidinal) drive clearly motivates the characters, and
the work itself, through an interplay of desire and satiation.

In the process, Yamada inverts many phallocentric paradigms
dominant in modern Japanese discourses of heterosexual relationships. Yamada's primary project seems to be the representation of
women independent and defiant of such common contemporary Japanese depictions as woman as mother, woman as passive (surrendered) object, and woman as male property. Simply writing sexual
pleasure as a woman (suggesting the possibility of woman-as-subject)
begins the process of inversion. Japanese narratives of sexual pleasure, most notably modern pornography, overwhelmingly portray
women as the victims of rape (or at least as the reticent objects of male
sexual desire) (see Terawaki). Standing in obvious contrast are the
women of Yamada's fictional world, women with overtly expressed
and powerful sexual desire. Yet do these inversions rewrite the heroines as somehow differently gendered subjects? Do they truly differ
from the dominant performance of gender in contemporary Japan?

As an American feminist, I find that some moments of Yamada's
tales of passion have spoken to my own sexuality with a rare honesty
and directness. In her afterword to *Hāremu wārudo* (Harem world;
1990; hereafter *Harem*),[6] she writes, "I want men to read my works.
You won't lose anything by it. Really. And it will definitely improve
your skills as lovers. And I want women to laugh. Laugh and laugh"
(198). I cannot comment on her qualifications as a sex therapist for
men, but she has successfully made me laugh with her audacious as-
saults on constructions that empower men in patriarchal societies. Yet
I have found Yamada's narratives to be slippery ones; although she
frames them in a deceptive simplicity, she exhibits a profound am-

bivalence toward her own (limited) reconstruction of gender, approaching moments of liberation only to ultimately retreat to familiar notions of difference.

Yamada's tentative gesture toward rewriting "womanhood" (and possibly enacting a personal liberation) celebrates her positioning at the margins of society and manipulates power relationships along the axis of dominance/submission. The adaptations are varied: woman is written as polygamous or powerful, as gazer-stalker, as aggressor; and sexuality is centered upon the vagina and principles of incorporation. The modifications evolve from women who are subsumed in their physicality, which, as I will argue, is that of a traditionally engendered body.

Protagonist Kim of *Bedtime* is all-body. Groping to satisfy her desire for Spoon, the man she has just seen for the first time, she exhibits no hesitation, no shame, and less resistance to sexual desire than the man:

> I fumbled to unbutton his shirt, clutching his jacket desperately.
> —I want to know this man's smell, now.
> The man was, in contrast to my reckless abandon, rather precisely and methodically stripping me. (13–14)

In the dim boiler room of a bar, they have sexual intercourse standing up. It is the man who suggests that they continue "making love" in a more comfortable and private setting. There are no post-passion musings by Kim over her reckless actions. Sex, for Kim, and for most of Yamada's female protagonists, is like eating when hungry. Kim sees Spoon, she desires Spoon, she embraces him (suggesting also an element of power in her gaze).

Harem, in Yamada's words, purports to depict "a woman who behaves like a man" by surrounding herself with smitten lovers (199). The impossibly naive heroine, Sayuri, is confused when one lover, Kobayashi, demands that she appear more chaste in public. In outraged response, she proclaims: "I despise men who don't appreciate clothes that bare the back. I can't see my own back, but everyone says its beautiful. What is wrong about showing off something beautiful?" (72).

Sayuri is a fanciful, independent character who lives in defiance of social definitions of "how a lady should comport herself." Repeatedly, she asserts her right to define herself and control the parameters of her own life, as is clear from the following exchange with Kobaya-shi:

> "You are my woman now."
> "I don't belong to anyone. One could rephrase: you are now my man." (72)

Kobayashi's need to control and possess backfires: Sayuri dumps him. Unable to understand the concept of male propriety, Sayuri amuses herself with multiple sexual partners. The narrator of "X-Rated" conversely limits herself to one man: if it's not George, then "it just won't do for me" (50). The women come together, however, in a shared celebration of sexual need. As the narrator of "X-Rated" muses, regarding her sexual desire: "I think that using the phrase 'in love' is appropriate. I believe that it is ok to use such lofty words for something that is an absolute necessity" (52).

Liberation does not halt at a mere acceptance of sexual arousal for these heroines. Yamada's women caress, sanction, and stoke their sexuality in much the same way piety, altruism, and morality enshrine more conventional heroines. Sayuri and Kim are decidedly, contentedly lusty, unafraid of their fierce passions. For both women, sexual pleasure is not dependent upon the immediate presence of a lover. In the absence of a lover, they pleasure themselves as naturally as they are pleasured by others, temporarily displacing the centrality of the phallus. Yamada offers readers an unusual (outside of the confines of pornography), graphic description of female masturbation: "I whisper that name [George], and my legs open of themselves; I place my hand there, inside, churning what is about to ooze out. I blend this self, a self excited by a finger. And so in a delicious state a delicious concoction is served up" ("X-Rated," 50).

Descriptions of sexual interludes, sexual yearnings, eating, and sleeping are punctuated by ruminations on love or banal conversations. Only one conversation interrupts the sensual tapestry of impassioned physicality in "X-Rated":

> "All we do is make love."
> "We can't help it. We have to make love."
> "Why do we have to make love?"
> "Because I love you." (52)

The conversation merely reframes the physical in a verbal equivalent. The body, thus written, gives birth to appetites that emanate from the body in rapid succession: sex is followed by eating, and eating is followed by sex, which may be followed by sleeping, or more eating, or drinking, or more sex. Sometimes the appetites entwine:

> Spoon's sharp teeth scraping the meat off the bone. A drop of grease dripping from his lips to float on the surface of the red wine. . . .
>   One by one I take his sauce-stained fingers in my mouth, all the while watching him. Oh, yes, Spoon wants to do it with me, now, I think. He has that sort of look on his face. (*Bedtime*, 126)

These varied instinctual appetites, which dominate the lives of Yamada's women with a tactile urgency, can be described as conventionally "female" in their presentation of women as creatures of nature and of a sexual appetite that turns insatiable once it has been unleashed. In her discussion of gender difference, Wendy Hollway has noted that in some cultural systems (and possibly underlying other systems' insistence on female asexuality), women's sexuality is believed to be "rabid and dangerous and must be controlled" (232). The dangerous, lusty woman (frequently associated with nature and the bestial) is a familiar figure to readers of Japanese myth and legend. The archetypal "woman of the mountains" (the *yamamba*) is a classic example.[7] Other appetites (such as hunger) collude to tether Yamada's women securely to their bodies and sever them from acculturation. Beasts to male humanity, Yamada's heroines make a theater of their bodies, publicly and defiantly caressing their sexuality.

The expression of female sexuality employed by Yamada situates women in the teleological narrative of incorporation. Lips (labial or facial) encircle fingers, penises; mouths ingest food, drinks, semen, flesh. This principle of engulfment (the vagina) is defined in oppositional relation to the "male" principle of penetration (the penis), determining her representations of women. Although she privileges the "female" principle (in metaphor, the bodies of water that symbolize woman), her view of this principle is determined by an all-too-familiar configuration of female anatomy. Biological axioms (formed within phallocentric sciences) frame the concept of the natural: the vagina is seen as the organ that incorporates the phallus (the site of empowerment) rather than having an existence and a significance independent of it. Sayuri's lover Teien pays homage to her vagina, situating himself both figuratively and literally at her feet:

> "What have I done to deserve a relationship with you? I can never thank God enough."

"If you are thanking someone, then thank this sensitive, understanding pussy."

Sayuri opened her legs in front of his face. He buried his face
there, kissing that sensitive, understanding, living thing, over and
over. (*Harem*, 49)

Possessor of this transcendental vagina, the powerful Sayuri nevertheless turns weak and pathetic as her lovers reject her one by one.
Comforting her, Teien has an epiphany: she is powerless without her
harem: "Now, he understood clearly. It was the indulgent attentions
of those men that had brought fullness and body to her hair. Hair that
had completely concealed the smallness of her head, the thinness of
her neck. She had chosen men capable of doing that" (*Harem*, 195).

Deprived of the phallus, the vagina is devalued. Sayuri's vagina
is empowered by the homage paid it by male lovers. The narrator of
"X-Rated" likewise confesses, "If I were not enwrapped by George's
body, my life would probably be ruined by my fretfulness. Even if I
am left breathless by the onslaught of pleasure, without him I could
have no tranquillity" (52). For these women, the vagina is severed
from any association with the womb; representations of woman-as-
mother are strikingly rare within Yamada's repertoire of female characters.[8] The first definition of "woman" in Yamada's work is thus
mired in a single, repeated representation of "woman as penis-
incorporating physical entity." Sexual bravado and fluid orgasms
aside, Yamada's narratives reproduce conventionally, socially engendered representations of female sexuality.

In seeking out sexual partners, many of Yamada's women play
stalker-gazer-subject. It is Kim who spots Spoon first in *Bedtime*, and
Sayuri who notices the handsome Stan in *Harem*. Sayuri follows Stan
to the telephone of the bar where she caught sight of him. Gazing at
him, her eyes note parts of his body with great satisfaction and anticipation. She concludes her visual inspection with an appreciative sigh
(24). A further narrative appropriation of the gaze depicts sexual interludes through the agency of the woman's consciousness, which
mirrors that of the stalking-women by reversing dominant configurations of power-by-gender. Yet the operation of the gaze is still characterized by objectification. Men and women alternate in offering
themselves for visual inspection.

Although Yamada thus threatens the absolute construction of
male as dominant, in control of a gaze that carries power, her methodology merely inverts a (maintained) structure. As E. Ann Kaplan

argues in *Women and Film*, reversals of roles along the axis of dominance/submission (masculine/feminine) do not affect the underlying antipodal structure:

> Our culture is deeply committed to myths of demarcated sex differences, called "masculine" and "feminine," which in turn revolve first on a complex gaze apparatus and second on dominance-submission patterns. This positioning of the two sex genders in representation clearly privileges the male (through the mechanisms of voyeurism and fetishism, which are male operations, and because his desire carries power/action where woman's usually does not). However, as a result of the recent women's movement, women have been permitted in representation to assume (step into) the position defined as "masculine," as long as the man then steps into her position, thus keeping the whole structure intact. (29)

If to operate the gaze, regardless of gender, is to be in the masculine position (30), Yamada's heroines temporarily step into the male position when they gaze, thereby situating the object (here, biologically male, engendered in the female role) in a submissive, receptive moment.[9]

Moreover, even this limited attempt to rebalance the power of female/male control of the gaze is temporary and ambivalent. Yamada's heroines spot their targets, reverse the gaze paradigm, but then collapse into the dominant model as, once the male's gaze is engaged, the women offer themselves as spectacle, exciting the agentive male voyeur who propels the text toward sexual gratification. Yamada's attempts to write-the-woman as subject instead reinstate the woman engendered as object: "The moment our eyes met, I felt as though he had discerned my thoughts and I looked down. When I raised my head again, he seized my line of vision and shifted it toward the exit. As though bewitched, I simply stood up, leaving my male companion with some excuse about the ladies room" (*Bedtime*, 10–11). Kim's brief moment of power as stalker is swiftly annihilated by the male (re)assumption of power. Similarly, in "X-Rated" the woman written as subject promptly turns into spectacle: "The doorbell rings; I fly to the door. . . . Together with the outside air George's eyes nestle into my body. I receive, catch his tumbling gaze. Before being touched by fingers or lips, all of me is licked by his eyes" (51).

♋

The visual feast of women's bodies is graphically extended to include that of women's sexual ecstasy (once again, mirroring pornography). There is a scene of female masturbation in *Harem*, but, unlike that in "X-Rated" (quoted above), it provides scopophilic pleasure for the male voyeur in text (not only for the reader). Teien travels to a beachfront cottage for a tryst with Sayuri. He finds her seated on a bed, facing windows flung open to the sea. In the passage that follows, reported to the reader through the medium of Teien's thoughts, Sayuri remains unaware of Teien's presence.

> Sayuri's back was barely moving, the muscles taut. He knew that she was staring straight at the ocean. The sun was setting. Face to face with the sun, Sayuri was only a black shape. Teien's gaze traced all the contours of her body. Slender arms extended from white silk. Just then, her body bent forward a little. Just before Teien called to her. He saw. Her hand was buried between her legs, moving in short, rapid motions, as though it had a life of its own quite separated from her still, hushed shoulders and back.
>
> Teien watched motionless. A sigh leaked from her mouth, as she slowly lay down. . . .
>
> Both hands between her legs, certain fingers began to thoroughly take her pleasure. (*Harem*, 59)

Voyeur Teien is overcome with feelings of exclusion, helplessness, and self-pity—at first glance, feelings incommensurate with his position of power as voyeur. The unaware Sayuri's absorption in her moment of pleasure seems to render Teien inconsequential and thereby return a measure of power to Sayuri herself. His desire to possess her produces a seething jealousy over her communion with the ocean, which he is afraid pleasures her as might a man. (Reaffirming woman as inseparable from nature.) Still, Teien is not so wounded as to be rendered unstimulated: the erotic, lingering, and graphic three-page description of Sayuri masturbating culminates when *he* ejaculates against the wall. Ultimately, the text adheres to accepted gender roles: the readers participate in the scopophilic titillation (tinged with masochism) enjoyed by Teien of furtively viewing Sayuri as masturbating-spectacle.

In this depiction of masturbation (as elsewhere), Yamada appropriates a hard-core pornographic focus on the vagina. In the following scene, for example, ambling through a park one early evening, Sayuri makes use of a swing to offer her vagina as spectacle for a prurient Stan:

> Sayuri swung vigorously, her legs stretched out and her upper body thrown back. Presently, the swing was above Stan's line of vision.

Her dress flipped up. She was not wearing panties. Stan's eyes were riveted. He didn't move. But his head bobbed like a pendulum. Nonplused, he stared fixedly at her skirt hem, which alternately exposed and hid her crotch. Her pussy was dancing! Stan's eyes turned into opera glasses. He thought, I don't care if I die. (*Harem*, 42)

The vagina thus challenges the penis as the centralized location of sexual desire and pleasure, yet it is always linked to its role as penis-incorporating organ. Yamada's approach to "vagina-power" reminds me of a cartoon I saw many years ago in a pornographic magazine: a little girl and a little boy are comparing genitals. The little boy proudly points out her "lack," telling her that she doesn't have one of "these." She icily responds, "So what? With one of these I can get as many of those as I want." For Yamada, the vagina remains employed in the role of ensnaring the penis. There is no equilibrium in power relations between Yamada's couples, only shifting positions of dominance and submission, predicated on who controls the phallus. In the narrative resistance to a shift to a description of male penetration, this (frightening and exciting) spectacle of the vagina weakens the male voyeur, in a masochistic capitulation to her sexual powers. In Yamada's work, woman thus temporarily occupies the subject position in relation to the male object while retaining the basic structure of the genitalia as centralized site of empowerment.

Fluctuating positions of power further suggest Yamada's ambivalence. Some stories depict men in classically dominant positions; others reverse this paradigm. Whichever positioning is chosen, however, narrative tension and motivation for character and narrative movement stem from the vacillation of power relations between lusting partners.

In an example where power-by-gender is inverted, Sayuri is depicted as the embodiment of sexual fantasy. One of her lovers, Klaus, muses: "He had known a great many women. He had enjoyed sex with many different women. He had quite fulfilled his desires and had assumed that the days of lusting after some woman or another were quite behind him. But then along came Sayuri, continually shattering that equilibrium" (*Harem*, 50).

Sayuri demands that her (willing) male partners attend diligently to her appetites: the amorous Teien may be instructed to cook for Sayuri while she reclines in bed, rather than being treated to the feast of her sexual favors. He complains:

Embracing her, or being embraced by her, the rule was that it was up to her. When she was neither hungry, nor sleepy. When all she desired was sex.

That was when her long, curling lashes framed pupils glistening with a plea for passions of the flesh. In the room dark with night, Sayuri demanded Teien's body, incessantly, until the daylight turned their bodies distinctly visible again. How Teien suffered. (*Harem*, 12)

Even when Teien is allowed to possess her sexually, he suffers from the intensity of her physicality. Lamenting Sayuri's dominance and the infrequency of her visits, the male lovers of *Harem* accept the passive, masochistic role traditionally assigned to the "ever-waiting" woman. Here *Harem* inverts the Japanese classical romantic paradigm. as exemplified by *The Tale of Genji*. Yamada replaces the romantic ideal (the shining Genji) with the stunning Sayuri, who makes a sexual playground of her life, and the predominant narrative voices are the laments of waiting, yearning men, who assume the role of the ladies awaiting the infrequent visits of the errant Genji.

Moreover, once the men are engendered in female roles of passivity, their desire is transformed into a "colonized" desire. Yielding their sexual gratification under the mantle of pleasuring Sayuri, they are reduced to reflections of her erotic imagination—a position that disallows their unmediated desire.

Destabilizing the positioning of women as dominant subjects is a subtext of reprisals that await the masculine heroines. Kim, who has for the first time given herself wholly to one man, is deprived of him by the police (society/norm/law), who arrest him. In another inversion of the classic romance, Sayuri is haunted by the ghost of spurned lover Kobayashi, who committed suicide after her rejection of him and who here takes the place of conventional jealous and vengeful female archetypes such as Lady Rokujō of *The Tale of Genji*. Although the classical model is thus overturned, Kobayashi's ghost threatens Sayuri's independence, driving her to seek solace from yet another lover, Teien. In the end, Sayuri's lovers leave her one by one, ultimately refusing the passive position. Only Teien remains, now empowered by the increasingly violent reprisals of Kobayashi's ghost that have transformed Sayuri from powerful goddess into pathetic victim.

The price Kim of *Bedtime* must pay for following her instinctual needs places her firmly in the submissive/masochistic position. Kim becomes the victim of Spoon's unfocused rage:

I was assaulted by fumes of cheap gin and absinthe wafting up from Spoon's leather jacket.

"What a stench, Spoon!"

"Shut up, bitch."

He grabbed my glass and hurled it at the floor. A fragment broke, ricocheted, and cut my cheek.

"You said I stink. How do I stink? Tell me! Huh? Spit it out." Spoon began choking me.

"I meant . . . let me go . . . I'll die . . ."

He let go abruptly and threw me against the wall. His eyes were muddied and unfocused. Once again, today, he had overindulged in narcotics. (54)

Typical of Yamada's ambivalence, *Harem* reverses this model of male violence when Sayuri pays an (as always) unannounced, spontaneous visit to Teien, only to discover another woman in his bedroom:

Then, Sayuri, who had been silently observing the two of them, strode forcefully into the room, resoundingly slapping Se's cheek a good ten times. Her eyes rounded, and silenced in surprise, broken capillaries stained Se's swollen cheeks bright red.

Sayuri seized Se by the front of her blouse and flung her against the wall. Se landed loutishly, with a loud bang, on her bottom. Sayuri straddled her and, seizing a nearby teabox, began to use it to beat Se. Striking wildly, she did not care where the blows fell — on her face, or her shoulders — so long as they connected somewhere to her body. (178)

Even in this transposition of a man with a woman as the violent abuser (who assumes exclusive access and ownership of her lover's body), the role reversal is incomplete. Brutality is directed not at Teien, but at the other woman / competitor.

Yamada thus colludes with prevailing power organizations in her portrayals of heterosexual relationships, as characters are engendered in the classical binary structures of dominance/submission. Regardless who assumes the dominant role, she is mired in the hegemony of a system in which one term must dominate the other. The temporary balance of power tends toward mutual objectification, situating both the heroine and her lovers in a definition of self-as-body. Limited to counteracting male dominance with female, Yamada's texts reproduce women engendered according to conventional configurations of power.

Moreover, as I argue below, Yamada figuratively and concretely pays homage to the phallus as the ultimate symbol of power, regardless of her labor to control it with an inversion of its centrality (the vagina). For her heroines, power is wrought through control of this transcendental marker of empowerment, which ushers in a similarly problematic racial hegemony that permeates her work and introduces the second part of this chapter, for her symbol of the ultimate "bearer of phallic power" is repeatedly an African-American male.

Race

Yamada is most famous in Japan for her overt engagement with African-American male lovers, in life and in fiction. She uses African-American men as already eroticized icons of phallic potency. Reversing the immediate postwar paradigm of black American soldier serviced (only) by Japanese prostitutes, Yamada's heroines lay claim to black lovers. Her texts, which are songs to the purely physical, are also ripe with ambivalent dissolutions of difference. Yamada's toppling of Japanese (and white) men from any position as bearers of · phallic power and her inversion of dominant gender-power structures depend upon the incorporation of existing, stereotypical images of black men (as well as those of sex/gender).

This textual employment of black male lovers is not simply the choice of an individual and should not be separated from past and present imagistic and stereotypical representations of African-American men in Japanese prose. As John Russell has noted:

> Recent trends in Japanese literary representations of the black Other tend to portray blacks as sexual objects, studs, fashion accessories and quintessential performers, images that imported American media reinforce daily. . . .
>
> A brief survey of literary and visual representations of blacks in contemporary Japan reveals the persistence of racial stereotypes which ascribe to blacks the following characteristics: (1) infantilism, (2) primitivism, (3) hypersexuality, (4) bestiality, (5) natural athletic prowess or physical stamina, (6) mental inferiority, (7) psychological weakness, and (8) emotional volatility. ("Race and Reflexivity," 19, 6)

Yamada's portrayals of the black male, which, as I will show, generally mirror those listed above, are also employed by advertisers in the selling of commodities marketed mostly to youth, and they function, in Russell's words, as a "symbolic counterpoint to modernity, rationalism, and civility" ("Race and Reflexivity," 22). In Yamada's work, as in advertising, one subtext is thus resistance to societal norms.

The contemporary popularity of black American urban "styles" in Japan provides a context against which Yamada's black male characters take on additional dimensions. Wolfgang Haug has argued convincingly that contemporary (one can add global) marketing techniques rely on an erotic sensualism (or libidinal urge) to sell commodities, which are increasingly divorced from any utilitarian value and compete on the level of illusion and appearance (56). In present-day Japan, African-Americans, and what is perceived to be the African-American style, are actively sought for commercials and other organs of the mass media. Already associated with the natural, the physical, and the sexual, black American men function symbolically in narrative and advertising as icons for physical performance (sexual or athletic).[10] As do commodities, the black male in Yamada's work enwraps the targeted consumer-reader in an incited desire, simultaneously promising (illusory) satiation through identification with the created icon. This icon also acts as a sign of resistance, or challenge, to dominant Japanese racial and gender evaluative norms.

The stud stereotype employed (and taken for granted) in Yamada's narratives, however, did not burst forth spontaneously in present-day Japan. The association of African-American males with primal sexuality reproduces earlier Japanese racialist discourses. A brief discussion of the history of Japanese racialism is therefore necessary to contextualize Yamada's writing of the black male.

In the introduction to this chapter, I mentioned Japanese racial separation of the (perceived) pure Japanese male from others within Japan, but focused exclusively on how women are "othered." Japan has also historically made distinctions between Japanese (male and female) "self" and non-Japanese "other," as John Dower has argued, through recourse to theories of blood purity related to ancient Shinto and Buddhist tenets regarding purity and pollution (275–77). These tenets have been reproduced in the discourse of Japan as a modern nation-state.

Racialism in Japan has thus been a mode of exclusion based on a belief in natural (or bodily) difference, which situates both the self and others in homogeneous, unified groups (Harootunian; Najita). In his essay "The Social Formation of Racist Discourse," David Goldberg has argued that this structure underlies racism in general through a hierarchical ordering of differences based on a value of purity—whether interpreted biologically (in terms of "blood" or "genes"), hygienically (in terms, for instance, of body odor), culturally (for example, language as signifying the evolution of thought patterns and rational capacity), or even environmentally (character, like nose shape and size, as determined by climate). Impurity, dirt, disease, and pollution are expressed as functions of the transgression of classificatory categories. (306)

Japan has identified itself as Asian in opposition to non-Asian nations in the modern period. Yet this alliance has been characterized by a concurrent conviction of Japanese supremacy, most vehemently from the time of the Meiji Restoration (1868) through the Pacific War. This distinction, an outgrowth of the ideology of Japanese racial purity, has also marked portions of the Japanese population as other. Included in the varied markers of difference is an association of purity and culture with light complexions. John Dower has said that "the Japanese themselves looked down on all the other 'colored' races. . . . They had esteemed 'whiteness' since ancient times" (12). The valuation of whiteness, which was also employed to distinguish the non-laboring, dominant Heian aristocracy from the working classes, has been reinforced in the modern period by the assimilation of European and American racialism.

Early modern Japanese interactions with Africans and Europe-an/American people of African descent were limited primarily to interactions with the slaves and servants of European and American traders. According to Russell, "the dichotomy that the West had drawn between 'European Culture and Civilization' on the one hand and 'African Barbarity and Savagery' on the other . . . provided a conceptual base upon which Japan could erect its own hierarchy of racial otherness" ("Race and Reflexivity," 6). I would rephrase the statement to stress that the European and American association of the black man with nature reinforced (but did not initiate) a similar, extant Japanese racialism that labeled darker Asians as inferior along the same nature/culture axis of demarcation and produced (and continues to reproduce) a *hybrid* discourse. One can thus call Japanese racialism "classical" because it marks difference along what Etienne Balibar terms the anthropological universal axis of humanity (culture) and animality (nature) (290–91).

Black Americans were among the soldiers who occupied Japan in the immediate postwar period. Shortly thereafter, the centralization of the military in Okinawa created a "colonized" site where black and white Americans constituted (to some degree) an other within. But conceptually, Okinawa (and Okinawans) stands excluded from "pure" Japan and is situated among the other within (Buraku Liberation Research Institute, 207–19). Interracial liaisons between soldiers and native Okinawan women were common, yet did not threaten the racial purity of the "real" Japanese. Moreover, the soldiers, because they stood outside the Japanese economy proper, offered no economic threat to the dominant (pure) class.

Black jazz musicians who toured Japan in the postwar period have been followed in recent times by other performers and entertainers. The racialist structures of European and American mainstream societies limit the realms in which blacks are seen to excel and reinforce Japanese association of blacks with music and athletic achievement to the exclusion of intellectual, political, and other arenas. These individuals still pose no internal economic threat to dominant structures; on the contrary, Japanese media, corporations, and so forth profit handsomely from the popularity of African-American performers. Unlike the laborers from other Asian nations who form a growing subclass of others within Japan, black Americans continue on the whole to be celebrated guests and do not impinge on social, political, or economic structures (outside of the soldiers confined primarily to Okinawa).

In Japan, the foreignness of blacks facilitates the borrowing of elements of style sundered from content. Attitudes toward American blacks are not a direct outgrowth of social tensions (although earlier discourses of racial purity were). Japanese representations and appreciation of the American black (sub)culture are thus limited and operate on the level of signs split from their referents, thus increasing the potential for reductive mythic images. This is apparent in some fairly recent racialist pronouncements by Japanese public officials, including the infamous comment by Prime Minister Nakasone Yasuhiro in 1986.[11] Japan's contemporary black myth further negates the (actual) presence of black women by their (general) absence in representation, and stagnates at the symbolic level of phallic potency. Yet the recent popularity of black male lovers among young Japanese women (not Okinawans, but Tokyoites) creates new challenges to discourses of Japanese racial purity, constituting a site of resistance to Japanese male standards of propriety for Japanese women, as well as to myths of homogeneity. Yamada's best-selling narratives, which eroticize the black male, testify to this site of resistance.

Japanese and American eroticization of black men as the bearer of mythic phallic potency is based on an association of the black man with the "natural" (primal) (Stepan; Fanon). This is because black men are ideologically constructed to be "closer to nature." The primal is only one of many metaphors employed in racialist portrayals of blacks that have also appeared in various discourses on women. As Nancy Leys Stepan has argued, scientists in the nineteenth century interpreted the biological differences between the sexes by placing women in an analogous position with so-called lower races, locating both women and non-whites in the category of inferior other:

> Women and lower races were called innately impulsive, emotional, imitative rather than original and incapable of the abstract reasoning found in white men. Evolutionary biology provided yet further analogies. Woman was in evolutionary terms the "conservative element" to the man's "progressive," preserving the more "primitive" traits found in lower races.
>
> In short, lower races represented the "female" type of the human species, and females the "lower race" of gender. (40)

The stereotypical images of black men in Yamada's narratives resemble her depictions of women; as lusty, volatile, physical beings held captive by overpowering appetites and marginalized by dominant (Japanese and white male) economic power. The partial view of the African-American male thus mirrors the representation of "gendered female" that permeates Yamada's narratives. In her works, likeness works magnetically, alternating between fierce, irresistible attraction and powerful repulsion. A struggle then ensues, between the similar and disparate natures of black male / Japanese female—a struggle fought along the same axis of dominance/submission. This power struggle is perhaps most obvious in Yamada's renditions of the affairs between black American soldiers and their Japanese lovers.

Black American soldiers appear in postwar prose, as do white Americans, as part of a conquering force that occupied Japan at the end of the Pacific War. Narratives and films often portrayed male American servicemen (white and black) as conquerors, and Japanese women as prostitutes. Rumors circulated regarding the mythic size and power of American (black and white) penises.[12] During a period when Japan was wartorn and economically shattered, the images portrayed an imbalance of power characterized by figurative rape and colonization and by Japanese humiliation and subjugation.

The rising value of the yen is mentioned by Yamada's contemporary, the writer Shimada Masahiko, as related to the type of writing bartered in a late-stage capitalist consumer society (Inoue et al., 447–50). He cites Yamada's work as an example of easily accessible, easily circulated, and easily consumed prose. On the level of myth, her works reinforce the commodity aesthetic of the African-American as stud. One can also frame Shimada's argument in the concrete arena of the Japanese economy. As the yen exchange rate rose and Japanese women became more prosperous, the image changed: both *Bedtime* and *Harem* portray Japanese women as the purchasers of black lovers. In *Harem*, a peripheral character, Junko, describes the black men gathered at a bar in Japan:

> Junko pointed out a group of worthless black men kept by prostitutes who indulged them. It's because of men like those that all black men in Japan are regarded with suspicion. . . .
> The black people she had known so far were slick gigolos. Worthless pimps. Talentless musicians. (*Harem* 82)

Although the passage maintains the (now classical) association of black man with prostitute in Japan, there is a fundamental shift. The prostitutes support their black lovers. Here, both the black man and the Japanese woman are linked through the commodity value of their (sexual) bodies. A similar economic arrangement between American soldier and Japanese lover (not prostitute) is reported by Kim in *Bedtime*:

> The military had a special term for runaway soldiers: U.A. The women who gathered at the discos frequented by soldiers responded to being told that a guy was U.A. in one of two ways. Either they maintained distance for their own personal safety, or else they contemplated purchasing and supporting the man as a pet to be played with however they pleased. (112)

Japanese women at clubs, bars, and discotheques frequented by African-Americans in Japan use their greater economic means to buy sexual partners (both texts refer to the practice using the Japanese word *kau*, to raise, keep, or take care of an animal or pet). Elsewhere in *Harem*, however, this arrangement is partially transposed. Stan impoverishes himself to purchase gifts for Sayuri. Because Stan's livelihood is linked to a meager American soldier's salary, he cannot compete economically with, for example, Sayuri's Japanese lover, Shin'ichi. As Stan is forced by circumstances into criminality, Yamada's writing cloisters him securely in an ever-increasing social marginality.

Most of the inversions in Yamada's work are characterized by fluctuations of power; different positions along the power axis afford alternating degrees of power. Some women buy men, some men buy women, but the struggle for dominance is never static. In Yamada's narratives there are thus ambivalent representations of the (im)balance of power between Japanese prostitute and black soldier. The struggle along the axis of dominance/submission, however, need not be framed in economic terms. Similar alternations of power by virtue of degree of emotional investment constitute another plane on which Yamada constructs battles of power. Whereas in *Bedtime* Spoon stands firmly in the power position vis-à-vis his smitten Japanese lover, *Harem* reverses the paradigm:

> Struck by sensation, Stan raised his head to see Sayuri at the crosswalk. Stan always felt something special as she approached, akin to the quickened heartbeat of a child about to embark on a school excursion—a confusion of expectation and unease.
>
> He had been basically indifferent about his lovers. Until the night when he met Sayuri. Thoughts of her made his breast race with passion. Whenever he was with her, he felt a hot enduring hardness melt away. . . .
>
> It was completely unlike how he had handled affairs previously, when he had been convinced that life was easier when one was single. (38, 40–41)

The economic and sexual dominance of the postwar black soldier is thus alternately threatened and reinstated by Yamada's renditions. In keeping with modern trends, however, her representations of black men are not limited to soldiers and include a variety of stereotypes. A sampling of various African-American characters from the anthology *I Am Beat* offer further examples of how Yamada writes of black men. "Kuroi kinu" (Black silk; 1988) introduces jazz-musician Percy as follows: "Lately, Percy is Maria's exclusive property. He escorts her everywhere. Decked out in a linen suit, Panama hat on his head, he's dressed like a good old-time sax-player. But he doesn't look old-fashioned, because Percy is a very young black man with a superfine, beautiful body" (43). Note that Percy is called Maria's property. Another example from *I Am Beat*, "Boku no ai wa in o fumu" (My heart in rhyme; 1988), describes a black American who is both rap artist and jazz musician (a composite figure of African-American musical forms):

> Moving to the music, Barney began to rap. A year ago he fell in love with a fine woman, but then his life got totally crazy and that was that. Even though he loved her sooo much, jealousy got in the way and it didn't go well at all. The words went something like that. Barney performed it in front of Phyllis, gesturing and posturing, making her laugh. (73–74)

No survey of black characters would be complete, it seems, without the requisite association of African-American men with certain forms of music, dance, and of course, drugs, which appears in the story "Daburu jointo" (Double joint; 1988):

> . . . not just gambling. You probably remember Dealer Victor. It so happened that there was some fine coke at his house, and we had a party and got high. If I try to remember how many white lines I sniffed, there's this fantasy in my head. The fantasy is, I bring along these two cute girls who take me to bed, sandwiched in between them, too much. (96)

The sadistic, accusatory voice of the drug abuser in "Double Joint" degenerates in the course of the narrative. By the conclusion, it has been reduced to that of a broken, jilted lover, begging the woman to come back to him, inverting the power premise that opens the story. Each of these tales reproduces partialized representations of black men culled from the repertoire of popular media images—men who then function as the erotic object for the female protagonist.

Two other short tales in the collection, "X-Rated" and "Boku no aji" (Taste of . . . ; 1988), are soliloquies on the pleasures of lovemaking from, respectively, a woman's and a man's points of view. Although neither narrative explicitly identifies the object of passion ("X-Rated") or the narrator ("Taste of . . .") as black, it can be easily inferred. The narrator of "Taste of . . ." plays the harmonica and smells like barbecue sauce, and the yearned-for George in "X-Rated" has a voice described as "like a southern melody" (54). In Yamada's work, however, that which clearly identifies a male character as black is his excellence as a lover. For it is black men who, in Yamada's words, possess the "genius" of lovemaking; repeatedly she compares the sexual skill of lovers in text through reference to their race: "Stan expressed affection toward Sayuri very ingenuously. When affection became sexual desire, he exhibited a colossal genius, marshaling fingers, tongue, sighs, and words to suit his purposes" (*Harem*, 149).

The word translated above as "ingenuously" is *sunao*, used repeatedly by Yamada to describe the naive, unstudied sexuality of both Japanese women and their black lovers. The reproduction of a social discourse of black male sexual mystique is further affirmed by comments Yamada attributes to Japanese male characters. Sayuri brings her black lover Stan to her Japanese lover Shin'ichi's house, whereupon Shin'ichi muses anxiously:

> A black man—the so-called very incarnation of sexuality. He had heard that once a woman tasted that, she would never return to Japanese men. [Sayuri] had said that the size of his [Shin'ichi's] penis was not a problem, but if she knew how good that one [the black man's penis] was, then she surely would switch [to a black lover]. (*Harem*, 100)

The supreme mark of difference, or demarcation, perceived in Yamada's work as the inverter of the conventional superior/inferior dyad (that places Japanese men in the empowered position), is the "perfect penis" of black men, which puts that of white men and Japanese men to shame: "His dick bore no resemblance to those reddish, nasty cocks that white men have; and it was also different from Japanese men's child-like, pathetic ones that were completely incapable of self-assertion unless they were stuck inside some helpless Japanese pussy" (*Bedtime*, 14). Although Sayuri claims it is more than the size of the sexual organ that defines sexual prowess, talented lovemaking remains the province of African-Americans; this is partly related to their purported simplicity and separation from the rational and intellectual: "The only solution he knew was fucking. How are we going to do it? How can I satisfy you? What do you mean there are other methods besides fucking? She was sure this was what Spoon was saying to himself. An immature child framed in a big body. My adorable Spoon" (*Bedtime*, 61).

Spoon's appetite for sex (he is also frequently portrayed as childlike, as in the preceding quotation) is matched only by his heavy drinking and cocaine sniffing. It is his animality, opposition to culture, and lack of restraint that attract his Japanese lover Kim, as is evident in the depiction of their first embrace, as quoted by John Russell: "From his arm pits came a strange smell. A corrupt odor, but definitely not unpleasant. As if by being assaulted by a dirty thing, I am made aware I am a pure thing. That kind of smell. His smell gives me a sense of superiority. It makes me yearn like a bitch in heat driven by the smell of musk" ("Narratives of Denial," 423).

Although this passage would suggest that Yamada's taste for black men is inseparable from a desire to affirm her own difference, her non-blackness, there are more ambivalent statements elsewhere in her fiction, in which her female narrators attempt to dissolve this difference through incorporation of the male phallus: "I realize that this body draped over mine is a completely different type of body. I move my hips, raise my voice, trying to transform his type into the same type as mine" ("X-Rated," 53). Elsewhere she celebrates the physical in passages that challenge those who would denigrate this as bestial: "All we do is make love. . . . Maybe people will say we are like animals. But do animals desire their partners like this? Can they know the art of feeling the flesh tingle even as one is satisfied? Every bit of him is enveloped in smooth skin. There, in that core, he is. Can an animal hunger to taste that, as though sipping broth?" ("X-Rated," 52).

In *Harem*, the attempt to dissolve difference takes the form of incorporation of the (black) male body into the (Japanese) female. Sayuri pays homage to the phallic superiority of black men in the same breath as she claims kinship with African ancestors. Boasting of a prior tryst, Sayuri proclaims:

> "His dick is the best!"
> "He's black?"
> "Well, of course. Do you think white people have dicks? My African blood [kokujin no chi] was all stirred up. My ancestors were certainly not slaves. They were African nobility, royalty." (8–9)

Yamada's African-American male is placed on a pedestal or transformed into an icon as the bearer of bestial, phallic potency, which she may then appropriate for her own erotic impulses, ensnaring him with her (empowered) vagina. When one of Sayuri's longtime Japanese lovers is shocked to learn that she is half-black, her black lover Stan responds, "You make love with Sayuri, don't you. You should have known [that she was part black]—no one should have had to tell you such a thing" (*Harem*, 150).

Sayuri's status as sex goddess, queen of sensuality, the woman before whom all men kneel, is inseparable from this hidden, yet all important alliance by blood with the black race. Her power to entrance men brings even the black male (the original object of phallic power) under her sway. Thus, the African-American Stan descends into a desperate life of thievery in his obsession to have the economic means to purchase pretty items for Sayuri, debasing and situating himself firmly outside the confines of socially acceptable activity.

Alienation from society proper thus produces another link between Yamada's heroines and their black lovers. Repeatedly in *Harem*, racist commentary attributed to Japanese men stresses black marginality in Japan. For example, Shin'ichi complains that "the black men in Japan are all trash. Those bastards think they can fuck Japanese women as soon as they meet them" (22). Elsewhere, Shin'ichi notes that "black people have hot bodies. Apparently they were savages, after all" (101). When Sayuri leaves Stan (who is hiding from the police) at Shin'ichi's apartment, Shin'ichi is seized with the fear that Stan will steal something (105).

Yamada's women, however, occupy socially marginal arenas as well. Kim sings in a cabaret that is frequently raided by the police for prostitution, and Shinobu of *Hizamazuite ashi o oname* (Kneel down and lick my feet; 1988; hereafter *Kneel*)[13] is employed as a dominatrix. Their liminal position in society through their occupation, which comprises an arena of shared marginality with black men, abets the connection through nature and appetite of Yamada's women to their black lovers. Stan's descent into crime and Spoon's much more serious violation of law—the selling of military secrets—firmly isolate and alienate them from society proper. Yamada's heroines act in opposition to subordination to Japanese male-centrism by choosing African-American sexual partners. This freedom, nonetheless, is limited to ambivalent inversions of extant constructions of both race and gender.

Yamada's textual treatment of Japanese men is quite different from that given her black lovers, and can be brutal and sadistic. Although undertones of sadism may color her treatment of black men (unavoidable given the vacillation along the power axis), when it comes to Japanese men, sadism is no longer mere suggestion. Emasculation begins at the site of empowerment, as apparent in the comparisons of penises quoted above. The symbol of black masculinity operates to threaten and shame Japanese men. Thus, *Harem*'s Shin'ichi feels disempowered when confronted by Sayuri's black lover: "[Shin'ichi] seethed with violent jealousy toward the black man confronting him. Lurking deep inside his breast was a powerful conviction of his inferiority—in comparison to their [black men's] legendary physical prowess and large sexual organs" (117).

In *Kneel*, in terms far removed from the enshrined phallic icons associated with Yamada's black studs, dominatrix Shinobu describes her (Japanese) clients' penises: "They just look like a bunch of wriggly vegetables out of some cartoon" (191). Referring to her clients repeatedly with words like "pathetic," "jerk," and "slave," Shinobu has a decidedly negative opinion of men in general, but her sharpest criticism is reserved for Japanese men:

> I think men are quite delicate. If I say the wrong thing at the wrong moment, it's all over for them. If there were a man who could talk to a woman in bed the way I talk, women would come just listening to him. But there aren't many men like that, men who can say enough of the right things in bed. Relatively speaking, foreigners are better at it. Men who can speak in a way that is both obscene and refined, crude and sincere. Most Japanese men don't have it in them. (195)

Boasting that her line of work affords her a peek into the most natural male state—one that the wives and girlfriends of her clients are sadly ignorant of—she gleefully admits to finding pleasure in the (temporary) power reversal. Quite to the point, she asks rhetorically, "Show me another job where you can abuse men and have them thank you" (189). Contemptuously she compares her job to that of bar hostesses, concluding that not only do hostesses have to serve their clients but they also make less money. Shinobu's pleasure in the power reversal is abundantly clear in the following description of her session with a Mr. Yamamoto:

> I sit on the red velvet throne with my legs crossed. Stark naked, the man approaches. He sits at my feet. He sure does look like a slave. In real life, the guy is president of a big company and spends his time bullying his employees.
> "Queen Shinobu, it is an honor to be your humble plaything today."
> "You are a despicable little slave." (190)

As she hammers away at Japanese men, both in her asides and in the depicted tortures, the scornful tone with which Sayuri attacks the symbol of masculine identity reaches its zenith in a scene that consists of an extremely graphic description of needles being inserted into the penis of a pathetic, paying (Japanese) client.

More conscientious considerations of these power metatheses reveal that Shinobu is solidly dependent on men: she is paid to fulfill their sexual perversions. Shinobu's economic survival is predicated on a male need to be tortured—a sexual perversion that requires female compliance with male directives. The senior queen, called Mama, is the only one not too shocked and revolted to satisfy the client who requests needles inserted in his penis. Shinobu narrates, "Mama began to speak in a loving voice, in that dim room oozing with insanity. It was enough to make me shiver, in spite of myself. Times like this, I really admire Mama. She's a real pro" (201).

Mama's capacity to repress revulsion or distaste, to suppress her own needs and sexuality in the interests of fulfilling those of her paying client, is what marks her as a professional. The power wielded by the "queens" of *Kneel* is thus inseparable from male economic supremacy, a facade that reinforces (in a disguised format) the subordination of women. In society proper, client Yamamoto is a powerful man. The private world of the club, which (temporarily) transposes power roles at the request of the male, does not affect his position in society.

Yamada's narratives go beyond the confines of a genteel, familiar, and acceptable fictional topography, into the midst of a world dictated by (often illicit and shockingly perverse) desire. Vacillating between awe of the black man's penis and contempt for men in general, she uses her sexuality as a means to effect at least a temporary appropriation of male power. The myth of the black American male that permeates Japanese culture is the already present icon that she can utilize in a re-creation of herself in his image.

Ultimately, however, the lover in "X-Rated" is revealed to be a reflection of the woman's own desire. The source of the female narrator's inspiration is her own mirror, and her own desire: "Twisted, I am wet; water floods high enough to wet my eyes. That's how I clearly recognize my own desire when I look in the mirror" (7). Alone in her bathroom, she looks at herself and sees the reflection of both her own desire and her sexual liaisons with her lover George, much in the manner that Wolfgang Haug claims commodities reflect the inner desire of the consumer (52). Moreover, just as the desire inflamed by advertisements' manipulations of the libido cannot be sated through the acquisition of goods, so too Yamada's narrator confesses: "As the sensation of satiation fills me—the satisfaction of having at last become one—I savor an intense pleasure tinged already with the mingling of a new, ongoing hunger" ("X-Rated," 14). Chained to the bina-

ries of absence/presence and dominance/submission, Yamada's narratives produce alternations that reinforce images of others (female
and black) as mirrors of each other's desire, and ultimately, as distorted mirrors of the (pure) Japanese male.

Moreover, Yamada's unique form of sexual expression — the incorporation of the black Other — is facilitated by her use of *katakana*
(the syllabary used to write foreign words of non-Chinese origin).
Frequently, the voices of characters in texts are expressed in New
York African-American vernacular slang written in *katakana*. The
flexibility of the Japanese language, particularly its ability to absorb
other languages in *katakana* — a process that often renders the words
unrecognizable to the country of origin — complements Yamada's
writing of African-American culture. In the following example of
Yamada's Japanese prose, English loanwords are translated back into
English:

> Diira [dealer] bikutā [Victor] o oboete iru darō. Aitsu no ie de wa ta-
> matama suteki na, kōku [coke/cocaine] ga haitte pātii [party] hiraite
> gettohai [get high]. Howaito [white] rain [line] o nanbon hiita ka
> omoidasōto sureba, atama no naka wa fantajii [fantasy]. ("Double
> joint," 96)

This is no longer American urban slang, but Japanese. Although
katakana is becoming the syllabary of choice for many of today's
young writers and is used to transliterate most words of non-Chinese
foreign origin (which account for increasingly larger proportions of
the written text), Yamada's renditions can also be read as an attempt
to appropriate the linguistic idioms of (New York urban) African-
Americans. In her works, reference to the genitals — male or female —
are almost exclusively in *katakana* renditions of American slang, as are
most of the names of her male characters and the titles of her works
(Spoon or Stan as character names, and "Double joint" or *Harem World*
as titles, for example). Japanese proper — relational, hierarchical, and
gender-based — does not provide her with a voice for her special
brand of sexual bravado. Yet *katakana* is both part of the Japanese language and suggestive of the foreign. Vocabulary lifted from its context is slipped into Japanese syntax, which gives it the appearance and
atmosphere of American slang, while, in fact, it remains Japanese.

The manner in which Yamada incorporates the black other in text
parallels the structures that inform *katakana* usage in the modern period. While signaling the presence of the other in text (or indicating

emphasis, much like italics), *katakana* simultaneously orders what is written within the parameters of Japanese linguistic structure and pronunciation. African-Americans likewise function to mark a difference, catalogued by a reproduction of marginality. Yamada's ambivalent "othering" of African-American men also marks a desire for racial slippage, supplementary to the Western black/white binarism that does not represent Asian "yellowness."[14]

$\wp$

Although Yamada's literary intention appears to mirror Cixous's personal and political sexual liberation, by not challenging the underlying binaries of patriarchal society, she instead reproduces sex/gender and racial discourses dependent on existing structures of empowerment and resistance. Vacillating between an embrace of marginality and the replacement of male centrality with female-as-subject, the organization of power relations between men and women in her narratives does not transcend the axis of dominance/submission. Aligned with the African-American man through racialist and gendered marks of difference, Yamada labors at incorporation, laying claim to a kinship, yet is reduced to writing battles for power between two colonized (subordinate) categories of people. These characters then objectify and dominate each other, reproducing a discourse of colonization. Desire in Yamada's texts is thus never more than the desire of the Other. Culture and society imprison and restrain Yamada's heroines and their black lovers, and her characterizations reproduce the "engendered body" and the "racialized body" of the very culture to which they stand in opposition. It is the production of her "engendered" self as woman-body that leads to Yamada's depiction of an association with self-as-black (colonized); in both cases, the end result is (perhaps unwanted) collusion with dominant Japanese racialism and patriarchal ideology. Her writing of Japanese woman and African-American male remains locked inside the conventional dominance/submission dialectic that underlies both.

Notes

1. Ishikawa, 54; quoted in Niwa, 72. Two important sources on the history of women and the women's movement in Japan are Joseishi sōgō kenkyū kai, *Nihon joseishi*; and idem, *Nihon josei seikatsu shi*. Despite similarities in modern structures, sex/gender roles and the status of women in contempo-

rary Japan diverge in many ways from Western patterns. Nor should the reader assume a correlation between premodern or modern Western and Japanese gender politics, and the class issues that inform these politics. Sources in English that offer a good general introduction to political, economic, social, literary, and other contemporary and historical positionings of women in Japan, modern and premodern gender roles, women's status, and sexual politics include Bernstein; Ueno; and Sievers.

2. See, e.g., Niwa; and Wakita. Wakita argues for revised readings of women's subordination during the medieval period, and Niwa theorizes that the Japanese myth of motherhood, which is often thought of as historically transcendental, was absent during the Edo period and was reproduced as a modern construct through Meiji period social transformations.

3. For historical and sociological studies that describe and analyze Japanese phallocentrism in its premodern and contemporary manifestations, see *Nichi-bei josei jānaru*, which also publishes an English supplement under the name *The U.S.-Japan Women's Journal*. For additional sources, see notes 1 and 2 above.

4. See, e.g., Tajima Yōko's (44–47) discussion of woman and nature in Kawabata's *Snow Country* from Komako's point of view; and Ningen bunka kenkyūkai, *Josei to bunka*; and idem, *Josei to bunka II & III*.

5. An English translation of "X-Rated Blanket" by Nina Cornyetz appears in Mitsios, *New Japanese Voices*, 50–54. The page references given in the text are to this translation.

6. The title, *Hāremu wārudo*, consists of two Japanese loan words. While *wārudo* is clearly "world," *hāremu* is used to transliterate two English words: "harem" and "Harlem." Although Yamada probably chose *hāremu* for its ambiguity, I have elected to translate it as *harem* because the word appears unambiguously as "harem" in the last sentence of the text. In the afterword, however, Yamada names Spike Lee's film "She's Gotta Have It" as the inspiration for the text, reinforcing the argument for double entendre.

7. See Chapter 7, pp. 239–61, by Meera Viswanathan, in this volume.

8. The French feminist celebration of self-as-mother is problematic for Japanese feminists because of the dominant myth of maternal-infant dualism that permeates much of classical Japanese literature. Many contemporary Japanese feminists and women writers find liberation in the refusal of the maternal position rather than in an embrace of it. For a discussion that contextualizes the issue of motherhood, see Lebra.

9. This construct cannot fully describe lesbian relations, which some feminists have argued involves a "gaze" supplemental to the male/female heterosexual, binary matrix. See Mayne; and de Lauretis.

10. See Russell, "Race and Reflexivity"; and idem, "Narratives of Denial." See also Jones for a description of the "borrowing" of African-American style by Japanese youth.

11. See Nakasone; Nakasone accused the United States of a low intel-

lectual average, which he attributed to the large numbers of African-Americans (*kokujin*), Puerto Ricans, and Mexicans.

12. See, e.g., Nosaka; Ōe, "Prize Stock"; the film *Setouchi shōnen yakyū dan*" (MacArthur's children; 1984) directed by Shinoda Masahiro; and popular magazines such as *Video-on-Stage*. An advice column in *Video-On-Stage*, called "Rūku no mi no shita sōdan," is written by a young black man named Luke. The column's title puns on the Japanese word *mi no ue*, which literally means "regarding the body," or in an even more literal rendering, "the upper body," but has the idiomatic meaning of "pertaining to circumstances." Replacing *ue* (upper) with *shita* (lower), the column offers advice on "matters pertaining to the lower half of the body." For example, both letters in the Nov. 1992 issue ask for advice on sexual matters. A young Japanese man writes of his endeavors to look and act "black" and of his feeling of being thwarted only by the smallness of his (Japanese) penis; and a young Japanese woman writes to ask where and how she might avail herself of (any) black male lover.

13. An excerpt, translated by Terry Gallagher, appears in the anthology *Monkey Brain Sushi*, 187–204. Further references are to the translation and are given in the text.

14. See Cornyetz, for an analysis of the meaning of "blackness" in Japan as a sign encoded with masculine, heterosexual *body* power, which simultaneously challenges Western (and dominant Japanese) racialism. Japanese youths' reproduction of themselves in black style, and Japanese women's desire for black lovers, also signifies a potential transnational identity, supplementary to a previously introjected, Western imperialist black/white antipodal paradigm, revelatory of a desire and a propensity for racial identificatory slippage.

Works Cited

Balibar, Etienne. "Paradoxes of Universality." In Goldberg, *Anatomy of Racism*, 283–94.

Bernstein, Gail Lee, ed. *Recreating Japanese Women, 1600–1945*. Berkeley: University of California Press, 1991.

Buraku Liberation Research Institute. *Long-Suffering Brothers and Sisters, Unite!* Osaka: Buraku kaihō kenkyūsho, 1981.

Butler, Judith. *Bodies That Matter: On the Discursive Limits of "Sex."* New York: Routledge, 1993.

Cixous, Hélène, and Catherine Clément. *The Newly Born Woman*. Trans. Betsy Wing. Minneapolis: University of Minnesota Press, 1986.

Cornyetz, Nina. "Fetishized Blackness: Hip Hop and Racial Desire in Contemporary Japan." *Social Text*, no. 9 (Dec. 1995): 29–58.

de Lauretis, Teresa. "Sexual Indifference and Lesbian Representation." In *The Lesbian and Gay Studies Reader*, ed. Henry Abelove, Michèle Aina Barale, and David M. Halperin. New York: Routledge, 1993, 141–58.

Dower, John. *War Without Mercy: Race and Power in the Pacific War*. New York: Pantheon Books, 1986.

Fanon, Frantz. "The Fact of Blackness." In Goldberg, *Anatomy of Racism*, 108–26.

Goldberg, David Theo, ed. *Anatomy of Racism*. Minneapolis: University of Minnesota Press, 1990.

———. "The Social Formation of Racist Discourse." In idem, *Anatomy of Racism*, 295–318.

Harootunian, Harry. "Visible Discourses / Invisible Ideologies." *South Atlantic Quarterly* 87, no. 3 (Summer 1988): 445–74.

Haug, Wolfgang. *Critique of Commodity Aesthetics: Appearance, Sexuality and Advertising in Capitalist Society*. Trans. Robert Bock. Minneapolis: University of Minnesota Press, 1986.

Henriques, Julian et al., eds. *Changing the Subject: Psychology, Social Regulation, and Subjectivity*. New York: Methuen, 1984.

Hollway, Wendy. "Gender Difference and the Production of Subjectivity." In Henriques et al., 227–63.

Inoue Hisashi, Takahashi Gen'ichirō, and Shimada Masahiko. "Soshite, ashita wa dō naru ka." *Shinchō*, special issue: "Kono issatsu de wakaru Shōwa no bungaku" (Feb. 1989): 440–62.

Ishikawa Matsutarō, ed. *Onna daigaku-shū*. Tokyo: Heibonsha, 1977.

Jones, Andrew. "Black Like Me." *Spin* 9, no. 7 (Oct. 1, 1993): 74–78.

Joseishi sōgō kenkyūkai, ed. *Nihon josei seikatsu shi*. Tokyo: Tōkyō daigaku shuppankai, 1990.

———, ed. *Nihon joseishi*. 5 vols. Tokyo: Tōkyō daigaku shuppankai, 1982.

Kaplan, E. Ann. *Women and Film: Both Sides of the Camera*. New York: Methuen, 1983.

Lebra, Takie S. "Fractionated Motherhood: Status and Gender Among the Japanese Elite." *U.S.-Japan Women's Journal, English Supplement* 4 (1993): 3–25.

Mayne, Judith. "Lesbian Looks: Dorothy Arzner and Female Authorship." In Bad Object-Choices, ed., *How Do I Look? Queer Film and Video*. Seattle: Bay Press, 1991, 103–35.

Najita Tetsuo. "On Culture and Technology in Postmodern Japan." *South Atlantic Quarterly* 87, no. 3 (Summer 1988): 401–18.

Nakasone Yasuhiro. "Zensairoku: Nakasone shushō chiteki suijun kōen." *Chūō kōron* 101 (Nov. 1986): 142–62.

Newton, Judith, and Deborah Rosenfelt, eds. *Feminist Criticism and Social Change: Sex, Class and Race in Literature and Culture*. New York: Methuen, 1985.

Ningen bunka kenkyūkai, ed. *Josei to bunka (I)*. Tokyo: Hakuba shuppan, 1979.

———. *Josei to bunka (II) & (III)*. Tokyo: JCA, 1984.

Niwa Akiko. "The Formation of the Myth of Motherhood in Japan." *U.S.-Japan Women's Journal, English Supplement* 4 (1993): 70–82.

Nosaka Akiyuki. "American *Hijiki.*" Trans. Jay Rubin. In *Contemporary Japanese Literature: An Anthology of Fiction, Film, and Other Writing Since 1945,* ed. Howard Hibbett. New York: Knopf, 1977, 435–68.

Ōe Kenzaburō. "Prize Stock" ("Shiiku"). Trans. John Nathan. In idem, *Teach Us to Outgrow Our Madness.* New York: Grove Press, 1977, 111–68.

Russell, John. "Narratives of Denial: Racial Chauvinism and the Black Other in Japan." *Japan Quarterly* 38, no. 4 (Oct. 1991): 416–28.

———. "Race and Reflexivity: The Black Other in Contemporary Japanese Mass Culture." *Cultural Anthropology* 6, no. 1 (Feb. 1991): 3–25.

Sievers, Sharon L. *Flowers in Salt: The Beginnings of Feminist Consciousness in Modern Japan.* Stanford: Stanford University Press, 1983.

Stepan, Nancy Leys. "Race and Gender: The Role of Analogy in Science." In Goldberg, *Anatomy of Racism,* 38–57.

Tajima Yōko. "A Rereading of *Snow Country* from Komako's Point of View." *U.S.-Japan Women's Journal, English Supplement* 4 (1993): 26–48.

Terawaki Kiyo. "Shin pinku eiga jihyō." *Eiga geijutsu* 360 (Winter 1991): 111–13.

Ueno Chizuko. "The Position of Japanese Women Reconsidered." *Current Anthropology* 28 (1987): 575–84.

Wakita Haruko. "Women and the Creation of the *Ie* in Japan: An Overview from the Medieval Period to the Present." *U.S.-Japan Women's Journal, English Supplement* 4 (1993): 83–105.

Yamada Eimi. *Beddotaimu aizu.* Tokyo: Kawade shobō shinsha, 1987.

———. "Boku no ai wa in o fumu." In idem, *Boku wa biito,* 67–92.

———. "Boku no aji" In idem, *Boku wa biito,* 189–210.

———. *Boku wa biito.* Tokyo: Kadokawa shoten, 1988.

———. "Daburu jointo." In idem, *Boku wa biito,* 93–115.

———. *Hāremu wārudo.* Tokyo: Kōdansha bunko, 1990.

———. *Hizamazuite ashi o oname.* Tokyo: Shinchōsha, 1988.

———. *Kneel Down and Lick My Feet* (*Hizamazuite ashi o oname* [excerpt]). Trans. Terry Gallagher. In *Monkey Brain Sushi: New Tastes in Japanese Fiction,* ed. Alfred Birnbaum. Tokyo: Kōdansha International, 1991, 187–204.

———. "Kuroi kinu." In idem, *Boku wa biito,* 43–66.

———. "Seijin-muki no mōfu." In idem, *Boku wa biito,* 5–15.

———. "X-Rated Blanket" ("Seijin-muki no mōfu"). Trans. Nina Cornyetz. In *New Japanese Voices: The Best of Contemporary Fiction from Japan,* ed. Helen Mitsios. New York: Atlantic Monthly Press, 1991, 50–54.

Reference Matter

Selected Bibliography of Japanese Women's Writing

COMPILED BY JOAN E. ERICSON
AND MIDORI Y. McKEON

This bibliography is designed as an aid to further study for readers of this volume. It contains a selection of translations and studies of fiction by Japanese women writers published in English, and since it is not intended to be an exhaustive survey of the field, we have chosen mainly material readily available in North American libraries. Translations and studies of poetry are largely excluded, consistent with the volume's focus on fiction.

The bibliography consists of two parts: Section 1, "English Translations of Modern Japanese Fiction by Women," lists individual writers alphabetically and includes translations of works published from 1868 to the present. (For annotated listings of translations, we recommend Mamola's two-volume *Annotated Bibliography*, Mulhern's *Japanese Women Writers*, and the chapters by Kathryn Sparling in Huber's *Women in Japanese Society*.) Section 2 lists bibliographies, studies, translations of classical works by Japanese women, collections, journal articles (1980–95), and book reviews (1980–95).

For complete data on works cited in abbreviated form in Section 1, see Section 2.

1. *English Translations of Modern Japanese Fiction by Women*

Amino Kiku (1900–1978)
  "Wakare" (1976). "Breaking Up." Trans. Chieko M. Ariga. *Mānoa: A Pacific Journal of International Writing* 3, no. 2 (Fall 1991): 28–30.

Ariyoshi Sawako (1931–84)
  "Eguchi no sato" (1958). "The Village of Eguchi." Trans. Yukio Suwa and Herbert Glazer. *Japan Quarterly* 18, no. 4 (1971): 427–41.

Hanaoka Seishū no tsuma (1966). *The Doctor's Wife.* Trans. Wakako Hironaka and Ann Siller Konstant. Tokyo: Kōdansha, 1978.

Izumo no okuni (1972). *Kabuki Dancer.* Trans. James R. Brandon. Tokyo: Kōdansha, 1994.

"Jiuta" (1956). "Jiuta." Trans. Yukio Sawa and Herbert Glazer. *Japan Quarterly* 22, no. 1 (1975): 40–58.

"Kazunomiya-sama otome" (1978). "Her Highness Princess Kazu." Trans. Mildred Tahara. *Translation* 17 (Fall 1986): 164–83.

Ki no kawa (1959). *The River Ki.* Trans. Mildred Tahara. Tokyo: Kōdansha, 1980.

"Kitō" (1959). "Prayer." Trans. John Bester. *Japan Quarterly* 7, no. 4 (1960): 448–81.

Kōkotsu no hito (1972). *The Twilight Years.* Trans. Mildred Tahara. Tokyo and New York: Kōdansha, 1984.

"Sumi" (1961). "The Ink Stick." Trans. Mildred Tahara. *Japan Quarterly* 22, no. 4 (1975): 348–69.

"Tomoshibi" (1961). "The Tomoshibi." Trans. Keiko Nakamura. In Ueda, 241–57.

Enchi Fumiko (1905–86)

"Kikuguruma" (1967). "Boxcar of Chrysanthemums." Trans. Yukiko Tanaka and Elizabeth Hanson. In Tanaka and Hanson, 69–86.

"Mekura oni" (1962). "Blind Man's Bluff." Trans. Beth Cary. In Ueda, 165–77.

"Nise no en—shūi" (1958). "A Bond for Two Lifetimes—Gleanings." Trans. Phyllis Birnbaum. In P. Birnbaum, 25–47; "Love in Two Lives: The Remnant." Trans. Noriko Mizuta Lippit. In Lippit and Selden, *Stories by Contemporary Japanese Women Writers,* 76–91. Reprinted in Lippit and Selden, *Japanese Women Writers,* 97–111.

Onna men (1958). *Masks.* Trans. Juliet Winters Carpenter. New York: Aventura, 1983.

Onna-zaka (1957). *The Waiting Years.* Trans. John Bester. Tokyo: Kōdansha, 1971.

"Otoko no hone" (1956). "Skeletons of Men." Trans. Susan Matisoff. *Japan Quarterly* 35, no. 4 (Oct.–Dec. 1988): 417–25.

"Yō" (1957). "Enchantress." Trans. John Bester. *Japan Quarterly* 5, no. 3 (1958): 339–57.

Gō Shizuko (1929–)

Rekuiemu (1975). *Requiem.* Trans. Geraldine Harcourt. Tokyo: Kōdansha, 1985.

Harada Yasuko (1928–)

"Banshō" (1960). "Evening Bells." Trans. Chia-ning Chang and Sara Dillon. In Ueda, 47–69.

Hayashi Fumiko (1903–51)

"Bangiku" (1948). "Late Chrysanthemum." Trans. John Bester. *Japan*

Quarterly 3, no. 4 (Oct.–Dec. 1956): 468–86; "A Late Chrysanthemum." Trans. Lane Dunlop. In Dunlop, *A Late Chrysanthemum*, 95–112.

"Boruneo daiya" (1946). "Borneo Diamond." Trans. Lane Dunlop. *Translation* 22 (Fall 1989): 181–96. Reprinted in Dunlop, *Autumn Wind*, 161–82.

"Hone" (1949). "Bones." Trans. Ted T. Takaya. In Saeki, 133–54.

Hōrōki (1928–30). *Vagabond's Song* (excerpt). Trans. Elizabeth Hanson. In Tanaka, *To Live and to Write*, 105–25. Trans. Joan E. Ericson. *Diary of a Vagabond*. In Ericson, *Hayashi Fumiko*.

"Shitamachi" (1949). "Downtown." Trans. Ivan Morris. In I. Morris, *Modern Japanese Stories*, 349–64. Also in Keene, *Modern Japanese Literature*, 415–28.

"Suisen" (1949). "Narcissus." Trans. Kyoko Iriye Selden. In Lippit and Selden, *Stories by Contemporary Japanese Women Writers*, 49–61. Reprinted in Lippit and Selden, *Japanese Women Writers*, 46–57. Trans. Joan E. Ericson. "'Narcissus'—A Short Story by Hayashi Fumiko." *Asian Cultural Studies* 21 (Apr. 1995): 71–84.

Ukigumo (1949–51). *The Floating Clouds*. Trans. Koitabashi Yoshiyuki and Martin C. Collcutt. Tokyo: Hara shobō, 1965.

"Uruwashiki sekizui" (1947). "Splendid Carrion." Trans. Shioya Sakae. *Western Humanities Review* 6, no. 3 (Summer 1952): 219–28.

Hayashi Kyōko (1930–)

"Eki" (1990). "Stations." Trans. Margaret Mitsutani. *Mānoa: A Pacific Journal of International Writing* 3, no. 2 (Fall 1991): 81–93.

"Futari no bohyō" (1975). "Two Grave Markers." Trans. Kyoko Iriye Selden. *Bulletin of Concerned Asian Scholars* 18, no. 1 (Jan.–Mar. 1986): 23–35.

"Kōsa" (1977). "Yellow Sand." Trans. Kyoko Iriye Selden. In Lippit and Selden, *Stories by Contemporary Japanese Women Writers*, 197–207. Reprinted in Lippit and Selden, *Japanese Women Writers*, 207–16.

"Kū kan" (1977). "The Empty Can." Trans. Margaret Mitsutani. In Ōe, *The Crazy Iris*, 127–43.

Hayashi Mariko (1954–)

"Wain" (1985). "Wine." Trans. Dawn Lawson. In Mitsios, 138–51.

Higuchi Ichiyō (1872–96)

"Jūsanya" (1895). "The Thirteenth Night." Trans. Robert Lyons Danly. In Danly, *In the Shade of Spring Leaves*, 241–53.

"Koto no ne" (1893). "The Sound of the Koto." Trans. Robert Lyons Danly. In Danly, *In the Shade of Spring Leaves*, 178–81.

"Nigorie" (1895). "Troubled Waters." Trans. Robert Lyons Danly. In Danly, *In the Shade of Spring Leaves*, 218–40.

"Ōtsugomori" (1894). "On the Last Day of the Year." Trans. Robert Lyons Danly. In Danly, *In the Shade of Spring Leaves*, 205–17.

"Takekurabe" (1895–96). "Child's Play." Trans. Robert Lyons Danly. In

Danly, *In the Shade of Spring Leaves*, 254–87; "Growing Up." Trans. Edward Seidensticker. In Keene, *Modern Japanese Literature*, 70–110.

"Wakare michi" (1896). "Separate Ways." Trans. Robert Lyons Danly. In Danly, *In the Shade of Spring Leaves*, 288–95. Also in Arkin and Shollar, 139–43.

"Yamiyo" (1894). "Encounters on a Dark Night." Trans. Robert Lyons Danly. In Danly, *In the Shade of Spring Leaves*, 182–204.

"Yamizakura" (1892). "Flowers at Dusk." Trans. Robert Lyons Danly. In Danly, *In the Shade of Spring Leaves*, 167–73.

"Yuki no hi" (1893). "A Snowy Day." Trans. Robert Lyons Danly. In Danly, *In the Shade of Spring Leaves*, 174–77.

Hikari Agata (1943–)

"Hōmu pātei" (1986). "A Family Party." Trans. Yukiko Tanaka. In Tanaka, *Unmapped Territories*, 84–119.

Hirabayashi Taiko (1905–1972)

"Azakeru" (1927). "Self-Mockery." Trans. Yukiko Tanaka. In Tanaka, *To Live and to Write*, 75–96.

"Haha to iu mono" (1966). "A Woman to Call Mother." Trans. Richard Dasher. In Ueda, 211–23.

"Hito no inochi" (1950). "A Man's Life." Trans. George Saito. In I. Morris, *Modern Japanese Stories*, 365–82.

"Kishimojin" (1946). "The Goddess of Children." Trans. Ken Murayama. *Pacific Spectator* 6, no. 4 (1952): 451–57.

"Kuroi nenrei" (1963). "The Black Age." Trans. Edward Seidensticker. *Japan Quarterly* 10. no. 4 (1963): 479–93.

"Mō Chūgoku hei" (1946). "Blind Chinese Soldiers." Trans. Noriko Mizuta Lippit. In Lippit and Selden, *Stories by Contemporary Japanese Women Writers*, 44–48. Reprinted in Lippit and Selden, *Japanese Women Writers*, 41–45.

"Watakushi wa ikiru" (1947). "I Mean to Live." Trans. Edward Seidensticker. *Japan Quarterly* 10, no. 4 (1963): 469–79.

Hiraiwa Yumie (1932–)

"Yūgao no onna" (1979). "Lady of the Evening Faces." Trans. Patricia Lyons. In Ueda, 259–77.

Kanai Mieko (1947–)

"Puraton-teki ren'ai" (1975; 1979). "Platonic Love." Trans. Amy Vladeck Heinrich. In Gessel and Matsumoto, 361–68.

"Tama ya" (1986–87). "Tama." Trans. Mark Jewel. *Japanese Literature Today* 14 (Mar. 1989): 5–12.

"Usagi" (1976). "Rabbits." Trans. Phyllis Birnbaum. In P. Birnbaum, 1–23.

Kizaki Satoko (1939–)

"Aogiri" (1985). "The Phoenix Tree." Trans. Carol A. Flath. In Kizaki, *The Phoenix Tree*, 143–242.

"Kaenboku" (1981). "Flame Trees." Trans. Carol A. Flath. In Kizaki, *The Phoenix Tree*, 47–121.

"Mei howa ru" (1987). "Mei Hua Lu." Trans. Carol A. Flath. In Kizaki, *The Phoenix Tree*, 123–42.

The Phoenix Tree and Other Stories. Trans. Carol A. Flath. Tokyo: Kōdansha , 1990.

"Rasoku" (1980). "Barefoot." Trans. Carol A. Flath. In Kizaki, *The Phoenix Tree*, 7–46.

Shizumeru tera (1987). *The Sunken Temple*. Trans. Carol A. Flath. Tokyo: Kōdansha International, 1993.

Kōda Aya (1904–1990)

"Hina" (1955). "Dolls." Trans. Alan M. Tansman. In Tansman, 184–92.

"Kami" (1951). "Hair." Trans. Alan M. Tansman. In Tansman, 162–65.

"Kunshō" (1949). "The Medal." Trans. Alan M. Tansman. In Tansman, 153–61.

"Kuroi suso" (1955). "The Black Hems." Trans. Alan M. Tansman. In Tansman, 166–83; "The Black Skirt." Trans. Edward Seidensticker. *Japan Quarterly* 3, no. 4 (Oct.–Dec. 1956): 196–211; reprinted in *Modern Japanese Short Stories*. Tokyo: Japan Publications Trading, 1960, 118–40.

Kometani Fumiko (Foumiko; 1930–)

"Enrai no kyaku" (1985). "A Guest From Afar." Trans. Kometani Foumiko. In Kometani, *Passover*, 87–148.

Passover. New York: Carroll & Graf, 1989.

"Sugikoshi no matsuri" (1985). "Passover." Trans. Kometani Foumiko. In Kometani, *Passover*, 1–86.

Kōno Taeko (1926–)

"Ari takaku" (1964). "Ants Swarm." Trans. Noriko Mizuta Lippit. In Lippit and Selden, *Stories by Contemporary Japanese Women Writers*, 105–19. Reprinted in Lippit and Selden, *Japanese Women Writers*, 112–25.

"Hone no niku" (1969). "Bone Meat." Trans. Lucy Lower. In Hibbett, 41–52.

"Kani" (1963). "Crabs." Trans. Phyllis Birnbaum. In P. Birnbaum, 99–131.

"Saigo no toki" (1966). "The Last Time." Trans. Yukiko Tanaka and Elizabeth Hanson. In Tanaka and Hanson, 43–67.

"Shuken" (1980). "Crimson Markings." Trans. Yukiko Tanaka. *Literary Review* (Fairleigh Dickinson University) 30, no. 2 (Winter 1987): 184–93.

"Tetsu no uo" (1976). "Iron Fish." Trans. Yukiko Tanaka. In Gessel and Matsumoto, 348–60.

"Yōji gari" (1961). "Toddler-hunting." Trans. Lucy North. *Mānoa: A Pacific Journal of International Writing* 3, no. 2 (Fall 1991): 42–57.

Kurahashi Yumiko (1935–)
"Kakō ni shisu" (1970). "To Die at the Estuary." Trans. Dennis Keene. In Hibbett, 247–81.
"Kyosatsu" (1961). "The Monastery." Trans. Carolyn Haynes. In Gessel and Matsumoto, 218–31.
"Natsu no owari" (1960). "The End of Summer." Trans. Victoria V. Vernon. In Vernon, *Daughters of the Moon*, 229–40.
"Parutei" (1960). "Partei." Trans. Yukiko Tanaka and Elizabeth Hanson. In Tanaka and Hanson, 1–16.
"Shūma-tachi" (1965). "Ugly Demons." Trans. Lane Dunlop. In Dunlop, *Autumn Wind*, 201–21.
Sumiyakisto Q no Bōken (1969). *The Adventures of Sumiyakist Q.* Trans. Dennis Keene. Queensland, Australia: University of Queensland Press, 1979.

Makino Eri (1953–)
"Spring" (1987). Trans. Mona Tellier. In A. Birnbaum, 29–48.

Masuda Mizuko (1948–)
"Chinka chitai" (1982). "Sinking Ground." Trans. Yukiko Tanaka. In Tanaka, *Unmapped Territories*, 39–68.

Miura Ayako (1922–)
Hyōten (1964–65). *A Heart of Winter.* Trans. Mark Caprio and Clyde Moneyhun. Littleton, Colo.: OMF Books, 1991.
Shiokari tōge (1966). *Shiokari Pass.* Trans. Bill Fearnehough and Sheila Fearnehough. London: OMF Books, 1975. Reprinted—Rutland, Vt.: Tuttle, 1987.

Miyamoto Yuriko (1899–1951)
Banshū heiya (1946). *The Banshū Plain* (chap. 1). Trans. Brett de Bary. "After the War: Translations from Miyamoto Yuriko." *Bulletin of Concerned Asian Scholars* 16, no. 2 (1984): 41–45; also in *Journal of the Association of Teachers of Japanese* 19, no. 1 (Apr. 1984–85): 29–33.
Fūchisō (1946). *The Weathervane Plant* (chap. 4). Trans. Brett de Bary. "After the War: Translations from Miyamoto Yuriko." *Bulletin of Concerned Asian Scholars* 16, no. 2 (1984): 46–47.
"Koiwai no ikka" (1938). "The Family of Koiwai." Trans. Noriko Mizuta Lippit. In Lippit and Selden, *Stories by Contemporary Japanese Women Writers*, 3–21. Reprinted in Lippit and Selden, *Japanese Women Writers*, 3–19.
Nobuko (1926). *Nobuko* (excerpt). Trans. Yukiko Tanaka. In Tanaka, *To Live and to Write*, 47–64; Trans. Brett de Bary. In Arkin and Shollar, 368–73.

Mori Reiko (1928–)
"Mokkingubādo no iru machi" (1979). "Desert Song." Trans. Noah Brannen. *Japan Christian Quarterly* 51, no. 4 (1985): 232–44; 52, no. 1 (1986): 25–44.

Mori Yōko (1940–)
"Beddo no otogibanashi" (1984–85). "Two Bedtime Stories." Trans. Makoto Ueda. In Ueda, 117–32.

Mukōda Kuniko (1929–81)
"Daikon no tsuki" (1980). "The Daikon Moon." Trans. Adam Kabat. In Mukōda, *A Deck of Memories*, 84–97; "Half-Moon." Trans. Tomone Matsumoto. In Mukōda, *The Name of the Flower*, 130–39.

"Daradara-zaka" (1980). "Small Change." Trans. Tomone Matsumoto. In Mukōda, *The Name of the Flower*, 17–27.

"Dauto" (1981). "Doubt." Trans. Dan Seymour. *Japan Quarterly* 31, no. 3 (1984): 281–87; "I Doubt It." Trans. Adam Kabat. In Mukōda, *A Deck of Memories*, 126–40; "I Doubt It." Trans. Tomone Matsumoto. Mukōda, *The Name of the Flower*, 28–38.

"Funa" (1981). "Mr. Carp." Trans. Tomone Matsumoto. In Mukōda, *The Name of the Flower*, 108–20.

"Hamekoroshimado" (1980). "The Upstairs Window." Trans. Adam Kabat. In Mukōda, *A Deck of Memories*, 22–36; "The Window." Trans. Tomone Matsumoto. In Mukōda, *The Name of the Flower*, 140–49.

"Hana no namae" (1980). "The Name of the Flowers." Trans. Adam Kabat. In Mukōda, *A Deck of Memories*, 112–25; "The Name of the Flower." Trans. Tomone Matsumoto. In Mukōda, *The Name of the Flower*, 7–16.

"Inugoya" (1980). "The Doghouse." Trans. Adam Kabat. In Mukōda, *A Deck of Memories*, 54–68; "The Doghouse." Trans. Tomone Matsumoto. In Mukōda, *The Name of the Flower*, 75–84.

"Kawauso" (1980). "The River Otter." Trans. Marian E. Chambers. *Japan Quarterly* 33. no. 3 (July–Sept. 1986): 320–27; "The Otter." Trans. Adam Kabat. In Mukōda, *A Deck of Memories*, 7–21; "The Otter." Trans. Tomone Matsumoto. In Mukōda, *The Name of the Flower*, 39–49.

"Manhattan" (1980). "Manhattan." Trans. Adam Kabat. In Mukōda, *A Deck of Memories*, 37–53; "Manhattan." Trans. Tomone Matsumoto. In Mukōda, *The Name of the Flower*, 50–61.

"Mimi" (1981). "Ears." Trans. Tomone Matsumoto. In Mukōda, *The Name of the Flower*, 121–29.

"Otokomayu" (1980). "Men's Brows." Trans. Adam Kabat. In Mukōda, *A Deck of Memories*, 69–83.

"Sankaku nami" (1981). "Triangular Chop." Trans. Tomone Matsumoto. In Mukōda, *The Name of the Flower*, 97–107.

"San-mai niku" (1980). "Beef Shoulder." Trans. Tomone Matsumoto. In Mukōda, *The Name of the Flower*, 62–74.

"Suppai kazoku" (1980). "The Sour-Smelling Family." Trans. Adam Kabat. In Mukōda, *A Deck of Memories*, 98–111.

"Usotsuki tamago" (1981). "The Fake Egg." Trans. Tomone Matsumoto. In Mukōda, *The Name of the Flower*, 85–95.

Murata Kiyoko (1945–)
"Kōsaku densha" (1980). "The Cable Cars." Trans. Mark Jewel. *Japanese Literature Today* 16 (Mar. 1991): 6–18.
"Nabe no naka" (1987). "In the Pot." Trans. Kyoko Iriye Selden. In Lippit and Selden, *Japanese Women Writers*, 217–64.

Nakamoto Takako (1903–)
"Suzumushi no mesu" (1929). "The Female Bell-Cricket." Trans. Yukiko Tanaka. In Tanaka, *To Live and to Write*, 135–44.

Nakayama Chinatsu (1948–)
Koyaku no jikan (1980). *Behind the Waterfall.* Trans. Geraldine Harcourt. London: Virago Press, 1990.

Nogami Yaeko (1885–1985)
"Kaijin-maru" (1922). "The Neptune." Trans. Ryōzō Matsumoto. In Matsumoto, 119–76.
"Kata ashi no mondai" (1931). "A Story of a Missing Leg." Trans. Yukiko Tanaka. In Tanaka, *To Live and to Write*, 153–58.
"Kitsune" (1946). "The Foxes." Trans. Ryōzō Matsumoto. In Matsumoto, 177–242.
"Mado to onboro gakki" (1977). "Windows and an Out-of-Tune Instrument." Trans. Juliet Winters Carpenter. *Literary Review* (Fairleigh Dickinson University) 30, no. 2 (Winter 1987): 224–31.
"Meigetsu" (1942). "The Full Moon." Trans. Kyoko Iriye Selden. In Lippit and Selden, *Stories by Contemporary Japanese Women Writers*, 22–43. Reprinted in Lippit and Selden, *Japanese Women Writers*, 20–40.
"Subako" (1970). "Birdhouses." Trans. Juliet Winters Carpenter. In Gatten and Chambers, 223–34.

Ōba Minako (1930–)
"Aoi kitsune" (1973). "The Pale Fox." Trans. Stephen W. Kohl. In Gessel and Matsumoto, 337–47.
"Higusa" (1969). "Fireweed." Trans. Marian Chambers. *Japan Quarterly* 28, no. 3 (July–Sept. 1981): 403–27.
Naku tori no (1985). *Birds Crying* (chap. 1). Trans. Michiko N. Wilson and Michael K. Wilson. *Chicago Review* 39, nos.3–4 (1993): 186–95.
"Rōsoku uo" (1986). "The Candle Fish." Trans. Yukiko Tanaka. In Tanaka, *Unmapped Territories*, 18–38.
"San biki no kani" (1968). "The Three Crabs." Trans. Yukiko Tanaka and Elizabeth Hanson. In Tanaka and Hanson, 87–113; "The Three Crabs." Trans. Stephen Kohl and Ryōko Toyama. *Japan Quarterly* 25, no. 3 (July–Sept. 1978): 323–40.
"Shiroi kaze" (1989). "White Wind." Trans. Joel Cohn. *Mānoa: A Pacific Journal of International Writing* 3, no. 2 (Fall 1991): 12–16.
"Tankō" (1978). "Sea-Change." Trans. John Bester. *Japanese Literature Today* 5 (Mar. 1980): 12–19.
"Tori no uta" (1987). "Birdsong." Trans. Seiji M. Lippit. *Review of Japanese Culture and Society* 4 (Dec. 1991): 84–93.

Urashimasō (1977). *Urashimasō*. Trans. Ōba Yū. Tokyo: Center for Inter-Cultural Studies and Education, Josai University, 1995.

"Yamauba no bishō" (1976). "The Smile of a Mountain Witch." Trans. Noriko Mizuta Lippit. In Lippit and Selden, *Stories by Contemporary Japanese Women Writers*, 182–96. Reprinted in Lippit and Selden, *Japanese Women Writers*, 194–206.

"Yorozu shūzen-ya no onna" (1974). "The Repairman's Wife." Trans. Tomoyoshi Genkawa and Bernard Susser. In *The Kyoto Collection: Stories from the Japanese*. Osaka: Niheisha, 1989, 87–132.

Ōhara Tomie (1912–)

En to iu onna (1960). *A Woman Called En*. Trans. Kazuko Furuhata and Janet Smith. London: Routledge & Kegan Paul, 1986.

Okamoto Kanoko (1889–1939)

"Boshi jojō" (1937). "A Mother's Love." Trans. Phyllis Birnbaum. In P. Birnbaum, 49–97.

"Hana wa tsuyoshi" (1937). "Scarlet Flower." Trans. Edward Seiden-sticker. *Japan Quarterly* 10, no. 3 (1963): 331–48; "A Floral Pageant." Trans. Hiroko Morita Malatesta. In Tanaka, *To Live and to Write*, 205–25.

"Michinoku" (1938). "North Country." Trans. Kazuko Sugisaki. In Okamoto, *The Tale of the Old Geisha*, 65–78.

"Rōgi shō" (1938). "The Old Geisha." Trans. Kazuko Sugisaki. In Okamoto, *The Tale of the Old Geisha*, 38–64.

"Sushi" (1939). "Sushi." Trans. Kazuko Sugisaki. In Okamoto, *The Tale of the Old Geisha*, 14–37.

"Tsuta no mon" (1938). "Ivy Gates." Trans. Lane Dunlop. In Dunlop, *Autumn Wind*, 95–108.

Ōta Yōko (1903–63)

"Hotaru" (1953). "Fireflies." Trans. Kōichi Nakagawa. In Ōe, *The Crazy Iris*, 85–111.

"Shikabane no machi" (1945). "City of Corpses." Trans. Richard Minear. In Minear, 147–273.

"Zanshū tenten" (1954). "Residues of Squalor." Trans. Kyoko Iriye Selden. In Lippit and Selden, *Japanese Women Writers*, 58–83.

Ozaki Midori (1896–1979)

"Mokusei" (1929). "Osmanthus." Trans. Miriam Silverberg. *Mānoa: A Pacific Journal of International Writing* 3, no. 2 (Fall 1991): 187–90.

Saegusa Kazuko (1929–)

"Rokudō tsuji" (1987). "The Rain at Rokudō Crossing." Trans. Yukiko Tanaka. In Tanaka, *Unmapped Territories*, 3–17.

Sata Ineko (1904–)

"Chiisai yama to tsubaki no hana" (1986). "Camellia Blossoms on the Little Mountain." Trans. Mark Jewel. *Japanese Literature Today* 12 (Mar. 1987): 5–14.

"Iro no nai e" (1961). "The Colorless Paintings." Trans. Shiloh Ann Shimura. In Ōe, *The Crazy Iris*, 113–25.

Kurenai (1936). *Crimson.* Trans. Yukiko Tanaka. In Tanaka, *To Live and to Write*, 167–80.

"Yoru no kioku" (1955). "Memory of a Night." Trans. Kyoko Iriye Selden. In Lippit and Selden, *Stories by Contemporary Japanese Women Writers*, 62–75. Reprinted in Lippit and Selden, *Japanese Women Writers*, 84–96.

"Yuki no mau yado" (1972). "The Inn of the Dancing Snow." Trans. Victoria V. Vernon. In Vernon, *Daughters of the Moon*, 217–28.

Setouchi Harumi (1922–)

Bi wa ranchō ni ari (1966). *Beauty in Disarray.* Trans. Sanford Goldstein and Kazuji Ninomiya. Rutland, Vt.: Tuttle, 1993.

"Kiji" (1963). "Pheasant." Trans. Robert Huey. In Ueda, 189–209.

"Miren" (1963). "Lingering Affection." Trans. Mona Nagai and Akiko Willing. In Tanaka and Hanson, 17–42.

Natsu no owari (1962–63). *The End of Summer.* Trans. Janine Beichman, with Alan Brender. Tokyo: Kōdansha, 1989.

"Waremokō" (1983). "The Burnet Plant." Trans. Nancy Andrew. *Japanese Literature Today* 10 (Mar. 1985): 6–11.

Shibaki Yoshiko (1914–)

"Hamon" (1970). "Ripples." Trans. Michael C. Brownstein. In Gessel and Matsumoto, 317–36.

"Kazahana" (1984). "Snow Flurry." Trans. Mark Jewel. *Japanese Literature Today* 11 (Mar. 1986): 6–16.

Sono Ayako (1931–)

"Fuji" (1975). "Fuji." Trans. Phyllis Birnbaum. In P. Birnbaum, 17–26.

Kami no yogoreta te (1979). *Watcher from the Shore.* Trans. Edward Putzar. Tokyo: Kōdansha, 1990.

"Mura no funade" (1983). "Village Embarcation." Trans. Charles M. DeWolf. *Japan Christian Quarterly* 50, no. 4 (1984): 225–28.

Takahashi Takako (1932–)

"Byōshin" (1978). "Invalid." Trans. Van C. Gessel. *Mānoa: A Pacific Journal of International Writing* 3, no. 2 (Fall 1991): 132–40.

"Ningyō ai" (1976). "Doll Love." Trans. Mona Nagai and Yukiko Tanaka. In Tanaka and Hanson, 197–223.

"Otsuge" (1977). "The Oracle." Trans. Nina Blake. *Review of Japanese Culture and Society* 3, no. 1 (Dec. 1989): 97–110.

"Sōji kei" (1971): "Congruent Figures." Trans. Noriko Mizuta Lippit. In Lippit and Selden, *Stories by Contemporary Japanese Women Writers*, 153–81. Reprinted in Lippit and Selden, *Japanese Women Writers*, 168–93.

Takenishi Hiroko (1929–)

"Gishiki" (1963). "The Rite." Trans. Eileen Kato. In Ōe, *The Crazy Iris*, 169–200.

Tamura Toshiko (1884–1945)

"Eiga" (1916). "Glory." Trans. Yukiko Tanaka. In Tanaka, *To Live and to Write*, 19–38.

"Onna sakusha" (1913). "A Woman Writer." Trans. Yukiko Tanaka. In Tanaka, *To Live and to Write*, 11–18.

Tawada Yōko (19–)

"Inu muko iri" (1993). "The Bridegroom Was a Dog." Trans. John Munroe. *Japanese Literature Today* 19 (1994): 17–39.

Tomioka Taeko (1935–)

"Hatsumukashi" (1975). "Hatsumukashi." Trans. Kyoko Iriye Selden. *Review of Japanese Culture and Society* 5, no. 1 (1993): 84–91.

"Inu ga miru fūkei" (1974). "Scenery Viewed by a Dog." Trans. Noriko Mizuta Lippit. *Japan Quarterly* 28, no. 2 (Apr.–June 1981): 271–84.

"Jikoku hyō" (1975). "Time Table." Trans. Kyoko Iriye Selden. *Review of Japanese Culture and Society* 1, no. 1 (Oct. 1986): 110–23.

"Meido no kazoku" (1974). "Family in Hell." Trans. Susan Downing Videen. In Tanaka and Hanson, 141–77.

"Oka ni mukatte hito wa narabu" (1971). "Facing the Hills They Stand." Trans. Kyoko Iriye Selden. In Lippit and Selden, *Stories by Contemporary Japanese Women Writers*, 120–52. Reprinted in Lippit and Selden, *Japanese Women Writers*, 138–67.

"Sūku" (1980). "Straw Dogs." Trans. Yukiko Tanaka. In Tanaka, *Unmapped Territories*, 120–51.

Tsuboi Sakae (1900–1967)

"Jūgoya no tsuki" (1942). "The Moon of the Fifteenth Night." Trans. William B. Giesecke. *Japan Quarterly* 27, no. 3 (July–Sept. 1980): 390–98.

"Kaki no kino aru ie" (1948). "Under the Persimmon Tree." Trans. Kiyonobu Uno. *Reeds* 10 (1965): 49–63.

"Natsu-mikan" (1948). "Summer Oranges." Trans. William B. Giesecke. *Japan Quarterly* 27, no. 3 (July–Sept. 1980): 387–90.

Nijūshi no hitomi (1952). *Twenty-Four Eyes*. Trans. Akira Miura. Tokyo: Kenkyūsha, 1957. Reprinted—Rutland, Vt.: Tuttle, 1983.

"Tsukiyo no kasa" (1953). "Umbrella on a Moonlit Night." Trans. Chris Heftel. In Ueda, 83–95.

Tsumura Setsuko (1928–)

"Gangu" (1965). "Playthings." Trans. Kyoko Evanhoe and Robert N. Lawson. *Japan Quarterly* 27, no. 1 (Jan.–Mar. 1980): 87–107.

"Shiroi tsubo" (1960). "White Urn." Trans. Shoichi Ono and Sanford Goldstein. *Mānoa: A Pacific Journal of International Writing* 3, no. 2 (Fall 1991): 154–70.

"Yakō dokei" (1969). "Luminous Watch." Trans. Elizabeth Hanson and Yukiko Tanaka. In Tanaka and Hanson, 115–40.

Tsushima Yūko (1947–)
  Chōji (1978). *Child of Fortune.* Trans. Geraldine Harcourt. Tokyo: Kōdansha, 1983.
  "Danmari ichi" (1982). "The Silent Traders." Trans. Geraldine Harcourt. In Gessel and Matsumoto, 400–411.
  "Fucho" (1981). "Auguries." Trans. Elizabeth Wood. *Mānoa: A Pacific Journal of International Writing* 3, no. 2 (Fall 1991): 67–74.
  "Hana o maku" (1977). "To Scatter Flower Petals." Trans. Lora Sharnoff. *Japan Quarterly* 27, no. 2 (Apr.–June 1980): 249–62; "Scattering Flowers." Trans. Phyllis I. Lyons. In Arkin and Shollar, 1024–36.
  "Hatsujōki" (1974). "A Sensitive Season." Trans. Geraldine Harcourt. In Tsushima, *The Shooting Gallery,* 1–21.
  "Hōyō" (1984). "An Embrace." Trans. Geraldine Harcourt. *Translation* 17 (Fall 1986): 97–114.
  "Kikumushi" (1983). "The Chrysanthemum Beetle." Trans. Geraldine Harcourt. In Tsushima, *The Shooting Gallery,* 45–79.
  "Kusamura" (1976). "Clearing the Thickets." Trans. Geraldine Harcourt. In Tsushima, *The Shooting Gallery,* 107–21.
  "Kusa no fushido" (1977). "A Bed of Grass." Trans. Yukiko Tanaka and Elizabeth Hanson. In Tanaka and Hanson, 225–87.
  "Minami kaze" (1978). "South Wind." Trans. Geraldine Harcourt. *Japan Quarterly* 33, no. 1 (Jan.–Mar. 1986): 72–79.
  "Mizube" (1978). "Water's Edge." Trans. Gillian Kinjo and Susan Bouterey. *Review of Japanese Culture and Society* 6, no. 1 (Dec. 1994): 54–60.
  "Mugura no haha" (1975). "The Mother in the House of Grass." Trans. Sara Dillon. *Literary Review* (Fairleigh Dickinson University) 30, no. 2 (Winter 1987): 265–96.
  "Numa" (1981). "The Marsh." Trans. Yukiko Tanaka. In Tanaka, *Unmapped Territories,* 152–63.
  "Shateki" (1975). "The Shooting Gallery." Trans. Geraldine Harcourt. In Tsushima, *The Shooting Gallery,* 91–106.
  The Shooting Gallery and Other Stories. Trans. Geraldine Harcourt. New York: Pantheon, 1988.
  Yama o hashiru onna (1980). *Woman Running in the Mountains.* Trans. Geraldine Harcourt. New York: Pantheon Books, 1991.
  "Yorokobi no shima" (1977). "Island of Joy." Trans. Lora Sharnoff. *Japan Quarterly* 27, no. 2 (Apr.-June 1980): 263–69.
  "Yukue fumei" (1973). "Missing." Trans. Geraldine Harcourt. In Tsushima, *The Shooting Gallery,* 80–90.

Uno Chiyo (1897–1996)
  Aru hitori no onna no hanashi (1971). *The Story of a Single Woman.* Trans. Rebecca L. Copeland. London: Peter Owen, 1992.
  Irozange (1933–35). *Confessions of Love.* Trans. Phyllis Birnbaum. Honolulu: University of Hawaii Press, 1989. "Passion and Repentance" (excerpt). Trans. Phyllis Birnbaum. *Translations* 17 (Fall 1986): 43–60.

"Kaze no oto" (1969). "The Sound of the Wind." Trans. Rebecca L. Copeland. In Copeland, *The Sound of the Wind*, 138–207.

"Kōfuku" (1970). "Happiness." Trans. Phyllis Birnbaum. In P. Birnbaum, 133–47.

"Kono oshiroi ire" (1967). "This Powder Box." Trans. Rebecca L. Copeland. In Copeland, *The Sound of the Wind*, 208–36.

"Mohō no tensai" (1934). "A Genius of Imitation." Trans. Yukiko Tanaka. In Tanaka, *To Live and to Write*, 189–96.

"Ningyōshi Tenguya Kyūkichi" (1942). "The Puppet Maker." Trans. Rebecca L. Copeland. In Copeland, *The Sound of the Wind*, 105–37.

"Ohan" (1947–57). "Ohan." Trans. Donald Keene. In Keene, *The Old Woman, the Wife, and the Archer*, 51–118.

"Sasu" (1963–66). "To Stab." Trans. Kyoko Iriye Selden. In Lippit and Selden, *Stories by Contemporary Japanese Women Writers*, 92–104. Reprinted in Lippit and Selden, *Japanese Women Writers*, 126–37.

Yamada Eimi (1959–)

"Hizamazuite ashi oname" (1988). "Kneel Down and Lick My Feet." Trans. Terry Gallagher. In A. Birnbaum, 187–203.

"Otoko ga onna o aisuru toki" (1987). "When a Man Loves a Woman." Trans. Yukiko Tanaka. In Tanaka, *Unmapped Territories*, 69–83.

"Seijin muki mōfu" (1988). "X-Rated Blanket." Trans. Nina Cornyetz. In Mitsios, 50–54.

Trash (1991). *Trash*. Trans. Sonya Johnson. Tokyo: Kōdansha, 1995.

Yamamoto Michiko (1936–)

"Ame no isu" (1972). "Chair in the Rain." Trans. Geraldine Harcourt. In Yamamoto, *Betty-san*, 115–52.

Betty-san: Four Stories. Tokyo: Kōdansha, 1983.

"Betei-san no niwa" (1972). "Betty-san." Trans. Geraldine Harcourt. In Yamamoto, *Betty-san*, 7–67.

"Kusa o karu otoko" (1972). "The Man Who Cut the Grass." Trans. Yukiko Tanaka and Elizabeth Hanson. In Tanaka and Hanson, 179–95.

"Mahō" (1972). "Powers." Trans. Geraldine Harcourt. In Yamamoto, *Betty-san*, 83–67.

"Rōjin no kamo" (1972). "Father Goose." Trans. Geraldine Harcourt. In Yamamoto, *Betty-san*, 69–114.

Yamazaki Toyoko (1924–)

Bonchi (1960). *Bonchi*. Trans. Harue Summersgill and Travis Summersgill. Honolulu: University of Hawaii Press, 1982.

Fumō chitai (1976). *The Barren Zone*. Trans. James T. Araki. Honolulu: University of Hawaii Press, 1985.

Yoshida Tomoko (1934–)

"Mumyō chōya" (1970). "The Long Night of Illusion." Trans. James Kirkup and Eiko Harvey. *Japan Quarterly* 24, no. 1 (1977): 57–95.

"O-sonae" (1991). "The Offering." Trans. John Munroe. *Japanese Litera-ture Today* 18 (1993): 46–62.

Yoshimoto Banana (1964–)
   Kitchin (1987). *Kitchen*. Trans. Megan Backus. Yoshimoto, *Kitchen*. New York: Grove Press, 1993; *Kitchen* (excerpt). Trans. Ann Sherif. In Mitsios, 152–71.
   "Mūnraito shadō" (1988). "Moonlight Shadow." Trans. Megan Backus. In Yoshimoto, *Kitchen*, 107–50.
   N. P. (1990). *N. P.* Trans. Ann Sherif. New York: Grove Press, 1994.
   Tokage (1993). *Lizard*. Trans Ann Sherif. New York: Grove Press, 1995.

Yoshiyuki Rie (1939–)
   "Chiisana kifujin" (1981). "The Little Lady." Trans. Geraldine Harcourt. *Japanese Literature Today* 7 (Mar. 1982): 5–18.

2. Bibliographies, Studies, Translations of Classical Works by Japanese Women, Collections, Journal Articles (1980–95), and Book Reviews (1980–95)

Akazome Emon (?). *A Tale of Flowering Fortunes: Annals of Japanese Aristo-cratic Life of the Heian Period* (*Eiga monogatari*). Trans. William H. McCullough and Helen C. McCullough. 2 vols. Stanford: Stanford University Press, 1980.

Aoyama Tomoko. "Male Homosexuality as Treated by Japanese Women Writers." In *The Japanese Trajectory: Modernization and Beyond*, ed. Gavan McCormack and Yoshio Sugimoto. Cambridge, Eng.: Cambridge University Press, 1988, 186–204.

Ariga, Chieko. "Dephallicizing Women in *Ryūkyō shinshi*: A Critique of Gender Ideology in Japanese Literature." *Journal of Asian Studies* 51, no. 3 (Aug. 1992): 565–86.

———. "Who's Afraid of Amino Kiku? Gender Conflict and the Literary Canon in Japanese Literature." *International Journal of Social Education* 6, no. 1 (Spring 1991): 95–113.

"Ariyoshi Sawako, 1931–1984." (Obituary.) *Monumenta Nipponica* 39, no. 4 (Winter 1984): 453.

Arkin, Marian, and Barbara Shollar, eds. *Longman Anthology of World Litera-ture by Women 1875–1975*. New York and London: Longman, 1989.

Arntzen, Sonja. "Getting at the Language of *The Tale of Genji* Through the Mirror of Translation." In Kamens, *Approaches*, 31–40.

———. Review of *String of Beads: Complete Poems of Princess Shikishi*, trans. by Hiroaki Sato. *Journal of the Association of Teachers of Japanese* 29, no. 1 (Apr. 1995): 69–73.

———. Review of *The Buddhist Poetry of the Great Kamo Priestess: Senshi Daisaiin and Hosshin wakashū*, by Edward Kamens. *Monumenta Nipponica* 46, no. 3 (Autumn 1991): 372–75.

[Review of] *As If It Never Happened* (*Naki ga gotoki*), by Hayashi Kyōko. *Japanese Literature Today* 7 (Mar. 1982): 24–26.

Backus, Robert. Review of *Murasaki Shikibu: The Tale of Genji*, by Richard Bowring. *Journal of the Association of Teachers of Japanese* 23, no. 1 (Apr. 1989): 98–100.

Bardsley, Jan. Review of *Noh Drama and "The Tale of Genji,"* by Janet Goff. *Journal of the Association of Teachers of Japanese* 27, no. 2 (Nov. 1993): 259–65.

Bargen, Doris G. "The Problem of Incest in *The Tale of Genji.*" In Kamens, *Approaches*, 115–23.

———. "The Search for Things Past in the *Genji monogatari.*" *Harvard Journal of Asiatic Studies* 51, no. 1 (June 1991): 199–232.

———. "Spirit Possession in the Context of Dramatic Expressions of Gender Conflict: The Aoi Episode of the *Genji monogatari.*" *Harvard Journal of Asiatic Studies* 48, no. 1 (June 1988): 95–130.

———. "Twin Blossoms on a Single Branch: The Cycle of Retribution in *Onnamen.*" *Monumenta Nipponica* 46, no. 2 (Summer 1991): 147–71.

[Review of] *Bedtime Eyes*, by Yamada Eimi. *Japanese Literature Today* 11 (Mar. 1986): 20–21.

Beichman, Janine. "Akiko Goes to Paris: The European Poems." *Journal of the Association of Teachers of Japanese*, special issue: *Yosano Akiko (1878–1942)*, ed. Laurel Rasplica Rodd, 25, no. 1 (Apr. 1991): 123–45.

———. "Yosano Akiko: Return to the Female." *Japan Quarterly* 37, no. 2 (Apr.-June 1990): 204–28.

———. "Yosano Akiko: The Early Years." *Japan Quarterly* 37, no. 1 (Jan.-Mar. 1990): 37–54.

Bernstein, Gail Lee. "The Model Japanese Woman." Review of *The Waiting Years*, by Enchi Fumiko, trans. John Bester; and *The Doctor's Wife*, by Ariyoshi Sawako, trans. Hironaka Wakako and Ann Siller Kostant. *Journal of Japanese Studies* 6, no. 2 (Summer 1980): 354–59.

———. Review of *The River Ki*, by Ariyoshi Sawako, trans. Mildred Tahara. *Journal of the Association of Teachers of Japanese* 16, no. 1 (Apr. 1981): 105–8.

———. Review of *The Twilight Years*, by Ariyoshi Sawako, trans. Mildred Tahara. *Journal of the Association of Teachers of Japanese* 19, no. 2 (Nov. 1984–85): 287–88.

Birnbaum, Alfred, ed. *Monkey Brain Sushi: New Tastes in Japanese Fiction.* Tokyo: Kōdansha, 1991.

Birnbaum, Phyllis, trans. *Rabbits, Crabs, Etc.; Stories by Japanese Women.* Honolulu: University of Hawaii Press, 1982.

Bowring, Richard. "The Female Hand in Heian Japan: A First Reading." In *The Female Autograph: Theory and Practice of Autobiography from the Tenth to the Twentieth Century*, ed. Domna C. Stanton. Chicago: University of Chicago Press, 1987, 49–56.

———. *Murasaki Shikibu: The Tale of Genji.* The Landmarks of World Literature Series. Cambridge: Cambridge University Press, 1988.

————. Review of *The Poetic Memoirs of Lady Daibu*, trans. Phillip Tudor Harries. *Journal of Japanese Studies* 7, no. 2 (Summer 1981): 447–53.

Bowring, Richard, trans. *Murasaki Shikibu: Her Diary and Poetic Memoirs: A Translation and Study*. Princeton: Princeton University Press, 1982.

Brazell, Karen. Review of *New Leaves: Studies and Translations of Japanese Literature in Honor of Edward Seidensticker*, eds. Aileen Gatten and Anthony Hood Chambers. *Monumenta Nipponica* 49, no. 1 (Spring 1994): 99–102.

————. Review of *The Poetics of Nikki Bungaku: A Comparison of the Traditions, Conventions, and Structure of Heian Japan's Literary Diaries with Western Autobiographical Writings*, by Marilyn Jeanne Miller. *Journal of Asian Studies* 46, no.2 (May 1987): 414–15.

Brewster, Jennifer. Review of *The Tale of Nezame: Part Three of "Yowa no Nezame Monogatari,"* trans. Carol Hochstedler. *Monumenta Nipponica* 36, no. 1 (Spring 1981): 93–94.

Brown, Janice. "Hayashi Fumiko: Voice from the Margin." *Japan Quarterly* 43, no. 1 (1996): 85–99.

Buckley, Sandra. "En-gendering Subjectivity in *The Tale of Genji*." In Kamens, *Approaches*, 88–94.

————. "Reading Women's Texts." Review of *Stories by Contemporary Japanese Women Writers*, trans. and ed. by Noriko Mizuta Lippit and Kyoko Iriye Selden; and *This Kind of Woman: Ten Stories by Japanese Women Writers, 1960–1976*, trans. and ed. by Yukiko Tanaka and Elizabeth Hanson. *Bulletin of Concerned Asian Scholars* 20, no. 3 (1988): 63–68.

Bundy, Roselee. "Japan's First Woman Diarist and the Beginning of Prose Writing by Women in Japan." *Women's Studies* 19 (1991): 79–91.

Carpenter, Juliet Winters. "Enchi Fumiko: 'A Writer of Tales.'" *Japan Quarterly* 37, no. 3 (July–Sept. 1990): 343–55.

————. "Tawara Machi: 'To Create Poetry Is to Live.'" *Japan Quarterly* 36, no. 2 (Apr.–June 1989): 193–99.

————. Review of *This Kind of Woman*, trans. and edited by Yukiko Tanaka and Elizabeth Hanson. *Japan Quarterly* 30, no. 3 (July–Sept. 1983): 320–22.

————. "Uno Chiyo: Writer and *Femme Fatale*." Review of *The Sound of the Wind: The Life and Works of Uno Chiyo*, by Rebecca L. Copeland. *Japan Quarterly* 39, no. 4 (Oct.–Dec. 1992): 502–5.

Carter, Steven D. "'The End of a Year — the End of a Life As Well': Murasaki Shikibu's Farewell to the Shining One." In Kamens, *Approaches*, 124–31.

————. Review of *Noh Drama and "The Tale of Genji": The Art of Allusion in Fifteen Classical Plays*, by Janet Goff. *Harvard Journal of Asiatic Studies* 54, no. 2 (Dec. 1994): 567–71.

Chambers, Marian E. "Ōba Minako: Rebirth in Alaska." *Japan Quarterly* 38, no. 4 (Oct.–Dec. 1991): 474–83.

Chang, Chia-ning. Review of *The Shōwa Anthology*, ed. Van C. Gessel and Tomone Matsumoto. *Journal of the Association of Teachers of Japanese* 21, no. 1 (Apr. 1987): 106–12.

[Review of] *Child of Wrath (Ikari no ko)*, by Takahashi Takako. Trans. Charles M. DeWolf. *Japanese Literature Today* 11 (Mar. 1986): 16–18.

Childs, Margaret H. Review of *The Aesthetics of Discontent: Politics and Reclusion in Medieval Japanese Literature*, by Michele Marra. *Harvard Journal of Asiatic Studies* 53, no. 1 (June 1993): 185–87.

Chisholm, Julianne Kaui. "The Steel-Belted Radial of Karma: The End of Genji." *Journal of the Association of Teachers of Japanese* 28, no. 2 (Nov. 1994): 183–93.

Coats, Bruce A. "Buildings and Gardens in *The Tale of Genji.*" In Kamens, *Approaches*, 52–59.

Cooper, Michael. Review of *Eigo taiyakuban: Sarada kinenbi*, trans. Jack Stamm; and *Salad Anniversary*, by Tawara Machi, trans. Juliet Winters Carpenter. *Monumenta Nipponica* 45, no. 1 (Spring 1990): 106–9.

Copeland, Rebecca L. "The Made-up Author: Writer as Woman in the Works of Uno Chiyo." *Journal of the Association of Teachers of Japanese* 29, no. 1 (Apr. 1995): 3–25.

———. "Motherhood as Institution." *Japan Quarterly* 39, no. 1 (Jan.–Mar. 1992): 101–10.

———. Review of *Postwar Japanese Women Writers: An Up-to-date Bibliography with Biographical Sketches*, comp. Sachiko Shibata Schierbeck; ed. Soren Egerod. *Monumenta Nipponica* 45, no. 3 (Autumn 1990): 365–66.

———. "Shimizu Shikin's 'The Broken Ring': A Narrative of Female Awakening." *Review of Japanese Culture and Society* (Dec. 1994): 38–47.

———. *The Sound of the Wind: The Life and Works of Uno Chiyo*. Honolulu: University of Hawaii Press, 1992.

———. "Uno Chiyo: Not Just 'A Writer of Illicit Love.'" *Japan Quarterly* 35, no. 2 (Apr.–June 1988): 176–82.

Cornyetz, Nina. "Bound by Blood: Female Pollution, Divinity, and Community in Enchi Fumiko's *Masks.*" *U.S-Japan Women's Journal: English Supplement* (forthcoming).

Cranston, Edwin A. Review of *The Ink Dark Moon*, by Ono no Komachi and Izumi Shikibu, trans. Jane Hirschfield with Aratani Mariko. *Journal of Asian Studies* 47, no. 3 (Aug. 1988): 646–48.

Daibu, Lady. *The Poetic Memoirs of Lady Daibu*. Trans. Phillip Tudor Harries. Stanford: Stanford University Press, 1980.

Danly, Robert Lyons. *In the Shade of Spring Leaves: The Life and Writings of Higuchi Ichiyō, a Woman of Letters in Meiji Japan*. New Haven: Yale University Press, 1981.

———. Review of *The Sound of the Wind*, by Rebecca L. Copeland. *Journal of Japanese Studies* 20, no. 1 (Winter 1994): 234–38.

Daughter of [Sugawara no] Takasue. *As I Crossed the Bridge of Dreams: Recollections of a Woman in Eleventh-Century Japan (Sarashina nikki)*. Trans. Ivan Morris. New York: Dial Press, 1971.

——— (?). *A Tale of Eleventh-Century Japan: Hamamatsu Chūnagon Monogatari*. Trans. Thomas H. Rohlich. Princeton: Princeton University Press, 1983.

——— (?). *The Tale of Nezame: Part Three of "Yowa no Nezame Monogatari."* Trans. Carol Hochstedler. Cornell University Asian Papers, no. 22. Ithaca, N.Y.: Cornell University, 1979.

de Bary, Brett. "Wind and Leaves: Miyamoto Yuriko's *The Weathervane Plant.*" *Journal of the Association of Teachers of Japanese* 19, no. 1 (Apr. 1984–85): 7–28.

Dunlop, Lane, trans. *Autumn Wind and Other Stories.* Rutland, Vt.: Tuttle, 1994.

———. *A Late Chrysanthemum: Twenty-one Stories from the Japanese.* San Francisco: North Point Press, 1986.

Eiga monogatari, see Akazome Emon

Enomoto Yoshiko. "Breaking out of Despair: Higuchi Ichiyō and Charlotte Bronte." *Comparative Literature Studies* 24, no. 3 (1987): 251–63.

———. "*Machiko* and *Pride and Prejudice.*" *Comparative Literature Studies* 28, no. 3 (1991): 245–58.

Ericson, Joan E. *Hayashi Fumiko and Japanese Women's Literature.* Honolulu: University of Hawaii Press, forthcoming.

———. "Hayashi Fumiko and the Transformation of Her Fiction." In *Essays on Translations and Transformations in Japanese Culture,* ed. Amy V. Heinrich. New York: Columbia University Press, forthcoming 1996.

Fahy, David. Review of *The Shōwa Anthology,* ed. Van C. Gessel and Matsumoto Tomone. *Journal of Asian Studies* 46, no. 2 (May 1987): 404–7.

Field, Norma. *The Splendor of Longing in "The Tale of Genji."* Princeton: Princeton University Press, 1987.

Fischer, Felice. "Murasaki Shikibu: The Court Lady." In *Heroic with Grace: Legendary Women of Japan,* ed. Chieko Irie Mulhern. Armonk, N.Y.: M. E. Sharpe, 1991, 77–128.

Fujino Yukio, comp. *Modern Japanese Literature in Western Translations: A Bibliography.* Tokyo: International House of Japan, 1972. Reprinted as *Modern Japanese Literature in Translation: A Bibliography.* International House of Japan Library. Tokyo: Kōdansha International, 1979.

Fujiwara no Nagako. *The Emperor Horikawa Diary (Sanuki no suke nikki).* Trans. and with an introduction by Jennifer Brewster. Honolulu: University of Hawaii Press, 1977.

Gardner, Richard. Review of *Noh Drama and "The Tale of Genji,"* by Janet Goff. *Monumenta Nipponica* 47, no. 1 (Spring 1992): 107–9.

Gatten, Aileen. "Criticism and the *Genji.*" Review of *The Splendor of Longing in "The Tale of Genji,"* by Norma Field; and *The Bridge of Dreams: A Poetics of "The Tale of Genji,"* by Haruo Shirane. *Journal of the Association of Teachers of Japanese* 22, no. 1 (Apr. 1988): 69–95.

———. "Death and Salvation in *Genji monogatari.*" In Gatten and Chambers, 5–27.

———. "Murasaki's Literary Roots." Review of *Murasaki Shikibu: Her Diary and Poetic Memoirs,* by Richard Bowring. *Journal of the Association of Teachers of Japanese* 17, no. 2 (Nov. 1982): 173–91.

———. Review of *Classical Japanese Prose: An Anthology,* comp. and ed. Helen Craig McCullough. *Monumenta Nipponica* 46, no. 3 (Autumn 1991): 367–72.

———. Review of *A Tale of Eleventh-Century Japan: Hamamatsu Chūnagon*

Monogatari, trans. Thomas. H. Rohlich. *Journal of Asian Studies* 43, no. 2 (Feb. 1984): 336–39.

———. "Three Problems in the Text of 'Ukifune.'" In Pekarik, *Ukifune*, 83–111.

———. "Weird Ladies: Narrative Strategy in the *Genji monogatari.*" *Journal of the Association of Teachers of Japanese* 20, no. 1 (Apr. 1986): 29–48.

Gatten, Aileen, and Anthony Hood Chambers, eds. *New Leaves: Studies and Translations of Japanese Literature in Honor of Edward Seidensticker.* Ann Arbor: University of Michigan, Center for Japanese Studies, 1993.

Gessel, Van C. "Due Time: Modern Japanese Women Writers." Review of *Daughters of the Moon*, by Victoria V. Vernon; *To Live and to Write*, ed. Yukiko Tanaka; *A Woman Called En*, by Ohara Tomie; *Masks*, by Enchi Fumiko; and *The Shooting Gallery*, by Tsushima Yūko. *Journal of Japanese Studies* 15, no. 2 (Summer 1989): 439–47.

———. "Echoes of Feminine Sensibility in Literature." *Japan Quarterly* 35, no. 4 (Oct.–Dec. 1988): 410–16.

———. "The 'Medium' of Fiction: Fumiko Enchi as Narrator." *Contemporary Japanese Literature. World Literature Today*, special issue, 62, no. 3 (Summer 1988): 380–85.

———. Review of *This Kind of Woman*, eds. Yukiko Tanaka and Elizabeth Hanson; and *Stories by Contemporary Japanese Women Writers*, trans. and edited by Noriko Mizuta Lippit and Kyoko Iriye Selden. *Journal of the Association of Teachers of Japanese* 18, no. 1 (Apr. 1983): 97–102.

Gessel, Van C., and Matsumoto Tomone, eds. *The Shōwa Anthology: Modern Japanese Short Stories (Part I, 1929–1961; Part II, 1961–1984).* Tokyo: Kōdansha International, 1985.

Goff, Janet. *Noh Drama and "The Tale of Genji": The Art of Allusion in Fifteen Classical Plays.* Princeton: Princeton University Press, 1991.

———. "The Pleasure of Reading the *Genji.*" Review of *The Splendor of Longing in "The Tale of Genji,"* by Norma Field; *The Bridge of Dreams: A Poetics of "The Tale of Genji,"* by Haruo Shirane; and *Murasaki Shikibu: "The Tale of Genji,"* by Richard Bowring. *Journal of Japanese Studies* 17, no. 2 (Summer 1991): 345–58.

———. Review of *Beauty in Disarray*, by Setouchi Harumi, trans. Sanford Goldstein and Kazuji Ninomiya. *Japan Quarterly* 41, no. 1 (Oct.–Dec. 1994): 519–20.

———. Review of *Kitchen* by Yoshimoto Banana, trans. Megan Backus. *Japan Quarterly* 40, no. 2 (Apr.–June 1993): 226.

———. Review of *New Leaves: Studies and Translations of Japanese Literature in Honor of Edward Seidensticker*, eds. Aileen Gatten and Anthony Hood Chambers. *Japan Quarterly* 41, no. 1 (Jan.–Mar. 1994): 115–16.

Grafflin, Dennis. "A Short Term with *The Tale of Genji.*" In Kamens, *Approaches*, 41–44.

Hamamatsu chūnagon monogatari, see Daughter of (Sugawara no) Takasue

Harper, T. J. "From the Original, from the Start." In Kamens, *Approaches*, 70–76.

―――. "Genji Gossip." In Gatten and Chambers, 29–44.

―――. "More Genji Gossip." *Journal of the Association of Teachers of Japanese* 28, no. 2 (Nov. 1994): 175–82.

Harries, Phillip Tudor, trans., *see* Daibu, Lady

Heinrich, Amy Vladeck. "Blown in Flurries: The Role of the Poetry in 'Ukifune.'" In Pekarik, *Ukifune*, 153–71.

―――. "Double Weave: The Fabric of Japanese Women's Writing." *World Literature Today*, special issue: "Contemporary Japanese Literature," 62, no. 3 (Summer 1988): 408–14.

Hibbett, Howard, ed. *Contemporary Japanese Literature: An Anthology of Fiction, Film, and Other Writing Since 1945*. New York: Knopf, 1977.

Hochstedler, Carol. Review of *A Tale of Eleventh-Century Japan: Hamamatsu Chūnagon Monogatari*, trans. Thomas H. Rohlich. *Monumenta Nipponica* 38, no. 4 (Winter 1983): 429–31.

Horton, H. Mack. "Fashioning Personality: Text, Context, and Interpretive Strategy." Review of *The Buddhist Poetry of the Great Kamo Priestess*, by Edward Kamens. *Journal of the Association of Teachers of Japanese* 26, no. 1 (Apr. 1992): 25–46.

―――. "They Also Serve: Ladies-in-Waiting in *The Tale of Genji*." In Kamens, *Approaches*, 95–107.

―――. Review of *Travelers of a Hundred Ages: The Japanese as Revealed Through 1,000 Years of Diaries* by Donald Keene. *Journal of the Association of Teachers of Japanese* 24, no. 2 (Nov. 1990): 201–5.

Huber, Kristina Ruth. *Women in Japanese Society: An Annotated Bibliography of Selected English Language Materials*. Westport, Conn.: Greenwood Press, 1992.

Hulvey, Shirley Yumiko. "The Nocturnal Muse: Ben no Naishi Nikki." *Monumenta Nipponica* 44, no. 4 (Winter 1989): 391–413.

Ichikawa, Chihiro. "Yosano Akiko and *The Tale of Genji*: Ukifune and Midaregami." Trans. G. G. Rowley. *Journal of the Association of Teachers of Japanese* 28, no. 2 (Nov. 1994): 157–74.

Inada, Hide Ikehara. *Bibliography of Translations from the Japanese into Western Languages: From the 16th Century to 1912*. A *Monumenta Nipponica* Monograph. Tokyo: Sophia University, 1971.

Iwamoto, Yoshi, and Yoshiko Yokochi Samuel. "Introduction." *Literary Review* (Fairleigh Dickinson University), special issue: "Japanese Writing, 1974–1984," 30, no. 2 (Winter 1987): 133–40.

Izumi Shikibu (?). *The Izumi Shikibu Diary (Izumi Shikibu nikki)*. Trans. Edwin Cranston. Cambridge, Mass.: Harvard University Press, 1969; "The Diary of Izumi Shikibu." Trans. Earl Miner. In Miner, *Japanese Poetic Diaries*, 95–153.

Jackson, Earl, Jr. Review of *Ukifune: Love in "The Tale of Genji,"* ed. Andrew Pekarik. *Journal of Asian Studies* 43, no. 2 (Feb. 1984): 333–36.

Kagerō nikki, see Mother of [Fujiwara no] Michitsuna

Kamens, Edward, ed. *Approaches to Teaching Murasaki Shikibu's "The Tale of*

Genji." Approaches to Teaching World Literature, 47. New York: MLA, 1993.

———. "Genshin's 'Shadow.' " In Kamens, *Approaches*, 132–41.

Keene, Donald. "The Diary of Higuchi Ichiyō." *Japan Quarterly* 36, no. 2 (Apr.–June 1989): 167–78.

———. "The Revival of Writing by Women." *Dawn to the West*, vol. 1, *Fiction.* New York: Holt, Rinehart & Winston, 1984, 1113–66.

———. *Travelers of a Hundred Ages: The Japanese as Revealed Through 1,000 Years of Diaries.* New York: Henry Holt, 1989.

Keene, Donald, ed. *Anthology of Japanese Literature: From the Earliest Era to the Mid-nineteenth Century.* New York: Grove Press, 1955.

———. *Modern Japanese Literature: From 1868 to the Present Day.* New York: Grove, 1956.

Keene, Donald. trans. *The Old Woman, the Wife, and the Archer.* New York: Viking Press, 1961.

Keiser, Elizabeth B. "Team Teaching the Literary and Visual *Tale of Genji."* In Kamens, *Approaches*, 60–69.

Kerkham, H. Eleanor, and Janet A. Walker. "Introduction to Japan" and "Bibliographical Entries: Japan." In *Women Writers in Translation: An Annotated Bibliography, 1945–82*, ed. Margery Resnick and Isabelle de Courtivron. New York: Garland Press, 1984, 171–87.

Kleeman, Faye Yuan. "Sexual Politics and Sexual Poetics in Kurahashi Yumiko's *Cruel Fairy Tales for Adults."* In *Constructions and Confrontations: Changing Representations of Women and Feminisms East and West*, ed. Cristina Bacchilega and Cornelia N. Moore. Literary Studies East and West, vol. 12. Honolulu: University of Hawaii, College of Languages, Linguistics, and Literature; and the East-West Center, forthcoming, 1996.

Knapp, Bettina Leibowitz. "Fumiko Enchi's *Masks*: A Sacred Mystery." In idem, *Women in Twentieth-Century Literature: A Jungian View.* University Park: Pennsylvania State University Press, 1987, 183–207.

Komashaku, Kimi. "Murasaki Shikibu's Message: A Reinterpretation of *The Tale of Genji."* Trans. Tomiko Yoda. *U.S.-Japan Women's Journal, English Supplement* 5 (July 1993): 28–51.

Kornicki, P. F. Review of *In the Shade of Spring Leaves: The Life and Writings of Higuchi Ichiyō*, by Robert Lyons Danly. *Journal of Japanese Studies* 9, no. 2 (Summer 1983): 353–56.

Kristeva, Isvetana. "The *Genji*-intext in *Towazu-gatari."* In *Contemporary European Writing on Japan: Scholarly Views from Eastern and Western Europe*, ed. Ian Nish. Kent, Eng.: Paul Norbury, 1988, 251–57.

———. "Japanese Lyrical Diaries and the European Autobiographical Tradition." In *Europe Interprets Japan*, ed. Gordon Daniels. Kent, Eng.: Paul Norbury, 1984, 155–62.

Larson, Phyllis Hyland. "Yosano Akiko and the Re-creation of the Female Self: An Autogynography." *Journal of the Association of Teachers of Japanese*, special issue: "Yosano Akiko (1878–1942)," ed. Laurel Rasplica Rodd, 25, no. 1 (Apr. 1991): 11–26.

Lewell, John. *Modern Japanese Novelists: A Biographical Dictionary.* Tokyo: Kō-dansha International, 1993.

Linhart, Sepp. Review of *The Twilight Years,* by Ariyoshi Sawako, trans. Mildred Tahara. *Journal of Japanese Studies* 11, no. 2 (Summer 1985): 423–30.

Lippit, Noriko Mizuta. *Reality and Fiction in Modern Japanese Literature.* White Plains, N.Y.: M. E. Sharpe, 1980.

———. Response to Sandra Buckley, "Reading Women's Texts." *Bulletin of Concerned Asian Scholars* 20, no. 3 (1988): 68–70.

Lippit, Noriko Mizuta and Kyoko Iriye Selden, trans. and eds. *Japanese Women Writers: Twentieth Century Short Fiction.* Armonk, N.Y.: M. E. Sharpe, 1991.

———. *Stories by Contemporary Japanese Women Writers.* Armonk, N.Y.: M. E. Sharpe, 1982.

Loui, Shirley M. "The Akashi Lady: When Second Is Best." In Kamens, *Approaches,* 155–61.

———. *Murasaki's "Genji" and Proust's "Recherche": A Comparative Study.* Lewiston, N.Y.: Edwin Mellen Press, 1991.

Lyons, Phyllis I. "Cultural Myths and Comic Book Heroes." Review of *Requiem,* by Gō Shizuko, trans. Geraldine Harcourt; and *The Barren Zone,* by Yamasaki Toyoko, trans. James Araki. *Journal of the Association of Teachers of Japanese* 21, no. 1 (Apr. 1987): 77–84.

———. " 'Modern Girl': The Shishōsetsu Revisited." Review of *Confessions of Love: A Novel by Uno Chiyo,* trans. Phyllis Birnbaum. *Journal of the Association of Teachers of Japanese* 24, no. 2 (Nov. 1990): 219–24.

———. Review of *The Mother of Dreams and Other Short Stories,* ed. Makoto Ueda. *Monumenta Nipponica* 43, no. 1 (Spring 1988): 104–6.

Makura no sōshi, see Sei Shōnagon

Mamola, Claire Zebroski. *Japanese Women's Writings in English Translation: An Annotated Bibliography.* 2 vols. New York: Garland, 1989, 1992.

Marra, Michele. *The Aesthetics of Discontent: Politics and Reclusion in Medieval Japanese Literature.* Honolulu: University of Hawaii Press, 1991.

Matheson, William H. "Madness in Literature: Reading the 'Heartvine' Chapter and Its Descendants." In Kamens, *Approaches,* 162–68.

Matsumoto Ryōzō, trans. and ed. *Japanese Literature New and Old.* Tokyo: Hokuseido Press, 1961.

McClain, Yoko. "Eroticism and the Writings of Enchi Fumiko." *Journal of the Association of Teachers of Japanese* 15, no. 1 (Apr. 1980): 32–46.

———. Review of *Confessions of Love: A Novel by Uno Chiyo,* trans. Phyllis Birnbaum. *Journal of Asian Studies* 48, no. 4 (Nov. 1989): 881–82.

———. Review of *Masks,* by Enchi Fumiko, trans. Juliet Winters Carpenter. *Journal of the Association of Teachers of Japanese* 20, no. 1 (Apr. 1986): 90–94.

———. Review of *This Kind of Woman,* ed. Yukiko Tanaka and Elizabeth Hanson; and *Stories by Contemporary Japanese Women Writers,* trans. and edited by Noriko Mizuta Lippit and Kyoko Iriye Selden. *Monumenta Nipponica* 38, no. 4 (Winter 1983): 442–45.

————. Review of *Twenty-four Eyes*, by Tsuboi Sakae, trans. Miura Akira. *Journal of the Association of Teachers of Japanese* 19, no. 1 (Apr. 1984–85): 111–16.

————. "A Writer as Steady as a Cow?" *Journal of the Association of Teachers of Japanese* 17, no. 2 (Nov. 1982): 153–72.

McCullough, Helen Craig. "The Seidensticker *Genji*." Review of *The Tale of Genji*, trans. Edward G. Seidesticker. *Monumenta Nipponica* 32, no. 1 (Sept. 1977): 93–110.

McCullough, Helen Craig, trans. and ed. *Classical Japanese Prose: An Anthology*. Stanford: Stanford University Press, 1990.

McCullough, William H., and Helen C. McCullough, *see* Akazome Emon

Meech-Pekarik, Julia. "The Artist's View of Ukifune." In Pekarik, *Ukifune*, 173–215.

Miller, Barbara Stoler, ed. *Masterworks of Asian Literature in Comparative Perspective: A Guide for Teaching*. Armonk, N.Y.: M. E. Sharpe, 1993.

Miller, J. Scott. "Teaching *The Tale of Genji* with Saikaku's *Life of an Amorous Man*." In Kamens, *Approaches*, 142–47.

Miller, Mara. "Canons and the Challenge of Gender: Women's Voices in the Japanese Canon." *Monist: An International Journal of General Philosophical Inquiry* 76, no. 4 (Oct. 1993): 477–93.

Miller, Marilyn Jeanne. *The Poetics of Nikki Bungaku: A Comparison of the Traditions, Conventions, and Structure of Heian Japan's Literary Diaries with Western Autobiographical Writings*. New York: Garland, 1985.

Minamoto, Gorō. "Fresh Insights into Human Nature: On Kōno Taeko's *Mira-tori ryōkitan*." Trans. Janet Goff. *Japanese Literature Today* 17 (Mar. 1992): 22–25.

Minear, Richard, trans. *Hiroshima: Three Witnesses*. Princeton: Princeton University Press, 1990.

Miner, Earl. "The Heroine: Identity, Recurrence, Destiny." In Pekarik, *Ukifune*, 63–81.

————. *Japanese Poetic Diaries*. Berkeley: University of California Press, 1978.

————. "Narrative Parts and Conceptions." In Pekarik, *Ukifune*, 231–50.

Mitsios, Helen, ed. *New Japanese Voices; The Best Contemporary Fiction from Japan*. New York: Atlantic Monthly Press, 1991.

Mitsutani, Margaret. "Higuchi Ichiyō: A Literature of Her Own." *Comparative Literature Studies* 22, no. 1 (Spring 1985): 53–66.

————. "Renaissance in Women's Literature." *Japan Quarterly* 33, no. 3 (1986): 313–19.

————. Review of *May You Now Rest in Peace* (*Yasuraka ni ima wa nemuritamae*, by Hayashi Kyōko. *Japanese Literature Today* 16 (Mar. 1991): 22–25.

Miyake, Lynne K. "The Narrative Triad in *The Tale of Genji*: Narrator, Reader, and Text." In Kamens, *Approaches*, 77–87.

————. Review of *Murasaki Shikibu: The Tale of Genji*, by Richard Bowring. *Monumenta Nipponica* 44, no. 3 (Autumn 1989): 349–51.

————. Review of *To Live and to Write*, ed. Yukiko Tanaka. *Journal of the Association of Teachers of Japanese* 23, no. 1 (Apr. 1989): 88–92.

————. "Women's Voice in Japanese Literature: Expanding the Feminine." *Women's Studies* 17 (1989): 87–100.

Miyamoto, Gorō. "Fresh Insights into Human Nature." Trans. Janet Goff. Review of *Miira-tori ryōkitan*, by Kōno Taeko. *Japanese Literature Today* 17 (Mar. 1992): 22–25.

Miyoshi, Masao. "Gathering Voices: Japanese Women and Women Writers." In idem, *Off Center: Power and Culture Relations Between Japan and the United States*. Cambridge, Mass.: Harvard University Press, 1991, 189–216.

————. "Translation as Interpretation." Review of *The Tale of Genji*, trans. Edward G. Seidensticker. *Journal of Asian Studies* 38, no. 2 (1978): 299–302.

————. "Women's Short Stories in Japan." *Mānoa: A Pacific Journal of International Writing* 3, no. 2 (Fall 1991): 33–39.

Mizuta Noriko. "Symbiosis and Renewal: Transformation of the Forest World of Ōba Minako." Trans. Julianne Komori Dvorak. *Review of Japanese Culture and Society* 5 (1993): 59–66.

Monnet, Livia. "Child of Wrath: The Literature of Takahashi Takako." *Transactions of the Asiatic Society of Japan* 4, no. 5 (1990): 87–121.

————. "In the Beginning Woman Was the Sun: Autobiographies of Modern Japanese Women Writers." *Japan Forum* 1, nos. 1–2 (1989): 55–75, 197–223.

————. "The Politics of Miscegenation: The Discourse of Fantasy in 'Fusehime' by Tsushima Yūko." *Japan Forum* 5, no. 1 (Apr. 1993): 53–73.

Mori, Maryellen T. "Cross-Cultural Patterns in the Quest Fiction of Okamoto Kanoko." *Comparatist* 20 (1996): 153–78.

————. Review of *Unmapped Territories: New Women's Fiction from Japan*, trans. Yukiko Tanaka; and Review of *Japanese Women Writers: Twentieth-Century Short Fiction*, trans. Noriko Mizuta Lippit and Kyoko Iriye Selden. *Belles Lettres: A Review of Books by Women* 7, no. 3 (Spring 1992): 35, 45.

————. "The Splendor of Self-Examination: The Life and Fiction of Okamoto Kanoko." *Monumenta Nipponica* 50, no. 1 (Spring 1995): 67–102.

————. "The Subversive Role of Fantasy in the Fiction of Takahashi Takako." *Journal of the Association of Teachers of Japanese* 28, no.1 (Apr. 1994): 29–56.

Morris, Ivan. *The World of the Shining Prince: Court Life in Ancient Japan*. New York: Penguin Books, 1964.

Morris, Ivan, ed. *Modern Japanese Stories: An Anthology*. Rutland, Vt.: Tuttle, 1977.

Morris, Ivan, trans., see Daughter of [Sugawara no] Takasue

Morris, Ivan, and Andrew Pekarik. "Deception and Self-Deception." In Pekarik, *Ukifune*, 139–51.

Morris, Mark. "Desire and the Prince: New Work on *Genji monogatari*." Review of *Murasaki Shikibu: The Tale of Genji*, by Richard Bowring; *The Splendor of Longing in "The Tale of Genji*," by Norma Field; and *The Bridge of Dreams: A Poetics of "The Tale of Genji,"* by Haruo Shirane. *Journal of Asian Studies* 49, no. 2 (May 1990): 291–304.

———. Review of *Traditional Japanese Poetry: An Anthology*, trans. Steven D. Carter. *Monumenta Nipponica* 48, no. 1 (Spring 1993): 116–19.

Mostow, Joshua S. "The Amorous Statesman and the Poetess: The Politics of Autobiography and the *Kagerō nikki*." *Japan Forum* 4, no. 2 (Oct. 1992): 305–15.

———. "*E no Gotoshi*: The Picture Simile and the Feminine Re-guard in Japanese Illustrated Romances." *Word & Image* 11, no. 1 (Jan.–Mar. 1995): 37–54.

———. "Japanese *Nikki* as Political Memoirs." In idem, *Political Memoir: Essays on the History, Nature and Functions of Polygenre*. London: Frank Cass, 1994, 106–20.

———. "On Becoming Ukifune: Autobiographical Heroines in Heian and Kamakura Literature." In *Contacts Between Cultures*, vol. 3, *Eastern Asia: Literature and Humanities*, ed. B. Luk and S. Steben. Lewiston, N.Y.: Edwin Mellen Press, 1993, 233–38.

———. Review of *The Buddhist Poetry of the Great Kamo Priestess: Daisaiin Senshi and the Hosshin Wakashū*, by Edward Kamens. *Journal of Asian Studies* 50, no. 3 (Aug. 1991): 691–92.

———. "Self and Landscape in *Kagerō Nikki*." *Review of Japanese Culture and Society* 5 (1993): 8–19.

———. "*Tales of Takamura*" (*Takamura monogatari*). *British Columbia Asian Review*, no. 3/4 (1990): 355–80.

Mother of [Fujiwara no] Michitsuna. *The Gossamer Years: The Diary of a Noblewoman of Heian Japan* (*Kagerō nikki*). Trans. Edward G. Seidensticker. Rutland, Vt.: Tuttle, 1964.

Mukōda Kuniko. *A Deck of Memories*. Trans. Adam Kabat. Tokyo: Kōdansha International, 1992.

———. *The Name of the Flower: Stories*. Trans. Tomone Matsumoto. Berkeley, Calif.: Stone Bridge Press, 1994.

Mulhern, Chieko Irie. "Japanese Harlequin Romances as Transcultural Woman's Fiction." *Journal of Asian Studies* 48, no. 1 (Feb. 1989): 50–70.

———. Review of *Rabbits, Crabs, Etc.*, trans. Phyllis Birnbaum. *Monumenta Nipponica* 38, no. 3 (Autumn 1983): 329–30.

———. Review of *To Live and to Write*, ed. Yukiko Tanaka. *Monumenta Nipponica* 43, no. 2 (Summer 1988): 239–41.

———. "Women's Literary Traditions: Regional Essays—Japan." In Arkin and Shollar, 1152–62.

Mulhern, Chieko Irie, ed. *Heroic with Grace: Legendary Women of Japan*. Armonk, N.Y.: M. E. Sharpe, 1991.

———. *Japanese Women Writers: A Bio-critical Sourcebook*. Westport, Conn.: Greenwood Press, 1994.

Murasaki Shikibu. *Murasaki Shikibu: Her Diary and Poetic Memoirs: A Translation and Study* (*Murasaki Shikibu nikki*). Trans. Richard Bowring. Princeton: Princeton University Press, 1982.

———. *The Tale of Genji* (*Genji monogatari*, abridged). *Genji and Heike: Selections from "The Tale of Genji" and "The Tale of the Heike."* Trans. Helen C. McCullough. Stanford: Stanford University Press, 1994, 3–242.

———. *The Tale of Genji* (*Genji monogatari*). Trans. Edward G. Seidensticker. New York: Knopf, 1976.

———. *The Tale of Genji: A Novel in Six Parts by Lady Murasaki* (*Genji monogatari*). Trans. Arthur Waley. New York: Random House, 1960. Reprinted— Rutland, Vt.: Tuttle, 1970.

Naff, William E. Review of *In the Shade of Spring Leaves: The Life and Writings of Higuchi Ichiyō*, by Robert Lyons Danly. *Monumenta Nipponica* 37, no. 2 (Summer 1982): 257–59.

Nakagawa, Victoria Vernon. Review of *Rabbits, Crabs, Etc.*, trans. Phyllis Birnbaum; *This Kind of Woman*, trans. and edited by Yukiko Tanaka and Elizabeth Hanson; and *Stories by Contemporary Japanese Women Writers*, trans. and edited by Noriko Mizuta Lippit and Kyoko Iriye Selden. *Journal of Asian Studies* 43, no. 1 (Nov. 1983): 155–58.

Nijō, Lady. *The Confessions of Lady Nijō* (*Towazugatari*). Trans. Karen Brazell. Stanford: Stanford University Press, 1973.

———. *Lady Nijo's Own Story: Towazu-gatari: The Candid Diary of a Thirteenth-Century Japanese Imperial Concubine*. Trans. Wilfrid Whitehouse and Eizo Yanagisawa. Rutland, Vt.: Tuttle, 1974.

Noguchi Takehiko. "The Substratum Constituting Monogatari: Prose Structure and Narrative in *Genji monogatari*." In *Principles of Classical Japanese Literature*, ed. Earl Miner. Princeton: Princeton University Press, 1985, 130–50.

North, Lucy. Review of *Daughters of the Moon* by Victoria V. Vernon. *Harvard Journal of Asiatic Studies* 52, no. 1 (June 1992): 370–90.

Ochner, Nobuko. Review of *Contemporary Japanese Literature*, special issue of *World Literature Today* 62, no. 3 (Summer 1988), ed. Ivar Ivask. *Journal of the Association of Teachers of Japanese* 23, no. 2 (Nov. 1989): 185–88.

Ōe Kenzaburō. "The Day Another Izumi Shikibu Was Born" ("Mō hitori Izumi Shikibu ga umareta hi"; 1984). Trans. Yoshio Iwamoto and Yoshiko Yokochi Samuel. *Literary Review* (Fairleigh Dickinson University) 30, no. 2 (Winter 1987): 232–44.

Ōe Kenzaburō, ed. *The Crazy Iris: and Other Stories of the Atomic Aftermath.* New York: Grove Press, 1985.

Okada, H. Richard. "Domesticating *The Tale of Genji*." Review of *The Splendor of Longing in "The Tale of Genji,"* by Norma Field; and *The Bridge of Dreams: A Poetics of "The Tale of Genji,"* by Haruo Shirane. *Journal of the American Oriental Society* 110, no. 1 (Jan.–Mar. 1990): 60–70.

———. *Figures of Resistance: Language, Poetry, and Narrating in "The Tale of Genji" and Other Mid-Heian Texts*. Durham: Duke University Press, 1991.

———. "Positioning Subjects Globally: A Reading of Yamada Emi." *U.S.-Japan Women's Journal: English Supplement*, no. 9 (1995): 111–26.

Okamoto, Kanoko. *The Tale of the Old Geisha and Other Stories*. Santa Barbara, Calif.: Capra Press, 1985.

Orbaugh, Sharalyn. Review of *Japanese Women Writers: Twentieth Century Short Fiction*, trans. and edited by Noriko Mizuta Lippit and Kyoko Iriye Selden. *Monumenta Nipponica* 47, no. 2 (Summer 1992): 281–83.

Peel, Ellen. "Mediation and Mediators: Letters, Screens, and Other Go-Betweens in *The Tale of Genji*." In Kamens, *Approaches*, 108–14.

Pekarik, Andrew. "Rivals in Love." In *Ukifune*, 217–30.

Pekarik, Andrew, ed. *Ukifune: Love in "The Tale of Genji."* New York: Columbia University Press, 1982.

Pekarik, Andrew, and Ivan Morris. "Deception and Self-Deception." In Pekarik, *Ukifune*, 139–51.

Pflugfelder, Gregory M. "Strange Fates: Sex, Gender, and Sexuality in *Torikaebaya monogatari*." *Monumenta Nipponica* 47, no. 3 (Autumn 1992): 347–68.

Pilgrim, Richard. "*The Tale of Genji* in a Religio-aesthetic Perspective." In Kamens, *Approaches*, 45–51.

Pounds, Wayne. "Enchi Fumiko and the Hidden Energy of the Supernatural." *Journal of the Association of Teachers of Japanese* 24, no. 2 (Nov. 1990): 167–83.

Puette, William J., ed. *Guide to "The Tale of Genji" by Murasaki Shikibu*. Rutland, Vt.: Tuttle, 1983.

Rabinovitch, Judith N. Review of *A Tale of Eleventh-Century Japan: Hamamatsu Chūnagon Monogatari*, trans. Thomas H. Rohlich. *Journal of the Association of Teachers of Japanese* 18, no. 2 (Nov. 1983): 211–21.

Ramirez-Christensen, Esperanza. "The Operation of the Lyrical Mode in the *Genji monogatari*." In Pekarik, *Ukifune*, 21–61.

———. "Resisting Figures of Resistance." Review of *Figures of Resistance*, by H. Richard Okada. *Harvard Journal of Asiatic Studies* 55, no. 1 (June 1995): 179–218.

Richard, Kenneth L. Review of *The Poetic Memoirs of Lady Daibu*, trans. Phillip Tudor Harries. *Monumenta Nipponica* 36, no. 3 (Autumn 1981): 341–43.

Rimer, J. Thomas. Review of *Self-Righting Lamp*, by Maruyama Kaoru, trans. Robert Epp; and *The Ink Dark Moon*, by Ono no Komachi and Izumi Shikibu, trans. Jane Hirshfield with Aratani Mariko. *Journal of the Association of Teachers of Japanese* 25, no. 2 (Nov. 1991): 304–7.

Rodd, Laurel Rasplica. Review of *Daughters of the Moon*, by Victoria V. Vernon. *Journal of the Association of Teachers of Japanese* 23, no. 1 (Apr. 1989): 85–87.

———. Review of *Japanese Women Writers: A Bio-critical Sourcebook*, ed. Chieko I. Mulhern. *Journal of Asian Studies* 54, no 2 (May 1995): 566–67.

———. "Yosano Akiko and the Bunkagakuin: 'Educating Free Individuals.'" *Journal of the Association of Teachers of Japanese*, special issue: "Yosano Akiko (1878–1942)," ed. Laurel Rasplica Rodd, 25, no. 1 (Apr. 1991): 75–89.

———. "Yosano Akiko and the Taishō Debate of the 'New Woman.'" In *Recreating Japanese Women, 1600–1945*, ed. Gail Lee Bernstein. Berkeley: University of California Press, 1991, 175–98.

Rogers, Lawrence. Review of *Reality and Fiction in Modern Japanese Literature*, by Noriko Mizuta Lippit. *Journal of the Association of Teachers of Japanese* 16, no. 1 (Apr. 1981): 101-4.

Rohlich, Thomas H. Review of *Genji and Heike: Selections from "The Tale of Genji" and "The Tale of the Heike,"* trans. Helen Craig McCullough. *Monumenta Nipponica* 50, no. 3 (1995): 387-89.

―――. Review of *Murasaki Shikibu: Her Diary and Poetic Memoirs*, by Richard Bowring. *Journal of Asian Studies* 43, no. 3 (May 1984): 539-41.

Rowley, G. G. "Making a Living from *Genji*: Yosano Akiko and Her Work on *The Tale of Genji*." *Journal of the Association of Teachers of Japanese*, special issue: "Yosano Akiko (1878-1942)," ed. Laurel Rasplica Rodd, 25, no. 1 (Apr. 1991): 27-44.

Ruch, Barbara. "Beyond Absolution: Enchi Fumiko's *The Waiting Years* and *Masks*." In B. Miller, 439-56.

―――. "A Book of One's Own: *The Gossamer Years*, *The Pillow Book*, and *The Confessions of Lady Nijō*." In B. Miller, 404-19.

Saegusa, Kazuko. "The Narcissism of Female Representation and the Professional Writer." Trans. Nina Blake. *Review of Japanese Culture and Society* 4 (Dec. 1991): 18-21.

Saeki Shōichi, ed. *The Catch and Other War Stories*. Tokyo: Kōdansha , 1981.

Sakaki, Atsuko. "Autobiographizing Fiction? Fictionalizing Autobiography?: A Contemporary Japanese Woman's Experimentations with Meta-Autobiography." In *Constructions and Confrontations: Changing Representations of Women and Feminisms, East and West*, ed. Cornelia N. Moore et al. Literary Studies East and West, vol. 12. Honolulu: University of Hawaii, 1996, 1-13.

―――. "Denaturalizing Nature, Dissolving the Self: An Analysis of Kurahashi Yumiko's *Popoi*." In *The Proceedings of the Conference on Nature and Selfhood in Japanese Literature*, ed. Kinya Tsuruta. Vancouver: Josai International University and University of British Columbia, 1993, 241-56.

―――. "A Gallery of 'Severed Heads': A Comparative Study of Kurahashi Yumiko's *Popoi*." In *Dramas of Desire/Visions of Beauty*, ed. Ziva Ben-Porat, Hana Wirth-Nesher, Roseanne Runte, and Hans Runte. Vol. 1 of *The Force of Vision*, ed. Earl Miner and Haga Toru. Tokyo: International Comparative Literature Association, 1995, 386-93.

Sanuki no suke nikki, see Fujiwara no Nagako

Sarashina nikki, see Daughter of [Sugawara no] Takasue

Sarra, Edith. *Fictions of Femininity: Literary Inventions of Gender in Japanese Court Women's Memoirs*. Stanford: Stanford University Press, forthcoming.

―――. "A Poetics of the Gaze in *Makura no sōshi*." In *The Desire for Monogatari: Proceedings of the Second Midwest Research/Pedagogy Seminar on Japanese Literature*, ed. Roger K. Thomas. Purdue University, 1994, 21-30.

Schalow, Paul Gordon. "Formulating a Theory of Women's Writing in 17th-Century Japan: Kitamura Kigin's *Ominaeshi monogatari* (Tales of the

Maidenflower)." *Early Modern Japan: An Interdisciplinary Journal* 5, no. 2 (Dec. 1995): 14–18.

Schierbeck, Sachiko. *Japanese Women Novelists in the 20th Century: 104 Biographies, 1900–1993*. Copenhagen: University of Copenhagen, Museum Tusculanum Press, 1994.

Schierbeck, Sachiko Shibata, comp. and Søren Egerod, ed. *Postwar Japanese Women Writers: An Up-to-date Bibliography with Biographical Sketches*. East Asian Institute Occasional Papers 5. Copenhagen: University of Copenhagen, 1989.

Sei Shōnagon. *The Pillow Book of Sei Shōnagon (Makura no sōshi)*. Trans. Arthur Waley. Boston: Houghton Mifflin, 1929; Trans. Ivan Morris. Suffolk, Eng.: Penguin Books, 1967.

Seidensticker, Edward. "Chiefly on Translating the *Genji*." *Journal of Japanese Studies* 6, no. 1 (Winter 1980): 15–47.

———. Review of *In the Shade of Spring Leaves: The Life and Writings of Higuchi Ichiyō*, by Robert Lyons Danly. *Journal of the Association of Teachers of Japanese* 17, no. 1 (Apr. 1982): 62–66.

———. Review of *Murasaki Shikibu: Her Diary and Poetic Memoirs*, by Richard Bowring. *Journal of Japanese Studies* 9, no. 2 (Summer 1983): 335–40.

———. "Rough Business in 'Ukifune' and Elsewhere." In Pekarik, *Ukifune*, 1–19.

Seidensticker, Edward, trans., *see* Mother of [Fujiwara no] Michitsuna

Seidensticker, Edward, and Haruo Shirane. "*The Tale of Genji*." In B. Miller, 390–95.

Sherif, Ann. "'The Bridge of Dreams' and *Masks*: Two Modern Responses to *The Tale of Genji*." In Kamens, *Approaches*, 148–54.

———. "The Canon with A Critical Difference." Review of *Complicit Fictions: The Subject in the Modern Japanese Prose Narrative*, by James A. Fujii; and *Reading Against Culture: Ideology and Narrative in the Japanese Novel*, by David Pollack. *Journal of the Association of Teachers of Japanese* 28, no. 2 (Nov. 1994): 195–208.

———. "Kōda Aya's *Nagareru* and the Literature of the Demimonde." *Journal of the Association of Teachers of Japanese* 28, no. 1 (Apr. 1994): 3–28.

———. Review of *Japanese Women Writers in English Translation: An Annotated Bibliography*, vols. I and II, by Claire Zebroski Mamola. *Journal of Asian Studies* 53, no. 1 (Feb. 1994): 221–22.

———. Review of *The Sound of the Wind: The Life and Works of Uno Chiyo*, by Rebecca L. Copeland. *Monumenta Nipponica* 47, no. 4 (Winter 1992): 535–37.

———. Review of *The Writings of Kōda Aya, a Japanese Literary Daughter*, by Alan M. Tansman. *Monumenta Nipponica* 48, no. 4 (Winter 1993): 493–96.

Shimer, Dorothy Blair, ed. *Rice Bowl Women: Writings by and About the Women of China and Japan*. New York: Mentor, 1982.

Shirane, Haruo. *The Bridge of Dreams: A Poetics of "The Tale of Genji."* Stanford: Stanford University Press, 1987.

————. Review of *Figures of Resistance*, by H. Richard Okada. *Journal of Japanese Studies* 20, no. 1 (Winter 1994): 221–28.

————. Review of *The Poetics of Nikki Bungaku*, by Marilyn Jeanne Miller. *Journal of the Association of Teachers of Japanese* 21, no. 1 (Apr. 1987): 98–102.

————. "The Uji Chapters and the Denial of the Romance." In Pekarik, *Ukifune*, 113–38.

[Review of] "Single Cell" ("Shinguru seru"), by Masuda Mizuko, trans. Mark Jewel. *Japanese Literature Today* 13 (Mar. 1988): 14–15.

Snyder, Stephen S. Review of *Monkey Brain Sushi: New Tastes in Japanese Fiction*, ed. Alfred Birnbaum; and *New Japanese Voices: The Best Contemporary Fiction from Japan*, ed. Helen Mitsios. *Journal of Japanese Studies* 19, no. 1 (Winter 1993): 271–75.

Sparling, Kathryn. "Modern Prose Writers: Fiction, Drama, Essays"; "Modern Poets"; "Premodern Prose Writers: Tales, Diaries, Miscellanies"; and "Premodern Poets." In Huber, 213–367.

Stinchecum, Amanda Mayer. "Who Tells the Tale? 'Ukifune': A Study in Narrative Voice." *Monumenta Nipponica* 35, no. 4 (Winter 1980): 375–403.

Strong, Sarah M. "Briefly Noted." Review of *Ono no Komachi: Poems, Stories, Nō Plays*, trans. Roy E. Teele, Nicholas J. Teele, and H. Rebecca Teele. *Journal of the Association of Teachers of Japanese* 28, no. 2 (Nov. 1994): 249–50.

————. "The Making of a Femme Fatale: Ono no Komachi in the Early Medieval Commentaries." *Monumenta Nipponica* 49, no. 4 (Winter 1994): 391–412.

————. "Passion and Patience: Aspects of Feminine Poetic Heritage in Yosano Akiko's *Midaregami* and Tawara Machi's *Salad kinenbi*." *Journal of the Association of Teachers of Japanese* 25, no. 2 (Nov. 1991): 177–94.

————. Review of *Noh Drama and "The Tale of Genji*," by Janet Goff. *Journal of Asian Studies* 52, no. 2 (May 1993): 449–50.

————. Review of *Self-Righting Lamp: Selected Poems*, by Maruyama Kaoru, trans. Robert Epp. *Monumenta Nipponica* 47, no. 1 (Spring 1992): 114–17.

————. Review of *The Shōwa Anthology*, ed. Van C. Gessel and Matsumoto Tomone. *Monumenta Nipponica* 41, no. 4 (Winter 1986): 499–502.

————. "Two New Anthologies for Teaching Premodern Literature." Review of *Classical Japanese Prose: An Anthology*, trans. and ed. Helen Craig McCullough; and *Traditional Japanese Poetry: An Anthology*, trans. Steven D. Carter. *Journal of the Association of Teachers of Japanese* 26, no. 2 (Nov. 1992): 193–209.

Tahara, Mildred. "Ariyoshi Sawako: The Novelist." In Mulhern, *Heroic with Grace*, 297–322.

Tajima, Yoko. "An Analysis of Kawabata's *Snow Country* from Komako's Perspective." Trans. Donna George Storey. *U.S.-Japan Women's Journal: English Supplement* 4 (Feb. 1993): 26–48.

Takahashi Yasunari. "'Kana-dehon Hamlet' ('Hamlet à la Kabuki'): A

Drama by Tsutsumi Harue" (synopsis). *Japanese Literature Today* 19 (1994): 94–97.

Takeda Katsuhiko. "The Inherent Significance of *Hana ni toe*: A Novel by Setouchi Jakuchō." Trans. John Munroe. *Japanese Literature Today* 18 (1993): 63–69.

———. Review of *The River Ki*, by Ariyoshi Sawako, trans. Mildred Tahara. *Japan Quarterly* 27, no. 3 (July-Sept.): 405–8.

[Review of] "A Tale of Snow Buddhas" ("Yuki no hotoke no monogatari"), by Tomioka Taeko. *Japanese Literature Today* 13 (Mar. 1988): 12–13.

Tanaka, Yukiko. Review of *The Mother of Dreams and Other Short Stories*, ed. Makoto Ueda. *Journal of Japanese Studies* 17, no. 2 (Summer 1991): 410–14.

———. Response to Sandra Buckley, "Reading Women's Texts." *Bulletin of Concerned Asian Scholars* 20, no. 3 (1988): 70–72.

Tanaka, Yukiko, trans. and ed. *To Live and to Write: Selections by Japanese Women Writers, 1913–1938*. Seattle: Seal Press, 1987.

———, trans. and ed. *Unmapped Territories: New Women's Fiction from Japan*. Seattle: Women in Translation, 1991.

Tanaka, Yukiko, and Elizabeth Hanson, eds. *This Kind of Woman: Ten Stories by Japanese Women Writers, 1960–1976*. Stanford: Stanford University Press, 1982.

Tansman, Alan M. *The Writings of Kōda Aya: A Japanese Literary Daughter*. New Haven: Yale University Press, 1993.

Taudin-Chabot, Jeanette. "The Feminine Tradition in Japanese Literature." In *Europe Interprets Japan*, ed. Gordon Daniels. Kent, Eng.: Paul Norbury, 1984, 162–67.

———. "A View of Tokugawa Women and Literature." *Women in Japanese Literature* (Netherlands Association for Japanese Studies) (1981): 55–66.

Teele, Roy E., Nicholas J. Teele, and H. Rebecca Teele. *Ono no Komachi: Poems, Stories, Nō Plays*. New York: Garland, 1993.

Thomas, Roger. Review of *Guide to "The Tale of Genji*," by William J. Puette. *Journal of the Association of Teachers of Japanese* 18, no. 2 (Nov. 1983): 212–14.

Torikaebaya monogatari. The Changelings. Trans. Rosette F. Willig. Stanford: Stanford University Press, 1983.

Towazugatari, *see* Nijō, Lady.

Treat, John Whittier. "Hiroshima and the Place of the Narrator." *Journal of Asian Studies* 48, no. 1 (Feb. 1989): 29–49.

———. Review of *Contemporary Japanese Literature*, special issue of *World Literature Today* 62, no. 3 (Summer 1988), ed. Ivar Ivask. *Monumenta Nipponica* 44, no. 1 (Spring 1989): 109–13.

———. "Yoshimoto Banana Writes Home: Shōjo Culture and the Nostalgic Subject." *Journal of Japanese Studies* 19, no. 2 (Summer 1993): 353–87.

Tsuruta, Kinya. Review of *The Shōwa Anthology*, ed. Van C. Gessel and Matsumoto Tomone. *Japan Quarterly* 33, no. 3 (July-Sept. 1986): 328–29.

Tyler, Royall. Review of *Noh Drama and "The Tale of Genji*," by Janet Goff. *Journal of Japanese Studies* 18, no. 2 (Summer 1992): 611–18.

Ueda, Makoto, ed. *The Mother of Dreams and Other Short Stories: Portrayals of Women in Modern Japanese Fiction.* Tokyo: Kōdansha International, 1986.

Ury, Marian. "The Real Murasaki." Review of *Murasaki Shikibu: Her Diary and Poetic Memoirs,* by Richard Bowring. *Monumenta Nipponica* 38, no. 2 (Summer 1983): 175–89.

———. Review of *Approaches to Teaching Murasaki Shikibu's "The Tale of Genji,"* ed. Edward Kamens. *Monumenta Nipponica* 50, no. 2 (1995): 269–71.

———. Review of *A Tale of Flowering Fortunes,* trans. William H. McCullough and Helen Craig McCullough. *Journal of the Association of Teachers of Japanese* 16, no. 2 (Nov. 1981): 208–12.

———. "Tales of *Genji.*" Review of *The Splendor of Longing in "The Tale of Genji,"* by Norma Field; *Murasaki Shikibu: The Tale of Genji,* by Richard Bowring; *The Bridge of Dreams: A Poetics of "The Tale of Genji,"* by Haruo Shirane; *Le Dit du Genji,* trans. René Sieffert. *Harvard Journal of Asiatic Studies* 51, no. 1 (June 1991): 263–308.

Vernon, Victoria V. *Daughters of the Moon: Wish, Will, and Social Constraint in Fiction by Modern Japanese Women.* Japan Research Monograph 9. Berkeley: University of California, Institute of East Asian Studies, 1988.

———. Review of *To Live and to Write,* ed. Yukiko Tanaka. *Journal of Asian Studies* 47, no. 3 (Aug. 1988): 652–53.

Videen, Susan Downing. Review of *Rabbits, Crabs, Etc.,* trans. Phyllis Birnbaum. *Journal of the Association of Teachers of Japanese* 17, no. 2 (Nov. 1982): 217–20.

Viswanathan, Meera S. Review of *Daughters of the Moon,* by Victoria V. Vernon. *Journal of Asian Studies* 48, no. 1 (Feb. 1989): 183–84.

Walker, Janet A. "The *Izumi Shikibu nikki* as a Work of Courtly Literature." *Literary Review* (Fairleigh Dickinson University) 22 (1980): 463–75.

———. "Poetic Ideal and Fictional Reality in the *Izumi Shikibu nikki.*" *Harvard Journal of Asiatic Studies* 37 (1977): 135–82.

———. Review of *In the Shade of Spring Leaves: The Life and Writings of Higuchi Ichiyō, a Woman of Letters in Meiji Japan,* by Robert Lyons Danly. *Journal of Asian Studies* 42, no. 1 (Feb. 1982): 160–62.

———. Review of *The Mother of Dreams and Other Short Stories,* ed. Makoto Ueda. *Journal of the Association of Teachers of Japanese* 23, no. 1 (Apr. 1989): 79–84.

———. Review of *The Poetic Memoirs of Lady Daibu,* trans. Phillip Tudor Harries. *Journal of the Association of Teachers of Japanese* 18, no. 1 (Apr. 1983): 94–96.

———. Review of *The Writings of Kōda Aya: A Japanese Literary Daughter,* by Alan M. Tansman. *Journal of Japanese Studies* 21, no. 2 (Summer 1995): 448–51.

Wallace, John R. "Fitful Slumbers: Nun Abutsu's *Utatane.*" *Monumenta Nipponica* 43, no. 4 (Winter 1988): 391–416.

Watanabe, Minoru. "Style and Point of View in the *Kagerō nikki.*" *Journal of Japanese Studies* 10.2 (Summer 1984): 365–84.

Waters, Virginia Skord. Review of *Ono no Komachi: Poems, Stories, Nō Plays*, trans. Roy E. Teele, Nicholas J. Teele, and H. Rebecca Teele. *Monumenta Nipponica* 49, no. 2 (Summer 1994): 235–37.

Willig, Rosette F., trans., *see Torikaebaya monogatari*

Yamamoto Kenkichi. "Ōhara Tomie: 'A Woman Called En.'" *Japan P.E.N. News* 5 (July 1960): 10–11.

Yowa no nezame monogatari, see Daughter of (Sugawara no) Takasue

[Review of] "A Year's Pastoral" ("Ichinen no bokka"), by Kōno Taeko. *Japanese Literature Today* 6 (Mar. 1981): 25–27.

Zolbrod, Leon. "The Four-Part Theoretical Structure of *The Tale of Genji*." *Journal of the Association of Teachers of Japanese* 15, no. 1 (Apr. 1980): 22–31.

———. Review of *Ukifune: Love in the Tale of Genji*, ed. Andrew Pekarik. *Journal of the Association of Teachers of Japanese* 19, no. 1 (Apr. 1984–85): 116–19.

Index

In this index, an "f" after a number indicates a separate reference on the next page, and an "ff" indicates separate references on the next two pages. A continuous discussion over two or more pages is indicated by a span of page numbers, e.g., "57–59." *Passim* is used for a cluster of references in close but not necessarily consecutive sequence.

Library of Congress Cataloging-in-Publication Data

The woman's hand : gender and theory in Japanese women's writing /
edited by Paul Gordon Schalow, Janet A. Walker.
    p.   cm.
  Includes bibliographic references and index.
  ISBN 0-8047-2722-8 (alk. paper). – ISBN 0-8047-2723-6 (pbk. : alk. paper)
  1. Japanese fiction — Women authors — History and criticism —
Congresses. 2. Japanese fiction — 20th century — History and criticism —
Congresses. 3. Japanese literature — Heian period, 794–1185 — History
and criticism — Congresses. 4. Gender identity in literature —
Congresses. 5. Sex role in literature — Congresses. 6. Feminism and
literature — Congresses. I. Schalow, Paul Gordon. II. Walker,
Janet A., 1942- .
PL725.W67   1997
895.6'3099287—dc20

96-12897
  CIP

⚝ This book is printed on acid-free paper

Original printing 1996

Last figure below indicates year of this printing
05   04   03   02   01   00   99   98   97   96